SUPPLEMENT VI
Don DeLillo to W. D. Snodgrass

AMERICAN WRITERS
A Collection of Literary Biographies

JAY PARINI
Editor in Chief

SUPPLEMENT VI
Don DeLillo to W. D. Snodgrass

Charles Scribner's Sons
An Imprint of the Gale Group
New York

Charles Scribner's Sons
1633 Broadway
New York, New York 10019

1   3   5   7   9   11   13   15   17   19   20   18   16   14   12   10   8   6   4   2

Library of Congress Cataloging-in-Publication Data

American writers; a collection of literary biographies. Leonard Unger, editor in chief.
    p. cm.
    The 4-vol. main set consists of 97 of the pamphlets originally published as the University of Minnesota pamphlets on American writers; some have been rev. and updated. The supplements cover writers not included in the original series.
    Supplement 2, has editor in chief, A. Walton Litz; Retrospective suppl. 1, ©1998, was edited by A. Walton Litz & Molly Weigel; Suppl. 5 has editor-in-chief, Jay Parini.
    Includes bibliographies and index.
    Contents: v. 1. Henry Adams to T. S. Eliot — v. 2. Ralph Waldo Emerson to Carson McCullers — v. 3. Archibald MacLeish to George Santayana — v. 4. Isaac Bashevis Singer to Richard Wright — Supplenment[s]: 1, pt. 1. Jane Addams to Sidney Lanier. 1, pt. 2. Vachel Lindsay to Elinor Wylie. 2, pt.1. W.H. Auden to O. Henry. 2, pt. 2. Robison Jeffers to Yvor Winters. — 4, pt. 1. Maya Angelou to Linda Hogan. 4, pt. 2. Susan Howe to Gore Vidal. 5. Russell Banks to Charles Wright.
    ISBN 0-684-19785-5 (set) — ISBN 0-684-13662-7
    1. American literature—History and criticism. 2. American literature—Bio-bibliography. 3. Authors, American—Biography. I. Unger, Leonard. II. Litz, A. Walton. III Weigel, Molly. IV. University of Minnesota pamphlets on American writers.

PS129.A55
810′.9
[B]   73-001759

ISBN 0-684-80623-1

Acknowledgment is gratefully made to those publishers and individuals who have permitted the use of the following material in copyright.

"Don DeLillo"
The Paris Review, v. 35, Fall, 1993. Copyright © 1993 The Paris Review, Inc. Reproduced by permission. DeLillo, Don. From *End Zone.* Houghton Mifflin, 1972. Reproduced by permission of Penguin Putnam Inc. DeLillo, Don. From *Libra.* Viking, 1988. Copyright © 1988 by Don DeLillo. Reproduced by permission of Viking, a division of Penguin Putnam Inc. DeLillo, Don. From *Mao II.* Viking, 1991. Copyright © 1991 by Don DeLillo. Reproduced by permission of Viking, a division of Penguin Putnam Inc.

"Annie Dillard"
Dale, Alan. *Observations and Experiments in Natural History.* Heinemann, 1960. Reproduced by permission.

"Stanley Elkin"
Elkin, Stanley. From *The Franchiser.* Farrar, Straus & Giroux, 1976. Copyright © 1976 by Stanley Elkin. Reproduced by permission of Farrar, Straus & Giroux, LLC. Elkin, Stanley. From *The Magic Kingdom.* Dutton, 1985. Reproduced by permission of Georges Borchardt, Inc. Elkin, Stanley. From *Criers and Kibitzers, Kibitzers and Criers.* Random House, 1966. Reproduced by permission of Random House, Inc. Elkin, Stanley. From *Searches and Seizures.* Random House, 1973. Reproduced by permission. *New York Times Book Review,* July 4, 1983. Copyright © 1983 by The New York Times Company. Reproduced by permission.

"John Gardner"
Carver, Raymond. From the foreword to *On Becoming a Novelist.* By John Gardner. Harper, 1983. Foreword copyright © 1983 by Raymond Carver. Reprinted by permission of HarperCollins, Inc.

"Robert Hass"
Atlantic Monthly, March, 1997 for "The Laureate as Onlooker" by Peter Davison. Reproduced by permission of the author. Hass, Robert. From *Twentieth Century Pleasures: Prose on Poetry.* Ecco Press, 1984. Copyright © 1984 by Robert Hass. Reprinted by permission of HarperCollins, Inc. Hass, Robert. From *Praise.* Ecco Press, 1979. Copyright © 1979 by Robert Hass. Reprinted by permission of HarperCollins, Inc. Hass, Robert. From *Human Wishes.* Ecco Press, 1989. Copyright © 1989 by Robert Hass. Reprinted by permission of HarperCollins, Inc. Hass, Robert. From *Field Guide.* Yale University Press, 1973. Reproduced by permission. Kunitz, Stanley. From the foreword to *Field Guide,* by Robert Hass. Yale University Press, 1973. Reproduced by permission. *New England Review,* v. 2, 1979 for "An Interview with Robert Hass," by Sydney Lea and Jay Parini. Copyright © 1979 by Middlebury College. Reproduced by permission of the authors. *Chicago Review,* v. 32, Spring, 1981. Copyright © 1981 by Chicago Review. Reproduced by permission.

"Irving Howe"
Commentary, v. 74, December, 1982 for "Socialism & Its Irresponsibilities: The Case of Irving Howe" by Midge Decter. Copyright © 1982 by the American Jewish Committee. All rights reserved. Reproduced by permission of the publisher and the author. *Dissent,* v. 14, May–June, 1967 for "Is This Country Cracking Up?" by Irving Howe. Copyright © 1967 by Dissent Publishing Corporation. Reprinted by permission of the publisher and The Estate of Irving Howe. Howe, Irving. From *World of Our Fathers.* Harcourt Brace & Company, 1976. Copyright © 1976 by Irving Howe. Reproduced by permission of Harcourt, Inc. Howe, Irving. From *William Faulkner: A Critical Study.* Random House, 1951. Copyright, 1951, 1952, by Irving Howe. Reproduced by permission of The Estate of Irving Howe.

"Richard Hugo"
Hugo, Richard. From *Making Certain It Goes On: The Collected Poems of Richard Hugo.* W.W. Norton & Company, 1984. Copyright © 1984 by The Estate of Richard Hugo. Reproduced by permission of W.W. Norton & Company, Inc.

"Susan Minot"
The Wall Street Journal, October 12, 1992. Reproduced by permission. *The Book Report,* 1998. Copyright © 1998 by Linworth Publishing, Inc., Worthington, Ohio. Reproduced by permission. Minot, Susan. From *Monkeys.* Dutton, 1986. Copyright © 1986 by Susan Minot. Reproduced by permission of Dutton, a division of Penguin Putnam Inc. Minot, Susan. From *Evening.* Knopf, 1998. Reproduced by permission of Alfred A. Knopf, Inc.

"Grace Paley"
Paley, Grace. From *Leaning Forward.* Reproduced by permission of the author.

"Robert Pinsky"
Pinsky, Robert. From *Jersey Rain.* Farrar, Straus & Giroux, 2000. Reproduced by permission of Farrar, Straus & Giroux, LLC. Pinsky, Robert. From *The Figured Wheel: New and Collected Poems.* Farrar, Straus & Giroux, 1996. Reproduced by permission of Farrar, Straus & Giroux, LLC. Pinsky, Robert. From *History of My Heart.* Ecco Press, 1984. Reproduced by permission of Farrar, Straus & Giroux, LLC. Pinsky, Robert. From *The Want Bone.* Ecco Press, 1988. Copyright © 1991 by Robert Pinsky. Reprinted by permission of HarperCollins, Inc. Pinsky, Robert. From *Sadness and Happiness.* Princeton University Press, 1975. Copyright © 1975 by Princeton University Press. Reproduced by permission of Princeton University Press. Pinsky, Robert. From *An Explanation of America.* Princeton University Press, 1979. Copyright © 1979 by Princeton University Press. Reproduced by permission of Princeton University Press.

"Reynolds Price"
The Paris Review, v. 121, Winter, 1991. Copyright © 1991 The Paris Review, Inc. Reproduced by permission. *Shenandoah,* v. 17, Summer, 1966 for "Notice I'm Still Smiling," by Wallace Kaufman. Reproduced by permission of the publisher and the author. Price, Reynolds. From *Vital Provisions.* Atheneum, 1982. Copyright © 1982 Reynolds Price. Reproduced by permission of the author. In North America by Scribner, a division of Simon & Schuster. Price, Reynolds. From *Clear Pictures.* Atheneum, 1998. Copyright © 1989 Reynolds Price. Reproduced by permission of the author. In North America by Scribner, a division of Simon & Schuster. *Time,* December 6, 1999. Copyright © 1999 Time Warner Inc. All rights reserved. Reproduced by permission of Time. *Chicago Sun-Times,* August 24, 1986 for "Staying Power of Reynolds Price," by Wendy Smith. Reprinted by permission of the author. *Washington Times,* February 1, 1983. Copyright © 1983 News World Communications, Inc. Reprinted by permission of *The Washington Times. Tobacco Road,* April, 1983 for "The Spy That Stayed: A Conversation with Reynolds Price" by Daniel Voll. Reproduced by permission of International Creative Management, Inc.

"Muriel Rukeyser"
Rukeyser, Muriel. From *Body of Waking.* Harper, 1958. Reproduced by permission. Rukeyser, Muriel. From *The Poetic Vision of Muriel Rukeyser.* Louisiana State University Press, 1980. Reproduced by permission of Louisiana State University Press. Rukeyser, Muriel. From *Collected Poems.* McGraw-Hill, Inc., 1978. Reproduced by permission of International Creative Management, Inc. Rukeyser, Muriel. From *Life of Poetry.* Paris Press, 1996. Originally published by Current Books, 1949. Reproduced by permission. Rukeyser, Muriel. From *A Turning Wind.* Viking, 1939. Reproduced by permission of Viking, a division of Penguin Putnam Inc.

"Jane Smiley"
Smiley, Jane. From *The Greenlanders.* Knopf, 1988. Reproduced by permission of Alfred A. Knopf, Inc.

Editorial and Production Staff

Managing Editors
AMANDA MATERNE
ANNA SHEETS NESBITT

Copyeditors
MELISSA DOBSON
JUDITH A. V. HARLAN
LOUISE B. KETZ
INGRID STERNER

Proofreader
CAROL HOLMES

Indexer
IMPRESSIONS BOOK AND JOURNAL SERVICES, INC.

Publisher
KAREN DAY

List of Subjects

Introduction

This series has its origin in the famous Minnesota Pamphlets on American Writers, which were published by the University of Minnesota Press between 1959 and 1972. The sharply conceived, concise, and popular monographs treated 97 American writers—mostly poets and novelists. Not surprisingly, they attracted a following, and the series proved invaluable to a generation of students and teachers, who could depend on reliable and interesting critiques of major literary figures. (I myself grew up on these pamphlets, prizing their condensed wisdom and critical rigor.) The idea of reprinting these essays occurred to Charles Scribner, Jr. (1921–1995). The series appeared in four volumes entitled *American Writers: A Collection of Literary Biographies* (1974).

Since then, five supplements to the original series have appeared, treating 141 additional American writers: poets, novelists, playwrights, essayists, and autobiographers. The idea has been consistent: to provide lucid, informative essays aimed at the general reader. Written by critics of considerable talent and expertise, these essays often rise to a high level of craft and critical vision, yet they are meant to introduce a writer of some importance in the history of American literature, and to provide a sense of the scope and nature of the career under review. A certain amount of biographical context for the work is also offered, so that readers can appreciate the historical ground that provided the texts under review with air and

light, soil and water. When necessary, the critics provide relevant historical backgrounds and culture settings.

Most of the contributors to these supplements are professionals: teachers, scholars, and writers. As anyone glancing through this volume will see, they are held to the highest standards of good writing and sound scholarship. Critical jargon is discouraged, and the essays are meant to appeal to a wide range of general readers. Each essay concludes with a select bibliography for further study.

This volume is mostly about contemporary writers, many of whom have received little sustained attention from critics. For example, William Gass, Charles Johnson, Irving Howe, Susan Minot, Grace Paley, Reynolds Price, Stanley Elkin, and Jane Smiley have been written about in the review pages of newspapers and magazines, but their work has yet to attract significant scholarship. The essays included here constitute a beginning. In other cases—as with Don DeLillo, John Gardner, Annie Dillard, and Zora Neale Hurston, for example—a significant body of critical writing has already accrued, and the authors of these essays have had to sift through this material in order to take a critical position. In each case, they have done so with admirable clarity, and their bibliographies reflect the current scholarship.

The poets included here, such as Robert Hass, Richard Hugo, W. D. Snodgrass, and Muriel Rukeyser, have each won a secure place in the tradition of American poetry, and their work in each case has been honored in various ways. But the real work of assimilation, of discovering the true place of each writer in the larger world of American literature, has only begun.

Supplement VI is a rich and varied collection that treats authors from a wide range of ethnic, social, and cultural backgrounds. The critics who contributed to this collection in themselves represent a range of voices and critical approaches. The work of culture involves the continuous assessment and reassessment of major texts produced by its writers, and our belief is that this supplement performs a useful service here, providing substantial introductions to American writers who matter to readers, and who will be read well into the next century.

—JAY PARINI

Contributors

Lindsay Pentolfe Aegerter. Associate Professor of English, University of North Carolina at Wilmington. Author of critical essays in such journals as *College English, College Literature*, and *Tulsa Studies in Women's Literature*. SUSAN MINOT

Carolyn Alessio. Deputy Literary Editor, *Chicago Tribune*. Editor of *Las Voces de la Esperanza/The Voices of Hope*, a bilingual anthology of Guatemalan children's writing. GRACE PALEY

William D. Atwill. Associate Professor of English, University of North Carolina at Wilmington. Author of *Fire and Power: The American Space Program as Postmodern Narrative*. JOHN GARDNER

Charles R. Baker. Poet, short story writer, and essayist. Author of *Christmas Frost* and *What Miss Johnson Taught*. REYNOLDS PRICE

Josie P. Campbell. Professor of English and Women's Studies, University of Rhode Island. Editor of *Popular Culture in the Middle Ages;* author of *John Irving: A Critical Companion* and numerous articles on drama, popular culture, women's literature, and comparative literature. JOHN IRVING

Joseph Dewey. Associate Professor of American Literature, University of Pittsburgh. Author of *In a Dark Time: The Apocalyptic Temper in the American Novel of the Nuclear Age* and *Novels from Reagan's America: A New Realism*. WILLIAM GASS

Nancy Coffey Heffernan. Author (with Ann Page Stecker) of *New Hampshire: Crosscurrents*

in Its Development and *Sisters of Fortune: being the true story of how three motherless sisters saved their home in New England and raised their younger brother while their father went fortune hunting in the California Gold Rush.* JANE SMILEY

Brooke Horvath. Professor of English, Kent State University. Editor with the *Review of Contemporary Fiction;* author of *Consolation at Ground Zero* and *In a Neighborhood of Dying Light;* coeditor of books on William Goyen, Henry James, and Thomas Pynchon, among others. WILLIAM GASS

Steven G. Kellman. Professor of Comparative Literature, University of Texas at San Antonio. Author of *Loving Reading: Erotics of the Text, The Plague: Fiction and Resistance, The Self-Begetting Novel,* and *The Translingual Imagination;* editor of *Perspectives on Raging Bull;* coeditor of *Into The Tunnel: Readings of Gass's Novel, Leslie Fiedler and American Culture,* and *Torpid Smoke: The Stories of Vladimir Nabokov.* DON DELILLO

Karen L. Kilcup. Professor of American Literature, University of North Carolina at Greensboro and Davidson Eminent Scholar Chair at Florida International University. Author of *Robert Frost and Feminine Literary Tradition;* editor of *Nineteenth-Century American Women Writers: An Anthology,* and *Soft Canons: American Women Writers and Masculine Tradition.* ANNIE DILLARD, MURIEL RUKEYSER

Jerome Klinkowitz. Professor of English and University Distinguished Scholar, University of

Northern Iowa. Author of *Literary Disruptions: The Making of a Post-Contemporary American Fiction, Structuring the Void: The Struggle for Subject in Contemporary American Fiction*, and forty other books on contemporary literature, art, music, philosophy, sport, and military historiography. STANLEY ELKIN

James Longenbach. Joseph Henry Gilmore Professor of English, University of Rochester. Author of *Threshold*, a volume of poems, and several books of literary criticism, including *Stone Cottage: Pound, Yeats, and Modernism, Wallace Stevens: The Plain Sense of Things*, and *Modern Poetry after Modernism*. ROBERT PINSKY

Molly McQuade. Contributing editor for Graywolf Press, a correspondent for *Booklist*, and a board member of the National Book Critics Circle. Founder and former editor of the poetry review column of *Publishers Weekly*, her poetry has appeared in *The Paris Review, The American Scholar, The North American Review, Pequod*, and elsewhere. Author of *Stealing Glimpses: Of Poetry, Poets, and Things in Between*, a collection of her essays, and editor of *By Herself: Women Reclaim Poetry*, an anthology of essays about poetry. ROBERT HASS

William R. Nash. Assistant Professor of American Literature and Civilization, Middlebury College. Author of critical essays on Gloria Naylor, John A. Williams, Walter Mosley, Frances Ellen Watkins Harper, and Charles Johnson, including

articles in the *Oxford Companion to African American Literature* and an interview in *New England Review*. CHARLES JOHNSON

Sanford Pinsker. Shadek Professor of Humanities, Franklin and Marshall College. Author of *The Catcher in the Rye: Innocence under Pressure, Jewish-American Fiction, Understanding Joseph Heller*, and numerous articles, reviews, poems, and stories. IRVING HOWE

David R. Slavitt. Poet, novelist, translator, and editor of such works as *The Book of the Twelve Prophets, The Latin Odes of Jean Dorat, The Sonnets of Love and Death of Jean de Sponde*, and a collection of poems, *Falling From Silence*. Coeditor of the *Johns Hopkins Complete Roman Drama* and the *Penn Greek Drama*. W. D. SNODGRASS

Stephen Soitos. Author of *The Blues Detective: A Study of African American Detective Fiction* and numerous works centering on German expressionist painting, Brazilian art, and African American art and literature. ZORA NEALE HURSTON

Richard Wakefield. Professor of English, Tacoma Community College and the University of Washington, Tacoma. Poetry critic, *The Seattle Times*. Author of articles and poetry in various publications, including *American Literature, The Robert Frost Review, Midwest Quarterly, Tampa Review, Light*, and *Edge City Review*. RICHARD HUGO

SUPPLEMENT VI
Don DeLillo to W. D. Snodgrass

Don DeLillo

1936—

*F*EW AMERICAN NOVELISTS have been as ambitious or playful as Don DeLillo in recording the complex currents of our time, an era in which electronic images have usurped primal reality, and society has become organized around the consumption of commercial commodities. "What I try to do," DeLillo said in a 1993 *Paris Review* interview, "is create complex human beings, ordinary-extraordinary men and women who live in the particular skin of the late twentieth century. I try to record what I see and hear and sense around me—what I feel in the currents, the electric stuff of the culture. I think these are American forces and energies. And they belong to our time." In a rich fictional oeuvre whose characters inhabit the microcosms of advertising, sports, pop music, science, espionage, academe, and waste management, among others, DeLillo sketches vast, arcane patterns that tantalize with the promise of deciphering America in the era following World War II.

"The world is full of abandoned meanings," contends Jack Gladney, narrator of *White Noise* (1985). "In the commonplace I find unexpected themes and intensities." DeLillo's are commonplace books, texts that invite intimacy with the detritus of popular culture and that are created in a quest for what the author once called, in a 1988 *Rolling Stone* interview, "radiance in dailiness." In the Gladney household, which contains a litter of half siblings, offspring thrown together from several marriages by Jack and his third wife, Babette, DeLillo records the instability of the contemporary family. He casts a stranger's eye on ordinary consumer culture, defamiliarizing its rituals of shopping and eating. Elsewhere, the rites of sports, business, and academic life are rendered absurd by that same outsider's gaze. For some authors, particularly those Latin American novelists who have been called magical realists, such as Isabel Allende, Julio Cortázar, Mario Vargas Llosa, and Gabriel García Márquez, discovering luminosity in everyday life induces awe. But for DeLillo, the suggestion of divinity in a supermarket aisle is comically uncanny. The humor in his fictions is unsettling, and sober laughter is an understandable reaction to disruptions that defeat understanding.

"To be understood is faintly embarrassing," declares a character in *Ratner's Star* (1976):

> What you want to express is the violence of your desire not to be read. The friction of audiences is what drives writers crazy. These people are going to read what you write. The more they understand, the crazier you get. You can't let them know what you're writing about. Once they know, you're finished.

Although DeLillo himself is not quite as wary of his reader, he is, for all his immersion in the stuff of mass culture, a difficult author, in print and in person. Avoiding the conventional pleasures of linear plot, driven more by language and theme than coherent, stable characters, his dark, elliptical fictions are a challenge to the casual reader. And DeLillo himself is notoriously elusive, extremely reluctant to grant interviews, write blurbs, give readings, conduct workshops, and in general engage in most of the promotional activities expected of successful authors at the turn of the twenty-first century. Whereas much contemporary American writing is overtly confessional, DeLillo refrained from mining materials from his own Bronx childhood until the eleventh novel published under his name, *Underworld* (1997), when he invented a raffish childhood in the Bronx for Nick Shay (né Nicholas Costanza).

Although not as reclusive as J. D. Salinger, Thomas Pynchon (who breached his own scrupulous privacy to contribute a blurb to the cover of DeLillo's 1991 novel, *Mao II*), and Cormac McCarthy, DeLillo, whose stories often expose the treacherous machinery of publicity, has become famous for evading the trappings of fame. He even published one novel, *Amazons: An Intimate Memoir by the First Woman to Play in the National Hockey League* (1980), pseudonymously, as Cleo Birdwell. "Fame and secrecy are the high and low ends of the same fascination, the static cackle of some libidinous thing in the world," notes DeLillo's J. Edgar Hoover, who in *Underworld* savors the secret files he keeps on celebrities. If so, Greta Garbo, declaring ostentatiously that she wants to be alone, is a kindred spirit to Madonna, voracious for publicity. Both strategies are a tribute to the power of mediated images.

Bill Gray, the novelist at the center of *Mao II,* lives in shielded seclusion, having vanished from public view more than twenty-three years earlier, when he began writing the novel that he refuses to publish. Perhaps it is necessary for this fictional author, who was born Willard Skansey, to blanch the color out of himself, to become "Gray," in order to write iridescent prose. In DeLillo's first novel, *Americana* (1971), a would-be writer named Bobby Brand, who dreams of "writing the novel that would detonate in the gut of America like a fiery bacterial bombshell," also aims to make himself "colorless." In *Libra* (1988), DeLillo's Lee Harvey Oswald convinces himself that "the only safety was in facelessness." In *Great Jones Street* (1973), Bucky Wunderlick, once the world's most famous rock star, retreats from clamorous public appearances to anonymous, ascetic solitude in a bare New York apartment. And his impulse toward self-extinction seems akin to three-hundred-pound Anatole Bloomberg's attempt in *End Zone* (1972) both to shrink and to "unjew" himself by entering Logos College in gentile West Texas. "True greatness always involves a period of complete withdrawal," declares Chester Greylag Dent, the "Supreme Abstract Commander" in *Ratner's Star.* Possibly undermining his own standards, DeLillo signed a lucrative contract with Charles Scribner's Sons for publication of *Underworld* that obligated him to assist in the book's promotion; nevertheless, he remained uneasy when interest in the fiction was deflected to interest in its author. DeLillo does not encourage biographical investigation.

CAREER

Donald Richard DeLillo was born on November 20, 1936, in the New York City borough of the Bronx, the son of Catholic immigrants from Italy. The family lived briefly in Pottsville, Pennsylvania, but DeLillo spent most of his childhood in the Arthur Avenue section of the Bronx. He graduated from Cardinal Hayes High School, a neighborhood parochial school, in 1954 and received a bachelor's degree in communication arts from Fordham University, a Catholic institution, in 1958. DeLillo has attributed some of his literary preoccupation with asceticism and apocalypse to his religious background in general and to his Jesuit education in particular, remarking in the *New York Times Magazine* in 1991: "I think there's a sense of last things in my work that probably comes from a Catholic childhood."

Following his graduation from Fordham, DeLillo worked as a copywriter for the Ogilvy and Mather advertising agency in Manhattan. It was in 1960, during his stint in advertising, that his first published short story, "The River Jordan," appeared in *Epoch,* the literary magazine of Cornell University. Others followed in *Epoch* and two other small academic periodicals, *Carolina Quarterly* and *Kenyon Review.* In 1964 DeLillo resigned from his advertising job and became a full-time writer, supporting himself with freelance nonfiction commissions. In 1966 he began work on *Americana,* a novel that was completed and published five years later. The story of David Bell, a twenty-eight-year-old network television executive who leaves his job after seven years to travel across the United States in a red Mustang convertible, making a film about America, *Americana* drew indirectly from DeLillo's experience in advertising and directly from his aspirations to create an encyclopedic work that would embody the enormity of the country. As he explained in 1993 in *Paris Review:* "It's no accident that my first novel was called *Americana.* This was a private declaration of independence, a statement of my intention to use the whole picture, the whole culture. America was and is the immigrant's dream, and as the son of two immigrants I was attracted by the sense of possibility that had drawn my grandparents and parents." Although it was favorably, even enthusiastically, reviewed, the book's reception did not match its immense ambition. Although his second novel, *End Zone,* the story of a ragtag group of athletes assembled to play football at a college in West Texas, eventually became a standard of American sports fic-

tion, neither it nor his third novel, *Great Jones Street,* initially gained a wide following. Until 1985 DeLillo, like his contemporaries James McElroy and William Gaddis, remained the object of a small but devoted cult of readers.

In 1975 DeLillo married Barbara Bennett, a banker who later turned to landscape design. When she was assigned to the Toronto office of Citibank, the couple moved to Canada for a year. *Ratner's Star,* a dauntingly erudite science fiction novel about the adventures of Billy Twillig, a fourteen-year-old mathematics prodigy, at a think tank called Field Experiment Number One, appeared in 1976. *Players,* an espionage novel about a Wall Street broker, Lyle Wynant, who becomes a double agent for the FBI and a group of terrorists plotting to blow up the New York Stock Exchange, followed in 1977. *Running Dog,* another novel about covert operations, this time about a CIA mole, Glen Selvy, who works both on the staff of a United States senator and as a procurer of pornography, appeared in 1978. In 1979 DeLillo was awarded a Guggenheim Fellowship; he used the grant money to live in Greece and travel from there to the Middle East and India, doing research for a new book, *The Names.* The story of an American expatriate, James Axton, a risk analyst for a multinational corporation who becomes intrigued by a series of mysterious ritual murders throughout the region, *The Names* was published in 1982. In that year DeLillo and his wife returned to the United States, moving to a suburb just north of New York City.

With an award in literature from the American Academy of Arts and Letters in 1984, DeLillo began to receive wider recognition, but the major breakthrough in the public's awareness of his work came with *White Noise* in 1985. A dark comedy about Jack Gladney, a professor of Hitler Studies at fictional College-on-the-Hill, and his patchwork family, *White Noise* received the American Book Award for fiction and extensive journalistic and scholarly attention. In 1998 it was reissued by Viking in a critical edition designed for classroom use. DeLillo's position in contemporary American literature was consolidated by the 1988 publication of *Libra,* a speculative fiction about the life of Lee Harvey Oswald, who happened to have grown up a few blocks away from DeLillo in the Bronx, although the two apparently never met. A finalist for the National Book Award and the winner of the *Irish Times*–Aer Lingus International Fiction Prize, *Libra,* which had its origins in a nonfiction piece on the Kennedy assassination that DeLillo wrote for *Rolling Stone* in 1983, was chosen as a main selection by the Book-of-the-Month Club. It also became the first DeLillo book to reach the *New York Times* best-seller list.

Although his greatest distinction is as a novelist, DeLillo was writing a number of plays that were produced or published during this time. *The Engineer of Moonlight,* a two-act drama about an aging mathematician that offers echoes of the dangers of abstraction found in *Ratner's Star,* was published in 1979. *The Day Room,* an absurdist metadrama set in a bizarre hospital in which it is impossible to distinguish the doctors from the patients, was first performed in 1986 and published in 1987. *Valparaiso: A Play in Two Acts,* which is about a man who sets out on a business trip to Indiana but ends up in Chile, was performed and published in 1999.

In 1989, when the Iranian leader Ayatollah Khomeini issued a *fatwa,* an Islamic decree, condemning the writer Salman Rushdie to death for his novel *The Satanic Verses,* DeLillo took an uncharacteristically public stand against the threat. And he began conceiving *Mao II,* a book that deals in part with the relationship between novelists and terrorists. With fellow novelist Paul Auster, he later issued a pamphlet in defense of Rushdie (1994). Published in 1991, *Mao II* received the PEN/Faulkner Award for Fiction. In 1992 *Harper's* magazine published a DeLillo no-

vella, *Pafko at the Wall,* an account of the drama in the stands during the legendary 1951 playoff game between the Brooklyn Dodgers and the New York Giants that concluded with a home run hit by the Giants' Bobby Thomson. That novella became the dazzling opening chapter of *Underworld,* which proceeds to follow the fate of the game-winning ball and of American culture during the next four decades. A finalist for both the National Book Award and the National Book Critics Circle Award and a main selection of the Book-of-the-Month Club, the 827-page *Underworld,* at the close of the twentieth century, was DeLillo's biggest book and his greatest critical and commercial success. In 1999 he became the first American to win the Jerusalem Prize, bestowed biennially on a leading international literary figure.

REPRESENTING THE ABSURD

In an oft-quoted essay, "Writing American Fiction," Philip Roth bemoans the predicament of contemporary novelists who are compelled to compete with a reality that is so grotesque it exceeds their most extravagant gifts of invention: "It stupefies, it sickens, it infuriates, and finally it is even a kind of embarrassment to one's meager imagination." Since 1960, when Roth published his essay and DeLillo was breaking into print with his first short story, "The River Jordan," reality—or at least the version of it that is mediated by electronic devices—seems to have grown even more fantastic. A writer could not contrive a plot more preposterous than Watergate, the O. J. Simpson trial, or the Monica Lewinsky scandal. And with the marginalization of print culture, writing has come to seem less critical to our collective task of making sense. "We knew that nothing is too absurd to happen in America," says Gary Harkness, the brooding running back who narrates *End Zone.* Rather than compete with the absurdities of contemporary society, DeLillo shifts his strategy to representing the absurdity of representing the absurd. The life of Lee Harvey Oswald, as portrayed in *Libra,* is a skein of implausible accidents and coincidences, and in *Underworld* as in life, the Soviets detonate their first atomic bomb on October 3, 1951, just as slugger Bobby Thomson hits the explosive "shot heard round the world." DeLillo draws on and competes with a world of improbable gestures. One of his fundamental preoccupations is with the ways in which fiction, as a representation of contemporary realities, is doomed to distortion and inadequacy.

In *Mao II,* when fundamentalist guerrillas hold a Western poet hostage in Beirut, Bill Gray, a famous novelist with a famous case of writer's block, resolves to redeem his unproductive life by offering himself in exchange. Gray, who used to be Willard Skansey before submerging his public identity entirely in his writing, observes that writers and terrorists are locked in a zero-sum game: "What terrorists gain, novelists lose. The degree to which they influence mass consciousness is the extent of our decline as shapers of sensibility and thought. The danger they represent equals our own failure to be dangerous." In DeLillo's novel the novelist loses. "Years ago I used to think it was possible for a novelist to alter the inner life of the culture," notes Gray elsewhere. "Now bomb-makers and gunmen have taken that territory. They make raids on human consciousness. What writers used to do before we were all incorporated." DeLillo's postmodernist fiction is reduced to recording its inability to make raids on human consciousness, though that recognition can in itself profoundly alter the inner life of the culture.

In *Libra,* Nicholas Branch, a retired CIA officer, has been commissioned by the agency to write a confidential, definitive report on the assassination of John F. Kennedy. Placed in a sealed room with thousands of documents and relics, the prospective author reels before the impossible task of imposing a coherent narrative on all the data before him:

> Everything belongs, everything adheres, the mutter of obscure witnesses, the photos of illegible documents and odd sad personal debris, things gathered up at a dying—old shoes, pajama tops, letters from Russia. It is all one thing, a ruined city of trivia where people feel real pain. This is the Joycean Book of America, remember—the novel in which nothing is left out.

From *Americana* onward, DeLillo, too, has been attempting to write the all-encompassing Joycean Book of America, while recognizing that America defeats the efforts of its authors. Although the epic *Underworld* is the most crammed of DeLillo's chambers, all of his works together constitute an archive of America in the last half of the twentieth century that resists attempts at cataloging.

THE THEME OF DEATH

"All plots tend to move in one direction," Jack Gladney tells his wife, Babette, a woman who is paralyzed by the fear of death. *White Noise,* the novel in which they appear, itself moves inexorably toward Gladney's murderous confrontation with a man named Mr. Gray who, in exchange for sex, has been supplying Babette with Dylar, a drug that stifles the fear of death. If death is the ultimate closure, conventional plots are deadly; they are fables of mortality. Readers of *Libra* know in advance that a story about the confluence of John F. Kennedy, Lee Harvey Oswald, and Jack Ruby is, inevitably, going to conclude with the deaths of all three. And in this particular story, when Win Everett, a veteran intelligence officer intent on sabotaging American policy toward Castro's Cuba, sets in motion a clandestine operation deploying Oswald as a failed assassin, the plot takes on a life—and death—of its own. "Plots carry their own logic," reflects Everett, echoing Gladney:

> There is a tendency of plots to move toward death. He believed that the idea of death is woven into the nature of every plot. A narrative plot no less than a conspiracy of armed men. The tighter the plot of a story, the more likely it will come to death.

DeLillo, who claims that his inspiration comes more directly from jazz, European film, and abstract expressionist painting than other novels, resists traditional linear narratives, as if imposing a definitive beginning, middle, and end on his fiction would kill it. His original working title for *White Noise* was *The American Book of the Dead.* And it—like *Death Is Just Around the Corner,* the title of a radio program in *Americana*—could double as the title for most of DeLillo's other works, preoccupied as they are with individual extinction and global catastrophe.

DeLillo came of age during the cold war, an era of potentially deadly rivalry between two nuclear powers that dominated the planet and possessed the technological prowess to destroy it. *Libra,* whose title is derived from the astrological sign of balance and Lee Harvey Oswald's oscillation between East and West, is certainly focused on the symmetries of Moscow and Washington poised for mutual destruction. And so is the espionage that drives *Running Dog* and *Players.* But even *Mao II* and *Underworld,* novels that DeLillo published after 1989, when the Berlin Wall fell and the cold war in effect ended, evoke the period when two hostile superpowers were plotting the possibility of an end to the universal narrative. In *End Zone* Gary Harkness takes a course in "modes of disaster technology," and he derives perverse pleasure from reading about the prospects for thermonuclear conflict:

> I liked reading about the deaths of tens of millions of people. I liked dwelling on the destruction of great cities. Five to twenty million dead. Fifty to a hundred million dead. Ninety percent population loss. Seattle wiped out by mistake. Moscow demolished. Airbursts over every SAC base in Europe. I liked to think of huge buildings toppling, of firestorms, of bridges collapsing, survivors roaming the charred countryside. Carbon 14 and strontium 90. Escalation ladder and subscrisis situation. Titan, Spartan, Poseidon. People burned and unable to breathe. People being evacuated from doomed cities. People diseased and starving. Two hundred thousand bodies decomposing on the roads outside Chicago.

DeLillo's apocalyptic fiction is haunted—and oddly animated—by the post-Hiroshima realization that for the first time in history human beings have the ability to annihilate life on earth.

In the exquisitely orchestrated opening chapter of *Underworld,* a torrent of improvised confetti descends on the Polo Grounds as the Giants clinch the pennant. Among those showered by discarded scraps of paper is J. Edgar Hoover, who happens to be present for the game, accompanied by Jackie Gleason, Toots Shor, and Frank Sinatra. Two pages ripped from the current issue of *Life* magazine cling to the shoulders of the FBI director; peeling them off, he is fascinated by the image pictured there: "It is a color reproduction of a painting crowded with medieval figures who are dying or dead—a landscape of visionary havoc and ruin." It is, Hoover learns, a work by the sixteenth-century Flemish master Pieter Brueghel the Elder called *The Triumph of Death,* but it is a title that could as well apply to DeLillo's novel, stalked by the specters of nuclear annihilation, the AIDS pandemic, and random serial murder— or even his entire corpus, as anxious as Babette Gladney to find a literary Dylar to overcome the fear of death.

During the years that followed the Cuban Missile Crisis, when the world teetered on the brink of a cataclysmic war, DeLillo (who evokes that nuclear confrontation in both *Libra* and *Underworld*) was, like Brueghel, painting strangely alluring, visionary landscapes of havoc and ruin. But it is not only the danger of nuclear holocaust that provokes apocalyptic dread and rapture in DeLillo's fiction. Other perils during the second half of the twentieth century—the accelerated pace of technological enterprise, global warming, eradication of the ozone layer, and the greenhouse effect, among other consequences of unchecked industrial development—also threatened the viability of the earth as human habitat.

In the second section of *White Noise,* an "airborne toxic event" descends on the region and forces mass evacuation of Blacksmith, the Gladneys' hometown; this chemical plague is another symptom of the millennialist, end-of-life zeitgeist that DeLillo's works articulate. When, on December 3, 1984, toxic gas leaked from a Union Carbide insecticide plant in Bhopal, India, killing more than two thousand in the worst industrial chemical accident in history, the timing, just one month before the publication of *White Noise,* seemed like the kind of grotesque coincidence that only DeLillo might have invented. By immersing himself in the worst atrocities of the century, as a specialist in the discipline called Hitler Studies, Jack Gladney cauterizes himself against the fear of death. "Death was strictly a professional matter here," notes the professor about a lecture he delivers. "I was comfortable with it, I was on top of it." Other people in Gladney's life seem similarly saturated in death. His fourteen-year-old son, Heinrich, revels in the spectacle of automobile accidents. His colleague Murray Jay Siskind, a scholar of Elvis Presley, prefers American movies over foreign ones because of their depiction of violent highway smashups: "It is a high-spirited moment like old-fashioned stunt flying, walking on wings. The people who stage these crashes are able to capture a lightheartedness, a carefree enjoyment that car crashes in foreign movies can never approach," says Siskind. Depicting those moviemakers and other connoisseurs of doom, DeLillo is himself a comic dys-topian, intent on making mirth out of images of apocalyptic horror.

THE THEME OF AUTHENTICITY

Mao II derives its title from a famous Andy Warhol serigraph of Mao Tse-tung; in the novel, the serigraph is purchased by Bill Gray's assistant, Scott Martineau. Like similarly mass-produced Warhol prints of Jacqueline Kennedy, Marilyn Monroe, and Elvis Presley, this appropriated image of the Chinese leader transforms a unique human being into a duplicable commodity. In the culture of the photocopy, Mao I is supplanted by Mao II, Mao III, Mao IV, and an endless supply of further facsimiles. Perhaps it is more accurate to say that the distinction between original and facsimile has lost its significance; there is no Mao I in the world that DeLillo depicts. As David Bell remarks in *Americana,* "one thinks of an image made in the image and likeness of images."

In an influential 1935 essay called "The Work of Art in the Age of Mechanical Reproduction," the German philosopher Walter Benjamin observed that original artifacts manifest an "aura," an emanation we sense in the physical presence of an object that is unique, that occupies specific coordinates in space and time. The replicas that are increasingly available through the technologies of photography, cinematography, and audio and video recording lack aura. Whereas Benjamin hails the democratization of cultural experience facilitated by mechanical reproduction, when images are no longer the exclusive possession of wealthy patrons, DeLillo mocks a world of counterfeits, in which nothing can be said to exist except in replica. In *White Noise,* when the refugees from the "airborne toxic event" realize that their ordeal is not being covered by television camera crews, they are sorely disappointed, and the experience seems less real than the emergency rehearsals engineered by a state agency called

SIMUVAC, which uses the actual disaster as an occasion to practice its simulated evacuations. Unless an image is broadcast, and thereby duplicated in living rooms throughout the nation, it lacks validation. In the words of another great German philosopher, Friedrich Nietzsche, "einmal ist keinmal" (once is never).

That nothing is singular is the postmodern condition, as defined by Jean Baudrillard, the French cultural theorist. In contemporary society, Baudrillard contends, the real and that which represents the real have been inverted; simulacra take precedence over originals, if such can be said even to exist. DeLillo, who began his career in advertising, again and again presents a world saturated with mediated images, in which mimesis becomes the dominant or even only reality. Mr. Gray, the object of Jack Gladney's quest for relief from the dread of death, turns out to be addicted to the flow of visual phenomena across his TV screen, as is Lyle Wynant, the stock broker–terrorist in *Players.* In *Mao II,* Brita Nilsson, an internationally active photographer, recalls meeting an editor in Chile who was sent to prison because his magazine published caricatures of the country's military dictator, General Augusto Pinochet. "The charge was assassinating the image of the general," she explains.

In *Libra* Lee Harvey Oswald is captured in a Dallas movie theater, amid flickering images of Van Heflin in combat in the Philippines in *Cry of Battle*; Oswald, whose presence in Dealey Plaza on the day the presidential motorcade passes through is motivated by TV images of JFK, is himself immediately translated into a figure on newsreels and radio and TV broadcasts. "Everybody knew who he was now. This charged him with strength"; approaching death, Oswald derives life from the propagation of the electronic versions of himself. He recirculates throughout the culture in endless replays of the Zapruder home-movie footage of the assassination and of his own execution by Jack Ruby. Film figures prominently in several of the DeLillo novels,

starting with *Americana,* where David Bell undertakes his cross-country journey in order to film it. *Players* begins with a prologue, titled "The Movie," that situates the characters in an airplane watching a film before the body of the novel begins. *Running Dog* features a home movie of Adolf Hitler, in his final Berlin bunker, impersonating Charles Chaplin. *Underworld* derives its name in part from the title of an imaginary film by Sergei Eisenstein. In each of these cases, DeLillo emphasizes the mediated lives of the movie viewers in knowing English prose that further mediates its readers.

Early in *White Noise,* Jack Gladney drives Murray Jay Siskind to an attraction located about twenty miles from their town, called "THE MOST PHOTOGRAPHED BARN IN AMERICA." Abundant publicity about the structure has rendered the site itself invisible. "Once you've seen the signs about the barn," says Siskind, "it becomes impossible to see the barn." The building is utterly undistinguished, insignificant in itself except as the occasion for thousands of tourists to set up their cameras in front of it, because thousands of other tourists have also set up their cameras in front of it. "They are taking pictures of taking pictures," observes Siskind about the barn, a ghostly monument to the age of exponential simulacra. In *Underworld,* where Brian Glassic's daughter, Brittany, participates in "Apartheid Simulation Day" at her school, a sociopath referred to as "The Texas Highway Killer" seems to exist in and for his TV coverage, which is continuous and repetitive. Like *Underworld* itself, the novel in which he appears, Nick Shay, a waste management specialist, ponders the archaeology of garbage, how civilizations are displaced by their own factitious trash.

The celebrities who flit through the pages of DeLillo's novels—historical figures such as Lenny Bruce (*Underworld*), Lee Harvey Oswald (*Libra*), and Sun Myung Moon (*Mao II*); and fictional notables such as Bill Gray (*Mao II*), Bucky Wunderlich (*Great Jones Street*), and Klara Sax

(*Underworld*)—are simulated beings, functions of mechanical reproduction. A prominent piece in *Time* magazine promotes Klara Sax, the environmental artist who reappropriates mothballed B-52 bombers into a sculptural installation in the southwestern desert. And each of the others is likewise seized and recycled, again and again, through the machinery of publicity.

Though Bill Gray has attempted to elude the consequences of his own literary renown, becoming ever more famous for his rejection of celebrity, he eventually invites noted photographer Brita Nilsson to capture and propagate his image. Posing in front of her camera, he realizes that she is altering something fundamental about his identity:

> I've become someone's material. Yours, Brita. There's the life and there's the consumer event. Everything around us tends to channel our lives toward some final reality in print or on film. . . . Everything seeks its own heightened version. Or put it this way. Nothing happens until it's consumed.

Much of *Underworld* is organized around the quest to achieve a consumer event: purchase of a baseball. The dramatic victory of the Giants over the Dodgers in the 1951 playoffs has been reduced to a commodity, the home run ball that Bobby Thomson hit to end the game, but there is no certainty that the spherical object offered for sale for $34,500 by Marvin Lundy, a reclusive vendor of baseball memorabilia, is any more authentic than dozens of other ersatz versions. Not lost on DeLillo is the further irony that his critique of consumer culture is packaged in a printed book, mass-produced for rapid sale.

THE CROWD VERSUS THE INDIVIDUAL

Mao II begins with a kind of parody of unrestrained duplication. Some 6,500 couples, dressed identically—men in blue suits, women in lace-and-satin gowns—and smiling uniformly, are assembled on the field of Yankee Stadium for a mass wedding conducted by the Reverend Sun Myung Moon. Sitting in the stands, Rodge Janney focuses his binoculars on one bride in particular, his daughter, Karen, who has chosen to surrender her individuality by marrying Kim Jo Pak, a Korean who cannot speak English and whom she barely knows. Watching Karen and the 12,999 other new spouses submerge themselves in the nubile mass, Rodge broods over this brave new world of multiple versions of a single identity:

> All things, the sum of the knowable, everything true, it all comes down to a few simple formulas copied and memorized and passed on. And here is the drama of mechanical routine played out with living figures. It knocks him back in awe, the loss of scale and intimacy, the way love and sex are multiplied out, the numbers and shaped crowd. This really scares him, a mass of people turned into a sculptured object.

Karen's yearning to make herself part of a vast, collective pattern is shared by many other DeLillo characters, just as other characters—and the reader—are teased by the challenge of deciphering the pattern. The disturbing spectacle of throngs inspires some of DeLillo's most lyrical prose, as if the very process of writing imaginative prose were a guerrilla action aimed at keeping crowds at bay. At the beginning of *Underworld*—which, like *Libra,* opens at a sports facility, Yankee Stadium rather than the Polo Grounds—Cotter Martin, a street-smart young black, skips school to see the National League playoff:

> This is just a kid with a local yearning but he is part of an assembling crowd, anonymous thousands off the buses and trains, people in narrow columns tramping over the swing bridge above the river, and even they are not a migration or a revolution, some vast shaking of the soul, they bring with them the body heat of a great city and their own small rev-

eries and desperations, the unseen something that haunts the day—men in fedoras and sailors on shore leave, the stray tumble of their thoughts going to a game.

If, as we are told in *Underworld,* "Longing on a large scale is what makes history," attentiveness to the degrees within that large scale is what makes DeLillo's fiction distinctive.

In the epigraph to *Libra,* taken from an actual letter to his brother, Oswald declares: "Happiness is not based on oneself, it does not consist of a small home, of taking and getting. Happiness is taking part in the struggle, where there is no borderline between one's own personal world, and the world in general." In another example of the paradox of reclusive celebrity, the urge toward anonymity is a different manifestation of the desire to be exceptional; and of all of DeLillo's characters, Oswald, the nondescript loner, is the most successful at both submerging himself in history and standing out from it. Confined to a Marine brig in South Korea, he ruminates:

> Maybe what has to happen is that the individual must allow himself to be swept along, must find himself in the stream of no-choice, the single direction. This is what makes things inevitable. You use the restrictions and penalties they invent to make yourself stronger. History means to merge. The purpose of history is to climb out of your own skin.

And the purpose of fiction is to reassert the self, to step back from history and make fine distinctions. If, as he says in *Mao II,* "the future belongs to crowds," DeLillo's novels belong to those readers who, in the here and now, refuse to relinquish individual sensibilities.

LANGUAGE

In the 1993 *Paris Review* interview, DeLillo addresses the contention that his novels are gloomy and the implicit premise that it is the responsi-

bility of the novelist to provide solace for a troubling world. Insisting on the primacy of language in the shape that writing takes, DeLillo calls attention to the nuances of style and structure that some critics, intent on reading him exclusively for his somber themes, neglect:

> I don't offer comforts except those that lurk in comedy and in structure and in language, and the comedy is probably not all that soothing. But before everything, there's language. Before history and politics, there's language. And it's language, the sheer pleasure of making it and bending it and seeing it form on the page and hearing it whistle in my head—this is the thing that makes my work go.

DeLillo stands out from other contemporaries who depict a similar landscape by his playful deployment of and anxious attentiveness to the English language—from the depersonalized jargon of bureaucracy in *White Noise* and of football in *End Zone* to the Italian-inflected street patois of immigrants and their children in the final section of *Underworld.* The story of *End Zone* takes place in an institution in West Texas called Logos College, and there is a sense in which *logos*—the word—is the inspiration and not just the medium for all of DeLillo's work. The word is very often even the engine of the plot. In *The Names,* whose title testifies to the arcane power of words, a homicidal cult (whose password is: "How many languages do you speak?") allows language—a congruence of initial letters in personal and place names—to determine the location and victim of each of its operations. Since Michaelis Kalliambetsos is killed in Mikro Kamini and Hamir Mazmudar in Hawa Mandir, James Axton is in mortal danger while in Jebel Amman. Such deadly verbal games—like the ball games in *End Zone* and *Underworld* and the mathematical puzzles in *Ratner's Star*—are a bid to contain and explain chaos.

It is a telling paradox that the late founder of Logos College, Tom Wade, was mute, and that a school named for the word offers a course in the untellable, in which students are required to memorize and recite long poems in a language they do not understand. When he arrives at Logos from upstate New York, narrator Gary Harkness is disturbed by the menacing silence of the bare West Texas terrain:

> It hung over the land and drifted across the long plains. It was out there with the soft black insects beyond the last line of buildings, beyond the prefabs and the Quonset hut and the ROTC barracks. Day after day my eyes scanned in all directions a stunned earth, unchangingly dull, a land silenced by its own beginnings in the roaring heat, born dead, flat stones burying the memory. I felt threatened by the silence.

The fact that it can inspire such lyricism in Harkness demonstrates that silence is not only the negation of language but also its necessary context. At the conclusion of *Great Jones Street,* sinister conspirators inject Bucky Wunderlick with a drug that neutralizes the sector of the brain that processes and generates speech. But the novel's final pages recount how, one by one, words—and the world—begin to return, as Wunderlick is slowly restored to "the mad weather of language" in which the reader lives. Each of DeLillo's verbally ingenious fictions is explicitly a victory over the stubborn muteness of the nonhuman.

Harkness has come to Logos in order to play football, and much of the sport is conceived of as shaped by language—the vapid motto that their martinet coach, Emmett Creed, uses to motivate players ("It's only a game but it's the only game"), the insults, imprecations, and incantations employed by players ("Nigger kike faggot"), and the names of plays ("Middle-sift-W, alph-set, lemmy-2") that dictate action on the field. Though he admits to knowing nothing about football, Wally Pippich, Logos College's sports information director, promotes the team by coining catchy nicknames, phrases, and slogans. But it is Coach Creed who rules absolutely, and he derives his authority from his control of words.

"This was his power," observes Harkness, "to deny us the words we needed. He was the maker of plays, the name-giver."

According to Harkness, football "is the one sport guided by language, by the word signal, the snap number, the color code, the play name." Like the novel itself, football is a matter of negotiating a linguistic system. In his own interpolation, DeLillo explains that in writing about football in *End Zone* he has rendered it as verbal play:

> The author, always somewhat corrupt in his inventions and vanities, has tried to reduce the content to basic units of language and action. . . . Much of the appeal of sport derives from its dependence on elegant gibberish. And of course it remains the author's permanent duty to unbox the lexicon for all eyes to see—a cryptic ticking mechanism in search of a revolution.

The same might be said about any of the other subjects that DeLillo has tackled throughout his writing career. It is worth noting particularly how, in *Underworld,* baseball is manifestly another sport guided by language. Russ Hodges, the play-by-play announcer for the New York Giants, recalls his work of simulation, the years he spent sitting in a radio studio re-creating major league games from information coming off a teletype:

> Somebody hands you a piece of paper filled with letters and numbers and you have to make a ball game out of it. You create the weather, flesh out the players, you make them sweat and grouse and hitch up their pants, and it is remarkable, thinks Russ, how much earthly disturbance, how much summer and dust the mind can manage to order up from a single Latin letter lying flat.

DeLillo constructs his universe out of just such bits of language, even as the deconstruction of the elegant gibberish—the white noise—that defines our lives has been the continuing project of his texts.

Consider the absurdist drama *Valparaiso,* in which Michael Majeski's destination is determined by the linguistic accident of geographical homonymy; intending to visit Valparaiso, Indiana, he ends up in Florida and Chile as well—and achieves world fame—because in those locations, too, are cities by that name. In *White Noise,* Jack Gladney provides a similarly comic example of how language both facilitates and constrains experience. Though he is a professor of Hitler Studies, Gladney is embarrassed enough over his inability to speak the language of the Nazi führer that he takes private lessons in German. As host of a conference in his field held at the College-on-the-Hill, Gladney at first officially welcomes the other scholars in a halting, inexpressive version of the language and then retreats to the safety of his office, afraid to attempt any further communication in German.

Neither does Billy Mast know German, but in *End Zone* the football player relieves his anxieties over the violent game by reciting German words whose meaning he does not understand. What is for him gibberish has the effect of a team prayer. It serves the same function as the nonsense syllables "pee-pee-maw-maw" (in *Great Jones Street*), to which the prolific musician Bucky Wunderlick has reduced his lyrics, and the trade name "Toyota Celica," which Jack Gladney's young daughter Steffie repeats in her sleep as "part of a verbal spell or ecstatic chant." Beneath a conscious level, the child has appropriated the catchwords of consumer culture, its white noise, as a kind of verbal talisman against her fears of environmental disasters and other, unnamed terrors. This is language that consoles and protects—both despite and because of the fact that it ceases to signify. It is the kind of rapture induced by transcending language that Bucky Wunderlick experiences when listening to that "music of a dead universe" that is the telephone dial tone: "Source of pleasure and fear never before explored. It was always the same, silence endowed with acoustical properties." It is what the adolescent Gary Harkness experienced when staring at the banal aphorism "When the Going Gets Tough the Tough Get Going," which his father had posted on his bedroom wall:

> The sentiment of course had small appeal but it seemed that beauty flew from the words themselves, the letters, consonants swallowing vowels, aggression and tenderness, a semi-self-re-creation from line to line, word to word, letter to letter. All meaning faded. The words became pictures. It was a sinister thing to discover at such an age, that words can escape their meanings. A strange beauty that sign began to express.

It is a signature moment in DeLillo's fiction, when a strange beauty is born through language deployed to transcend the merely linguistic.

That moment echoes in the epiphany that Jack Gladney experiences early in *White Noise* when, walking through a supermarket, he senses some ultimate meaning just beyond the conventional sounds of commercial clamor:

> I realized the place was awash in noise. The toneless systems, the jangle and skid of carts, the loudspeaker and coffee-making machines, the cries of children. And over it all, or under it all, a dull and unlocatable roar, as of some form of swarming life just outside the range of human apprehension.

David Ferrie, too, in *Libra,* claims intimations of a truth just beyond language, beyond both what has been told and what can be told. As he tells Oswald: "There's always more to it. Something we don't know about. Truth isn't what we know or feel. It's the thing that waits just beyond." Truth is what lies beyond the numerical language that mathematicians participating in the Logicon Project in *Ratner's Star* rely upon but which they realize is irremediably flawed: "They'd had to confront the terror of the irrational, this everlasting slit in the divinity of whole numbers." DeLillo's fiction is veritably gnostic in its premise that truth is ineffable and in its use of words to dramatize their own inadequacy.

As if respecting the reticence of metaphysical mysteries, the rootless international businessmen who wander through *The Names* find elemental reassurance in the fact that they do not understand the babel of ambient tongues, a kind of Levantine white noise, spoken in the Mediterranean and Asian countries through which they travel. The novel concludes with a flashback to archaeologist Owen Brademas's childhood in the Midwest. Both disturbed and intrigued by a rapturous church service, in which the congregants are given to ecstatic utterance, Brademas is described as "tongue tied" over the phenomenon of speaking in tongues. "The gift was not his, the whole language of the spirit which was greater than Latin or French was not to be seized in his pityfull mouth"—the odd spelling of "pitiful" simulating the boy's awkwardness. In the final sentence of *The Names,* young Brademas runs outside the church into the rain, into "the nightmare of real things, the fallen wonder of the world," forced, like all flawed authors and readers, to make do with words inadequate for the language of the spirit.

PATTERNS

DeLillo concludes David Bell's cross-country journey and his own first novel, *Americana,* with a drive through downtown Dallas, past the Texas Book Depository, Dealey Plaza, and Parkland Hospital. The three sites have been familiar landmarks since John F. Kennedy was shot on November 22, 1963. DeLillo was still working for an advertising agency in New York at that time, and in a sense all of his subsequent books are a gloss on the lingering enigma of the national trauma of presidential assassination. *Libra* is an explicit attempt to make sense of the events; his other works aim indirectly at that same goal, each a parable of frustration in the quest for coherence.

In *Underworld* Marvin Lundy pores through a vast array of evidence to ascertain which was the authentic baseball hit by Bobby Thomson to clinch the pennant for the Giants in 1951. "I looked at a million photographs," he tells Brian Glassic, "because this is the dot theory of reality, that all knowledge is available if you analyze the dots." Like a pointillist painter, DeLillo constructs his elaborate fictions less in terms of straight lines stretching from beginning to middle to end than as isolated dots dependent on an active reader for integration into a complete, coherent design. Yet this "figure in the carpet," to use one of Henry James's metaphors, remains elusive, if not illusory, a tantalizing possibility that seems to linger just beyond the grasp of characters and readers.

Underworld, for example, is constructed out of several overlapping fields of action. Like an old movie plot tied together by the penny, violin, or pistol that passes through very different hands, *Underworld* finds such unity as it has in the very different people who have touched or been touched by the Thomson baseball. Not least among them is Nick Shay, who in 1951 was a young Bronx thug. At seventeen Nick had a brief dalliance with the wife of his high school physics teacher, thirty-two-year-old Klara Sax, now a renowned artist creating environmental installations in the desert by covering 230 abandoned military planes with paint. Nick's life was profoundly altered when his father, a minor Mafioso, walked out for cigarettes and never returned; so too was he changed when he himself slew a poolhall hustler with a gun that the hustler had handed to him with assurances that it was not loaded. Now living near Phoenix, he works with corporate colleagues as "cosmologists of waste." "What we excrete comes back to consume us," says Nick, in a commentary not only on his own experiences but on postwar America and on the structural principle of DeLillo's elliptical text.

The novel mixes separate riffs on a mysterious drive-by murderer called the Texas Highway Killer; Esmeralda, a twelve-year-old Bronx waif beatified by popular culture after her violent demise; J. Edgar Hoover and his companion, Clyde Tolson, cavorting at Truman Capote's 1966 Black and White Ball; a genius of subway graffiti who signs his creations Moonman 157; and the comedian Lenny Bruce, rapping about the deadly forces that converge to create the Cuban Missile Crisis. Nick notes that Ralph Branca, the Dodger hurler who served Thomson his home run pitch and won 13 games that year, wore the number 13 on the fateful day, 10/3. The winning hit occurred at 3:58, another variation on 13 if you add the last two digits. Does numerology explain the enigmas of Nick Shay's life and times, and ours? Or does the conjunction of numbers indicate mere happenstance?

"Find the links," insists Hoover to his aide and companion, Clyde Tolson. "It's all linked." A quest for links will turn readers into rereaders of *Underworld,* a paradigm of the postmodernist renunciation of master narratives that resolve everything in a single thread. If, as its narrator contends, history is made by large-scale longing, *Underworld* makes history into an immense, engaging puzzle of unfulfilled desire. Connecting the dots is no simple task, and reading DeLillo is often like looking at one of M. C. Escher's visual riddles offering multiple perspectives that are mutually exclusive. A viewer can make sense of Escher's inky lines by processing them as a flock of birds or else as a school of fish, but not as both simultaneously. According to Bucky Wunderlick: "Life itself is sheer ambiguity. If a person doesn't see that, he's either an asshole or a fascist." Whether or not sheer ambiguity is a quality of life, it certainly characterizes DeLillo's fiction. The "asshole" is incapable of seeing additional possibilities for connecting the dots, and the "fascist" insists on asserting only one connection. Jack Gladney's author is, like him, an expert in Hitler Studies: so many of DeLillo's books are parables of fascist reading, works that encourage us to read intricate systems of signs more flexibly than do many of the characters in them, to recognize more than one valid way to connect the dots.

A DeLillo novel is typically a quest for a unified theory that would make sense of disparate data, a quest that is shared by the reader and the characters. The typical DeLillo protagonist is a solitary seeker who is set against a vast, inscrutable landscape—the desert Southwest in *Underworld,* the continental United States in *Americana,* the cosmos in *Ratner's Star.* In *Ratner's Star* Billy Twillig attempts to decipher radio messages from space, and beyond him, Jean Sweet Venable attempts to make sense of his attempts within the novel she is writing. In *The Names* James Axton tries to discover a pattern to ritual murders in the Middle East. In *Libra* Marguerite Oswald and Nicholas Branch separately seek some single explanation for all the sundry facts of the Kennedy assassination. In these and other instances, DeLillo suggests caution in how we choose to connect the dots, as well as resistance to the fascistic perspective of those who would impose exclusive patterns on us.

Conspiracy is another way of talking about imposed patterns, and the DeLillo universe is rife with intimations of conspiracy. Large, clandestine, coercive organizations such as the CIA, the FBI, and the KGB are prominent players in several of the novels, including *Players, Running Dog,* and *Underworld.* Tightly organized groups of spectral terrorists dominate the plots of *The Names* and *Mao II.* Billy Twillig's Field Experiment Number One falls victim to a hostile takeover by a Nazi megacorporation named ACRONYM in *Ratner's Star.* Reflecting on the media conglomerates that seem to control everything in *Great Jones Street,* Bucky Wunderlick, who is unsuccessful in his bid to opt out of the music industry, coins the term "Transparanoia"—"for our spreading inkblot of holding companies, trusts, acquisitions, and cabals." A DeLillo novel is itself just such a spreading inkblot; that a single inkblot can be interpreted in myriad ways is the basis for Hermann Rorschach's famous diagnostic test. The spectacle of unconnected dots could inspire panic, pride, or imaginative agility, depending on whether the spectator is distressed by the lack of structure, insistent on connecting the dots in only one way, or open to several possible patterns. Even as he diagnoses paranoia as a reasonable reaction to the collusion of large, insidious forces, DeLillo liberates us from fascists with designs on us, by imagining alternative ways of seeing patterns.

Of course the touchstone for American speculation about conspiracy is the Kennedy assassination, which has spawned innumerable theories to counter the facile conclusions of the official Warren Commission Report. DeLillo's David Ferrie speaks for all conspiracy theorists when, upset over the possibility of clandestine collusion between Washington and Havana, he posits secret machination as a universal principle: "There's something they aren't telling us. Something we don't know about. There's more to it. There's always more to it. This is what history consists of. It's the sum total of all the things they aren't telling us." The reader of a DeLillo novel, which demands that readers be rereaders, is always left with the feeling that there's more to it. And no omniscient author intercedes to tell us what to make of things. Unfounded suspicion of hostile collusion is paranoia, but the reader can reasonably found such suspicion on patterns that have been planted in the text.

Or are they mere coincidence? On September 9, 1963, Oswald, working in New Orleans with both pro- and anti-Castro forces, makes a mental list of all the odd concurrences in his life—among them, the fact that Guy Banister was searching for him when Oswald walked through his door and asked for an undercover job, the fact that the revolver and the carbine that he ordered six weeks apart arrived on the same day, the fact that both he and John Kennedy had brothers named Robert and wives who were pregnant. The ex-

perience of reading DeLillo's fictions simulates paranoia, except for the fact that he allows multiple interpretations to compete for our credence—as well as the possibility that, ultimately, the dots cannot be connected at all. Haunting all of the stories is the plausibility of Win Everett's radical skepticism: "He believed that nothing can be finally known that involves human motive and need. There is always another level, another secret, a way in which the heart breeds a deception so mysterious and complex it can only be taken for a deeper kind of truth."

Yet, according to Sister Alma Edgar: "Everything is connected in the end." At the end of *Underworld,* the Bronx nun dies in her sleep, but instead of being transported to Christian heaven finds herself in an electronic one, cyberspace, where everything is linked to everything else: "Everything is connected. All human knowledge gathered and linked, hyperlinked, this site leading to that, this fact referenced to that, a keystroke, a mouse-click, a password—world without end, amen." In her posthumous meditations, Sister Edgar, a gentle doppelgänger to J. Edgar Hoover, the FBI director who is professionally inclined to find connections, concludes *Underworld* by tying together the disparate threads of that book. Her musings from and about the Internet also recapitulate themes from throughout DeLillo's work—the quest for connection, the replacement of reality by electronic simulation, the generative power of language, the specter of violence. In the book's final line, one word in particular—*peace*—is sent coursing through the circuits of the World Wide Web, to make its way out into the world.

With more than a dozen distinctive texts, DeLillo has planted brilliant dots on the canvas of contemporary literature. But it would be presumptuous to connect those dots in pen rather than pencil, to proclaim a definitive pattern to the career of a living author who is still in the midst of production. Yet certain situations and themes, as we have seen, clearly resurface from work to work. And in general, DeLillo's power to articulate those situations and themes has grown steadily since publication of his first short story, "The River Jordan," in 1960. Though the early novels offer scattered flashes of brilliance and opportunities to observe the author rehearsing materials for later use, the most mature, enduring work stands in the sequence that he published between 1985 and 1997: *White Noise, Libra, Mao II,* and *Underworld.* Of these, *White Noise* is the most manically inventive, *Mao II* the most pointed and poignant in its exploration of the writing life, and *Underworld* the most ambitious.

Yet *Libra* is in many ways the touchstone of the DeLillo oeuvre, the "nonfiction" novel he seems to have been born—in the Bronx—to write. It is a book that deals compellingly with the unresolved mystery of the Kennedy assassination, which continued to haunt American culture at the close of the second millennium. In *Libra,* as in other DeLillo novels, contemporary life is shaped by the simulations of electronic media, eruptions of irrational violence, and intimations of conspiracy. Nonlinear, constructed out of several strands that the active reader is invited to try to reconcile (including the life of Lee Harvey Oswald; the attempt by Win Everett and Larry Parmenter to mount a covert, rogue operation that will scuttle rapprochement between the United States and Castro's Cuba; the speculations by Alek Kirilenko, Oswald's KGB interrogator; the effort by Nicholas Branch to make sense of it all; and Marguerite Oswald's urgent questions), *Libra* is the exemplary DeLillo narrative. In search of a coherent political system that will endow his life with meaning, Oswald oscillates between Washington and Moscow. "Which way will Leon tilt?" asks David Ferrie about Oswald, again recalling the astrological sign, represented by a pair of scales, that gives the book its title. *Libra* ends up creating *Oswald II,* as well as a telling instance of DeLillo's ambiguous and agile art.

Selected Bibliography

WORKS OF DON DELILLO

NOVELS

Americana. Boston: Houghton Mifflin, 1971.
End Zone. Boston: Houghton Mifflin, 1972.
Great Jones Street. Boston: Houghton Mifflin, 1973.
Ratner's Star. New York: Knopf, 1976.
Players. New York: Knopf, 1977.
Running Dog. New York: Knopf, 1978.
Amazons: An Intimate Memoir by the First Woman to Play in the National Hockey League. New York: Holt, Rinehart, 1980. Published under the pseudonym Cleo Birdwell.
The Names. New York: Knopf, 1982.
White Noise. New York: Viking, 1985.
Libra. New York: Viking, 1988.
Mao II. New York: Viking, 1991.
Underworld. New York: Scribners, 1997.

PLAYS

The Engineer of Moonlight. Cornell Review 1:21–47 (1979).
The Day Room. American Theatre, September 1986, pp. 1–12.
The Rapture of the Athlete Assumed into Heaven. South Atlantic Quarterly 91:241–242 (1992).
Valparaiso: A Play in Two Acts. New York: Scribners, 1999.

ARTICLES AND ESSAYS

"Total Loss Weekend." *Sports Illustrated,* November 27, 1972, pp. 98–101.
"Notes Toward a Definitive Meditation (by Someone Else) on the Novel Americana." *Epoch* 21, no. 3:327–329 (spring 1972).
"Notes on 'The Uniforms.' " In *Cutting Edges: Young American Fiction for the '70s.* Compiled by Jack Hicks. New York: Holt, Rinehart, 1973. Pp. 532–533.
"American Blood: A Journey through the Labyrinth of Dallas and JFK." *Rolling Stone,* December 8, 1983, pp. 21ff.
"Silhouette City: Hitler, Nason and the Millennium." *Dimensions* 4, no. 3:29–34 (1988).

Salman Rushdie Defense Pamphlet. With Paul Auster. New York: Rushdie Defense Committee USA, February 14, 1994.

"The Artist Naked in a Cage." *New Yorker,* May 26, 1997, pp. 6–7.

"The Power of History." *New York Times Magazine,* September 7, 1997, pp. 60–63.

SHORT STORIES AND NOVELLA

"The River Jordan." *Epoch* 10:105–120 (1960).

"Take the 'A' Train." *Epoch* 12:9–25 (1962).

"Spaghetti and Meat Balls." *Epoch* 14:244–250 (1965).

"Coming Sun. Mon. Tues." *Kenyon Review* 28:391–394 (1966).

"Baghdad Towers West." *Epoch* 17:195–217 (1968).

"The Uniforms." *Carolina Quarterly* 22:4–11 (1970).

"In the Men's Room of the Sixteenth Century." *Esquire,* December 1971, pp. 174ff.

"Creation." *Antaeus* 33:32–46 (1979).

"Human Moments in World War III." *Esquire,* July 1983, pp. 118–126.

"The Runner." *Harper's,* September 1988, pp. 61–63.

"The Ivory Acrobat." *Granta* 25:199–212 (autumn 1988).

Pafko at the Wall. Harper's, October 1992, pp. 35–70.

"The Black-and-White Ball." *New Yorker,* December 23, 1996, pp. 80ff.

"Sputnik." *New Yorker,* September 8, 1997, pp. 76ff.

CRITICAL AND BIOGRAPHICAL STUDIES

BOOKS

Civello, Paul. *American Literary Naturalism and Its Twentieth-Century Transformations: Frank Norris, Ernest Hemingway, Don DeLillo.* Athens: University of Georgia Press, 1994.

Hantke, Steffen. *Conspiracy and Paranoia in Contemporary American Fiction: The Works of Don DeLillo and Joseph McElroy.* Frankfurt: Peter Lang, 1994.

Keesey, Douglas. *Don DeLillo.* New York: Twayne, 1993.

LeClair, Tom. *In the Loop: Don DeLillo and the Systems Novel.* Urbana: University of Illinois Press, 1987.

Lentricchia, Frank, ed. *Introducing Don DeLillo.* Durham, N.C.: Duke University Press, 1991. Reprint of *South Atlantic Quarterly* 89, no. 2 (spring 1990), special DeLillo issue.

———, ed. *New Essays on White Noise.* New York: Cambridge University Press, 1991.

Phillips, Dana. *Don DeLillo's Postmodern Pastoral.* Moscow: University of Idaho Press, 1998.

ARTICLES AND ESSAYS

Bawer, Bruce. "Don DeLillo's America." *New Criterion* (April 1985), pp. 34–42.

Begley, Adam. "Don DeLillo: *Americana, Mao II,* and *Underworld.*" *Southwest Review* 82, no. 4:478–505 (1997).

Bell, Pearl K. "DeLillo's World." *Partisan Review* 59, no. 1:138–146 (winter 1992).

Bryson, Norman. "City of Dis: The Fiction of Don DeLillo." *Granta* 2:145–157 (1980).

Edmundson, Mark. "Not Flat, Not Round, Not There: Don DeLillo's Characters." *Yale Review* 83, no. 2:107–124 (April 1995).

Johnston, John. "Generic Difficulties in the Novels of Don DeLillo." *Critique* 30:261–275 (1989).

Kucich, John. "Postmodern Politics: Don DeLillo and the Plight of the White Male Writer." *Michigan Quarterly Review* 27, no. 2:328–341 (spring 1998).

McClure, John A. "Postmodern/Post-Secular: Contemporary Fiction and Spirituality." *Modern Fiction Studies* 41:141–163 (1995).

Modern Fiction Studies 45, no. 3 (September 1999). Special DeLillo issue.

Mottram, Eric. "The Real Needs of Man: Don DeLillo's Novels." In *The New American Writing: Essays on American Literature Since 1970.* Edited by Graham Clarke. New York: St. Martin's, 1990. Pp. 51–98.

Nadeau, Robert. *Readings from the New Book on Nature: Physics and Metaphysics in the Modern Novel.* Amherst: University of Massachusetts Press, 1981, pp. 161–181.

Oriard, Michael. "Don DeLillo's Search for Walden Pond." *Critique* 20:5–24 (1978).

Weinstein, Arnold. "Don DeLillo: Rendering the Words of the Tribe." In his *Nobody's Home: Speech, Self, and Place in American Fiction from Hawthorne to DeLillo.* New York: Oxford University Press, 1993. Pp. 288–315.

INTERVIEWS

Begley, Adam. "Don DeLillo: The Art of Fiction CXXXV." *Paris Review* 35, no. 128:274–306 (fall 1993).

Connolly, Kevin. "An Interview with Don DeLillo." In *The Brick Reader.* Edited by Linda Spalding and Michael Ondaatje. Toronto: Coach House Press, 1991. Pp. 260–269.

DeCurtis, Anthony. "Matters of Fact and Fiction." *Rolling Stone* 17 (November 1988):113–122, 164.

Howard, Gerald. "The American Strangeness: An Interview with Don DeLillo." *Hungry Mind Review* 43:13–16 (fall 1997).

LeClair, Tom. "An Interview with Don DeLillo." In *Anything Can Happen: Interviews with Contempo-rary American Novelists.* Edited by Tom LeClair and Larry McCaffery. Urbana: University of Illinois Press, 1983. Pp. 79–90.

Nadotti, Maria. "An Interview with Don DeLillo." *Salmagundi* 100:86–97 (fall 1993).

Passaro, Vince. "Dangerous Don DeLillo." *New York Times Magazine,* May 19, 1991, pp. 36ff.

Remnick, David. "Exile on Main Street." *New Yorker,* September 15, 1997, pp. 42–48.

—STEVEN G. KELLMAN

Annie Dillard

1945–

I N PITTSBURGH, PENNSYLVANIA, on April 30, 1945, Meta Ann Doak was born into a nation at war. Only a month before her birth, the United States had occupied Iwo Jima; although it would be several months before the bombing of Hiroshima and the surrender of Japan, the war in Europe would end in days. With its many industries, especially steel, Pittsburgh played a pivotal role in the success of the American war machine. The arrival of peace began a long period of national prosperity coupled with intense social repressiveness emblematized by Senator Joseph McCarthy's domestic war against Communists, by the actions of the Ku Klux Klan, and by the development of what the feminist writer Betty Friedan would call "the feminine mystique," a set of confining norms for American women. In her autobiographical narrative *An American Childhood* (1987), Dillard intimates that many of these tensions haunted her early life, observing, "The theaters of war . . . and the death camps in Europe, with their lines of starved bald people . . . were the settings in which our imaginations were first deeply stirred." At the same time, she affirms in *Encounters with Chinese Writers* (1984) that "my life has set me at little risk, put me under no hardship." Focusing first on Dillard's life history through a discussion of *An American Childhood,* this essay will examine her work from the perspective of several literary contexts and explore some of her characteristic concerns. As Dillard readers quickly learn, however, her work is so densely textured, with themes and perspectives so intricately interwoven, it is difficult to separate the various strands.

"I WOKE IN BITS, LIKE ALL CHILDREN": PERSONAL HISTORY, PLACE, AND PEOPLE

"I woke in bits, like all children," affirmed Dillard in *An American Childhood,* and a wakeful stance, an openness to experience and attention to her own perceptions, is what she brought to the pages of this book. The oldest of three daughters, Dillard was fortunate to have parents who encouraged nonconformity and creativity. *An American Childhood* reveals that her mother, Pam (Lambert) Doak, was a gifted, imaginative woman who spurned unthinking acceptance of others' opinions and who—like her husband, Frank Doak—loved jokes. Dillard tells us that "remembering jokes was a moral obligation" and that "people who said, 'I can never remember jokes,' were like people who said, obliviously, 'I can never remember names,' or 'I don't bathe.'" Pam delighted in unsettling complacent, inflexible people; when playing cards with friends, if the game became too serious, she would show her opponents her hand or toss her cards over her shoulder.

Frank Doak kept a little black notebook to record memorable jokes. This playful environment, which made the young Dillard familiar with the diverse possibilities of language, contributed to her unparalleled ability to catch readers delightfully off balance with her combination of humor and intensity.

Dillard's father, Frank Doak, was a manager in the family business, American Standard Corporation, which had been founded by his great-grandfather. Very much his own person, Doak resigned from the firm when Dillard was ten to take a long-desired solo voyage in his twenty-four-foot cabin cruiser down the Ohio to the Mississippi River and New Orleans. A devotee of Mark Twain's *Life on the Mississippi,* Doak loved jazz and had, before he married, "halfheartedly played the drums; he had smoked marijuana, written poems, begun a novel, painted in oils, imagined a career as a riverboat pilot, and acted for more than ten seasons in amateur and small-time professional theater" in New York. His trip down the river proved disappointing, however: "He wasn't free so much as loose," Dillard writes. After only six weeks, missing his wife and daughters, he sold the boat at Louisville, Kentucky, and returned home. The idea of life's preciousness and the necessity of mindfulness to one's true calling threads through all of Dillard's work, a legacy from both parents.

Dillard was also fortunate to have loving paternal grandparents who fostered her imagination and sense of self. The grandmother for whom she was named, Meta Waltenburger Doak, was a large, self-confident woman whom Dillard describes as "an imperious and kindhearted grande dame of execrable taste, a tall, potbellied redhead, the proud descendant and heir of well-to-do Germans in Louisville, Kentucky, who boasted that she never worked a day in her life." At the family's summer home at Lake Erie, in Ohio, "Oma" relaxed; at home in Pittsburgh, "she wore jewelry by the breastful, by the armload: diamonds, rubies, emeralds. She wore big rings like engine bearings, and vast, slithering mink coats." Dillard's paternal grandfather, "an uncommonly kind and good-natured man," was of Scotch-Irish descent and devoted to his wife and grandchildren. Dillard and her sisters often summered at the lake with her grandparents, up until her grandfather's death of a brain tumor when Dillard was thirteen. She registers her horror at his gradual diminishment, describing how, lying in his hospital bed, this proper man was reduced to responding to all questions in anger, with the single word "balls." The simultaneous presence in the world of profound love and profound pain is often found in Dillard's writing.

Surrounded by love and humor—as well as this early grief and the resonant anxieties of the era—the writer suggests that an important element in her early environment was the tension between conformity and resistance to social norms. For example, Dillard's parents insisted that their daughters attend the Shadyside Presbyterian Church, although they themselves chose not to go. Dillard also describes participating in Presbyterian church camp for four years; it was "cheap, wholesome, and nearby. . . . If our parents had known how pious and low church this camp was, they would have yanked us." Dillard conveys the incommensurability of her wealthy girlhood Pittsburgh world with that depicted in the Bible, wondering why adults made children read and even memorize large portions of Scripture, highlighting "the vivid danger that we would, through repeated exposure, catch a case of its wild opposition to their world." This questioning attitude is one that Dillard's parents, especially her mother, would foster: "Torpid conformity was a kind of sin; it was stupidity itself, the mighty stream against which Mother would never cease to struggle. If you held no minority opinions, or if you failed to risk total ostracism for them daily, the world would be a better place without you."

Dillard's reflections on her high school years suggest the mood of the period and reveal once again the elite company in which she grew up. The boys whom she and her schoolmates met at dancing school as young adolescents later became their partners at country club subscription dances: "Those froggy little beasts had elongated and transformed into princes and gods." Although she was initially dazzled by the atmosphere of these social events, her descriptions of Pittsburgh society elsewhere in *An American Childhood* suggest her eventual rejection of this world, with its rigid rules and predictable lives. A rebellious teenager, she was suspended from school for smoking; she also resisted what she saw as the hypocrisy of the church, quitting briefly, although she returned after reading the work of C. S. Lewis, which her minister had loaned her. Emerging from her sometimes contradictory early experiences, her narratives as a whole reveal the ability of the writer to hold opposites in balance, to find value in and admire what she simultaneously critiques. As she observes after having described a woman at the country club who refused to wash her face all summer in order to maintain her tan, "There was real beauty to the old idea of living and dying where you were born. You could hold a place in a kind of eternity."

In all of this childhood experience, place, and in particular Pittsburgh, provides an important home ground, "a great town to grow up in." Embodying the American myth of the self-made man, the famously wealthy industrialist Andrew Carnegie funded many great public works projects in the city, including libraries, a museum of natural history, music hall, and art gallery. Dillard describes her fondness for rummaging about in the natural history museum, where children could lose—or find—themselves; she highlights the role of Carnegie's gifts in the creation of the imagination. In addition Pittsburgh provided a strong sense of history. Dillard describes how,

wherever one dug, it was possible to find traces of the city's prior inhabitants: under the paved city streets lay cobblestones; under that, treacherous nineteenth-century mud; deeper still, pioneer tracks and Indian trails.

While Pittsburgh offered many attractions, it also possessed contradictions. Dillard reminds her readers that the city had the country's highest death rate at the turn of the twentieth century. Public health projects were often scrapped or delayed because of powerful business interests. And Carnegie himself was generous only on his own terms; in 1892, while Carnegie was on a trip to Scotland, his manager ordered security police to beat striking workers in the city, breaking not only the strike but steel unions nationwide. On a more personal level, Pittsburgh was carefully divided by religious and class barriers. The young Annie might fall in love with "a red-haired fourth-grade boy named Walter Milligan . . . [who] was tough, Catholic, [and] from an iffy neighborhood," but everyone, herself included, understood that such relationships could never actually materialize.

Similarly, racial and ethnic boundaries were well-policed, sometimes even by those who were socially marginalized. When a Catholic boy tells the young Annie to call her maid a "nigger" and she complies, she learns both the presence of and necessary resistance to social hierarchies: Dillard's mother became furious, "steely," insisting that such language and those who used it were forbidden. When Dillard reached the age for dancing school lessons, she learned that "we were all on some list. We were to be on that list for life, it turned out, unless we left." Ominously conjuring the memory of World War II, this "list" turns out to exclude Dillard's friend Ellin Hahn, who was half Jewish. Dillard also learned about differences and connections between people in her many visits to the library of Pittsburgh's black Homewood section. It was at this library that she discovered a compelling book, *The Field*

Book of Ponds and Streams by Ann Haven Morgan, which teaches her as much by its full checkout card as by its contents; having passed through the crowded and ruined Homewood neighborhood on the way to the library, she is forced to envision people who shared her hopes and imaginative flights but were far less likely to realize them—Homewood lacked a pond or stream. Describing her thoughts on one such occasion she concludes, "The Homewood residents whom I knew had little money and little free time. The marble floor was beginning to chill me. It was not fair."

Dillard's parents, especially her mother, resisted social and class barriers with all her energy: "She asserted, against all opposition, that people who lived in trailer parks were not bad but simply poor. . . . Her profound belief that the country-club pool sweeper was a person, and that the department-store saleslady, the bus driver, telephone operator, and housepainter were people . . . this was a conviction common enough in democratic Pittsburgh, but not altogether common among our friends' parents, or even, perhaps, among our parents' friends." Dillard's early experiences prompted her to cross all kinds of borders, both in her writing and in her life. As a girl, she was tomboyish, hanging out with boys to play baseball and to throw snowballs at cars passing through the neighborhood. Her difficult, rebellious high school years led her parents to send her to Hollins College in Virginia, where she flourished, being named to Phi Beta Kappa in her junior year. According to Nancy C. Parrish, Hollins provided an environment that was at once competitive and collaborative, enabling Dillard's writing to flourish and initiating a community of women writers that would be important throughout her life. Here too she met Louis J. Rubin Jr., a writer and scholar of southern literature who was a crucial influence on her work. Crossing another border, she married her creative writing teacher, Richard Henry Wilde Dillard, in 1964.

A poet, critic, and novelist, Richard Dillard was nine years her senior; according to Dillard, he was extremely influential in shaping her writing, especially her poetry, while she was an important source for his own work. After her marriage and the completion of her undergraduate degree, she stayed on at Hollins, receiving her M.A. in 1968. Her thesis, "Walden Pond and Thoreau," indicates the admiration she felt for her predecessor, Henry David Thoreau, whose work has inspired her own. During the next few years, she placed poems in journals that included *The Atlantic Monthly* and *The American Scholar;* she also suffered from a nearly fatal case of pneumonia that may have sparked her to reconsider her life goals. Soon after her recovery, she began to take camping trips, often by herself, reading voraciously and working on a journal of reflections that she had begun about 1970. This work, parts of which were published in the *Atlantic* and *Harper's,* generated immediate attention and ultimately came together in a book-length essay, *Pilgrim at Tinker Creek* (1974), which was awarded the Pulitzer Prize for general nonfiction in 1975. *Tickets for a Prayer Wheel,* her first book of poetry, was published the same year.

Pilgrim at Tinker Creek became a Book-of-the-Month Club selection; its wide distribution and recognition in reviews made Dillard an instant celebrity. Young and physically attractive, Dillard expressed dismay at being co-opted by the marketing machine of contemporary publishing: as she commented cynically to the interviewer Robert Lindsey in 1977, "You feel maybe your success is partly because you have yellow hair and beautiful legs." When the book was being completed, Dillard's marriage to Richard Dillard was in the process of breaking up, and the couple divorced in 1975. Always a private person, Dillard has not discussed the reasons for this split, but it is clear that it caused her considerable pain. To absent herself from the publicity surrounding her literary success, and perhaps also to help subdue the loss in her personal life, she moved to Washington State in 1975, taking up a position at Western Washington University in Bellingham, living in a small cabin on an island in Puget Sound, and writing *Holy the Firm* (1977). Shortly after the move west, she met and, in 1980, married novelist Gary Clevidence, an anthropology professor at Fairhaven College.

Dillard moved back to the East Coast in 1979 to become visiting professor at Wesleyan University in Connecticut for two years, where she taught creative writing. She then lived again in Washington for two years, but after separating from Clevidence, she returned to Connecticut and Wesleyan. During this time, she published two books, *Teaching a Stone to Talk: Expeditions and Encounters* (1982), a well-received collection of essays, and *Living by Fiction* (1982), a literary theory volume. In 1982 she joined a State Department cultural delegation to China; back in the United States, she participated in the organization of a conference and hospitality for visiting Chinese writers. From these experiences, she published *Encounters with Chinese Writers* in 1984, the same year in which her daughter, Cody Rose, was born to her and Clevidence. Her daughter's birth prompted the self-reflection that resulted in *An American Childhood* in 1987. Shortly after this time, she was divorced from Clevidence and married Robert D. Richardson Jr., moving to Middletown, Connecticut. Sometime during this period, she converted to Roman Catholicism.

In 1989 Dillard published *The Writing Life*, a characteristically elegant and witty set of reflections on the challenges of being a writer, with her only novel, *The Living*—a revision and expansion of a 1978 short story—appearing in 1992 and a collection of her work, *The Annie Dillard Reader*, appearing in 1994. A collection of "found" poems, *Mornings Like This: Found Poems,* emerged in 1995, and an extended meditative essay, *For the Time Being,* in 1999. Having received grants from the Guggenheim Foundation and the National Endowment for the Humanities, in 2000 Dillard was adjunct professor of English at Wesleyan. Reticent about her personal life and guarding her privacy carefully, she restricted public appearances. In a 1987 interview with Alvin Sanoff she observed, "I want enough sanity to keep on writing literature because it's literature that I love—and that means not being too famous."

"COMING AWAKE AND DISCOVERING A PLACE": *PILGRIM AT TINKER CREEK* AND AMERICAN AUTOBIOGRAPHY

Much of Dillard's writing represents a version of spiritual autobiography that emerges from such diverse sources as the Bible and, as Linda Smith points out, "medieval alchemy, Jewish cabalism and Hasidism, various Eskimo spiritual traditions, and Islamic Sufism." Beyond what it adds to our understanding of her life, Dillard's autobiographical writing also merits consideration within a long tradition of American personal writing, which includes both the Puritans' spiritual autobiographies, with which Dillard's work shares strong affinities, and poetry such as Walt Whitman's "Song of Myself." Like her predecessors', Dillard's writing explores such subjects as humans' relationships with nature and with God, the simultaneous presence of beauty and suffering, the relationship of the writer to his or her imagined audience, the connections between the body and the spirit, and the role of gender in personal writing.

Steven Kagle has suggested a feature of diary literature that resonates for autobiographical literature more broadly, that the primary impulse for such writing is often "an imbalance, disorder, or dislocating change in the world of its author," who attempts to negotiate a correction of this imbalance, disorder, or change through his or her writing. Such a generalization was certainly true of one of the earliest genres in American literary history, the captivity narrative. The best known of these stories was Mary Rowlandson's spiritual autobiography, which established a pattern for the early genre: the writer speaks of hardships as a captive among the Indians and of the important role of God in effecting her release. Rowlandson's narrative focuses on the "howling wilderness" surrounding her and on the "savages" among whom she found herself; she tells of the violent deaths of members of her family and neighbors and the difficulties that she endured.

Dillard's personal narratives explore the savagery in nature, a savagery from which humans are not, she implies, exempt. Some of the most memorable instances emerge in her study of Tinker Creek (located near Hollins), where she oversees the "natural" cycles of life and death with fascination and horror. For example, on one occasion she is walking beside the creek and spots a frog. Usually frogs are jittery about her presence, but this frog doesn't jump; instead, as she looks, "he slowly crumpled and began to sag. . . . His skin emptied and drooped. . . . Soon, part of his skin, formless as a pricked balloon, lay in floating folds like bright scum on top of the water: it was a monstrous and terrifying thing." The culprit responsible for literally draining the frog's life is a giant water bug, which punctures its victims with a single bite, poisons it with enzymes that liquefy all internal organs and bones, and sucks the resulting juice from the skin. As Sandra Humble Johnson observes, such graphic descriptions permeate Dillard's writing, generating both wonder and fear. Like Rowlandson's experiences in nature, Dillard's transform her understanding of the world and her place in it.

Facing painful psychological (as well as physical) dangers, Mary Rowlandson turns to her faith in God to sustain her and to give meaning to her chaotic and confusing experiences. Similarly, Dillard turns to ponder—though with less certain acceptance—divinity's place in such a horrifying universe. Interestingly, she turns not just to sacred texts but also to science for an explanation of the place of divinity in the world's mysteries, quoting Albert Einstein: "Nature conceals her mystery by means of her essential grandeur, not by her cunning." Expanding on Einstein's comment, Dillard suggests that, enacted in nature on a scale often too large to be perceived by human beings, "It could be that God has not absconded but spread, as our vision and understanding of the universe have spread, to a fabric of spirit and sense so grand and subtle, so powerful in a new way, that we can only feel blindly of its hem." "It's rough out there and chancy," she acknowledges, but then describes the deliberate, wings'-folded drop and last-minute graceful landing of a mockingbird, concluding "that beauty and grace are performed whether or not we will or sense them. The least we can do is try to be there."

This first section of *Pilgrim at Tinker Creek,* "Heaven and Earth in Jest," embodies a number of Dillard's characteristic conceptual, imagistic, and vocal gestures. First, she repeatedly poses the question of being's paradoxes. In *An American Childhood,* she sees one night from a window a neighboring Catholic girl from a working-class family illumined magically under a street lamp, skating on the icy street; the next morning, the girl reappears in her ordinary school uniform. The girl's outsider status—both Catholic and working class—in Dillard's mind enhanced the aesthetic performance to create a moment of mysterious attraction. Such attraction was counterbalanced by the girl's mundane appearance on her way to school the next day, teaching the young Annie that the transcendent resides even in the most ordinary activity. In the water bug scene, we sense the presence of horror and danger juxtaposed with wonder and beauty. Like many of Dillard's works, *Pilgrim at Tinker Creek* often counterposes great beauty and great suffering; as she works through the meaning of such paradoxes she also invites the reader to come to terms with them.

The water bug scene also reveals Dillard's use of imagery to suggest parallels between disparate worlds; that is, to invoke a poetic interpretation. The water bug is unseen, virtually invisible, detected only by means of a passing shadow; the hidden presence of danger in everyday life is terrifying. Similarly, the mockingbird Dillard describes surpasses the image of a bird in flight to suggest the writer as trickster; Dillard's prose invites us to wonder why the bird envisioned is not a starling or a robin. Just as the mockingbird "mocks" the earthbound expectations of the writer, the writer plays with the similarly stolid perspective of the reader. Finally, this scene intimates Dillard's wry and athletic humor; she not only records the violence in life but undercuts the horror of her descriptions—here, with Einstein's humorous observation that "God is subtle . . . but not malicious." We see her effort, as in much American autobiographical narrative, to bring her—and the reader's—consciousness back to a balanced state.

Autobiographical narratives invite a consideration of their complex audiences. Although the earliest diaries, for example, began as private documents, as Kagle observes, there is "no such thing as a totally private diary." Autobiographies can range from personal, private writing, intended to preserve for the writer an "earlier" sense of self, to clearly public self-presentation. From this perspective, we might compare Dillard's *An American Childhood* to Walt Whitman's "Song of Myself," both of which are presented as public documents. Whitman repeatedly emphasized the important role of the reader in the creation of his narrative—and, at the same time, the world—by paradoxically invoking himself. Although the tone of the texts varies substantially, the two share many perspectives, including the appreciation of paradox and of the compensations present in human existence. Whitman's famous assertion, "Do I contradict myself? Very well then, I contradict myself," anticipates the acceptance in Dillard's work of life's complexities and nuances. For instance, describing a school of sharks momentarily visible within the curve of a Florida wave, Dillard concludes, "The sight held awesome wonders: power and beauty, grace tangled in a rapture with violence."

Like Whitman, Dillard offers her readers a form of autobiography that at once values the spirit and insists on its embodiment. She opens *Pilgrim at Tinker Creek* with a description that underscores this necessary linking of the mind with the body: an old tomcat, who would occasionally climb in through her open window at night, purring and "stinking of urine and blood," leaves paw prints on her body that give the appearance that she had been "painted with roses." Washing the blood away, Dillard ponders the difficulty of knowing "whether I'd purified myself or ruined the blood sign of the passover." Like many American autobiographers, Dillard presents herself and her own experience as in some ways representative—in spite of the privilege of her upbringing—and hence possessing the ability for others to share in her struggles and learn from her experiences. On the other hand, like many prior American women autobiographers, she may have been prompted to record her own history not only as paradigmatic but also to preserve community and family history for her daughter.

We should recognize that, although Dillard has frequently resisted being labeled a "woman writer"—and with good reason, given the past usage of this term to diminish women's literary accomplishments—her autobiography, like much of her other writing, is sometimes subtly gendered. As Suzanne Clark and others have observed, Dillard's autobiographical writing—which encompasses virtually everything she has done—expands the tradition of autobiography by blending such genres as nature writing, philosophy, science writing, and fiction. Crossing "the boundaries between fiction and nonfiction," she "rais[es] questions about the status of both." Moreover, as Clark points out, "When we read Annie Dillard, we don't know who is writing." She interprets this "absence" as Dillard's transformation into narrative practice of the traditional social silencing of women, and she argues that this silencing parallels the objectification of nature. Thus, Dillard's writing becomes "the inscription of otherness, with the receptivity of a female author-ity." Nancy C. Parrish concurs, comparing Dillard's persona to Emily Dickinson's "supposed person" and observing that "the literary 'Annie Dillard' has become as much a metaphor as the creek she once portrayed." In Dillard's ecstatic visions we are required to see from a female perspective closely allied with nature.

More concretely, Leigh Gilmore argues of autobiography that an exploration of the body is one potential source of gendered female identity; male writers are expected to concentrate on the life of the mind. Interestingly, in *An American Childhood* Dillard frequently describes herself in neutral or even boyish terms, as we see her playing football, collecting bugs and rocks, and throwing snowballs with the local boys. Of her baseball experience, she recalls, "I had, through enthusiastic practice, what was weirdly known as a boy's arm. In winter . . . there was neither baseball nor football, so the boys and I threw snowballs at passing cars. I got in trouble throwing snowballs, and have seldom been happier since." Although she is fascinated early on by the tanning rituals of her mother's contemporaries, it is not until adolescence that she experiences a sense of being embodied female, as she describes her experience at formal dances, feeling the warmth of a boy's palm on her white-gloved hands. More painfully, it also brings an unrelenting self-consciousness, both physical and psychological, which she describes with brilliant metaphoric precision: "I was a dog barking between my own ears, a barking dog who wouldn't hush."

"THE DREAMING MEMORY OF LAND": DILLARD AND AMERICAN NATURE WRITING

Dillard's writing has most frequently been compared with that of Henry David Thoreau. In "Living Like Weasels," in *Teaching a Stone to Talk,* she echoes Thoreau's language explicitly: "I would like to learn, or remember, how to live." *Pilgrim at Tinker Creek* shares many similarities with *Walden, or Life in the Woods* (1854). Both chart the passing of the seasons over the course of a year, although Dillard's book begins in January and Thoreau's in the summer. Both see beyond the visible, scanning with a transcendental vision the divinity in nature. And both center their visions on a body of water—Walden Pond and Tinker Creek—as the principal image for the transcendent. Linda Smith reminds us that Dillard characterized *Pilgrim at Tinker Creek* to her publisher as "a theology book," and she describes how Dillard the artist negotiates between good and evil in the world via her creative imagination, which indicates a "via creativa" that must be followed by the spiritual aspirant. Acknowledging Dillard's resistance to being characterized as a woman writer, Smith also suggests that Dillard nevertheless participates in a long tradition of spiritual quest by women in which they have emphasized connection and community over individualism, and a search for a renewed sense of self. Other contemporary critics such as John Tallmadge highlight Dillard's connections with the Thoreauvian tradition of American nature writing, "in which nature has often been viewed as a source of religious revelation or a standard of moral value." Tallmadge emphasizes Dillard's view that "nature reveals a God who is powerful, fascinating, violent, and inscrutable. Dillard goes out into nature seeking encounters with power and mystery."

As we also see in *Walden,* Dillard's emphasis on science—and the horrors as well as the beauties of nature—attempts to bring together human and divine, whether one focuses on a small or a large scale. Like Thoreau's study of the motion of sand and water in a thawing hillside, Dillard's "scientific" description of her place in the universe captures some of her sense of marvel. Of the aftermath of one particularly captivating afternoon and early evening at Tinker Creek, she comments:

> Later I lay open-mouthed in bed, my arms flung wide at my sides to steady the whirling darkness. At this latitude I'm spinning 836 miles an hour round the earth's axis. . . . In orbit around the sun I'm moving 64,800 miles an hour. The solar system as a whole, like a merry-go-round unhinged, spins, bobs, and blinks at the speed of 43,200 miles an hour along a course set east of Hercules. . . . I close my eyes and I see stars, deep stars giving way to deeper stars, deeper stars bowing to deepest stars at the crown of an infinite cone.

Through many detailed descriptions such as this, Dillard suggests that science is not incommensurate with transcendence or wonder; in fact, the more we know of science, the more wonderful, full of wonder, the world becomes. A later work, *For the Time Being,* would also reveal her awe of numbers, as she describes the place of human beings in the galaxy and the universe.

Dillard's female precursors in nineteenth- and early-twentieth-century American literature include such nature writers as Lucy Larcom, Celia Thaxter, and Mary Austin. Of these, Austin (1868–1934) anticipates and parallels Dillard's work in particularly powerful ways. Born in Illinois, Austin moved west to California at the age of twenty; there she found ample sources for her imagination. Much of her work, which was firmly rooted in nature and the western landscape, sought both directly or indirectly to preserve that landscape. Like that of Dillard and other American nature writers, Austin's writing encompasses the paradoxes and admires the adaptations of nature, revealing a precision that echoes Dillard's, as in

this quote from her best-known work, *The Land of Little Rain* (1903): "The desert floras shame us with their cheerful adaptations to the seasonal limitations. Their whole duty is to flower and fruit, and they do it hardly, or with tropical luxuriance, as the rain admits. It is recorded in the report of the Death Valley expedition that after a year of abundant rains, on the Colorado desert was found a specimen of Amaranthus ten feet high. A year later the same species in the same place matured in the drought at four inches."

Austin records the paradox of life in the desert in another way when she affirms in the same text: "Go as far as you dare in the heart of a lonely land, you cannot go so far that life and death are not before you. Painted lizards slip in and out of rock crevices, and pant on the white hot sands. Birds, hummingbirds even, nest in the cactus shrub; woodpeckers befriend the demoniac yuccas; out of the stark, treeless waste rings the music of the night-singing mockingbird." Bringing together "life and death," Austin affirms the diversity and potential of life in the most hellish conditions. Austin's work, like that of Dillard, operates on both a literal and metaphorical level, urging the seeker to take the broad picture and, implicitly, to understand divinity as part of an enormous pattern that can occasionally be perceived in its tiny details. Like Austin, one of Dillard's regular narrative strategies is to focus readers' attention on the minute—on insects, or even on the microscopic life evident in a drop of pond water.

Austin also shares Thoreau's and Dillard's interest in water, acknowledging its renewing and transcendent qualities. Dillard speaks of the mystery of Tinker Creek's constant self-reinvention, its perpetual newness. Similarly, in "Water Borders" in *The Land of Little Rain,* Austin describes the mystery of mountain springs: "The origin of mountain streams is like the origin of tears, patent to the understanding but mysterious to the sense. They are always at it, but one so seldom catches them in the act." With such descriptions Austin anticipates a rhetorical strategy that Dillard often uses: the juxtaposition of elevated images with (in the next sentence) everyday language. One effect of this juxtaposition, in Austin's work as in Dillard's, is humor. Another effect is the translation of the transcendental for the reader, making it accessible and familiar.

Like Dillard, Austin insists on the constant presence of both human agency and divinity, asserting in *The Land of Little Rain* that "since it appears that we make our own heaven here, no doubt we shall have a hand in the heaven of hereafter." Such affirmations often appear in the conclusions of chapters, as Austin moves from the descriptive to the inspirational; one of the most delicate examples occurs at the end of "Water Borders," where she imagines the mountain stream calmed "when once free of the rifted cañon walls; the high note of babble and laughter falls off to the steadier mellow tone of a stream that knows its purpose and reflects the sky." In a similar fashion, Dillard often concludes her chapters with an elevated tone and image; in "Heaven and Earth in Jest," she feels "the delicate air of twilight" on her face as she watches the surface of Tinker Creek crinkle into "running sheets of light": "The sight has the appeal of the purely passive, like the racing of light under clouds on a field, the beautiful dream at the moment of being dreamed. The breeze is the merest puff, but you yourself sail headlong and breathless under the gale force of the spirit." Although neither Austin nor Dillard is explicitly invested in the environmental movement, we cannot fail to see their work as an indirect argument for the preservation of the natural world in the face of human intervention and indifference, in part because that natural world parallels an invisible, transcendent one.

Dillard has been criticized by some, as Gary McIlroy observes (in *Earthly Words: Essays on Contemporary American Nature and Environmental Writers,* edited by John Cooley), for the "virtual neglect of society" in *Pilgrim at Tinker Creek.* Yet careful attention to this volume reveals an intense interest in human relations, though this interest is often figured in natural images. For example, early in the volume Dillard echoes Thoreau's concern with the encroachment of technology as she describes a group of black steers: "They are all bred beef: beef heart, beef hide, beef hocks. They're a human product like rayon. They're like a field of shoes. They have cast-iron shanks and tongues like foam insoles."

Readers can more readily understand the connections in *Pilgrim at Tinker Creek* between nature and society by turning to Dillard's essay collection *Teaching a Stone to Talk.* Here the writer extends her account of her time at Tinker Creek with "On a Hill Far Away," an essay on religious fundamentalists who live nearby. She also provides her unique, questioning, and questing vision in essays like "Total Eclipse," "The Deer at Providencia," "God in the Doorway," and several ruminations on the Galápagos Islands, but she more often peoples these essays explicitly instead of conjuring the reader as her only witness. As always, humor informs her perspective, engaging us in the work of re-visioning the world. A passage from "Total Eclipse" is representative: "A partial eclipse is very interesting. It bears almost no relation to a total eclipse. Seeing a partial eclipse bears the same relation to seeing a total eclipse as kissing a man does to marrying him, or as flying in an airplane does to falling out of an airplane. Although the one experience precedes the other, it in no way prepares you for it." All of Dillard's work shows her fundamental investment in reinventing the relationship between nature, divinity, and humans.

"THIS BOOK IS THE STRAYING TRAIL OF BLOOD": AESTHETICS, PASSION, AND VISION

Although Dillard has written two books explicitly about writing, virtually all of her work maps out the necessary and difficult journey of the writer. First and foremost, the writer must be a visionary, able to see beyond the everyday and mediate between divine and human. Like Whitman, Dillard seeks to apprehend the harmony in disparates, bringing together beauty and ugliness, pain and transcendence, to create meaning in a modern world that threatens meaninglessness. Like Emily Dickinson, Dillard values both intensity and humor as measures of the creative artist's vision. With styles ranging from the concrete and restrained to the elevated and lush, Dillard emphasizes the necessary courage of the writer and the need for him or her to connect with an audience. Finally, the measure of a writer is his or her ability to inspire readers to live life fully and consciously.

In concert with her intensity and sense of the writer's elemental task, Dillard often uses powerful metaphors in her representation of the artist. In *Pilgrim at Tinker Creek,* describing grooved arrows that certain Indians used to ensure that wounded game would eventually bleed to death and that the hunter could follow its track "into whatever deep or rare wilderness it leads," she compares herself to "the arrow shaft, carved along my length by unexpected lights and gashes from the very sky." That is, in some sense the artist is a hunter out for blood—for meanings connected to life and death. At the same time, the artist is a seer, and "the secret of seeing is . . . the pearl of great price." Vision and spirituality are irrevocably connected for Dillard.

In *Holy the Firm,* which, like *Pilgrim at Tinker Creek,* is a form of spiritual autobiography, Dillard struggles to construct meaning from an event that left a little girl disfigured. The girl, the child of a couple Dillard lived near in Washington, suffered severe burns on her face after the small airplane she was flying in with her father crashed; her father walked away from the accident unscathed. Named Julie Norwich after the medieval woman mystic Julian of Norwich, the child, be-

fore the accident, would often play with Dillard's cat, which she dressed up in a black dress like a "nun." The child fascinated Dillard "because we look a bit alike and we both knew it." Or, as Dillard reminds herself, "We *looked* a bit alike. Her face is slaughtered now, and I don't remember mine." Imagining the child in excruciating pain from the burns, pain that cannot be relieved by drugs, which merely leach out of the skinless face, Dillard questions the presence of God in the world: "The question is then, whether God touches anything. . . . Did Christ descend once and for all to no purpose, in a kind of divine and kenotic suicide, or ascend once and for all, pulling his cross up after him like a rope ladder home?" Figuring God's coldness, she imagines him as "a glacier."

Near the beginning of the book, Dillard describes for the reader another burning: a moth drawn to her candle is quickly consumed by the flame, yet is transformed into a kind of wick, burning side by side with that of the candle. By the end of the book, she converts these striking images that structure the volume into a reaffirmation of faith, in spite of the horrible suffering of an innocent child. Such a reaffirmation is possible, she indicates explicitly, only through the transformative powers of the artist: "What can any artist set on fire but his world? . . . What can an artist use but materials, such as they are? What can he light but the short string of his gut, and when that's burnt out, any muck ready to hand?" In this conception, the artist becomes a visionary transformed by the kind of love embodied by seraphs, who are "aflame with love for God"; she affirms, "love is greater than knowledge." To be great—and to live in this world of suffering—the artist must be able to mediate between the divine and the everyday: The artist's "face is flame like a seraph's, lighting the kingdom of God for the people to see." Although *Holy the Firm* addresses more directly some of the same questions about theology as *Pilgrim at Tinker Creek* and *For the*

Time Being, it is also fundamentally a book about the artist's role in the world.

Reviewers praised *Holy the Firm* as intensely and sustainedly beautiful. As in *Pilgrim at Tinker Creek,* Dillard's prose approaches the status of poetry, with its dense clusters of images, careful attention to sound, and rhythmic power. In the passage of questions cited above, for example, she uses the technique of anaphora, the repetition in successive lines of a beginning word or phrase, to establish increasingly intense emphasis; the questions simultaneously invite the reader to internalize these difficult questions in much the same way that Whitman uses the technique in "Song of Myself." Dillard also recalls here Whitman's explicit project: to provide readers with a vision of unity in spite of the world's disharmony. Her work performs a contemporary version of Whitman's assertion, "I am large, I contain multitudes." It also echoes his indirect affirmation that the artist must both share and transcend suffering: "I am the man, I suffer'd, I was there."

Dillard's use of such images as the moth (in *Holy the Firm*), the collapsing frog and the red-winged blackbird tree (in *Pilgrim at Tinker Creek*), and the hidden penny and the illuminated skater (in *An American Childhood*) underscore the poetic qualities of Dillard's prose. In terms of theme, image, and intensity, she is perhaps best compared not to Thoreau or Whitman but to Emily Dickinson, who was the subject of Dillard's undergraduate thesis at Hollins College. In her many explorations of suffering Dickinson anticipates Dillard, affirming "I like a look of agony / Because I know it's true." Much of Dickinson's work explores the relationship between human suffering and the presence of God in the world. Dillard's images also seem often to recall Dickinson's poetry. For example, in poem 291 Dickinson describes a sunset in flamboyant and passionate terms: "How the old Mountains drip with Sunset / How the Hemlocks burn." It is "the Wizard Sun" who sparks this show, but the artist who must describe it, the poet suggests, as she asks, "Have I the lip of the Flamingo / That I dare to tell?" In *Pilgrim at Tinker Creek* Dillard describes a sunset on the mountains with similar poetic precision: "The sun in the west illuminates the ground, the mountains, and especially the bare branches of trees, so that everywhere silver trees cut into the black sky like a photographer's negative of a landscape. . . . the mountains are going on and off like neon signs." Describing the "dizzying" feeling that this panorama inspires, Dillard parallels Dickinson's description of the artist who is "paralyzed, with Gold" by his vision.

Intensity is a prominent feature of both Dickinson's and Dillard's work, and of their conception of the artist. Dickinson affiliates poetry, love, and God in poem after poem; the results of this affiliation can be apocalyptic, as in poem 1247: "To pile like Thunder to its close / Then crumble grand away / While Everything created hid / This—would be Poetry—." Poetry arrives simultaneously with love, and experiencing either causes one to "consume"—that is, to endure a death that is also a consummation and a vision of divinity. Dickinson describes a similarly intense and potentially destructive vision in poem 601, which begins, "A Still—Volcano— Life," and poem 754, "My Life had stood—a Loaded Gun." Just as Dickinson often describes herself as a nun or the bride of God, in *Holy the Firm,* Dillard concludes by imagining the vision of Julie Norwich and affirming to both the burned girl and the reader the redemptive role of the artist: "So live. I'll be the nun for you."

For both Dickinson and Dillard science is not incommensurate with vision or art; more often, it enables the artist's transcendent vision. A careful observer of the particular, Dickinson frequently transforms the everyday into art. A snake, in poem 986, is "a narrow Fellow in the Grass" who provokes "a tighter breathing / And Zero at the Bone," a chill forecasting eternity as much as death. She describes without sentiment in poem

328 a bird that "bit an Angleworm in halves / And ate the fellow, raw." Similarly, in *Pilgrim at Tinker Creek* Dillard describes an incident in which a teacher brought the egg case of a praying mantis to school so that the children could watch the eggs hatch; over the course of a few hours, two of the new mantises consumed the other siblings: "Tiny legs were still kicking from the mouths of both." Finally, the two survivors fight and die of the injuries; Dillard observes, "I felt as though I myself should swallow the corpses, shutting my eyes and washing them down like jagged pills, so all that life wouldn't be lost."

In spite of the horror provoked by both these descriptions, the eye of the writer transforms the sacrifice into something lovely and again transcendent. In Dickinson's poem 328, the bird has a "Velvet Head"; after the poet's sighting—or because of it—the bird departs: "He unrolled his feathers / And rowed him softer home— / Than Oars divide the Ocean, / Too silver for a seam." Just as the image of the bird mutates into a rower that magically becomes part of the mysterious, divine ocean, so too do Dillard's hatching mantises mean more than their literal, voracious presence: "They trailed from the egg case to the base of the Mason jar in a living bridge that looked like Arabic calligraphy, some baffling text from the Koran inscribed down the air by a fine hand." Similarly, Dickinson's "certain Slant of light" (poem 258) gives the viewer an "internal difference," "an imperial affliction"; in *Pilgrim at Tinker Creek* Dillard's "slant of light" confirms her understanding that "living is moving; time is a live creek bearing changing lights."

Any comparison between Dickinson and Dillard must acknowledge the wry humor of both writers. After Dickinson's description in poem 328 of the bird's raw feast, she continues with comic images: "Then he drank a Dew / From a convenient Grass— / And then hopped sidewise to the Wall / To let a Beetle pass—." Suddenly we see the voracious bird transformed into a gen-

tleman sipping a cocktail and standing decorously aside. Imagination, Dickinson suggests, can transform the most violent act to a humorous one in the turn of a phrase.

In spite of her affirmation in *An American Childhood* that "I grew up in Pittsburgh in the 1950s, in a house full of comedians, reading books," Dillard has received far too little credit for her humor. We see this humor sprinkled liberally throughout her writing; even in the poignant *Holy the Firm* and *Encounters with Chinese Writers,* Dillard insists on the necessary, salvific function of humor. She delights in telling stories, such as the one in *Pilgrim at Tinker Creek* about the man who found starlings roosting incorrigibly in the large sycamore tree near his house; frustrated by ineffective attempts to remove the noisy, dirty birds, he killed three with a shotgun. "When asked if that discouraged the birds, he reflected a minute, leaned forward, and said confidentially, 'Those three it did.' " In the same text, when speaking about the seasonal dropping of tree leaves each fall, she affirms, "Don't believe them when they tell you how economical and thrifty nature is, whose leaves return to the soil. Wouldn't it be cheaper to leave them on the tree in the first place? This deciduous business alone is a radical scheme, the brainchild of a deranged manic-depressive with limitless capital." Both Dickinson and Dillard use various forms of humor—stories, understatement, and overstatement—to affirm the visionary role of the creative artist.

In different ways, Dillard's collection of literary critical essays on contemporary fiction, *Living by Fiction,* her autobiographical collection of sketches, *Encounters with Chinese Writers,* and her extended meditation on the creative artist's life, *The Writing Life,* all consider the complexities of writing and the life of the mind. Although she is principally an essayist, Dillard poses questions and makes observations in *Living by Fiction* that parallel her own life and work. Like Dickinson, who proclaimed in poem 435 that the "Majority" determines what is "sane" and what is "dangerous— / And handled with a Chain—" Dillard interrogates the line between creativity and insanity: "Where do those of us who are not in asylums draw the line—by tacit agreement—between the humanly meaningful and meaningless? . . . What is (gasp) the relationship between the world and the mind? Is *knowledge* possible? Do we ever discover meaning, or do we always make it up?"

One of Dillard's projects in *Living by Fiction* is to "cry foul" the aims of some contemporary modernist fiction to "[recreate] . . . the meaninglessness of the modern world." She asks her reader, "When is a work 'about' meaninglessness and when is it simply meaningless?" Believing in the responsibility of art to generate fire as well as smoke—"any art, including an art of surface, must do more than dazzle"—she calls for a more serious contemporary criticism. Although, as she points out, much contemporary fiction concerns itself with art—and with distinguishing itself from merely popular writing—she emphasizes her belief that "our knowledge is contextual and only contextual." In some sense, this assertion indirectly underscores the changing fortunes of fiction and nonfiction over time; in the recent past, novels were considered "junk entertainment," while nonfiction was "significant literature." Finally, whether she composes fiction or nonfiction, Dillard affirms the need for writing to provide interpretations of the world rather than merely to reflect the self-absorbed playfulness of the writer. Such an ethic is reflected profoundly in *For the Time Being.*

Dillard's comments on style in prose fiction provide a window through which to view her nonfiction. She describes, for example, the nonlinear progression of much contemporary fiction, its sometimes trendy use of "narrative collage"; yet her books and many of her essays—such as "An Expedition to the Pole" in *Teaching a Stone to Talk*—make powerful use of this technique. In that book, she moves readily between such disparate objects as "a snail, a sea lion, or a systems analyst" ("Life on the Rocks: The Galápagos") via the flight of her imagination. In celebrating the merit of contemporary prose style (while again disparaging style for its own sake), she identifies two strands of style, the "plain" and the "fancy," both of which she employs effectively. Fine writing, she affirms in *Living by Fiction,* "is at once an exploratory craft and the planet it attains"; paradoxically, such prose can both "penetrate and dazzle." Dillard asks, "How can it call attention to itself, waving its arms as it were, while performing metaphysics behind its back?" She then describes a prose that is "a wrought verbal surface" that "changes subjects as often as it changes moods; it presents us with an array of the world's objects moving so fast they spin." Yet this kind of performance is precisely what we see, over and over, in Dillard's own powerful prose style.

At the same time, she also uses the kind of "plain," spare, almost ascetic style that in *Living by Fiction* she calls "useful": it is "not an end in itself, but a means"; it controls experience and renders difficult ideas with firmness and control. Such prose does not require metaphor: "No angelic systems need be dragged in by the hair to sprinkle upon objects a borrowed splendor." She celebrates such writing in *Encounters with Chinese Writers,* observing that "what interests me here, and elsewhere, is the possibility for a purified nonfiction narration—a kind of Chekhovian storytelling which might illuminate the world with a delicate light—coupled with humor in the American tradition and no comment." Dillard makes effective use of this restrained style, especially in certain situations where (as in "The Deer at Providencia" in *Teaching a Stone to Talk*) great suffering is involved. Paradoxically, however, other similar situations (as in *Holy the Firm*) might require the elevated prose style that enables the writer and the reader to construct meaning from disorder. As Dillard herself acknowledges, the "fancy" and "plain" styles can be used together. One of her best descriptions of the world-view that each style embodies makes clear for us their relationship in her own writing: "If we call fancy experimental prose 'poetry' and plain prose 'science,' then again we see that most prose falls somewhere in the middle," she writes in *Living by Fiction.* In Dillard's work, the exuberant, soaring "fancy" style is often counterbalanced and grounded by the "plain" style.

The idea of "usefulness" re-emerges in *Encounters with Chinese Writers,* where she describes writing in terms beyond individual self-expression. For the Chinese, representing a collective understanding of the world is more important than presenting "an individualistic and anarchic mentality" that is "too selfish for us," as one of her Chinese colleagues insists. In characteristic Dillard fashion, one of the most prominent descriptive details assumes metaphoric significance. Everywhere she goes in China, Dillard sees trees, a precious national resource, carefully watered and protected in an environment that is hostile at best, "a kind of packed dust. Every day, another of us notices this dust and asks the guide, How can these trees live?" By contrast, in the United States, trees are so common they are ignored, needing little care. Visiting America, the Chinese writers express a similar amazement: "Who takes care of all these trees?" The tactful image of the trees evokes the differences between the two countries: in the poor country, life flourishes in spite of the hostile environment; in the wealthy one, life flourishes although people are unconscious of its lushness and their own neglect.

In *The Writing Life,* Dillard emphasizes a characteristic that emerges elsewhere in her work: the necessary courage of the writer, whether to carry on in the face of inevitable failure, to cut inessential matter, to make imaginative leaps, to connect meaningfully with an audience, or to be patient and persevering. Writing is difficult, she emphasizes, requiring time, concentration, self-awareness (and, paradoxically, the loss of self-awareness) and, perhaps most important, faith. In a passage reminiscent once again of Emily Dickinson's affirmation of the writer's volcanic power to destroy and create, Dillard imagines her typewriter "erupting": "The old green Smith-Corona typewriter on the table was exploding with fire and ash. Showers of sparks shot out of its caldera—the dark hollow in which the keys lie. Smoke and cinders poured out, noises exploded and spattered, black dense smoke rose up, and a wild, deep fire lighted the whole thing. It shot sparks." Comic in its hyperbole, this passage simultaneously signals the author's understanding of writing's explosive power.

Finally, for Dillard writing must be useful to others in ways that enable them to transcend and live fully their daily lives: "Why are we reading if not in hope that the writer will magnify and dramatize our days, will illuminate and inspire us with wisdom, courage, and the possibility of meaningfulness, and will press upon our minds the deepest mysteries, so we may feel again their majesty and power?" For her own life—and, by extension, for her reader—she seeks the intensity, passion, tenacity, and vision that she celebrates at the end of "Living Like Weasels" (in *Teaching a Stone to Talk*) as she recalls Ernest Thompson Seton's story of a man shooting an eagle out of the sky and finding "the dry skull of a weasel fixed by the jaws to his throat":

I think it would be well, and proper, and obedient, and pure, to grasp your one necessity and not let it go, to dangle from it limp wherever it takes you. Then even death, where you're going no matter how you live, cannot you part. Seize it and let it seize you up aloft even, till your eyes burn out and drop; let your musky flesh fall off in shreds, and let your very bones unhinge and scatter, loosened over fields, over fields and woods, lightly, thoughtless, from any height at all, from as high as eagles.

"OURS IS A PLANET SOWN IN BEINGS":
LATER WORK

Dillard's mature work has continued the themes and perspectives of her earlier writing, with some interesting variations. More accessible than her first collection of poems, *Tickets for a Prayer Wheel,* her 1995 book of "found" poems, *Mornings Like This,* constructs poems out of a wide range of Dillard's reading, from Mikhail Prishvin's *Nature's Diary* (1925) to D. C. Beard's *The American Boys Handy Book* (1882), the letters of Vincent Van Gogh (1873–1890), Charles H. Cugle's *Practical Navigation* (1936), Elizabeth A. Ryan's *How to Make Grammar Fun—and Easy!* (1992), and Max Picard's *The World of Silence* (1946). Although this eclectic collection might at first glance seem to diverge from Dillard's earlier concerns, in fact it highlights many of those interests. In its very construction—"making" poems out of prose—it emphasizes the importance of seeing the world in new ways. The book also embodies Dillard's central intellectual and spiritual task of constructing alliances and coherences where none ostensibly exist.

Encompassing perspectives from the playful to the profound, *Mornings Like This* also continues Dillard's strong emphasis on surprise and humor. The titles of the sources from which she draws set up expectations that the writer delights in undercutting or transforming. A book called *The Friendly Stars* (1907), which suggests a book introducing children to astronomy, yields a poem called "An Acquaintance in the Heavens," which surveys the night sky over the year with poignant personal detail, ending with a description of "Fomalhaut the lonely": "Just after dark, one sees it, trailing / Over the small arc of its circle / With no companion near it, and no need." "Observations and Experiments," another poem about seeing, comes from a book called *Observations and Experiments in Natural History* (1960), which sounds technical and dry as dust. But in the second section of "Observations," Dillard draws

from the prose her own characteristic gallows humor: "Trout seem to learn that danger / Is associated with artificial flies; / Perhaps it is the hook in them." As with her earlier work, literal description effortlessly spills over into resonant metaphor.

As its title suggests, Dillard's 1999 work *For the Time Being* also continues the author's earlier themes of vision, the search for spiritual significance, courage in the face of great suffering, and the place (in many senses) of humans in the universe and in time. Her prose, however, is more ascetic, with fewer flights of the imagination and a quieter sense of humor. Although she reiterates the necessity to maintain faith in a troubled and troubling world, her vision in this book seems less optimistic and less exuberant, and her questioning of God more intense. This questioning begins aggressively as Dillard graphically describes medical-textbook photographs of deformed children. Picturing for us two bird-headed dwarfs, she comments on her own misapprehension of a girl, who seemed initially "amused and haughty," but given her mental retardation was "likely neither haughty nor bright." She pictures for us another girl, in "a dress with a polka dot collar," whose "eyes are far apart, and under each one is a nostril. She has no nose at all, only a no-man's-land of featureless flesh and skin, an inch or two wide, that roughly bridges her face's halves. You pray that this grotesque-looking child is mentally deficient as well. But she is not. 'Normal intelligence,' the text says." Returning to these children later in the book, Dillard signals the profound difficulty of describing them by quoting from the notebooks of the French painter Edgar Degas: "There are, naturally, feelings that one cannot render."

The structure of *For the Time Being* parallels the associative, nonlinear shape of *Pilgrim at Tinker Creek,* though without the latter's seasonal organization. As in her essay "An Expedition to the Pole," from *Teaching a Stone to Talk,* Dillard provides bones for the narrative by dividing it into recurring sections, such as "Sand," "Clouds," "Encounters," "Birth," and "Numbers." In addition, the meandering structure is anchored by Dillard revisiting several places (Israel, China) and people (the paleontologist priest and philosopher Pierre Teilhard de Chardin; the eighteenth-century Ukrainian peasant Baal Shem Tov, founder of modern Hasidism; and a nurse named Pat Eisberg, who washes newborns). Reflecting the conjunction of science, art, and mysticism that characterize her earlier works, *For the Time Being* is a meditation not only on human suffering but also on human indifference to suffering. Addressing the reader directly on many occasions, fostering self-questioning, Dillard asks such questions as "Shall we contemplate Chinese scholars' beheadings twenty-three centuries ago? It hurts worse to break a leg." Here as elsewhere we see her dark humor emerge; she reflects on an ancient Chinese emperor's order to make use of dead bodies, "It is never easy to find good fill for construction. Many workers died building the Great Wall; no one knows if millions died or mere thousands." Of the brother and sister bird-headed dwarfs—he, five years old and grim; she, three and untroubled—she comments, "The confident girl and the sorrowing boy, facing each other on opposite pages, make it appear as if, at some time between the ages of three and five, these kids catch on. Their legs are short, and it is going to be more of a problem than buying clothes."

Dillard's reflections on clouds, sand, and numbers suggest the transience of human existence, its fragility and its relative insignificance. At the same time that Dillard ponders the idea of individuality—figured, for example, in unique clouds—she also situates individuals in the stream of life, in a human community existing over thousands of years. Just as in her earlier works, Dillard invites readers to take the large, transcendent view. More directly here, however, she assumes an activist position in the face of suffering. For example, she invites us to consider the size of Los Angeles airport, with its twenty-five thousand parking spaces, in far from neutral terms:

> This is one space each for two years' worth of accidental killings from land mines left over from recent wars. . . . If you propped up or stacked four bodies to a car, you could fit into the airport parking lot all the corpses from the firestorm bombing of Tokyo in March, 1945, or all the world's dead from two atomic bombs, or the corpses of Londoners who died in the plague, the corpses of Burundians killed in civil war since 1993. You could not fit America's homeless there, however, even at eighteen or nineteen to a car.

Ending her paragraph here, Dillard opens a space for self-reflection. She also implicitly invites readers to reconsider her earlier, ostensibly "non-political" writing, which is clearly impelled by such concerns as the materialism, excessive speed, and injustice in American society.

In spite of the violence that she sees as endemic to life, and in spite of her contention that "God *per se* is wholly invisible" and "his voice is very still, very small," Dillard highlights a belief system called "pan-entheism." Pan-entheism holds that "not only is God immanent in everything, as plain pantheists hold, but more profoundly everything is simultaneously in God, within God the transcendent." Finally, she concludes, though "doubt and dedication often go hand in hand," "the absolute is available to everyone in every age. There never was a more holy age than ours, and never a less." Dillard's passion, and her passionate understanding of the paradoxes of faith, urges readers to share her perspective, her vision.

Selected Bibliography

WORKS OF ANNIE DILLARD

BOOKS
Pilgrim at Tinker Creek. New York: Harper's Magazine Press, 1974.

Tickets for a Prayer Wheel. Columbia: University of Missouri Press, 1974.

Holy the Firm. New York: Harper and Row, 1977.

The Weasel. Claremont, Calif.: Rara Avis Press, 1981. (A limited edition of 190 copies.)

Living by Fiction. New York: Harper and Row, 1982.

Teaching a Stone to Talk: Expeditions and Encounters. New York: Harper and Row, 1982.

Encounters with Chinese Writers. Middletown, Conn.: Wesleyan University Press, 1984.

An American Childhood. New York: Harper and Row, 1987.

The Writing Life. New York: Harper and Row, 1989.

The Living. New York: HarperCollins, 1992.

The Annie Dillard Reader. New York: HarperCollins, 1994.

Mornings Like This: Found Poems. New York: HarperCollins, 1995.

For the Time Being. New York: Knopf, 1999.

ESSAYS

"Thinking About Language." *Living Wilderness* 38:2–3 (Autumn 1974).

"Winter Melons." *Harper's* 248:87, 89–90 (January 1974).

"Some Notes on the Uncertainty Principal." *New Lazarus Review* 1:49–50 (1978).

"A Speech on Socks." *New York Times,* December 12, 1978, sec. A, 23.

"The Joys of Reading." *New York Times Magazine,* May 16, 1982, pp. 47, 68–69, 78–81.

"Is There Really Such a Thing as Talent?" *Seventeen,* June 1979, p. 86. Reprinted in *The Elements of Writing,* edited by Peter D. Lindblom. New York: Macmillan, 1983.

"The Purification of Poetry—Right Out of the Ballpark." *Parnassus* 11:287–301 (1984).

"Why I Live Where I Live." *Esquire* 101:90–92 (March 1984).

"How I Wrote the Moth Essay—and Why." In *The Northern Sampler.* Edited by Thomas Cooley. New York: W.W. Norton, 1985.

"Postscript on Process." In *The Bedford Reader.* Edited by X. J. Kennedy and Dorothy M. Kennedy. New York: St. Martin's Press, 1985.

"Writing 'God in the Doorway.'" In *Writing from Start to Finish.* Edited by Jeffrey L. Duncan. New York: Harcourt Brace, 1985.

"The French and Indian War in Pittsburgh: A Memoir." *American Heritage* 38:49–53 (July/August 1987).

"To Fashion a Text." In *Inventing the Truth: The Art and Craft of Memoir.* Edited by William Zinsser. New York: Book-of-the-Month Club Press, 1987.

"Making Contact." *Yale Review* 72:615–22 (October 1988).

POETRY

"The Sign of Your Father." *Field* 11:23–24 (autumn 1974).

"The Heart." *Poetry* 125:260 (February 1975).

"A Natural History of Getting through the Year." *Poetry* 125:261 (February 1975).

"Quatrain of the Body's Sleep." *Poetry* 125:262 (February 1975).

"Monarchs in the Field." *Harper's* 253:104 (October 1976).

"Metaphysical Model with Feathers." *Atlantic* 242:82 (October 1978).

"Language for Everyone." *Southwest Review* 71:488–92 (1986).

SHORT STORIES

"Life Class." *Carolina Quarterly* 24:23–27 (spring 1972). Expanded and revised version reprinted in *Antaeus* 36:52–60 (winter 1980).

"Five Sketches." *North American Review* 260:30–31 (summer 1975).

"The Doughnut." *Antioch Review* 34:22–25 (fall–winter 1975/1976).

"A Christmas Story." *Harper's* 292:58 (January 1976).

"Utah." *Triquarterly* 35:96–98 (spring 1976).

"At Home with Gastropods—A Nineteenth Century Interior, in Translation." *North American Review* 263:50 (spring 1978).

"The Living." *Harper's* 257:45–52, 57–64 (November 1978).

"Forest and Shore." *Harper's* 270:24 (January 1985).

OTHER WORKS

The Best American Essays. (Guest editor.) New York: Ticknor and Fields, 1988.

"Tales of Grandeur, Tales of Risk." *Harper's* 249:122 (November 1974).

"Critics' Christmas Choices." *Commonweal,* December 7, 1979, pp. 693–694.

Foreword to *Moments of Light*. By Fred Chappell. New York: New South, 1980.

"Reading for Work and Pleasure." *New York Times Book Review,* December 4, 1983, p. 66.

"First Taste of America." *American Heritage* 36:26 (December 1984).

"The Good Books: Writers' Choices." Edited by Karen Fitzgerald. *Ms.* 14:80–81 (December 1985).

"Natural History: An Annotated Booklist." *Antaeus* 57:283–289 (1986).

"The Meaning of Life." *Life* 11:93 (December 1988).

CRITICAL AND BIOGRAPHICAL STUDIES

BOOKS

Cooley, John R., ed. *Earthly Words: Essays on Contemporary American Nature and Environmental Writers.* Ann Arbor: University of Michigan Press, 1994.

Johnson, Sandra Humble. *The Space Between: Literary Epiphany in the Work of Annie Dillard.* Kent, Ohio: Kent State University Press, 1992.

Kagle, Steven. *Early Nineteenth-Century American Diary Literature.* Boston: Twayne, 1986.

Parrish, Nancy C. *Lee Smith, Annie Dillard, and the Hollins Group: A Genesis of Writers.* Baton Rouge: Louisiana State University Press, 1998.

Smith, Linda L. *Annie Dillard.* New York: Twayne, 1991.

ARTICLES AND ESSAYS

Baker, John F. "Story Behind the Book: *Pilgrim at Tinker Creek.*" *Publishers Weekly,* March 18, 1974, p. 28.

Becker, John E. "Science and the Sacred: From Walden to Tinker Creek." *Thought—A Review of Culture and Idea* 62:400–413 (1987).

Bischoff, Joan. "Fellow Rebels: Annie Dillard and Maxine Hong Kingston." *English Journal* 78:62–67 (December 1989).

Cantwell, Mary. "A Pilgrim's Progress." *New York Times Magazine,* April 26, 1992, p. 34.

Clark, Suzanne. "Annie Dillard in Nature and the Subject of Nonfiction." In *Literary Nonfiction: Theory, Criticism, Pedagogy.* Edited by Chris Anderson. Carbondale: Southern Illinois University Press, 1989.

Elder, John. "Structures of Evolving Consciousness." In *Imagining the Earth: Poetry and the Vision of Nature.* Urbana: University of Illinois Press, 1985.

Felch, Susan M. "Annie Dillard: Modern Physics in a Contemporary Mystic." *Mosaic* 22, no. 2:1–14 (1989).

Keller, Joseph. "The Function of Paradox in Mystical Discourse." *Studia Mystica* 6:3–19 (fall 1983).

Koenig, Rhoda. "About This Issue." *Harper's* 248:14 (February 1974).

Lea, Sydney. " 'I recognize thy glory': On the American Nature Essay." *The Sewanee Review* 106:478–485 (summer 1998).

Lavery, David L. "Noticer: The Visionary Art of Annie Dillard." *Massachusetts Review* 21:255–270 (summer 1980).

McClintock, James I. "Annie Dillard: Ritualist." In *Nature's Kindred Spirits: Aldo Leopold, Joseph Wood Krutch, Edward Abbey, Annie Dillard, and Gary Snyder.* Madison: University of Wisconsin Press, 1994.

———. " 'Pray Without Ceasing': Annie Dillard among the Nature Writers." In *Earthly Words: Essays on Contemporary American Nature and Environmental Writers.* Edited by John R. Cooley. Ann Arbor: University of Michigan Press, 1994.

McConahay, Mary Davidson. "Into the Bladelike Arms of God: The Quest for Meaning through Symbolic Language in Thoreau and Annie Dillard." *Denver Quarterly* 20:103–116 (fall 1985).

McIlroy, Gary. "Pilgrim at Tinker Creek and the Burden of Science." *American Literature* 59:71–84 (March 1987).

———. "Pilgrim at Tinker Creek and the Social Legacy of Walden." *South Atlantic Quarterly* 85:111–122 (spring 1986). Reprinted in *Earthly Words: Essays on Contemporary American Nature and Environmental Writers.* Edited by John R. Cooley. Ann Arbor: University of Michigan Press, 1994.

Messer, Richard E. "The Spiritual Quest in Two Works by Annie Dillard." *Journal of Evolutionary Psychology* 9:321–330 (August 1988).

Reimer, Margaret Loewen. "The Dialectical Vision of Annie Dillard's *Pilgrim at Tinker Creek.*" *Critique: Studies in Modern Fiction* 24:182–191 (spring 1983).

Ronda, Bruce A. "Annie Dillard and the Fire of God." *Christian Century* 100:483–486 (May 18, 1983).

Scheick, William J. "Annie Dillard: Narrative Fringe." In *Contemporary American Women Writers: Nar-*

rative Strategies. Edited by Catherine Rainwater and William J. Scheick. Lexington: University Press of Kentucky, 1985.

Smith, Pamela A. "The Ecotheology of Annie Dillard: A Study in Ambivalence." *Cross Currents* 45:341–358 (fall 1995).

Tallmadge, John. "Beyond the Excursion: Initiatory Themes in Annie Dillard and Terry Tempest Williams." In *Reading the Earth: New Directions in the Study of Literature and the Environment.* Edited by Michael P. Branch et al. Moscow: University of Idaho Press, 1998.

INTERVIEWS

Caldwell, Gail. "Pilgrim's Progress." *Boston Globe Magazine,* May 8, 1983, pp. 10–11, 32–37, 42, 48.

Chambers, Andrea. "Annie Dillard: Her Pilgrimage This Time Is into Her Past." *People,* October 19, 1987, pp. 99–100, 105.

Hammond, Karla M. "Drawing the Curtains: An Interview with Annie Dillard." *Bennington Review* 10:30–38 (April 1981).

Krauth, Laurie. "Diving into Life with Annie Dillard." *Toledo Blade,* February 14, 1988, sec. F, 1–2.

Lindsey, Robert. "Annie Dillard: Far from Tinker Creek." *New York Times,* November 9, 1977, sec. C, 1, 7.

Major, Mike. "Annie Dillard: Pilgrim of the Absolute." *American* 138:363–364 (May 6, 1978).

Sanoff, Alvin P. "Remembrances of Things Past." *U.S. News and World Report,* November 16, 1987, p. 78.

Trueheart, Charles. "Annie Dillard's Pilgrim's Progress." *Washington Post,* October 28, 1987, sec. D, 1–3.

Weber, Katherine. "Annie Dillard." *Publishers Weekly,* September 1, 1989, pp. 67–68.

Yancey, Philip. "A Face Aflame: An Interview with Annie Dillard." *Christianity Today* 5:958–963 (May 1978).

BOOK REVIEWS

PILGRIM AT TINKER CREEK (1974)
Kiser, Jo Ann. "Pilgrim at Tinker Creek." *Village Voice,* May 2, 1974, pp. 50–51.

Lehmann-Haupt, Christopher. "The Bloody Veil of Nature." *New York Times,* March 12, 1974, p. 35.

Maddocks, Melvin. "Terror and Celebration." *Time,* March 18, 1974, p. 92.

Welty, Eudora. "Meditation on Seeing." *New York Times Book Review,* March 24, 1974, p. 4.

TICKETS FOR A PRAYER WHEEL (1974)
Randolph, Leonard. "*Tickets for a Prayer Wheel.*" *Living Wilderness* 38:37 (summer 1974).

HOLY THE FIRM (1977)
Buechner, Frederick. "Island Journal." *New York Times Book Review,* September 25, 1977, pp. 12, 40.

Lemontt, Bobbie Burch. "*Holy the Firm.*" *Western American Literature* 13:274 (November 1978).

Phillips, Robert. "In Brief." *Commonweal,* February 3, 1978, p. 94.

LIVING BY FICTION (1982)
Bourjaily, Vance. "Contemporary Modernists—A Dreadful Mouthful." *New York Times Book Review,* May 9, 1982, pp. 10, 22–23.

Kilgore, Kathryn. "Metaphysics in a Teacup." *Village Voice,* July 13, 1982, pp. 40–41.

Sundelson, David. "Matthew Arnold She's Not." *Nation,* November 20, 1982, pp. 535–536.

TEACHING A STONE TO TALK (1982)
Bevington, Helen. "Tranquil and Trembling." *New York Times Book Review,* November 28, 1982, pp. 13, 19.

Hancock, Wade. "Transmuting the Invisible into Prose." *Christian Science Monitor,* November 5, 1982, sec. B, 3.

Lehmann-Haupt, Christopher. "Books of the Times." *New York Times,* September 21, 1977, sec. C, 17.

ENCOUNTERS WITH CHINESE WRITERS (1984)
Broughton, Diane. "Mission Inscrutable: Omission." *Los Angeles Times Book Review,* November 18, 1984, p. 11.

Herbert, Rosemary. "University Presses." *Christian Science Monitor Book Review,* December 7, 1984, sec. B, 14.

Silver, Ron. *"Encounters with Chinese Writers."* *Saturday Review,* March–April 1985, pp. 64–65.

AN AMERICAN CHILDHOOD (1987)

Hawkins, Peter S. *The Christian Century,* June 7, 1989, pp. 592–595.

Hazo, Samuel. "Attention Must Be Paid." *Commonweal,* November 6, 1987, pp. 636–638.

Perrin, Noel. "Her Inexhaustible Mind." *New York Times Book Review,* September 27, 1987, p. 7.

THE WRITING LIFE (1989)

Bradbury, Malcolm. *Times Literary Supplement,* January 17, 1992, pp. 7–9.

Maitland, Sara. *New York Times Book Review,* September 17, 1989, p. 15.

Updike, John. *The New Yorker,* December 25, 1989, pp. 106–108.

THE LIVING (1992)

Keneally, Thomas. *New York Times Book Review,* May 3, 1992, p. 9.

Kingsolver, Barbara. *Nation,* May 25, 1992, pp. 692–694.

Scheese, Don. *Georgia Review* 47:193–197 (spring 1993).

THE ANNIE DILLARD READER (1994)

Torrens, James S. *America,* November 19, 1994, pp. 2–3.

MORNINGS LIKE THIS: FOUND POEMS (1995)

Haines, John. *Hudson Review,* 48:663–671 (winter 1996).

FOR THE TIME BEING (1999)

Baumgaertner, Jill Palaez. *Christian Century,* May 19, 1999, pp. 572–573.

Lesser, Wendy. *New York Times Book Review,* March 28, 1999, p. 9.

Pickering, Sam. *The Sewanee Review,* 107: CXX–CXXIV (fall 1999).

—*KAREN L. KILCUP*

Stanley Elkin

1930–1995

"THERE IS IN literature an element of what I shall call 'crossover,'" Stanley Elkin stated during a conference of American fiction specialists in Nice, France, in 1982. Making a crossover, he explained, involves the "grafting of one condition upon another," so that what would be otherwise unremarkable in life becomes, in literary art, something noteworthy for its quirk, wrinkle, or slippage from one style of order into another. Giving examples from his own work and that of others, Elkin clarified how it is not the subject itself that must be idiosyncratic, strange, or mysterious, but rather the way in which the subject is portrayed; he referred to the "protuberant salience of the obliquely sighted"— a suddenly surprising view that puts the object in an unexpected light. That is what the crossover is: a clever move from one angle to another, a momentarily disorienting switch that catches the reader off guard.

Because such rhetorical switches or shifts are the stock in trade of comedians, the key technique with which they make their jokes, Elkin has been most readily appreciated as a comic writer. His fiction is given over to outspoken characters who defend their oddities with great verve; their verbal dexterity alone makes them seem like stand-up comedians. Himself like a nightclub comic, Elkin weaves narratives that proceed episodically (when they proceed at all). Rather than develop-

ing a plotline, he allows his protagonists to display themselves in an ongoing series of dramatized attitudes that seem most like vaudeville turns, the comic release of one providing the momentum that carries an audience into the next entertainment. Yet beneath the hilarity lies a distinctive view of life that characterizes Elkin's work as a whole. We are all orphans, he says, rootless dwellers in a new world that has itself been orphaned from securely nurturing tradition. What both we and the world have to do at every turn is make ourselves up from the materials our popular culture provides. Those materials, like the franchises that supply them, are often a crudely funny mix of the terrible and the sublime. Any combination will be radical, Elkin knows, and it is in his presentation of these that readers find humor, intelligence, and ultimately satisfaction with having learned something useful about their world.

BACKGROUND

The son of Philip Elkin, a salesman, and Zelda Feldman Elkin, Stanley Lawrence Elkin was born in New York City on May 11, 1930. Soon afterward the family moved to Chicago, where Elkin was raised. In his childhood he was enthralled by his father's colorful storytelling, and he developed an appreciation for his family's Jewish American heritage during vacation-time visits back to New York. Elkin attended the University of Illinois, where he earned his bachelor's (1952), master's (1953), and doctoral (1961) degrees, the last pushed back by Elkin's service in the army between 1955 and 1957. On February 1, 1953, he married Joan Marion Jacobson, a painter; they had three children (Philip Aaron, Bernard Edward, and Molly Ann). Elkin's doctoral dissertation on William Faulkner qualified him to teach modern fiction (as literature) and contemporary fiction (as creative writing). Except for occasional visiting professorships at other leading writing programs, he pursued an academic career at Washington University in St. Louis, Missouri, beginning as an instructor in 1960 and in 1983 becoming the Merle King Professor of Modern Letters, a position he held until his death (from a heart attack) on May 31, 1995.

Stanley Elkin's personal experiences assume a quiet but evident place in his fiction. His parents were a primary and quite specific influence, from his father's narrative proficiency (for both sales and anecdotes) to his mother's dedication to his career, personally funding residencies abroad (in Rome and in London), where Elkin had the freedom to write his first novel, *Boswell: A Modern Comedy* (1964). From his childhood in Chicago and time spent in New York, Elkin learned the nuances of the urban scene; from his study of modern writers at the University of Illinois he mastered intricacies of technique; and during his graduate student work on the little magazine *Accent* he was able to polish his own work and begin friendships with other novice writers, among them John Gardner and William H. Gass. During his service in the army Elkin was introduced to the wonders of radio, an interest he exploited in his third novel, *The Dick Gibson Show* (1971).

As a devoted family man, responsible college professor, and steadily productive author, Elkin was perhaps not a likely prospect for glamour or high adventure. But his genius would be to take the mundanely familiar prospects of personal and professional life and, by virtue of his clever literary shifts or crossovers, create engaging dramas. A demoralized salesman whipping up enthusiasm to sell an unwanted set of china can be a significant event for Elkin, not just realistically but in its deepest imaginative dimensions. Although there may not be a great deal of externally observable action in his work, the language Elkin employs is always enriched and exciting. When the most personally significant factor in his life became his battle with multiple sclerosis, which he was diagnosed with in the early 1970s, Elkin seized upon his illness as a way of identifying with human transience, not least of all in his writing of *The Magic Kingdom* (1985), a novel portraying the visit to Disney World of seven terminally ill children.

Although his characters have a great range of backgrounds and stretch from bail bondsmen to God himself, all of them are talented spokespersons, all of them masters of the sales job in which the product being pitched is themselves. Like performers in grand opera, Elkin's characters "sing" not so much to entertain an audience as to define themselves. Their songs, however, are familiar because they are made up of elements common to most late-twentieth-century Americans, albeit combined in funny and enlightening ways.

THE EARLY WORK: ARIAS OF INVENTION

"A Sound of Distant Thunder" was Elkin's first published fiction; it appeared in the little magazine *Epoch* in 1957. Not included in his major short story collections, it was reprinted with several other fugitive pieces in *Early Elkin,* a small-press volume appearing in 1985, at the height of his critical acclaim. The title is this story's most dramatic element. Within the narrative, not a great deal happens, and even when there is action, the focus is internal. On the story's surface, a shopkeeper named Feldman leaves home, stops for breakfast at the delicatessen where other neighborhood merchants are starting off their day, then opens his store for an uneventful morning and afternoon in which only one other person shows up, a customer who doesn't buy. But this surface is quiet because it should be. Feldman is in a gentle trade, selling fine china, where moving even a single expensive set would amount to an above average day of sales.

What does happen is initially subtle, nothing more than a vague threat, more imaginary than real, that by the story's end has grown to be not only profound but catastrophic. Quiet as the setting is, it seems inevitable that this peaceful order be destroyed by something almost completely unpredictable—this is the crossover that Elkin believes all successful literary art must have. Yet the concluding disruption (a riot, with looting and destruction) is not the story's point. Instead, the most interesting event turns out to be something that happens in between, when before Feldman's fears turn out to be true (because he makes them true), the man does what he is good at: he delivers a sales pitch. Not that the pitch is materially effective, for the customer it is aimed at is looking for a trendy name brand that Feldman doesn't stock. And not that this salesmanship does anything to relieve the ominous signs that since the story's beginning have been pressing all around. The day is still hot, traffic remains slow, vacated storefronts continue to define the neighborhood, presumably a result of growing racial tensions between white shop owners and the neighborhood's disfranchised African Americans. Feldman's sales pitch, however, is a thing unto itself, even as he tries selling his wary customer something the man doesn't want by telling him in compulsive detail things he doesn't need to know. Cut off from effective purpose and sundered from its context, the pitch becomes what Elkin, in the volume's introduction, calls one of "the arias my

characters often give themselves over to in my work."

It is this operatic quality of self-definition that becomes in later work the signal quality of Stanley Elkin's writing. As an argument for existence not by consequential action but in the very song of being, such performance demonstrates what the author, in the introduction to *Early Elkin*, praises as the "up-from-nothing quality about life which says a good word for human possibility." The contrast of this aria with the surrounding world suggests Elkin's vision, for without its projective energy life would be depressing indeed. Feldman himself is not morally superior; to anything good that comes his way he reacts with a chillingly mean spirit. His receptiveness to dim prospects distinguishes him as the most pessimistic person on the block. But unlike anyone else in the story, he can "create" himself, in a virtuoso display that eclipses customer and shop, business climate, and even the trade itself. There are declining neighborhoods and racial tensions everywhere, Elkin seems to say; it is a character like Feldman who can sustain a reader's interest in an otherwise actionless short story.

Ironically, it is the increasing popularity of china, in the form of the slickly marketed Noritake line, that costs Feldman the sale and contributes to his general demise. As an object of popular culture, Noritake becomes as much an attitude as a brand name, a lifestyle even as it functions as dinnerware. The culture, in fact, has made it a thing in itself—the customer's wife doesn't want china, she wants Noritake; absent the company's advertising campaign, however, one suspects that she would not have even considered acquiring new dishes.

Another story in this volume, "Fifty Dollars," first published in *Southwest Review* in 1959, introduces the commercial world that has replaced Feldman's commercial neighborhood; in it, as in so much of the America that came into being in the decades following World War II, people live in suburban developments and acquire goods in shopping centers. Like new brands of china, both suburbs and shopping centers have names, and the names are less pertinent to geography or demographics than to some projected theme. Elkin's character Mary lives and shops in just such an environment. Her husband dotes on the contrived artificiality of it all: how all the new homes are colonial in style, how the streets are named after the thirteen original colonies, and how the stores in the new mall express a Revolutionary era motif. Mary prefers to resist such trendiness. Yet she does have to shop, and when picking up groceries she gets herself involved in the new store's customer-appreciation promotion. By luck of the draw she becomes the five thousandth customer and is feted with a year's supply of bakery goods (ironic, as she had purchased only a single loaf of bread) and a fifty-dollar gift certificate, good anywhere in the mall.

How to spend this fifty dollars is the substance of the story. Like the crossover, it is another of Elkin's favorite devices, what film director Alfred Hitchcock called a MacGuffin, his nonsensical name for some happening, insignificant in itself, that nonetheless generates a subsequent narrative (in which the director or author could make any point desired). Elkin's point is the all-devouring nature of consumerism, accomplished through merchandising. Only because she has the gift certificate is Mary compelled to shop in the various stores. In them, she finds less substance than style, from the products available to the salespeople offering them. Herein she learns that shopping can yield an identity, a cause for being, even a purpose of sorts: exchanging the certificate for a material object will not only transform it but will change herself as well, making her the owner of a piece of jewelry, for example, rather than continuing on as the winner of a prize. Holding on to the certificate lets her maintain herself as a winner in the mall's world of impulses, signs, and signifiers, a realm in which stores are named after

images rather than for the things they sell and where young salesmen have more than good looks, "looks which stood at a slight remove from handsomeness for being so jauntily dapper." In such signs is found the song of existence, an aria of self-definition as stylistically removed from the real world as Feldman's free-floating pitch in "A Sound of Distant Thunder." In Elkin's fiction such songs become spiels, in the Jewish American tradition of self-spokesmanship by which manner alone can captivate attention and remove the listener or reader into language's own world, where things themselves are less important than a person's ability to be defined by and through them. One must be physically and economically powerful to manipulate things, but the simple mastery of a good spiel puts one in control of signs. Here is where both Elkin's and his characters' mastery lies.

Elkin's fiction owes its complexity to this dichotomous view of human existence: that the spiels so self-enhancing in an individual's life are consistent with the techniques by which popular culture itself becomes a construct of consumerism, driven by franchised images. What we treasure in interesting people we regret in our culture at large. This predicament characterizes the author's first novel, *Boswell.* As a protagonist, Boswell looks to both himself and his world for definition; not for nothing does Elkin name him for the eighteenth-century biographer who built his reputation by profiling the greatest living literary presence of his age, Dr. Samuel Johnson. The franchising nature of our modern Boswell's self-definition comes from two sources, his motivation and his methodology. Behind him stands a mentor, the psychiatrist Dr. Herlitz, who more like a fortune-teller than a shrink plots his patients' destinies (under the behavioralistic rubric of charting their aptitudes for success). Before him stands a world of celebrities, which he courts as a dilettante. Unlike James Boswell, he is presented with many personalities, not one Dr. Johnson, and he can't digest them all. But he does organize them into something he calls The Club, the founding principle of which is to replace Boswell's sense of vacancy with a purpose derived from the club members' collective fame. But Boswell's participation in The Club is contradictory. It lifts him from anonymity only to the extent that he remains an observer; were he to actively lead it, its prestige would dissolve, as he himself is not famous, reflector (rather than generator) that he is. When he becomes a professional wrestler, the same predicament obtains, for he is noteworthy only as a spectacular loser—to maintain this stature the matches must be fixed; he is not given a chance to compete and perhaps succeed on his own.

Boswell is less typical of the author's work than the stories collected in *Early Elkin,* mostly because the central character proves less successful at defining himself, and therefore presents a challenge for novel-length treatment. In time, Elkin would solve this problem by giving his novels' protagonists interesting professions that they could pursue with varying success but always with a relish for the job's shoptalk, which by itself could keep the action going for pages on end. His reputation as a fiction writer, however, was being established by his short stories, by now appearing in such prominent venues as *The Paris Review* (at the top of the literary journal market), *Esquire* (for stylish readers), and *The Saturday Evening Post* (where he had joined Kurt Vonnegut in tantalizing middle America with notions stretching the limits of popular acceptability). *Criers and Kibitzers, Kibitzers and Criers* (1966) is his first such collection, and would stand alone until much later in his career, when Elkin had already won respect as a novelist. The title piece is the volume's most representative of the author's success with voice and the manners of comedy. In it the protagonist Greenspahn learns that his shop has been pilfered—not just by the petty thieves he suspects, but by his own son, just

recently dead and still most lovingly mourned. The latter example, of course, is one of Elkin's crossovers, a mixing of unlike realms (bereavement and robbery, the intimacies of family versus the anonymity of crime). Yet for everything, Greenspahn has a verbal line; rather than crying, he prefers to kibitz, even when it comes to hectoring a customer he catches in a pathetic attempt to gain an economic edge:

> An old woman came into the store and Greenspahn recognized her. She had been in twice before that morning and both times had bought two tins of the coffee Greenspahn was running on a special. She hadn't bought anything else. Already he had lost twelve cents on her. He watched her carefully and saw with a quick rage that she went again to the coffee. She picked up another two tins and came toward the checkout counter. She wore a bright red wig which next to her very white, ancient skin gave her the appearance of a clown. She put the coffee down on the counter and looked up at Greenspahn timidly. He made no effort to ring up the sale. She stood for a moment and then pushed the coffee toward him.
>
> "Sixty-nine cents a pound," she said. "Two pounds is a dollar thirty-eight. Six cents tax is a dollar forty-four."
>
> "Lady," Greenspahn said, "don't you ever eat? Is that all you do is drink coffee?" He stared at her.
>
> Her lips began to tremble and her body shook. "A dollar forty-four," she said. "I have it right here."
>
> "This is your sixth can, lady. I lose money on it. Do you know that?"
>
> The woman continued to tremble. It was as though she were very cold.
>
> "What do you do, lady? Sell this stuff door-to-door? Am I your wholesaler?"
>
> Her body continued to shake, and she looked out at him from behind faded eyes as though she were unaware of the terrible movements of her body, as though they had, ultimately, nothing to do with her, that really she existed, hiding, crouched, somewhere behind the eyes. He had the impression that, frictionless, her old bald head bobbed beneath the wig. "All right," he said finally, "a dollar forty-four. I hope you have more luck with the item than I

had." He took the money from her and watched her as she accepted her package wordlessly and walked out of the store. He shook his head. It was all a pile of crap, he thought. He had a vision of the woman on back porches, standing silently at the back doors open on their chains, sadly extending the coffee.

He wanted to get out. Frank could watch the store. If he stole, he stole.

Though it doesn't reach the level of an aria, Greenspahn's verbal sparring defines himself more than it makes for any efficient communication with his customer. And why not? Because for the sake of his kibitzing he has transformed her from a customer into a fellow tradesperson, with whom he can engage in shoptalk. Wholesaler, peddling, margins of profits and loss, even the marketing device of a loss leader—what does a feeble old woman trying to save a few cents on her coffee bill know of all this? For all of her presence in the story, she is only able to master one line, repeated twice: the price of her paltry purchase. Her serial purchasing, however, is the MacGuffin of Elkin's narrative, the occasion, insignificant in itself, which invites the shopkeeper's spiel that makes low verbal comedy of his infuriation. The spiel victimizes the poor, uncomprehending old lady. But it hurts the spieler much more, for it propels him out of his shop, preventing him from keeping an eye on his distrusted employee, Frank, who is now positioned to steal many dollars instead of just a few cents.

Elkin's concern with death is another aspect of his later novelistic work that appears in these early stories. "In the Alley" features the character Feldman, who sold china in "The Sound of Distant Thunder" and who will appear in other works as well. As the author's emblem of suffering humanity, the man endures the worst this world has to offer but still manages to make it seem even worse. "In the Alley" finds him facing death, but in typical Feldman fashion the situation is even bleaker than that: having endured a terminal illness for over a year, he has outlived his predicted death date by several months and has become bored. Not terrified by mortality, not suffering unbearable pain, just exasperated with the tedious course of events and disappointed that his final exit will be less of a bang than a whimper. Feldman would like to be heroic, and wonders if the simple preference for life over death qualifies him for his culture's kudos. But society refuses to cooperate. Going against Feldman's wish that he be able to face death quietly and inconspicuously on his own terms, Feldman's doctor fails at keeping the secret and soon lets the dying man's family know the prognosis. Here at the very start the dying man's first hope for a well-played role is frustrated; to make it worse, his family misunderstands his reason for wanting the secrecy, frustrating him all the more. Worst of all, "He found himself suddenly an object," something to be visited on Sunday pilgrimages; now it becomes even harder to act heroically, for he's less of a person than a creature in the expectations of others. Death hasn't trapped Feldman, but life has. Hospitalized, he becomes the focus for the trials and tribulations (and occasional triumphs) of other patients' conditions, until he himself is "tired . . . of all this dying." Finally he leaves the hospital, where his own death has been denied him, to seek it directly. Here, he believes, will be true heroism.

The problem is that, outside, there are no challenges to face, much less dragons to slay or be slain by, just the humdrum world in all its insipidness. He sits on a bus stop bench, but cannot for the life of him sustain a friendly conversation. He boards the bus only to be thrown off after two circuits of its route, presumed by the driver to be nothing more than a drunk trying to sleep off a hangover. Ending up in a working-class bar, he's mistaken for an agent from the city's social services—why else would he be *here,* in a place so apparently remote from his own status? In fact, Feldman is a visitor from death, and the consequent estrangement shows all the more how his search for heroic resistance is a futile one. "I'm dying," he remarks to a vaguely attentive listener, only to be told in return that he should go see a doctor. When he reaches out for affection, his intentions are misread but easily enough served (this is the type of place where prostitutes work), but even here Feldman is denied a proper role and winds up being beaten up, dragged from the bar, and left for dead. This is where he does soon die, after better than a year of waiting, in the alley of the story's title, nestled in the detritus of a culture that has denied him the role of dying hero.

Feldman's quest for a heroic death, then, has rubbed his own (and the reader's) face in all that is disgusting about life, as he lies "by the waiting garbage, by the coffee grounds in their cups of wasted orange hemispheres, by the torn packages of frozen fish, by the greased, ripped labels of hollow cans, by the cold and hardened fat, by the jagged scraps of flesh around the nibbled bones, and the coagulated blood of cow and lamb." His struggle for something better has only led to this catalog of a back alley's refuse, with himself and his now-twisted vision in the center of it. Perhaps this does qualify as heroism, for Feldman has denied himself the comforts of family and hospital in order to perish among the dead things of life itself, amounting to an honest appraisal of his own mortality.

Another Feldman, Leo Feldman, is the protagonist of Elkin's second novel, *A Bad Man* (1967). Feldman is the bad man of the book's title, but only because of his own insistence—the novel's plot involves his wish to get himself imprisoned for doing illegal business favors, all so that he can act heroically in facing the more imposing challenges of prison life. Like his namesake of "In the Alley," this Feldman has been disappointed in life. Though economically successful (as not just a shopkeeper but a department store magnate), he regrets his place in an undistinguished family line that stretches from an overly idiosyncratic peddler of a father (interesting only for his immigrant Jewish culture) and the boredom of his son (who reflects the least imaginative aspects of American popular culture). In jail he sells something else: himself. His hardest customer

here is the warden, Fisher, who regards Feldman's Jewish heritage as a flaw. It is being Jewish that makes the prisoner a bad man, Fisher insists, believing that Jews are less concerned with community and more inclined to value the self.

Here lies the central tension of this novel, for in his quest to define himself as a strong individual Feldman has placed himself in the hands of an institutional authority who values group standards above all. For the warden, goodness is based on a rationality that denies the needs of self in favor of sacrifice to the better health of the commonwealth; badness is summed up by just what Feldman is trying to do—distinguish himself from the others by showing just how extraordinary his ambitions are. Fisher, in short, is a behavioralist at best and a bureaucrat at worst. The order he relishes is just what Feldman has rejected in the world and is seeking to exceed within the confines of the prison walls. As anyone with a bit of common sense can tell him, he has come to the wrong place.

Feldman's dispute with the warden is replicated in the subplot that recalls the department store magnate's dealings with a commercial developer. This latter figure is so deliberately stereotypical that he is never named; it is enough to say that he is the preeminent WASP businessman whose success in commerce serves as an index (according to Calvinist divine election) to his salvation, a doctrine that Feldman, as a Jew, is loath to share. Rather than being such a solidly located materialist, Feldman prefers to follow his father's advice in seeing the Jews' religious fate as "a destiny of emergency" that keeps them at move in a perpetual diaspora, a state far preferable to believing that they are effecting God's will at any place on earth.

THE ROLE OF POPULAR CULTURE

One of the major frustrations faced by Elkin's early heroes is the unavailability of a sympathetic audience. The author's next novel turns this condition into a challenge for its protagonist; in *The Dick Gibson Show* (1971) a radio announcer becomes a self-styled personality so that listenership can be both assumed and assured. He shares his earliest childhood memories of seeking out distant stations on the A.M. dial; late at night and lying abed, he takes advantage of clear-channel broadcasting, when the lesser local stations have signed off and the airwaves are clear for reception from over a thousand miles away. In such circumstances he once accomplishes the near impossible, pulling in a station from Seattle, Washington, beyond the supposedly impassable radio barrier of the Rocky Mountains. For the rest of the novel this becomes his ambition, to broadcast a show that draws listeners from everywhere, from places where he, Dick Gibson, has insinuated himself into their lives, for he himself is the show.

To accomplish this, the protagonist conducts his own marketing research and finds an appropriate slot. Elkin graphically displays the segmented, targeted nature of radio in the heading that begins part 2 of the novel, a reproduction of program listings from the daily newspaper:

Hartford Daily Intelligencer
Tuesday, March 3, 1959

WGR	WSQ	WMH	WHCN	WLLD
630	770	900	1320	1600

12:00 Midnight

WGR	Witching Hour (Music & News)
WHCN	The Dick Gibson Show (Talk)
WLLD	The World Tmrw

The offerings are appropriate to the hour: soft mood music and a wrap-up of the days events for those seeking to fall asleep, a discussion of upcoming happenings for those who wish to stay awake (yet for whom tomorrow is still "tmrw"), and soporific dialogue for listeners caught somewhere in between. It is only in our own age that masses of people take pleasure in listening to (or watching, given the medium of television) other people have conversations. Indeed, from a twenty-first-century perspective, the interactive medium of the Internet points out the peculiar nature of programming such as Dick Gibson's, in which audience members are content to merely overhear what is being said. But as a product of midcentury broadcasting "The Dick Gibson Show" becomes a staple entertainment.

The successive formats of Dick's show through the decades not only find him an audience but provide Elkin with a wide range of possibilities for character and plot development. Dick's first step is to play a certain style of music and create an on-air personality for its presentation; here can be found the first generation of late-night, clear-channel celebrities who've created themselves through manner alone, a decided advance over prewar evening broadcasting during which a noted swing band performing at a famous ballroom would have defined the show. By the 1950s Dick Gibson enlarges the entertainment vehicle to include more than himself, though he remains at the show's center. Here "The Dick Gibson Show" features a panel of experts, three or four authorities from widely disparate fields (a professor of English, a pharmacist concerned with the effects of flouridation, the proprietor of a charm school, and a disc jockey who had run for public office and been foiled by the political machine) who discuss a common topic of Dick's choosing (and which Dick himself can control). Finally with the 1960s and its newly personalized values comes the listener call-in show, where individuals around the country can phone Dick, be put on live radio, and share their intimacies with him as confessor while the country at large is eavesdropping. Here Elkin's fictive invention is truly unleashed, for the cast of characters is universal and their concerns encyclopedic.

In the process of telling his story Elkin rehearses old interests and develops new ones.

Once again, his protagonist creates and sells himself to the world as a product. Without a family of his own, Dick Gibson can relieve his sense of orphanhood by fashioning a virtual tribe of followers, to which he is an effective patriarch. Most successfully, "The Dick Gibson Show" becomes an artifact of American popular culture even as the show's format exploits that culture. Of all Elkin's novels, this one weaves itself most successfully from the signs and symbologies of day-to-day life for common Americans of the time. The talk reflects not just their speech idioms but their assumed values. As for his own ambitions, Dick's life takes on mythic proportions as he lives out the American dream in all phases of departure, initiation, and return.

Speaking to an audience liberated a great stream in Stanley Elkin's creative consciousness, and extending the narrative energy of *The Dick Gibson Show* is the triptych of novellas published in 1973 as *Searches and Seizures.* Together, "The Bailbondsman," "The Making of Ashenden," and "The Condominium" display great range, especially with respect to characterization. But all three share a narrative compulsion that can only be attributed to Elkin's security of voice. By the 1970s Elkin was more than well established as an author. He had been published steadily and consistently by a leading firm, Random House—a credit to any author but especially pleasing to someone who had written his doctoral dissertation on one of Random House's leading novelists and one of America's few Nobel laureates in literature, William Faulkner. Shorter works appeared in leading magazines, both popular and academic, and prestigious writing conferences at Breadloaf and elsewhere had drawn his presence and participation. At the time that *Searches and Seizures* was issued Elkin had enjoyed Guggenheim and Rockefeller fellowships and was about to be honored by the American Academy of Arts and Letters. At Washington University he was a full professor, and had been privileged with vis-

iting appointments at the University of California at Santa Barbara and at Yale. Most important in terms of the exercise of his literary art, Elkin had become a familiar face on the college reading circuit, where he delighted audiences with the type of verbal display evident in his works. Like Dick Gibson, he had developed a following, one before which he could act and react.

Alexander Main the bail bondsman tells his story in the present tense, much like a comedian delivering a monologue or a salesman making a pitch—or, and perhaps more suitable to Main's vernacular, like a fellow on the next bar stool telling you his life story in order to justify his existence. Main loves everything about his work, from the colorful characters he must track to the documents that make it legal:

> I love a contract like the devil, admire the tall paper and the small print—I mean the *print,* the lawful shapes and stately content. Forget word games, secret clause, forget hidden meaning and ambiguity, all those dense thickets of type where the fast ones lie like lost balls. Your forest-for-the-trees crap is myth, the sucker's special pleading. I'll fuck you in letters nine feet high if I've a mind. I beat no one with loophole. Everything spelled out, all clear, aboveboard as chessmen; truth in advertising and a language even the dishonest understand. No, I'm talking the *look* of the instrument, texture, watermark, the silk flourish of the bright ribbon, the legend perfected centuries (I'll tell you in a moment about the Phoenicians), the beautiful formulas simple as pie, old-fashioned quid pro quo like a recipe in the family generations. My conditions classic and my terms terminal. Listen, I haven't much law—though what I have is on my side, binding as clay, advantage to the house—but am as at home in replevin, debenture and gage as someone on his own toilet seat with the door closed and the house empty. I have mainpernor, bottomry, caution and hypothecation the way others might have a second language. I have always lived by *casus foederis;* do the same and we'll never tangle assholes.

The words beg to be spoken aloud; it is as if Elkin wrote them with an eager listenership in mind.

Terms of a kind flow together with alliteration and assonance; language clashes with itself in a riot of diverse associations; conditions of law mix with references to lavatory functions—all of it delivered in a cascading stream of the vulgar and familiar. "The Bailbondsman" continues this way for 126 pages, monologue growing into dialogues as the protagonist encounters others, until a conventional narrative of people, places, and things emerges to take its rightful place on the page. Soon universes of experience are encompassed, the only problem being that crime comes to nothing, and Alexander Main is prevented from obtaining the clue to existence that he has been seeking. What Elkin as author seems to be telling us is that there is no clue to life, just its ongoing energy. The only sense consists in learning how to speak: Main through his mastery of shoptalk, legal jargon, and the patois of petty crime, Elkin thanks to his fashioning of a simulacrum of this world that proceeds by virtue of its perpetual energy.

"I've been spared a lot," admits Brewster Ashenden, the narrator of Elkin's next novella, "one of the blessed of the earth, at least one of its lucky, that privileged handful of the dramatically prospering, the sort whose secrets are asked, like the hundred-year-old man." Ashenden's good station in life has been assured by his maternal grandmother, who devised the way to store oxygen in tanks, and by his father, who helped pioneer the matchbook industry and invented the phrase "Close Cover Before Striking." Although there is a hint of the ridiculous here—especially when Ashenden's father undercuts the butane lighter industry by coining another phrase, "For Our Matchless Friends"—Elkin's new protagonist is, in terms of background and socialization, miles away from Alexander Main, with his bail-skipping clients and gutter language. What begins as a lampooning of the aristocratic lifestyle develops into a love story of sorts, inasmuch as there can be romance within the mating rites of the very

rich, where so much wealth and tradition rides on each match. To this first half of the story Elkin adds a second, where Ashenden turns from human intercourse to fascination with the animal world (comfortably accommodated by the convenience of a private zoo). Here he is attacked by a bear in heat, something Alexander Main could have described with vulgar dexterity but which in "The Making of Ashenden" is sustained in the same cultivated tones that distinguish the novella's opening sentence. Because he can understand the bear, Ashenden learns how to survive the occasion and also how to live his life more fruitfully, even if that involves succumbing to the temptations of luxury.

"The Condominium" presents the volume's third protagonist, but this character is in the act of writing rather than speaking. Marshall Preminger has inherited a condominium, part of his father's legacy that soon becomes his own. Preminger's profession is an academic one: he is engaged in a study of the human compulsion to build a home. In the resort where he and his parents once summered, he notes a decay of social structure as the facility's recreation sites fall into disrepair. The modern conception of homemaking involves people withdrawing into themselves, he learns. But on inheriting the condominium he finds that financial conditions draw him out of himself and into his late father's lifestyle, beginning with a move into the old man's quarters and developing into a hoped-for seduction by his father's former companion. A universe of rules pertains to the condominium's occupancy and operation. There is a committee that superintends its corporate rules, and Preminger's delight with the sense of community this fosters soon turns to dismay when he learns of the group's exclusivity—the residents are mostly Jews, and rather than feeling sympathy for victims of prejudice they organize themselves to keep others out, specifically Asians, African Americans, and Puerto Ricans. When in the process of revising the rules for the use of the swimming pool the residents play with technicalities as a way of excluding their own bothersome relations, including children, Preminger protests. When his father's last companion trivializes the son's interest, he becomes dismayed; her offhand descriptions of the old man's bizarre death (in which she cooperated) drives Preminger to despair for the human condition in general and for himself in particular, leaving suicide as the sole option.

Here is where Elkin's understanding of popular culture comes into play, effecting the plot and articulating its theme. The recent development of condominiums as a form of housing had initially reversed the trend Preminger had regretted seeing among old-time family resorts. Social decay could be arrested by the need for cooperation among residents who owned their own property within the larger corporate entity of the building itself. But such organization has only provided a way for further withdrawal, from other groups and even from family. Sexuality, once the founding principle of kinship, now becomes an adjunct of finance and an agent of exclusion and ultimately death. As Preminger leaps to his death from a twelfth-floor balcony, he makes one last attempt at speaking, delivering his lecture on the motives for human habitation. But the conditions of his fall smother his words. There is neither time nor space for a convincing spiel, even for a self-defining aria. The banal language of these condominium dwellers, who discuss Mike Nichols' movies and Philip Roth's novels with the same nonchalance that has horrified Preminger in their commentaries on his father's death, remains the lingua franca of this realm, where sordidness is eclipsed only by the insipidly dull.

If Marshall Preminger feels orphaned, this only qualifies him as a typical Elkin protagonist. His fate, though, is among the harshest in this author's canon. More typically comic is the life of Ben Flesh, whose occupation gives Elkin's fourth novel, *The Franchiser* (1976), its title. Ben has

no reason to feel abandoned. Instead, he has been raised by a wonderful man named Julius Finsberg, who has succeeded in the field of musical comedy, one of America's most beloved forms of popular entertainment. The large family in which Flesh grows up consists of eighteen twins and triplets, all suffering from rare diseases, yet whose Jewish American culture and musical-comedy heritage encourages them to be happily assimilated into the broad American mainstream.

The specifics that Ben Flesh inherits are remarkable in their pertinence to how the country has been developing since Ben's own childhood in the Great Depression. The core of Ben's wealth comes from his godfather's theatrical costume business, while its growth is guaranteed by something else the godson has inherited: the right to borrow investment capital at a low rate of interest. Beyond the Finsberg family, Ben would still like to feel at home, and so he uses the advantages it has given him to undertake a franchising business—not as an end in itself, but rather to help America become a country in which anywhere and everywhere feels like home. Elkin's entrepreneur would like to unify everything, have it all function together like a team. He has seen Broadway musicals produced this way and admires their success. He appreciates how brilliantly applied advertising techniques can marshal support for charity appeals: "The United Way" is not just a name or a slogan, but represents the man's deepest and most sincere philosophy. His own work ethic fits the same bill. How ironic, then, that Ben Flesh himself is battling an uncommon disease, a legacy he shares with his variously afflicted stepbrothers and stepsisters: multiple sclerosis.

By the time of his writing of *The Franchiser* Elkin himself had been diagnosed with MS. If his own association with the disease motivated his choice to have Ben Flesh suffer from it as well, then giving his character the occupation of franchiser may have derived from frustration. For how efficiently does multiple sclerosis undo for the human body what franchising seeks to accomplish for the country. Its degenerative effects undermine the central control a body needs to work harmoniously among its parts; a person ravaged by MS is a sadly apt metaphor for a collapsing organization. Yet as with the best of Elkin's comic protagonists there remains a verbal energy; MS may disorganize muscles and limbs, but it cannot quell Ben's speech or his ability to perform an aria, even if it be concerning the sorry state of current credit, as evidenced in this discussion he has with an associate:

"But the credit checks, Ben, we run credit checks, we know exactly—"

"Yesterday's newspapers, kid, history. Yesterday's news, last year's prospecti. The times have changed on them, their mood has, their disposition. A depression comes, the first thing that goes, after the meat on the table, after the fruit in the bowl, the first thing that goes is optimism, the belief they can pay back what they owe."

"We can garnishee—"

"What? *What* can we garnishee? Their unemployment checks? Their workman's compensation? What can we garnishee? Their allowance from the union? What, *what* can we garnishee? The widow's mite? The plastic collateral? What can we garnishee? We going to play tug-of-war with the dealer to repossess the car? We take their furniture? Their color TV? And do what? We got a warehouse? We got storage facilities? Tracts of land in the desert for all the mothball fleet of a bankrupt's detritus? *Credit checks!* On what? Old times? The good old days? It doesn't make you suspicious white-collar guys come to you for dough? College graduates? The class of '58? *That* doesn't bother you? Your ear ain't to the ground? Take your credit checks in the men's toilet. Hear what they're saying in *those* circles. Sneak up behind them where they eat their lunch, taking their sandwiches from a paper bag, their milk from mayonnaise jars, because these are the people never owned a lunch pail, a pencil box of food, who wouldn't recognize a thermos unless it was beside a Scotch cooler on a checkered cloth spread out on the lawn for a picnic. Fuck your credit checks, cancel them they bounce. Overhear the rumors they overhear—the layoffs, the open-ended furloughs coming just after the Christmas upswing, the plants closing down in this industry and that, and only a skeleton crew to bank the furnaces, only the night-watchman industry booming because we live in the time of the looters, of the plate-glass smashers, in the age of the plucked toaster from the storefront window and somebody else snitches the white bread. This is the credit you're running down? No no. They won't pay. They can't. And they don't care."

Elsewhere in this novel Ben can use his voice to rhapsodize over all the states he's worked in, all the cities he's helped make uniform with chain restaurants and motels. But even in this jeremiad against the loss of credit standards his voice takes on an energy of its own, enumerating like a prophet and adding serial emphases like a revival tent preacher. Despite the country's energy crisis, Ben Flesh feels no depletion in his own reserves. Energy is what keeps him going. In the end MS will kill him, if his competitors don't beat the disease to it. But for now, all there is, is life.

ULTIMACIES

The work Elkin published from 1979 through the 1980s is the most consistent of his career, thanks to its focus on the ultimate question of death and its purpose in otherwise ongoing human existence. Even the titles of his three stories from the beginning of this period—"The Conventional Wisdom," "The Bottom Line," and "The State of the Art"—suggest a state of finality, reinforced by the collection's title, *The Living End* (1979). For the protagonist Ellerbee in the first piece, the end certainly seems near. Ellerbee has a habit of dropping things: change under seat cushions, glass bottles on the floor, and way too much money in the stock market. His main business, a liquor store, suffers from its location in a decaying neighborhood; but it has become a site not only of disrespect, as Feldman's shop was in Elkin's first story, but of murder—two of Ellerbee's clerks have been shot, leaving one of them crippled and the other dead. Even as he does his best to rectify matters, Ellerbee himself is killed in an armed robbery, although the story does not stop there. Instead, the angel of death takes him into the afterlife, beginning with a visit to the gates of heaven. Here, he's found lacking, and Elkin takes the opportunity to craft one of his simplest but situationally funniest lines: " 'Go to Hell,' Saint Peter said beatifically." After a trial period down below Ellerbee is summoned before God for final judgment. He prays that hell will end in death. God scoffs at this notion. Ellerbee is left with the stark realization that everything he had heard about the afterlife was true:

> Even the conventional wisdom, perhaps especially the conventional wisdom—that which had made up Heaven like a shot in the dark and imagined into reality halos and Hell, gargoyles, gates of pearl, and the Pearl of Great Price, that had invented the horns of demons and cleft their feet and conceived angels riding clouds like cowboys on horseback, their harps at their sides like goofy guitars. Everything. Everything was. The self and what you did to protect it, learning the house odds, playing it safe—the honorable percentage baseball of existence.

Except for the gross physicality of particular punishments, hell is little different from life; eternity is simply the stuff of temporality without end. "The Bottom Line" picks up where "Conventional Wisdom" leaves off, as Ellerbee and his murderer pass the time as equals. God comes to visit them in hell, giving Elkin the chance for another once-in-a-lifetime line: "Hot enough for you?" Practicing in his role of being ubiquitous, God visits with these condemned souls like a royal prince touring the colonies. Some unkind questions from his subjects lead to a surreal display of nightmares that only God can end. Like the first of these three stories, the bottom line of

"The Bottom Line" is that existence continues in afterlife much as it did on earth, with the hoodlum acting now as bagman for and petty accomplice to the Creator of the Universe.

"The State of the Art" is even more surreal, and is consequently less successful as an example of Elkin's darkly comic sensibilities. Here God the Father and God the Son engage in a family argument of sorts, a bit of vulgarity that builds to the point where God begs the son's forgiveness. When Christ intercedes in the affairs of hell (because he remains sympathetic to humanity by virtue of all he learned during life on earth), Creation seems out of control—but only as would any mismanaged household. Meanwhile one of the liquor store's murdered clerks decides to redeem hellish eternity by dividing it into units of time, second-guessing his old employer's comic repudiation of God. All in all, the afterlife seems little different from a bad neighborhood in Minneapolis. Although not articulated as such, the implication from these three stories is clear and recalls comedian W. C. Fields's classic line on being dead: "All the same, I'd rather be in Philadelphia," undoubtedly part of Elkin's childhood storehouse of American popular culture treasures.

For *George Mills: A Novel* (1982) Elkin returned to earth, but maintained his focus on ultimate concerns by writing a narrative that spans one thousand years of history, a millennial stretch from the Middle Ages to the end of the twentieth century. The consistent element here is the name George Mills; George himself appears as distinctive personalities in diverse periods of history and takes part in half a dozen or more separate plot actions. By producing the novel in this manner Elkin may well have been seeking membership with the writers critically grouped as meganovelists (or authors of the novel of excess): Thomas Pynchon, William Gaddis, and his university colleague and close friend William H. Gass, all of whom crafted massive novels distinguished by informational overkill and monumental narrative scope. *George Mills* tops five hundred pages, totaling close to a quarter of a million words. Oddly enough, the novel's length and great historical span work to curb some of the author's other excesses, most notably his pleasure with letting language run loose (certainly well ahead of the story's development) and his disinclination to closely manage plot. In *George Mills* readers will find Elkin's most unified book; though it has several actions, those actions reflect each other, reinforcing the theme that lives can well take similar form. One asks, however, is it the lives that are similar or the writing about them that follows parallel tracks? Indeed, is life itself being played out according to a larger structural plan? To listen to the leader of the earliest incarnation of George Mills, on a tenth-century Crusade, one certainly suspects this may be true:

> Listen to me, my Mills. I'm your superior, just as that barbarian we saw was mine. Learn this, Mills. There are distinctions between men, humanity is dealt out like cards. There is natural suzerainty like the face value on coins. Men have their place. Even here, where we are now, at large, outside of place, beyond it, out of bounds and offside, loosened from the territorial limits, they do. It's no accident that Guillalume is the youngest son for all it appears so, no more accident than that you are the Horseshit Man. It isn't luck of the draw but the brick walls of some secret, sovereign Architecture that makes us so. It's as simple as the scorn in my voice when I talk to you like this, as natural as the italics my kind use and your kind don't. Now do as I tell you, get on your horse.

In all of George Mills's historical appearances, he remains a "horseshit man" of sorts, just as God's petty hoodlum in *The Living End* continues that role in the afterlife. The difference is that each successive George Mills knows just what his fate is. Some fight against it, while others cooperate, but all join together in the author's wry explanation of how someone is always expendable, someone can always be spared to do the job nobody else wants to do—reminiscent of another

saying that was presumably included in Elkin's childhood treasury of Americana: "Let George do it." Sadness comes only when heirs of this blue-collar tradition earn the momentary privilege of looking into contexts of a better life, only to realize that it is not for them. Instead, classic forms of human organization consign them to the lower level. In the tenth century, that form is religion. In the eighteenth century, the operative structure is politics. Finally, our late-twentieth-century George Mills, so much like other Elkin characters, is given the short end of things thanks to this new age's ruling passion, psychology. It is the ruling class in each period that comes out on top of such structures, while the George Millses of the world remain at the bottom.

An interesting compromise between the methodological extremities of *The Living End* and *George Mills* gave Elkin a rare opportunity in *The Magic Kingdom* (1985). Its title page contains an interesting qualifier: there the book's name appears as *Stanley Elkin's The Magic Kingdom,* to compound the impression that this short novel is a work of the imagination at double strength. Not only does it take place in Walt Disney's Magic Kingdom of Disney World, but it is a fictive narrative about a land already given over to fantasy. It becomes Stanley Elkin's kingdom as well because of the use he puts it to: a man named Eddy Bale takes seven terminally ill children to the world's greatest amusement park in Orlando, Florida, a trip that's all the more exceptional because they are coming from England to an America that is itself very much an imaginative construct. On their visit to the Magic Kingdom these children see plenty of fantasy, but in the process Elkin treats his readers to one of his most heartfelt treatises about how death remains at the center of things, as the sick though still young travelers are exposed to the legions of old people visiting the park:

> "It breaks your heart," Colon said. "Imperfection everywhere, everywhere. Not like in nature. What,

you think stars show their age? Oceans, the sky? No fear! Only in man, only in woman. Trees never look a day older. The mountains are better off for each million years. Everywhere, everywhere. Bodies mismanaged, malfeasanced, gone off. Like styles, like fashions gone off. It's this piecemeal surrender to time, kids. You can't hold on to your baby teeth. Scissors cut paper, paper covers rock, rock smashes scissors. A bite of candy causes tooth decay, and jawlines that were once firm slip off like shoreline lost to the sea. Noses balloon, amok as a cancer. Bellies swell up and muscles go down. Hips and thighs widen like jodhpurs. My God, children, we look like we're dressed for the horseback! (And everywhere, everywhere, there's this clumsy imbalance. You see these old, sluggish bodies on thin-looking legs, like folk carrying packages piled too high. Or like birds puffed out, skewed, out of sorts with their foundations.) And hair. Hair thins, recedes, is gone. Bodies fall away from true. I don't know. It's as if we've been nickel-and-dimed by the elements: by erosion, by wind and water, by the pull of gravity and the oxidation of the very air. Look! Look there!"

Walt Disney's imagination would efface such blemishes, but when Elkin visits the Magic Kingdom reality stands out all the more, contrasted as it is with what the human imagination and the protagonist's intentions would hope to achieve.

Religion is imagination's last refuge in the face of death, but in Elkin's *The Rabbi of Lud: A Novel* (1987), the Judaism of his heritage seems mostly a laughing matter. The rabbi himself, Jerry Goldkorn, has little more than mail-order credentials for practicing his faith. He earns a living among the dead, conducting funerals on an operational basis in an East Coast town that provides for little else; everything about Lud, New Jersey, is styled for the culture of death, its prime industry—if one wants to learn Hebrew, the only reading material is on the tombstones. The people he buries are themselves as anonymous as the lobsters filling the tank at a nearby seafood restaurant. This last image is surely chosen for its outrageousness. In "The Condominium" Elkin had paid homage to the styles and themes of Philip Roth by having his narrative's own characters cite the famous author, but for this novel the imitation is patently transparent, right down to the familiar geography of Roth's novels. The ethnic references are laid on much stronger than anywhere else in Elkin's work, and when the characters exchange their hilariously shocking lines it seems as if shorthand references to works like *Portnoy's Complaint* and *Goodbye, Columbus* are meant to suffice as indictments of contemporary Judaism's ineffectiveness with ultimate concerns.

BEYOND LAST WORDS

Stanley Elkin died in 1995, just twenty days past his sixty-fifth birthday and thus unable to experience the coda to life's narrative that retirement is supposed to be. Yet his last three books read as an epilogue of sorts, even as his work of the 1980s had tested various earthly responses to spiritual concerns and found them wanting. His novel *The MacGuffin,* which appeared in 1991, calls back the energetic voice that so ably carried his earlier works. A devotee of shoptalk, the author finds some of the best in the vocabulary of his new hero, a city streets commissioner named Bobbo Druff. The novel's 283 pages of action are jammed into thirty-six hours of Druff's customary routine. In this late-middle-aged man's world, everything seems in helpless decline. Were one to follow the logic of syntax, only final words could be pronounced. But Bobbo's linguistic world is one of non sequiturs and mixed metaphors, riotous slang carrying listeners down a path that no reasonably oriented mind could follow. The man relishes life, and as long as he can perpetuate his spiel he holds purchase on it. A MacGuffin, we recall, is the technique Elkin admired in director Alfred Hitchcock's repertorie, something inconsequential in itself that nevertheless is the device that gets a narrative rolling. *The MacGuffin* is just that for Elkin at this stage in his career: an excuse for maintaining the story-teller's art, even once the ultimacies of existence have had their say.

Elkin also continued to write novellas, for him a more comfortable format than the short story because his exercises in language demanded more room. Among the three pieces that fill *Van Gogh's Room at Arles* (1993) are numerous reminders that linguistic virtuosity is more than just display; it is a disciplined exercise in getting the most out of words without losing track of their essential meanings. Elkin's spokespersons are thus never simply verbose. Their cascading verbiage is always articulate, and more than anything they distrust imprecision and false assumption. One of the author's characters suffers from MS, just as he does, and like him he's a professor. Physically disabled, the man can still teach—and teach he does, especially about the clarities of language. He's a political geographer, and so is adept at charting his laborious progress throughout a variety of realms, each with their unique challenge: bathroom, hallway, and bedroom. When a student warns him about depleting his energy, he objects that he's not a turbine or generator but rather a person, for whom "energy" is not a helpful term. "Her Sense of Timing" thus opens the collection with the sad spectacle of man facing the loss of almost everything, from muscle control to his wife, yet left with the two great materials of his work: his language and his students.

"*Town Crier* Exclusive, Confessions of a Princess Manqué: 'How Royals Found Me "Unsuitable" to Marry Their Larry' " is this volume's second novella. Its narrator is a young woman who had been engaged to marry a future king of England, but who seems to have talked herself out of the position. Her recounting of this event is a reminder of what Elkin does best: giving center stage to someone with a case to make about themselves. The third novella, "Van Gogh's Room at Arles," returns to academia for some trivial fun as well as insightful moments, when a community college instructor, hardly one of the world's leading scholars, finds himself ensconced in the room Vincent Van Gogh slept in before he died. As always, it is what people have to face in doing their jobs that interests Elkin the most; in the novellas of this collection he provides exceptional range for the topic.

The title character of Elkin's last novel, *Mrs. Ted Bliss* (1995), is eighty-two years old. During her husband's life she existed quietly behind his name, as she does now in widowhood. She kept a neat house, economized on purchases, and helped prepare for what should have been an ideal Florida retirement, just what the American system promises for a hardworking Chicago butcher and his wife. Now she is alone in their Florida condominium. On the inside, life is quiet to the point of tedium. But because this is Florida in the late twentieth century, outside threats make their presence felt. Is there involvement among people around her with drug-dealing South Americans? At the very least, are there crooked deals afoot involving the lifetimes of wealth accumulated in such unspectacular fashion by these retirees who have come south to await death? Elsewhere Stanley Elkin has made his thoughts clear about the living end, and here there seems little joy in anticipating its coming. What society there is among these condo dwellers is artificial and unfulfilling; not even a meal can be reasonably enjoyed, as food prepared in one's toaster oven or microwave is always a safer bet than what will be served in the cafeteria.

Against this deteriorating world whose lapsed ethics are familiar from Elkin's "The Condominium" and whose declining old folks are reminiscent of those cited in his *The Magic Kingdom,* Dorothy Bliss would protest. "What fools old people were!" she laments. "The crazy things they fell for! Wisdom? You thought *wisdom* came with the territory? It was a myth of the young. Only terror came with the territory." Such terrors have become the unstated theme of her last years, and she is angry:

> There ought to be a law, she thought, against all the song and dance they foist on you if you live past sixty. The victims they turn you into, the scams they run. It was on all the programs. Bunco squads working around the clock every day of the year didn't make a dent in it. They were easy pickings, old folks. Mrs. Bliss was, easy pickings. Old as she was, she could have been born yesterday.

Complaints alone, however, are futile, serving only to exhaust the speaker. Dorothy is at a greater disadvantage than most of Elkin's protagonists because she doesn't have much of a self to sell, having existed for most of her life as Mrs. Ted Bliss. But the novel that bears her name gives her something to do. For the first time in her life she takes notice, and it is this receptivity (rather than the customary projective spieling) that provides Elkin with his MacGuffin. Although what motivates her to act is minor—a disputed personal property tax bill on her late husband's Buick LeSabre (the car he loved best because its radio would pull in White Sox broadcasts from almost anywhere)—it does give her the chance to assert herself. In doing so she joins the ranks of Elkin characters who define themselves by their speech. Once defined, she can make the most of what involvements she has, orphan that she is— even if it only comes down to comforting a confused woman looking for her mother in the aftermath of a hurricane. Stroking the woman's hair, Dorothy realizes that she has no choice but to help the woman. Why so? "Because everything else falls away. Family, friends, love fall away. Even madness stilled at last. Until all that's left is obligation."

With these last words Stanley Elkin's literary canon came to a close. Finding a proper place for his oeuvre in America's literary history, critics have had to shift their ground with each new development in the author's career. At first, a novel like *Boswell* seemed to place Elkin among the group of writers from the late 1950s described as black humorists. From the distance of almost a half century later, the term has become far too limiting (and is, in fact, no longer used in this context). Those authors who were black humorists—that is to say, those who scored comic points by outrageous themes alone, without making similar advances in technique and form— failed to grow with the times; little is said these days about Terry Southern, Hughes Rudd, and Bruce Jay Friedman, even though they were once linked as equals with Stanley Elkin and Kurt Vonnegut. What distinguishes Elkin's work, and Vonnegut's too, is not just the ability to make daring comments but to draw the language for them from the great storehouse of American vernacular speech, and most crucially to let that speech stretch the confines of narrative until a genuinely new form comes into being.

As readers learned more about Elkin's style of work, there were thoughts that he might be another Bernard Malamud. From the character Feldman in his first published story through the beleaguered shopkeeper Greenspahn in the title piece of *Criers and Kibitzers, Kibitzers and Criers,* all the necessary components are there. Everything needed to create another Morris Bober (the protagonist of Malamud's classic novel of just a few years earlier, *The Assistant*) is available—but also something more, specifically the character's richer sense of articulation when talking of himself. Malamud's grocer is content to shrug, thinking that this is his luck, admitting that others have better. Elkin's speaks out.

It is because his characters speak so volubly that Elkin's narratives achieve something other than the mannered moralism that readers came to expect of Malamud. Conventions exist only to be broken, it is implied. Anything but bourgeois, Elkin is rarely predictable; you never know what he is going to say next, and hence his fictions sacrifice the socially stable comforts of John Updike and John Cheever in favor of a much more disorderly world. Order exists in the minds of his protagonists, whose roles become sellers of persuasive accounts. Although his unconventionality made him appeal to readers of innovative fiction (by such formally iconoclastic writers as Donald Barthelme and Richard Brautigan), Elkin's privileging of characterizational integrity made him stand apart from the more radical practitioners of this style, authors such as Ronald Sukenick and Raymond Federman, for whom character was just one more device whose artifice should be displayed at every turn. Yet neither was Elkin the advocate of a reenvisioned humanism, as was his friend the philosopher-novelist William H. Gass. Intellectual themes are present in Elkin's work, but only as they emerge naturally from the popular culture. For the author of "The Bailbondsman" and *The Franchiser*, humanity is the issue, without any isms attached.

Are Elkin's fictions, then, just entertainments? They do entertain. But as his character Professor Schiff does in "Her Sense of Timing," Elkin's fictions teach even as they humorously chide. In writing such books as *The Living End, The Magic Kingdom,* and *Mrs. Ted Bliss,* the author completed a canon that encompassed the broader range of developments in fiction in the four full decades after World War II. There is dismay at the apparent deteriorations in a changing world, but also sufficient wryness to make the commentary engaging. The commentators will say outrageous things, but are never egregious—their point of view is rarely indecipherable to the herd, but instead grows from its culture and is surprising only because of its sudden turnaround of judgment. In the end, there's a moral to the story. But in articulating it, even God himself must speak the language of the crowd. And what a crowd it is, from conscientious liquor store owners to small-time hoodlums from the Twin Cities who wouldn't last a day in Harlem or the Bronx.

But, much like Mrs. Ted Bliss at the end, they are driven by an obligation—first to be themselves, then to justify that being in self-defining song. In the fiction of Stanley Elkin, the stage is theirs.

Selected Bibliography

WORKS OF STANLEY ELKIN

NOVELS, NOVELLAS, AND SHORT STORIES

Boswell: A Modern Comedy. New York: Random House, 1964.

Criers and Kibitzers, Kibitzers and Criers. New York: Random House, 1966. (Contains "Criers and Kibitzers, Kibitzers and Criers," "I Look Out for Ed Wolfe," "Among the Witnesses," "The Guest," "In the Alley," "On a Field, Rampant," "A Poetics for Bullies," "Cousin Poor Lesley and the Lousy People," and "Perlmutter at the East Pole.")

A Bad Man. New York: Random House, 1967.

The Dick Gibson Show. New York: Random House, 1971.

Searches and Seizures. New York: Random House, 1973. (Contains "The Bailbondsman," "The Making of Ashenden," and "The Condominium.")

The Franchiser. New York: Farrar, Straus & Giroux, 1976.

The Living End. New York: Dutton, 1979. (Contains "The Conventional Wisdom," "The Bottom Line," and "The State of the Art.")

George Mills: A Novel. New York: Dutton, 1982.

Early Elkin. Flint, Mich.: Bamberger, 1985. (Contains "A Sound of Distant Thunder," "The Party," "Fifty Dollars," and "The Graduate Seminar," plus an introduction and the essay "Where I Read What I Read.")

The Magic Kingdom. New York: Dutton, 1985.

The Rabbi of Lud: A Novel. New York: Scribners, 1987.

The MacGuffin. New York: Linden Press/Simon & Schuster, 1991.

Van Gogh's Room at Arles. New York: Hyperion, 1993. (Contains "Her Sense of Timing," "*Town*

Crier Exclusive, Confessions of a Princess Manqué: 'How Royals Found Me "Unsuitable" to Marry Their Larry,' " and "Van Gogh's Room at Arles.")

Mrs. Ted Bliss. New York: Hyperion, 1995.

OTHER WORKS

Stories from the Sixties (editor). New York: Doubleday, 1971.

The Best American Short Stories: 1980 (coeditor, with Shannon Ravenel). Boston: Houghton Mifflin, 1980.

Why I Live Where I Live. University City, Mo.: Contre Coup, 1983.

The Coffee Room. Louisville, Ky.: Contre Coup, 1987. (Radio play)

The Six-Year-Old Man. Flint, Mich.: Bamberger, 1987. (Screenplay)

Pieces of Soap: Essays. New York: Simon & Schuster, 1992.

MANUSCRIPTS

Elkin's papers are housed in Special Collections at the John M. Olin Library, Washington University, St. Louis, Missouri.

CRITICAL STUDIES

Bailey, Peter J. *Reading Stanley Elkin.* Urbana: University of Illinois Press, 1985.

Bargen, Doris G. *The Fiction of Stanley Elkin.* Bern, Switzerland: Lang, 1980.

Chénetier, Marc. *Beyond Suspicion: New American Fiction Since 1960.* Translated by Elizabeth A. Houlding. Philadelphia: University of Pennsylvania Press, 1996.

Dougherty, David C. *Stanley Elkin.* Boston: Twayne, 1990.

Gorak, Jan. *God the Artist: American Novelists in a Post-Realistic Age.* Urbana: University of Illinois Press, 1987.

Guttmann, Allen. *The Jewish Writer in America: Assimilation and the Crisis of Identity.* New York: Oxford University Press, 1971.

LeClair, Thomas. "The Obsessional Fiction of Stanley Elkin." *Contemporary Literature* 16:146–161 (spring 1975).

O'Donnell, Patrick. *Passionate Doubts: Designs of Interpretation in Contemporary American Fiction.* Iowa City: University of Iowa Press, 1986.

Olderman, Raymond M. *Beyond the Waste Land: A Study of the American Novel in the Nineteen-Sixties.* New Haven, Conn.: Yale University Press, 1972.

Saltzman, Arthur M. *Designs of Darkness in Contemporary American Fiction.* Philadelphia: University of Pennsylvania Press, 1990.

———. *The Novel in the Balance.* Columbia: University of South Carolina Press, 1993.

Wilde, Alan. *Middle Grounds.* Philadelphia: University of Pennsylvania Press, 1987.

INTERVIEWS

Chénetier, Marc. "Stanley Elkin: An Interview." *Delta* 20:15–35 (February 1985).

Duncan, Jeffrey. "A Conversation with Stanley Elkin and William H. Gass." *Iowa Review* 7:48–77 (winter 1976).

Heide, Ziegler, and Christopher Bigsby, eds. *The Radical Imagination and the Liberal Tradition: Interviews with English and American Novelists.* London: Junction Books, 1982, pp. 93–110.

LeClair, Thomas. "Stanley Elkin: The Art of Fiction LXI." *Paris Review* 66:54–86 (summer 1976). Reprinted in Thomas LeClair and Larry McCaffery, *Anything Can Happen: Interviews with Contemporary American Novelists.* Urbana: University of Illinois Press, 1983. Pp. 106–125.

Sanders, Scott. "An Interview with Stanley Elkin." *Contemporary Literature* 16:131–145 (spring 1976).

—JEROME KLINKOWITZ

John Gardner

1933–1982

*I*N HIS FIRST published novel, *The Resurrection* (1966), John Gardner has his character James Chandler, a dying philosopher, come to understand that "in Art a gifted consciousness simplifies, extends, or reorders categorization and choice for the rest of us, speeding up the painfully slow process of evolution toward what, hopefully, we *are.*" In light of the tremendous outpouring of fiction, scholarship, and criticism by Gardner during his short life, this could very well serve as his epitaph. His was a gifted consciousness wherein "painful" modified not only the pace of that process of evolution but the process itself.

John Champlin Gardner Jr. was born July 21, 1933, in Batavia, New York. On the morning of April 4, 1945, when World War II was winding down in Europe, eleven-year-old Gardner accidentally crushed his seven-year-old brother, Gilbert, beneath a cultipacker on the family farm in Batavia. Tragedy ripples out from the center through the lives of everyone touched by it; at the vortex of the loss, where culpability collides with guilt, John Gardner received the wound that would shape his writing life. He spent the next thirty-seven years exploring the nature of "accident" until his own life ended, on September 14, 1982, in a motorcycle mishap that was never fully explained.

In the sense that, with artists, all deaths are premature, we are left wondering where Gard-

ner's art might have taken him (and us) in subsequent years. As a teacher, scholar, editor, translator, poet, librettist, novelist, and essayist, he was a prolific writer whose strong opinions were often, but not exclusively, mediated through the lives of his fictional characters. At the time of his death he had published eight novels, a book-length epic poem, two collections of stories, eight works of scholarship or criticism, lyric poetry, children's books, and a coauthored textbook. Including posthumous publications, his literary and critical output totals more than thirty titles.

Gardner's death at age forty-nine was particularly untimely because it occurred while the controversy over his attempts to be a moral arbiter of late-twentieth-century fiction still simmered. In 1978 he published a book-length manifesto, *On Moral Fiction,* decrying what he saw to be the sorry state of contemporary fiction and calling for a return to a view of art that was morally instructive in its efforts faithfully to explore the dilemmas of humanity. This had always been Gardner's take on the redemptive power of art, but he had never made his point so stridently. In the four years after the publication of *On Moral Fiction,* his public role as cultural critic so polarized colleagues and reviewers that both his older and new creative works were inevitably read through the lens of his own polemic. Now that the years have put sufficient distance between his art and that debate, it is easier to trace John Gardner's journey through America's literary landscape.

One of four children born to John Champlin Gardner and Priscilla Jones Gardner, Gardner spent his formative years living and working on the family farm. In addition to farming, his father served as a lay reader in the Presbyterian church and had a local reputation as an orator, often reciting poetry at the local Grange. Gardner's mother taught high school English. He often credited the combination of his father's public recitations and his mother's love of literature as the spark to his early interest in the possibilities of language.

The stories Gardner grew up hearing, and then learned to tell himself, were performance pieces, spoken aloud to pass the time while doing repetitive chores around the farm or performed during moments of rest. As Robert Frost dramatizes in many of his early poems, the moment of aesthetic consciousness for workers is often found during those brief pauses in the act of labor. To reach this audience for whom literature was a welcome diversion from physical labor, Gardner learned that stories must focus on clear plot and action and rise out of conflicts familiar to those who have little time for leisure; but they must also transcend the mundane to move the listener or reader in some way. The audience Gardner first encountered was composed of people who understood that danger and death are part of the landscape of this world; they could accommodate that understanding within some sort of theological outlook, but disorder was not something easily accommodated.

Disorder destroyed the coherence of things, threatened foundations. Gilbert Gardner's death is the inescapable instance: Gardner's parents were devastated by the farm accident but grieved within the ordered understanding of a tragedy stemming from both children's lapses of judgment. For Gardner, the violent disorder of this accident had no connection to any world he imag-

ined; his guilt was ineradicable. For him the world was now divided between those who are able to find meaning and order in the world and those who have seen "the skull behind the mask." His novels and much of what he wrote about the role of artists in society focus on that divide between a consciousness that can accept a tragic order to the world and a consciousness that despairs and seeks to destroy any illusion of order.

THE THEME OF PERSONAL TRAGEDY

In virtually all of Gardner's fiction, flight from personal tragedy becomes a journey toward knowledge. Indeed, two of the recurring themes that run through his work are culpable negligence that results in the death of a family member and flight from those actions that bring one to the edge of the abyss on one's path to redemptive vision. Gardner enacts through his fiction the two courses that pulled him in life—despair: fleeing from the originating accident along paths that lead to alcoholism, sex, and self-destruction; or affirmation: the self-conscious ordering of chaotic accident into the structured aesthetic of art. His fiction explores the fine tension between tragedy and redemption—specifically, the redemptiveness of art.

Early in his career Gardner acted the part of the formal academic, in dark suits and with close-cropped hair, who kept disorder at bay through carefully structured forms. In midcareer he became the eccentric, long-haired visionary in a leather jacket, railing against the old social and aesthetic norms. His fictions called into question the stylistic constraints of novelistic form. In the years just before he died, Gardner pushed his own limits as a writer and tested the limits of his life. Taking as his operative metaphor the flat-track motorcycle racer's technique of going "flat out," by laying the torso low against the gas tank to lower the drag coefficient at the expense of being able to see very far ahead, Gardner drove head-long into his creative endeavors. It was on his beloved Harley-Davidson that he was fatally injured by some sort of impact with the bike itself as he exited on a curve on his way to teach a class at the State University of New York at Binghamton. No one witnessed the accident.

Gardner's fiction is filled with characters driving "darkly thundering" motorcycles, rattling pickups, and an assortment of cars, tractor trailers, and farm machinery into the "farther darkness." Like Gardner, these characters travel through landscapes illuminated by headlights only, in more than one sense of the word. They think too much; they rely on their own rationality until it can no longer penetrate the stillness and shadows that surround them. They seem most acutely aware of their mortality when they are en route somewhere, usually toward a moment when they must embrace some fusing vision of the world or give in to tragic disconnectedness. Most often the setting is rural, western New York, as in *The Resurrection, The Sunlight Dialogues* (1972), and *Nickel Mountain: A Pastoral Novel* (1973), or adjoining states, as in *October Light* (1976) and *Mickelsson's Ghosts* (1982), which take place in Bennington, Vermont, and Susquehanna, Pennsylvania, respectively. Even those narratives not located in an American fictional landscape, novels such as *The Wreckage of Agathon* (1970), *Grendel* (1971), or the modernized epic *Jason and Medeia* (1973), chronicle characters whose flights carry them back to their actual or philosophical points of departure. Indeed, the tragic figures in nearly all of Gardner's fictions are characters that fail to apprehend the cyclic nature of these patterns.

TRADITION AND EXPERIMENT

Even in his most experimental fiction, Gardner follows traditional modes that are centered on solid development of plot and character and that use structure and sentence rhythms as the means to reveal character. In his writings on fiction, whether the Arthur or Gilgamesh myths or the modern novel, he is consistently concerned with how events are represented through the point of view of the narrator. Gardner's literary devices were influenced by his translating and teaching of Old English poetry. He acknowledges his debt to Geoffrey Chaucer in his introduction to *The Poetry of Chaucer* (1977):

> I write about Chaucer because I believe profoundly what he says in his poetry about human life, and believe his ideas are more significant right now, in the twentieth century. He knew, for instance, about "uncertainty"—knew from having thought about the arguments offered by the philosophical position called nominalism, that quite possibly all truth is relative (if we use "truth" in, say, the moralist's sense) and knew that quite possibly, there can be, in the end, no real communication between human beings. He played with those ideas throughout his career, and toward the end of his life he played even with such particularly, if not exclusively, modern aesthetic problems as the unreliable narrator and the paradox of . . . speech denying the validity of speech.

In his fiction Gardner delves into that paradox and by extension the uncertainties of literary creations; he often does so by means of the unreliable narrative voice, whether the point of view is first or third person, or by the metafictional technique of having the author intrude into his tale. The technique of the unreliable narrator adds a dual dimension of proximity and possible fallibility in the relation of the story to the reader. Particularly in some of the early novels, the causally related events that unfold in a gray area between deterministic and random worldviews force the reader to decide whether or not the narrator can be trusted. The reader is compelled to engage in an act of interpretation, thinking continually about alternative explanations for events.

Gardner leads us to view this interpretive act as a reflection of how we act in the real world we inhabit; his approach suggests that fictional narratives that hold up a mirror to the reader in this way achieve an authenticity that omniscient narrative practices cannot.

All stories are subjective and contingent, but that is not necessarily cause for despair, he would have us see. What arcs across the divide between individual isolate lives is the redemptive spark of imagination and, in it, order. Merely because the connectedness of all things cannot be shown, there is no reason to presuppose randomness. It might be that the connections are outside the realm of human understanding. Those who embrace despair, Gardner says, are those who cannot make the leap of faith.

But Gardner did not initially pursue the harrowing task of creating order out of the disorder of language. After graduating from Batavia High School in 1951, he enrolled at DePauw University in Indiana, intending to major in chemistry. Two years later he married his second cousin, Joan Patterson, and transferred to Washington University in St. Louis, where he studied philosophy and literature and graduated Phi Beta Kappa in 1955. Receiving a Woodrow Wilson Fellowship, he next enrolled in the Ph.D. program at the University of Iowa, where he concentrated on both creative writing and studies in early English literature. His master's thesis and Ph.D. dissertation were both creative projects. Parts of the stories submitted for the master's degree would be reworked as sections of *Nickel Mountain,* but his doctoral thesis, "The Old Men," was never published.

After taking the Ph.D., Gardner followed a fairly predictable trajectory for a young assistant professor trying to secure his academic tenure. After a one-year appointment at Oberlin College, he taught at Chico State College (now California State University at Chico) from 1959 to 1962. One of his first students at Chico was the then-unknown writer Raymond Carver, who, in his introduction to the posthumous publication of Gardner's *On Becoming a Novelist* (1983), recalls that the young "Gardner had a crewcut, dressed like a minister or an FBI man, and went to church on Sundays. But he was unconventional in other ways." Of his literary beliefs, Carver writes:

It was a basic tenet of his that a writer found what he wanted to say in the ongoing process of *seeing* what he'd said. And this seeing, or seeing more clearly, came about through revision. He *believed* in revision, endless revision; it was something very close to his heart and something he felt was vital for writers, at whatever stage of their development.

No publishers were interested in his manuscripts in their workshop forms from his Iowa days, so he was forced to "see more clearly" what he wanted to say in order to discover those narrative devices that impressed publishers enough to take a chance on an unknown writer. This process of discovering how writers shape their writing led to his first published work, *The Forms of Fiction* (1962), coauthored with his colleague Lennis Dunlap.

That same year Gardner moved to San Francisco State University, where he taught from 1962 to 1965, publishing scholarly articles in journals and finishing *The Complete Works of the Gawain-Poet* (1965). In the fall of 1965 Gardner, with his wife and children, Joel (b. 1959) and Lucy (b. 1962), moved back to the St. Louis area after he was hired by Southern Illinois University. His first published novel, *The Resurrection,* appeared in 1966.

EARLY NOVELS

The Resurrection, like Gardner himself, cloaks its iconoclastic character in an outwardly formal appearance. It uses an omniscient narrator and features a prologue followed by three sections of twelve chapters each. The plot traces the final weeks in the life of James Chandler, a young philosophy professor diagnosed with incurable leukemia. No longer able to live his comfortable life of "pedantic abstraction" in the face of his still-incomprehensible death, Chandler has packed up his wife and three small children and left California to return to his childhood home in Batavia, New York. Back home with his aging mother and family, Chandler sees the unbridled growth of Batavia as the same sort of rampant spread perpetrated by disease in his body. Though he wants desperately to abandon philosophy and live fully in the tangible dailiness of his family, his illness will not allow it. Chandler is troubled by dreams that defy the empirical rigor of his training and feels he must write one last treatise. As he works against the cancer's clock, Chandler is also drawn into the tragic world of Viola Staley, an orphan who has been raised by three spinster aunts. Viola has never known family life as she sees it between James and Marie Chandler and their children. Her life has been stifled until the Chandlers come home to Batavia.

After Chandler's visit to the Staleys' home, where he has a powerful emotional response to a painting of an old mill done by the now-senile Emma Staley, he begins to draft an essay on aesthetics, using the painting of the mill as an image of "the soul's sublime acceptance of lawless, proliferating substance." Gardner goes on to have Chandler paraphrase the philosopher Edmund Burke's distinction between the beautiful and the sublime as he builds toward his own aesthetic epiphany: "All that belongs in Burke's realm of *the Sublime* (the large, the angular, the terrifying, etc.) we may identify with *moral affirmation;* that is to say, with human *defiance of chaos,* or the human assertion of *the godlike magnificence of human mind and heart.*"

Near the end of his battle with leukemia, Chandler is shocked and embarrassed by Viola Staley's unexpected declaration of love for him.

He misses his chance to say something appropriate to Viola, and she flees in embarrassment. His own feelings surprise him, and he realizes how much of the world he has cut himself off from over the years. Chandler also comes to understand another price exacted by Viola's declaration. In order to come to Chandler, Viola has left her aging aunt alone and her aunt has wandered from the unlocked house into the unknown. Faced with his own imminent death, Chandler has learned that there are worse fates, among them a life shut off from the world the way Aunt Emma's has been and Viola's will be. Chandler exhausts his remaining strength to drag himself to the Staley home, hoping to console Viola. What he has learned and wishes to transmit to her is that "it was not the beauty of the world one must affirm but *the world,* the buzzing blooming confusion itself. He had slipped from celebrating what was to the celebration of empty celebration. . . . *One must make life Art.*"

The Resurrection received only a few reviews, lukewarm at best and at worst, like that of Granville Hicks, dismissive. For the next few years Gardner concentrated his energies on mentoring young writers at Southern Illinois University and on his scholarly writing. In 1967 he wrote two editions of Cliff's Notes, the bright-yellow booklet summaries ever popular among undergraduates. Both *Le Morte D'Arthur Notes* and *The Gawain-Poet Notes* are still in print. Gardner did not publish another novel until 1970, but the drafts and manuscripts that he had been revising assiduously over the intervening years were waiting in the wings. For the next twelve years he published more than one title a year.

His next novel, *The Wreckage of Agathon* (1970), is much more reflective of Gardner's interest in the metafictional experiments that were current in the late 1960s. This novel can be read as a political allegory of cold war America displaced to ancient Greece. Using a double-stranded narrative alternating between the aging philosopher and seer Agathon and his young disciple Demodokos, also called Peeker, Gardner allows us a glimpse of Athens under Solon and of Sparta under Lykourgos. Again, Gardner's dialectic tension between freedom unconstrained and restrictive order is at the center of the novel. Athens is depicted as a kind of classical precursor to California in the late 1960s—casually, amorally, democratically decadent—and Sparta as a society rigidly controlled by law and order but at terrible cost. Whether the maintenance of law and order is worth the toll it takes on freedom and dignity is a question that Gardner would return to time and again as it was played out in the cultural turbulence of the United States during the Nixon years.

The narrative begins in the final days of Lykourgos' rule, with the arrest and imprisonment of Agathon and Demodokos on no particular charge. While they are being held, they record their thoughts on parchment supplied to them. Both are first-person accounts, alternating between Agathon's efforts to trace his own ascendancy and decline during Lykourgos' rise to power and Demodokos' naive visions of what Agathon has become. Throughout, the novel depends on dramatic irony, an ever-widening gulf between what the narrators tell the reader and what the reader knows to be true, if in fact truth can ever be discerned merely from knowing what is not true. Again, the conflicts and debates grow out of interrogation of the philosophical foundations of western culture.

Not that *The Wreckage of Agathon* is a novel of plodding seriousness. Gardner balances comedy and tragedy with deft pacing of plot and development of character. Agathon, although he was once revered as a seer whose prophecies foretold the fate of Athens and Sparta, has become a comical figure of lust and lechery. The reader is lulled by tragicomic lamentations over lost lovers and social positions to the point that reasons for loss are often missed. As in *The Res-*

urrection, which explores the protagonist's failed philosophical system, Gardner exposes the consequences for a society of "bad faith." Agathon is in a position to influence policy by means of how he shapes his narrative; thus the personal and political failures that have embittered him have larger consequences.

We learn—without being surprised—that Agathon's despair is rooted in the accidental death of his brother, killed by a horse in a riding accident when he was ten. What Agathon cannot tell us and what we must learn from his wife very late in the novel, after his death, is that it was Agathon who rode his brother down. Embittered by a world where gods would allow that sort of accident, Agathon deploys his philosophical training and rhetorical skill to help Solon rise to power through deception and treachery and at the expense of honor and dignity. Disillusioned by that extreme, Agathon is at first attracted to the orderly structure of Sparta's rule of law but soon learns the oppressive cost. Now, near the end of his life, viewing the "wreckage" his despair has brought to all about him, his last task is to prevent Peeker from falling under the influence of flawed systems.

After Agathon's death Demodokos, freed and left to pick up the chaotic threads of his life, takes his biographical account to Tuka, Agathon's wife, who knows that it is a distortion of the truth; nevertheless, she finds herself embellishing it as well. In the end they all opt for the ordering power of imagination over fact, and this act of limited affirmation is a stay to chaos for a while longer.

GRENDEL

With *The Alliterative Morte Arthure, The Owl and the Nightingale, and Five Other Middle English Poems* (1971), Gardner further solidified his scholarly reputation as a translator and popularizer of Old and Middle English poetry. Arguing for the narrative power of this version of the Arthurian cycle over the more familiar version by Sir Thomas Mallory, Gardner emphasizes the poet's understanding of mutability in human affairs. Fortune is cyclic, as Arthur must discover, and when the wheel starts down, by whatever accident, tragedy unfolds. There is always culpability, either direct or indirect. On an epic level Gardner once again draws the reader into a moral conflict that ends in the fratricidal deaths of Arthur and his brother Mordred.

That saturation in medieval literature found a more experimental outlet in the other book Gardner published in 1971. As a clever retelling of the Beowulf legend from the monster's point of view, *Grendel* has become one of Gardner's most enduring novels. In it he revisits the consequences of failed moral systems in western thought. *Grendel* was not initially a publishing success, but over time it became a cult classic that built its reputation on the enthusiasm of friends recommending it to friends.

The central conflict in *Grendel* is between the mythmaking vision of the Shaper, who is constructing the epic poem of Hrothgar's reign (which he recites nightly in Mead Hall and which we as readers know will come down to us as the Caxton manuscript of Beowulf), and the monster Grendel's first-person counter-narrative, which deconstructs the noble motives of the Danes but can offer only a bleak existentialism in its place. The monster's voice of alienation and the seeming moral righteousness he represents against the avarice and greed of the Danes initially hold sway over the reader. Grendel recounts his early life and his painful moment of awareness when, trapped in a tree and attacked by a bull, he discovers how indifferent the world is: "I understood the world was nothing: a mechanical chaos of casual, brute enmity on which we stupidly impose our hopes and fears."

His encounter with humans leads him to discover their power as pattern makers, creating through the imaginative force of Hrothgar's court poet, the Shaper, a usable past. The Shaper fabricates a myth of heroism and destiny that even includes Grendel, but only as enemy, outcast, cursed by God as a son of Cain. Though he knows the truth about the Danes, Grendel is seduced by the linguistic power of the Shaper even though it implicates him. Again, Gardner presents a central character who bears the consequences of fratricide, however untrue and distant that guilt might be. But because Grendel prefers the beautiful falsity of the Shaper's poem to the ugly disorder of the truth, he tries to reconcile his place in this narrative.

Driven out violently by the Danes, Grendel next visits the dragon's lair. The role of the dragon in *Grendel* is to offer up a nihilistic cynicism weary of anything local and historical. For the dragon the universe is a grand chaotic design of entropic decay so beyond our ability to alter it that the only thing to do with one's life is find a suitable material diversion—seek out gold and hoard it. Trapped between the ordering influence of the Shaper and the absolute disorder of the dragon, Grendel chooses chaos and destruction.

The arrival of Beowulf changes all that. Beowulf, Gardner would have us believe, is able to embrace the contradictions of the Shaper's order and the dragon's chaos by positing a universe that is cyclic in its process of creating and destroying. The key is that the world does renew itself. Beowulf drives Grendel to a small act of imagination, a painful creation of a poem that moves from the decay of the dragon's view to the limited affirmation of Beowulf's:

> The wall will fall to the wind as the windy hill
> will fall, and all things thought in former times:
> Nothing made remains, nor man remembers.
> And these towns shall be called the shining towns!

But Grendel cannot grant this affirmation its full power as the ordering force of art. He will only concede it as unplanned: "Poor Grendel's had an accident, I whisper. *So may you all.*"

THE SUNLIGHT DIALOGUES

The Sunlight Dialogues (1972) was Gardner's first best-seller. Thematically, it continues the conversation of his previous novels, focusing on the tension between the cost to personal freedom of an ordered society and the inevitable disorder that results whenever a group attempts to subsume the individual. Its setting, like that of *The Resurrection,* is Batavia, and the year is 1966. In formal terms *The Sunlight Dialogues* is Gardner's most traditional novel: it is essentially a saga over three generations of the once-powerful Hodge family, numerous prominent townspeople, and many more minor characters involved in subplots that echo and add texture to the central conflict. The conflict between police chief Fred Clumly and Taggert Hodge, a.k.a. the Sunlight Man, captured for the novel's contemporary readers the moral and social upheavals of the 1960s and early 1970s, when every newscast was filled with accounts of civil disobedience and anarchy.

Fred Clumly, the aging police chief of Batavia, frets over the decay of social order in the world. He reads disturbing accounts daily and sees the images of chaos on television. In Clumly's mind, the epicenter of this decadence is California, a new Babylon. When he arrests a vandal for painting LOVE in large letters across Main Street and that man begins to act bizarrely in jail, Clumly's immediate sense is that this wild-eyed character must hail from California. The anarchic Sunlight Man then becomes accessory to murder when he stages a jailbreak that results in the death of a young guard. Clumly now pursues him in what becomes an allegory of every epic struggle of a culture to preserve itself. Old, pale, and hairless as a mole, limited in imagination, Clumly pursues what turns out to be the flamboyant and despairingly brilliant son of the town's patriarch. Taggert Hodge, the Sunlight Man, has returned to destroy the objects of the social order that he feels has betrayed him.

Throughout this richly layered novel, we find Hodge's worldview borrowed from ancient Babylon and presented to a befuddled Clumly as a better alternative than the crumbling order he has embraced. According to Hodge, the Babylonians had a cosmology superior to western civilization's classical and Judeo-Christian system of law. In his secret meetings with the powerless Clumly, held while he remains at large in Batavia, Hodge presents a series of dialogues that instruct Clumly on the radical separation between the spiritual world and the material world in Babylon. Delighting in this material world, since the spiritual remained unknowable, Babylonians lived for immediate pleasure without the guilt and constraint of law as it has been handed down in western civilization. However, like the dragon's cynicism in *Grendel,* the Babylonians and Taggert Hodge live with the knowledge that, ultimately, "all systems fail," that death will conquer all and "Hell's jaws will yawn and the cities will sink, and there will not be a trace." All Clumly has to counter this despair is his plodding faith in the necessity of order as preserved by law. That, and his gift for empathy. It is this empathy that sustains him in the face of the chaotic world represented by Hodge. And empathy will lead Clumly to a final, limited act of imagination that provides the affirmative ending of *The Sunlight Dialogues.*

OTHER NOVELS

Two very different narratives were published in 1973. *Jason and Medeia* is Gardner's effort at a long epic poem; *Nickel Mountain* is a pastoral novel that grew out of stories originally written for his master's thesis more than a decade earlier. *Jason and Medeia* is among Gardner's most ambitious but flawed works. Written in unrhymed, sprung hexameters and rich in its use of epic simile, *Jason and Medeia* allows Gardner to interweave the classical past with the present. In it he borrows from the primary texts of Apollonius of Rhodes's *Argonautica* and Euripides' *Medeia* to explore the shaping power of myth in the formation of culture. Gardner's desire in *Jason and Medeia* is to revisit one of those formative epics through the postmodern lens of late-twentieth-century consciousness. In an age of indeterminacy, no longer assured that the past speaks in one voice if it speaks at all, Gardner once again develops a multistrand narrative that presents radically different points of view.

In the faithful borrowing and embellishing of the voyage of the Argonauts taken from Apollonius, Gardner presents Jason as classical epic hero, representing the cultural values of a western male. Jason is rational, pragmatic, opportunistic, and a fabricator. Language for him is rhetorical power. From Euripides, Gardner develops the more eastern female depiction of Medeia as someone whose devotion, commitment, and intuition border on the irrational. Language for her is unambiguous, fixed, and objective. Hers is a ceremonial view of the world in which words and the loyalties pledged in words shimmer with substance.

The tragedy in this epic is Jason's betrayal of the moral precepts of the artist for cynical gain. He abandons Medeia and his children to contend for the throne of Corinth by winning the hand of Pyripta, Kreon's daughter. He does this by creating a self-justifying narrative of his voyage to Colchis in search of the Golden Fleece; although this narrative enthralls the court, in fact his art offers nothing affirmative or redemptive in its fabrication. It betrays the trust of his listeners, estranges Medeia, and leads to the tragic death of innocents. At the end of this modern epic, the image of Jason wandering in despair in search of Medeia evokes the bleakness of Agathon's, Grendel's, or Taggert Hodge's failed vision.

Nickel Mountain: A Pastoral Novel, on the other hand, solidified Gardner's reputation as a philosophical novelist who could cross over into the popular readership. The eight interwoven stories that map the Catskill Mountains in and around Henry Soames's Stop-Off cafe celebrate that same pastoralism present in *The Resurrection* and certain sections of *The Sunlight Dialogues.* Henry Soames is very much a part of his landscape. He is large, unkempt, and inarticulate compared with previous voices through which Gardner has spoken. Soames has to grow into the affirmation of the world that Gardner wants to celebrate. Looking out into the darkness that surrounds the Stop-Off halfway up Nickel Mountain, Soames fears dying alone and unloved. The arrival at the Stop-Off of unmarried, pregnant Callie Wells shakes Soames loose from his alienation and begins to reintegrate him, and those around him, into some version of community. As the character who represents some fusing vision between Calvinism and nihilism, Henry Soames dramatizes Gardner's belief that wholeness in art and life comes from a faith in order, however limited our understanding of it. Married to Callie, father to her son, still fat, and likely to die from his ailing heart, over time "he became in reality what he was, his vision not something apart from the world but the world itself transmuted."

In 1974 Gardner was invited to be one of the writers in residence at the Bread Loaf Writers Conference in Vermont along with his friend the novelist William Gass. The next few summers at Bread Loaf he held forth at cocktail debates over the direction and craft of fiction; those debates served as rehearsals for Gardner's attack on popular fiction as unfaithful to the mission of true art.

OCTOBER LIGHT

In fall 1974 Gardner began teaching at Bennington College in southern Vermont. In 1976 he published his novel *October Light,* set in this rural landscape. Gardner said that he conceived the novel as a work that would celebrate the traditional New England values that shaped the nation's revolutionary sense of exceptionalism, "good workmanship, independence, unswerving honesty, and so on," in order to contrast those values with the decadent material culture of the late twentieth century. What Gardner discovered in the process of writing the novel was that a rigid adherence to celebrating those values was no more possible for the author than for the character of James Page.

Seventy-two-year-old James Page is enraged at the intrusion of the modern world into his insular, rural farm life. His eighty-year-old sister, Sally Abbot, has returned to live with him in the family home after the death of her husband. Years of solitude and habit cannot easily accommodate the return of his sister, particularly her incessant interaction with television. The bombardment of images from the modern world angers and disturbs Page's sense of the world, much as Clumly is disturbed in *The Sunlight Dialogues*. In a fit of rage that has already occurred before the opening of the novel, Page has taken his shotgun and blasted the television. Sally's outrage at the act angers him further, and he has driven her upstairs into a bedroom. Locked inside the bedroom, Sally decides to go on "strike," refusing to leave the room despite pleas from family and friends. Provisioned with a basket of apples stored in the room and diverted by a trashy paperback novel she has found, Sally takes her stand.

What ensues in this poignant and funny novel is nothing less than an exploration of American values some two hundred years after the founding of the country. James Page, champion of self-sufficiency, independence, and the agrarian idealism of the framers of the Constitution, is contrasted to the more malleable Sally Abbot. His rugged code of self-reliance has come at great cost. His son Richard, unable to live up to his father's harsh expectations or live with the blame Page placed on him for the accidental death of

his brother, was a suicide. Sally, for whom television is a form of travel, embraces change. In her view, mass production has eliminated scarcity; nuclear plants might provide cheap electricity; and the United States should enact the Equal Rights Amendment. In short, everything Sally sees as new and exciting is a serious threat to James Page.

Gardner stylistically contrasts the primary fictional narrative that frames *October Light*—the day-to-day reality of Sally Abbot's and James Page's lives—with the sensational fictional lives of the interpolated story developed in the novel Sally is reading. In that contrast lies the novel's power. *The Smugglers of Lost Soul's Rock* is Gardner's satire of postmodern fiction—lurid, facile, and filled with cynical characters whose violent exploits offer nothing but titillating diversion. At first Sally Abbot is offended by this sort of trash novel, but, having nothing else to do while she waits out her battle of wills with Page, she reads on. Eventually, the seductive power of this novelistic cynicism drives her to act out that kind of violence, and she sets a trap to kill her brother. Her plotting takes a terrible turn when she nearly kills her niece instead, and the shock retrieves Sally from the seductive lure of believing that one can lead a life without constraints and consequences.

James Page, too, must learn the cost of believing in a world of narrowly constrained order, grim, cyclic, and darkening. His fierce adherence to his code has contributed to the suicide of his son, the injury of his friends, and his estrangement from the community. Just as Clumly's plodding devotion to law and order must be leavened by some creative anarchic mystery in the vision of the Sunlight Man, or Grendel's nihilism be modified by Beowulf's celebration of the world's renewal, James Page and Sally Abbot must be lifted out of various forms of despair. Trapped as Page is on one end of the continuum and as intractable as Sally has become on the other, it remains for one of Gardner's moral arbiters to resolve the conflict in this novel. Estelle Parks is the character who shares that deeper understanding of the world's purpose and meaning. She organizes a community potluck dinner at Page's home in hopes of luring Sally down from her room to reconcile with James. The party is a huge success for all but James and Sally, but Estelle is able to articulate to James the central vision of what is missing in his life:

> It's a fragile life. One moment we're happy and wonderfully healthy and our children are all well, and it seems as if nothing can possibly go wrong, and the next some horrible accident has happened, and suddenly we see how things really are and we cling to each other for dear life.

October Light was Gardner's biggest critical and commercial success. Nominated for the National Book Critics Circle Award, it won the prize, after acrimonious disagreement among the judges as to whether it or Renata Adler's *Speedboat* ought to have been their choice, in a split vote.

CHALLENGES AND CONTROVERSIES

Life imitated art for Gardner in 1977, during his stint as writer in residence at George Mason University in Washington, D.C. He was diagnosed with colon cancer and underwent surgery at Johns Hopkins Medical Center. Although the prognosis was not as grim as for James Chandler, the disease was serious. Other parts of Gardner's life were equally unhappy. He separated from his wife of twenty-four years; his National Book Critics Circle Award was tainted by the judges' acrimonious disagreements; and a minor academic controversy over sloppy attribution in his Chaucer books was being misrepresented in the press as plagiarism. By his own admission, he was hurting both physically and emotionally.

In 1978 he joined the English department at the State University of New York at Binghamton. Forty-four years old, faced with the prospect that he might not survive the cancer and his voice would be silenced while other writers would go on publishing, Gardner poured his frustration into *On Moral Fiction.* It is a manifesto so strident and dismissive in places of nearly all Gardner's literary contemporaries that the notoriety it achieved overshadowed his fiction; worse, the book opened up his own fiction to the same criticisms he leveled at others. What he calls for in *On Moral Fiction* is what he had been dramatizing in the conflicts between faith and despair in his characters: that art instructs, that moral art affirms life and offers models for our lives. There is not much new here that Sir Philip Sidney, Samuel Johnson, Leo Tolstoy, or Matthew Arnold, to name a few literary giants, had not already stated, but Gardner was determined to demonstrate his thesis against the postmodern tendencies that he saw as having eclipsed a higher vision of the artist. The metafictional techniques he had experimented with—parody of earlier forms, calling attention to the constructedness of the text, decentering the point of view, calling into question the reliability of the narrator—are not incompatible with a moral vision. Experimentation with form is not the problem; rather, it is the lack of seriousness of purpose. Gardner argues for fiction as another form of philosophy, a way of trying out ideas about the world that might be too dangerous to attempt in one's own life. Therefore, the artist is obligated to be truthful and honest in the creative process, asking at every turn what a character would truly do or say if the fiction is to have integrity. The smoke and fire of that debate can be detected in the number of essays, such as those by Marilyn Edelstein, Bo G. Ekelund, and Stephen Singular, that continue to be published on Gardner.

Throughout 1979 Gardner was in demand as a public speaker. He lectured at universities, was interviewed several times, and engaged in lively debates in print and in person with his friend William Gass. Unable to find the time to work through the intricacies of a novel, Gardner turned to opera and radio theater, publishing librettos for *Rumpelstiltskin* (1978), *Frankenstein* (1979), and *William Wilson* (1979). The following year he married the poet Liz Rosenberg, who also taught at Binghamton, and wrote an award-winning radio play, *The Temptation Game* (1980). Later that year he published his last novel, *Freddy's Book.*

Freddy's Book is another frame tale in the manner of *October Light,* but it marks a return to Gardner's love of national myth. In the extended frame tale that begins the novel, Professor Jack Winesap meets the odd Professor Aagard while lecturing at the University of Wisconsin. As a "psycho-historian," Winesap expounds on the topic of "monstrosity" in the public imagination. The talk visibly agitates Aagard, and afterward he approaches Winesap to tell him that he has a son who is a monster. They arrange for Winesap to visit the Aagards at their rural home, where he can meet Freddy. After some delay Winesap is introduced to an adolescent who is incredibly tall—eight feet—and terribly shy. Reclusive, hiding his monstrous bulk from the taunting world, Freddy has been writing a book for two years.

He leaves this book in the guest room for Winesap to read. What Freddy has written is a heroic tale, "King Gustav and the Devil," based on the sixteenth-century historical accounts of Gustav Vasa's rise to power in 1520. In Freddy's narrative Gustav is aided by his cousin, the giant Lars-Goren, and by the opportunistic cleric Bishop Brask. Gustav's rule as king is threatened from without and within, but the faithful knight Lars-Goren is there to protect him. Predictably, Freddy foregrounds Lars-Goren as the real hero of the story. We see how he fulfills Freddy's dreams of strength and courage, and we know what Lars-Goren fears more than anything. In-evitably, King Gustav asks Lars-Goren to undertake the most harrowing quest of all: he is to venture into the dark regions of his greatest fear and slay the Devil. Gustav sends the villainous Bishop Brask along, too.

At the edge of the world, where snow blurs all form and substance, the faithful Lars-Goren overcomes his terror and scales the looming bulk of the Devil, stabbing him in the eye with his bone knife. Brask is stunned by the courage and loyalty that Lars-Goren has displayed in the face of almost insurmountable difficulty. His despair and cynicism are laid bare in contrast. What we would expect of such a heroic story would be the triumphant return of Lars-Goren to the palace, but instead the novel ends on a more ambiguous note. King Gustav is standing at a window: "Darkness fell. There was no light anywhere, except for the yellow light of cities."

This lack of affirmation after heroic sacrifice seemed deeply troubling to the novel's critics. As the first novel published after *On Moral Fiction,* *Freddy's Book* was analyzed in the context of the earlier work's arguments. Many critics felt Gardner was using Freddy as a grotesque misfit to say something about the marginalized voice of the artist in our time. Through Freddy, Gardner is able to explore the self-fashioning of artists in a hostile world. It is the redemptive act of creating that leads to some limited apprehension of the world's order.

The 1981 publication of *The Art of Living and Other Stories* is notable for the inclusion of Gardner's heavily autobiographical "Redemption," a story that first appeared in *The Atlantic Monthly* in 1977. "Redemption" dramatizes how music, in the form of his devotion to the French horn, saves Jack Hawthorne from the hopeless despair his father has suffered in the years after Jack accidentally killed his brother. Changing few of the actual facts of his life, Gardner is spare and poignant, holding in check the expansive dialectics usually playing through his prose. Other important stories in the collection are "Nimram," "Vlemk the Box Painter," and "Come on Back."

By 1982, the last year of his life, Gardner was working hard to repair some of the damage from his broadsides in *On Moral Fiction.* In interviews and in his drafts of *The Art of Fiction,* he takes pains to acknowledge his facile judgments and misreading of his contemporaries. His marriage to Liz Rosenberg had ended, and he had become something of a Susquehanna local, staying active in little theater while still mentoring young writers in and out of his classes at SUNY Binghamton. The painful excesses of the last four years seem to have been cathartically rendered into the fictional life of Peter Mickelsson, the hero of his last complete novel.

MICKELSSON'S GHOSTS

In *Mickelsson's Ghosts* we have an ironic closure to Gardner's writing career. He has come back to the professional philosopher as central character, as in *The Resurrection.* This time, the philosopher has lived long enough to see his academic star reach its apogee and begin its downward arc. Mickelsson has slipped from the privileged world of the elite private university to the public state college. Once an ethicist of some reputation, he has separated from his wife and children, drinks to excess, shirks his teaching, and hides from the Internal Revenue Service. In short, Mickelsson's current life is a repudiation of his whole academic career.

Just how far he has slipped becomes brutally evident when he clubs to death a neighbor's dog that frightens him one night as he is walking. Shocked by his actions, he blames them on his living situation and begins to search the country-side for somewhere to live beyond the city. When he buys a run-down old farmhouse across the state line in Pennsylvania, the pastoral pattern seems all too familiar to Gardner's readers. Once

again, a character retreats from the deadening city to the country, where nature and the rustic community will heal the disorder of his life.

Yet Gardner is not having any of that in this novel, at least not in any easy way. Mickelsson soon finds that his old house harbors more than rats in the basement. People tell him the house is haunted, that a murder took place there, that there is a troubled history to the place that goes back to Joseph Smith and the roots of Mormonism. The present does not seem much better. Strange sounds, strange lights, and vandals destroy what little serenity the place might hold. Nor do the good country people fit the stereotype. At worst they are avaricious, deceitful, and mean, at best aloof.

By this time Mickelsson's life is in a death spiral. As he works late into the night remodeling the old house, he works equally hard to shut out the sordidness of his most grievous error. A teenage prostitute has told him that she is pregnant by him and wants money for an abortion. Firm in his antiabortion ethics, Mickelsson tries to dissuade her by promising her money to have the baby. To get the money he robs a petty thief, who then has a heart attack and dies. Now certain that he is under suspicion for murder, Mickelsson holes up in his house. In his isolation and misery he is haunted by both the local ghosts of the house and the larger philosophical ghosts of his profession. The novel plays the philosophical positions of Friedrich Nietzsche, Karl Marx, and Martin Luther into Mickelsson's paranoid decline. Then a greater insanity than his saves Mickelsson from his hell of self-destruction.

Gardner puts Mickelsson at the mercy of a Mormon zealot who thinks the house hides evidence of a Mormon scandal. The religious fanatic forces Mickelsson systematically to dismantle the house he has remodeled. This outrage to his house, the one thing that he has done well lately, finally drives Mickelsson to action. By tearing out all of his handiwork to prevent the zealot from killing him, Mickelsson chooses to destroy the symbol of his isolation and seek help from his community. His Susquehanna neighbors answer his plea for help and literally save his life. Later, he moves back into the larger community, just as James Chandler attempts to do in going to Viola in *The Resurrection.* Mickelsson seeks out the woman who might best comprehend his new awareness of life's interdependence—Jessica Stark, a sociology professor whose friendship he had rejected earlier. With his declaration of love to Jessica, surrounded by party goers inside and a more surreal world of ghosts and life tumbling outside, Mickelsson redeems the sorry state of his life and is lifted back into some limited affirmation of his world.

Technically and ethically, Gardner seemed poised to take his fiction further over the next few years. He spoke hopefully of the breakthrough that would dazzle his readers in *Stillness,* but that work and *Shadows,* published together posthumously, show little evidence of his once-fervent belief in revision. *Mickelsson's Ghosts* will stand as the point of departure for Gardner. He remained true to his complicated faith in the redemptive power of art and the fundamental mysteries of this world that challenge our belief. His moral vision was not a simple didactic embrace of grace and order. It was, rather, a cosmology filled with uncertainty, rooted in the medieval nominalism of William of Ockham, but holding nonetheless that there is a pattern and orderliness to the universe, even if it stands outside humankind's ability to comprehend it. Throughout his fiction we are told by characters that "systems fail," that "language fails," and yet things happen in ways that suggest more then mere randomness.

What Gardner is saying, then, when he points up the failure of man-made systems is that these systems fail to explain accurately and adequately what various characters "know" to be true on some inexpressible level. We see this in James

Chandler's attempt to refute the claims of Horne, in Agathon's tortured choices between the views of Lykourgos and Solon, in Grendel's fatal apprehension of Beowulf's message, in Clumly's small act of imagination, in Henry Soames's redemptive act, in the "unlocking" of James Page, or in the redemptive chance allowed Peter Mickelsson. The larger, inexplicable system is intact, unavailable to any adequate representation by narrative act, knowable only by intuitive glimpses, oracular visions, and in those acts of imagination that bridge the separateness of lives.

Selected Bibliography

WORKS OF JOHN GARDNER

NOVELS AND SHORT STORY COLLECTIONS
The Old Men. Ann Arbor, Mich.: University Microfilms, 1959.
The Resurrection. New York: New American Library, 1966. Rev. ed., New York: Ballantine, 1974.
The Wreckage of Agathon. New York: Harper and Row, 1970.
Grendel. Illustrated by Emil Antonucci. New York: Vintage, 1971.
The Sunlight Dialogues. Illustrated by John Napper. New York: Knopf, 1972.
Jason and Medeia. New York: Knopf, 1973.
Nickel Mountain: A Pastoral Novel. Illustrated by Thomas O'Donohue. New York: Knopf, 1973.
The King's Indian: Stories and Tales. Illustrated by Herbert L. Fink. New York: Knopf, 1974.
October Light. Illustrated by Elaine Raphael and Don Bolognese. New York: Knopf, 1976.
In the Suicide Mountains. Illustrated by Joe Servello. New York: Knopf, 1977.
Vlemk the Box-Painter. Northridge, Calif.: Lord John Press, 1979.
Freddy's Book. New York: Knopf, 1980.
The Art of Living and Other Stories. New York: Knopf, 1981.
Mickelsson's Ghosts. New York: Knopf, 1982.

Stillness; and, Shadows. Edited and with an introduction by Nicholas Delbanco. New York: Knopf, 1986.

ANTHOLOGIES, CRITICISM, AND EDITED WORKS

Gardner, John, and Lennis Dunlap. *The Forms of Fiction.* New York: Random House, 1962.

The Construction of the Wakefield Cycle. Carbondale: Southern Illinois University Press, 1974.

The Construction of Christian Poetry in Old English. Carbondale: Southern Illinois University Press, 1975.

The Life and Times of Chaucer. New York: Random House, 1977.

The Poetry of Chaucer. Carbondale: Southern Illinois University Press, 1977.

On Moral Fiction. New York: Basic Books, 1978.

Gardner, John, and L. M. Rosenberg, eds. *MSS: A Retrospective.* Dallas, Tex.: New London Press, 1981.

Gardner, John, and Shannon Ravenel, eds. *The Best American Short Stories 1982.* Boston: Houghton Mifflin, 1982.

The Art of Fiction: Notes on Craft for Young Writers. New York: Knopf, 1983.

On Becoming a Novelist. New York: Harper, 1983.

On Writers and Writing. Edited by Stewart O'Nan, with an introduction by Charles Johnson. New York: Addison-Wesley, 1994.

Lies! Lies! Lies! A College Journal of John Gardner. Rochester, N.Y.: University of Rochester Press, 1999.

TRANSLATIONS

The Complete Works of the Gawain-Poet. Chicago: University of Chicago Press, 1965.

The Alliterative Morte Arthure, The Owl and the Nightingale, and Five Other Middle English Poems. Carbondale: Southern Illinois University Press, 1971.

Tengu Child: Stories by Kikuo Itaya. Trans. John Gardner and Nobuko Tsukui. Carbondale: Southern Illinois University Press, 1983.

Gilgamesh: Translated from the Sîn-Leqi-Unninni Version. Translated by John Gardner and John Maier with Richard A. Henshaw. New York: Knopf, 1984.

CHILDREN'S BOOKS

Dragon, Dragon and Other Tales. Illustrated by Charles Shields. New York: Knopf, 1975.

Gudgekin the Thistle Girl and Other Tales. Illustrated by Michael Sporn. New York: Knopf, 1976.

A Child's Bestiary. With additional poems by Lucy Gardner and Eugene Rudzewicz and drawings by Lucy, Joel, Joan, and John Gardner. New York: Knopf, 1977.

The King of the Hummingbirds and Other Tales. Illustrated by Michael Sporn. New York: Knopf, 1977.

POETRY AND LIBRETTOS

Poems. Northridge, Calif.: Lord John Press, 1978.

Rumpelstiltskin. Dallas, Tex.: New London Press, 1978.

Frankenstein. Dallas, Tex.: New London Press, 1979.

William Wilson. Dallas, Tex.: New London Press, 1979.

The Temptation Game. Dallas, Tex.: New London Press, 1980.

Death and the Maiden. Dallas, Tex.: New London Press, 1981.

BIBLIOGRAPHIES

Howell, John M. *John Gardner: A Bibliographical Profile.* Carbondale: Southern Illinois University Press, 1980.

Morace, Robert A. *John Gardner: An Annotated Secondary Bibliography.* New York: Garland, 1984.

CRITICAL STUDIES

BOOKS

Butts, Leonard. *The Novels of John Gardner: Making Life Art as a Moral Process.* Baton Rouge: Louisiana State University Press, 1988.

Cowart, David. *Arches and Light: The Fiction of John Gardner.* Carbondale: Southern Illinois University Press, 1983.

Henderson, Jeff, Leonard C. Butts, and Kathryn Van Spanckeren, eds. *Thor's Hammer: Essays on John Gardner.* Conway: University of Central Arkansas Press, 1985.

Howell, John M. *Understanding John Gardner.* Columbia: University of South Carolina Press, 1993.

Morris, Gregory L. *A World of Order and Light: The Fiction of John Gardner.* Athens: University of Georgia Press, 1984.

Nutter, Ronald Grant. *A Dream of Peace: Art and Death in the Fiction of John Gardner.* New York: Peter Lang, 1997.

Winther, Per. *The Art of John Gardner: Instruction and Exploration.* Albany: State University of New York Press, 1992.

ARTICLES AND ESSAYS

Allen, Bruce. "Settling for Ithaca: The Fictions of John Gardner." *Sewanee Review* 85:520–531 (1977).

Barrow, Craig. "On a Moral Fiction Writer's Last Novel: Gardner's *Mickelsson's Ghosts.*" *Critique: Studies in Contemporary Fiction* 26, no. 2:49–56 (winter 1985).

Daly, Robert. "John Gardner and the Emancipation of Genres." *Georgia Review* 37, no. 2:420–428 (summer 1983).

Des Pres, Terrence. "Accident and Its Scene: Reflections on the Death of John Gardner." *Yale Review* 73, no. 1:145–160 (autumn 1983).

Edelstein, Marilyn. "Ethics and Contemporary American Literature: Revisiting the Controversy over John Gardner's *On Moral Fiction.*" *Pacific Coast Philology* 31, no. 1:40–53 (1996).

Ekelund, Bo G. "The Alien in Our Midst: Trash Culture and Good Americans in John Gardner's *October Light.*" *Novel: A Forum on Fiction* 30, no. 3:381–404 (spring 1997).

Fawcett, Barry, and Elizabeth Jones. "The Twelve Traps in John Gardner's *Grendel.*" *American Literature* 62, no. 4:634–647 (December 1990).

Fitzpatrick, W. P. "John Gardner and the Defense of Fiction." *Midwest Quarterly* 20:405–415 (1979).

Henderson, Jeff. "The Avenues of Mundane Salvation: Time and Change in the Fiction of John Gardner." *American Literature* 55, no. 4:611–633 (December 1983).

———. "John Gardner's *Jason and Medeia:* The Resurrection of a Genre." *Papers on Language and Literature* 22, no. 1:76–95 (winter 1986).

Johnson, Charles. "John Gardner as Mentor." *African American Review* 30, no. 4:619–624 (winter 1996).

Larsen, Eric. "Writing and Nostalgia: Hiding in the Past." *New England Review and Bread Loaf Quarterly* 5, no. 4:461–477 (summer 1983).

McCaffery, Larry. "The Gass-Gardner Debate: Showdown on Main Street." *Literary Review* 23:134–144 (1979).

Merrill, Robert. "John Gardner's Grendel and the Interpretation of Modern Fables." *American Literature* 56, no. 2:162–180 (May 1984).

Milosh, Joseph. "John Gardner's *Grendel:* Sources and Analogues." *Contemporary Literature* 19:48–57 (winter 1978).

Morace, Robert A. "Something Happened." *Literary Review* 28, no. 4:617–633 (summer 1985).

Murr, Judy Smith. "John Gardner's Order and Disorder: *Grendel* and *The Sunlight Dialogues.*" *Critique: Studies in Modern Fiction* 18, no. 2:97–108 (1976).

Singular, Stephen. "The Sound and the Fury over Fiction." *New York Times Magazine,* July 8, 1979, pp. 12ff.

"Special Feature on John Gardner: A Tribute." *MSS* 4:1–2 (fall 1984).

Stansberry, Domenic. "John Gardner: The Return Home." *Ploughshares* 10:2–3, 95–123 (1984).

Strehle, Susan. "John Gardner's Novels: Affirmation and the Alien." *Critique: Studies in Modern Fiction* 18, no. 2:86–96 (1976).

Stromme, Craig J. "The Twelve Chapters of Grendel." *Critique: Studies in Modern Fiction* 20, no. 1:83–92 (1978).

INTERVIEWS

Bellamy, Joe David. *The New Fiction: Interviews with Innovative American Writers.* Urbana: University of Illinois Press, 1974.

Chavkin, Allan, ed. *Conversations with John Gardner.* Jackson: University Press of Mississippi, 1990.

Christian, Ed. "An Interview with John Gardner." *Prairie Schooner* 54, no. 4:70–93 (winter 1980).

Harvey, Marshall L. "Where Philosophy and Fiction Meet: An Interview with John Gardner." *Chicago Review* 29:73–87 (spring 1978).

LeClair, Tom, and Larry McCaffery. *Anything Can Happen: Interviews with Contemporary American Novelists.* Urbana: University of Illinois Press, 1983.

Mitchell, Judson, and William Richard. "An Interview with John Gardner." *New Orleans Review* 8, no. 2:125–133 (summer 1981).

Suplee, Curt. "John Gardner, Flat Out." *Washington Post,* July 25, 1982, sec. H1, pp. 8–9.

—WILLIAM D. ATWILL

William Gass

1924–

"W̶E MUST TAKE our sentences seriously," William Gass wrote in his essay "The Ontology of the Sentence" (collected in *The World within the Word: Essays,* 1978), "which means we must understand them philosophically." Few figures in American literary history have taken sentences as seriously as William Gass or have commented as eloquently on the implications of the writing enterprise itself. Gass defies the conservative assumption that writing ought to work diligently to obscure its "madeness," boldly dismissing the efforts of strictly representational literature as clumsy legerdemain that inevitably diminishes the sheer craftsmanship of literary expression. Life, Gass has argued, is highly overrated, raw experience like heavy stones that drop forgotten into deep water. "Life really doesn't have any power until it gets put into language," he remarked during a colloquy with Brooke Horvath and others in 1983. Trained in aesthetics and word theory, Gass has long insisted that a text is not a reflection of the world but an addition to it, an entity that commands attention not because of its "truthfulness" (such concerns, in Gass's mind bogus when applied to literature, always merit placement in quotation marks in his vision) but because of the rightness of its construction—its beauty, its order. Eager for characters to cheer on or hiss; desperate, given the unvaryingness of their lives, for the thrill of stage-managed suspense; and addicted, given a chaotic world, to the compact resolution of themes, unschooled readers have long insisted on ignoring the obvious: that a book is a fashioned artifact, a world-system with its own internal logic, its own design—and its own designer.

In a public career that spans nearly half a century Gass has produced remarkably few such artifacts—two novels (his first not published until he was forty, his second more than thirty years later); a handful of startlingly original short stories and novellas; a perverse conceit-qua-novella (*Willie Masters' Lonesome Wife,* 1968); a book-length essay on the color blue (*On Being Blue: A Philosophical Inquiry,* 1976); translations of the German poet Rainer Maria Rilke; and four compilations of essays. Although Gass has audaciously pushed each genre into radically new directions, what sustains his place in contemporary literature is not his output as much as his abiding—and very public—interrogation of language and the aesthetics and mechanics of fiction making. His often daunting prose is the product of a sedulous process of shaping his sentences until they fold together in stunning matrices, with a rhythm, a sound that delights and challenges readers willing to accept the responsibility not merely of reading a text—which Gass dismisses as joyless passivity—but of performing it, of playing out self-consciously and exuberantly the intricate designs of sound and silence.

THE ANTIMIMETIC MOVEMENT

Gass's work can be seen as a single-minded investigation into the shock and stroke of language. Whatever his subject, it is his prose that Gass foregrounds. Indeed, he refers to himself as stylist rather than a writer. As he states in *On Being Blue,* for Gass, literature is not about the "language of love, but the love of language." Although he often eroticizes the writing/reading process, there lurks an unsettling loneliness at the heart of his work. Gass's writings remind us that the radical formalism of modernist landmarks such as Marcel Proust's *Remembrance of Things Past* and James Joyce's *Finnegans Wake* (both touchstone volumes for Gass) gave the twentieth century its most fabulous—and most desperate—act of love: the love of language itself and the oxymoronic relationship of isolates, those who meet only within the lexical landscape of the text-site: a nameless reader toiling lovingly beside an inaccessible writer-maker, each gratifying a selfish indulgence, each apart from yet a part of the process. Modernism's elevation of articulation, its consecration of consciousness, demands that the reader move into the great edifice of the text-site itself, where words matter more than the dreary world that occasions them. The problem then becomes clear: what to do with the troubling immediate that awaits the moment we step out from the contained world of ink on paper. Gass's career-long disdain for moral crusades (despite writing during decades of dramatic social upheaval), indeed his dismissal of the tedium of everyday life and the fiction that records it, opens his work to charges of elitism and irresponsibility. But to question style over substance misses the obvious: in Gass's conception, that question has

been irrelevant since poets first fashioned words, the thin stuff of conversation, into literature: style has always *been* substance.

William Howard Gass, who has expressed pleasure in the American ability to generate aesthetic wonder in modest sites, was himself born in Fargo, North Dakota, on July 30, 1924. Within six months, his family moved to Warren, Ohio—which Gass described in a 1977 *Paris Review* interview with Tom LeClair as a "dirty, tense, industrial city"—where his father, William Bernard Gass, taught mechanical drawing at a local high school. Gass's recollections of his Depression-era childhood suggest the sort of loneliness that centers his fiction: a father who was a semiprofessional baseball player, crippled by arthritis; a distant, alcoholic mother (Claire Sorensen Gass); and the constant moving from house to house and school to school in the struggle to meet the rent. Gass has written movingly of the refuge he found as a child within the hermetic environment of books and writing, privately through poetry and more publicly by means of his experience as a high school journalist. His departure for Kenyon College in Gambier, Ohio, shortly after the outbreak of World War II—he planned to follow his father's career as a teacher—marked for Gass a clean break from this troubled home life. "I just fled," he told LeClair. "It was a cowardly thing to do, but I simply would not have survived."

His studies at Kenyon—interrupted by a two-year stint as a naval ensign in the Far East theater—coincided with John Crowe Ransom's tenure as a professor of poetry there and the heyday of the formalist thinking of New Criticism. Gass was introduced to the then revolutionary notion of the text as an autonomous artifact and the belief that commentary about its author and cultural context was intrusive, even irrelevant. Although a student in philosophy, Gass audited literature courses and pursued an aggressive independent investigation into the works of modernist literature that would so influence his own work (he has repeatedly called himself a "purified modernist"), particularly the esoteric game-texts of Gertrude Stein, the imposing structural experiments of Joyce and Proust, and the enclosing rhetoric and intricate symbolic patternings of Henry James and William Faulkner.

In 1947 Gass began graduate work in philosophy at Cornell University. Studying aesthetics, he became intrigued by the dense, often unsettling language theories of the Vienna-born British philosopher Ludwig Wittgenstein (he has called his participation in the seminars conducted by Wittgenstein a turning point in his intellectual life). He was drawn specifically to Wittgenstein's investigation into the process of language, how combinations of words come to represent a fact, and how sentences do not record reality but are, in fact, models of it. After accepting a teaching position in 1954 in philosophy at the College of Wooster in Ohio, Gass completed his dissertation, "A Philosophical Investigation of Metaphor," which not only centered on the literary construct that would become his signature stylistic device but also marked his emerging interest in the speculative interplay between the word and the world. The following year he accepted a teaching position in philosophy at Purdue University in Lafayette, Indiana. A gifted classroom presence, he was the recipient of numerous teaching citations both at Purdue and at Washington University in St. Louis, where he moved in 1969; in 2000 he continued to teach at Washington University as the David May Distinguished University Professor in the Humanities, an appointment he received in 1979, and as the director of the university's International Writers Center.

While at Wooster, Gass began to experiment with serious fiction and, beginning in 1958, to publish short works in elite academic journals. These early pieces were striking experiments in narration, lacking linear plot, the engine of suspense, and characters that readers could identify with. Set against the mass-market stories of the postwar boom in magazine fiction, these unsettling works were different in content, vision, argument, and—most dramatically—their use of language, in how they sounded. They caused a considerable buzz within academic circles and brought Gass immediate recognition.

Gass conducted these rigorous experiments in craftsmanship amid a radical mid-century upheaval in narrative theory. Drawing on the self-reflective *ficciones* of Jorge Luis Borges, the self-conscious game-texts of Vladimir Nabokov, and the language theories of French intellectuals such as Alain Robbe-Grillet and Nathalie Sarraute, a generation of American avant-garde writers sought to overthrow the traditional elements of realistic narrative: plot, theme, and character. Their vision would be engendered within the closed world of academia, and their experimental fictions and fulminous manifestos would be appreciated largely by an academic audience. For these young writers—among them Donald Barthelme, John Barth, Robert Coover, William Gaddis, and John Hawkes—contemporary fiction had become little more than a conduit for relaying action, maintaining suspense, rendering dialogue, and imposing themes. Suddenly, the very premise of mimesis, of representational, "realist" fiction, was exposed as naive; words themselves were seen as objects, evocative and layered; theme was discounted as the reader's act of intrusive translation; and ethical conundrums and social agendas were deemed irrelevant to fiction's aesthetic enterprise. Within the turbulent countercultural movement of the 1960s, these combative writers reminded an audience, often befuddled, at times shocked, that the text was a made thing, a structure-system of sounds playing off each other, an artifact as mathematical as a machine, as scored as music. But these writings, for all their deliberate innovations, were in many ways the logical extension of the works of Proust, Joyce, and Faulkner that had so enthralled the young Gass.

Empowered by an aesthetic that demanded awareness of the craftedness of fiction, these writers fashioned within the self-enclosed world of the text the order unavailable in their unsettling century. Fiction, as Gass would tirelessly theorize, is not a description but a construction, not a message but an artifact. Although these writers (most of them a generation younger than Gass) would turn to progressively more outlandish experiments in their decade-long guerrilla war on mimetic fiction, Gass, perhaps because of sobering life experiences during the Depression and World War II, would never wholly abandon the realist's curiosity for exploring the immediate and for sifting through raw experience to find within it the illumination of epiphany. Yet Gass would become a leading proponent, in many ways the public voice, of this radical shift in literary perspective. His training in language theory; his distinctive prose line; his vast erudition; his caustic wit; his eagerness during an era of reclusiveness among prominent writers to engage in public forums (particularly a series of point-counterpoint kitchen debates with the realist novelist/moralist John Gardner) and grant interviews established Gass as an eloquent and unapologetic theoretician of this subversive literature.

Since his emergence in the 1960s, Gass has shifted between fiction and nonfiction, between a handful of genre-busting experiments in narrative and his far more copious theoretical investigations into the process itself. Is Gass then a philosopher who writes fiction or a novelist fascinated by the mechanics of his own trade? He has long maintained that fiction writers and philosophers share more than they dispute: both draw on a facility with language to construct convincing, airtight systems, sonic models that are ambitious contrivances of the reaching imagination attempting to fashion not only order through design but beauty (readers are immediately struck by the indulgent elegance of Gass's prose line; detractors bemoan its hyperexcess). It is that tension—irresolvable and suggestive—between the word and the world that centers Gass's work, fiction and nonfiction. If the essays celebrate the kinetic prowess of the mind, the elegant structures of the creative imagination, the sacred space of the articulated consciousness, the aural stun of language, in the fiction we meet central characters who generously indulge such intellection, who exercise just such a need for order and beauty, and find themselves inhumed ultimately within the echoing chamber of their own rhetoric, isolated and denied the simplest interaction with the accessible immediate and the tonic bond of compassion.

OMENSETTER'S LUCK

Gass's exploration of the seductive danger of eloquence began with *Omensetter's Luck,* a work of such originality—it has been compared with *Moby-Dick* and *Ulysses*—that its publication in 1966 justified Gass's reputation as a first-rank novelist for the almost thirty years until his second novel appeared. The work itself was nearly twelve years in the making, and then suffered a series of rejections at the hands of perplexed editors, as well as theft by a Purdue colleague, forcing Gass to begin virtually from scratch, before being taken on by New American Library. The novel's complex narrative design, dense sonic play, and intricate networking of interior monologues recalls the watershed experimental works of Faulkner and Joyce. It draws on a theme so central to the American literary imagination that it risks cliché: the tension between nature and civilization, specifically between sensuality—unexamined and intuitive—and speculation, the human need to domesticate experience, make it meaningful, using the awkward signs of language.

Despite its structural complexity and dense prose, the plot of *Omensetter's Luck* is straightforward. In the closing years of the 1890s, Brackett Omensetter, his pregnant wife, and his two daughters move to Gilean, a sleepy Ohio river town. From the moment he persuades the town blacksmith to hire him, the charismatic Omensetter upsets the town's quiet. Like a prelapsarian Adam or a figure out of frontier folk literature—shaggy-haired, handsomely muscled, he emerges from the deep woods with a laugh that is "deep, loud, wide, and happy"—Omensetter effortlessly manages a profound harmony with the natural world. Supremely, he is man with little use for language. His intuitive ease—his luck—allows him the deep joy of living, without the crushing burden of self-awareness.

Thus, Omensetter comes to the reader only secondhand, as perceived by three characters who, in an accidental conspiracy that recalls Faulkner's *The Sound and the Fury,* structure the narrative. We hear first from Israbestis Tott, a senile and thoroughly unreliable storyteller who ruminates about Omensetter in a rambling first-person account to whomever he can collar, during a town auction long after the family has moved away. Despite (or perhaps because of) the seductive colloquialism of this self-proclaimed town historian, the reader must be skeptical of the veracity of his recollections. Tott is deliberately "(re)creative," the first of Gass's lonely creatures of the imagination. Indeed, he confesses that he finds most enthralling the "mysterious geography" of the wallpaper in his bedroom, with its grease stains, plaster cracks, and swirling rose print.

On the other hand, Henry Pimber, Omensetter's landlord, who provides the narrative center for the novel's second section, struggles to connect. When Pimber comes to the Omensetter farm to collect the rent, Omensetter tells him that a fox has fallen into an abandoned well on the property. Omensetter sees no reason to interfere in the natural order, but Pimber insists on shooting several rounds into the well to put the starving animal out of its misery. A chance ricochet nicks Pimber,

and within days he develops lockjaw, which the local doctor is helpless to treat. It is Omensetter who, with a crude poultice made from beets, saves Pimber's life. Pimber, who had initially thought the stranger "foolish, dirty, careless," immediately comes under his suasion.

As Pimber heals, he sees how closely he has come, in his loveless marriage to a barren woman and his unrewarding job, to suggest the trapped fox. He convinces himself that the easygoing Omensetter possesses the tantalizing secret of "how to be," of how to live without anxiety. But in a poignant conversation with Omensetter in the remote midwoods, Pimber struggles to articulate his feelings only to be drowned out by the roaring wind and the tumbling river. Unable to return to his routine, unable to elicit any "secret" from Omensetter, a frustrated Pimber determines his only choice: in a remote section of the woods, he hangs himself from the highest branches of an oak tree, an inverted image of the fox in the well.

If Pimber cannot square the tantalizing premise of Omensetter with the squalid reality of his own compromised life, the town clergyman, Jethro Furber, initially entertains no such inner conflict. Furber commands the closing three-fourths of the novel, a dense weave of symbolic language and at times impenetrable subtleties. Furber offers, in his eccentric fascination with words, a striking example of Gass's sense of both the power and the curse of those who traffic in language. Furber, isolated and unloved, is a creature of words. A preacher, he is passionately involved not with the salvation of his congregation or with theological consistency but rather with the polished rhetoric of his sermons, the satisfying stroke of his sentences. Estranged from his own animal nature, he indulges in vivid onanistic fantasies involving girls in the town and even Omensetter's young wife. A sickly and unloved child, he now tends the church's walled-in garden in a dark suggestion of a lifetime spent in deliberate retreat—there he befriends his only confidant: the conjured ghost of an earlier pastor. Furber reveals to the reader the power of the engine of language: his section is an often mesmerizing tour de force of dense explication, intricate wordplay, and the accelerating energy of his facile reasoning. Satisfied by the virtual realities of language, Furber avoids the direct brush of experience, indeed the slightest movement toward the complication of connection. "Joy," he says icily at one point, "to be a stone." Furber is trapped—and yet sustained—inside the suffocating constructs of his own voice, the isolating barrier of language.

Confronted by the bare animal ease of Omensetter, Furber characteristically fashions the stranger into a convenient sign—labeling him evil, a threat to the community—and manipulating language, he stirs up the townspeople, convincing them that the stranger had a hand in Pimber's disappearance. When Omensetter discovers Pimber's body in the woods and innocently confides in Furber, Furber comprehends the true nature of the guileless Omensetter, who had so casually imparted information that Furber could use to convince the town of Omensetter's guilt. After a life of negotiated retreats, Furber suddenly engages a man simply, face to face. Stunned by the power of the confrontation, he tries to help Omensetter, who is himself engaged in a crisis: his newborn son has contracted diphtheria and, rather than pursue medical help, he has told his fretful wife that they must trust his luck. But thus verbalized, Omensetter's rich intuitive nature is corrupted. He has fallen into language. Consequently, he must watch his son slip toward death. Furber, charged by the raw emotions surrounding the boy's sickbed, wants to be of use and convinces Omensetter to go for medical help.

But the doctor arrives too late. Overcome by his epiphanic realizations of the inevitability of despair, the cold absence of God, and the dark blessing of awareness, Furber suffers a winter-long mental collapse. When he recovers, Furber finds that the heartbroken Omensetter clan has long since departed. Thus, Furber is left alone at narrative's end, without Omensetter, without his pulpit. But in a gesture commensurate with Omensetter's impact on him, Furber donates to the church the rent money Pimber had collected long ago from Omensetter, a modest gesture save that it is executed by a character unwilling to demonstrate even the slightest interest in the welfare of others. That church is now under the direction of a minister who, in his simple love of his congregation and his unaffected sickbed conversations with Furber, brings to the novel a restorative sense of language as a means of connecting, a modest exercise of the word that is sufficient in a brutal world.

How tempting to simply depart the text with this theme in hand. But such "translation" ignores the reading experience itself. *Omensetter's Luck* is a narrative about narration, about the process of composition. The reader must perform this text, must manage the intricate sound of each section as each exercises a different verbal cunning in an attempt to compose into words the figure of Omensetter, who like Ishmael's white whale, the Surveyor's scarlet letter, and Benjy Compson's sister, eludes definition. The unsettling implication of a text in which the title character stays beyond the reach of words and the character most sustained by language collapses into despair is ultimately that however we aspire to fashion a world into words, that world cannot, finally, be manipulated by language.

IN THE HEART OF THE HEART OF THE COUNTRY AND WILLIE MASTERS' LONESOME WIFE

Like *Omensetter's Luck*, the five stories Gass collected in *In the Heart of the Heart of the Country* (1968) conjure characters who "live *in*," as the narrator of the book's title story puts it: within a consciousness characterized by verbal inwardness. With its publication, Gass enhanced his place at the fore of the antimimetic movement. As Arthur Saltzman argues, the central characters in these stories "trade life for language" and can be read as artist-figures whose retreat from the world—like Furber's into his garden—is simultaneously life-enhancing and solipsistically isolating. These are tales of lonely, disappointed, misanthropic men and women driven by their own overwhelming isolation to tell stories and thereby to fashion a self-sustaining sense of order that is at the very heart of the fiction enterprise.

However, it is arguably largely within the context of Gass's prefatory comments, later fiction, and other critical pronouncements that these stories call attention to themselves as innovative antimimetic work. The novella-length "The Pedersen Kid," for instance, is strongly plot-driven, a mock-detective story that deals with the discovery of a strange boy who almost freezes to death during a North Dakota blizzard and the story the boy tells of a mysterious intruder who has murdered his family, a tale that sends the narrator Jorge (himself a boy), his alcoholic father, and his family's hired hand across the storm-driven countryside in a grudging, unheroic effort to ascertain the truth of the story. "Mrs. Mean" and "Icicles" present disgruntled middle-aged men increasingly lost in the warp and woof of their diddling imaginations—the former by voyeuristically entering into the lives of his neighbors, the latter while seeking compensation for his lonely life as a lackluster real-estate salesman. Less conventional is the brief and Kafkaesque "Order of Insects," which offers the reflections of a housewife increasingly fascinated by the dead cockroaches she finds each morning on the carpet of her home. "In the Heart of the Heart of the Country" is the most manifestly experimental of the stories (it is told in thirty-six vignettes bearing headings such as "Politics," "Business," and "My House") but has nonetheless managed over its author's continual objections to earn, in the words

of Arthur Saltzman, a reputation as a "clinically precise depiction of Middle America."

Each of these stories, all but "Icicles" told in the first person, gives voice to a misanthropic consciousness alienated from self and others: "I no longer own my own imagination," the woman in "Order of Insects" despairs, and the lawn-tending fantasist of "Mrs. Mean" reflects, "I am not myself. This is not the world." Although each might covet relations in and with the world, they all refuse the stories that would bind them to others. "I forget my friends, associates, my students, and their names," the voice of the title story boastfully laments while from the safe cell of his imagination telling off the one neighbor who does visit: "Shut your fist up, bitch, you bag of death; go bang another door." And of his neighbors, the narrator of "Mrs. Mean" observes that they expected his scrutiny of them to yield gossip, expected "that I would soon be round with stories":

> I would tell Miss Matthew of Mr. Wallace, and Mr. Wallace of Mrs. Turk, and Miss Matthew and Mr. Wallace and Mrs. Turk would take the opportunity to tell me all they knew of one another, all they knew about diseases, all they thought worthy of themselves and could remember of their relatives, and the complete details of their many associations with violent forms of death. But when I communicated nothing to them; when I had nothing, in confidence, to say to anyone; then they began to treat my eyes like marbles and to parade their lives indifferently before me.

Whereas "The Pedersen Kid" suggests the danger of stories told and believed—although ambiguous, the story leaves open the possibility that Jorge has gone mad and that several people may have died as a result of believing the kid's "fancy tale"—this passage indicates Gass's elitist lack of interest in the conventional ends of narrative. It is an indifference that, in the book's preface, Gass says caused him to "[write] these stories without imagining there would be readers to sustain them." The self-deprecation here is faux, for Gass has received ample proof of these stories' success: "In the Heart of the Heart of the Country," for instance, has been anthologized or reprinted twenty-four times. Nevertheless, Gass tells us that he continues to imagine an ideal reader, one "whose heartbeat alters with the tenses of the verbs" and whose "brow wrinkle[s] with wonder at the rhetoric" and at "thoughts found profound." These readers, Gass affirms, come "from that other, less real world of common life and pleasant ordinary things" to be confronted with the greater reality of his fully imagined texts.

Gass has long been skeptical of securing such trained readers. As he told Tom LeClair, "One problem is that the reader isn't conditioned, hasn't the time, intelligence, patience to perform the work," to engage a text boldly and fully. The problem of the inept reader is very much at the center of the conceit that dominates Gass's wildly eccentric novella published the same year as *In the Heart of the Heart of the Country.* Even in the context of the aesthetically turbulent 1960s, *Willie Masters' Lonesome Wife* is a *tour d'extremis.* If the characters of *In the Heart of the Heart of the Country* each unspool a lisle of language, Willie Masters' wife, Babs, is language herself, awaiting a lover-author-reader worthy of her charms; her body is Gass's text, her story her debasement as well as her passionate potential, and the consummation of her desire the book's construction word by word.

Here, to dissuade readers from looking through or past his words to some "reality" upon which his text merely comments, Gass draws attention to the fact that books are about their forms and about the imagination such forms contain like cows their cud. Toward such corrective ends, Gass disrupts narrative conventions and deploys multiple reminders that what we are holding in our hands are nothing more—or less—than pages upon which the signifying stains of language shape the figures of our inner lives. Unpaginated and divided into four sections (in the first edition distinguished by the different colors and kinds of paper used), *Willie Masters' Lonesome Wife* contains multiple texts in a variety of typefaces and page layouts (including word balloon, marginalia, and lines that bend and sag as they depart the page) interrupted by black-and-white photographs of a nude woman and marked by brown rings meant to represent where Gass set down his coffee cup. The text of one page is shaped like an evergreen tree, another page printed backward as though reflected in a mirror, while footnotes to one stretch of prose lag so far behind the text they annotate that it becomes increasingly difficult to match note to passage glossed; part of the novella assumes the form of a play, and in one section competing narrative lines vie for attention as they move across the top, middle, and bottom of the pages, forcing the reader to decide whether to read each page top to bottom or to track each text to its end, then backtrack.

To guarantee the reader's removal from the rut of habit, the text mixes Victorian pornography and salacious burlesque (for instance, one character finds his penis baked in a bun) with content misogynistic, anti-Semitic, and abusive of the dully plodding reader. This assault on readerly expectations is compensated for by the skillfulness and originality of the prose. In a 1983 colloquy with Brooke Horvath and others, Gass spoke of the novelist John Hawkes's choice of "depraved" subjects, observing that the point of such a tactic is "to show that the subject matter can be disarmed, can be transmuted," because transmutation is anyway art's end, driven by an imagination whose "acts," as Gass in his novella averred, "are our most free and natural" creations, dared "for no better reason" than the pleasure they give.

Willie Masters' Lonesome Wife is, then, a paean to prose, a love song to language, a fondling of form, a seduction of sentences: a celebration and demonstration of "imagination imagining itself imagine," quite unconcerned with whatever stories it might painstakingly plot, whatever truths it might illuminate, whatever moral it might muster. Books are artful words artfully arranged, and what these words do, as Gass states in *Willie Masters' Lonesome Wife,* is "brood upon . . . the world," in the process creating the consciousness within which we live today. The book's peroration remains a touchstone passage in Gass's work, as it makes clear his antimimetic commitment while salvaging that commitment from charges of arid formalism and disengagement:

> Then let us have a language worthy of our world, a democratic style where rich and well-born nouns can roister with some sluttish verb yet find themselves content and uncomplained of. . . . Our tone should suit our time: uncommon quiet dashed with common thunder. It should be as young and quick and sweet and dangerous as we are. Experimental and expansive . . . it will give new glasses to new eyes. . . . It's not the languid pissing prose we've got, we need; but poetry, the human muse, full up, erect and on the charge, impetuous and hot and loud and wild like Messalina going to the stews, or those damn rockets screaming headstrong into stars.

Unlike *In the Heart of the Heart of the Country,* Gass's aesthetic concerns are explicit, flagrant, in *Willie Masters' Lonesome Wife.* They are concerns he will elaborate over the next thirty years in his nonfiction, the first collection of which, *Fiction and the Figures of Life,* was to appear two years later.

EXPLICATING THE WORD

In 1970 Gass released the landmark essay collection *Fiction and the Figures of Life.* Although the volume moves about a variety of topics—provocative appreciations of the literary innovations of Stein, Robert Coover, Borges, Nabokov, and James, among others—the first section reprints four stunning position papers on the fiction process ("Philosophy and the Form of Fiction," "The Medium of Fiction," "The Concept of Character in Fiction," and "In Terms of the Toenail: Fiction and the Figures of Life") that together offer a compelling seminar in Gass's conception of literature.

The terms "essay" and "philosophy" can be misleading when applied to Gass's nonfiction works if we understand those terms to imply rigorous reasoning and tight unfolding of logical processes. Like Ralph Waldo Emerson, in his nonfiction Gass is emphatic and assertive, metaphoric, not mathematical. He does not seek to convince with arid proofs but to stun, to provoke not only by the audacity of his uncompromising insistence on the primacy of the text but also by a compelling prose line whose playful architecture, the pitch and flow of puns, metaphors, and alliteration, offer the best evidence of that primacy. And unlike Gass's dark fictions where characters find their lives compromised by their uncompromising pursuit of the private order of words, the nonfiction is expansive, exuberant, brash. Whatever Gass's subject, the emphasis is on language—his. He wants us to be aware that we are reading. What Gass says of James's prose style in "In the Cage" could describe his own nonfiction offerings: "His sentences have such complex insides, they amaze. . . . The object we sought to have explained seems obscured by the explanation; it is no longer a scene we see, it is a sentence we experience."

But amid the polished surfaces of his prose, Gass argues with verve and bite. He reminds us in "The Medium of Fiction" that "literature is language, that stories and the places and the people in them are merely made of words as chairs are made of smoothed sticks and sometimes of cloth or metal tubes." He understands that a reader merely intent on plot and character might feel humiliated by his books, like a man who discovers that the woman he has loved is a contrivance of inflated rubber. But Gass's tone is irrepressibly celebratory. His aim is to reveal how writers take words, whose currency as casual conversation so radically tarnishes their shine, and recovers them until within the design system of the page, they electrify with their beauty.

We are then to be readers who move about the text not like department store shoppers mindlessly grabbing what we fancy, but rather like admirers touring an architectural marvel (Gass, himself married to a prominent architect, has long been drawn to architectural metaphors). In "The Concept of Character in Fiction," Gass refutes the emotional need readers have to identify with characters, to accord fictional representations a life outside the text. Great characters from Hamlet to Molly Bloom cannot leave the text on the arm of the reader, a most unseemly gesture of familiarity that Gass likens to a sordid motel rendezvous. A literary character, Gass reminds us, is a noise, a word-chord, a proper name on a page, an "instrument of verbal organization," a "source of verbal energy"—not a person. Only by freeing characters from the dreary existence alongside our own and allowing them their verbal space can they shine, like essence, and "purely Be."

Thus, the structured energy and cool passion of a text cannot point to anything beyond itself. In the reading of Malcolm Lowry's *Under the Volcano* (1947) that closes the first section, Gass bristles that the Mexico we enter in this book is not a real Mexico with "menacing volcanoes" but rather a model Mexico composed of "menacing phrases." Shattering the illusion of realistic fiction, Gass reminds us that fiction is incurably figurative, that every vivid setting is not a rendering—an inventory—but rather a private, tightly controlled zone of verbal ingenuity that merely creates the illusion of context. Narratives are objects where the intrusive stroke of circumstance is choreographed into plot; they are splendidly enclosing contrivances, lovingly crafted sentence by sentence by a lonely artisan eye-deep in the brutal vacuousness of a wasteland immediate.

As if to demonstrate such a theory, Gass published a mesmerizing volume that would be in many ways a companion to *Willie Masters' Lonesome Wife.* To step into the splendid enclosure of Gass's slender disquisition *On Being Blue* (1976) is unnerving; it is to witness, at last, Gass ravishing language boldly and unapologetically. It is a speculation over the mystery of how meanings come to gather "softly" about words "the way lint collects." As in *Willie Masters' Lonesome Wife,* this is Gass at his most eccentric, his most playful, his most intense as he indulges the only erotic interplay he cautions any writer can indulge: "there's one body only whose request for your caresses is not vulgar, is not unchaste, untoward . . . the body of your work itself." The subject here is not merely the color blue, although surely Gass's speculations recast the word into a dazzling suggestiveness as he investigates things that are blue, things that are called blue, things that make us feel blue. Rather the subject is surely the sentences we read about the color blue, the mesmerizing shine of Gass's voluptuous prose. We must love words, Gass inveighs, for themselves, not for what they record. Pornography, he warns, happens whenever words are mistaken for what they signify.

Thus, Gass celebrates the extravagant impulse to indulge language the only way he can: by indulging it. What in his fictions is darkly suggestive of a harrowing isolation, here is intoxicating play. Gass restructures the word "blue" into a text site of meanings that range from the chilling hue of rigor mortis to the romantic rendering of the transcendent infinite, the very color of the imagination; it is our word both for the Christian heavens and for the debased images of our animal cravings. We are impressed by how unexamined the word is, how easily we have ignored the structures that lurk within the apparently simple edifice of a word. Like Israbestis Tott slipping into his wallpaper world, we move into the mysterious verbal geography of blue.

As Gass urgently lavishes love on his word, executes the swollen catalogs of accumulated evidence, we sense that at last Babs has found a lover equal to her rich premise. There is Gass—both lost and found—at the center of a lexical landscape of his own fashioning, there in the country of blue, in the lonely company of his words. Readers are as irrelevant as a hushed audience at a jazz improv session or, more appropriately, as Reverend Furber's dazzled congregation. Style becomes substance, and excess, at last, its own theme. In its closing pages Gass invites other authors (those "wretched writers") to forsake the simple banalities of the quotidian, the "blue things of this world," to indulge the "words which say them," the very move that, ironically, dooms characters in Gass's fictions.

That celebration of the word centers as well Gass's second collection of essays, *The World within the Word* (1978). Again, Gass hotly celebrates the word and the enclosing edifice of the text and relegates the "spit and cough and curse of daily life" to irrelevancy and distraction. We are, Gass concludes in "Groping for Trouts," system makers; we hypermanage the motion all about us into explanation and order. We conjure such systems—and the novel is manifestly a system of systems—because we cannot live easily within the untidy immediate with its "unstimulating bumps, its teaseless, enervating grinds." Thus we fashion models, whether theology, physics, astronomy, history, mathematics, or fictional narratives, that provide us, despite their evident artificiality, the comfort of meaning, the security of management.

In this selection of fifteen previously published pieces, Gass affirms familiar tenets: words are not signposts but rather things themselves; a novel is not commentary on life but rather a system of intricate design; an author (he uses Proust) lives only within a text; a text is a created space as wide as the mind—here Gass borrows from Emily Dickinson, yet another lonely architect. In this book Gass tirelessly reminds us that the reader and writer separately conspire to perform a text. Consider his intricate response, complete with

flowcharts, to the enigmatic verbal surfaces of Gertrude Stein. In "Gertrude Stein and the Geography of the Sentence," Gass detects within Stein's dense constructs highly charged sexual confessions, language that entices like the "promise of the nipple through the slip." This is the sweet gamesmanship of language, how words can be both code and confession, enigma and declaration. Gass does not "translate" Stein but rather participates in the tonic play of the text's possibilities.

And Gass wants us to appreciate that play. He wants us to be aware. In "Carrots, Noses, Snow, Rose, Roses," one of Gass's most frequently cited essays, he argues that words introduced into the energy field of a text are involved in an ontological transformation. The words we use in the reckless blather of the everyday become the "passionately useless rigmarole that makes up literary language." Gass uses the elaborate conceit of a snowman to argue his point. Like a text, a snowman is obviously constructed. And just as a carrot, in the context of a snowman, becomes a nose—its very essence if not its appearance altered—so words within a text are transformed. Within a text, a word's arbitrary properties—sound, spelling, length—all become dramatically essential. Words can tap unsuspected meaning within connections fashioned by the writer; grammatical categories are no longer secure. Words, freed from their tiresome responsibility to bear witness, can tangle, touch, and enfold into sentences never before imagined. Only this "inner constitution . . . will guarantee [a text's] right to be read."

In reading this lavish construction of essays, the reader willingly suspends doubt, forgets the nagging pull of the irredeemable immediate, the danger of indulging eloquence faced by Gass's fictional characters beginning with Reverend Furber in *Omensetter's Luck*. Whatever the subject, we linger in Gass's seductive essays, stroll (as he suggests readers ought to in reading Proust) as if on a country walk, compelled by the confident audacity of the author's execution, persuaded by the exuberant music of syllable-perfect pitch, that the world of words is, for the moment, world enough, beauty enough, order enough.

The twelve essays Gass gathered seven years later in *Habitations of the Word* (1985)—which won Gass his first National Book Critics Circle Award—cover similar concerns. Gass clings tenaciously to the core convictions that he first articulated in the mid-1950s, but with each collection the prose line that he fashions to make his declarations startles anew. Gass still centers on the textness of a text and on the role of the performing reader. In "Tropes of the Text" Gass speaks of the novel as an "intense interior"; it is, he explains in "On Reading to Oneself," sung into being by worthy readers who attend to it so carefully that it becomes "nothing but feeling and pure response." In "Representation and the War for Reality" he reflects upon the reasons behind the "reader's reluctance to submit to the novel's transforming power" and dismisses novels that would merely offer realistic commentary upon the world. In "The Soul inside the Sentence," he details the nature of the creative process and the novelist's need to master the medium, and he catalogs what "all the finest writing strives for: energy, perception, passion, thought, music, movement, and imagination."

These rigorously playful pieces move from appreciations of Emerson and Ford Madox Ford to a tour-de-force twenty-five-page examination of the word "and" from elegant engagements with theoretical debates of the late 1970s and early 1980s (specifically, the rejection of the idea that authors are invariably mastered by language and what it will and will not permit them to say) to an exploration of culture as an unavoidable grammar that "completes us as persons by creating a common consciousness" ("Culture, Self, and Style"). Throughout, Gass's remarks shed light on his own fictional aims and assumptions. For instance, it is as true of Gass's fictions as of the novels he names (by Coover, Carlos Fuentes,

Michel Butor, and others) that one reads them the first time primarily "to ready oneself to read [them]" and that although their length and difficulty may "eventually be forgiven them," they may never see the day when they will be forgiven "their intelligence" and the "cultivation they require" ("Tropes of the Text"). One of the more self-reflexive topics that the volume broaches is the nature of the essay itself, which according to Gass "interests itself in the narration of ideas"—wherein the "conflict between philosophies or other points of view becomes a drama" and "systems are seen as plots and concepts as characters"—while the essayist strives to be a "self worthy to be spoken of, and a self capable of real speech." The essayist is preoccupied by the "essay's special art," Gass continues, the essence of which is meditation, which "exfoliates," "browses," "enjoys an idea like a fine wine" ("Emerson and the Essay"). So described, the essay, although it might narrate ideas, is as little concerned with sustained argument as Gass's fictions are concerned with sustained plotting.

To observe that these essays succeed in large part because of how they articulate their ideas is not, however, to trivialize Gass's accomplishment because his performances are more than endless bons mots: "[Emerson] spent himself freely, but he counted his change" ("Emerson and the Essay"); children unable yet to read or write are puppies who "go to school to be paper trained" ("The Soul inside the Sentence"). For when in another self-revealing moment Gass observes that the sentences of Henry James are "not informations, placations, injunctions, improvements, vacations" but "celebrations" of consciousness, his reason for valuing such celebration is clear: "consciousness is all the holiness we have" ("Culture, Self, and Style"). Human consciousness, Gass believes, both minds the world and determines the quality of existence for ourselves and the world. "Things have a life, a presence, a value in consciousness which they can possess nowhere else," Gass writes, because it is we who infuse the world with feeling and meaning, "arrange it rationally" and cause it to "solidify as spirit." As he says in "The Origin of Extermination in the Imagination":

> When we fail to see whatever is plainly put before us; when we deny the existence of certain concepts, and will not entertain them; when we refuse to draw necessary inferences, and continue to cherish our beliefs long after their infamous, false, and misleading nature has been disclosed . . . when our evils go unspoken, unconfessed, cynically rewarded: then we are polluting, distorting, maiming, killing consciousness, that space which should be most sacred to us. . . .

To read a text properly—soulfully, performatively—is not only to make what is dead live again; it is also to live more fully ourselves, to feel, as he states in "On Reading to Oneself," the "pure passage of the spirit past the exposed skin."

THE TUNNEL

Even as Gass published these essays, which comprise a stirring apologia for the word, he was preparing a probing, disturbing examination of the isolation that had long lurked at the heart of his vision. This work would be little less than a critique of the claustrophobic logic of modernism itself, of the world fashioned by words. To do so, Gass required scale. Despite his public admiration of the modernist masterworks, heavy tomes with epical ambitions such as *Finnegans Wake* and *Remembrance of Things Past,* Gass long shied away from capacious constructions, even as his contemporaries from Thomas Pynchon to Norman Mailer routinely indulged the monumental. "My natural length," he asserted in a 1976 interview with Jeffrey L. Duncan, "runs about forty pages."

Yet starting in 1969 Gass began to publish lengthy stories in academic journals, densely woven narratives that centered on a single character, a middle-aged history professor in a nameless midwestern university, a complex figure with ties to Nazi Germany who, in his role as historian, was attempting to make sense of the depthless evil of the Third Reich—and as a corollary enterprise of the petty insignificance of his own life and misspent loves. For nearly twenty-five years, Gass published more than twenty such fragments, teasing curious interviewers with this work-in-progress and providing commentary on the book's argument until its ongoing evolution became the subject of intense speculation. How would Gass, the aesthete, the word-drunk defender of the primacy of language, handle the moral horror of the Holocaust, which the twentieth century's most eloquent commentators had long agreed beggared language? Conjecture was fueled by Gass himself, who asserted repeatedly that his published works were mere preparation for this evolving text.

The Tunnel, at more than 650 pages Gass's most involved and compelling work, was published in February 1995. Immediately it touched off a galestorm of critical response that ran from awed admiration (it was awarded the American Book Award and the PEN/Faulkner Award for fiction); to frank bewilderment over its often unapproachable density, exasperating detailing, loose and meandering plot; to indignation over its apparent trivializing of the Holocaust by placing the narrative of that event in the hands of a thoroughly vulgar character, a misogynist and anti-Semite who as the narrative opens is just completing his own magnum opus, *Guilt and Innocence in Hitler's Germany,* which applied moral relativism to a historical analysis of the Third Reich.

But William Frederick Kohler, Professor of History, is surely the monster that has lurked in the back shadows of each of Gass's text-edifices, a darkling presence anticipated by characters beginning with Reverend Furber. Here, however, we are entombed within this character's consciousness for interminable periods of reading: we share his extensive rantings, his rationalizing, the facile spew of his overheated intellect. Trapped within the "sacred" space of this character's mind, we realize that consciousness can be a profane space indeed. Drawing on the sympathetic bond assumed by first-person narration, Gass uses the rhetorical strategy of the interior monologue to trap us within the tunnel vision of Kohler, to compel us to think like this monster, to share his vile logic.

The premise of this massive book is oddly simple: Professor Kohler wants to write an introduction to his completed treatise. But he is a consummate craftsman who, exiting his own massive text-site, faces the unwanted return to the dreary dailiness of his unexamined life. And so he lingers. Kohler finds himself drawn to examining his own life (and thus the reader becomes entrenched in this exercise): a lonely childhood in the Midwest; his student days in Germany shortly before the war where, caught up in the nationalist rhetoric of a charismatic teacher, he participates in the Kristallnacht pogrom—considered the beginning of the Holocaust—before returning to America to complete his studies. He returns to Europe as an American soldier and serves in postwar Europe as a consultant during the Nuremberg Trials. Since the war, he has taught history, barely tolerating the lackluster students who pass anonymously through his classes. His marriage, his family, has settled into cool arrangements; his two brief long-ago affairs with students have left his heart sere. Kohler excavates this life, burrows into its dirt; the text we read is like the tunnel to nowhere in particular that Kohler begins to dig in his basement.

Historian, career wordsmith, Kohler determines that he will fashion in some fascistic enterprise explanation for the roiling untidiness of his life. Even as Kohler moves with deliberation and ruthless honesty through his experiences, it is clear that Gass is principally interested in the exertion of language to create meaning. Kohler is

a weak sort, passive and unable to muster sufficient presence to act; rather he bunkers behind words. History and autobiography are both imperfect world-systems of manipulation that impose—rather than recover—design.

It is an unsettling argument, of course, because Gass tackles the most heinous exercise of the human will: genocide. But there is Kohler determining the ineluctable nature of right and word, how good and evil are arbitrary sign systems fashioned after the fact, Kristallnacht and Nuremberg both systems for clarifying events into meaning. Amid the tortuous indulgence of introspection, even as he struggles to fashion his life (and the twentieth century) into plot, even as he composes himself sentence by sentence, Kohler sentences himself to the sort of loneliness that the life of the confessing mind has accepted since Proust. Kohler cannot adhere to any group, cannot bond. Alone in his university office, alone in his basement tunnel, alone amid colleagues he mocks, alone in the bed he shares with his wife Martha, Kohler constructs his private lexical landscape sustained by his detachment, comforted only by his eloquence. Unable to enjoy his spare stretch of time, Kohler investigates it, casts his wasted opportunities and diminishing expectations (he dreams of starting a Party of the Disappointed) into the hardening shape of word designs.

As with Gass's earliest experimental texts, we are never allowed the easy privilege of reading—we must maneuver through long pages of dense stream-of-consciousness prose, encountering a steady repertoire of printing and graphics "tricks" such as smudges, typeface alterations, and crude drawings. *The Tunnel* is then a narrative about narrating. Like the townsfolk in Gilean, Kohler must understand phenomena and he has only language. Thus, we are educated into the deep process of consciousness as it deploys words to make sense of what, in the darker moments of history, we fear is bald contingency. Gass reveals that whatever the subject—from assessing (as Kohler/

Gass does with unblinking honesty) the titanic horrors of the Jewish persecution to cataloging the texture of the bristles on Kohler's toothbrush—our every effort to create awareness represents the inexplicable cooperation of the muscle of intellection and the music of language—and by definition a wholesale retreat from experience. Joy, we recall, Reverend Furber claimed to be stone. Kohler, misanthrope, loves only one thing: the sound of his own steady voice, and language, should it cease, would leave only insignificance and a cold burial in silence.

LATER WORKS

A year after *The Tunnel*'s appearance, Gass, now past seventy, selected nineteen essays as part of *Finding a Form: Essays* (1996), his fourth essay collection, which brought him his second National Book Critics Circle award for criticism. These essays present no radical change of position; rather they refine and elaborate Gass's aesthetic and philosophical beliefs, extending longstanding concerns into new subject areas. He remains an elitist, a word-drunk formalist, and foe of anything (literary prizes, creative writing programs, ideologies) that suggests that art succeeds and ultimately matters on any but aesthetic grounds. The collection ranges from the mediocrity of the Pulitzer Prize to the autobiographer's difficult art, from the disjunction between ethics and art to the book as "container of consciousness," from the failures of Ezra Pound and Ford Madox Ford to how the lives of Wittgenstein and Friedrich Nietzsche shaped their thought, from recollections of Gass's own childhood to vituperative asides on what weasels have made American culture go pop.

Throughout, polished opinions, gemlike metaphors in alliterative settings, and sometimes brash, sometimes susurrant assertions confetti down upon his obsessions: how language works and why words shaped into art matter. Gass as-

serts in "Finding a Form" that his "stories are malevolently anti-narrative," his essays "maliciously anti-expository" and in "The Vicissitudes of the Avant-Garde" contends that to succeed in the realm where Paul Valéry, Rainer Maria Rilke, and Gertrude Stein permanently reside, the artist must "shake things up, and keep things moving; offer fresh possibilities to a jaded understanding; encourage a new consciousness; revitalize the creative spirit of the medium" —comments that do much to clarify the aims and methods of his own work.

The notion of conjuring consciousness is key for Gass. It is the centrality of consciousness that makes his essays contiguous with his fiction, for he wishes those essays no less than the fiction to be literature, and he knows that "ideas aren't literature, any more than remarks are, or plots, or people, or noble truths, or lively lies." Rather, as "The Language of Being and Dying," an essay on Serbian writer Danilo Kiš, concludes, "It is the consistent quality of the local prose that counts. It is how, sentence by sentence, the song is built and immeasurable meanings meant. It is the rich regalia of his rhetoric that leads us to acknowledge his authority."

These nineteen essays, each rich as a Sacher torte, manifest that sentence-by-sentence song, that rich regalia of metaphor and voice their author applauds in the works of others. Of his own work, Gass has this to say in "Finding a Form": "I often think, overhearing myself at work, that I do not write; I mumble, I whisper, I declaim, I inveigh. My study is full of static when it is full of me." Yet it is a tuneful static, a melodious murmur, whose modulated song, like that of any prose able to carry a tune, "is . . . far from frivolous decoration; it embodies Being" ("The Music of Prose").

Each text ought then to be, according to Gass, a shapely "repository for moments of awareness, for passages of thought—states which, we prefer to believe, make us most distinctly us" ("The Book as a Container of Consciousness") and "whose end is contemplation and appreciation" ("The Baby or the Botticelli"). But because "the word is all the soul is, ever was, or wants to be" ("Exile"), books are where consciousness, where the soul, may be held in one's hands. Artists "add to the world's objects and ideas those delineations, carvings, tales, fables, and symphonic spells which ought to be there," and through well-wrought words, sounds, images admit us to a "higher level of reality" ("The Baby or the Botticelli") where both the self and the slovenly, indifferent world might find redemption. In every musical page of every carefully constructed textual reality can be found "the show of taste and care and good custom—what a cultivated life is supposed to provide" ("The Book as a Container of Consciousness"). Writing therefore aims at perfection because, let the ear once go tin, let a ruckus interrupt the music, and what we will hear is a "sardonic reminder of how little gold can do to rescue ruck when ruck can ruin whatever it rubs against" ("The Book as a Container of Consciousness").

Cartesian Sonata and Other Novellas (1998) remains true to the bifurcated aesthetic vision that characterizes Gass's earlier works. For if *Finding a Form* and *Reading Rilke,* which bracket this collection, continue the task of lauding artfully shaped words as the embodiment of Being, the four novellas comprising *Cartesian Sonata* present characters isolated, attenuated, defeated, or deformed by language that ensnares or evades them.

The title *Cartesian Sonata* refers to Gass's concern with the dualism of mind and matter as expounded by the French philosopher René Descartes, and to the sonata structure of the collection, its exposition, development, and recapitulation (or perhaps simply to the notion of a work characterized by contrasting movements). As did Descartes, the volume's title novella finds a place for God in the narrator of its opening section, but his efforts to get his story of Ella Bend Hess un-

der way quickly collapse into noodling accounts of tangential characters, riffs on his own artistic fumblings, and fascinated coloratura on restroom graffiti. With the novella's second part, Ella finally appears, a woman so clairvoyant she "was almost totally attention and antennae," almost entirely mind and vision without a corresponding ability to live in the world or to shape what she confusedly perceives. Against Ella's aesthetic impotence is set part three, wherein her husband, a clod so alienated from his wife he wishes her dead but can do no more than hang like a dim bulb above her sickbed, rants against her other-worldliness on behalf of his own unimaginative being, "none of that's real, you hear me? I'll tell you what's real. I am. I AM REAL."

If "Cartesian Sonata" poses aesthetic incompetence—the artist who cannot control his material or articulate his character's vision—against the equally unforgiving matter-mired realist, the following novellas play variations on the theme of aesthetic consciousness. In "Bed and Breakfast," itinerant accountant Walt Riff makes a meager living doctoring the debits of small businesses while fantasizing in sleazy motel rooms about a woman named Eleanor, who may or may not exist. Chance delivers him to a cozy Illinois bed-and-breakfast overseen by devout Bettie Ambrose. In Bettie's busy rooms of doilies and needlework samplers, figurines and decorative candies, Riff discovers that art called craft, which he comes to hope might save him from himself, could he only find the words to articulate fully what he sees, until in the back of a bedroom drawer he discovers an abandoned G-string that belies Bettie's marmalade moralism and, reviving thoughts of Eleanor, makes mockery of any hopes for a new and richer life. As Riff's story closes, his tenuous hold on goodness is reduced to a muffled "Ummm" as second-rate art's redemptive promise—like language itself—fails him, and he buries "his face in the satin" of that "thong of Satan."

In "Emma Enters a Sentence of Elizabeth Bishop's," the title character does not make Riff's mistake of seeking in pious kitsch redemption from her miserable existence (here a drab and crippling life on a small Iowa farm). Rather, Emma turns to art, eventually deciding to stop eating and live on the poems of Elizabeth Bishop until she grows "thin enough . . . to slip into a sentence of the poet's like a spring frock." For Emma, "words redeemed the world," and reading "was making love the way she imagined it would be if it were properly done." If Riff's strained responses to "art" completely unravel at the sight of a pair of panties, Emma knows that only words "will outwear every weakness," that her soul was nothing more or less than "all the eyelighted ear-heard words" accumulating upon her soul's floor "year after year from the first *no* to final *never.*" The price she pays is a self so slight in its relation to others and to the world that it weighs "little more than shade on lawn."

If Emma recalls the narrator of "In the Heart of the Heart of the Country" in her retirement from love and life, the same cannot be said of Luther Penner in "The Master of Secret Revenges." Penner's aesthetics are in the service of corrupt worldly ends; his story is narrated by a friend as unfortunately captivated by Penner's vision as Ella Bend's husband was alienated by hers. An inferior person given to "many smirks of superiority," Penner wields language skills both phony and self-serving; he pretends to know languages he does not, mispronounces words, and writes "with all the featureless precision of analytical philosophy." He is, however, also in possession of visionary powers that reveal to him the dirtiness of others' souls and consequently help him in his life's work: to wreak vengeance upon everything and everyone. Working his way through various methods of revenge, Penner ultimately hits upon the idea of propagating a spurious aesthetics raised to the level of religion, by means of which he would convince the world that

its most ordinary and useless objects are "full to the brim with Being." Merely pretending to believe that the "world was a work of art," Penner propagates a worldview that transforms things into what they are not and thereby infects his victims with a false consciousness: the opposite of a true artist's aims.

Even as each novella marshals its resources toward what Gass in "Finding a Form" called the "construction of a verbal consciousness," cumulatively *Cartesian Sonata* recognizes the pitfalls of the aesthetic act the artist is perforce compelled to perform: its difficult mastery, its fragility, its siren-like allure, its adaptability to nefarious ends. These concerns are likewise at the center of Gass's study of the Austrian poet Rainer Maria Rilke. If *Reading Rilke* involves, moreover, the reconstruction and habitation of the consciousness of another, this is what, according to Gass, reading and especially translation always entail. Although the book includes forty-eight Rilke poems (including *Duino Elegies*) as rendered by Gass, *Reading Rilke* is more than a selection of translated poems, more even than what its subtitle promises—"reflections on the problems of translation"—despite two chapters devoted to this topic. Equal parts biography and thematic analysis, subjective response and meditation on what an apprenticeship to inspiration can cost, *Reading Rilke* is likewise more than a contribution to Rilke studies or a demonstration of Gass's penchant for pushing at genre boundaries and conventions.

Perhaps each of his many essays devoted to admired writers finds Gass scoring their work so that it harmonizes with his own writerly preoccupations. *Reading Rilke* is ultimately Gass's occasion for articulating an aesthetic that is both Rilke's and his own. In doing so, Gass offers readers an eloquent if indirect explanation of the texts he himself has labored to write and why he has thought the effort worthwhile. Readers familiar with Gass's earlier criticism may find little in this book that is startlingly new, but familiar ideas are here fully orchestrated.

In creating a verbal artifact that aspires to be art, Gass contends, a writer's ideas may be (as Gass feels Rilke's in the *Elegies* often are) "more than a bit balderdashy": their "truthfulness" matters less, however, than that in their construction they are "splendid" and well-formed. If assertions such as these risk advocating an art-for-art's-sake aestheticism, they acquire consequence in the context of art's larger agenda: to effect the world's transformation by putting "the world into words, and, in that way, hold[ing] it steady for us."

The Rilkean artist who accomplishes this metamorphic task is someone free of "human distraction . . . indifferent to the point of divinity, absorbed in himself like all noumena are, and at one with the work and the world of the work, its radiant perfections"; he or she is someone who creates a permanent and "complex bit of human awareness of the world" capable of preventing a little of what is from becoming what is not by transforming it into what never was before. "We only live once," Gass observes,

and everything that fills this life, we shall have only once—once and no more. And what is this life but our awareness of ourselves and our awareness of the world? If the world awaits our seeing, if our duty is to give consciousness to things, that consciousness will disappear with bitter quickness, for we are the most fragile of all. So what is to be done? Leave that consciousness behind as a quality of our created things; deposit it in the forms and textures we give to objects.

It is fitting that at the turn of the twenty-first century Gass's oeuvre culminated in *Reading Rilke,* a book about a poet who claimed that "singing is being" (*Sonnets to Orpheus*) and whom Gass imagines enjoining us, "Life is not a song . . . so sing!" The song that is the poem or novel or essay is, Gass believes, finally "a state

of the soul" and among the most fully realized things we manage in the "unrealized life." Works of art, Gass affirms in conclusion, exist intensely; they "*are—are* with a vengeance; because, oddly enough, though what has been celebrated is over, and one's own life, the life of the celebrant, may be over, the celebration is not over. The celebration goes on." Just so, the celebration of language that is *Reading Rilke* or *The Tunnel,* "In the Heart of the Heart of the Country" or *On Being Blue* goes on, raucous and refined, in every complex bit of awareness that is the fiction and criticism of William Gass.

Selected Bibliography

WORKS OF WILLIAM GASS

FICTION

Omensetter's Luck. New York: New American Library, 1966.

In the Heart of the Heart of the Country. New York: Harper and Row, 1968. (Contains a preface by Gass, "The Pedersen Kid," "Mrs. Mean," "Icicles," "Order of Insects," and "In the Heart of the Heart of the Country.") A paperback edition published by Pocket Books (1977) includes a revised preface by Gass; in a 1981 edition from David R. Godine that preface was revised again. Quotes in this essay are from the 1981 edition.

Willie Masters' Lonesome Wife. Evanston, Ill.: Northwestern University Press, 1968.

The Tunnel. New York: Knopf, 1995.

Cartesian Sonata and Other Novellas. New York: Knopf, 1998. (Contains "Cartesian Sonata," "Bed and Breakfast," "Emma Enters a Sentence of Elizabeth Bishop's," and "The Master of Secret Revenges.")

NONFICTION

Fiction and the Figures of Life. New York: Knopf, 1970.

On Being Blue: A Philosophical Inquiry. Boston: David R. Godine, 1976.

The World within the Word: Essays. New York: Knopf, 1978.

Habitations of the Word: Essays. New York: Simon & Schuster, 1985.

Finding a Form: Essays. New York: Knopf, 1996.

Reading Rilke: Reflections on the Problems of Translation. New York: Knopf, 1999.

BIBLIOGRAPHY

Saltzman, Arthur M. "A William Gass Checklist." *Review of Contemporary Fiction* 11:150–158 (fall 1991). Supersedes earlier bibliographies; includes listings of uncollected short fiction, selected uncollected essays, book reviews and book introductions, interviews, and selected criticism.

CRITICAL STUDIES

Allen, Carolyn J. "Fiction and Figures of Life in *Omensetter's Luck.*" *Pacific Coast Philology* 9:5–11 (1974).

Bassoff, Bruce. "The Sacrificial World of William Gass: 'In the Heart of the Heart of the Country.' " *Critique* 18:36–58 (summer 1976).

Boyers, Robert. "Real Readers and Theoretical Critics." In his *After the Avant Garde: Essays on Art and Culture.* University Park: Pennsylvania State University Press, 1988. Pp. 81–90.

Bruss, Elizabeth W. "William H. Gass." In her *Beautiful Theories: The Spectacle of Discourse in Contemporary Criticism.* Baltimore: Johns Hopkins University Press, 1982. Pp. 139–202.

Busch, Frederick. "But This Is What It Is to Live in Hell: William Gass's 'In the Heart of the Heart of the Country.' " *Modern Fiction Studies* 19:97–108 (spring 1973).

Caramello, Charles. "Fleshing Out *Willie Masters' Lonesome Wife.*" *SubStance* 27:56–69 (1980).

Eckford-Prossor, M. "Shattering Genre/Creating Self: William Gass's *On Being Blue.*" *Style* 23:280–299 (summer 1989).

French, Ned. "Against the Grain: Theory and Practice in the Work of William H. Gass." *Iowa Review* 7:96–107 (winter 1976).

Guttenplan, Donald. "The Wor(l)ds of William Gass." *Granta* 1:147–160 (1979).

Hadella, Charlotte Byrd. "The Winter Wasteland of William Gass's 'In the Heart of the Heart of the Country.' " *Critique* 30:49–58 (fall 1988).

Haley, Vanessa. "Egyptology and Entomology in William Gass's 'Order of Insects.' " *Notes on Contemporary Literature* 16:3–5 (May 1986).

Hassan, Ihab. "Wars of Desire, Politics of the Word." *Salmagundi* 55:110–118 (winter 1982).

Holloway, Watson L. *William Gass.* Boston: Twayne, 1990.

Kane, Patricia. " 'The Sun Burned on the Snow': Gass's 'The Pedersen Kid.' " *Critique* 14:89–96 (fall 1972).

Kaufmann, Michael. "The Textual Body of William Gass's *Willie Masters' Lonesome Wife.*" In his *Textual Bodies: Modernism, Postmodernism, and Print.* Lewisburg, Penn.: Bucknell University Press, 1994. Pp. 87–105.

Kellman, Steven G., and Irving Malin, eds. *Into "The Tunnel": Readings of Gass's Novel.* Newark: University of Delaware Press, 1998.

Klein, Marcus. "Postmodernizing the Holocaust: William Gass in *The Tunnel.*" *New England Review* 18:79–87 (summer 1997).

McCaffery, Larry. "William H. Gass: The World within the Word." In his *The Metafictional Muse: The Work of Robert Coover, Donald Barthleme, and William H. Gass.* Pittsburgh: University of Pittsburgh Press, 1982. Pp. 151–250.

Merrill, Reed B. "The Grotesque as Structure: *Willie Masters' Lonesome Wife.*" *Criticism* 18:305–316 (1976).

Rodrigues, Eusebio L. "A Nymph at Her Orisons: An Analysis of William Gass's 'Order of Insects.' " *Studies in Short Fiction* 17:348–351 (summer 1980).

Saltzman, Arthur M. *The Fiction of William Gass: The Consolation of Language.* Carbondale: Southern Illinois University Press, 1985.

———, ed. *Review of Contemporary Fiction* 11:7–158 (fall 1991).

Schneider, Richard J. "The Fortunate Fall in William Gass's *Omensetter's Luck.*" *Critique* 18:5–20 (summer 1976).

Shorris, Earl. "The Well-Spoken Passions of William H. Gass." *Harper's,* May 1972, pp. 96–100.

Tanner, Tony. "On Reading 'Sunday Drive.' " In *Facing Texts: Encounters between Contemporary*

Writers and Critics. Edited by Heide Ziegler. Durham, N.C.: Duke University Press, 1988, pp. 205–214.

———. "William Gass's Barns and Bees." In his *Scenes of Nature, Signs of Men.* Cambridge: Cambridge University Press, 1987. Pp. 248–273.

Unsworth, John M. "William Gass's *The Tunnel:* The Work in Progress as Post Modern Genre." *Arizona Quarterly* 48:63–85 (spring 1992).

Waxman, Robert E. "Things in the Saddle: William Gass's 'Icicles' and 'Order of Insects.' " *Research Studies* 46:215–222 (1978).

White, Ray Lewis. "The Early Fiction of William H. Gass: A Critical Documentary." *Midamerica* 7:164–177 (1980).

INTERVIEWS AND PANEL DISCUSSIONS

Brans, Jo. "William Gass: Games of the Extremes." In *Listen to the Voices: Conversations with Contemporary Writers.* Edited by Jo Brans. Dallas: Southern Methodist University Press, 1988. Pp. 193–214.

Castro, Jan Garden. "William H. Gass." *Bomb* 51:58–61 (spring 1995).

Domke, Lorna H. "An Interview with William Gass." *Missouri Review* 10:53–67 (1987).

Duncan, Jeffrey L. "A Conversation with Stanley Elkin and William Gass." *Iowa Review* 7:48–77 (winter 1976).

Gass, William H., and Lorin Cuoco, eds. *The Writer in Politics.* Carbondale: Southern Illinois University Press, 1996. (In addition to Gass's formal talk/ essay "The Writer in Politics: A Litany," this collection, which grew from a conference sponsored by the International Writers Center of Washington University, includes transcriptions of two panel discussions in which Gass, the center's director, participated.)

Horvath, Brooke K., and others. "A Colloquy with William Gass." *Modern Fiction Studies* 29:587–608 (winter 1983).

LeClair, Tom. "An Interview with William Gass." In *Anything Can Happen: Interviews with Contemporary American Novelists.* Edited by Tom LeClair and Larry McCaffery. Urbana: University of Illinois Press, 1983. Pp. 152–175.

LeClair, Tom, and Larry McCaffery, eds. "A Debate: William Gass and John Gardner." In their *Anything Can Happen: Interviews with Contemporary American Novelists.* Urbana: University of Illinois Press, 1983. Pp. 20–31.

McCauley, Carole Spearin. "Fiction Needn't Say Things—It Should Make Them Out of Words." In *The New Fiction: Interviews with Innovative American Writers.* Edited by Joe David Bellamy. Urbana: University of Illinois Press, 1974, pp. 32–44.

McKenzie, James. "Pole-Vaulting in Top Hats: A Public Conversation with John Barth, William Gass, and Ishmael Reed." *Modern Fiction Studies* 22:131–151 (summer 1976).

Morrow, Bradford. "An Interview with William Gass." *Conjunctions* 4:14–29 (spring/summer 1983).

Mullinax, Gary. "An Interview with William Gass." *Delaware Literary Review* 1:81–87 (1972).

" 'Nothing but Darkness and Talk?': Writers' Symposium on Traditional Values and Iconoclastic Fiction." *Critique* 31:233–255 (summer 1990).

Saltzman, Arthur M. "An Interview with William Gass." *Contemporary Literature* 25:121–135 (summer 1984).

———. "Language and Conscience: An Interview with William Gass." *Review of Contemporary Fiction* 11:15–28 (fall 1991).

Spatz, Ronald. "Something in the World Worth Having." *Alaska Quarterly Review* 15: 9–14 (1997).

"A Symposium on Fiction: Donald Barthelme, William Gass, Grace Paley, Walker Percy." *Shenandoah* 27:3–31 (winter 1976).

Ziegler, Heide. "Interview with William H. Gass" In *The Radical Imagination and the Liberal Tradition: Interviews with English and American Novelists.* Edited by Heide Ziegler and Christopher Bigsby. London: Junction, 1982. Pp. 151–168.

—JOSEPH DEWEY
—BROOKE HORVATH

Robert Hass

1941—

SINCE THE PUBLICATION of his first collection of poetry, the prize-winning *Field Guide,* in 1973, Robert Hass has been regarded as a leading poet of his generation. Critics have commended various poetic strengths as forming Hass's literary signature, from "a range of emotion combined with a steadiness of style" and "a rich, almost philosophical brooding," in the words of Charles Molesworth, to what Linda Wagner calls a "sonorous" music and "the pleasure that he brings to lists of foods and objects, the loving emphasis on the very thingness of his images." Hass's natural inclination is to open himself up to a series of greatly diverse influences; in effect, he offers himself as a medium to various literary traditions and styles even as he seizes them as his own medium. This inclination, a sign both of his sensibility and his skill, can be regarded as Asian in its aesthetic overtones, in that it values keenness of insight in a fleeting present moment, a moment that the self does not insist on dominating. Hass's reading and translation of haiku reflect his sympathies.

Hass's willingness as a writer to be acted on and altered by influences in a consensual spirit may originate in his lifelong habit of close observation of nature in his native California, with its congenial climate. This intimate proximity to abundant nature, beginning in childhood, has helped, arguably, to give Hass the sense of a hab-

itat in which many beings can and should mingle with relative freedom and ease—that is, naturally. Even so, the landscape and the lives supported by it are forever sensitive to changes wrought by humans, with all the attendant risks, and sometimes losses, of change. To know nature in such a close mingling is also to be known by nature; the observer is also the observed, and as such perhaps not finally dominant. Hass's poetry demonstrates in many respects a heightened consciousness of this complex and nuanced interplay, such as in the poetry's dynamic meditative movement; in a narrator's ability to disappear and reappear in a poem's body; and in the author's seeming response to or reception of outside influences, literary or other, in his poetry.

His knowing susceptibility to artistic traditions unlike those into which he was born marks Hass as the rare master who might rather not be one, who continues to write as an inspired and gifted student of other words and other worlds. His eagerness to be molded by such influences suggests a literary stance distinctly different from the more common American ambition to imitate, compete with, and ultimately prevail over one's immediate or direct native progenitors. Hass's avid and abiding openness to Asian literary traditions, in particular; his devotion, as a cotranslator, colleague, and friend of the Polish poet Czeslaw Milosz; his forays into other translation projects; and his accomplishments as an anthologist, nationally syndicated poetry columnist, critic, essayist, and editor combine to set him apart from his peers, not only in his work but also in his approach to the work. As Hass told David Remnick in an interview published in *The Chicago Review* in 1981, "In order not to get trapped, I think an artist has to keep trying to enrich his means so that all the different ways he or she feels about things are available as materials for the art. . . . Otherwise, you just get locked into a particular way of seeing and speaking and feeling."

The diversity of Hass's interests and influences represents less a rebellion against the American poetic tradition than an augmentation of it. His lasting enthusiasms for Wallace Stevens, Walt Whitman, Robinson Jeffers, William Carlos Williams, Ezra Pound, and Theodore Roethke, among others, are evident in his poetry over the long span, and he shares this American literary inheritance with other American poets of his age. Hass has said that his earliest boyhood poems were written as rhymed verse after models supplied by Robert Service and Vachel Lindsay. Later, as a high school student, he discovered Allen Ginsberg's *Howl,* which had recently appeared, and the novels of Jack Kerouac; he then felt moved to reconsider his poetic prospects and choices in light of those writers. Ginsberg and Kerouac's acknowledged debt to Walt Whitman and Ezra Pound led Hass in turn to those poets; as a result, he began to explore the particular urgencies of free verse, for which he is now well known. It was in his midtwenties, after trying his hand at fiction, that he began to consider himself a poet. Hass notes in the preface to the 1998 reissue of *Field Guide:* "I belong to the last generation of American poets who did not automatically get the training of a poetry workshop. I taught myself what I could about the art mostly in isolation." This isolation stands, perhaps paradoxically, alongside his openness to influence as a formative condition for his work.

BACKGROUND

Hass, whose paternal great-grandfather had settled in California in the 1880s, was born in San Francisco on March 1, 1941 to Fred Hass, a businessman, and Helene Dahling Hass; he grew up in San Francisco and in Marin County. Hass earned a bachelor of arts in 1963 from St. Mary's College of California, then an all-male school; he received his Ph.D. in English in 1971 from Stanford University. He taught at the State University of New York at Buffalo from 1967 to 1971, then returned to California to teach at St. Mary's through 1989 before accepting a teaching job at the University of California at Berkeley. Hass's professional honors have included a Woodrow Wilson fellowship (1963–1964); a Danforth fellowship (1963–1967); the William Carlos Williams Award (1979); a Guggenheim fellowship (1980); the National Book Critics Circle Award (1984); a MacArthur fellowship (1984); and the position of Poet Laureate of the United States (1995–1997). His own teachers included Stanford's legendary Yvor Winters, the influential literary critic and poet described by Hass, in a 1979 interview with Sydney Lea and Jay Parini, as "the bad father who would never give you approval until you became like him and liked yourself for what you'd become." Stanford at that time "was full of people who went around writing poems in tetrameter and reciting them in a barrel voice like his. . . . Winters . . . subjected everything to such furious rational scrutiny, because he was so frightened of feeling." While in graduate school Hass edited a newspaper dedicated to investigating and reporting on Stanford's research efforts on behalf of the American military; over the years the poet's leftist political leanings have played an important role in both his life and his writing.

A turning point occurred early in his life as a writer when, for a college assignment in a great books course, he was asked to observe nature with field glasses and commit his observations to paper after reading essays by Charles Darwin and Aristotle. "At the end of the term," Hass told Remnick, "we had to turn in our notebooks of observation and an essay on whether looking at things and classifying them was real knowledge or not. . . . In the meantime, I kept huge notebooks full of soul-searching and things like that." In effect, *Field Guide* merged Hass's practice of nature observation with his spiritual habit of self-seeking.

Hass's outlook on nature, whatever the setting, has always been that of a Westerner, and in his view, West Coast and East Coast attitudes to nature diverge. "I think that West Coast poets have a different relation to Nature," Hass told Lea and Parini. Unlike Western poets such as Kenneth Rexroth, Michael McClure, Gary Snyder, and Winters, "none of the important East Coast poets have been notably interested in botany. . . . I'm talking . . . about particulars, the interest in particulars." But like Ralph Waldo Emerson, an Eastern observer of nature, Hass feels "that Nature [is] the symbol of the spirit." And he shares in the general sense that "wilderness is the religion of Americans." Commenting on Hass's immersion in nature, the poet Stanley Kunitz, who selected *Field Guide* as the winner of the prestigious Yale Series of Younger Poets Prize, noted that Hass's poetry

is permeated with the awareness of his creature self, his affinity with the animal and vegetable kingdoms, with the whole chain of being. The country from which he has his passport is the natural universe, to which he pledges his imagination. . . . Natural universe and moral universe coincide for him, centered in a nexus of personal affections, his stay against what he describes as "the wilderness of history and political violence."

THE THEME OF NATURE

As a poet, Hass finds a home for himself in scenes of natural order. These scenes may or may not situate him directly in nature in the effort to take its measure. His understanding of nature and his own relation to it is characteristically subtle. Hass is not a documentarian of nature, not a tourist of natural places, not an outsider to nature's mysteries or harmonies. Rather, he dwells within nature and gives himself to it. The balance struck by Hass between himself and nature also suggests that poetry itself can become a medium of nature, for a poem can embody the balance struck in nature by the poet or by his speakers.

Examples of Hass's approach to nature in his poetry and to poetry as a medium of nature are abundant. One such is "Measure," from *Field Guide.* The poem is composed of six stanzas of three lines each, regular though not identical in length and rhythmic impact. While "Measure" seems to be set indoors at a writer's desk that is accessible to nature, the poem's locale, like its time of day (sunset), is transitional. The desk is present; so is a plum tree; so is the play of closing light. Conventional borders of a room have receded, or at least are not observed by the poem's speaker. To evoke a transitional scene with borders dissolved or dissolving, Hass justly employs an impressionistic technique in offering readers a view of outside mingling with inside. His technique suggests that little or nothing divides the natural world from the human.

Recurrences.
Coppery light hesitates
again in the small-leaved

Japanese plum. Summer
and sunset, the peace
of the writing desk

and the habitual peace
of writing, these things
form an order I only

belong to in the idleness
of attention. Last light
rims the blue mountain

and I almost glimpse
what I was born to,
not so much in the sunlight

or the plum tree
as in the pulse
that forms these lines.

Observing his writing desk bathed in the "coppery light" of a sunset that seems characteristically Californian, the speaker remarks, with inconspicuous grace, on "an order" implicit in the scene, even though he is observing it at a moment of change, day's end, when order might be assumed to disperse or soften. The poem quietly salutes the writer's vocation as a daily pleasure and seeks a destiny in the larger natural order for the writer sitting at his desk. However, the poem is remarkable for the absence of an informing self. The speaker makes so few overt claims on our attention that, like the evening light, he seems to glow while he ebbs, to sidle into an ineffable knowledge of himself and the moment without the customary ego or arrogance of human effort. The poem is written during and as a pause between seasonal and circadian "recurrences," in between the rhythms of a day and its writing. For as long as the pause can endure, man and nature mingle. The poem does not propose writing or the writing life as being worthy of worship—there is neither a god nor a subservient self on the premises. But it is a song of hopeful praise, seeking no more glory than can be found in a day turning slowly to dusk.

The restraint of Hass's imagery, which avoids a buildup of descriptive detail, achieves a harmony, like nature's, that does not hoard its beauties. Instead, "Measure" remains serenely unencumbered as a lyric expression, faithful to an implicit order. The closing light that "hesitates / again in the small-leaved / Japanese plum" is as much description as the poet will allow in the poem. (In another poem in *Field Guide*, "Palo Alto: The Marshes," Hass's eye only reluctantly

"performs / the lobotomy of description." Description seems for him to falsify the thing described and the relation of a witness to it.) All but two of his lines are enjambed with a gentleness that rests and eases the mind. Such easefulness appears lustrously tentative. Despite "the habitual peace of writing" that is savored by the speaker, the poem marks a moment of "almost glimps-[ing]," not of premonitory insight or insistent conclusion.

In part, the speaker is painting a still life of the true nature of the poet's calling: desk, mountain view, plum tree, and, as an element of this picture, his own longing to say what is needed—and no more. But he is also declining to take credit for the larger natural order he senses; he neither has designs on nor plans to possess this order, yet will, if he can, dwell peaceably within it—without the imposition of his own will, if that is possible. To witness a scene without embroidering on it one's whims or ambitions seems a habit demanding uncommon attention from the witness, demanding a love of the still life quite apart from the viewer's contributions to creating it. The speaker's "idleness of attention" is thus a boon, for that idleness has allowed him to avoid mastering a place or time; instead, he can slip into their rhythm, best known on the rhythm's own terms. To master the rhythm would suggest an alternative scenario of human willfulness and separation from nature, which ultimately binds all living things. To master the rhythm might also suggest a willful separation from the true nature of writing. For Hass, to "idle" with all of nature is a necessary idyll. The beauty of the poem can be recognized in the secure looseness of its bindings.

The longing for a place in the natural order of things, expressed humbly in "Measure," gets turned on its side and translated into the tone of mega-ego and worldly wit in "Applications of the Doctrine," which follows "Measure" in a pleasing dialectical pairing in *Field Guide.* "Applications of the Doctrine" portrays a professor of French who has set up a virtual altar to the self. He has built a place for that self in the scheme of things and dwells there becalmed but busy; in order to maintain this place, however, he tends to ignore everything and everyone else. An irony of his self-celebration is the cultivation of doubt: the professor is able and willing to question the moorings of the self, superficially, if only to better protect it in the long run. With doubt as one of his intellectual mainstays, his self is safe from most assaults. His longing for safety has actually grown obsolete; he is now totally lost, stranded on an island of his own making. Ratiocination is his seductively unreliable god, and he worships it:

> The self is probably an illusion
> and language the structure of illusions.
> The self is beguiled, anyway,
> by this engine of thought.

Unlike the peaceful rhythmic continuities of "Measure," the nine stanzas of "Applications of the Doctrine" are marked by a flashy, assertive swagger. The spaces between stanzas are ignited by asterisks; an asterisk also follows the last stanza, thereby concluding the poem with an emphatic jolt. Many of the lines end with words carrying hard or crackly consonants, so that even enjambed lines appear, by force of their sound, to call with peremptory dispatch for a temporary halt, as in the lines "The self has agreed to lecture / before a psychoanalytic study group." The lines strive for an authority like the professor's, and as he does, they claim too much. Hass, by exposing this overweening tendency, achieves a witty flourish ("The deck includes / an infinite number / of one-eyed jacks"). The determined asperity of tone in "Applications of the Doctrine" mimics and mocks the professor's self-command and the confident narcissism of his fashionably intricate thoughts ("The self botanizes. / He dreams of breeding, one day, / an odorless nar-

cissus"). Hass's dance of merrily deprecating syllables ("There is a girl the self loves. / She has been trying to study him for days / but her mind keeps / wandering") sympathetically lampoons an intellectual order that has nothing to do with nature's. He leaves the scholarly egotist to his own devices, unknowingly isolated by his self-serving longings.

Thematically, Hass's four major collections of poetry to date range recurrently between the poles suggested by "Measure" and "Applications of the Doctrine." That is, there are times when he finds a home in scenes of natural order, and times when he finds occasion for reflection in other kinds of scenes, in realms and in people alien to or alienated from nature. However, the theme of nature seems primary and definitive in much of Hass's writing. His work suggests that to live in nature demands more than will or mind; no one, not even a thoughtful professor, can break nature's code—no one can master our natural heritage. The inadequacy of human tools for mastery means that our sense of ourselves as beings inhabiting nature calls for constant readjustment and reassessment. That inadequacy also calls for a measured, ongoing humility that requires continual rethinking and musical retuning. For Hass, those who worship nature get it wrong; instead, we owe nature faithful, not lavish or obsequious, attention. No organism counts for more than another, except in the sense that the avid, accurate glance, when cast on nature, rewards the observer with a more certain and complete sense of nature's particulars.

INFLUENCE OF ASIAN LITERATURE

Hass's reading and translation of Chinese and Japanese literature may have confirmed, rather than given rise to, the humble realism of his view of nature as a panorama of particulars, without a deity, where no self can or should want to hold sway if to be natural means to be happy. One forfeits happiness as a human in nature by trying to hold sway; holding sway crosses nature, falsifying the complicated links and balances underlying the natural order. To see nature with any kind of clarity demands that one cease to compete with its power and cease, too, to regard oneself as a corollary or potential center of power. The self dissolves except as a means of insight.

That dissolving self, the bearer of insight, may seem paradigmatically Asian. And as a Californian, Hass has faced the Orient as readily as, or more readily than, he has faced the American heartland and the more distant Atlantic horizon. His readings of other American writers shaped by Asian literature, including Ezra Pound, Gary Snyder, and Kenneth Rexroth, also may have helped to "orient" him. The particularity and purity of his images evoke Asian poetry, as does Hass's mystic cleanliness and swiftness of perception. Some of his poems, in *Field Guide* and other volumes, seem notably formed by a haiku aesthetic. One fruit of Hass's literary Asian explorations is his 1994 annotated anthology *The Essential Haiku,* which collects haiku written by Bashō, Buson, and Issa as rendered into English by various poets and translators. *Field Guide* also features some of Hass's own renderings of these poets.

"In Weather," a poem included in *Field Guide,* is composed as a long diary of unmet desires and endless desiring. The poem begins as follows:

> What I wanted
> in the pearly repetitions of February
> was vision.

It continues:

> All winter,
> grieved and dull,
> I hungered for it.

Typically, Hass expands the poem with a Whitmanian list of things desired or actively desiring, ranging from "lightning- / stricken trees" that absorb the narrator's attention to "the russet cores of apples" to "long, inch-thick / sea worms / . . . writhing in the sun" and filled with desires of their own. Hass's source of examples, characteristically, is nature, and he takes care to observe them in detail. (As the American poet and translator Sam Hamill, a Buddhist, has noted in his book *The Essential Basho,* Confucius once commented: "All wisdom is rooted in learning to call things by the right name." As a professional poet and an amateur botanist, Hass too is fascinated with names and the act of naming.)

The speaker of the poem next considers misogynistic violence as a tendency of human nature, before he returns to a natural scene and searches again for solace. When he returns, the time of year is March. While watching owls mate at night, the speaker, until recently a mostly solitary figure, feels compelled to imitate the "ecstatic" calls of the birds. The poem closes with three lines, written in three terse declarative sentences:

> I drew long breaths.
> My wife stirred in our bed.
> Joy seized me.

Although their combined syllable count falls slightly short of the seventeen prescribed by tradition, in spirit and in form the lines veer unmistakably near to haiku.

"In Weather" echoes Whitman's use of catalogs—of things seen, heard, touched, tasted, and felt—to motivate and illustrate a meditation as though pursued informally, on the run; but more tellingly, the poem exemplifies Hass's debt to the Japanese poets for the chasteness and rapt brevity of his images. Another sign of this influence is the stance assumed by the narrator with regard to the world of sensory experience and knowledge. To a degree he seeks knowledge, and to a degree he also awaits the arrival of knowledge, which keeps to its own mysterious schedule; for instance, he regards the mating of the owls passively before echoing their calls. The owls gain or regain a sense of creaturely gladness before he does, because they know more than he can. In Hass's view of things, animal initiative and human responsiveness follow here in an appropriate sequence. Moreover, the speaker's stance, common to Hass's work, is one of mutuality. The speaker of "In Weather" sensuously sifts the things of the world while also offering himself and his sensations to the world to be sifted. Poetry thus supplies a meeting place, or a near meeting place, for subjective and objective viewpoints.

In his essay "Images," included in his 1984 prose collection *Twentieth Century Pleasures: Prose on Poetry,* which won a National Book Critics Circle Award, Hass writes about the haiku poet Bashō (1644–1694): "Basho told a disciple that the trouble with most poems was that they were either subjective or objective, and when the disciple said, 'You mean, too subjective or too objective?' Basho said, 'No.' " Elsewhere in the same essay, Hass, in a thoughtful personal aside, reveals that "it is possible to feel my life, in a quiet ecstatic helplessness, as a long slow hurtle through the forms of things." He tends to resist the hurtle as too passive a mode of living and of thinking. However, one is never more aware of the relative positions of subject and object than during an experience of action felt "passively." Such an awareness comes naturally to the reader of "In Weather." In the poem's culminating three lines, as in haiku, we enter sensation through the sensibility of a witness. Yet we finish by forgetting the witness and instead accepting the absolution of the sensation given. As "In Weather" demonstrates, there are times when we ought to await the arrival of knowledge. At those times, to seek is not to find anything.

Critics have not always admired the stance of permeability or willingness to await and witness rather than act. Reviewing Hass's fourth major collection of poetry, *Sun Under Wood,* which appeared in 1996, in *The Atlantic Monthly,* Peter

Davison voices his sense that poems in Hass's second book, *Praise* (1979), tend "to blur into a haze of contemplative passivity . . . in which states of mind and feeling [are] rendered reflexively with passive, copulative, or auxiliary verbs and the present tense, as though poems were to be merely tickled into existence, instead of animating themselves as self-propelled, self-motivating creations." Of *Sun Under Wood,* Davison wrote that

the charm and modesty remain, but these poems keep relaxing into the voice of an onlooker rather than taking on the energy of full participation—as though they came to the poet through a window, a filter, a screen of white noise and unscented air. It would seem that the verbs that Hass employs have not willingly enlisted in the fight for meaning.

The fighting metaphor favored by Davison may be revealing of this critic's assumptions about merit in poetry. Hass usually refuses to "fight" and prefers instead to resist, when necessary; resistance is his moral creed where poetry is concerned. In the play of Eastern and Western sensibilities in his work, perhaps no fight is possible. Thus, one might see Hass as culturally ambidextrous or as culturally ambivalent or undecided and thus in a way passive. The quintessential meditative movement of Hass's poems also shows the influence of Asian poets and their sense of what is natural.

In "Maps," from *Field Guide,* another Whitmanian catalog of sensuous things gives the poem its essential shape. Asterisks separate the stanzas, suggesting that each stanza should be savored individually as a singular experience:

Sourdough french bread and pinot chardonnay
                *

Apricots—
the downy buttock shape
hard black sculpture of the limbs
on Saratoga hillsides in the rain.
                *

These were the staples of the China trade:
sea otter, sandalwood, and bêche-de-mer

*

The long ripple in the swamp grass
is a skunk
he shuns the day

By naming the sensory array that floats about him in the Californian scene, Hass's "eye owns what is familiar," as he puts it in the poem, "felt along the flesh." But for him, as well as for a reader, the array also molds our experience of it. Unlike the errant brutalities committed by the early California settlers, mentioned in the poem, Hass's contribution to the landscape, as well as to the landscape of the poem, is to dwell within it as one of many inhabitants, alert to the "eyes of fish" and the "intelligence of crabs." He is unwilling to impose a mastering narrative upon the poem or to "fight for meaning," in the words of Davison; instead, he would rather allow for gaps to show between the fragmentary stanzas.

The resting and slipping actions of man and animal in the poem seem typically Japanese, for the essence of haiku is to enable speed of insight, fast traveling along an interstice between a witness and the things witnessed. Increasingly, as his work has continued, Hass has fathomed that interstice—flown to, from, and within it associatively in order to feel and think fully as a poet. His increased freedom as this roving interstitial soul has led him to become a witness to inner as much as to outer worlds, especially in his later books. Over the years influences other than Asian poetry, such as the poetry of Rainer Maria Rilke, have tempered and redirected the meditative moment in Hass's work. This writer can travel in between the poem and the world. Moreover, when the writer can also sidle in between the poem and its speaker, reflecting on both or either, he often emerges with challenging and artful literary craft and insights into human nature.

THEMES OF LANGUAGE AND KNOWING

One of Hass's best-known poems, "Meditation at Lagunitas," centers thematically his second book of poetry, *Praise,* and also suggests some of the growing freedoms claimed by the poet in his travels about the interstices. This meditation considers the presumed inadequacies of language and the human longing to remedy or transcend them. "Meditation at Lagunitas" opens:

All the new thinking is about loss.
In this it resembles all the old thinking.
The idea, for example, that each particular erases
the luminous clarity of a general idea. That the clown-
faced woodpecker probing the dead sculpted trunk
of that black birch is, by his presence,
some tragic falling off from a first world
of undivided light. Or the other notion that,
because there is in this world no one thing
to which the bramble of *blackberry* corresponds,
a word is elegy to what it signifies.

As the poet and critic Alan Shapiro has pointed out, Hass's first "idea" originates in "the scholastic notion of haecceity—that each particular, by its presence, represents a falling away from a realm of seamless purity, of 'undivided light.' " Hass's second "notion" derives from "the nominalist notion that in the representation of the thing the word is, at best, 'elegy to what it signifies.' " The first-person voice in "Meditation at Lagunitas" is troubled by these abstract concepts that he has talked about with a friend; he tries in the poem to give words back their meanings and to wrest some affirmation out of the sense of "loss."

The meditation in "Lagunitas" is offered as an intimate baring of the soul by a speaker who questions the value of abstraction. Instead, he prefers to cultivate a sense of wonder provided partly by memories from childhood—e.g., "the little orange-silver fish" and "silly music from the pleasure boat." The speaker also engages with the things connoted by words he does not want to let "dissolve"—*"justice, / pine, hair, woman, you* and *I."* Longing to revive erased correspondences, hoping to live in the word as in the thing it might have signified, the speaker suggests that memory can offer us a limited redemption at auspicious moments. However, the union or reunion of word and thing, spirit and body, is a rare occurrence, and so the speaker arrives at a consoling emotion, tenderness

The emotional ferocity of "Santa Lucia," another poem in *Praise,* should not blind us to its tenderness. The poem is narrated in the first person by a woman. According to a note provided by Hass to "Santa Lucia II," a poem-sequel included in *Human Wishes* (1989), the woman "apparently . . . writes about art professionally." A gallery stroller and an urbanite, she is certainly desirous—she is singed by desire—yet she seems to live ascetically, surrounded by dubious plenty without partaking directly of it: "He wants to fuck. Sweet word. / All suction. I want less." She is an onlooker, a scrupulous witness, who says of wildflowers, which sport "fierce little wills rooting," that "they have intelligence / of hunger." Her own intelligence seems to have betrayed her, seems turned recklessly to the pursuit of images, which punish her. She is particularly haunted, even molested, by the figure of her nemesis, which opens the poem. Here the woman's voice ushers us into the poem with her finely realized tone of besieged, struggling cynicism:

> Art & love: he camps outside my door,
> innocent, carnivorous. As if desire
> were actually a flute, as if the little song
> *transcend, transcend* could get you anywhere.
> He brings me wine; he believes in the arts
> and uses them for beauty.

The notion of exploitative usage gives "Santa Lucia" its thematic burden; the poem follows the woman's efforts to contend for and with that bur-

den. Used and exploited, fearful, sickened by her knowledge of sensual "glut & desperation," the woman yearns to defy the truism *"All women / are masochists."* She wants to evade "male eyes and art," and yet "I see / my body is his prayer . . . / . . . He sees me like a painter." She also hears herself described, just as any muse would. But Hass presents her as a spiritual and artistic muse of an uncommon kind who can gaze at what the men themselves gaze upon: herself. She can see herself as they do, then gaze with horror upon them. Her role is thus both male and female, stuck in the strain of conflicting perceptual traffic. Her searching eye itself ensures her captivity. Paradoxically, the writer's searching eye reveals her.

"Santa Lucia II" in *Human Wishes* offers a more quietly mournful soliloquy. In the absence of even a nemesis, the woman here, resembling T. S. Eliot's Prufrock, seems resigned to her loneliness and far more solitary. She is deeply fatigued spiritually, as though there were no longer anything to subsist on but herself. And although memory can retrieve long-gone happiness, as shown in "Meditation at Lagunitas," this poem begins by failing to recall or honor what, palpably, she needs most: pleasure. "Pleasure is so hard to remember," Hass writes. "It goes / so quick from the mind." The woman's spiritual depletion has led her to become the sort of masochist that she had scorned in "Santa Lucia"—a masochist who finds all the torment she desires close at hand in herself. No longer craving the "intelligence / of hunger," she concludes instead that hunger is best understood as "a form of suffering." And so she suffers, only dimly alive to anything else. In that important sense, her hunger for suffering remains true to her, as she does to her hunger. Would this faithfulness give the woman an unexpected integrity, even a late-twentieth-century nobility of status? The saint for whom both poems are named was persecuted for refusing a man in marriage, though she miraculously survived attempts made on her life as a consequence. By legend, she either removed her own eyes voluntarily in order to take revenge on a suitor, or else they were torn punitively from her. (In Hass's poem, the power of the woman's gaze does pose a danger to her.) When translated from Italian, the saint's name means light; the melancholy compassion of Hass, who is Catholic, in evoking the travail of hunger for the hungry casts a fiercely clear yet still swaddling light on a woman who seems to do without too much, too often.

Human Wishes as a whole is a more doleful book than *Praise* or *Field Guide,* expansively and richly so. The poetry suggests a generosity of temperament that extends well beyond the qualified Whitmanian joy taken by an earlier Hass from nature. The book's emotional range also avoids the spare exigencies of haiku, its faintly predictable jolts and unremitting elegance, for a more expansively human breadth of perception and form. The poems do not necessarily cluster around nature as a primary theme. For instance, although the woman in "Santa Lucia II," like any good Californian, leaves her perch in the city from time to time to venture into nature, she goes as a fairly alienated observer of "dunes," "turban snails," and "brown kelp," named and evoked with the peculiar punctiliousness of one so sad that names can hardly matter. "I wanted to be touched / and didn't want to want it. And by whom?" the woman asks plaintively, recoiling later from the cry of "a gull's hunger bleeding off the wind." Instead of traveling from solitude to community, instead of translating herself into one anemone among many (or even just into somebody's ordinary girlfriend), she makes a home resolutely in solitude, as though guided by bodily instinct. And although her home is furnished in gloom, it does belong to her. Oddly and persuasively, she takes her place there with the sense of fitness that sends any species home. As Hass writes in an essay in *Twentieth Century Pleasures* about poetic form, "It is this forming, this coming into existence of imagination as a shaping power,

that 'irradiates and exalts all objects' and makes the forms of nature both an echo of that experience and a clue to the larger rhythms of a possible order in which the human mind shares or which it can make." The woman of the Santa Lucia poems forms her life by dint of a darkening and potent—if desperate—moral imagination.

ESSAYS AND PROSE POEMS

As *Twentieth Century Pleasures* makes clear, Hass is a searching and subtle prose stylist, and one who is eager to steer clear of certain conventions of criticism so as to stay closer to the poetry in question. Commenting in the essay "One Body," in *Twentieth Century Pleasures,* on a poem by Randall Jarrell, Hass argues that Jarrell has failed to enter and fulfill the poem's rhythm; he "has not found for himself the form of being in the idea":

> Criticism is not especially alert to this matter [the form of being in the idea]. It talks about a poet's ideas or themes or imagery and so it treats all the poems of Stevens or Williams equally when they are not equally poems. The result is the curiosity of a huge body of commentary which has very little to do with the art of poetry. . . . What gets lost is just the thing that makes art as humanly necessary as bread. Art is an activity of the spirit and when we lose track of what makes an art an art, we lose track of the spirit.

Incidentally, the same cannot be said of the woman in the Santa Lucia poems; whatever her disappointments, she has not lost track of the spirit. Is this as good a way as any to explain her embattled, apparently unlikely, heroism?

In another essay in the same volume, Hass applies his intuitive and associative intelligence to the subject of the Polish poet Czeslaw Milosz, many of whose books Hass has helped to translate into English. Of Milosz's early poetry Hass writes:

It seems to be beautifully made—critics would speak of a reckless freedom of imagination in his early work, combined with a surprisingly classical strength in the phrasing—it rehearses lifelong themes and preoccupations, and more crucially it is choral. The poet does not speak in one voice but in many, none of them quite his own. And it has an intensity, an emotional nakedness.

Some of these observations seem equally true of Hass himself in *Human Wishes,* notably in the second section, which consists of fourteen prose poems, themselves emotionally expansive. The prose poems reveal his resourceful, even ingenious attentiveness to a set of human situations not easily or logically linked to one another. He writes with the cunning insinuation of a man who appears able to speak in many different tones or lingos. Hass himself, the interstitial soul, seems inclined to disappear into the bodies of his prose poems, claiming a new imaginative freedom and an observational restraint even while some of his characters are laid bare with an intensity that borders on the shocking. Although their links as prose poems are indirect, the impact of the group eventually sounds "choral."

A thematic undercurrent tugs tenderly and in a sidelong manner at the fourteen prose poems. All are nicked, nudged, touched by an oncoming knowledge of mortality, even when the situation seems to indicate a safer, simpler story. "Museum," the second prose poem in the sequence, and one of the most sunny, begins with an account of a rather routine urban weekend outing:

On the morning of the Käthe Kollwitz exhibit, a young man and woman come into the museum restaurant. She is carrying a baby; he carries the air-freight edition of the Sunday *New York Times.* She sits in a high-backed wicker chair, cradling the infant in her arms. He fills a tray with fresh fruit, rolls, and coffee in white cups and brings it to the table. His hair is tousled, her eyes are puffy. They look like they were thrown down into sleep and then yanked out of it like divers coming up for air.

The almost reportorial flair of the writing gradually summons poignancy from the young family's apparent indifference to the nearby art of Kollwitz, which portrays "faces . . . carved in wood of people with no talent or capacity for suffering who are suffering the numbest kinds of panic: hunger, helpless terror." Although the narrator of the prose poem has "fallen in love with" his Sunday vision of commonplace familial well-being, which suggests to him that "everything seems possible," the timelessness of the haunted art would seem to contradict the innocent family's prospects. The fact that the young family appears to have no knack for or knowledge of suffering marks their affinity with the people Kollwitz portrays, who once—tragically—resembled them. Unprotected happiness—fearless happiness, unaware even of itself—may seem to promise nothing but more of the same, yet it remains absurdly vulnerable. Hass's grace in presenting the reader with the perfume of a fate but not the fate itself, without allegory, without the presence of imagery crafted in support of his theme, is typical of the prose sequence as a whole. He writes with convincing confidence of what happens, of how the world works.

In much of Hass's work, words can serve as the most delicate moral registers, embodying (rather than merely naming) difficulties and dilemmas of the human. "A Story About the Body," the twelfth piece in the prose sequence, exemplifies this tendency. Just one paragraph in length, it tells from a third-person point of view of a young composer at an artist's colony who develops an erotic interest in an older Japanese painter: "He loved her work, and her work was like the way she moved her body, used her hands, looked at him directly when she made amused and considered answers to his questions." He almost propositions her. She tells him that she knows he wants her, and that she is willing, but also informs him that she has been through a double mastectomy. "The radiance that he had carried around in his belly and chest cavity—like music—withered very quickly. . . ." The composer returns to his cabin. We hear no more about the two of them, but after their mutual revelation, the painter leaves a bowl on the composer's doorstep. The prose poem concludes, "It looked to be full of rose petals, but he found when he picked it up that the rose petals were on top; the rest of the bowl—she must have swept them from the corners of her studio—was full of dead bees."

"A Story About the Body" explains nothing: its impact derives from the economy of a form that holds meaning yet will not spill it. After reading about the encounter, we are compelled to try to enter the feelings of the sage and the innocent and to think ourselves, also, into the piece's artful interstices. The closing image of rose petals blanketing dead bees is only one of the goads we feel bound to respond to. Though not described and not pictured, the meeting of the man and woman as they trade their revelations is in some respects still more graphic than the image of the bowl and its contents. The figure of death and the figure of love approach each other in a certain place, at a certain time; in so doing, they finally shed their abstractness and the tiresome legibility of most parables. Still, as always in such a tale, love must flee death's image—by nature, love cannot help it. The placatory violence of the dead bees conciliates and ravages, with no further words shared. In a sense, the image of the bowl arrives as a poem inside of Hass's poem—tacit, beautiful, pained, and wondrously implicative.

The idiosyncratic mastery of story in this prose sequence may show the impact of Hass's close working relationship of many years with Milosz, whose fascination with myth and tale informs both his prose and his poetry. The American writer's appetite, though, for inventing his writing anew has also found fresh impetus in the work and the working methods of his wife, the poet Brenda Hillman. In an unpublished public conversation held as an event on the program of the 1996 Geraldine R. Dodge poetry festival in Waterloo, New Jersey, Hass and Hillman spoke to a large audience about the collaborative nature of their lives as writers.

LATER WORK

Hass and Hillman began to share their lives in 1986, after both had seen their first marriages end in divorce. (Hass married Earlene Leif, a psychotherapist, in 1962; they had three children.) Neither Hillman nor Hass had been married to a poet. During their public conversation, each acknowledged the other's literary influence. Hass said in particular that Hillman had helped him to learn from the techniques of hypnosis and meditation how to write more inwardly, how to travel farther from the well-known world and into the unknown self. Hillman also led Hass as a reader into a renewed involvement with famously inward poets, such as Emily Dickinson and Sylvia Plath. "Though I had read them," Hass said, "I was a Whitman person, not a Dickinson person. . . . I'm extroverted, I love the world." For that matter, Hillman's own poetry altered his work. "Her work," he commented, "has an interiority that I have envied." He "hungered for more interiority in my own work." Moreover, "Mine felt crude to me when I read Brenda's. I felt like I was dumb on the subject of my own interior movements."

Perhaps partly as a consequence of his relationship with his wife, Hass's 1996 collection of poems, *Sun Under Wood,* is probably his most frankly personal and elaborately playful book, allowing memories not just of happiness but also of woe to arise in poems and be probed. The book's exhilarating willingness to turn around and comment on or question some of its constituent poems and their foundations also points to Hass's reawakened sense of poetic possibilities.

An element of Hass's poetry from the beginning has been its dynamic meditative movement.

An example of his zealous, joyful efforts to extend this movement can be found in "Layover," a poem in *Sun Under Wood,* and in "Notes on 'Layover,' " a postscript or fraternal literary twin to "Layover" that takes shape as a prose poem. "Layover," a poem of geographic, cultural, and political witness, observes the airport in Anchorage, Alaska, during a change of planes. Although the speaker seems to be addressing us in the first person, with a directness and immediacy that could not be accounted for otherwise, the pronoun "I" never appears in the poem, as though too oppressed by the surroundings to surface. The scene is dreary: gray, dry, desultory, with native workers, subservient to the territory's "colonizers," toiling on the runway, and with fuel exhaust polluting nearby "pre-Cambrian forests." The landscape seems to have capitulated to the worst forces in American capitalism, and that is not all; on this anticlimactic "day of diplomatic lull," Iraq has decided to cooperate and withdraw from invaded Kuwait. Declares the unseen narrator, "It won't happen." Like those around him, he is lost in a lassitude of diminished moral expectation.

By contrast, "Notes on 'Layover' " actively considers alternative approaches to the same subject and alternative utterances. The piece begins, "I could have said that I am a listless eye gazing through watery glass on a Friday afternoon in February." The conditional tone continues, yet Hass moves to contradict that, too, with a series of adamant declarations and confessional disclosures. Rather than lazily imagine the rote contents of other people's luggage, as in "Layover" ("Flowerburst ties, silky underwear"), the unmuzzled "I" of "Notes on 'Layover' " singles out for his attention "that woman with the baby" whose ovarian cyst, our eavesdropper reports, was recently removed; he thinks of "her body, and then of her underwear." The prose poem ultimately steps out of its own increasingly liberal confines, seeking to characterize its own flights of mind reflexively. As a means of doing so, the meditative voice utters this sentence fragment: "A way of locating itself that even the idle mind works at." Although when read out of context the self-characterization may seem static, we know from Hass's earlier history of poetic meditation that an "idleness of attention" is by no means a bad thing. Rather, "idleness" of attention can serve to love the world and the word. In fact, the "idle mind" at large in "Notes on 'Layover' " is just idle enough to wander free, through the dross of a featureless airport and up to the heights of the imagined cry of an Alaskan raven, "ruthless and playful spirit of creation." Confirming that spirit of play, Hass concludes that "all crossings over are a way of knowing, and of knowing we don't know, where we have been."

Consciously wayward, irreverently playful, the poet can also rethink himself, not just the terms of the world. In "My Mother's Nipples," a confessional poem in *Sun Under Wood* whose subject was suggested to Hass by the poet Sharon Olds, he revisits with mixed emotions scenes from his childhood, when he acted alternately as a caretaker and a victim of his alcoholic, sometimes hospitalized mother. The poem is diverted into prose from time to time; includes carefree doggerel along with painful personal revelations of a family's struggle to save itself; and undercuts the poem's own dramatic momentum, for the better. "My Mother's Nipples" thrives on a series of permissions and refusals, including the poet's refusal to envision or construct an improved plot, a falsely construed course of human progress. Instead, he crosses unfriendly territory and thoughtfully recrosses it. Meanwhile, we ride the exposed interstices of Hass's family lament, voiced in the emotional plural.

"The mind, in the act of recovery, creates," wrote Hass in *Twentieth Century Pleasures,* as if to explain his own resurgence as a poet. "Because rhythm has direct access to the unconscious, because it can hypnotize us, enter our bodies and make us move, it is a power. . . . Repetition makes us feel secure and variation makes us feel free. What these experiences must touch in us is the rhythm of our individuation." Although Hass began his writing life as an intimate witness of this tree and not that one, of the world's fully specified natural panoply, the observer has come full circle to assume a position as his own observed creation. Perhaps therein lies a sort of poetic justice. For Hass has offered himself to nature, and nature has given him back.

Selected Bibliography

WORKS OF ROBERT HASS

POETRY AND PROSE

Carroll, Paul, comp. *The Young American Poets* (contributor). With an introduction by James Dickey. Chicago: Follett, 1968.

Field Guide. New Haven, Conn.: Yale University Press, 1973. (Reissued edition with a new preface by the author, 1998.)

Winter Morning in Charlottesville. Knotting, Eng.: Sceptre Press, 1977.

Five American Poets (contributor). Introduction by Michael Schmidt. Manchester, Eng.: Carcanet, 1979.

Praise. New York: Ecco Press, 1979.

Twentieth Century Pleasures: Prose on Poetry. New York: Ecco Press, 1984.

Human Wishes. New York: Ecco Press, 1989.

Sun Under Wood: New Poems. Hopewell, N.J.: Ecco Press, 1996.

EDITED ANTHOLOGIES

Hass, Robert, ed. and trans. *The Essential Haiku: Versions of Basho, Buson, and Issa.* Hopewell, N.J.: Ecco Press, 1994.

———, ed. *Poet's Choice: Poems for Everyday Life.* Hopewell, N.J.: Ecco Press, 1998.

———, ed. *Rock and Hawk: A Selection of Shorter Poems by Robinson Jeffers.* New York: Random House, 1987.

———, ed. *Tomas Tranströmer: Selected Poems, 1954–1986.* Translated by Robert Bly et al. New York: Ecco Press, 1987.

Hass, Robert, Jorie Graham, and Bill Henderson, eds. *The Pushcart Prize XII.* Wainscott, N.Y.: Pushcart Press, 1987.

Hass, Robert, and Stephen Mitchell, eds. *Into the Garden: A Wedding Anthology: Poetry and Prose on Love and Marriage.* New York: HarperCollins, 1993.

TRANSLATIONS: WORKS BY CZESLAW MILOSZ

The Collected Poems, 1931–1987. Translated by Robert Hass, Louis Iribarne, and Peter Scott. New York: Ecco Press, 1988.

Facing the River: New Poems. Translated by the author and Robert Hass. Hopewell, N.J.: Ecco Press, 1995.

Provinces. Translated by the author and Robert Hass. New York: Ecco Press, 1991.

Roadside Dog. Translated by the author and Robert Hass. New York: Farrar, Straus & Giroux, 1998.

The Separate Notebooks. Translated by Robert Hass and Robert Pinsky with the author and Renata Gorczynski. New York: Ecco Press, 1984.

Unattainable Earth. Translated by the author and Robert Hass. New York: Ecco Press, 1986.

CRITICAL AND BIOGRAPHICAL STUDIES

BOOKS

Contemporary Literary Criticism. Vol. 18. Detroit: Gale, 1981.

Dictionary of Literary Biography. Vol. 105: *American Poets Since World War II,* Second Series. Detroit: Gale, 1991.

Contemporary Poets. Chicago: St. James Press, 1991.

Contemporary Authors on CD. Detroit: Gale, 1991.

ARTICLES AND ESSAYS

Adams, Susan, and Joshua Levine. "Why Not a Sonnet?" *Forbes* 163, no. 10:344–348 (May 17, 1999).

Baker, David. "Romantic Melancholy, Romantic Excess." (Review of *Sun Under Wood.*) *Poetry* 170, no. 5:288–302 (August 1997).

Billington, James. "Writing for the Mind and the

Heart." *Civilization* 3, no. 1:91 (January/February 1996).

Bogen, Don. "A Student of Desire." *Nation,* December 11, 1989, pp. 722–723.

Bond, Bruce. "The Abundance of Lack: The Fullness of Desire in the Poetry of Robert Hass." *Kenyon Review* 12, no. 4:46–54 (fall 1990).

Clines, Francis X. "A Poet's Road Trip Along Main Street, U.S.A." *New York Times,* December 9, 1996, pp. A1, B8.

Davie, Donald. "A Clamor of Tongues." *New Republic,* March 16, 1992, pp. 34–37.

Davis, Dick. "Arguing in Unknown Quantities." *Times Literary Supplement,* March 15, 1985, pp. 293–295.

Davison, Peter. "The Laureate as Onlooker." (Review of *Sun Under Wood.*) *Atlantic Monthly,* March 1997, pp. 100–103.

Ford, Mark. "Reality Bites." (Review of *The Essential Haiku.*) *New Republic,* October 31, 1994, pp. 48–52.

Hirsch, Edward. "Praise." (Review of *Twentieth Century Pleasures.*) *Poetry,* March 1985, pp. 345–348.

Hofmann, Michael. "At the Center of Things." *New York Times Book Review,* April 27, 1997, p. 13.

Kizer, Carolyn. "Necessities of Life and Death." *New York Times Book Review,* November 12, 1989, p. 63.

Lea, Sydney, and Jay Parini. "An Interview with Robert Hass." *New England Review* 2, no. 2:295–314 (1979).

Libby, Anthony. "Criticism in the First Person." *New York Times Book Review,* March 3, 1985, p. 37.

Molesworth, Charles. "Some Recent American Poetry." *Ontario Review* 11:91–102 (fall/winter 1979–1980).

Pollock, Sarah. "Robert Hass." *Mother Jones,* March–April 1997, pp. 18–22.

Remnick, David. "A Conversation with Robert Hass." *Chicago Review* 32, no. 4:17–26 (spring 1981).

Schmidt, Elizabeth. "Ill Paid, Ill Defined and Nearly Irresistible." *New York Times Book Review,* December 17, 1995, p. 39.

Shapiro, Alan. " 'And There Are Always Melons': Some Thoughts on Robert Hass." *Chicago Review* 33, no. 3:84–90 (winter 1983).

Shillinger, Kurt. "New Laureate Wields Bully Pen for Poetry." *Christian Science Monitor,* October 12, 1995, p. 1.

Vendler, Helen. "Looking for Poetry in America." *New York Review of Books,* November 7, 1985, pp. 53–60.

Wagner, Linda. "Four Young Poets." *Ontario Review* 1:89–97 (fall 1974).

—MOLLY MCQUADE

Irving Howe

1920–1993

*B*EST KNOWN FOR *World of Our Fathers: The Journey of the Eastern European Jews to America and the Life They Found and Made* (1976), an encyclopedic study of New York's Lower East Side and the immigrant Jewish population that settled there in the late nineteenth century, Irving Howe was a man of letters in the best sense of that old-fashioned term. As an editor, he founded *Dissent* magazine in 1954 and was responsible for a handful of influential anthologies on Yiddish poetry and prose, American Jewish literature, and literary modernism. As a prolific book reviewer and critic, he wrote about literature and politics for such magazines as *Time, Partisan Review, Commentary,* and the *New York Times Book Review.* Perhaps most important of all, as a New York intellectual (a term he both defined and embodied) and a man on the left, he helped sharpen cultural debate during the second half of the twentieth century.

In the essay "The Lost Young Intellectual," written for *Commentary* in October 1946, when he was just launching his public career, the twenty-six-year-old Howe describes his vision of the representative marginal man this way: *"He is a victim of his own complexity of vision:* even the most harrowing of his feelings, the most intolerable aspects of his alienation, he must still examine with the same mordant irony he applies to everything else." Howe takes some pains to explain that the young Jewish intellectual being ex-

amined is a pastiche rather than an actual person, but few were fooled. His savviest readers always insisted that Howe was talking about himself—his subsequent writing would give eloquent testimony to his ongoing quarrel with the world. In personal terms, the conflict often manifested itself in an apparent split between political activism and literary contemplation, but one needs to look no further than *Politics and the Novel* (1957) to see, in fact, how fused were Howe's twin sensibilities. In less obvious ways the same thing is true whether his ostensible subject was the Yiddish culture on New York's Lower East Side, Thomas Hardy's heath or William Faulkner's Yoknapatawpha County, the prospects for democratic socialism in the United States, or the fate of contemporary literary criticism, there was an identifiable Howe thumbprint on every paragraph. Whatever topics happened to fall under his pen were rendered with equal measures of engagement and clarity. Few contemporary critics were tougher—or more eloquent—about the necessity of critical dissent within the larger folds of American culture.

THE LONELY YOUNG INTELLECTUAL

Howe's *A Margin of Hope: An Intellectual Autobiography* (1982) describes how it was that a generation of bright immigrant Jewish sons, attending the City College of New York (CCNY) during the late 1930s, changed the shape (and pedigree) of American intellectual life. Among Howe's CCNY classmates were such future public intellectuals as the sociologist Daniel Bell, the educational theorist Nathan Glazer, and the neoconservative spokesperson Irving Kristol. If the formal instruction offered in CCNY classrooms was often mediocre, the debates that raged in its alcoves eventually became the stuff of legend and numerous scholarly studies. In that time and that place, young communists pitted themselves against young socialists as the larger world lurched toward totalitarianism—first from the fascism then gathering steam in Nazi Germany and then from the Stalinism of Soviet Russia. In such heady times, it is hardly surprising that Howe was drawn to a cosmopolitanism that seemed the very antithesis of the parochialism and restraint he associated with growing up in the Bronx, New York.

Vivid memories of a dispossessed family's belongings scattered on the sidewalk turned Howe into a socialist at the tender age of fourteen, but it was the addition of avant-garde modernism that gave a mythic dimension to his left-leaning politics. In the depths of the Great Depression, Howe was hardly alone in feeling that capitalism had failed; the marvel is that he became a socialist and then a staunch anti-Stalinist, rather than a communist. Never one given to pretentious, overexplanations, he put the matter of his youthful politics this way: "They [the socialists] simply got to me first."

Irving Horenstein was born on June 11, 1920, to David and Nettie Goldman Horenstein. David Horenstein ran a grocery store, then worked as a peddler and later as a presser in a dress factory. Nettie also worked in the dress trade as a machine operator. As was customary at the time, political radicals often adopted "party names"; the young Irving Horenstein went through a series of them until he legally changed his name to Irving Howe

in 1946, the same year that he was publicly announcing himself as an alienated young intellectual. When Howe was ten years old, his father's grocery store failed and the family was forced to move downward in the pecking order of Bronx society. Howe never entirely forgot the trauma. An insistence on social justice and radical economic reform remained a vital part of his career, however he much later modified his early Marxism and so watered down his socialism that it often seemed to be based on moral rectitude rather than on economic theory.

In addition, Howe was destined to be an intellectual of a rather special sort: unflinchingly honest, given to testing ideas against the gritty surface of experience, and, perhaps most of all, conflicted. The wide net of his loyalties—to the idea of family, if not always to its grating reality; to a radical politics that could be as burdensome as bracing; to a life of the mind often more European in style and content than American; to literature that liberated the human spirit; and to the beauty and power of the word—did not, indeed could not, come without enormous costs. Howe outlined some of them in "The Lonely Young Intellectual," but he continued to ruminate about his ambiguous status as a Jewish immigrant son in books such as *World of Our Fathers* and *A Margin of Hope*—the first, a barely covert effort to extend a loving hand to his father, and the second, an intensely personal effort to assess his place in the political-cultural struggles that surrounded him.

In his 1946 essay, however, Howe worked mightily to keep the autobiographical inclination of his essay at arm's length, often writing paragraphs that read like sociology rather than personal statement. As with many others of his generation, he eschewed the word "I" (now a required staple of autobiographical tell-all books), preferring to couch his observations in a collective "we." But when he describes fathers who literally work themselves to death so their sons can attend college or when he describes a "second friend"—a leader of a small radical group—whose father berates him for wasting his time ("All right, go change the world, but can you make a living from it?"), one suspects that Howe himself is the source of both portraits. True enough, the ambition of immigrant fathers was encapsulated in the wish, often little more than a desperate hope, that "My son shouldn't have to work in a shop," and Howe's father was hardly the only case of somebody worrying about such practical matters as how to butter one's bagel, but Howe clearly felt the tensions more deeply than most. Exaggerate the outlines of the immigrant Jewish family—with its contradictory fears and ambitions, its yearning to be fully American, balanced against its deep loyalties to an Old World past—and the result is a string of Jewish mother–terrified son jokes that stretches from the mean immigrant streets to the Borscht Belt (Catskill Mountain resorts) comics and to such contemporary examples as the author Philip Roth's character Alexander Portnoy or nearly any film comedy by the director and actor Woody Allen. But Howe was not especially interested in handing anybody a laugh—not in 1946 and not in the decades that followed. He always found it difficult to be a Jew and just as difficult not to be one, and especially difficult to make jokes about the difficulty. As he put it in "The Lost Young Intellectual," with a seriousness only slightly tempered by a taste for irony he could never entirely shake:

> He [the mythical young Jewish intellectual] cannot surrender himself to events or moods or people, for he is always searching for meanings and examining himself while he acts. And this self-examination, this split into participant and observer—in which he watches his own personality as if it belonged to someone else—is the core of his lack of spontaneity. For spontaneity requires a total reaction, and that the Jewish intellectual cannot find.

One possibility is that Howe is being entirely too hard on himself (a characteristic that would only deepen in the following decades); another is that his exercise in the mythos of alienation is a part—albeit a significant part—of the young Jewish intellectual's psychological profile rather than the whole story. Indeed, was the young Jewish intellectual, in truth, really as isolated, riddled with angst, neurotic, and just plain grim as Howe's essay suggests? Or were there unguarded moments when he sat at his father's table without sulking and without shame, when a Sabbath meal contained moments that did not fit his tidy script, when talk at the corner candy store fixed on the Dodgers rather than on Marxist dialectics?

Howe may be protesting a bit too much when he insists (with italics no less) that the lost young intellectual *"has inherited the agony of his people; its joy he knows only second-hand."* Perhaps it is fairer to say that traditional Jewish beliefs and practices had little place in Howe's upbringing. He could never put much credence in the well-meaning advice put forth by those who felt that every dilemma—including the ones troubling his lost young intellectual—has its "solution." Indeed, the very definition of an authentic "dilemma" is that it is not available to palliatives such as Zionism or a return to traditional religious practice, Jewish education, or a reconstruction of the Jewish community. Such options may be the official raison d'être of Jewish organizations, but, for Howe, the sermons—whether delivered from the pulpit or at the podium—fell on deaf ears. If anything, their predictable, often glib assessments only deepened Howe's commitment to a politics of universalism and to an unfettered life of the mind.

Howe's extended portrait of tortured young intellectuals, torn between an insular Jewish environment more smothering than protective and a larger world hostile to everything they held dear, so blends the heroic and antiheroic, the grandiose and the banal, that one can never be sure if his alienated constituency is crowing or whining. Will their doting, anxious parents ever see them as the independent beings they presumably yearn to be? Will society at large recognize their incipient greatness? In a 1982 essay in *Commentary,* "Socialism and Its Irresponsibilities: The Case of Irving Howe," the neoconservative critic Midge Decter throws cold water on Howe's romantic mythmaking, especially since Howe remained a man of the left long after many other young Jewish intellectuals had moved toward the right:

> Together they roamed the neighborhoods, and from there the city, distributing leaflets, arguing till the wee hours over cups of coffee in cafeterias, going to foreign films on 42nd Street (how much of the history of contemporary intellectual life is bound to memories of *Grand Illusion* and *Alexander Nevsky* on 42nd Street?), preaching Marxism and revolution at street corners, and no doubt—though [Howe] is elegantly discreet about this—fumbling around with the female comrades.

No doubt Howe's reply would be to remind Decter that each age has its own burdens and its own ways of dealing with them. Thus, consciousness turned out to be all—although what Howe's mythic intellectual is ultimately conscious of is how isolated, alienated, and hopeless is his situation. Decter would call this self-pitying of the first order; and there are reasons to believe that even Howe might agree. "The Lost Young Intellectual," Howe's first essay to appear in a magazine of wide circulation and influence, has not been included in any of his subsequent collections, and careful readers of *World of Our Fathers* will note, first, that selected paragraphs from "The Lost Young Intellectual" have been elbowed into the text without calling attention to the fact that the words are from Howe himself.

Still, the sheer ambition and unflinching honesty of "The Lost Young Intellectual" makes the essay important—not only because it represents, in effect, Howe's intellectual debut (previous review articles in *Tomorrow* and Dwight Macdonald's *Politics* were more akin to warm-ups than a sustained performance), but also because it put the conflicts and sensibilities of an entire gener-

ation on the map. To his credit, Howe soon moved beyond the rhetoric of alienation (he was soon writing copy for *Time* magazine and, in effect, put the kibosh on the notion that American culture had no time or place for the likes of him) and into a series of studies on literary modernism that established his reputation as one of America's savviest critics.

ENTERING A WIDER STAGE

The collapse of *Politics,* Dwight Macdonald's magazine, in 1949, the bitter debates that followed the decision to honor Ezra Pound with the Bollingen Prize that same year, and the publication by Howe of *Sherwood Anderson: A Biographical and Critical Study* in 1951 and *William Faulkner: A Critical Study* in 1952, may seem to be entirely unrelated events, but, taken together, they indicate certain cultural trends and certain delicate shifts in position and emphasis that mark a difference between the Howe who thought of himself as lost, marginal, and young in 1946 and the Howe whose literary criticism aimed for (and received) national attention a short six years later.

One way of explaining the difference is to say the obvious, namely, that Howe was a young man in a hurry (sometimes this was noted with admiration, sometimes in wry amusement, and sometimes with a distinctly anti-Semitic spin); another explanation is to recognize that F. Scott Fitzgerald's test of intelligence ("the ability to hold two contradictory ideas in one's head at the same time") applies to Howe more deeply and over a longer span of time than it ever did to Fitzgerald. Still, even at the age of seventy, Howe felt obliged to defend the curious twists and turns of his long career at the writing desk. He admitted that *Selected Writings, 1950–1990* (1990) "may raise a question in the minds of some readers: What are we to make of a writer who divides his time and energy among several interests rather than confining himself to one? How does it affect a writer's work if he shuttles between literary and cultural criticism, on the one hand, and political commitment on the other?" The truth is that Howe's twin interests in literature and politics had been there all along; moreover, the contemplative pleasures of literature provided a welcome respite for the fractious business of polemical debate. But, in the final analysis, Howe saw precious little difference between the literature that interested him and the moral-political vision of what his 1963 collection called "a world more attractive." But those who live and die by "categories" were not easily convinced; Howe still seemed to be an odd duck. Was he an activist or a literary essayist? Was he a radical formed by Karl Marx and Leon Trotsky or an English professor formed by the classical writers of what the English literary critic F. R. Leavis grandly pronounced in 1948 as the "Great Tradition"?

During the Spanish Civil War, Howe's utopian idealism, like that of George Orwell, came in for rude shocks and radical reassessment. Both writers saw the nightmare of our century against a backdrop of catastrophe: "Nothing else," Howe asserts somberly in *A Margin of Hope,* "reveals so graphically the tragic character of those years than that the yearning for some better world should repeatedly end in muck, foul play, murder." If history has taught us anything, it is to distrust those with a programmatic reading of "history"—whether it comes as garden variety utopianism or with a full head of ideological steam.

Small wonder, then, that the New York intellectuals themselves had cause to reassess what the old battles meant—some by way of setting the record straight, for example Lionel Abel's *The Intellectual Follies* (1984), and others by way of justifying their drift toward neoconservatism, such as William Barrett's *The Truants* (1982). The magazines around which writers cluster are one way to gauge the changes in the mental landscape. For what are intellectual quarterlies if not the shapers of "taste"—whether it is the *Hudson Review, New York Review of Books, Salmagundi,* or *Raritan*? And from this perspective, the gradual decline of *Partisan Review* as the preeminent vehicle for the New York intellectuals and the concomitant rise of *Commentary* (from 1960, under the editorship of Norman Podhoretz) puts the issue of where New York intellectuals stand in bold relief. Those who embraced, or at least accommodated themselves to, the affluence and the conformity of the 1950s (most notably, the influential Columbia University professor and critic Lionel Trilling) drew sharp rebukes from the likes of Howe and Norman Mailer. At stake was nothing less than dissent itself, and, as such, Howe felt compelled to start a journal of his own in 1954, to name it *Dissent,* and to write "The Age of Conformity," an essay that many thought was an attack on Trilling's accommodation with post–World War II affluence.

But if the days of what Trilling called "the adversary culture" were numbered, they returned—with something of a vengeance—during the countercultural, antiwar protests of the late 1960s and early 1970s. This time, however, Howe sharply differed from those on the New Left bent on overturning what they called "the Establishment." Howe's quarrel with them centered around what he regarded as their insufficient grasp of all that an older generation of radicals had achieved, coupled with what he regarded as a dangerous attraction to totalitarianism. In a series of essays and debates, Howe came off as a moral scold to a younger generation hardly of a mind to listen. He was saddened by the personal attacks hurled his way, but they did not deter him. After all, Howe had been a political infighter for more than four decades, and his skills as a fearsome debater and rapier-sharp writer had been honed to perfection. Others were simply made uncomfortable by the swipes Howe often took against those whose "crime" seemed to be that they were of a younger generation, one unfortified by immigrant milk:

> What, for "emancipated" people, is the surviving role of moral imperatives, or at least moral recommendations? Do these retain for us a shred of sanctity or at least of cohesive value? . . . Are we still to give credit to the idea, one of the few meeting points between traditional Christianity and modern Freudianism, that there occurs and must occur a deep-seated clash between instinct and civilization, or can we now, with a great sigh of collective relief, dismiss this as still another hang-up, perhaps the supreme hang-up, of Western civilization?

That these words from "The Age of Conformity" were written when Howe found himself under relentless attack by the New Left, is true enough, but even if one makes allowance for those tensions that the counterculture brought to a boil, the fact remains that Howe always favored social action over individualist excess. As he put it, in a memoir about his earliest encounters with American literature, "the idea of an individual covenant with God, each man responsible for his own salvation; the claim that each man is captain of his soul . . . the notion that you not only have one but more than one chance in life, which constitutes the American version of grace; and the belief that you rise or fall in accord with your own merits rather than the will of alien despots—these residues of Emersonianism seemed not only strange but sometimes even a version of that brutality which our parents had warned was intrinsic to Gentile life." By contrast, what rang true, then and now, were the inevitable entanglements of history; the anchoring character of social reality, which the best of literature reflected and the best of politics meant to change; the abiding force, for good or ill, of one's family; and a sense of commandment usually transmogrified into aspects of moral idealism.

Whatever else may be said of the New York Jews who scratched their way through City College in the mid-1930s and, to their enormous surprise, ended up holding down jobs as academics and wielders of considerable intellectual power, they thought of themselves as engaged in the defining cultural-political battles of the modern period: the totalitarian threat of Stalin as well as Hitler; the moral bankruptcy of capitalism and the large promises of socialism; the explosion of cultural modernism in all its dizzying variety of complicated forms; and, perhaps most of all, the exhilaration of argument in essays that were simultaneously polemical, brilliant, and, in a new sense of the term, "literary."

The art critic Harold Rosenberg once argued that "for two thousand years the main energies of Jewish communities in various parts of the world have gone into the mass production of intellectuals" (quoted in *World of Our Fathers*). Those usually numbered in this admittedly loose group include Philip Rahv, Meyer Schapiro, Sidney Hook, Daniel Bell, Delmore Schwartz, Lionel Trilling, Alfred Kazin, and Irving Howe—each, in his fashion, a New York Jew and an intellectual who ranged widely among cultural matters. They became specialists in being nonspecialists. In addition, there were powerful minds and fiercely polemical writers who were not Jewish at all: Mary McCarthy, Dwight Macdonald, and, perhaps most spectacularly, Edmund Wilson.

Still, with all that separated them and all that broke out in periodic spats, those writers and critics who identified themselves with the *Partisan Review* knew full well what they were not. They were not, for example, members of the Ivy League establishment, nor were they ever likely to be—although that, too, came to pass as their prestige and power reached its crest in the 1950s. Nor were they numbered among the Southern Agrarians who huddled at Vanderbilt University and perfected the New Criticism that was ultimately to change the way that literature was taught in American colleges and universities—although here, too (and despite the considerable cultural and political differences), they found themselves making common cause with the likes of John Crowe Ransom and Allen Tate and found their articles appearing in journals of the New Criticism such as the *Kenyon Review* and *Southern Review*. Indeed, as Marian Janssen's estimable 1989 history of the *Kenyon Review* points out:

> The New York intellectuals and the New Critics shared a deep concern for literature as literature and a belief in the value and necessity of literary criticism. This formed a strong if uneasy bond between them, a measure of agreement often obscured by the disproportionate attention paid to their disagreements and differences. The antipathies that existed were mainly political and rather one-sided to boot: the New York intellectuals found grave fault with the alleged conservatism of the New Critics; most of the time, the New Critics could not care less about the political beliefs of the New Yorkers. In general, there was more that drew these two groups together than kept them apart. The common concern for literature proved such a firm bond that when the "Protofascists" actually met the "Communists," they recognized "with almost ludicrous rapidity that they were very close together indeed in literary matters and felt alike on an astonishing number of social issues."

In this regard, Howe provides an instructive example. Whatever his politics, he long held the now-unfashionable view that critical reading required little more than a focused concentration and a sharpened pencil. Others in the bad, old days were less sanguine, not because Howe eschewed "theory" (academia's current obsession), but because he sprang from immigrant stock. And what the raised eyebrows and whispers of the 1940s came down to was this: Could such a person be trusted to teach and to write about American literature?

HOWE, FAULKNER, AND THE SOUTH

Still, there must have been a sense that some southern critics had squatter's rights to Faulkner, while northern critics like Howe had to learn about grits in the library stacks. Howe grew up among people who drank celery tonic, not Dr. Pepper, and while there certainly must have been other Irvings in his neighborhood, there probably was not a single Joe Bob. In short, there must have been some hangers-on in Nashville, Tennessee, who regarded Howe as something of a literary carpetbagger and his critical study of William Faulkner as somewhat dubious.

Granted, none of this should matter, and it did not for the best of the New York intellectuals and for the most impressive of the New Critics. Both groups agreed wholeheartedly with T. S. Eliot's position that all a critic really needs is "intelligence." Howe might miss a southern nuance here, a whiff of verbena there, but even his most grudging critics would admit that he was a perceptive reader and a persuasive writer. If the central question for southern apologist writers was, "How could God allow us to lose the war?," and if the agony that modernist southern writers struggled with was, "Why do you hate the South?," Howe had been pondering similar questions—albeit, with respect to Jewish history—all his life.

Not surprisingly, then, the Faulkner who most interested Howe was the one who shared his passion for elegy, for missions of retrieval and rescue. For what are novels such as *The Sound and the Fury* or *Absalom, Absalom!* if not exercises in lamentation, written at the moment when the residue of a culture faced, for better or worse, extinction? And, for that matter, what is Eliot's *The Waste Land,* literary modernism's quintessential epic, but an extended lament for the redemptive rhythms that haunt industrial societies in the ambivalent space between "memory and desire"?

The energy Howe plowed into ambitious, and pointedly Jewish American, projects such as *World of Our Fathers* was not unlike that which he expended on behalf of Faulkner in *William Faulkner: A Critical Study* (1952) or what he called the "idea of the modern." Here again Howe found himself attracted—or perhaps, more correctly, chosen—by subjects he came to late. It was a tendency that he shared with other New York Jewish intellectuals, and that he explains this way:

> The great battles for Joyce, Proust, and Eliot had been fought in the twenties and mostly won; now, while clashes with entrenched philistinism might still occur, these were mostly mopping-up operations. The New York intellectuals came toward the end of the modernist experience, just as they came at what yet have to be judged the end of the radical experience, and as they certainly came at the end of the immigrant Jewish experience. One quick way of describing their situation, a cause of both their feverish brilliance and recurrent instability, is to say that *they came late.*

No one has described the "style"—now fixed in the collective consciousness as the very signature of the New York intellectuals—better than Howe himself. Speculative, assertive, freewheeling—its rhythms not only came naturally to those who had read their way through the public libraries, but they also seemed a perfect vehicle for tweaking the noses of stuffy, Ivy League types who had not. After all, the generation Howe describes so vividly in pieces such as "The New York Intellectuals" and "Strangers" (collected in *Selected Writings*) argued about everything (Marx, Russian novels, Walt Whitman, the Brooklyn Dodgers, Hollywood films) around kitchen tables and at corner candy stores. Small wonder that their prose struck the early readers of *Partisan Review* as brilliant, dazzling, and altogether a new note in American criticism. As Howe characterizes the phenomenon in "The New York Intellectuals":

> The kind of essay they wrote was likely to be wide-ranging in reference, melding notions about literature and politics, sometimes announcing itself as a study of a writer or literary group but usually taut with a pressure to "go beyond" its subject, toward some encompassing moral or social observation. It is a kind of writing highly self-conscious in mode, with an unashamed vibration of bravura. Nervous, strewn with knotty or flashy phrases, impatient with transitions and other concessions to dullness, calling attention to itself as a form or at least an outcry, fond of rapid twists, taking pleasure in dispute, dialectic, dazzle—such at its best or most noticeable, was the essay cultivated by the New York writers. Until recently its strategy of exposition was likely to be impersonal (the writer did not speak much as an "I") but its tone and bearing were likely to be intensely personal (the audience was to be made aware that the aim of the piece was not Judiciousness, but, rather, a strong impress of attitude, a blow of novelty, a wrenching of accepted opinion, sometimes a mere indulgence of vanity).

Howe, unlike many of his New York contemporaries, soon developed a manner of his own, one that eschewed buzz words such as "alienation" in favor of paragraphs seared free of fat and rigorously tested against plain, human sense. Others could not so easily escape the fate of first becoming an affectation and then hardening into a "fashion." In its most predictable incarnations those who cracked their heads trying to outdazzle the likes of Philip Rahv, Delmore Schwartz, or Isaac Rosenfeld, ended as ever-paler carbon copies. But for the best of the bunch—and here Howe is a case study in powers that grew more refined and more subtle, even as they retained a kinship with the sheer exuberance of earlier times and those places—the beat has continued to enliven public discourse and sharpen the terms of our debate.

WORLD OF OUR FATHERS

For Howe, the tension between advocacy and disinterested scholarship reached its zenith with *World of Our Fathers,* a study that more than justified his belief that "a sense of natural piety toward one's origins can live side by side with a spirit of critical detachment." His project was nothing less than to capture the immigrant Jewish world in all its various manifestations: tenement squalor and Yiddish newspapers, sweatshops and labor unions, Yiddish theater and the Yiddish language, synagogues and settlement houses. At the same time, however, Howe's ambitious project was also a species of autobiography, a way of coming to grips with the father he battled against and so often disappointed. The result is arguably the most balanced, most reliable, and certainly the most humanely rendered account of the world that immigrant Jews found and made on New York's Lower East Side, but it is also a quintessentially American story.

Americans are a restless people. Their collective history seems always to begin somewhere else, with the dream of an America that will collapse the distance between idealistic visions and quotidian reality. Most arrive as immigrants, as strangers in a strange land, only to find their wanderings slowly metamorphosed into native forms. To cross an ocean is, in effect, to end the journeys of one generation and simultaneously begin those of another. Fathers yearn for the stability promised at dockside; their sons seek out the dizzying possibilities of the New World. In short, immigrant parents tend to produce migratory sons.

World of Our Fathers is the mythos seen in sharp relief. But it is also a drama fashioned from gritty, human particulars, from the internecine warfare and familial anguish of people caught within the sweep of history. Social scientists often race past such tensions as they heap fact upon dry fact. By contrast, Howe understands that the grip of ideas has a context in the heart as well as the brain, and that the whirligig of social forces comes to individual men and women wearing very human faces. The result is a book that tells not only "the story of those east European Jews who, for several decades starting in the 1880's, undertook a massive migration to the United States" but that also suggests something about the inevitable conflicts between ethnicity and acculturation. The focus of *World of Our Fathers* may be the culture that Yiddish-speaking fathers established on New York's Lower East Side, but it is also bordered at one extreme by the hostility of an American past and at the other by the homogeneity of an American present.

The year 1881 had an impact on modern Jewish history analogous to that of the destruction of the Temple in Jerusalem in 70 A.D. or the expulsion of Jews from Spain in 1492. With the assassination of the Russian tsar Alexander II on March 1, 1881, it was no longer possible for east European Jewry to sustain itself on the glimmers of liberality that had characterized his reign. Alexander II may not have embodied Jewish fears at their worst, but the pogroms that initiated his reign were evidence enough that Russian "needs" would never be compatible with *Yiddishkeit* (roughly translated as Jewish culture). Jewish folk wisdom could hardly have been more correct. In 1880 there were approximately 80,000 Jews in New York City; by 1910 the number had mushroomed to 1,100,000. Howe's encyclopedic study brushes in the fine strokes of their adjustment, not only to a New World, but also to the modernity they discovered there. If such stories can be said to have definable beginnings, the rippling effect set in motion on March 1, 1881, deserves that special remembering associated with Jewish history.

By contrast, the year 1953 was a beginning of a very different sort, for in that year Howe received a note from the Yiddish poet Eliezer Greenberg proposing that they become "partners." Greenberg had seen a piece about Sholom Aleichem titled "Sholom Aleichem: Voice of Our Past" that Howe published in the pages of *Partisan Review* and was obviously impressed. No doubt the destruction of European Jewry had something to do with Howe's decision to take up Greenberg's offer, but it also could be argued that

World of Our Fathers is the culmination of Howe's efforts to reclaim at least a portion of the joy he felt had eluded his generation. Howe's work with Greenberg in compiling anthologies began in the act of "translation," in the research that identified the best writing produced by Yiddish culture and then introduced it to a wider audience. In this sense, the impulse to compile such anthologies is necessarily a popularizing one, and, as such, the collections of Yiddish poetry, stories, and essays edited by Howe and Greenberg made Yiddish studies possible for those whose knowledge of the language was minimal or nonexistent.

At the same time, however, the Howe-Greenberg anthologies have an even greater importance as a necessary corrective, for all too often Yiddish literature has been the victim of its well-meaning friends, including those who would sentimentalize the shtetl (Jewish town), make extravagant claims for its literature, or simply confuse special pleading with critical judgment. As Howe pointed out in his piece on Aleichem, here was a writer whose "genius was acknowledged, but his importance skimped." Howe's essay did much to create a climate in which readers could respond to Aleichem's work with a new attention to his "moral poise and his invulnerability to ideological fashions." Put another way, the anthologies that Howe and Greenberg cobbled together struck exactly the right balance between the virtues of a coherent worldview and the tremendous costs that such a Jewish parochialism exacted. What Howe and Greenberg understood, as seen in this text from *World of Our Fathers,* was nothing more nor less than history itself:

> The east European Jews [had] a conscious sense of being at a distance from history, from history as such and history as a conception of the Western world. Living in an almost timeless proximity with the mythical past and the redeeming future . . . the Jews could not help feeling that history was a little ridiculous; a trifling, though often troublesome trifling, of the frivolous gentile era. . . . They enjoyed, as it were, a perspective from the social rear.

By maintaining a delicate balance between the integrity that Yiddish culture deserves and that wider perspective demanded by responsible scholarship, the world of east European Jewry began to emerge both steady and whole.

The virtue of Howe's balanced portrait of east European villages is not because it looms large in *World of Our Fathers* (indeed, only a scant twenty pages are devoted to "origins"), but because many of the tendencies to falsify history have attached themselves to selective "memories" of the Lower East Side. Howe has little patience with characterizations of an idyllic life that no Old World Jews, in fact, ever lived. As he puts it, conditions in the shtetl were "rarely picturesque," adding that abject poverty and political oppression seldom are. Much the same thing can be said about the squalor of the Lower East Side, with its crowded tenements, its collective fear of tuberculosis (known as the "tailors" disease), and, of course, its nearly overpowering smells:

> Perhaps worst was the assault of smells: the odors of human waste only intermittently carried away from back-yard privies by a careless sanitation department, the stench of fish and meat starting to rot on pushcarts, the foulness of neglected sewers and gutters. Life was abrasive, clamorous. Even if the immigrants had arrived with impeccable sanitary habits, they could not have won the battle against dirt and decay.

These are the harsher truths that such sanitized portrayals of Jewish life as the Broadway musical *Fiddler on the Roof* and the film *Hester Street* consciously leave out.

At the same time, however, one can also err on the side of muckraking exposé. The slums of the Lower East Side housed more than a collection of shabby immigrants exploited in sweatshops and befuddled by an America they could not quite understand. They were also a locus for *Yiddish-keit,* a term Howe describes as

> that phase of Jewish history during the past two centuries which is marked by the prevalence of Yiddish as the language of the east European Jews and by the growth among them of a culture resting mainly on that language. The culture of *Yiddishkeit* is no longer strictly that of traditional Orthodoxy, yet it retains strong ties to the religious past. It takes on an increasingly secular character yet it is by no means confined to the secularist elements among Yiddish-speaking Jews. It refers to a way of life, a shared experience, which goes beyond opinion or ideology.

Howe writes about *Yiddishkeit* with an eloquence and an intensity that borders on the elegiac, for this was a world that could not compete with the English language of America's majority culture, much less survive unscathed against the dizzying possibilities of mobility and success offered by the American Dream. Indeed, the world Howe recaptures may have passed its high point when Howe was still wearing short pants.

Nonetheless, the sheer range of Howe's concerns—whether it be the development of the union movement or the Yiddish press or the impact of "borders" on family life—is staggering. Among the things that Howe's study proved is that the scholarly imagination need not wear the robes of pedantry, nor must the heart shrivel if the mind is engaged. Moreover, Howe's translation of *Yiddishkeit* into English reminds us, again and again, that writing matters, that it is still worth the effort and agony required to turn thought into well-chosen words:

> As immigrants, they could be embarrassed by their failure with English, their awkwardness with American friends, and the incongruities they might sense between the kind of personal relations they took for granted and the prevailing romantic ethos of the new world, especially when it was declared by their children. But toward the primary, root emotions of their life—toward the joy of bringing children into the world, the gratification of seeing them securely married, the grief of persecution, the despair of death—they felt no embarrassment. . . . They were not controlled by the visions of the Gentlemen, the Protestant, the Intellectual. Mostly their lives consisted of long stretches of denial and once in a while an outburst. If they laughed, it was with sardonic glee; if they cried, it was to the heavens. Letting loose their grief was, in [Michael] Gold's wonderful phrase, a way to "unpack their hearts."

Howe's special genius with regard to bringing the essential rhythms and complexities of Yiddish culture to American readers has always been an ability to absorb the very best that New York City has to offer. In this sense, his contribution is less a matter of pioneering research than it is of crystallizing great heaps of material into a coherent book, one with equal measures of large vision and critical acumen. This is true of Howe's work in general (it would apply to, say, his writings on socialism as well as to his various treatises on literary modernism), but in the case of *World of Our Fathers,* the job of sifting must have been enormous. One would be hard-pressed to think of sources, either primary or secondary, that he missed. But it is Howe as filter, as the mediator between intellectual process and *dos folk* ("the people"), that makes the difference. Good sense triumphs as it seldom does in weighty tomes, for Howe not only has the uncanny ability to frame his discussions with the right questions but also how to respond to them with the full measure of his own humanity:

> Was the Atlantic crossing really as dreadful as memoirists and legend have made it out to be? Was the food as rotten, the treatment as harsh, the steerage as sickening? One thing seems certain: to have asked such questions of a representative portion of Jews who came to America between 1881 and 1914 would have elicited stares of disbelief, suspicions as to motive, perhaps worse. The imagery of the journey as ordeal was deeply imprinted in the Jew-

ish folk mind—admittedly, a mind with a rich training in the imagery of ordeal. Of the hundreds of published and unpublished accounts Jewish immigrants have left us, the overwhelming bulk can still communicate a shudder of dismay when they recall the journey by sea and the disembarkation at Castle Garden or Ellis Island. Only a historian sophisticated to the point of foolishness would dismiss such accounts as mere tokens of folk bewilderment before the presence of technology, or of psychic disorientation following uprooting, journey, and resettlement.

Indeed, some questions are a matter of understanding history as an all-too-human conflict, as crossed purposes and messy, intersecting lines. Hindsight requires that one walk a delicate line between the arguments that reduce genuine passions to the level of petty squabble and those that serve up pat solutions or easy judgments across the divide of history itself. Nothing illustrates this vexing problem more than the deeply ambivalent relationship between the east European Jews crowded into the Lower East Side and their wealthier, more Americanized German counterparts:

How to educate immigrants in both the English language and American customs became an issue that agitated the East Side for decades. A clean, ruthless sweep of everything they had brought with them? A last-ditch resistance to each and every new influence they now encountered? . . . By the turn of the century, the tensions between the established German Jews and the insecure east European Jews had become severe, indeed, rather nasty—a glib condescension against a rasping sarcasm. The Germans found it hard to understand what could better serve their ill-mannered cousins than rapid lessons in civics, English, and the uses of soap. But even as they seemed maddeningly smug to the east Europeans, they were bound to them by ties they might have found hard to explain yet rarely wished to deny. A struggle ensued, sometimes fraternal, sometimes fractious, about the best ways to help the hordes of east Europeans find a place in the new world.

Under the humane directorship of David Blaustein, the Education Alliance, founded in 1889,

represented a kind of "answer" in compromise, one that substituted service for polemics. Memoirs of this organization, which was located in a five-story building on East Broadway and Jefferson Street, differ sharply, but Howe is probably closest to the truth when he suggests that the German Jews felt a need to wipe the noses of Lower East Side brats and that, quite naturally, east European Jews would resent the intrusion: "Out of such friction came a modest portion of progress."

Irony lies at the very core of what made *Yiddishkeit* possible, and then impossible. No aspect of Lower East Side culture illustrates the phenomenon more clearly than the Yiddish press. Howe describes the newspaper *Jewish Daily Forward* as a "large enclosing mirror," one which "replicated the whole of the world of Yiddish—its best, its worst, its most ingrown, its most outgoing, its soaring idealism, its crass materialism, everything." In Abraham Cahan, its extraordinary editor, one can feel the fullest expression of what Howe calls "the overarching paradox of Yiddish culture in America: that the sooner it began to realize its visions, the sooner it would destroy them." As Cahan imagined it, his task was "simultaneously to educate them [the immigrant masses] in Yiddish culture and tear them away from it in behalf of American fulfillment." Cahan's instincts were correct, but it is one of *Yiddishkeit*'s continuing realities that the education program should have taken so long and should have generated so much of its own distinctive culture in the process. Evidently the ironies of history can cut in both directions. That which cannot be must be; that which must be cannot be.

The story of *Yiddishkeit* can only be retold; the surfaces and textures of the life itself cannot be recaptured, much less remade. Howe surely knew this, even as he inched his large, unwieldy manuscript forward. He felt it important that successive generations not glamorize poverty, suffering, or deprivation as if those things alone make for rich experiences. Rather, it was, for him, the ethical considerations, the code of *menschlichkeit* (ideals over self), which blossomed despite, or because of, such conditions that merit consideration. Nostalgia merely luxuriates in the warm baths of its own falsification. *World of Our Fathers* reminds us that history is made of richer, sterner stuff.

MAN OF LETTERS AS MORAL CONSCIENCE

Howe retains a position as moral conscience almost unparalleled in contemporary letters. Granted, there are those who find his hectoring insufferable. Sometimes, as is the case with Philip Roth, bruised feelings about a Howe essay account for the impulse to turn him into Milton Appel, the pornographer of his novel *The Anatomy Lesson* (1983) and to have Nathan Zuckerman, his alter ego, resident ventriloquist, and literary hit man, imagine the sweet revenge an article titled "Right and Rigid in Every Decade" might wreak. However, literature, for Howe, has always been too important, too serious, in the best sense of the word, to be left to pedants, symbolmongers, or thin-skinned contemporary writers. One could sense intimations of this no-nonsense posture from the beginning. Commenting in *William Faulkner* on the character Quentin Compson's visit to the watchmaker in Faulkner's *The Sound and the Fury,* Howe suggests that the scene is flawed because it "contains almost nothing but symbolism" and, moreover, that critics do Faulkner, and literature itself, a disservice by overly ingenious efforts to turn a defect into a virtue:

> More could be said about Faulkner's use of symbols; it may be better to say that they are often a mare's nest for critics. The contemporary eagerness to interpret works of literature as symbolic patterns is often due to a fear or distaste of direct experience—sometimes, of direct literary experience. It is supposed that a symbol is always deeper and more profound than the object or condition it symbolizes, hence the kind of readings we have recently had, in which virtually every noun in *The Sound and the Fury* is elevated to symbolic significance.... Symbolic patterns certainly appear in the novel, and important ones; but their importance depends on the primary presence of represented objects and people.

Howe was thirty-two years old when he wrote those lines, but they show a sophistication—yea, a wisdom—far beyond his years. It is not merely that Howe was part of an intellectual milieu that gave overly clever close readings the fish eye or that he brought a high regard for the "direct experience" that symbol hunters backed away from, but that he simply had a better, richer feel for the way literary textures work. There are times, he was fond of pointing out, when a kitchen pan is simply a pan; and what we need pay attention to is not its symbolism (Freudian or otherwise), but rather to what is, or is not, being cooked. People need to eat, and pans are one of the ways they accomplish this. Moreover, the kind of pan it actually is reveals far more about the social landscape—with its class structure, subtle family codes, and "history"—than empty literary talk.

To set up shop as a literary critic did not strike Howe as akin to becoming a brain surgeon. One was neither examined by a board nor required to hang out a shingle. Critics simply declared that they were critics, and if enough people were persuaded, they were. As he put it in *A Margin of Hope,* becoming a writer—a real writer—was quite another matter. That would take time (he figured, in the bravado of the young, at least several decades), but to make one's way as a critic, that would be, comparatively speaking, a snap: "All you needed to be called a literary critic, it seemed, was a determination to read with charged attention and a pencil in the clutch of your fingers." In fairness, Howe was part of a generation not given to methodology, much less to the current infatuation with literary theory. What mattered to him was the shape and ring of sentences out to capture the elusive character of a piece of writing. When he took the measure of Faulkner's greatness, he used the standard set by writers such as George Eliot, Stendhal, or Fyodor Dostoyevsky: "Where Faulkner disappoints, whether in whole books or in parts of them, it is usually through a failure of intellect." Faulkner—despite his spectacular achievements in novels such as *The Sound and the Fury* (and especially in the Benjy section, which Howe reckoned as the equal of any piece of experimental writing done anywhere), *As I Lay Dying, Absalom, Absalom!,* or *Light in August*—remained limited by all that delimits modern American writing:

> It is in this department of the novel [that is, an ability to handle general ideas with a dramatic cogency equal to his ability in rendering images of conduct], as important in its way as the delineation of character and the heightening of drama, that so many gifted American novelists conspicuously fail, particularly those "natural talents" of Faulkner's generation who are unstained by the imprint of training or tradition. Their failure is a failure in the explicit, in precise statement and intellectual coherence.

Only Hawthorne and Melville, the great novelists of the American Renaissance, escaped such reservations; by contrast, their twentieth-century American counterparts usually settled for Howe's tempered judgment and guarded praise.

At the same time, however, Howe did not quite number himself among those critics who first championed the cause of difficult modernist texts (for example, *The Waste Land, Ulysses, The Sound and the Fury*) and then made them the benchmarks against which undergraduate English majors measured themselves. Howe looked upon the curious circumstance of modernism becoming part of the very establishment it once sought to overturn with skepticism and worry. Literary modernism, as Howe imagined it, could triumph over everything except its own success.

What replaced Howe's cautions about modernism was, at least for him, much worse—postmodernism. When its leading theorists threatened to make traditional literary criticism obsolete, Howe had had enough—and he said so, again and

again, in a posthumous collection of short pieces titled *A Critic's Notebook* (1994). Perhaps no one was more skeptical than Howe about indulgent collections cobbled together by aging critics or more skittish about the risks of self-repetition. A lifetime at the writing desk had set a high standard, and perhaps even higher expectations. Small wonder, then, that he must have worried about the growing number of short, often quirky pieces he wrote during the last five or six years of his life. Would they add up to a satisfying whole? Even more important, was there sufficient reason to believe that they added a measure of hard-won truth, however provisional, to a lifetime of brooding about what fiction is and does?

Howe was, of course, one of the twentieth century's great cultural worriers, and it is hardly surprising that he should worry about what he called his *shtiklakh,* a Yiddish word suggesting "little pieces" or "morsels." That he eventually convinced himself that his mounting stack of virtuoso turns (originally published in the pages of magazines such as *New Republic, Pequod, Threepenny Review,* and *Salmagundi*) merited hard covers is testament to the triumph of sound judgment over undue caution. Unfortunately, Howe did not live long enough to complete the project himself. Before his death on May 5, 1993, he imagined some twelve or thirteen *shtiklakh* yet to be written, and one suspects that he would have come up with even more had he been granted additional time to ruminate about matters most contemporary critics never think about at all.

In his introductory remarks to *A Critic's Notebook,* Nicholas Howe, Irving's son, quotes a line from his father's 1979 essay on *Daniel Deronda* entitled "George Eliot and the Jews": "Toward the end of their careers, great writers are sometimes roused to a new energy by thoughts of risk. Some final stab at an area of human experience they had neglected or at a theme only recently become urgent." The same spirit can rightly be applied to the forty mini-essays that, taken together, constitute *A Critic's Notebook.*

Consider, for example, the opening sentence from "Anecdote and Storyteller": "You won't find much about the anecdote in studies of literary genre: it seems too humble a form to attract the eye of the theorist." What follows are Howe's reflections about a small, but crucial matter in the prenovelistic fiction of pre-urban societies: the provincial Russia of the storyteller Nikolay Leskov, the Missouri villages of Mark Twain, the shtetl according to Sholom Aleichem, and Ignazio Silone's town of Abruzzi. Much the same willingness to raise basic, albeit thorny questions finds its subject in discussions about how literary characters are and are not like real people; what, exactly, is meant by slippery terms such as "tone" or "taste"; or why a novel's apparently gratuitous detail matters greatly; or how it is that farce can work effectively on stage and in film, but generally not in fiction. In each case, Howe brings full measures of his long experience as patient teacher and clear writer to the subject at hand. The result is, well, authority—admittedly a fighting word in the age of indeterminacy—but one always tempered by Howe's willingness to admit that certainties are few and doubts many.

No doubt the grim reality of his failing health prompted Howe to mingle memory with a renewed sense of literary-political engagement. Memory evidences itself in his return to the formative writers of his youth—Anton Chekhov, Nikolay Gogol, Sir Walter Scott, and, perhaps most of all, Leo Tolstoy. Literary-political engagement is evident in the side blows Howe directs to those bloodless literary theorists who insist that characters are nothing more nor less than verbal constructs, signs that exist only on the page. Why, Howe rightly wonders, should such critics push so hard against open doors, and with such solemn, heavyweight language?:

> The great fictional characters, from Robinson Crusoe to Flem Snopes, from Tess to Molly Bloom, cannot quite be "fitted" into or regarded solely as functions of narrative. *Why should we want to*? What but the delusions of system and total grasp do we gain thereby? Such characters are too interesting, too splendidly mysterious for mere functional placement. (Who'd even look at Emma Woodhouse if she were just an "it"?) Severe critics say that characters "exist only on the page"—but why do critics want to be so severe? They are wrong, too: all that exists on the page are black marks. As symbols for language, these marks stimulate impressions in our minds which lead us to suppose—though we "know better"—that characters exist in their own right, apart from the page. They refuse to be banished. They will not be driven back between covers.

To talk about fiction in these ways is to risk being written off as a "naive reader" by those who come at texts armed to the teeth with the best that continental theorists such as Michel Foucault, Roland Barthes, and Jacques Derrida have thought and said, but that is precisely the political point Howe felt pressed upon to make. At a time when the very idea of a democratic culture was under relentless attack, when many fashionable critics cared not a fig for the common reader and not a whit for fiction qua fiction, Howe could not entirely resist scoring a few well-turned polemical points:

> A number of those drawn to deconstructionist theory, for example, feel that their writings have political implications, though that does not lead them, so far as I can tell, to any viable politics available in the United States. A small academic group describes itself as Marxist, but that strikes me as a bit comic: whatever Marxism may have been, it always saw itself attached to, or in search of, a mass movement for the working class. It was not merely a "method" for literary criticism. But Marxism has gone to universities to die in comfort.

Those who have found it convenient to separate Howe the indefatigable political animal from Howe the insightful literary critic may well change their view after reading even a handful of the *shtiklakh* in *A Critic's Notebook.* One could argue that, at the end, the democratic socialism he fiercely defended in the pages of *Dissent* came to little more than a species of moral humanism. The same might be said of his literary criticism, despite its large stake in social criticism and the enduring residue of what he himself defined as the New York Jewish intellectual style.

In the concluding pages of *Irving Howe: Socialist, Critic, Jew* (1998), the literary critic and biographer Edward Alexander sums up the legacy of Howe's multifaceted career as the chronicle of his devotion "to lost causes, forsaken beliefs, and impossible loyalties," but he goes on to insist that this is also to chronicle "a kind of heroism." Alexander is hardly the first critic to make this observation about Howe's penchant for arriving at utopian visions just as they were crumbling. At one point in *A Margin of Hope,* Howe speaks of himself as "moving closer to the secular Yiddish milieu at the very moment it was completing its decline" and then he wonders, almost as an afterthought, if this newfound passion—one that ended with a series of anthologies of Yiddish literature in translation that helped to popularize its long forgotten writers—is not perhaps "another lost cause added to my collection." Such candor on Howe's part, long before Alexander points out the ambivalence, was hardly ever in short supply, for it is precisely Howe's ability to look upon both the world and the self with a critical, often skeptical detachment and to report the results with an unflinching honesty that had been his trademark from the beginning. For Howe, nothing quite succeeded as the intellectually bracing aroma of fallen grandeur. In his words, "Trying to keep alive a tradition," accurately describes the zigzagging arc of Howe's involvement with democratic socialism, secular Jewishness, southern writing, and literary criticism. As with most things about Howe, his own words put it best: "American intellectuals seem capable of almost anything except the ultimate grace of a career devoted to some large principle or value, modulated by experience and thought, but firm in purpose." Irving Howe's career was a study in grace under the pressure of history's cunning and an example of how modulated principles can simultaneously change and stay the course.

Selected Bibliography

WORKS OF IRVING HOWE

BOOKS

The U.A.W. and Walter Reuther. With B. J. Widick. New York: Random House, 1949.

Sherwood Anderson: A Biographical and Critical Study. New York: William Sloane, 1951.

William Faulkner: A Critical Study. New York: Random House, 1952. Enlarged and revised editions, New York: Vintage Books, 1962, 1975, and 1991.

A Treasury of Yiddish Stories. With Eliezer Greenberg. New York: Viking, 1954.

The American Communist Party: A Critical History, 1919–1957. With Lewis Coser. Boston: Beacon Press, 1957.

Politics and the Novel. New York: Horizon Press, 1957.

A World More Attractive: A View of Modern Literature and Politics. New York: Horizon Press, 1963.

Steady Work: Essays in the Politics of Democratic Radicalism, 1953–1966. New York: Harcourt, Brace and World, 1966.

Thomas Hardy. New York: Macmillan, 1967.

World of Our Fathers: The Journey of the Eastern European Jews to America and the Life They Found and Made. New York: Harcourt Brace Jovanovich, 1976.

Leon Trotsky. New York: Viking, 1978.

The Critical Point: On Literature and Culture. New York: Horizon Press, 1973.

Celebrations and Attacks: Thirty Years of Literary and Cultural Commentary. New York: Harcourt Brace Jovanovich, 1979.

A Margin of Hope: An Intellectual Autobiography. New York: Harcourt Brace Jovanovich, 1982.

Socialism and America. New York: Harcourt Brace Jovanovich, 1985.

The American Newness: Culture and Politics in the Age of Emerson. Cambridge, Mass.: Harvard University Press, 1986.

Selected Writings, 1950–1990. New York: Harcourt Brace Jovanovich, 1990.

A Critic's Notebook. Edited by Nicholas Howe. New York: Harcourt Brace, 1994.

EDITED ANTHOLOGIES

Classics of Modern Fiction: 10 Short Novels. New York: Harcourt Brace and World, 1968.

Voices from the Yiddish: Essays, Memoirs, Diaries. Edited with Eliezer Greenberg. Ann Arbor: University of Michigan Press, 1972.

Israel, the Arabs, and the Middle East. Edited with Carl Gershman. New York: Quadrangle, 1972.

The New Conservatives. Edited with Lewis Coser. New York: Quadrangle, 1974.

Jewish-American Stories. New York: New American Library, 1977.

Ashes Out of Hope: Fiction by Soviet-Yiddish Writers. Edited with Eliezer Greenberg. New York: Schocken, 1977.

SELECTED CRITICISM

"The Dilemma of *Partisan Review.*" *New International* 8:22–24 (February 1942).

"The Lost Young Intellectual." *Commentary* 2:361–367 (October 1946).

"The Jewish Writer and the English Literary Tradition." *Commentary* 8:364–365 (October 1949).

"Does It Hurt When You Laugh?" *Dissent* 1:4–7 (January 1954).

" 'The New Yorker' and Hannah Arendt." *Commentary* 36:318–319 (October 1963).

"Is This Country Cracking Up?" *Dissent* 14:259–263 (May–June 1967).

"Why Should Negroes Be above Criticism?" *Saturday Evening Post,* December 14, 1968, pp. 10, 14–15.

"Literary Criticism and Literary Radicals." *American Scholar* 41:113–120 (winter 1971–1972).

"Israel: A Visitor's Notes." *Dissent* 24:359–363 (fall 1977).

"George Eliot and the Jews." *Partisan Review* 3:359–375 (1979).

"The Burden of Civilization." *New Republic,* February 10, 1982, pp. 27–34.

"Again: Orwell and the Neoconservatives." *Dissent* 31:236 (spring 1984).

"Immigrant Chic." *New York Magazine,* May 12, 1986, pp. 76–77.

"American Jews and Israel." *Tikkun* 4:71–74 (December 1988).

CRITICAL STUDIES

Alexander, Edward. *Irving Howe: Socialist, Critic, Jew.* Bloomington: Indiana University Press, 1998.

Alter, Robert. "Yiddishkeit." *Commentary* 61:83–86 (April 1976).

Decter, Midge. "Socialism and Its Irresponsibilities: The Case of Irving Howe." *Commentary* 74:25–32 (December 1982).

Hindus, Milton. "Milton Hindus vs. Irving Howe." *New Boston Review* 2:7–10 (January 1977).

Hux, Samuel. "Uncle Irving." *Modern Age* 37:330–336 (summer 1995).

Kramer, Hilton. "Irving Howe at Seventy." *New Criterion* 9:69 (October 1990).

Pinsker, Sanford. "Lost Causes/Marginal Hopes." *Virginia Quarterly Review* 65:215–230 (Spring 1989).

"Remembering Irving Howe." Special issue of *Dissent* 40:515–549 (fall 1993).

Rosenfeld, Alvin. "Irving Howe: The World of Our Fathers." *Midstream* 22:80–86 (October 1976).

Simon, John. "Irving Howe: A Triple Perspective." *New Leader* 21:1921 (May 1979).

Wieseltier, Leon. "Remembering Irving Howe, 1920–1993." *New York Times Book Review,* May 23, 1993.

Wisse, Ruth R. "The New York (Jewish) Intellectuals." *Commentary* 84:28–38 (November 1987).

ARCHIVAL SOURCES

Lewis Coser Collection. Boston College Archives, Boston, Mass.

Albert Glotzer Collection. Hoover Institution Archives, Stanford University, Stanford, Calif.

Sidney Hook Papers. Hoover Institution Archives, Stanford University, Stanford, Calif.

Dwight Macdonald Papers. Yale University Library, New Haven, Conn.

—SANFORD PINSKER

Richard Hugo

1923–1982

RICHARD HUGO WAS a poet of place. The Pacific Northwest was his point of obsessive return. Although he often set poems elsewhere, most of his major poems are windows on the damp, gray landscape at the edge of Puget Sound. They are also, of course, windows inward to a self intimately attuned to his region.

Hugo was born December 21, 1923, in White Center, a working-class community south and west of Seattle, Washington. The general prosperity of the 1920s had bypassed the area. The population was a few thousand, and the jobs were factory or seasonal work—fishing, logging, agriculture. After prospering during World War I, the economy declined, with cutbacks at the shipyards and other defense-related sites. For White Center, the Depression began ten years early.

On the west bank of the Duwamish River, White Center's location reflected its economic malaise. The Duwamish runs north into Puget Sound, and as it passes White Center it is so near sea level that at high tide saltwater flows upriver; the sluggish, turbid river runs backward for a few hours, carrying flotsam upstream. Although most Seattle neighborhoods are hilly, much of White Center lies in the river's ancient flood plain between two hills, east and west, which impinge upon the sunrise and the sunset. Hugo refers to these hill shadows in "West Marginal Way," published in his first book, *A Run of Jacks* (1961):

"Some places are forever afternoon." The shortened days and the chronic overcast of western Washington resulted in what Hugo once claimed was one of the highest suicide rates in the world. Whatever else there was to see, his eye was drawn to poverty, alcoholism, repressed anger, and violence. No poet could have been born into a place richer in metaphors suited to his temperament. The title "West Marginal Way" is a powerful metaphor: the western margin of America's westering impulse and the marginalized lives of the people Hugo writes about; but it is also the real name of the road on the west bank of the Duwamish.

Hugo's name at birth was Richard Franklin Hogan. As his parents' marriage foundered, he was handed over to his maternal grandparents, Fred and Ora Monk, at twenty months. The Monks had failed at farming in Michigan, and Fred now worked at various menial jobs for the Seattle Gas Company. Hugo's grandparents' house was cold: Hugo claimed he heard his grandfather laugh only a few times, and his grandmother, scarred by her own father's suicide, was emotionally distant and given to talking to herself. Hugo's mother, Esther, soon remarried, but he never lived with his mother and her second husband, except for a few extended visits. Still, when he was eighteen, he took his mother's new name, Hugo.

Hugo attended high school in nearby West Seattle. Within walking distance of his grandparents' house, it was a long emotional and economic journey. West Seattle sweeps down the western slope of the hill that blocks White Center's sunsets and was solidly middle class in the late 1930s. At West Seattle High, Hugo mixed with a distinctly different economic stratum, young people at ease with relative prosperity. What he called, in *The Real West Marginal Way: A Poet's Autobiography* (1986), the "social superiority" of his new schoolmates had a sexual dimension as well: He found the girls more attractive and less approachable. He seldom had the courage even to speak to them, and his various humiliations remained vivid memories.

Hugo grew more aware of his emotional deprivation at a party, where he saw boys and girls kissing; in *The Real West Marginal Way* he writes, "I had never seen a man kiss a woman before except in the movies, and I'm not putting anyone on when I say that I really thought people kissed only in films. I can never remember being kissed as a child, nor did I ever see any show of affection between my grandparents." He felt incapable of loving or being loved, and he believed his alcoholism had its beginnings in his intense emotional isolation. Writing of the aftermath of his experience at that party, he says, "At home, my grandparents were already asleep, and I sat alone, as I did so many times in that still house, and stared into the solitary void I was certain would be my life."

A bright spot was baseball. It became an "obsession," and in his teenage years on the baseball field Hugo felt himself the equal of young men who were elsewhere his superiors. Even after his success as poet and teacher, he wrote in the poem "Missoula Softball Tournament" about seeing the players' wives in the stands and realizing that the game, for him an antidote to loneliness, was for the other players merely part of a full life.

Hugo enlisted in the Army Air Force in 1943. He flew thirty-five missions as a bombardier and was decorated, but his military service did not increase his self-esteem. "I had volunteered for the Army Air Corps for the cheapest kind of romantic personal reasons," he writes in *The Real West Marginal Way;* "I felt weak and inadequate, and foolishly thought facing and surviving danger would give me spiritual depth and a courageous dimension I lacked and desperately wanted." Rather than ameliorating his sense of inadequacy, combat made it even harder to evade: "The panic in my belly was physiologically real. Every morning explosive diarrhea and phlegmatic choking." It was during the war that he began drinking heavily.

Hugo returned to college on the GI bill and attended the University of Washington in Seattle, beginning in June 1948 and majoring in creative writing. Theodore Roethke, a new professor there, had just published *The Lost Son and Other Poems* (1948), establishing him as an important poet. (*The Waking: Poems, 1933–1953* won the Pulitzer Prize in 1953, and *Words for the Wind* [1957] received the Bollingen Prize and National Book Award in 1958.) Hugo was a student in Roethke's first class, and while many writers were intimidated by him, Hugo flourished. He completed his bachelor's degree and, in June 1950, his master's degree, although unpaid fees delayed his receiving it for two years.

In 1952 Hugo married Barbara Williams. They shared a predisposition for the down and out, the derelict, and they rented shabby houses in deteriorating neighborhoods even after they were both working and could afford better. While their contemporaries spent weekends house-hunting, he and Barbara made a hobby of what they called "house haunting." From these excursions grew many poems expressing both fascination with the hard life and his resentment toward anything that would sweep away its evidence. In "What the Brand New Freeway Won't Go By," for example,

Hugo sees people like himself in the neighborhoods condemned for freeway construction: "To live here you should be a friend of rain, / and fifty with a bad job on the freights, / knowing the freeway soon will siphon / the remaining world away." Another poem, "Letter to Matthews from Barton Street Flats," explains his need for physical evidence of suffering. Addressed to Hugo's friend and fellow poet William Matthews, its title refers to an area in White Center where Nisei (Japanese Americans) farmed until they were interned during World War II; later, the flats were bulldozed to make way for a shopping center. Bitter over the treatment of the Nisei, Hugo longs for tangible proof of even the painful past. He has lost "my faith that change (I really mean loss) / is paced slow enough for the blood to adjust." Change takes away the "evidence to support our claim / our lives really happened." He and Barbara shared this need to dwell in a desolate past, and their marriage could not survive Hugo's later success and a resulting move to a teaching post in Missoula, Montana. They were divorced in 1965.

In the first years of his marriage, Hugo was a technical writer at the Boeing Aircraft Company. For almost ten years he worked at a plant across the Duwamish from White Center. The plant was old and poorly maintained, and squatters lived in squalid shacks on company land between the chain link fence and the river. The work was a distraction from his poetry, but Hugo felt at home in these surroundings, and he identified as much with those at the margin—the literal margin of the riverbank—as with his coworkers. In "The Squatter on Company Land," celebrating the desperate dignity of a man evicted from a shack on the riverbank, he empathizes with the compulsion of the poor to hold on to the very tokens of their deprivation.

The publication of Hugo's first book, *A Run of Jacks,* by the University of Minnesota Press in 1961 established him as a poet. The book was favorably reviewed, and he began to place poems more easily and in more prestigious publications. He and Barbara decided to spend a year in Italy, to gather material for more poems. Hugo applied for a grant from the Guggenheim Foundation but was turned down.

The trip was a gamble on Hugo's future as a writer. He and his wife would have no jobs upon their return, but the trip enabled Hugo to revisit, as a mature poet, a place that deeply influenced him. Over the next six years he reworked the material, supplemented with another visit (alone) in 1967, until the release of *Good Luck in Cracked Italian* (1969). Hugo wrote in *The Triggering Town: Lectures and Essays on Poetry and Writing* (1979) that good writers have "learned to submit to their obsessions," and the six years of writing and revising would be his own long submission.

On Hugo's return to the United States, he was hired as visiting lecturer at the University of Montana at Missoula. Hugo had no confidence in his ability as a teacher, and some of his early teaching confirmed his low opinion of himself, as did his breakup with Barbara soon after they arrived in Missoula. His growing dependence on alcohol was both cause and symptom of his increasing despair.

Death of the Kapowsin Tavern was issued by a major commercial press, Harcourt, Brace and World, in 1965. Within two years Hugo was the subject of a documentary film and the recipient of a Rockefeller fellowship in creative writing, which financed his second visit to Italy, in 1967–1968. After returning, he became an associate professor at the University of Montana. Now in his mid-forties, it was his first permanent academic job. He was soon offered and accepted a position as visiting poet at the University of Iowa (1970–1971), which was followed by a summer occupying the Roethke Chair at the University of Washington (1971). The Roethke Chair was a high honor, especially for a former Roethke student.

Success precipitated a crisis more intense than any brought on by failure. In Iowa City, Hugo had a breakdown. His alcoholism became acute, and there was concern over whether he would be able to fulfill his duties the following summer at the University of Washington. He resigned and drove alone back to Montana in a daze of self-contempt. Then, in Montana, he was evicted from his rental house so it could be torn down for a new development. For a man obsessed with holding on to the evidence of his own past, this was a serious blow, and he was literally helpless. His friends packed his belongings while he drank and wept. The episode sent him back to the psycho-analysis he had pursued a few years before, but he already suspected that his very success was the trigger for his new difficulties. Acclaim—and especially the admiration and respect of women—terrified him. As he recalled in *The Real West Marginal Way,* he had developed the habit of "dwelling on painful episodes of my past," especially those involving women, convinced that failure represented his true self. "Success and popularity," he continued, "constituted an interruption. . . . The louder the acclaim, the stronger my urge to overcome the interruption."

The crisis was a turning point. He stopped drinking, and after the summer of teaching in Seattle, he bought a house in Missoula, his first, a symbol of rootedness and a new phase in his life. He was promoted to the rank of full professor and appointed director of creative writing. His next book, *The Lady in Kicking Horse Reservoir* (1973) was nominated for the National Book Award. He accepted his success gracefully. His sense of self-worth also allowed him to enter the relationship that sustained him for the rest of his life. He met Ripley Schemm Hansen in the autumn of 1973, and they were married the following summer.

The remaining decade of Hugo's life was an almost uninterrupted series of successful publications and awards. He served as visiting professor at the University of Colorado in 1974, and in 1975 W. W. Norton published *What Thou Lovest Well Remains American* (1975), which was nominated for the National Book Award. The next year he received the Theodore Roethke Memorial Poetry Prize, and in 1977 a Guggenheim fellowship, which made it possible for him to spend a year on Skye, an island off Scotland. In one year, 1980, Hugo published two books, *The Right Madness on Skye* and *White Center,* the second of which is one of his strongest. Also in 1980, Hugo spent a term as visiting distinguished professor at the University of Arkansas, and he suffered no self-doubt, looking with humor rather than horror upon honors so disproportionate to his older sense of himself. At the age of forty-eight he turned to novel writing with the mystery *Death and the Good Life* (1981), which was nominated for the Pulitzer Prize. That same year he was awarded a fellowship by the Academy of American Poets, and in 1982 he received an honorary doctorate and the Distinguished Scholar Award from the University of Montana.

In the summer of 1982 Hugo was diagnosed with leukemia. He declined rapidly and died in Seattle in late October of that year.

A RUN OF JACKS

By the time he published *A Run of Jacks* in 1961, Hugo had been publishing for more than a decade, and he was very much aware of his technique and his dominant themes. It is a fully realized work. None of the poems in *A Run of Jacks* would seem out of place in any later book. (Curiously, the phrase "a run of jacks" does not appear in the book but does appear in his second book, *Death of the Kapowsin Tavern.*) "Jack" is a type of fish typically caught for food, not sport. Hugo's recurring subjects are laid out in the book: rivers, the oppressive gray of the northwest sky, economic hardship.

Also laid out clearly are Hugo's poetic techniques: strong alliteration and assonance, unexpected turns from literal to subjective, abrupt shifts from indicative to imperative mood. Lines from the second stanza of "Trout" demonstrate all three: "I wedged hard water to validate his skin— / call it chrome, say red is on / his side like apples in a fog." The repeated vowel and consonant sounds of "wedged hard water," "call it chrome, say red . . . / side," and "side like" tie the words into a sequence that is more than grammatical and more than simply pleasing to the ear. The "r" and "c" sounds in particular suggest an assertive voice and a forceful, intrusive gaze, a search for something beyond the physical particulars of a trout. But what? To "validate" the fish's skin is not to verify or merely observe it; it is to ascertain some higher truth. It is a way of forcing the world to divulge something.

That forcefulness is verbalized when the mood shifts to imperative: "call it . . . say." The command is directed at the poet himself, an order to find the word that will "validate" the fish's colors. As we overhear the poet's conversation with himself, there is a peculiar tension. Poet and reader are intimate, and yet the relationship is contentious, because the poet's stance toward himself is also contentious.

"West Marginal Way" is titled for the road that runs along the west bank of the Duwamish River. Validating the road no less than "Trout" does the fish, "West Marginal Way" explores margins and convergences of the outer and inner worlds. The first stanza describes a tugboat pulling a boom of logs as the shadows of Pigeon Hill bring early afternoon, and people fish from a pier near a run-down chapel. All are seen in the light not of the afternoon sun but of the poet's vision. The log boom is "an afternoon / of logs," the shadow of the hill "crawls" as it advances, and the derelict church is a "crackpot chapel."

This tour of West Marginal Way, a literal place, is also a tour of the poet's metaphorical west marginal way, where emotions occupy a narrow margin between helplessness and violence. In the

third stanza, Hugo notes that the local men are at sea on fishing boats, and that the end of the fishing season is the beginning of the drinking season. It is "forever afternoon," the margin of the workday, of the season. The river, too, is at its margin, and twice a day backs up with seawater, as the returning fishermen are backed up with unspent emotion.

Another theme throughout Hugo's work is his private metaphor of the direction north. A brief, cryptic poem in *A Run of Jacks* is titled "North," but the word and its associated images can be found in many poems over many years. The Duwamish runs north, except when high tide backs saltwater southward; his grandparents' house bordered woods to the north, where he played but which he also feared. North represents outflow: fulfillment, release, promise—but also death, oblivion, dispossession. "North" recalls the war, when death was a constant possibility, but is impossible to place geographically, because north for Hugo is a state of mind, the direction he turns in fear and yearning for ultimate release.

"Alki Beach" describes a spot a few miles from White Center; it is also the place where the first white settlers came ashore to found Seattle. For Hugo, it is a place of beginnings and of loss. He describes young lovers playing in the water, then turns to see flotsam from a passing ferry, the abandoned picnic area, and "one man, / his coat too dark for the day" who "remembers / what descended where the bubbles are." The lone man cannot literally see below the surface, but his memory informs the scene with loss. What was lost? The poem suggests the loss of a deeper connection with the natural world, but the specifics of "what descended" are not as important as the fact that only one person remembers it. "Alki Beach" is a powerful example of how distinctly Hugo's landscape is a place of loneliness.

"Neighbor" further expresses the compulsion to hold on to the past. An account of the death of an alcoholic who lived across the street from Hugo's grandparents' house, the poem enacts the need to keep the past close at hand. "I admit my envy," he says of the man, because "in that dim warm mind" the past is present. No matter whether the retained past is pleasant or horrible—the poet says it could be either—it is the saving itself that matters. He admits that he will have to practice his show of disapproval for when they carry away the man's corpse, but he believes that the dead man will be smiling.

The drunk he remembered from his childhood was transformed by Hugo's own experience: here were his own desires left to run their course. The picture was simultaneously horrifying and attractive. It was also very immediate, very relevant to his own alcoholism, so the first part of the poem is in the present tense. Time collapses into a continuous now that makes no literal sense but suggests that even death is no match for the revivifying force of imagination. "Neighbor" asserts the transforming power of the poet's memory and the validating force of his voice.

"Duwamish" is the centerpiece of *A Run of Jacks* and central to all of Hugo's work. In five stanzas the poem flows gradually from contemplation of the river to the problem of finding words for its meaning. We see the river flow with saltwater from tidal wash, the impoverished and abandoned mills and lumberyards, the poor people who live along the banks. Early in the poem, the river links these scenes. In the second stanza the river links past and present, when the poet notes that the name of the river is an Indian word, although the Indians in a nearby tavern ignore it; it is too strong a reminder of loss. The Indian myths remain unspoken as the men continue their drinking.

In the third stanza the river absorbs the sky, reflecting clouds and sun. Reflection also joins its fish with the vegetation along its banks. The river becomes a metaphor for the poet's transforming imagination, as we see that its year-round gray gives all it reflects the hue of the Northwest win-

ter, in the same way that the poet's temperament shades all he sees. In the final two stanzas the poet realizes that his emotions and memories are the forces that create the scene. Variations on the word "cold" dominate, but the physical cold is incidental. The poet's emotional isolation is his coldness; he is made cold by the knowledge that "this poverty / is not a lack of money but of friends." He comes to the river "looking for a word," which he discovers: "cold." But he must distinguish his coldness from its other forms, and he concludes the penultimate stanza by choosing three images of cold linked by the river: the cold of the water, the cold of a late Sunday afternoon, the cold of a dead and decaying fish.

The fifth and final stanza acknowledges that no word fully expresses his emotions. His isolation is painful, but the river's joining of everything into a gray sameness carried seaward is a frightening anodyne. None of the languages spoken by those living their marginalized lives along the river expresses the promise and threat that it represents. The nearest any comes is not his own word at all but is rather the Indian name for the river, which he takes to mean "love," "madness," and "home." The name unites people, river, history, and is finally the word—not his, but available to him—for his own relationship to it.

DEATH OF THE KAPOWSIN TAVERN

Many poems in Hugo's second book are meditations on rivers and on his struggle to discover and express their meaning. The opening section bears the collective title "Duwamish, Skagit, Hoh," rivers that drain, respectively, the central Cascades, the North Cascades, and the Olympic Mountains. Each is named for the indigenous people who lived along its banks. Each becomes for Hugo an exploration of the limits of language to link himself to the world.

"Introduction to the Hoh" notes that the river rises in glacial melt, that it changes course during flood season and then returns to its channel. The river's correspondence to the poet's inner life is hinted at, the cold of his own past, his tendency to cast about for new directions for his life, his perennial return to his old ways. The poem takes the familiar turn to the imperative mood, and for the three remaining stanzas the poet commands himself to see, to think, and to remember, Hugo's three concerns in the writing of a poem. All three are continuing actions, for the flow of the river is both constant and constantly changing; the symbol of continuity is also a symbol of flux. The last concern, to remember, is the most important and the most difficult, for the current sweeps the past away: "Remember famine as these broken leaves / ride away like Indians from you."

Hugo was troubled by success. The world seemed to efface his past, and so how permanent could his success be, particularly when it seemed so poorly to suit his deepest sense of himself? In "Introduction to the Hoh" he writes, "Think of stark abundance, a famous run of jacks / the vanished tribe at the mouth once bragged about." Here is his first use of the phrase that was the title of his first book. He has had a "famous run of jacks," both literally and figuratively, and he knows that those who would boast about such success have been swept away like "broken leaves" on the river.

In "Duwamish No. 2" Hugo finds that changes in the nearby city have not altered the river's essence. He looks at the "west hill" (which brings early dusk) and sees "a million / alders and five hundred modern homes." Alders, which grow where the first growth pine and fir have been cleared, are a sign, along with the new houses, of the assault on his past. Still the river flows north when the tide is ebbing or out. The symbolic weight remains: "North is easy. North is never love." He comes to the river "When the world hurts," and the verb can be transitive or intransitive: the world giving pain or in pain—or both. The river reminds him "there is one direction only— / north, and, though terror to believe, /

quickly found by river and never love," and in another telling equivocation, "by" can mean that the river finds or that the finding is done near the river—or both.

The ambiguities mirror the entrancing and terrifying confusion of poet and place. He seeks "north," just as the river does, and in their shared desire they come close to merging. But the river is also primordial; to merge with it is to lose himself. He yearns to succumb and fears the obliteration succumbing must bring. The place "makes me ready for the sea," the undifferentiated element that he longs for and fears: oblivion, rest, and loss of self but also loss of struggle.

"Death of the Kapowsin Tavern" commemorates a tavern on Lake Kapowsin, which lies in a forested area near Mount Rainier. Hugo frequented the tavern and loved its rundown, backwoods ambiance. The tavern burned down, and as the poet recalls the scene, he observes that the burned rubble is only the culmination of the trend visible in the whole area. An empty school has been for sale for years; most of the houses are empty and vandalized. "The fire," he says, "simply ended lots of ending."

A world that abandons this place is one in which wisdom is out of style, and he wonders if, "when wise men are in style again," one of them will tell of the beauty of the lake and the countryside and, "most of all," of the tavern itself, "the temple and our sanctuary there." The religious allusions are unmistakable. Like the birthplace of Christ, this humble place is passed over by the cosmopolitan, the ambitious. Hugo insists that something authentic and elemental dies along with these outposts of the poor in spirit.

GOOD LUCK IN CRACKED ITALIAN

Good Luck in Cracked Italian (1969) moves into a new-old landscape, and Hugo animates the new landscape with his old obsessions. "Docking at Palermo" challenges the poet himself, addressed in the second person, to understand Italy when "You never understood a cloudy north." Hugo recalls the invading forces during World War II, but the final line of the stanza, a fragment that lacks a finite verb and thus has no tense, suggests that the war continues: "On either side a cliff and raining guns." The conflict that brought him to Italy in his youth still shapes his view; the gunfire continues as naturally as rain.

Hugo imagines an emigrant returning to die in his native land, imagines the people awaiting him, and is reminded of his emotional alienation from his own home: "If you went home a bear would turn away." Others' warmth reminds Hugo of the cold world in which he grew up. Yet he concludes with hope that he can learn a new language of emotion here. "Learn the names / of streets or give them names to fight," he says, switching to his familiar imperative mood, addressing the necessity of accurately putting words to experience. But Hugo's goal is to pass beyond words. He imagines finding "a man who was a beggar then" and begging the former beggar to "show me how to cry."

Hugo sees through the novelty of these places (Padua, Naples, Tuscany, and many more) to his old obsessions; when he tries to see these places in their own terms, his vision rarely penetrates beneath the surface. The landscape often seems incidental, and much of the emotion is asserted rather than dramatized. In "G.I. Graves in Tuscany," for example, Hugo notes that even in death the soldiers are aligned uniformly, and he says, "The loss is so damn gross." Both observations are true but facile.

Although Hugo later expressed dissatisfaction with *Good Luck in Cracked Italian,* a few poems stand up. In "Tretitoli, Where the Bomb Group Was," he gazes upon the palimpsest of his experience: windswept fields of grain where bombers took off and landed, school buildings that were maintenance sheds, a pumphouse that was a brothel. Uncharacteristically, there is no regret at the changes as he tries to remember where each

feature was: "The runway's just a guess. I'd say, there." The poem never shifts to the imperative mood that Hugo uses elsewhere when he commands himself to look at something painful and articulate it accurately. The poem expresses an emotion rare in Hugo's work, satisfaction in the obliteration of the past.

Also rare in Hugo's work is a poem that departs from his familiar loose iambic pentameter lines, as does "Where We Crashed." Reexamining the site of a crash landing he experienced, he gives almost every word its own line, as if simultaneously mimicking his slow, deliberate steps through the grass and the panicky descent and impact twenty years earlier. He struggles for a half-dozen lines to impose continuity: "I was calling airspeed / christ / one-thirty-five and / pancake bam." The nonpattern of the emphatic "christ" soon exerts itself, crowding out mental discipline: "you end / now / here / explode / damn / damn / Steinberg / pilot / should / have found / more sky / you end." It is an explosion of words. Only in the last few lines does the return of form bring the relief of longer breaths: "and in this grass / I didn't die." "Where We Crashed" is a noteworthy example of Hugo's exploration of a new form that allowed him to discover new tonalities.

THE LADY IN KICKING HORSE RESERVOIR

By 1973, when he published *The Lady in Kicking Horse Reservoir,* Hugo owned his own home in Missoula and had a secure post at the University of Montana. Around the time the book appeared he entered the romantic relationship that sustained him for the rest of his life. As if to assert that satisfying relationships are now a part of his poetic landscape, he dedicates each of the book's first fifteen poems to a different friend. The poems are confident and polished. He writes as one secure in his ability and in his sense of belonging.

"A Map of Montana in Italy" demonstrates that Hugo is less oppressed by his old, crippling emotion. The map of Montana is "thick as a fist / or blunt instrument"; the lines marking roads are "red veins full of rage." But these are not his feelings. They are those of the self-defeating patrons of a bar, who have no release except through big talk and alcohol. The poet empathizes, but these emotions do not control his life: "There's too much / schoolboy in bars—I'm tougher than you— / and too much talk about money." Hugo distances himself from the insular, angry world of the drinkers.

Even the turn to the imperative mood serves a different purpose in this poem. "antelope sail / between strands of barbed wire and never / get hurt, west, I think, of Plevna, say near / Sumatra, or more west, say Shawmut, / anyway, on the right, east on the plains," he says, and the commands "say . . . say" are not the poet calling himself to the grueling task of accuracy; rather, they are the conversational voice of man willing to live with approximation.

"The Lady in Kicking Horse Reservoir" is the most densely textured and most psychologically telling in the book. A man has murdered his lover and submerged her body in a reservoir, but the poet works from anger back to love. The reservoir, like the rivers in Hugo's earlier books, is a metaphor for his deep reserves of repressed feelings, but a turning point comes in the fifth stanza, where we suddenly hear an account of a fight between two boys. The more cowardly of the two flees, humiliated, and drowns himself in a pond; the narrator tries in vain to recover the body. In an interview with Michael Allen (1982), Hugo explained that the two boys were the two sides of himself, and the "regressive, self-pitying side" had to be exorcised beyond return.

In the early stanzas the speaker imagines the drowned woman remaining unchanged: "Lie there lily still. The spillway's closed." In the final stanza, however, "The spillway's open and you spill out / into weather, lover down the bright canal / and mother, irrigating crops / dead Indians forgot to plant." The death of Hugo's self-pitying side has allowed the release of emotion. In the second stanza the water of the lake was described as "common gray," but now the woman has been transformed into a different kind of water: life-giving, changeable, and "bright." The opening of the spillway has drained away, even transfigured, Hugo's shame and regret.

A striking juxtaposition occurs with the poems "Montana Ranch Abandoned" and "2433 Agnes, First Home, Last House in Missoula." The first is a meditation on the many ways that the love and labor of making a home can come to nothing. The end may come from something as dramatic as "raiding bears" or as inconspicuous as "eel-worms," but it is no less final, and only wind animates the homestead.

Yet "Montana Ranch Abandoned" betrays no self-pity. Hugo sees loss, but he does not turn within to his own losses. The symbolic purging that occurred in "The Lady in Kicking Horse Reservoir" has freed him to see others' sorrows without sliding back into his own intertwined sorrow and guilt. A sympathetic, knowing observer, he is no longer an emotional victim.

Further indication of Hugo's new sense of himself comes in the poem immediately following "Montana Ranch Abandoned": "2433 Agnes, First Home, Last House in Missoula," the address of the house that Hugo bought in the fall of 1971, the first he ever owned. The title is ambiguous, despite the precision of the address: Does "in Missoula" modify "First Home" as well as "Last House"? That is, is this his first home anywhere, or only his first in Missoula? Does "last house" mean he lives on the outskirts of town, or that this will be his last house? The poem does not resolve the ambiguities, as perhaps Hugo could not resolve them. In any case, the poem suggests the triumph of his new sense of belonging over his old sense of abandonment. Just as he could look at the abandoned ranch and yet remain apart from its intimations of inevitable loss, in "2433 Agnes" he acknowledges the emotional difficulty of settling into a new home and a new life, and still decide in its favor.

"I'm somewhat torn," he says at the beginning of the final stanza, and explains his opposition to anyone's owning land. Ownership of land distorts our relationship with it; both the owner and the land are degraded. Nine of eleven lines in the stanza enumerate his reasons for his belief, but the first line signals a change of direction. To be "torn" is to be pulled by opposing forces, after all, and all of Hugo's reasons are prelude to his other feelings. "On the other hand, at least fifty buntings / are nervously pecking my lawn," he concludes. There is a joyful plenty in the phrase "at least fifty" and an unabashed self-satisfaction in the simple word "my." The word is the audible sign of his new relationship with the world and with himself.

Despite this improved sense of himself, "The Only Bar in Dixon" is a loving portrait of a bar that only a confirmed alcoholic could truly appreciate. "Home. Home. I knew it entering," he begins. He surveys the bar's destitute patrons and the impoverished landscape outside, and declares them the reasons this bar is "home." This moment of infatuation reveals parallels between Montana and White Center: "Home because / the Flathead goes home north northwest." The swift-flowing Flathead and the turbid Duwamish are as unalike as two rivers can be, but they share the similarity of running north, which has always been Hugo's orientation in his darkest moment. He concludes the poem, "Five bourbons / and I'm in some other home." That "other home" is White Center and the banks of the Duwamish. The poem traces how easily an alcoholic falls back into old associations. Alcohol is indeed "home," both the substitute for a real home and the thing that precludes his ever gaining a true and enduring one. Perhaps

in order to expunge the experience it records, Hugo excluded the poem from his *Selected Poems* (1979).

In *The Triggering Town* Hugo speculated that many poets drink too much because "alcohol keeps alive a self deserving of rejection"; they fear that an "acceptable" self might not be able to write. "The Only Bar in Dixon" displays Hugo's continuing attraction to "a self deserving of rejection."

WHAT THOU LOVEST WELL REMAINS AMERICAN

Hugo's fifth book, which was nominated for the National Book Award, continues his evolution away from the idiosyncrasies that created moments of obscurity in otherwise eloquent poems. In *What Thou Lovest Well* Hugo sets aside his most imperial acts of imagination and keeps the relationship between poet and place in focus.

"The House on 15th S.W." (the address of Hugo's grandparents' house in White Center) returns to a painful scene but suggests that he can revisit without losing all he has accomplished since leaving. He sees himself as a lonely, self-doubting child: "I watched my face / play out dreams of going north with clouds." Powerful as that image of northward movement is in all of Hugo's poetry, here it is experienced at a distance; not the mature poet, but the child dreams of pleasurable oblivion.

"North surely was soft. North was death / and women and the women soft," he continues, but the seductive images are in the past tense. The poet, in the present, looks back without losing his newfound poise. The poem resolves in favor of remaining outside the nexus of pain: "My pride in a few poems, my shame / of a wasted life, no wife, no children, / cancel out. I'm left neutral at this house, / not caring to go in." "To go in" would be to make present what the poem has established as past. Hugo can remain "neutral," a triumph.

A companion piece immediately follows: "A Snapshot of 15th S.W." The poet begins by demanding of himself, in his familiar imperative, that he obliterate the photographs that recall his painful past: "Burn this shot. That gray is what it is." He lists oppressive memories, many expressed in grammatical fragments and many associated with the oppressive gray of his childhood. The "it" in the line quoted above is the welter of dreary scenes punctuated with moments of crisis: "Shriek of siren. Red on cloud. The suicide." But in the final stanza he rewrites the first line: "Don't burn it. That gray is what it was." Hugo asserts the power of the past tense, changing the "is" to "was." He realizes that "out of camera range / the sun pulses on fields you still might run to, / wind a girl's hand on your ear." His escape has not been to the north but to where gray yields to sunlight and nature is tender.

"Again, Kapowsin" is a more direct declaration of liberation from the past, although not necessarily therefore a stronger poem. At the scene of "Death of the Kapowsin Tavern," Hugo reexamines impulses that gave much to his poetry but took much from his life. In "Again, Kapowsin" he releases the idealized representations of the scene and in doing so releases himself, even gaining a kind of permission from the scene itself to move on: "And whatever / I wave goodbye to, a crane waves back / slow as twenty years of lifting fog." As in "A Snapshot of 15th S.W.," Hugo was able to shift his vision to what lay outside the camera's range, where he sees what has been obscured by fog—the fog of alcoholism, of obsessive self-contempt.

"Again, Kapowsin" directly refutes "The Only Bar in Dixon" when he declares "From now on / bars will not be homes." The poem on which this one comments, "Death of the Kapowsin Tavern,"

was an elegy for a bar; "Again, Kapowsin" is an elegy (but almost certainly not a lament) for the man he was, who claimed identity with the derelict place: "The man who claimed he owned it is a stranger. / He died loud in fog and his name won't come." In this poem, like so many in *What Thou Lovest Well,* Hugo continues to free himself from the constraints of the past without obliterating it, even asserting in the phrase "twenty years of lifting fog" that only time and psychological distance allow an accurate vision of the past.

These poems are preparation for "What Thou Lovest Well Remains American," Hugo's declaration of poetic principle. Set on 15th S.W., it lists the losses and degradations of the old neighborhood. "Poverty was real, wallet and spirit," he says, and the economic improvements he sees now do not impinge upon his memories: "You still have need / to remember lots empty and fern." These are scenes he knows he "must play again / and again"; he must continue to bear "the gray / that was their disease." Even though Hugo blames the neighborhood for his "failure," it is also the source of his poetry, and the memories make him part of a "secret club" of similarly wounded souls. Hugo realigns himself with his past, recognizing that he is its product but declaring that he is no longer its victim. He makes the declaration through the use of the second person, addressing himself as "you." The distancing device dissociates Hugo from the suffering child he was when he lived in this neighborhood. He can own his past without in turn being owned by it.

31 LETTERS AND 13 DREAMS

If an evaluation of Hugo's work no longer places *31 Letters and 13 Dreams* (1977) at the pinnacle, it was nevertheless nominated for the Pulitzer

Prize and was finally voted a runner-up (to James Merrill's *Divine Comedies*), and it is perhaps his most coherent book, all the poems standing together in a volume. The title suggests a balance between self-absorption and friendship, the "dream" poems exploring Hugo's psychological depths, the "letter" poems seeking to make himself understandable to others. The balance, however, is not equal. As the title indicates, the letter poems outnumber the dream poems, and the poems are arranged into groups of two and three letters, followed by a dream and another group of letters. The dream poems therefore are isolated from one another by the poet's reaching outward. This pattern of two or three to one is Hugo's new ratio of self to society.

However, the book also blurs the distinction between letters and dreams. Because some of the letters are written in Hugo's earlier voice and place him back in the past, they probe his wounds as if they were still fresh. A look at the first four poems of the book illustrates both the pattern and the risks of any facile interpretation of it.

"Letter to Kizer from Seattle" is addressed to Carolyn Kizer, with whom Hugo taught in Missoula (and who was also the founding editor of *Poetry Northwest* and winner of the Pulitzer Prize for her book *Yin* in 1985). He calls her "Condor" (the Northwest poets in their circle called one another by animal names), and he thanks her for helping him through his breakdown at the University of Iowa. Back in Seattle now, he gives an overview of public and private issues of the early 1970s.

There was, for example, a city referendum on whether to tear down or rejuvenate the old Pike Place Public Market. For Hugo it was an intensely personal issue, as the market was a piece of the past threatened by progress. He characterizes the would-be destroyers as "the forces of evil" and the opposition as "the forces of righteousness, / me and my friends," who "are praying for a storm, one / of those grim dark rolling southwest downpours / that will leave the electorate sane." He wants nature to ally itself with a political cause (and his own nature); he prays that nature and righteousness will be aligned.

Hugo alludes to his position as holder of the Roethke Chair, and he gives accounts of mutual friends who are retiring or nearing retirement. Then, in an aside, he asks, "would you believe it / I've ignored the Blue Moon," a popular University District tavern that Hugo had frequented. Indirection is everything here. Having thanked Kizer for helping him through an alcoholic crisis, Hugo now almost casually assures her that his life is no longer ruled by his drinking. He then tells her of the places he has revisited, including White Center and Lake Kapowsin. "I tour old haunts," he says, but the Blue Moon Tavern, very much an "old haunt," is excluded.

Hugo lists his accomplishments: "One trout. One perch. One poem." As he had hoped that nature and human purposes would meld in a storm to influence the election, here he puts nature and art on an even footing: his poem parallels the fish he has caught. Hugo turns to nature for positive ways to think about himself and his poetry, in contrast to the obsession with grayness, stagnation, and north that had been the dominant symbols of his old emotional state.

The next two poems, "Letter to Bell from Missoula" and "Letter to Sister Madeline from Iowa City," work back toward his breakdown and, in the scheme of the book, toward the dream poem that will be a surrealistic account of the breakdown itself. In "Letter to Bell," addressed to fellow poet Marvin Bell, it is "Months since I left broke down and sobbing." He tells of his drive from Iowa City to Missoula, toward healing. "Until Sheridan / I took the most degenerate motels I saw because they seemed / to be where I belonged," he writes, as if westward movement had restored him. He assures Bell—indirectly, as he assured Kizer—that he has improved: "It's snowing / in Missoula, has been off and on for days but no fierce winds / and no regrets." The smooth conjunction of "no fierce winds / and no regrets" links nature with emotion, but tentatively.

Hugo concludes with a further tentative claim for his improving condition: "For no reason, I keep remembering my first woman / and how I said afterward happy, so that's what you do." Hugo located much of his distress in his habit of obsessively recalling betrayals and disappointments in his relationships with women, and in this poem he "managed to degrade myself / in front of waitresses so dumb I damn near offered them / lessons in expressions of disdain." So this new, positive memory of a woman is a change in the way his thoughts (and poems) habitually turn; his memory turns now, even if "for no reason," to a situation in which he was happy, even triumphant.

"Letter to Sister Madeline from Iowa City" approaches the brink of the collapse. "Sister Madeline" is Madeline DeFrees, fellow poet and professor. The letter-poem is a cry of despair, and the appellation "Sister" carries a suggestion of Hugo's need for both the biological closeness of a sibling (he was an only child) and the support of a spiritual guide. A "sister," whether biological or religious, is a safe confidante to whom he can confess his feelings of inadequacy without fear of repeating the pattern of romance and rejection.

He needs to feel close to a woman and yet protected from her. "I have a plan," he writes, "not serious, / for killing myself and leaving behind a beautiful note / in red paint on the ceiling, worded so the words would crawl / in the ears of women I have known like an ultrasonic hum. / And they would go mad, my life forever on their hands." The disclaimer "not serious" does not disguise the poet's despair, and he would sacrifice himself to get revenge against women, yet it is to a woman that he reveals his "plan." His "not seri-

ous" keeps her at a distance from his intimate confession. The poem concludes with a transition into the dream poem that follows: "Five A.M., and I'm wobbling off / to a dream of sea nymphs issued by the sea. Love always. Dick." Even his dreams will be of women, he confesses in an ironic tone that keeps his confidante at arm's length.

While "In Your Fugitive Dream" is not literally "a dream of sea nymphs," it involves Hugo's complicated relationships with women. Talking of himself in the second person, Hugo recounts a dream of a town closed up even at eleven A.M. on a Tuesday morning. "You break into a dress shop and imagine women / you've had in clothes the manikins wear. / You rip a dress from a plaster figure and roar. / The way you yell 'rape' it echoes about / the streets and comes back 'hope' as it dies," he says. Later, in a bar, the police catch up with him: "You watch them search your luggage. Then / you remember what you carry and start to explain."

The dream allegorizes Hugo's creative process: alienation, desperate and degrading grasping for intimacy, fear of being found out, and, finally, explanation. By the time of *31 Letters and 13 Dreams* he no longer believed this was his only possible process, but he believed that earlier in his career it had been both his curse and his deliverance.

No other book of Hugo's is as distorted by the omissions necessary for his *Selected Poems* as this one. The pattern of turning inward and outward is lost, and the reconciliation and optimism of the final poem, "In Your Good Dream," therefore seems less earned than when the book is read as a whole. The poem surveys what White Center could have been: idyllic houses and yards, friendly policemen, people who "marry forever." "Anger is outlawed," he writes; "The unpleasant get out." Hugo imagines that in this town there is a special process for inscribing granite that "cuts name, born date / and died too deep in the headstone to blur." This unnamed town is one where people are subject to the same old forces of life and death, but they are not forgotten; nature is subjugated to the small but comforting degree of being unable to efface the records of people lives.

Like the other dream poems, "In Your Good Dream" is in the second person, and the entire idealized town is observed from a "hill" where the poet is separate from these pleasant lives but sees them clearly. If one of the characteristics of despair, as Emily Dickinson claimed, is the inability to conceive of happiness, then Hugo declares himself to have reached a vantage point from which happiness is at least visible.

WHITE CENTER

White Center (1980), Hugo's strongest book, is his reexamination of his past from a place of relative safety. In "Second Chances," for example, he suggests that complete escape from the past is impossible but that there are palliatives in the redemptive work of the imagination. Writing in the first person, Hugo no longer needs the device of second person to distance his past; he has fully integrated his past. "I can't let it go, the picture I keep of myself / in ruin, living alone, some wretched town," he writes, imagining what he could have been. The image gives an ironic twist to the poem's title, a second chance being more often associated with opportunity than failure. For Hugo, there was but one chance for escape, and a second chance could have resulted only in this.

This alternative Hugo is a confirmed alcoholic, subject to the jibes of neighborhood children. While the second stanza describes his achievements—successful books, a happy marriage, respect of his peers—it also acknowledges what a small portion of his life it is: "Three years ago, I

wouldn't / have given a dime for my chances at life."

In the third and final stanza Hugo longs for the life that gave rise to the very poems that eventually allowed him to escape. A "vagabond" comes to his door and offers to take him where he will find "a million poems deep in your destitute soul." He sends the vagabond away but watches him walk to a group of children playing a game called "ghost": "a game where, according to the rules, you take / another child's name in your mind but pretend / you're still you while others guess your new name." His success notwithstanding, Hugo confronts the problem of his identity. His past old name persists (he had literally changed his name at the age of eighteen), and his new self seems a game that the children of his past (himself included) would see through.

"The River Now" reexamines the Duwamish River from Hugo's new emotional vantage point. "Hardly a ghost left to talk with," he begins, suggesting that he is no longer haunted, and he looks instead upon the mills, the water traffic, and the diminished salmon runs. In the absence of his ghostly self, the river is no longer a symbol of desolation. When Hugo says, "I can't dream anything, not some lovely woman / murdered in a shack, not saw mills going broke," he discovers that his imagination no longer turns toward violence and destitution.

Even what remains physically unchanged has a new emotional significance: "This river points / the way north to the blood," he says, but now "the bright bay north receives it all." Earlier poems associated north with death, always represented by the gray of the northern sky, but now the terminus is not death but "the bright bay."

In "White Center" Hugo walks with his grandmother's ghost to an empty lot where he recalls being bullied and afraid to fight, but the place is now grown up in roses. He recalls neighbors who suffered various degradations, but "it all comes back . . . in bites." The fragmented past no longer overwhelms him—even if it still "bites." The constant overcast no longer weighs upon him: "Clouds. What glorious floating. They always move on / like I should have early."

Hugo returns to the image of the neighborhood drunk, but while in "Second Chances" he returned in the present tense, expressing his persistent longing to give in to alcoholism, he now describes the drunk in the past tense: "I loved some terrible way / he lived in his mind and tried to be decent to others. / I loved the way we loved him behind our disdain." The verbs are emphasized by repetition and alliteration: "loved," "lived," "loved," "loved." His old feelings were strong, but they are past.

The final stanza begins, "And it isn't the same this time. I hoped forty years / I'd write and would not write this poem." The ambiguous phrasing expresses his ambivalence: The direct object of "I'd write" may or may not be "this poem." Poetry was his hope for escape from a place that was itself the only source for his poetry, and so he is deeply divided about writing "this poem," which lays his past to rest.

He hoped, he says, "your grave [would] never reopen. Or mine." Both have reopened, however. "Because I'm married / and happy . . . " he says, "I walk this past with you . . . / . . . certain I remember everything wrong." Again, the ambiguous phrasing is revealing: "wrong" can modify either "remember" or "everything." His memories may be distorted or highly selective, or his memories may be of wrongs done to and by him. The two readings do not exclude one another. His distorted memory does "remember everything wrong," so that the wrongness of the world and of the observer are one and the same. This double meaning clarifies an earlier passage in which Hugo used the present tense in this predominantly past tense poem: "I am the man / you beat into perversion." His habitual turning to the bad or wrong (the literal meaning of "perversion") is the product of the woman who raised him and the town in which he was raised. He indeed remembers "wrong," as that which is wrong within him habitually returns to the wrongs of his past.

THE RIGHT MADNESS ON SKYE

In 1977–1978 Hugo received a Guggenheim Fellowship that allowed him to live and write on the Scottish isle of Skye. His wife, Ripley, and daughter, Melissa, accompanied him, and they lived in a village called Uig, where they rented a cottage that overlooked the place where two rivers drained into the sea. While writing and revising the poems for *The Right Madness on Skye* (1980) in a new landscape, he also worked on the poems of *White Center,* and an irony of the two books is that while he found much new when he revisited the familiar town of his youth, he found much familiar when he journeyed to the new territory of Skye.

Hugo always celebrated the wisdom of the common people, especially of those most victimized by circumstances. On Skye he found peasant wit and integrity, bought at the cost of suffering dispossession when the feudal system of crofting (farmholding) evicted them during the famine years of the mid–nineteenth century. Hugo, who suffered a lifelong sense of dispossession, empathized deeply, but he did not plunge into his old suffering. In "The Semi-Lunatics of Kilmuir," for example, he says, "Imagine this lovely island warped ugly by tears." The tears are not his own; he must "imagine" the scene, and the words "lovely" and "ugly" balance one another.

That balance shifts in the second stanza as the scene changes from past to present. "Yesterday in Glasgow some magistrate ruled / feudal rights prevail"—a century after the great dispossession, the injustice continues, with legal sanction. The beauty is obscured by economic ugliness: "You pay and pay and own nothing." Only a "right madness" can make such injustice survivable, not the raving of the "real crazy" but the playful "clowning" of "con men," who are "crazy like dolphins."

The simile "like dolphins" implies that cutting oneself off from the land is a necessary prerequisite. It is a peculiar comparison, fittingly paradoxical as a description of salutary insanity. One survives on the land, it would seem, by making oneself capriciously indifferent to it. The "right madness," then, is to be simultaneously of the land and apart from it. This is Hugo's own salvation as well. As in "White Center," he achieved his new equanimity by accepting the influence of his hometown and yet separating his present self from it. Here, thousands of miles from White Center, Hugo confirms the rightness of his own journey toward integrating preservation and progress.

"Letter to Garber from Skye" portrays the landscape as a palimpsest. Old places show dimly through the new; old experiences are felt beneath the new. "The sky, water, vegetation and wind are Seattle," he writes to his friend Fred Garber, and "The panoramic bare landscape's Montana." He feels at home on two counts, and in more than the physical sense. Describing the area where he lived for the year on Skye, he notes that appearances can be sometimes deceiving, sometimes revealing. The streams, for example, "look trouty and aren't." The weather looks cold but isn't, as do the people, who are "Warmer than you think on first sight, with no throw-away charm / like in cities." Ironically, the deceptive appearance of the people proves their integrity; they do not display the superficial but false friendliness of city people. Hugo had loved this about the people of White Center, the way their poverty and isolation freed them from having to misrepresent themselves for economic gain.

"The fate of the Gael is to lose," he writes, and without the hope that leads to self-denying am-

bition, they have autonomy. "Up on the moors, the autonomous man is lost / in this autonomous land," Hugo observes—lost to him because Hugo is one of those "who need others, who / need a good time on a dock catching trout, in a cottage / writing a poem for a friend far away." Hugo embodies the paradox of loss and gain: "it is the fate of everyone to lose / the Gael." His security and his friendships have cost him the autonomy this landscape has made visible, at least to his imagination, and his loneliness, which is the cost of autonomy, is gone: "Did you hear the one / about the American who found so much quiet inside / he couldn't shut up, the way the lonely can't. I can."

"The Right Madness on Skye" asserts Hugo's own "right madness," the playful craziness he has been writing about. Dead and being taken to burial, his right madness allows him to speak from beyond death. His corpse will be taken by wagon to the grave, guided there by "Harry of Nothingham" (a pun on "Nottingham," and a telling one in this land of poverty). The refrain (sometimes with variations) "Tell Harry of Nothingham, slow" occurs in almost each of the ten stanzas as he orders how his gravestone shall be appointed, what of himself he bequeaths to the land, how his funeral services shall be conducted, and what route shall be taken to the cemetery.

The poem fuses Hugo's various selves: lonely child of White Center, respected poet, successful academic, and privileged visitor to Skye. Such fusion, never rational, requires the "right madness" that makes "all places . . . near and far selves . . . neighbors." Hugo is simultaneously a Scottish peasant and an American poet, the first bound toward his grave, the second asking that the cart detour for "a last look at Seattle and the way light / subtracts and adds miles to the journey."

Hugo can bring his own mythology and, through the synthesizing power of language, integrate it into this place: "Bury my wounded knee at Flodigarry," he says, punning on Wounded Knee, the place in South Dakota where, only seven years earlier, American Indians protested U.S. policies on Native American tribal governments, and the site, in 1890 of a massacre of unarmed Indians by government troops. It is a characteristic turn, seemingly far-fetched, and yet altogether apt; it asserts identity among dispossessed peoples everywhere, including Hugo. At a superficial level, it seems presumptuous for a world-traveling poet to imagine that he can identify with such suffering, but he claims that at some deeper level "far selves" are indeed "neighbors."

Finally, however, Hugo's empathy has limits. He reveals that he is not dead after all: "I want off at the crossroads. That's as far as I go," his last chance to curtail his exercise in empathy. He chooses not to go literally where he has already gone imaginatively. He commands, "Mail Harry of Nothingham home to his nothing." Let all things (including the poet) return to their places, no matter how impoverished. "Take my word. It's been fun," he concludes, offering his word, his poem, in place of his body.

"The right madness" is the ability to fuse disparities into coherence, but it is also the instinct for knowing how far to go. In this last line of his last book, Hugo extricates himself from the misery of the world.

Selected Bibliography

WORKS OF RICHARD HUGO

POETRY

A Run of Jacks. Minneapolis: University of Minnesota Press, 1961.
Death of the Kapowsin Tavern. New York: Harcourt, Brace and World, 1965.
Good Luck in Cracked Italian. New York: World, 1969

The Lady in Kicking Horse Reservoir. New York: Norton, 1973.
What Thou Lovest Well Remains American. New York: Norton, 1975.
31 Letters and 13 Dreams. New York: Norton, 1977.
Selected Poems. New York: Norton, 1979.
White Center. New York: Norton, 1980.
The Right Madness on Skye. New York: Norton, 1980.

PROSE
The Triggering Town: Lectures and Essays on Poetry and Writing. New York: Norton, 1979.
Death and the Good Life. New York: Norton, 1981.
The Real West Marginal Way: A Poet's Autobiography. Edited by Ripley S. Hugo, Lois Welch, and James Welch. New York: Norton, 1986.

CRITICAL AND BIOGRAPHICAL STUDIES

Allen, Michael S. *We Are Called Human: The Poetry of Richard Hugo.* Fayetteville: University of Arkansas Press, 1982.
DeFrees, Madeline. "In Madeline's Kitchen: Dick Talks about Writing." *Slackwater Review: Special Richard Hugo Issue* (1978), pp. 35–59.
Dillon, David. "Gains Made in Isolation: An Interview with Richard Hugo." In *American Poetry Observed: Poets on Their Works.* Edited by Joe David Bellamy. Urbana: University of Illinois Press, 1984. Pp. 101–113.
Driskell, Leon V. "What Thou Lovest Well Remains American." In *Survey of Contemporary Literature.* Edited by Frank N. Magill. Englewood Cliffs, N.J.: Salem Press, 1975. Pp. 8205–8208.
Friedman, Sanford. "Torn Divinities." *Modern Poetry Studies* 4.3:344–349 (1973).
Garber, Frederick. "On Richard Hugo and William Stafford." *American Poetry Review* 9:16–18 (1980).
Gardner, Thomas. "An Interview with Richard Hugo." *Contemporary Literature* 22.2:139–152 (1981).
Gerstenberger, Donna. *Richard Hugo.* Boise State University Western Writers Series, no. 59. Boise, Idaho: Boise State University, 1983.
Group, Bob. "Richard Hugo." In *American Poets since World War II.* Edited by Donald J. Greiner. Dictionary of Literary Biography series. Detroit: Gale Research, 1980.
Helms, Alan. "Writing Hurt: The Poetry of Richard Hugo." *Modern Poetry Studies* 9:106–118 (1978).

Hewitt, Geoff. "Richard Hugo." *Contemporary Poets,* 3d ed. Edited by James Vinson. New York: St. Martin's Press, 1980. Pp. 766–768.

Holden, Jonathan. "Instant Wordsworth." In his *The Rhetoric of the Contemporary Lyric.* Bloomington: Indiana University Press, 1980. Pp. 112–136.

Howard, Richard. "Richard Hugo: 'Why Track Down Unity When the Diffuse Is So Exacting?' " *Alone with America: Essays on the Art of Poetry in the United States Since 1950.* New York: Atheneum, 1980. Pp. 276–291.

Lieberman, Lawrence. "New Poetry: The Muse of History." *Yale Review* 63.1:113–136 (October 1973).

Myers, Jack, ed. *A Trout in the Milk: A Composite Portrait of Richard Hugo.* Lewiston, Ind.: Confluence Press, 1982.

Perloff, Marjorie. "Contemporary/Postmodern: The 'New' Poetry?" *Romanticism, Modernism, Postmodernism.* Edited by Harry R. Garvin. Lewisburg, Pa.: Bucknell University Press, 1980. Pp. 171–180.

Pinsker, Sanford. "Richard Hugo's Triggering Territory." *Three Pacific Northwest Poets: William Stafford, Richard Hugo, and David Wagoner.* Boston: Twayne, 1987. Pp. 55–96.

Young, William. "Traveling through the Dark: The Wilderness Surrealism of the Far West." *Midwest Quarterly* 39.2:187–202 (winter 1998).

—*RICHARD WAKEFIELD*

Zora Neale Hurston

1901–1960

ZORA NEALE HURSTON was one of the most mysterious and provocative writers of the early twentieth century. Over the course of her life, she published four novels, two collections of folklore, an autobiography, and more than fifty short stories, essays, and plays—more than any other black American woman of her period; yet by the time of her death in 1960, she had for years been a neglected figure, her works out of print. Beginning in the 1970s a critical reevaluation of Hurston's work brought her recognition as an influential pioneer in the African American women's literary tradition.

Born to a poor family in rural Florida at the beginning of the century, Hurston triumphed over many obstacles to achieve a unique place in the pantheon of African American creators as author, performer, songwriter, teacher, folklorist, and hoodoo priestess. The recipient of two Guggenheim Fellowships, she spent many years traveling throughout the South and the West Indies researching and recording black culture; she was one of the first in the field to recognize the value of African American folk and vernacular traditions and was a natural advocate of an Afrocentric culture. She was also one of the leading figures of the Harlem Renaissance (1920–1935), a period of tremendous growth and recognition for African American writers, musicians, and artists.

The major works published during Hurston's lifetime indicate the sometimes conflicting directions in which her talent and interests took her. The semiautobiographical novel *Jonah's Gourd Vine: A Novel* (1934) mined many of her own family secrets and problems in a symbolic tale of a black preacher's struggle against his natural urges. *Mules and Men* (1935), her first collection of folklore and oral tales, followed soon after, presenting black culture from an anthropological perspective. She continued to publish in the next two decades in both genres. *Their Eyes Were Watching God* (1937) is a work of powerful romantic folk fiction that continues to be her most famous and influential book. *Tell My Horse* (1938) is another collection of folklore that deals with hoodoo influences in Jamaican culture. *Moses, Man of the Mountain* (1939) is an adventuresome combination of fiction and folkloric reinterpretation of the Old Testament story told with black characters. Hurston's *Dust Tracks on a Road: An Autobiography* (1942) challenged accepted notions of autobiographical style and black politics. Her final novel, *Seraph on the Suwanee* (1948), forgoes black characters altogether in presenting an ironic narrative about marriage in a decaying southern landscape.

For many years after her death, Hurston's work was little known, and her personal reputation was often based on conjecture and judgmental evaluations of her life and its effect on her fiction. The novelist Alice Walker spurred the revival of interest in Hurston in the 1970s and 1980s. Since then Hurston's work has been reissued and reprinted and continues to be expanded. *The Sanctified Church* (1981), a collection of essays on spirituality and the black Baptist church, was written sixty years before its publication. Her short stories were gathered together for the first time in *Spunk: The Selected Stories* (1985). Lesser known essays and articles continue to be introduced to the reading public. Black feminist scholarship has been instrumental in identifying the unique qualities of Hurston's life and work.

EARLY YEARS

Zora Neale Hurston was born in Eatonville, Florida, on January 7, 1901, according to best estimates—her birth records are lost. This date is most commonly agreed upon by biographers, yet others insist she was born a decade earlier. Hurston gave conflicting dates of her birth and always kept certain details of her life shrouded in mystery. Her independent and outspoken nature, and her sometimes eccentric behavior, took her places no other black woman of that time had ventured, and often left both her admirers and critics befuddled. Like that of one of her contemporaries, the blues singer Bessie Smith, an equally gifted performer, Hurston's public persona often masked a deeply emotional and self-questioning interior life not often revealed outside her fiction.

Hurston was born to a family of five sons and three daughters; her mother, Lucy, died when Zora was nine. Her mother had been a great supporter of Zora's creative spirit. Her father, John Hurston, a Baptist preacher, remarried, and Zora quarreled with her stepmother. Dissatisfied with her small-town existence and frustrated by the lack of love and attention at home, Zora left at fourteen to join a theatrical troupe and traveled

with this group throughout the South for a year. Though she left no written record of what must have been a fascinating insider's view of the black music circuit worked by such luminaries as Ma Rainey, Charlie Patton, and Robert Johnson, the black tradition of the wandering troubadour had a powerful impact on her. Throughout her life Hurston traveled widely, presenting plays, dance and song revues, and comedic skits for black performers. In 1917, after leaving the troupe in Baltimore, Hurston attended Morgan Academy, now Morgan State University. She went on to Howard University in Washington, D.C., the following year. While studying English at Howard, she worked as a maid, a waitress, and a manicurist. She began writing stories and poems at this time.

In 1921 one of her early stories, "John Redding Goes to Sea," was published in *Stylus,* a Howard literary magazine. This folk story of hoodoo in a rural village engages some of the rich talents Hurston was to develop in coming decades—her lively and expressive language, a gift for humor, and the ability to capture and transmit folk wisdom. The story also established a persistent theme in Hurston's writing by presenting a sympathetic picture of an African American culture that at that time was not well known or accepted by the mainstream. One of the aspects of this culture was black hoodoo belief; the tenuous line between natural phenomena and supernatural significance was a boundary Hurston explored continuously in her stories.

Hurston's writing was soon recognized by editors and publishers. Charles S. Johnson, the editor of *Opportunity: A Journal of Negro Life,* published two of her early stories, "Drenched in Light" and "Spunk," and also a short play, *Color Struck,* about interracial color consciousness. Her second play, *The First One,* was also submitted to *Opportunity* in 1926. It was printed later in Johnson's *Ebony and Topaz* (1927). The play is a reinterpretation of the biblical Ham legend. This early effort indicates Hurston's interest in revising Old Testament stories in light of African American concerns. Her early years in Eatonville had exposed her to the great black oral storytelling tradition, in which biblical tales were often adapted and personalized.

"Drenched in Light" is one of the first stories in which Hurston uses Eatonville as a backdrop for her fiction. Incorporated in 1886, the town was one of a few self-governing, all-black townships that fostered pride, independence, and black self-improvement in a racially segregated environment. Eatonville was also a living repository of black folktales and oral traditions that helped define a unique community. Hurston's own father had helped write the town bylaws. "Drenched in Light" is a tale of a black girl growing up in Eatonville. Though she is poor, her life is far from tragic; indeed, she manifests joy and happiness in her origins, her color, and her emerging selfhood. The community imbues her with self-reliance and a love of her race.

THE HARLEM RENAISSANCE

In 1925 Hurston left Howard and moved to New York City, where she attracted the attention of Annie Nathan Meyer, a founder of Barnard College. Meyer arranged for a scholarship for Hurston, who became the only black student attending Barnard at that time. While studying English, history, and anthropology, Hurston participated in the Black Arts movement centered in Harlem, just uptown from the Columbia-Barnard campus. She met many of the writers and artists who later became famous figures in the Harlem Renaissance, including Langston Hughes, Countee Cullen, Claude McKay, Wallace Thurman, Jean Toomer, Rudolph Fisher, and the novelist Fannie Hurst, who hired Hurston to be her live-in secretary. Although Hurston was not the most efficient clerical assistant, Hurst kept her on as a paid companion and chauffeur. Hurston soon cut a

wide swath in the Harlem studios, clubs, and gathering places and was recognized as an influential Harlem Renaissance personality. Her lively and brash manner made her a natural entertainer who personified black pride, with generous doses of sarcastic and self-deprecating wit. She often dressed with an eye to African design and fabric and favored natural hairstyles. As a free-thinking and freely operating black woman, she assumed the role of a cultural revolutionary proudly committed to African American identity. She became friends with many people, both black and white, who were enjoying the resurgence of black creativity in New York's city within a city. Although she would later write only two paragraphs on the Harlem Renaissance in her autobiography *Dust Tracks on a Road,* Hurston was at the heart of this twentieth-century efflorescence of African American culture.

Hurston lived in Harlem for two and a half years. Much of her personal success was built around her storytelling. As a representative of the southern folk idiom, she helped contribute to the cultural forces that made the Harlem Renaissance part of American intellectual history. Part of the wave of southern blacks who had migrated to New York, Hurston held firmly to her southern folk perspective; this duality of rural folk and urban intellectualism, as well as her efforts to explain and represent the African American folk experience in a creative and positive light, made Hurston representative of what was being called the New Negro. Other black writers at the time, such as Claude McKay, who had come to New York from Jamaica, were working in a similar vein. Hurston was brought to the attention of the public when one of the leading lights in the movement, Alain Locke, reprinted her short story "Spunk" in his seminal book *The New Negro* (1925), an anthology of African American art and literature.

"Spunk," which takes place in Eatonville, is composed almost entirely of dialogue written in the black dialect of rural central Florida; the reliance on dialect signals Hurston's developing writing style. In the story, the title character, Spunk, carries on an affair with Lena, another man's wife. Much of the story is told as members of the community, gathered in a general store, offer their commentary on the affair; one suggests that Spunk acts with impunity because Lena's husband is "timid 'bout fighten'." Another responds to this remark:

> You wrong theah. . . . 'Tain't cause Joe's timid at all, it's cause Spunk wants Lena. If Joe was a passle of wile cats Spunk would tackle the job just the same. . . . he tole Joe right to his face that Lena was his. "Call her," he says to Joe. "Call her and see if she'll come. A woman knows her boss an' she answers when he calls."

Incorporating black folklore and hoodoo, the story features a supernatural force that rights the wrongs of the natural world. Hurston understood hoodoo rituals as expressions of religious belief that helped give blacks a hopeful worldview; that the outcome of the story is determined by benevolent magic powers is an expression of Hurston's ability to inhabit that worldview and an affirmation of the vibrancy of the black culture she wrote about.

Hurston's early work is characterized by this fusion of folklore and fiction. Her first short stories introduced an array of Eatonville's black characters, capturing their speech patterns and employing their vernacular in the exposition of the narrative. From early on in her personal life and in her writing, Hurston was interested in introducing Eatonville folklore to a wider audience. The complex spirit of the rural blacks she had known was also represented in the Harlem musicians and artists who were enjoying great success creating new African American art forms. In 1926 Hurston, Langston Hughes, Wallace Thurman, and Aaron Douglas created their own magazine, *Fire!!,* which lasted for only one issue. It was the implied intent of this magazine to express the pride and fascination with the black vernacular tradition that was inspiring the Harlem Renaissance. Hurston's short story in *Fire!!,* called "Sweat," is perhaps her best work of the period. A complex, allegorical tale of good and evil that concentrates on folk characters in a folk environment, it is a tragic story of a marriage gone bad between a hardworking and unloved washerwoman and her unemployed husband. The husband tries to kill his wife with the aid of a rattlesnake, but in the end it is he who is killed by the snake. The rattlesnake would appear again in Hurston's work; a symbol of retributive punishment, it represents a natural spirit or energy that infuses the world in ways sometimes good and sometimes bad.

"The Eatonville Anthology," published in *The Messenger* in 1926, is another of Hurston's fusions of folklore and fiction. This work consists of fourteen conversational vignettes. Some of the tales are *memorates,* stories based on memories of actual events special to the teller. The ninth vignette features a character sketch of Mrs. Joe Clarke, who would later become the protagonist of *Their Eyes Were Watching God.* With its perfect ear for dialect, "The Eatonville Anthology" may be the best early example of what might paradoxically be called Hurston's written oral art.

Hurston was interested in the retention and recalling of authentic elements of Africa in African American folklore. Her 1928 essay "How It Feels to Be Colored Me" explores the world of black jazz music. In this affirmative meditation on the joys of being an African American, Hurston relates how jazz touches on the racial memory of people of African descent through its use of African musical techniques and sounds. Hurston was in fact intensely interested in all aspects of black music. The article "Spirituals and Neo-Spirituals," which appeared in Nancy Cunard's anthology *Negro* (1934), stresses the importance of spirituals in black culture and affirms the beauty of their lyrical analogies. Like her friend James Weldon Johnson, a musician and songwriter who compiled two volumes of American Negro spirituals, Hurston supported black spiritual music in its unpretentious state as a transcendent expression of community survival. "Black Death," an unpublished story from the 1920s that tells of an Eatonville hoodoo man named Old Dan Morgan, shows Hurston's concern with African ancestral currents running through contemporary African American life.

In depicting an instinctual Africanism in black Americans, Hurston was attempting to generate racial pride. She believed that black Americans needed to understand better their unique culture and see how it reflected African origins. With its African roots, the historical and spiritual legacy of black people was distinct from that of whites, indicating a complex cultural consciousness. This was a theme she would proclaim often in life and write about in many of her later works.

FOLKLORE AND ANTHROPOLOGY

While at Barnard, from which she graduated in 1928, Hurston turned to the professional study of folklore as an alternative to writing fiction. Later she would return to fiction as a way to communicate the life of rural African Americans and their folk ethos to a wider audience. Hurston's work in anthropology at Barnard attracted the attention of Franz Boas, then the leading anthropologist in the United States and a professor at Columbia University. With his assistance, Hurston was awarded by the Association for the Study of Negro Life and History a fourteen-hundred-dollar fellowship to collect folklore in the South. Hurston would go on to become an authority on African American folklore and the first black female from the South to work in the

field. She later acquired a patron, Charlotte Osgood Mason, a rich white woman who supported many Harlem Renaissance artists, including Langston Hughes, as they struggled to build their careers. Hurston's eagerness to establish herself as a legitimate folklorist at one point led her into trouble. Her essay "Cudjo's Own Story of the Last African Slaver," published in the *Journal of Negro History* in 1927, includes an interview with Cudjo Lewis, the only survivor of the last known ship to bring African slaves to America in 1859. It appears that Hurston may have plagiarized some portions of this article from a previously published book on the subject.

Hurston had to make the difficult choice of subordinating art to science in becoming a professional folklorist. With her turn away from fiction and her plunge into anthropology, she became an enthusiastic recorder of folk customs. She hoped that the scientific record of her people's folk creations would make her a tradition bearer. Black folk culture was often criticized by whites as a primitive method of dealing with the world. But it was Hurston's conviction that there was nothing primitive about folk traditions that enabled black people to survive with strength and dignity the horrors of slavery and its aftermath.

During the period from 1927 to 1935, Hurston went on several folklore-gathering trips to the South and the West Indies, where she interviewed former slaves and migrant workers and recorded their tales. In 1931 she published some of the results of her expeditions in the *Journal of American Folklore.* Entitled "Hoodoo in America," her report was the first scholarly treatment of hoodoo by a black American folklorist. Her first book on folklore, *Mules and Men,* followed in 1935.

Hurston's pursuit of the authentic black folklore experience led her to New Orleans in August 1928, where she interviewed Samuel Thompson, a well-known hoodoo priest who was a student and descendant of the legendary hoodoo queen

Marie Leveau. Hoodoo as a synthesis of African religious retentions and Christian imagery fascinated Hurston, with its ancient history and its linking of African American and African Caribbean folklore. Her intrigue with hoodoo was not purely academic, and she became involved with the practice on a personal level. In the process of becoming a hoodoo priestess, she endured physical and psychic peril. As part of her ritual trial and ceremonial passage into the religion, she fasted and lay silent for three days. In the coming years she would enter into many more hoodoo ceremonies, endangering her own life in the process.

Some of Hurston's best nonfiction writing on folklore practices explores her personal journey through strange lands and secretive cults. She was capable of great sacrifice in her pursuit to record black culture in America. She undertook her travels in the West Indies and the Deep South at a time when unaccompanied single black women risked being victims of race-based violence. Hurston was urged on in her study by her mentor, the anthropologist Boas, who was deeply interested in the African survivals found in African American hoodoo culture.

In 1930 Hurston returned to New York City, where she collaborated with Langston Hughes on a play, *Mule Bone: A Comedy of Negro Life* (1991), which uses verbal improvisations and rhyming to create a theatrical experience of black expression. Unfortunately, her only known collaboration with another Harlem Renaissance artist was not a successful one. The relationship turned sour over a number of personal issues, and the play was not performed during the authors' lifetimes. Hurston and Hughes never worked together again. No consistent explanation has been given for this particular artistic fallout. Hurston's career was confrontational in many respects; she often did the opposite of what people expected her to do, manifesting an extreme individuality

and independence throughout her life. In 1991 Hurston and Hughes's play was published as *Mule Bone: A Comedy of Negro Life,* edited by George Houston Bass and Henry Louis Gates Jr.

After her travels, Hurston immersed herself in her book *Mules and Men,* a compilation of her major work on black folklore, which was published to considerable notice. The book includes pieces of pure folklore, narratives about collecting the material, and transcriptions of the tales people around her told as she was growing up. *Mules and Men* celebrates the art of the community. It is also a clever depiction of rural folk character, with trickster figures, in the African oral tradition, outwitting their adversaries. The tales from the John Marster cycle in the book are of this type, showing John's ingenuity in turning a situation to his advantage. The book establishes folklore as a dramatic vehicle for community expression.

RETURN TO FICTION

Even before *Mules and Men* was published in 1935, Hurston had returned to writing fiction. The Depression presented monumental obstacles for her. Unemployed and often sick, she could not rely on her published work for any significant income. During this period she attempted to break into the entertainment field by writing a musical revue called *The Great Day* (1932), which was later redone as *Sun to Sun* in Florida. From the descriptions of these and other song-and-dance musicals Hurston wrote, it is evident that she was trying to reinterpret the minstrel tradition by establishing an innovative black play form. None of her shows ever proved successful, perhaps a result of the conditions of segregated theaters at the time.

In 1933 *Story Magazine* printed Hurston's "The Gilded Six-Bits," which proved to be one of her most influential and most often anthologized stories. It analyzes a rural marriage shaken by infidelity and greed. Missie May, Joe's wife, falls under the spell of a black city slicker named Slemmons, who brandishes a ten-dollar gold piece as a watch fob. Lusting after the gold, Missie favors Slemmons. When Joe catches them in bed together, Slemmons narrowly escapes, dropping his watch fob as he runs away. Revealed as a gilded half-dollar, the phony gold piece represents the fickleness of human nature and the corrosive influence of materialism on human interactions. Joe, the outraged husband, insults Missie by leaving the coin under Missie's pillow for services rendered. In the end the marriage is damaged by Missie's greed and Joe's intolerance, but because of their joint efforts at reconciliation the story ends with images of a possible, if rocky, recovery.

Marriage problems form the basis of four of the five stories Hurston published between 1924 and 1933. The joys and sorrows of marriage would remain an important theme throughout her career. Her novels would also deal with marriage as a problematic state, a situation that haunted Hurston's personal life as well. (She was divorced from her first husband, whom she married in 1927, in 1931.) She began writing her first novel, *Jonah's Gourd Vine,* around this time. Gathering diverse ideas from folklore concerns and family history, this novel explores the conflict between African-based religious practices and Christianity through the struggles of the rural preacher John Pearson. The strictures of marriage and church intertwine with the natural urges of human beings, resulting in a potent and fatal mix.

John Pearson, sharecropper turned black preacher, has a gift for natural imagery and language in the black oral storytelling tradition. Laced with Pearson's rough-hewn poetry and sermons of magnificent energy that seem to decant from his being, the book captures the theatrical

richness and vitality of his speech, in passages such as the following:

I am the teeth of time
That comprehended de dust of de earth
And weighed de hills in scales
That pointed de rainbow dat marks de end of de
  parting storm
Measured de seas in de holler of my hand
That held de elements in a unbroken chain of
  controllment.

Yet the visceral life force that is the very source of Pearson's powerful creativity cannot be restrained by Christian morals. The temptations of the flesh prove too powerful: in conflict with himself and society, in and out of churches and marriages, Pearson succumbs to his desires to get drunk and sleep with other women. Blinded by mad rage at himself, deranged by the tension between the spiritual and the physical, he drives his car into a train and dies. While universal in theme, the book has a poignant personal aura of Zora's father's own reputed infidelities and their consequences for his marriage and family. Because of these resonances, the novel has often been called autobiographical.

In 1935 Hurston returned to the South and worked with Alan Lomax, collecting music for the Library of Congress. Because of contacts she had established in her folklore explorations, she was of great help in locating obscure black blues singers. She played an important part in the fieldwork aspect of this collection, which has become one of the most important records of early African American blues artists ever amassed. Her work also gave her the personal pleasure of introducing hidden areas of black culture to the researchers. In that year Hurston also worked on a number of different writing projects including *The Fiery Chariot,* a one-act comedic play that was never published. Experiencing financial difficulty, she joined the Works Progress Administration's Federal Theater Project in 1935. In 1936 she applied for and was offered a Guggenheim fellowship to collect folklore in the West Indies.

THEIR EYES WERE WATCHING GOD

By the spring of 1936 Hurston was in the Caribbean collecting material, with most of her time spent in Jamaica studying obeah, or black magic, and exploring the African survivals manifest in the native religion. *Tell My Horse* (1938), her second book of folklore, is Hurston's account of her trip and the time she spent living with the remote Maroons, descendants of black slaves who had fought their way out of bondage and lived in the high mountains of the island. Before finishing *Tell My Horse* she made another trip to Haiti, and under the romantic influence of a thwarted love affair, she wrote in seven weeks what was to become her most famous novel, *Their Eyes Were Watching God* (1937). Her most accomplished work, it is an authentic fictional representation of rural black Florida at the turn of the century. On this level the book captures the poignant loss of a part of rural culture that Hurston grew up with. But the book is much more: it is a celebration and exploration of woman's consciousness that traces a black woman's struggle to selfhood.

Hurston once again draws on Eatonville and the people she grew up with to form the basis of the novel. Told in flashback, the third-person narrative voice adheres closely to the natural voice and rhythms of its heroine, Janie Crawford, who acts out many roles in a variety of settings as she progresses toward individual womanhood. She breaks through two confining marriages to find momentary salvation in romantic and sensual love with Tea Cake, a young black migrant worker. In framing the novel as a tale told on a porch to Janie's good friend Pheoby, Hurston is obviously concerned with reflecting in her narrative the oral traditions of black Americans.

Finding a voice in which to articulate one's story—indeed, language itself—lies at the core of the novel's concerns. With its masterful use of dialect and folk idioms, the novel is a perfect marriage of Hurston's skills as folklorist and creative artist; its evocative natural imagery underlines the close connection between rural black life and the land. Two recurring metaphors, the blossoming pear tree and the beckoning horizon, represent Janie's quest for organic union with another and development of her self—themes that in Hurston's hands flow from the vernacular world of her heroine into the universal and back. This can be seen in the opening section of chapter 2:

> Janie saw her life like a great tree in leaf with the things suffered, things enjoyed, things done and undone. Dawn and doom was in the branches.
> "Ah know exactly what Ah got to tell yuh, [she said] but it's hard to know where to start at."

Laced with folktales, jokes, work songs, and dance, the novel pays tribute to the oral traditions of the early black community. Perhaps no other novel so skillfully and vibrantly re-creates a rural black woman's voice, rendering it as an emblem of the progression from slavery to the conditions of the early twentieth century. The book's characters speak convincingly of both the wisdom and the constraints of black southern life as they shake off the legacy of slavery to form a community of self-survival.

Janie's Grandmother Lucy, who raises her, was born into slavery. Her daughter, Janie's mother, was fathered by Lucy's white master. Janie knows neither her father nor her mother, both having deserted her. Before Grandmother Lucy dies, she forces Janie into marriage with an old black farmer. This loveless union and the man's material wealth fall far short of satisfying Janie's sense of self. Her search for her true identity starts early in her speculations on the true place of human beings in the natural world. Her second marriage, to Joe Starks, though it lasts twenty years, also proves inadequate and unfulfilling. Starks is instrumental in developing Eatonville as a black community, building a store, bringing the town its first public streetlight, and becoming its mayor. But Joe continues to subjugate Janie and uses physical violence to restrict her ability to speak her mind freely. Janie soon becomes dissatisfied with the male-dominated society that threatens to destroy her.

Janie's natural inclination to resist male domination through two mismatched marriages, to find the courage to break the bonds of her time and place, bespeaks her attempt to find a natural expression of her total being. When she falls in love with Tea Cake, a migrant worker and singer, Janie is allowed to participate as an equal. They share in their work and their lives. The organic union, the sense of completion, that Janie envisions early in the novel in the budding and blossoming pear tree is embodied in the natural connection between her and Tea Cake, who accepts her as a partner. Together they follow the harvest from one rural community to another, and as they do so Janie eventually finds her voice, telling stories in the best store-porch tradition. As she explains to Pheoby,

> Ah know all dem sitters-and-talkers gointuh worry they guts into fiddle strings till dey find out whut we been talkin' 'bout. Dat's all right, Pheoby, tell 'em. Dey gointuh make 'miration 'cause mah love didn't work lak they love, if dey ever had any. Then you must tell 'em dat love ain't somethin' lak uh grindstone dat's de same thing everywhere and do de same thing tuh everything it touch. Love is lak de sea. It's uh movin' thing, but still and all, it takes its shape from de shore it meets, and it's different with every shore.

The cyclical existence of Janie and Tea Cake, its simple values and deep community connections, provides its own rewards. In this environ-ment Janie blossoms into full womanhood. Hurston's rhythmically flowing language bursts with natural imagery, investing the world around Janie and Tea Cake with Afrocentric animism. Janie is liberated from structured gender roles and achieves a sense of fulfillment and creativity by claiming her place as an equal in the black folk tradition. In the end, the all-powerful and essentially mysterious force of the natural world bears down on the characters' fates: the novel ends in tragedy with a hurricane and Tea Cake's death from rabies. Yet there is redemption in Janie's return to her original Eatonville community and the powerful influence she will provide as an example of self-identified black woman.

The book met with a generally positive reception. At the time it was published, some criticism suggested that Hurston devoted too much of her talents to exploring intraracial folkloric situations rather than dealing with interracial confrontations. Critics writing in the 1990s have debated Hurston's gender definitions and the relationship between Janie and Tea Cake; some find the romantic folk aura of the novel facile and unrealistic. Undoubtedly the novel has earned an enduring place in American literature. Janie is one of the first heroic black women to appear in African American literature, and Hurston's themes of self-definition, autonomy, and liberation, arrayed against a rich panoply of black vernaculars, is unique in African American fiction from this period. The novel's folk imagery and uncanny capturing of a vanished way of life marks the work as an essential expression of African American culture in the twentieth century.

THE WANDERING YEARS

Following *Their Eyes Were Watching God,* Hurston renewed her Guggenheim fellowship and continued her research into hoodoo gods in Haiti. She became deathly ill with a mysterious ailment that was never fully explained; Hurston herself attributed it to a hoodoo priest's retribution for her prying activity into the mysterious religion. After recovering, she left Haiti and completed her cultural anthropological research into hoodoo in Florida. *Tell My Horse* was completed, for better or worse, in the spring of 1939. Extenuating circumstances such as her illness, her ever recurring financial difficulties, and her harried state of mind may have contributed to its uneven construction. Nevertheless, it remains important as an attempt to dignify the renegade religion.

Out of financial necessity, Hurston joined the Florida Federal Writers Project and reluctantly took a job as an editor of the American Guide series volume on Florida. Her main contribution was compiling a source guide called "The Florida Negro," which presented the history and current status of black populations in Florida; it remains unpublished. In the fall of 1939 she was hired to teach and organize a drama program at North Carolina College for Negroes in Durham. This experience proved to be a failure, as she was prevented by lack of financial support from producing a single play. However, it was at this time that she began work on her third novel, which she wrote at a feverish pace.

Moses, Man of the Mountain (1939) seemed to spring out of nowhere. Although indications of her interest in biblical themes exist in her early short fiction, such as "The Fire and the Cloud," *Moses* is a far more ambitious project. Completed in a matter of weeks, it was published soon after, mostly on the reputation of her two previous books. Immediately controversial, it elicited mixed responses from critics both black and white. The subject matter was a difficult jump for the general reader. By making Moses black and claiming his true birthright as African—an image and an idea far ahead of the times—Hurston foreshadowed revisionist Afrocentric theories of the 1980s and 1990s. Concerned with emancipation and the founding of African American identity,

Moses redefines the origins of African American culture and revises prevalent notions of black history, suggesting that the influence of Africa's past on African American consciousness cannot be overlooked. It is a work of myth and allegory that repositions Moses's identity as an African conjurer with tremendous spiritual power.

Hurston was married for the second time during this period. The marriage to a younger man lasted less than six months. Once again she overcame her sense of frustration in finding a workable union through travel and hard work. During the winter of 1940–1941 Hurston was back in New York, where she was encouraged by her publisher to write the first volume of what was projected to be a multivolume autobiography. She moved to California to stay with a friend and wrote most of the book there. She also worked as a story consultant for Paramount Studios without any recognizable success.

Moving back to Florida, near Eatonville, Hurston finished *Dust Tracks on a Road* (1942). Alice Walker has commented that the most unfortunate thing Hurston ever wrote is this autobiography. It is Walker's and other critics' impression that she was under too much pressure and too dependent on others while she wrote it. She has been accused of purposely watering down her reminiscences so as not to offend anyone and has been criticized for ignoring the race problem in this work, though excisions by her editor also affected the finished product. Other interpretations of the work, by Francoise Lionnet-McCumber ("Autoethnography: The An-Archic Style of Dust Tracks on a Road," in *Zora Neale Hurston: Critical Perspectives Past and Present,* edited by Henry Louis Gates Jr., and K. A. Appiah), for example, emphasize the aspect of the personal quest and the author's trickster qualities of blending picaresque narrative structure with mythic imagery and language. The matrix of Hurston's writing style is the front-porch, tall-tale tradition depicted in many of her folklore collections; by employing that style in her autobiography, she once again avoided revealing an inner self. Perhaps surprisingly, *Dust Tracks on a Road* was a publishing success. It sold well and won a literary award honoring books on race relations.

Partly as a result of the success of *Dust Tracks on a Road,* Hurston was well known during the 1940s and indeed may have been the most widely acclaimed black woman writer since Phillis Wheatley. She appeared on the cover of the *Saturday Review of Literature* in 1943 and the same year received the annual alumni award from Howard University. She was offered work writing for magazines, and between 1942 and 1945 she published articles in *American Mercury, The Saturday Evening Post, Negro Digest,* and *Reader's Digest.* Nonetheless, her early support for black cultural nationalists was often assailed as propaganda. This was a charge that other black writers also faced at the time. Contemporary critics judged her celebration of ethnic heritage as a failure to be universal. Her focus on Eatonville and its rural folklore characters provoked extended controversy over the nature and value of her work. Hurston chose to write of the positive effects of black experience and believed that folk expression was by far its most important element. In response, white critics blasted her for what they saw as propaganda, and black critics accused her of distorting the reality of black life by ignoring the exploitation of blacks and the misery of segregation and race riots.

Hurston's 1943 *American Mercury* article, entitled "The 'Pet Negro' System" expressed a hope for a mood of racial cooperation and recognition of black people's patriotism. Her comment in another essay that "the Jim Crow system works" drew a tremendous outcry from black critics. Yet Hurston proved herself a staunch supporter of black rights during World War II by joining the Negro Defense Fund and protesting the treatment of black servicemen at a military training school near her home in Florida.

Always in love with travel and adventure, Hurston lived for a time on a houseboat named the *Wanago.* At one point she brought it all the way to Manhattan and berthed it there. After collaborating in New York with Dorothy Waring on a musical comedy of black life in a sawmill camp that never made it to the stage, she turned to a project that stretched the bounds of her imagination. She was intrigued by a tale she had heard about an ancient undiscovered Mayan city in the jungle of Honduras. By May 1947 Hurston was in Honduras setting up an expedition to find the lost city. She also had a new contract with Charles Scribner's Sons to write another novel. The jungle expedition failed to work out, but she stayed on in Honduras writing what was to be her last novel. She moved back to New York for its appearance in the fall of 1948.

THE FINAL PERIOD

Seraph on the Suwanee, a puzzling novel that maintains an ironic stance while it explores the marriage between Arvay and Jim Meserve, poor southern white farmers, proved to be another controversial work. Hurston surprised her reading public by writing a novel about a white family. Many critics saw it as representing an irreversible decline in Hurston's literary abilities. However, the attitude of the third-person narrator toward the central character of Arvay deserves attention. In exploring Arvay's feelings of inferiority and incompleteness, Hurston offers insights into issues of sexuality and male domination within marriage.

In her last years Hurston wrote articles on political subjects that took an idiosyncratic approach to black-white relations, again espousing views that seemed at odds with black rights. Two controversial public problems marred this period of her life. In New York in September 1948, Hurston was arrested and charged with committing an immoral sexual act with a ten-year-old boy. She entered a plea of not guilty, and it was quickly proven that she was not even in New York City at the time the incident was alleged to have taken place. The accuser and his mother were found to be mentally disturbed. Moreover, it was disclosed that Hurston had quarreled with the mother over the previous two years; a vendetta was determined to be the cause of the charge, and Hurston was exonerated. But it was too late for her public reputation. The black newspapers had gotten hold of the story and milked it for its sensational value.

Disheartened by this betrayal, Hurston entered a period of deep depression and left New York for Florida. In March 1950 a white woman was amazed to discover that her black maid had published stories in *The Saturday Evening Post.* The revelation was picked up by the newspapers, and once again Hurston was exposed to public scrutiny.

Hurston then turned to politics, working for a conservative candidate in a primary race and publishing articles with controversial slants in *American Legion Magazine* and *The Saturday Evening Post.* Her comments concerning the Supreme Court desegregation decision of 1954 infuriated many black activists. Hurston appeared to enjoy exhibiting her cantankerousness. Yet her views can be traced to her experience in the all-black township of Eatonville, where the segregated lifestyles of the black community had worked very well. Eatonville was, however, an anomaly in a southern landscape of jim crowism and crippling prejudice and segregation.

By the winter of 1950–1951, Hurston was reduced to extreme poverty. A publication in *The Saturday Evening Post* of her article "A Negro Voter Sizes Up Taft" rescued her with a thousand-dollar check. She took the money and moved back to the cabin where she had written *Mules and Men* so many years before. She engaged in

her last literary task, an attempted retelling of the biblical story of Herod the Great. As in *Moses,* Hurston was intrigued by the dramatic potential inherent in the Herod story, especially if recast in a black perspective. Hurston saw the Jewish struggle as closely aligned to black independence movements. After years of work on the manuscript, she endured rejection by Scribner. The novel remains unpublished. Hurston had no luck interesting publishers with other ideas for books.

Although Hurston's life as a writer was over, she still gathered and preserved ideas that celebrated black culture. She made many friends in communities in Florida where she lived and enjoyed returning to a natural lifestyle, growing her own food and raising animals. Hurston had lived through many changes in black-white relationships in the United States, and through it all she remained committed to the survival of African Americans, striving to keep alive the promise of the Harlem Renaissance years. The sources of her spirit remained as always the music and speech, the energy and wisdom, the dignity and humor of the black rural southern folkways.

Over the next few years Hurston worked as a librarian on an air force base and as a reporter and writer for the *Fort Pierce Chronicle,* a local black weekly. Her health remained poor. She became overweight, and high blood pressure led to a stroke in 1959. She entered a county welfare home soon after and died of heart disease on January 28, 1960. She was laid to rest in an unmarked grave in Fort Pierce's segregated cemetery.

The critical reevaluation of Hurston's work undertaken in the 1970s through the 1990s, though not uniformly positive, brought proper recognition to her achievements. Feminists and multiculturalists recognized her groundbreaking status as an unabashed lover of black culture who saw black Americans as *creators* of culture. Her documentation of a lost oral tradition was of critical importance to early black consciousness. Distinguishing black culture from white forecast a direction that anticipated modern movements in African American literature. With her gift for capturing black vernaculars, for drama, humor, and the sheer joys of language, Hurston left her imprint on the American consciousness and helped establish the parameters for understanding the uniqueness of African American culture.

Selected Bibliography

WORKS OF ZORA NEALE HURSTON

BOOKS

Jonah's Gourd Vine: A Novel. 1934. Reprint, New York: HarperCollins, 1990.

Mules and Men. Preface by Franz Boas. 1935. Reprint, with a foreword by Arnold Rampersad. New York: HarperPerennial, 1990.

Their Eyes Were Watching God. 1937. Reprint, with a foreword by Mary Helen Washington. New York: Perennial Classics, 1999.

Tell My Horse. 1938. Reprint, with a foreword by Ishmael Reed, as *Tell My Horse: Voodoo and Life in Haiti and Jamaica.* New York: Perennial Library, 1990.

Moses, Man of the Mountain. 1939. Reprint, with a foreword by Deborah E. McDowell. New York: HarperPerennial, 1991.

Dust Tracks on a Road: An Autobiography. 1942. Reprint, with original chapters restored, edited and with an introduction by Robert Hemenway. Urbana: University of Illinois Press, 1984.

Seraph on the Suwanee. 1948. Reprint, with a foreword by Hazel C. Carby. New York: HarperPerennial, 1991.

The Sanctified Church. Foreword by Toni Cade Bambara. Berkeley, Calif.: Turtle Island, 1981.

Mule Bone: A Comedy of Negro Life (with Langston Hughes). Edited by George Houston Bass and Henry Louis Gates Jr. New York: HarperPerennial, 1991.

COLLECTED WORKS

I Love Myself When I Am Laughing . . . A Zora Neale Hurston Reader. Edited by Alice Walker. Old Westbury, N.Y.: Feminist Press, 1979.

Spunk: The Selected Stories. Berkeley, Calif.: Turtle Island, 1985.

The Complete Stories of Zora Neale Hurston. Introduction by Henry Louis Gates Jr., and Seiglinde Lemke. New York: HarperCollins, 1995.

Novels and Stories. Edited by Cheryl A. Wall. New York: Library of America, 1995.

Sweat. Edited by Cheryl A. Wall. New Brunswick, N.J.: Rutgers University Press, 1997.

BIBLIOGRAPHY

Davis, Rose Parkman, comp. *Zora Neale Hurston: An Annotated Bibliography and Reference Guide.* Westport, Conn.: Greenwood Press, 1997.

CRITICAL AND BIOGRAPHICAL STUDIES

Awkward, Michael, ed. *New Essays on Their Eyes Were Watching God.* Cambridge: Cambridge University Press, 1990.

Bloom, Harold, ed. *Zora Neale Hurston.* New York: Chelsea House, 1986.

Cronin, Gloria L, ed. *Critical Essays on Zora Neale Hurston.* New York: G. K. Hall, 1998.

Gates, Henry Louis, Jr., and K. A. Appiah, eds. *Zora Neale Hurston: Critical Perspectives Past and Present.* New York: Amistad Press, 1993.

Hemenway, Robert E. *Zora Neale Hurston: A Literary Biography.* Foreword by Alice Walker. Urbana: University of Illinois Press, 1977.

Holloway, Karla F. C. *The Character of the Word: The Texts of Zora Neale Hurston.* New York: Greenwood Press, 1987.

Howard, Lillie P. *Zora Neale Hurston.* Boston: Twayne, 1980.

Lowe, John. *Jump at the Sun: Zora Neale Hurston's Cosmic Comedy.* Urbana: University of Illinois Press, 1994.

Plant, Deborah G. *Every Tub Must Sit on Its Own Bottom: The Philosophy and Politics of Zora Neale Hurston.* Urbana: University of Illinois Press, 1995.

—*STEPHEN SOITOS*

John Irving

1942—

JOHN WINSLOW IRVING was born John Wallace Blunt Jr., on March 2, 1942, in Exeter, New Hampshire, to Frances Winslow. His biological father, whom Frances divorced before her son was born, was killed in World War II. When Irving was six, his mother remarried, and he was adopted by her second husband, Colin F. N. Irving, who taught Russian history at Exeter Academy.

Irving was an average student at Exeter (he suffered from dyslexia) and a better than average wrestler, earning a wrestling scholarship to the University of Pittsburgh. Although Irving left Pittsburgh after one year (1962), he never left the sport, later becoming a coach and a referee. Wrestling became a frequent topic in his writing, figuring centrally in *The 158-Pound Marriage* (1974) and *The World According to Garp* (1978).

Another early experience also shaped Irving's writing. In 1963 he left the United States to study at the Institute of European Studies at the University of Vienna. Vienna provides the setting for much of Irving's first novel, *Setting Free the Bears* (1969), and is significant in *The Water-Method Man* (1972), *The World According to Garp,* and *The Hotel New Hampshire* (1981). For Irving, Vienna represents the violence and decadence of the postmodern world—a "foreign country" that a number of his characters not only escape from but often return to.

Irving married Shyla Leary in 1964, and their first son, Colin, was born in 1965, while Irving was still in college. Irving completed his undergraduate degree, cum laude, at the University of New Hampshire. Under the writing instruction of the novelists John Yount and Thomas Williams, he wrote two short stories: "A Winter Branch" was published in *Redbook* in 1965 and "Weary Kingdom" appeared in *The Boston Review* in 1968. The stories, straightforward in development, lack the comedy and vitality of Irving's later works.

After college, Irving was a graduate student at the University of Iowa Writers' Workshop, where he studied with Vance Bourjaily and Kurt Vonnegut Jr., whom he imitated in his first novel, *Setting Free the Bears.* This book, based on Irving's master's thesis, received generally good reviews, and Irving earned enough money to purchase a home in Putney, Vermont, where he lived while he taught at Windham College. He sold the movie rights to *Setting Free the Bears* and returned to Vienna to collaborate with the director Irwin Kershner on a film version of the novel. Although the movie was never produced, the subject of filmmaking became an important aspect of his second novel, *The Water-Method Man.* In Austria, Irving's second son, Brendan, was born in 1970.

After publication of *The Water-Method Man,* Irving returned to the University of Iowa as a writer-in-residence for three years, during which he wrote short pieces for magazines and published what is generally considered his darkest novel, *The 158-Pound Marriage.* Although the reviews were favorable, the novel was hardly a best—or even good—seller, and he took a job as an assistant professor of English at Mt. Holyoke College. It proved to be his last "day job."

Irving's fourth novel, *The World According to Garp,* provided him the financial security to become a full-time writer; it not only sold extremely well, but it also won the American Book Award for the best paperback novel of 1979 and elevated Irving and his protagonist into cultural icons. In 1981, when his fifth novel, *The Hotel New Hampshire,* became a number-one fiction best-seller about the same time as the movie version of *The World According to Garp* was released, Irving's photo appeared on the cover of *Time* magazine. *Time*'s R. Z. Sheppard noted that "Garpomania" had hit the country.

Time proceeded to promote an Irving "cult," a process in which Irving himself cooperated, if reluctantly. In 1997, as a guest on a popular television talk show, "Politically Incorrect." Irving was stiff, awkward, even hostile as he responded to the interviewer's questions. Yet his very appearance on the show revealed his dogged determination to mediate between his art and popular consumption despite any personal cost. In this sense, Irving seems not far removed from Ernest Hemingway: both demonstrate an enormous tension between fame and financial success and critical approbation. Even though Irving often refuses to talk about his private life, seeming to want to guard it, at times he has played to the image makers with remarkable ease. Behind his cooperation with the media, however, lies a barely hidden hostility and contempt.

Attention from the media was fueled by the success of the film adaptations of *The World According to Garp* and *The Hotel New Hampshire.*

George Roy Hill, who directed the former film in 1982, reduced the novel to a series of funny and sometimes poignant vignettes; Robin Williams played the title role, but it was John Lithgow as the transsexual Roberta Muldoon who stole the movie (Irving had a cameo appearance as a wrestling referee). Tony Richardson directed the film *The Hotel New Hampshire* (1984) in interesting cinematic fashion, but in the process lost almost entirely the magic of the novel.

In 1981 Irving and Shyla Leary divorced, and Irving moved to New York City, where he wrote his most polemical novel, *The Cider House Rules,* published in 1985. It also became a best-seller and was a 1985 Book-of-the-Month Club selection. *The Cider House Rules* is perhaps Irving's most controversial novel because of its central issue, abortion.

The film version of the novel was released in 1999. Directed by Lasse Hallstrom, it was the most successful film adaptation of an Irving novel in the twentieth century. Irving, who wrote the screenplay and had a great deal of creative control over the making of the movie, provides a fascinating look into the world of movie production in *My Movie Business: A Memoir* (1999). Irving managed to capture the essence of his novel in the film, even though he had to cut, compress, and conflate the narrative in the process. Again here he made a cameo appearance, this time as the stationmaster.

In 1987 Irving and Janet Turnbull, a Toronto literary agent, married; their son Everett was born in 1991. They live in Dorset, Vermont, and Toronto.

A Prayer for Owen Meany (1989) followed *The Cider House Rules,* and in 1998, Mark Steven Johnson wrote and directed the movie *Simon Birch,* which was loosely based on Irving's book. The movie essentially rewrites the novel, reducing its twin themes of politics and religion to a young boy's search for his father. In contrast, *A Prayer for Owen Meany* offers a challenge of faith not only to its central characters—Owen and Johnny Wheelwright—but to readers as well. It is perhaps Irving's most profound novel, with the possible exception of *A Son of the Circus* (1994).

A Son of the Circus, like many of Irving's novels, has multiple intersecting plots with numerous characters, who seem at first disparate but who are actually linked in surprising ways. It is one of the few Irving novels to be set almost entirely outside of the United States (in India). Like *A Prayer for Owen Meany,* this novel is concerned with loss of innocence and the despair at the center of contemporary life, but also like the former novel, *A Son of the Circus* has to do with faith and hope.

A Widow for One Year followed in 1998. It marked Irving's first novel featuring a female protagonist (although it can be argued that Franny Berry is the coprotagonist of *The Hotel New Hampshire*). Irving reveals great sympathy for women in his earlier books, but *A Widow for One Year* is his most feminist novel.

In the memoir portion of *Trying to Save Piggy Sneed* (1996) Irving discusses, among other things, wrestling and writing. For him, both are related art forms, requiring control, discipline, and balance. These three qualities afford him great freedom to improvise and manipulate his prose, making it both flexible and graceful. "Strict toiling with the language," Irving explains in this book, leads to sentences that "sound as spontaneous as good conversation." In a 1996 talk at Boston's Arlington Street Church, Irving proved an eloquent speaker concerning his approach as a writer. He thinks of himself not as an intellectual but as a craftsman: "I'm a vehicle, not a thinker. I have no intellectual credentials. I attend to storytelling as a carpenter attends to making a good table" (quoted in Campbell). What interests Irving—and us, as readers—are the details of the storytelling itself: the plot with multiple situations and the development of character.

Irving's interests as a writer are remarkably similar to the nineteenth-century writers he so admires, especially Charles Dickens. It was Dickens' *Great Expectations,* he explains in *Trying to Save Piggy Sneed,* that made Irving want to be a writer, "to move a reader as I was moved then." Irving wanted to write intricately plotted, sad, and funny novels in the manner of Dickens, Hardy, Melville, and Hawthorne. Irving's father introduced him to the novels of Dostoyevsky, Turgenev, and Tolstoy, works that also contained grand sweeping plots and innumerable memorable characters. Even the contemporary writers Irving admires write novels in, more or less, the nineteenth-century tradition: Margaret Atwood, Gabriel García Márquez, Salmon Rushdie, Robertson Davies, and Günter Grass. Their novels tend to be plot- and character-driven, fast moving, and filled with energy, presenting characters whom we follow throughout their lives.

Although Irving claims to dislike William Faulkner's writing, perhaps because of Faulkner's use of stream-of-consciousness and his heavy liturgical style, both share common themes: family, issues of gender, violence, loss and reclamation, and despair and hope. Both are fond of irony, directing it particularly toward America's drive for acquisition and power and its lack of regard for individuals. Both write in the tradition of the tall tale, of broad—and often ribald—American humor, using jokes, farce, and the absurd. Both writers depict sexual relations as often funny, sometimes frightening, but ultimately as meaningful and profound. Both intertwine plots that at first may seem totally unrelated, and both juggle and juxtapose time frames, collapsing past, present, and future. For both Irving and Faulkner, comedy and tragedy are intermixed. Most significantly, perhaps, both are profoundly moral writers in a modern world that questions the meaning of morality and gives way to a sense of hopelessness. Both writers are finally life-affirming. Like Faulkner, Irving uses explicit Christian images and references (in *A Prayer for Owen Meany* and *A Son of the Circus,* for example), but neither author is doctrinal in any traditional sense. Irving focuses on the Gospels because in them he finds a wide range of humanity from the tragic to the comic; from arrogance to folly; from betrayal to the capacity to forgive and love beyond reason.

SETTING FREE THE BEARS

Irving's first novel, *Setting Free the Bears,* contains a plot that Irving would return to again and again: a plot of "becoming," one that concerns itself with origins, driven by the protagonist's attempt to discover the individual self. Although the plot is grounded in present time, it looks backward to the past and forward to the future. On its surface, *Setting Free the Bears* is deceptively simple, divided into three parts. The first and third parts comprise the "frame" of the novel and take place in the present time of the novel (1967), while the second part, literally the center and focus of the novel, juxtaposes and interlaces present and past time. Although set in Austria, with no American characters, *Setting Free the Bears* is a thoroughly American "buddy" or "on the road" novel, in which two young men join forces to seek freedom from what they perceive as the repressive authority of adults.

In part 1 of the novel, a university student in Vienna, Hannes Graff, at loose ends from having failed his final exam in history, meets Siegfried ("Siggy") Javotnik, a young man also at loose ends, who persuades Graff to leave Vienna with him to work their way south to the Riviera. Before leaving, however, they visit the Hietzinger Zoo. The zoo visit discloses Siggy's obsession to free the bears and also prepares us for the actual freeing of all the zoo animals in part 3. The frame of the novel affords Irving an opportunity to spin out often farcical and wildly comic scenes, filled with short, intense bursts of energy and action.

Indeed, in these scenes, Siggy reminds one of Buster Keaton, out of sync with time and place, confronting one near-death experience after another. Unlike Keaton, however, Siggy fails to escape death when his motorcycle collides with a truckload of beehives and he is fatally stung.

In part 2 of *Setting Free the Bears* lies the heart of the novel. Issues of history, as well as questions of birth, life, and death are raised. Here we find "The Notebook," Siggy's personal history, the events that led to his conception, birth, and life. If the Notebook is the center of Irving's novel, it is also central to our understanding of *Setting Free the Bears*. The Notebook details the past, the Nazi takeover in Austria, the tribal warfare in Yugoslavia, the Second World War, and the subsequent Russian occupation of Austria. Because of these elements, Gabriel Miller finds *Setting Free the Bears* to be Irving's "meditation on history," for here Irving writes not only of Hitler's takeover in Austria but also of the acquiescence and appeasement of Austria—and of England and the United States. Moreover, the brutality of the Nazis and others, as well as the collusion of the so-called freedom fighters, resonates in the Holocaust, in the bombing of Hiroshima and Nagasaki, and in American military involvement in Korea and Vietnam.

In part 3 of the novel, Graff carries out Siggy's plan and frees not only the bears but all the other animals from the Hietzinger Zoo. The liberation unleashes horrific and bloody violence and death, as Graff simply leaves the terrible mess behind him. He escapes to Kaprun, to find one of Siggy's old mentors, Ernst Watzek-Trummer, referred to throughout the novel as the "real historian," a "keeper of details."

For all the adolescent jokes and pranks in part 1 of *Setting Free the Bears,* Irving's coming-of-age novel is no lark. It is deadly serious in its aims and themes. Graff and Siggy's story questions not only the meanings of history, but also who "makes" history. Can historical forces set loose in the world be compared to fate, what Irving calls the "gale of the world," blowing away both guilty and innocent? And whose history is authoritative? The Nazi propaganda machine's, headed by Goebbels? Graff's history professor's, who failed his student? Watzek-Trummer's, the keeper of details—including graves? Or does "real" history come from the written recollections of people like Siggy, whose account is selective, personal, and subjective? The numerous allusions in the novel to wars preceding and following World War II suggest Irving's most troubling question about history: Can the lessons of history be transmitted from one generation to another, and, if so, do we learn anything from them?

THE WATER-METHOD MAN AND THE 158-POUND MARRIAGE

In 1972 Irving wrote *The Water-Method Man; The 158-Pound Marriage* followed in 1974. The two novels have many similarities: both have academic settings; both use Vienna as a significant location; both use architectural space to delineate character and plot development; both have powerful themes revolving around marriage and family; and both novels make use of art, literary or visual, to underscore those themes. At the same time, *The Water-Method Man* and *The 158-Pound Marriage* may be seen as polar opposites in terms of their narrative form. The first is an "absolute" comedy (as Irving calls it), a knockabout Oedipal farce, filled with elaborate narrative loops and extended comic riffs; the second is a cold, bitter, straightforward narrative, with only a few comic moments, laced with heavy irony.

The Water-Method Man is, like *Setting Free the Bears,* a coming-of-age novel, even though the major character, Fred "Bogus" Trumper, is older than either Hannes Graff or Siggy Javotnik. The story of Trumper tells of a man who grows from being irresponsible, incapable of making any

commitments or of completing any tasks, to one who devotes himself to family and work. Trumper's immediate problem has to do with a blocked urinary tract, which causes him pain both in urination and in his sexual life. His doctor offers two choices: an operation or the "water-method" treatment—drinking a great deal of water, especially before and after sex. Trumper chooses the water method. At the time, Trumper lives in New York City with Tulpen, having deserted his wife, Sue "Biggie" Kunft, and their son, Colm. He has also left the University of Iowa, where he had been a Ph.D. student in English, working on his dissertation, a translation of the Old Norse epic *Akthelt and Gunnel.*

In New York, Trumper works for Ralph Packer, making "art" films about various social and personal issues. One of Packer's films, *Fucking Up,* which is based on Trumper's life, becomes famous. Trumper's live-in girlfriend, Tulpen, who also works for Packer, not only loves Trumper but also wants to have a child with him. Through a bit of trickery, she becomes pregnant, and Trumper, afraid of any commitment, deserts her, just as he did Biggie. He runs off to Vienna and into his past to look for his best friend from his days as a student.

In Vienna, Trumper discovers that the friend has been dead for two years, drowned in the Danube while trying to impress an American girl he had picked up. Trumper has a nervous breakdown, somehow gets involved in a convoluted drug-smuggling plot, and is forced back to the United States by narcotics agents, who provide him with an airline ticket and money for a limousine ride into New York City. Instead of returning to Manhattan, Trumper convinces his driver to take him to Maine to see another boyhood friend, Cuthbert "Couth" Bennett, the caretaker of the Pillsbury estate.

At the estate, Trumper finds Biggie and Colm, who have moved in with Couth. Seeing Biggie and Colm with Couth pushes Trumper to return to the University of Iowa to complete his dissertation, which in turn leads to a reconciliation with his father, portrayed as a cold tyrant throughout the novel. In addition, Trumper ends the water-method treatment, which never really worked, and has a successful urinary tract operation. He returns to Tulpen, who by now has their child. Couth and Biggie marry and have a child of their own. Even Packer, the bohemian filmmaker, marries, and his wife soon becomes pregnant. The novel, then, is comic in the Shakespearean sense, which is to say that the book ends joyously, in celebration of marriage, fertility, and family. It also ends with song, with much feasting and drinking, as well as storytelling. Fittingly, the characters participate in the festival of "Throgsgafen," the Old Norse celebration akin to our Thanksgiving.

The Water-Method Man is much more than a pleasant and merry farce, however. Like Shakespeare, Irving depicts the Oedipal conflicts between parents and their children. Although on one level the family conflict may be wondrously funny, it is also profoundly serious in its generational and sexual conflicts with their connections not merely to individuals but to the larger community. Irving makes sure that we understand the seriousness by weaving the Old Norse epic *Akthelt and Gunnel* into his present-day comedy. Just as the word "water" in Irving's title is suggestive of transformation and rebirth, so the Old Norse epic is also a watery tale, but it moves in a totally different narrative direction. The epic tells a story of controlling fathers and rebellious sons, as well as of internecine warfare, of sexual power and lust, of "castration and murder, on which the lifeblood of nations depends" (quoted in Campbell).

By juxtaposing the horrendous tale of *Akthelt and Gunnel* with the novel's central story, Irving provides two narrative strands, pushing them in two different—and extreme—directions. Yet finally, both are epic struggles, both tales of tran-

sition and rebirth from one generation to another. We recognize, however, that the "happy" ending of *Akthelt and Gunnel* is momentary, perhaps even illusory. We hope that the joyous ending of *The Water-Method Man* is longer lived.

In *The Water-Method Man,* Irving creates for the first time comic scenes that loop in wide arcs from the main narrative yet continue to comment on the main action and characters. He uses setting—in particular, architectural space—brilliantly in this novel. Whether they be in Iowa City, New York City, Vienna, or Georgetown, Maine, houses and rooms effectively delineate character and enhance themes. For example, in Iowa, the house Trumper and Biggie share crumbles around them at the same time as their marriage is falling apart. In Vienna, Trumper lives in a hotel that doubles as a brothel, where he rents a room and tries to write order into his life. The hotel is a place for transients, men who merely float through as customers of the women; they represent Trumper's own lack of commitment to the women in his life. Only on the Pillsbury estate in Maine do Trumper and other characters discover the possibilities of life in the love they feel for others. Nature is restorative, similar to Shakespeare's Forest of Arden or Prospero's island.

Following hard on *The Water-Method Man,* Irving's third novel, *The 158-Pound Marriage,* uses a number of similar techniques: word puns on names, architectural space to delineate characters and reinforce themes, and underlying Oedipal conflicts. Both novels revolve around marriage, family, and children. Yet *The 158-Pound Marriage,* with its emphasis on power and leverage, has a different thrust from the novel that precedes it.

In the book the unnamed narrator speaks to his wife about the horror of the assassination of John F. Kennedy. The image of Jacqueline Kennedy remains in the background throughout the novel, making " 'voyeurs' of us all" as we "watch" her awful grief. In her blank face, we "see" the power struggles beneath society's surface, indeed the fragmentation of society and its lack of moral center. The epigraphs that open the novel, one from Ford Madox Ford's *The Good Soldier* (1915), the other from John Hawkes's *The Blood Oranges* (1971), deal with the same topic as Irving's work: spouse-swapping. All three novels look closely at the breakdown of moral values at a time of social collapse.

Although *The 158-Pound Marriage* makes use of flashbacks, its plot is direct and straightforward; absent here, for the most part, are the narrative loops and comic improvisations found in *The Water-Method Man* and in many of Irving's later novels. In the book, two couples, the narrator and his wife, Utchka (called Utch), and Severin Winter and his wife, Edith, decide to swap spouses, hoping to regain sexual excitement and romance in their marriages. Both husbands are academics at a New England university; the narrator, a history professor, writes popular historical novels; Severin, a German professor, coaches wrestling. The wives remain at home and take care of their children; Edith also attempts to write fiction. Severin and Utch share the terrible pasts of their survival of World War II. Both Severin and the narrator met their spouses and courted them in Vienna, and both couples by the end of the novel return there. The couples set certain rules and conditions for the spouse-swapping, which is looked at as an elaborate game or sport: no one is to get hurt, especially the children.

Of course, people do get hurt: the Winters' children in a freak accident, and Utch, who falls in love with Severin. In both situations, injuries occur because of carelessness and neglect. In both cases, the injuries, although not fatal, expose the irresponsibility, selfishness, and faithlessness of the adults. The children appear to recover better than the adults. Utch, in particular, finds no solace in her marriage and leaves her husband, taking her children to Vienna, where she grew up. The narrator, who has never paid attention to his wife or children, recognizes his loss and at the end of

the novel leaves for Vienna to find his family. Severin, who claims to have had doubts all along about spouse-swapping, tries to reconcile with Edith, and they also return to Vienna, hoping to regain their lost love.

The central metaphor in *The 158-Pound Marriage* is wrestling; indeed, the very title of the novel, as Edward C. Reilly has pointed out, refers to the weight class for both Severin and his star athlete, George Bender. Reilly also notes that seven of the ten chapters derive their titles from wrestling, linking the sport to birth, possible rebirth, and sexuality; the wrestling room in the gymnasium suggests the womb itself. For Irving, wrestling represents moral conflict. Moreover, wrestling has to do with leverage, with position and focus, with the throwing down, the riding, and the pinning of one's opponent. Wrestling is about control and power, not about love or even partnership, and thus is the perfect metaphor in a novel where couples view each other in terms of leverage. As Edith explains to the narrator about her marriage with Severin,

> "He thinks I have leverage on him," she said [to the narrator].
> "Leverage?"
> "He thinks he owes me something."
> "You never told me," [the narrator] said.
> [The narrator] didn't like the sound of leverage, of debts owed, at all.
> . . . . .
> Leverage? Another wrestling term.
> [The narrator] didn't like its application to couples.

The best that they can hope for, it seems, is that their "match" will end in a "draw," if only for the time being.

History in this novel is as significant as it is in *Setting Free the Bears*. Even though Irving's narrator is a historian, he seems to learn little from the past. For example, the histories of Utch and Severin not only tell us much about their characters, which the narrator totally fails to grasp, but these histories also point to the breakdown of social values during World War II and after. Of course, the spouse-swapping itself reflects the loss of these values. The ending of the novel merely tells us that the Winters are still together; the quality of their togetherness remains a question. And although the narrator sets out for Vienna to win back Utch, whether she will have him is an open question.

In *The Water-Method Man,* Irving used *Akthelt and Gunnel* to demonstrate the serious risks of Trumper and his familial comedy; in *The 158-Pound Marriage,* Irving uses Pieter Brueghel the Elder's painting "The Battle between Carnival and Lent" to demonstrate the moral questions the novel raises. Brueghel's painting, a print of which hangs in the narrator's kitchen, reveals a world seemingly divided between Lent, with its abstemious piety, and Carnival, with its gross self-indulgence. Careful examination of the painting, however, shows that life is not so neatly binary, that there is more than enough folly, enough games and sport, for those engaged in the activities of both Lent and Carnival. In Brueghel's satiric painting, his figures express fear, lust, and indifference, all the while remaining self-absorbed. So too do Irving's characters, with the possible exception of Utch, who seems to learn what it is to love and suffer loss.

THE WORLD ACCORDING TO GARP AND *THE HOTEL NEW HAMPSHIRE*

Although many critics view Irving's first three novels as a preamble to his "major" works, the early novels stand very well on their individual merits. Yet there is no denying that *The World According to Garp* was Irving's "breakthrough" novel, achieving for him not only fame but also financial security. Many of the themes in Irving's earlier novels recur in *Garp:* family and children;

sexuality and gender; random violence and death; and art and the artist, for examples. There are numerous echoes of Irving's life, as well: his education at Exeter Academy (called Steering Academy here), his wrestling, and his writing. In *The World According to Garp,* we also recognize the enormous flexibility and gracefulness of Irving's prose.

Garp's story follows a mythic curve, with the plot segmented by significant "moments" in his life, leading ultimately to the moment of his death and to his transcendent afterlife. His story begins with his conception in the 1940s when Sergeant Garp, a severely wounded ball-turret gunner lying near death in Boston's Mercy Hospital, impregnates his nurse Jenny Fields. Garp grows up at Steering Academy in New Hampshire, where Jenny takes a job as the school nurse. He has numerous adventures, especially sexual adventures with Cushie Percy, a faculty member's daughter. Garp desires to be a writer, becomes a wrestler, and meets Helen Holm, whom he later marries.

After Garp graduates from Steering, he and his mother travel to Vienna so that he can gain "experience" as a writer. Not only does he become a writer—he completes one of his "better" works, "The Pension Grillparzer"—so too does Jenny, who writes her autobiography, *A Sexual Suspect,* which becomes a feminist manifesto and an international bestseller.

Upon Garp and his mother's return to the United States, Jenny, now a controversial figure, retires from nursing to set up a home for abused women at Dog's Head Harbor. Among the women seeking refuge there is the redoubtable Roberta Muldoon, who before her sex change was Robert Muldoon, former football player for the Philadelphia Eagles. She becomes one of Garp's best friends and a failed bodyguard for the Garp family.

Garp's marriage to Helen Holm produces two children, Duncan and Walt. Garp remains at home—writing sporadically—and looks after the children, while Helen teaches. Although Garp has numerous affairs, it is Helen's affair with one of her students that turns out to be critical. In a bizarre accident, Duncan loses an eye, Helen's lover loses three-fourths of his penis, and Walt is killed. Helen and Garp are also injured physically, but their psychic wounds are profound.

The Garp family moves to Dog's Head Harbor, where healing takes place, and another child, Jenny, is born. Jenny's grandmother and namesake is assassinated, and Garp writes a novel, *The World According to Bensenhaver,* which reiterates the darkness of Garp's personal world, one of violence and sudden death. Helen, Garp, Duncan, and Jenny return to Steering Academy, where Garp, too, is assassinated by Cushie Percy's sister, who links his adolescent lust for Cushie to her death in childbirth.

In *The World According to Garp,* Irving reveals his indebtedness to Dickens and other nineteenth-century writers; added to a densely rich plot are complex situations and characters as well as social and psychological nuances: feminism, family conflicts, issues of gender and identity, random violence, and death. As in Dickens' novels, each chapter in the book tells a self-contained story, having a beginning, middle, and end, yet "hooks" into the next chapter. There are numerous comic riffs, wild comedic improvisations, that seem to make wide arcs, each with its own intense syncopation, only to return to the forward-driving rhythm of the novel itself.

Irving's use of narrative loops, swinging out from the main themes, underscore the role of memory; these loops—beautifully balanced and seemingly effortless—force readers to engage their own powers of recall as they progress through the text. For if *The World According to Garp* is a novel concerned with writing, it is also concerned with reading. Irving's inclusion of Garp's (and even some of Jenny Fields') writings in the novel reiterate many of the main themes of

the novel itself; through the stories within stories, we learn how to read and understand those themes. An especially poignant theme is the brevity of life. Even Garp's young son, Walt, recognizes the danger always threatening to snatch away life in an instant. He mistakenly calls the undertow at Dog's Head Harbor the "Under Toad," which becomes a catchphrase throughout the novel for any force that can quickly snuff out life.

> "I'm trying to see the Under Toad," Walt said.
> "The what?" said Garp.
> "The Under Toad," Walt said. "I'm trying to *see* it. How *big* is it?"
> And Garp and Helen and Duncan held their breath; they realized that all these years Walt had been dreading a giant *toad,* lurking offshore, waiting to suck him under and drag him out to sea. The terrible Under Toad.
> Garp tried to imagine it with him. Would it ever surface? Did it ever float? Or was it always down under, slimy and bloated and ever-watchful for ankles its coated tongue could snare? The vile Under Toad.
> Between Helen and Garp, the Under Toad became their code phrase for anxiety. Long after the monster was clarified for Walt ("Under*tow,* dummy, not Under Toad!" Duncan had howled), Garp and Helen evoked the beast as a way of referring to their own sense of danger. When the traffic was heavy, when the road was icy—when depression had moved in overnight—they said to each other, "The Under Toad is strong today."

In *The World According to Garp,* the fragility of life as emblematized by the Under Toad leads to an understanding of the value of memory, of how important it is "to remember everything."

Many of the issues and themes from Irving's earlier novels reappear here, but in richer combinations. At the end of the novel, Irving hurls his own challenge to death with the use of an epilogue. In the epilogue, Garp lives on—or at least his energy does. Indeed, his family agrees that Garp was energy, "Captain Energy"; as such he remains "full of life," quickening and energizing the lives of those he touched—and of the book's readers.

If *The World According to Garp* has energy, Irving's next novel, *The Hotel New Hampshire,* has magic. Indeed, the former novel prepared readers for the latter, as Garp plotted the book out in *The World According to Garp;* there, Garp called his novel *My Father's Illusions,* a title that becomes an identifying "tag line" for the character of Father in *The Hotel New Hampshire.* In an interview, Irving acknowledged that the idea for *The Hotel New Hampshire* came from "The Pension Grillparzer" in *The World According to Garp;* Irving wanted to write a "fairy tale" in which the novel "[operates] . . . on a symbolic level" (quoted in Miller). For all of its fairy-tale elements, however, *The Hotel New Hampshire* remains thoroughly anchored in the historical situations of World War II, including the Holocaust and the decadence of Vienna, followed by the postwar violence of terrorism.

The novel tells the story of Win Berry and Mary Bates, known as Father and Mother, and their children: Frank, Franny, John, Lilly, and Egg. It also features an array of memorable minor characters, including Win's father, Iowa Bob; "our Freud" (to distinguish him from the "real" Freud); the hateful Chipper Dove (who, with two other men, gang-rapes Franny); and the gallant Junior Jones, who attempts, but fails, to save her from rape and who later marries Franny; two magical bears, State O'Maine and Susie, the girl in the bear suit; and a dog named Sorrow. There is also the mysterious Arbuthnot, the man in the white suit, who owns the hotel where Mary and Win meet and fall in love. Arbuthnot, with his perfect clothes, represents money and power, in short, the American Dream.

The novel can be divided into three acts followed by an epilogue. In the first act, Win and Mary begin to raise their children in the bucolic town of Dairy, New Hampshire, where Win buys the Hotel New Hampshire. But the children, even in this country setting, begin their growing-up years with little exposure to innocence. Chipper Dove not only rapes Franny but brutally bullies Frank for being homosexual. The children's dog, Sorrow, must be put to sleep—though the animal is not put to rest. Frank stuffs him, and the sudden reappearance of Sorrow scares poor Iowa Bob literally to death.

The second act is more chilling as Father takes the children to Vienna. Mother and Egg follow separately, but their plane crashes in the Atlantic. A rescue operation finds no survivors, but does uncover a central truth of Irving's tale:

> It was Sorrow, of course, that the rescue planes saw. Searching for the sunken wreckage, trying to spot the first debris upon the surface of the gray morning water, someone saw a dog swimming. Closer examination convinced the rescue crew that the dog was just another victim; there were no survivors, and how could the rescue crew have known that *this* dog was already dead? This knowledge of what led the rescue crew to the bodies came as no surprise to my surviving family. We had learned this fact of Sorrow, previously, from Frank: Sorrow floats.

As Franny becomes a surrogate mother to the children, John and Franny, who had always been close to each other, find their love for each other increasing in intensity and desire. Father joins our Freud, blind from Nazi experimentation in a concentration camp, in a new hotel that Father also calls the Hotel New Hampshire. This second hotel turns out to be no safer for the children than the first; terrorists replace the menace of Chipper Dove. The terrorists, who plan to blow up the Vienna opera house, take the Berry family hostage and attempt to make our Freud drive the bomb car. In an explosive scene, Father kills one of the terrorists and John another, as our Freud drives the car into the hotel lobby, blowing up himself and the remaining terrorists and blinding Father.

The third act brings the return of the Berry family to the United States, where they settle in New York City, living in a series of hotels. Lilly, who cannot "grow" physically (the family euphemism for her dwarfism), discovers that she is also unable to grow as a writer. She published one book about her family life up to the point of Mother and Egg's deaths, but cannot proceed beyond that point. Eventually, however, she pens a short piece, a play that reenacts the rape scene between Chipper Dove and Franny, only this time Dove is the victim. As a result of the play, Franny is able to leave behind the trauma of rape. Moreover, she and John are able to leave behind their incestuous obsession with one another. Even the taciturn Frank is able to accept his homosexuality. Only Lilly cannot grow up; as a result, she is unable to "keep passing the open windows," a refrain from a favorite childhood folktale, "The King of Mice," in which a sorrowful performer jumps to his death from an open window.

The epilogue of *The Hotel New Hampshire* gathers all of the themes from the novel and reconciles them, mysteriously and magically as only a fairy tale or romance can. As in Shakespeare's romances, the young sustain and care for the older generation. The Berry children buy the old Arbuthnot Hotel from its owner, the man who seemed so perfect to Win Berry but who is now dying an ugly death from emphysema. In this final Hotel New Hampshire, renovated into a home at last, John and Susie the Bear marry and await the gift of a child, the child of Franny and Junior Jones. The novel's end, then, is really a beginning, with the expectation of a new generation.

Throughout the novel run the illusions of Father: his dreams of a perfect American family; of "making a go" of it in the future; of having the "obscene confidence" that comes from money. Father dreams what Gatsby dreams in F. Scott Fitzgerald's novel, itself a romance of America. It is not coincidental that Irving interlaces *The Great Gatsby* with the story of *The Hotel New Hampshire;* Fitzgerald's novel is read over and over to the children while they are in Vienna. Lilly notes that Father *is* Gatsby, that Father, too, believes "in the green light, the orgiastic future that year by year recedes before us."

The third Hotel New Hampshire might be seen to nourish Father's wrongheaded illusions. But in fact the hotel represents a transformation from a social milieu based on class and prejudice, from an institution that was itself filled with violence. The "new" hotel becomes a "great" hotel, democratic, spacious enough for all of its guests "to grow their own way." Even so, one is reminded of the more somber strains in the novel with the final exhortation that "you've got to get obsessed and stay obsessed. You have to keep passing the open windows."

THE CIDER HOUSE RULES AND *A PRAYER FOR OWEN MEANY*

The magical romance of *The Hotel New Hampshire* was followed by two far more polemical novels, *The Cider House Rules* and *A Prayer for Owen Meany,* both of which deal with controversial issues: abortion and the Vietnam War, respectively. *The Cider House Rules* takes place in the 1940s and recounts the parallel stories of Dr. Wilbur Larch and the orphan Homer Wells. The novel uses the orphanage at St. Cloud's, Maine, as its narrative frame. Larch, who is the director of the orphanage, is also an obstetrician who performs abortions (at a time when abortion is illegal). He brings up Homer as if he were his son, training him to deliver babies as well. But Homer, who sees an aborted fetus not as the deliverance of an unwanted pregnancy, what Larch calls "the Lord's work," but as a dead baby, makes it a rule never to perform abortions. He leaves St. Cloud's, not only because he is opposed to Larch's rules that allow for abortions, but also because he seeks the love and friendship of Candy Kendall and

Wally Worthington, who, ironically, had come to St. Cloud's seeking to terminate Candy's untimely pregnancy.

The first part of the novel concludes with Homer leaving St. Cloud's to become a member of the Worthington family. When Wally leaves to fight in World War II, Homer and Candy turn to each other for love. They have a child, Angel, at St. Cloud's. Eventually, however, Wally returns, paralyzed from an injury suffered in the war, and marries Candy, who continues to see Homer. Indeed, the three of them raise Angel, never telling the boy that Homer is his father. During this period of time, Larch carefully constructs a new identity for Homer, using the name of Fuzzy Stone, an orphan who died. As Larch ages, he hopes to persuade Homer to return to St. Cloud's and take his place. The new identity legitimizes Homer as a doctor—after all, Larch had trained him in obstetrics.

At the same time that Larch is creating a new identity for Homer, events transpire to change Homer's life with Candy and Wally. During apple-picking season at the Worthington's, rules are posted in the cider house; these rules are ignored by the foreman, Mr. Rose, who runs the migrant workers according to his own rules, often enforced with a knife. Mr. Rose also binds his daughter Rose Rose to his familial rules; he impregnates her. Angel, who is in love with Rose Rose, appeals to Homer to help, which he does by performing an abortion. Hard truths emerge from these events concerning Candy and Homer's affair; Angel learns that Homer is his father.

The end of the novel loops back to its beginning, with Homer, now Fuzzy Stone, returning home to St. Cloud's to replace Larch, who has died. Irving concludes the novel with a brief epilogue that ties up the loose ends of the story: Angel becomes a writer and divides his time between Homer and Candy and Wally. Homer now reads to a new generation of orphans, those "princes of Maine," the same novels read to him

as a boy: *David Copperfield* and *Great Expectations* (*Jane Eyre* was read to the girls). In addition to the epilogue, Irving adds an appendix of notes having to do with apples, Alzheimer's disease (which Wally's father, Senior Worthington, suffered), and abortion. This appendix not only provides scholarly authority for the novel, it reinforces the pro-choice tone of *The Cider House Rules.*

The central metaphor in *The Cider House Rules* is contained in the book's title. Larch sets and enforces the rules at St. Cloud's, rules that Homer rejects. He makes his own counter rule— not to assist or perform abortions. The Kendall and Worthington families continually reconstruct rules for family living. Candy has no mother; Wally has a father who is more child than adult. There are rules that govern relations among Candy, Homer, Wally, and Angel. And of course there are rules posted in the cider house, which are ignored. The migrant workers cannot read them, and Mr. Rose has his own set of enforced rules. He also brutally rules his daughter's body, until she breaks his rule over her by stabbing him to death.

In every case, Irving demonstrates that rules shift as individuals negotiate their way between them and their desires. Rules, Irving insists, are constantly in tension with "choice." The novel is set in a time when abortions were illegal, yet Larch pointedly tells Homer that the law—societal rules—conflicts with individual human choice, a woman's choice not to have a child.

> "I'm not saying it's *right,* you understand? I'm saying it's her choice—it's a woman's choice. She's got a right to have a choice, you understand?" Larch asked.

Indeed, Candy, Wally, and Homer negotiate family rules precisely because Homer and Candy chose not to abort Angel. The love that Angel brings to those around him suggests that the choice that Homer and Candy made was the right one. At the same time, Rose Rose's pregnancy as a result of incest shakes Homer's "absolute" rule that abortion is fundamentally wrong.

The Cider House Rules is a story not only about rules but about orphans: not only Homer Wells and the other orphans at St. Cloud's, but Dr. Larch, even Candy and Wally, and Rose Rose. Indeed, one of the points of the novel is that we are all orphans in one way or another, that we all yearn for a home and a family and a sense of belonging. Wilbur Larch's home is St. Cloud's, just as Homer is the son he never had.

In addition, Irving shows that we long for a sense of purpose: *The Cider House Rules* is also about "being of use." When Dr. Larch realizes that society considers it perfectly "right" to perform illegal abortions for wealthy women, but immoral to perform them for the poor, he determines that all women who come to him may choose whether to have a child. Thus, Larch decides to be of use in the world. Homer learns the same thing when he chooses to perform an abortion for Rose Rose; like his "father," Dr. Larch, Homer becomes of use. *The Cider House Rules* may seem to be one of Irving's bleakest novels because it offers no easy answers. At best, solutions turn out to be compromises: Homer returns to St. Cloud's; Wally and Candy stay together; Angel divides his time among the three adults. Still, at the end of the novel, Homer Wells is "delivered" from his rigid sense of rules. He chooses to go home to St. Cloud's, "to be of use."

Like *The Cider House Rules,* Irving's next novel, *A Prayer for Owen Meany,* deals with hard questions and offers no easy answers. Whereas the former book concerns itself with the moral and emotional debate surrounding abortion, *A Prayer for Owen Meany* raises issues about the Vietnam War and the Iran-contra affair of the 1980s, initiated by morally vacuous politicians and "powerful [but careless] men." Also like *The*

Cider House Rules, A Prayer for Owen Meany is about choices and the exercise of free will. Yet this novel moves into deeper territory. At the book's center, as both its title and opening sentence indicate ("I am doomed to remember a boy with a wrecked voice . . . because he is the reason I believe in God; I am a Christian because of Owen Meany") are themes of death and resurrection, belief and unbelief. *A Prayer for Owen Meany* is Irving's most profound exploration thus far of the difficulties of faith and the consequences of doubt.

The novel presents the coming-of-age story of Owen and his closest, perhaps only, friend, Johnny Wheelwright, the narrator of the novel. They prove an unlikely pair: Owen, the tiny (at maturity he is only five feet tall) son of a taciturn quarrier and his reclusive wife, a boy from a working-class family, and Johnny, the son of Tabitha Wheelwright, a boy from one of Gravesend, New Hampshire's, most prominent patrician families. Their respective quests bind them together: Johnny, to discover his father's identity and thus his own; Owen, to discover and live out his destiny.

Two deaths frame the narrative: first Johnny's mother is killed after being struck by a foul ball hit by Owen in a Little League game; Owen is later killed as a consequence of his own heroism. The two funerals, at the beginning and end of the novel—replete with hymns, scriptures, prayers, and ritual—afford the reader the opportunity for spiritual reflection. Between these two deaths, readers follow the boys' growing-up years in Gravesend: their studies and life at Gravesend Academy and at the University of New Hampshire; Owen's enlistment in the army, where he becomes a casualty assistance officer; his subsequent death during an attempt to save a group of Vietnamese children; and Johnny's departure for Toronto, Canada, in 1968, the year of Owen's death.

Interpolated into the history of the two boys are two other stories—dramas, really—the pageant of Christ's birth and a dramatization of Dickens' *A Christmas Carol*. In each story, readers encounter tales whose themes embrace issues of choice and destiny; each story is a tale of transformative power. When the boys are eleven years old, Owen is cast in pivotal roles in Gravesend's annual presentations of these dramas; as the Christ child in the Christmas pageant and as the Ghost of Christmas Yet to Come. In both cases Owen takes charge, transforming the roles; in Johnny's words, he becomes "both star and director" of these dramas presenting the meaning of Christmas. Both theater productions end in astonishment and near-disaster. Both foreshadow future events and at the same time underscore themes linked to characters, themes of belief and doubt, destiny, and free will. In the Nativity play, Owen is commanding, even demanding, as the Christ child; as Johnny Wheelwright says, Owen is "an unpredictable Prince of Peace," a "special Christ." Owen is equally special in *A Christmas Carol* as the Ghost of Christmas Yet to Come, a character who foresees the future. Owen sees his own future engraved on a tombstone, complete with his name and the date of his death.

In addition to these interpolations, *A Prayer for Owen Meany* also contains reports of the Vietnam War, of John Kennedy and Marilyn Monroe, of Lyndon Johnson, as well as news reports of Ronald Reagan and the Iran-contra scandal. Irving thus moves the narration both backward and forward in time, foreshadowing events in some instances, in others casting narrative loops that circle back to make connections that readers might otherwise miss. Although Johnny narrates the story of his boyhood with Owen, his account is based on dated entries from an adult narrator's diary. Many of the entries dated from 1987 allow Irving to demonstrate the political parallels between the Vietnam War, especially important to the main narrative, and the Iran-contra debacle making headlines as Irving wrote. The reportorial

voice commenting on the war makes its devastation all the more horrifying, as Gravesend, like many other American towns, changes forever. Johnny leaves his home for Canada; other hometown boys, including Owen, are killed. The violence in America and the moral confusion surrounding the war become all too apparent in the dirty men's room of the Phoenix airport, where Owen fulfills his destiny and dies. Later, Johnny finds the Iran-contra affair to be as sordid as the Vietnam War.

Yet there is also heroism in Owen's death. At the end of the novel, the meanings of Owen's life—and death—command our attention. His "wrecked voice" remains what we, along with Johnny, hear. The VOICE, presented throughout the novel in capital letters, indicates not only Owen's extraordinariness, but also his destiny as God's instrument (the capital letters function similarly to the red type used in various editions of the Bible to set off the words of Jesus). At Owen's funeral, the pastor follows the liturgical order of Easter and thereby emphasizes the hope of resurrection. Thus, the close of *A Prayer for Owen Meany* is not really an ending but a beginning. Indeed, the novel reiterates the structures and meanings of the story of Christ's Nativity and Dickens' *A Christmas Carol*. Like them, *A Prayer for Owen Meany* is a story of conversions, of beginnings.

A SON OF THE CIRCUS AND *A WIDOW FOR ONE YEAR*

With the exception of Sharon Locy, who understands that Irving's eighth novel, *A Son of the Circus* (1994), revolves around the theme of identity, many reviewers have misread and undervalued this book. In it, Irving pays homage to Graham Greene's *The Power and the Glory* (1940) and *The Heart of the Matter* (1948), using various crime novel and thriller formulae.

To say that Irving's plots are complex and often convoluted is a truism, but for *A Son of the Circus,* such a comment is an understatement. Plot in the novel appears to multiply, yielding numerous subplots and their spin-offs, with seeming digressions played out with their own loops and improvisations. Despite this congestion, the novel focuses on a murder, on the detection and capture of a killer—events that underscore issues of identity. The main narrative revolves around Dr. Farrokh Daruwalla and his sense of displacement in the world. Connected to this story is that of Vinod, Farrokh's driver, and his family, all circus dwarfs. Also related to Farrokh's narrative is the story of the twins John D. and Martin Mills, sons of an American film actress, who are separated at birth. All three of these plots, complicated in their own right, link in various ways to the murder that opens the novel.

Farrokh, who was born in Bombay and educated there by Jesuits, was trained as an orthopedic surgeon in Germany. Married, he and his wife live in Toronto but return "every few years" to Bombay, where he serves as an honorary consultant surgeon to the Hospital for Crippled Children. His main obsession, however, lies in his research for the genetic markers of achondroplasia, or dwarfism. To carry out his research, he collects blood samples from circus dwarfs, with whom Vinod is his direct link. Farrokh's research is not entirely altruistic; he hopes to make his "mark" in the medical world. When not engaged in medicine, Farrokh spends most of his time at the Duckworth Club, a vestige of British colonialism maintained now by Indians, who retain its former elitist and exclusionary practices.

Farrokh also writes movie scripts featuring the infamous Inspector Dhar, who is played by Farrokh's young brother, John D., who had been adopted by Farrokh's father at the behest of the boy's mother—one child was more than enough for her. John D. is young enough to be Farrokh's son, and he treats him as such, calling him his "dear boy." John D., too, is "displaced"; a stage actor in Zurich and a homosexual, he carries two passports, Swiss and Indian. He does not even "fit" the role he plays as Inspector Dhar; John D., fair-skinned, patronizes and insults the very Indian he portrays. His twin, Martin Mills, is just as much a misfit. Trained as a Jesuit priest, he comes to India, wearing Hawaiian shirts, to work at a mission outside Bombay. Although Martin wants to "save" India, one Indian at a time, he is totally incapable of saving anyone, including himself, until he realizes that he lacks a "calling" to the priesthood. Martin, like his twin, is a homosexual. The brothers finally meet on a plane to Zurich, and in this meeting come face to face with their individual identities.

Intersecting the above complex family structures are the families of Vinod, the dwarf, as well as of Inspector Patel and his wife Nancy. Patel, with Nancy's help, and Farrokh and John D.'s assistance, solves the murder that is at the center of the novel, committed at the Duckworth Club. The murderer, the transsexual Mrs. Dogar, formerly Rahul, also turns out to have been the feared "cage-girl" killer of prostitutes in Bombay, and a longtime admirer of John D. Fortunately these plots, as well as others, are sorted out in the epilogue to *A Son of the Circus.*

The book contains many of the same themes found in other Irving novels: the obsession with children; random violence and death; religious issues; and class structures as well as strictures. New to this novel is the emphasis on AIDS. The attention given to the circus and dwarfs is an expansion of the motif appearing in *The Hotel New Hampshire.* The overriding theme in the novel, however, has to do with identity, racial and ethnic as well as sexual. Farrokh is but one of the characters who has a sense of alienation: from country, family, origins, himself. Throughout the novel, whether in Bombay or Toronto, Farrokh feels that he does not belong. Only at the circus does he feel at home.

But Farokkh sees the circus as he wishes it to be: "The circus was an orderly, well-kept oasis surrounded by a world of disease and chaos." Unfortunately, the circus world reflects our own; both are filled with disease and chaos. Vinod's wife becomes sick, while Vinod himself is injured. The circus exploits children; they are bought, sold, contract AIDS, and die. The animals erupt with sudden violence. Their masters respond with "rehabilitative" beatings, and the animals, too, die. At the same time, the circus provides hope and even beauty in Farrokh's imagination, and this conception is extended to that of reader as well. The circus children become intrepid performers, able to "walk the sky" on their tightrope without a safety net, a symbol of human possibility.

In *A Son of the Circus,* Irving, like Graham Greene, gives us a fallen world in which landscape figures as importantly as character and situation. Indeed, the landscape encompasses the very brutality Irving portrays in his characters. Landscape not only ravages, it also absorbs the victims of violence and injustice—they simply disappear into the environs. Murderers blend into the landscape nearly unseen; Nancy Patel looks for the killer Rahul on every Bombay street. Bombay frightens with its noise and suffocates with its stench. Filth and poverty abound, even in pricey neighborhoods. Animals and people choke the streets. Even the "order" of the police station is fouled by the excrement of barking police dogs. Not even the Duckworth Club, with its manicured lawns and flowers, provides relief; the flowers are dying, and vultures feed on a corpse in the midst of the bougainvillea flowers.

The landscape reflects the brutality that cuts across all classes, from prostitutes and pimps to socially elite families and even to the law. The reader is unable to dismiss this brutality as limited to India, to a place foreign and exotic; Irving intends us to see Bombay as our own world and to recognize it in Toronto, with its "cold" land-scape, in its Little India, where Farrokh is roughed up by young toughs. The same viciousness exists in Hollywood and in Boston, where Martin's mother seduces his best friend and drives him to suicide. Even in Iowa, America's heartland, Nancy Patel's parents brutally judged her as evil because of an unwanted pregnancy. *A Son of the Circus* is much more than a "whodunit"; we are all guilty, for we have all "dunnit" (quoted in Campbell). In all of his novels, Irving points out that we are responsible *to* each other as well as *for* each other. Like Greene, Irving makes clear that we share a collective guilt as well as a lost innocence.

All of the characters in *A Son of the Circus* are displaced in such a world—a world fragmented by violence and lost innocence. All in one sense or another must come to terms with a divided self. The twins, John D. and Martin, doubly mark the split self that exists in the other characters, from Farrokh to the killer Rahul to Nancy Patel, who "embraced evil [and] found it lacking." Even her husband, Inspector Patel, whom she believes "incorruptible," is "far from home," "cut off" as much from his origins "as Nancy was from Iowa."

At the close of the novel, we feel Nancy's despair in her knowledge that she cannot "go home" again, and we hear it in "the exact degree of deadness in Nancy's voice" that John D. imitates so perfectly. Yet, for all the despair at the end of *A Son of the Circus,* we also find hope. Farrokh gives up his search for a genetic marker for dwarfism, and offers his services at an AIDS hospice. When he is asked by a caller to the clinic not only who he is but also "What are you," Farrokh answers, "I'm a volunteer." In Farrokh's answer we recognize his sense of ministry to those who are broken by illness and despair. We recall an earlier scene at the heart of the novel, when Farrokh visits a church he attended as a boy; Farrokh reads the lectionary text, from the Second Epistle of Paul to the Corinthians: "Therefore, since we have this ministry, as we have received mercy, we do not lose heart." He reads further in Paul's epistle that although we may be "perplexed," we are "not in despair . . . not destroyed—always carrying about in the body the dying of the Lord Jesus, that the life of Jesus may also be manifested in our body." Thus, there is a doubleness in the book's ending: deadness and despair but also hope in the service that individuals can offer one another. Although Irving's *A Son of the Circus* concerns human displacement in the fragmented, often alien, landscape of a fallen world, the novel also points out the transforming power of grace.

A Widow for One Year differs from Irving's previous novels in several ways. For the first time, he creates a female protagonist, Ruth Cole (although, as previously stated, it can be argued that Franny Berry shares the protagonist's role with her brother John in *The Hotel New Hampshire*). In other Irving novels, the father is often either dead or absent; in this book, Ruth's mother is the "lost" parent (again, *The Hotel New Hampshire,* in which the mother dies early in the novel, is similar).

A Widow for One Year tells the story of Ruth Cole, her discovery of both love and the self. Ruth, tough and unsentimental and thought "difficult" (by male standards) is a writer, she admits, before she is a woman. Yet Ruth wants both marriage and a child, despite her often bad relationships with men, beginning with her father. The novel follows her life at three different times: at four years old in the summer of 1958; at thirty-six, when a successful writer, in the fall of 1990; and at forty-one, when a widow, in the fall of 1995. Ruth is the daughter of Ted Cole, a writer of children's books, and his wife, Marion. In the first section, little Ruth "replaces" her brothers, killed in their teens in a horrible automobile accident. The brothers' deaths remain a memory that affects and changes the entire family. Marion hangs photographs of the boys throughout the

house and blames her husband, who was drunk at the time of the accident, not only for their deaths but also for persuading her to have another child. She does not hate Ruth; she merely ignores her, fearing her daughter will "catch" her grief, like a disease. Marion leaves her family when Ruth is four.

Ted Cole, a chronic womanizer and alcoholic, plots to be rid of Marion even before she leaves, hiring Eddie O'Hare, the same age as one of his sons, to be his driver and summer assistant; Ted anticipates that the thirty-nine-year-old Marion will have an affair with Eddie. She does, an affair neither recovers from for over thirty-seven years, and an affair Ruth witnesses when she is four, although she does not understand what she sees.

Later, Ruth meets Eddie O'Hare again, when she is an internationally known writer at thirty-six, and Eddie introduces her at a reading of her novel, which concerns a woman who was a widow for one year. Ironically, Ruth has no way of knowing that her fiction mirrors her future life; she too will be a widow for one year. Although Ruth has achieved success as a writer, her personal life remains a shambles. She has only one woman friend—her former roommate at school—and no men friends, only males who seem interested in Ruth as a bedmate. For example, Scott Saunders, her father's squash partner, charming on the surface and handsome, rapes and beats her on a first date. Ruth takes revenge by severely beating him with a squash racket. Eventually, she turns to Allan Albright, her editor, kind, loyal—and boringly safe. Ruth promises to marry him as soon as she returns from a promotional book tour in Europe.

Before leaving, Ruth beats her father in a game of squash, a game he had taught her. In addition, she tells him of Scott Saunders, linking his rape of her to pornographic Polaroids Ted had taken of various women. She also reveals that she found out how Ted plotted to be rid of Marion and that she knows of his one-night stand with her schoolmate, obviously a woman young enough to be Ted's daughter. Ruth's angry triumph over her father may be what leads to Ted's despair and suicide.

On her book tour in Amsterdam, Ruth plans her new novel, *My Last Bad Boyfriend,* which leads her to research the world of prostitutes in the city. While interviewing and observing the prostitute Rooie, Ruth witnesses her murder at the hands of a customer. Ruth saves herself by hiding in Rooie's closet and thinking about *A Sound Like Someone Trying Not to Make a Sound,* the title of one of her father's children's stories. Later she sends a letter describing the murder to Detective Harry Hoekstra. The murderer is finally caught, and several years later Hoekstra will meet Ruth, his missing and almost silent eyewitness.

After Ruth's brush with murder, she rushes home to Allan, marries him, and has a son, Graham. Allan dies when Graham is three and Ruth just thirty. Eventually Ruth returns to Amsterdam and meets Harry; they fall in love, and marry. Irving does not end the novel here, however; Marion returns to Eddie and to buy the Cole house. The novel closes on Thanksgiving weekend (we are reminded of the Throgsgafen family celebration in *The Water-Method Man*) with a family reunion and renewal. As mother, daughter, and grandchild meet, time seems to stop for this one significant moment.

A Widow for One Year is first of all a "love story," as Irving himself notes in his dedication of the novel to his wife. But it is also about storytellers and storytelling, about the public business of publishing and the private life of the writer, and about readers. It is not the first time that Irving has included in his novel characters who are writers, but in *A Widow for One Year* all of the major characters write: Ted writes and illustrates children's stories; Marion writes mystery novels; Eddie, romance; and Ruth writes the "real" thing.

She demonstrates control of language, of complex characters and situations, and of narrative. In short, Ruth writes much like Irving. Both begin with character and situation; both write comedies; both claim, for the most part, not to use autobiography in their fiction. In *A Widow for One Year,* however, Irving deliberately blurs the line between the "lived" part of Ruth's life, interlacing her personal postcards and diary entries within the fictions Ruth writes. In large measure, Ruth's life is her writing.

That we are our stories seems equally valid with Marion Cole, whose fictional detective, Margaret, remains obsessed with missing children, just like Marion. And Ted's children's stories, all cautionary tales, have to do with the loss of his sons, in one case, and with the desire to control his daughter in another. The story Ted writes for Ruth, *A Sound Like Someone Trying Not to Make a Sound,* is a story about a moleman, a creature who is half man, half animal, who captures little girls and takes them underground, where he keeps them. The psychological elements of the tale are clear: the aggression of the male, along with his desire to possess and punish the female and to bury her forever. The girl's fear and desire for the moleman are equally clear, as are Oedipal implications of her desire for her father/hero who "saves" her for himself. Ted's story links directly to the "real" moleman who captures Rooie and "keeps" her forever by killing her and photographing her dead body.

Ironically, Ruth saves herself from the moleman in Rooie's room by remaining silent, just as Ted's story cautions little girls to do. Rooie, who might not have remained silent about her attacker, has her throat crushed by the moleman, who then photographs her, using the same kind of camera Ted used to take his pornographic pictures of women.

Not only are stories and storytelling significant in *A Widow for One Year;* so too is the reader.

Irving demonstrated earlier in *The World According to Garp* the importance of "good" reading; Jillsey Sloper, a cleaning lady, recognizes worthwhile books by how "true" they are. In *A Widow for One Year,* Harry Hoekstra, the detective, is the model reader. He recognizes that just as no one answer exists to the world's violence, no one reading satisfactorily provides meaning to a novel; "plot summaries" merely distort novels. Harry would warn critics, one supposes, of the futility of summarizing John Irving's plots, any more than those of, say, Dickens. Their narratives are too rich, too complex, for any one "answer." Ruth falls in love with Harry precisely because he knows he can never know the whole story—or the only story—in her works or in her life, any more than we can in Irving's work.

CONCLUSION

Despite the difficulty of summing up Irving's work—and the risk of reducing its richness—one can say this: John Irving is not only one of America's most prolific writers, he is also one of its most moral. That is to say, he tackles difficult social and political issues and raises unflinchingly serious questions about human relationships. All of his novels deal in one way or another with origins, and thus ask the fundamental question of who we are. Often his characters seek, like Homer Wells, a place in which to belong—a home; in addition, they seek "to be of use" in the world, as Owen Meany is when he gives his life to save others, or as Farrokh Daruwalla is when he volunteers his service in an AIDS hospice.

Irving has been compared with Charles Dickens, especially in the use of plot and character, as well as in the exploration of social and political issues. In truth, however, Irving may be closer to Shakespeare in his ear for dialogue and in his intense intertwining of character, situation, and theme. Most of all, Irving, like Shakespeare, understands the uses of comedy. Comedy in an Irving novel, as in Shakespearean drama, helps to illuminate character, to further plot, and to enhance or reiterate themes. Comedy is never relief *from* anything; it always adds to the novel's meanings. Irving also recognizes, like Shakespeare, that comedy is profoundly social and that its inherent wellspring is life itself.

For all his indebtedness to Dickens and Shakespeare, Irving is a thoroughly American writer. His works embody the tension found in much of American literature: the pull toward individuality as well as the yearning for home and community. Like Whitman, Irving remains optimistic about the American people at the same time that he is deeply skeptical about America's political leaders. The sheer energy and rhythm of Irving's writing owe much to the pulse and beat of American jazz. Irving may grapple with language, trying to pin down the exact words for his stories, but he also "plays" language as eloquently as Duke Ellington played piano—with elegant swinging arcs, with effortless riffs, and seemingly endless improvisations. Just as we do not lose the melodic lines of Duke Ellington's music, we do not lose sight of the themes of John Irving's novels. In them we discover both our humanity and ourselves.

Selected Bibliography

WORKS OF JOHN IRVING

NOVELS
Setting Free the Bears. New York: Random House, 1969.
The Water-Method Man. New York: Random House, 1972.

The 158-Pound Marriage. New York: Random House, 1974.

The World According to Garp. New York: Dutton, 1978.

The Hotel New Hampshire. New York: Dutton, 1981.

The Cider House Rules. New York: Morrow, 1985.

A Prayer for Owen Meany. New York: Morrow, 1989.

A Son of the Circus. New York: Random House, 1994.

A Widow for One Year. New York: Random House, 1998.

OTHER WORKS

Trying to Save Piggy Sneed. New York: Arcade, 1996. (Memoir and short fiction.)

My Movie Business: A Memoir. New York: Random House, 1999.

UNCOLLECTED SHORT FICTION

"A Winter Branch." *Redbook,* November 1965, pp. 56–57, 143–146.

"Weary Kingdom." *Boston Review,* spring-summer 1968, pp. 8–35.

"Lost in New York." *Esquire,* March 1973, pp. 116–117, 152.

"Students: These Are Your Teachers." *Esquire,* September 1975, pp. 68, 156–159.

"Vigilance." *Ploughshares* 4, no. 1:103–114 (1977).

"Dog in the Alley, Child in the Sky." *Esquire,* June 1977, pp. 108–109, 158–162.

"A Bear Called State O'Maine." *Rolling Stone,* August 20, 1981, pp. 22–27, 50–55.

"The Foul Ball." *New Yorker,* January 30, 1988, pp. 28–56.

"The Courier." *New Yorker,* August 1, 1994, pp. 60–69.

CRITICAL AND BIOGRAPHICAL STUDIES

BOOKS

Campbell, Josie P. *John Irving: A Critical Companion.* Westport, Conn.: Greenwood, 1998.

Harter, Carol C., and James R. Thompson. *John Irving.* Boston: Twayne, 1986.

Miller, Gabriel. *John Irving.* New York: Frederick Ungar, 1982.

Reilly, Edward C. *Understanding John Irving.* Columbia: University of South Carolina Press, 1991.

ARTICLES AND ESSAYS

Beatty, Jack. "A Family Fable." *New Republic,* September 1981, pp. 37–38.

Cosgrove, William. "The World According to Garp as Fabulation." *South Carolina Review* 19:52–58 (spring 1987).

DeMott, Benjamin. "Domesticated Madness." *Atlantic Monthly,* October 1981, pp. 10l–106.

Drabble, Margaret. "Musk, Memory, and Imagination." *Harper's,* July 1978, pp. 82–84.

French, Marilyn. "The 'Garp' Phenomenon." *Ms,* September 1982, pp. 14–16.

Gussow, Mel. "John Irving: A Novelist Builds Out from Fact to Reach the Truth." *New York Times,* April 28, 1998, pp. B1, E1.

Korn, Eric. "Trying to Grow the Freudian Way." *Times Literary Supplement,* November 6, 1981, p. 1302.

Lehmann-Haupt, Christopher. "The Cider House Rules." *New York Times,* May 20, 1985, p. C20.

Locy, Sharon. "A Son of the Circus." *New York Times Book Review,* September 4, 1994, pp. 1, 22.

Marcus, Greil. "John Irving: The World of The World According to Garp," *Rolling Stone,* April 13, 1979, pp. 68–75.

Page, Philip. "Hero Worship and Hermeneutic Dialectics: John Irving's *A Prayer for Owen Meany.*" *Mosaic* 28:137–156 (September 1995).

Peterson, Eugene H. "Writers and Angels: Witnesses to Transcendence." *Theology Today,* October 1994, pp. 394–405.

Pritchard, William H. "A Widow for One Year." *New York Times Book Review,* May 24, p. 7.

Rockwood, Bruce L., and Roberta Kevelson. "Abortion Stories and Uncivil Discourse." In *Law and Literature Perspectives.* Edited by Bruce L. Lockwood. New York: Peter Lang, 1996.

Towers, Robert. "Reservations." *New York Review of Books,* November 5, 1981, pp. 13–15.

Walls, James M. "Owen Meany and the Presence of God." *Christian Century* 22:299–301 (March 1989).

INTERVIEWS

Bernstein, Richard. "John Irving: 19th Century Novelist for These Times." *New York Times,* April 25, 1989, pp. C13, 17.

Patterson, Nicholas. "Widow's Walk." *Providence Phoenix,* June 26, 1998, pp. 8, 10.

FILMS AND PLAYS BASED ON THE WORKS OF JOHN IRVING

The World According to Garp. Screenplay by Steve Tesich. Directed by George Roy Hill. Warner Bros./Pan Arts, 1982.

The Hotel New Hampshire. Screenplay by Tony Richardson. Directed by Tony Richardson. Orion Pictures, 1984.

The Cider House Rules. Screenplay by Peter Parnell. Directed by Jane Jones and Tom Hulce. Produced Seattle, 1996.

Simon Birch. Screenplay by Mark Steven Johnson, based on *A Prayer for Owen Meany.* Directed by Mark Steven Johnson. Buena Vista Pictures, 1998.

The Cider House Rules. Screenplay by John Irving. Directed by Lasse Hallstrom. Miramax, 1999.

—JOSIE P. CAMPBELL

Charles Johnson
1948–

*I*N RESPONSE TO separatist claims that fundamental differences lead inescapably to racial conflict, Charles Johnson presents a hopeful, inclusive vision of African American identity. Rejecting essentialist characterizations, he argues that there is no single definition of what it means to be black in America. Rather than rest with received assumptions about black being, he advocates an understanding of race that encompasses divergent viewpoints and recognizes that there are as many ways to be black in America as there are African Americans.

Johnson's position is one of many responses that African American artists have made since the late 1960s to questions about black identity. One of the most powerful, the Black Arts movement, and its cultural heir, Afrocentrism, counter Johnson's aesthetic goals by advocating artistic separatism. The Black Arts movement posits an aesthetic standard defined from within the African American community rather than by the white culture it views as dominant and hostile. Johnson, a practicing Buddhist, rejects this formulation on artistic and religious grounds. He brings these ideals to bear on his fiction by rejecting narrow definitions of racial identity. In disavowing the essentialist principles of the Black Arts movement and its monolithic version of African American life, often referred to as "the Black Experience," Johnson dramatizes the multiplicity of black experiences. This approach to black identity leads to a similarly broad interpretation of human experience, without regard to racial designation. It is this larger, transracial view that is the ultimate goal of Johnson's artistic quest.

BACKGROUND

Born April 23, 1948, in Evanston, Illinois, Charles Richard Johnson was the only child of Ruby Elizabeth (née Jackson) and Benny Lee Johnson, who came north as part of the great migration of African Americans from the southern states. In a 1998 interview Johnson described Evanston as "a very attractive community"; he told an interviewer in 1996 that he and his friends, both black and white, grew up believing that "bigotry, as we understood it then, was simply 'uncool.' " Certainly some elements of Evanston's history suggest the harmony he describes. The city's African American community developed during the antebellum period. Evanston's strong African American presence manifested itself in many ways. Evanston Township High School, for instance, has never been segregated at any time in its existence. Furthermore, Evanston's city government has been integrated since Edwin Jourdain's 1932 election as alderman.

Jourdain's election, however, suggests complexities in Evanston race relations that Johnson's comment obscures. Jourdain represented an all-black ward on the west side of the city, where most of Evanston's African American population was concentrated. Real-estate codes controlled where blacks could live for much of Evanston's history, and the effects of those codes continue to shape housing patterns in the city. Similarly, for years Evanston had separate black and white hospitals and black and white YMCAs; until 1962 it maintained a segregated swimming beach just south of Northwestern University, and until the mid-1950s no housing was available for black students at Northwestern. In the face of a situation with decidedly negative elements, the positive tone of Johnson's memory is noteworthy. His portrayal of Evanston's African American community in *Dreamer: A Novel* (1998) reflects the attitudes instilled by his upbringing. It is not that he downplays difficulty, but his emphasis is elsewhere: he refers to those Evanston citizens as "black men and women . . . so toughened by prejudice, by the rule of having to do twice as much to get half as far, that they regarded no problem as insurmountable." This emphasis on achievement rather than hardship, like his assertion of his friends' beliefs about bigotry, shows him enacting his community's resistance to definitions. Furthermore, as his writing reveals, he has continued to apply that same standard of resistance throughout his creative career.

Johnson's parents contributed other vital elements to his developing worldview and artistic approach. In a 1994 autobiographical essay, Johnson describes his father as "a quiet, deeply conservative, pro-black man with a fifth-grade education, who until the 1960s voted Republican" and his mother as "emotional, moody, a high school graduate who believed in integration, belonged to three book clubs, and always voted for Democrats." The tensions between their attitudes, especially his father's strong racial identity and

his mother's eclectic intellectual tastes, found their way into his writing as well. From his father, who at times had to work three jobs to provide for his family, Johnson learned the importance of a well-developed work ethic. A crucial episode in Johnson's life posed his passion for drawing against this work ethic. When Johnson told his father he wanted to become a professional artist, as he explains in his autobiographical essay, Benny Lee replied, "They don't let black people do that. You should think about something else." Initially frustrated, Johnson eventually wrote to a white artist, Lawrence Lariar, who would become his drawing teacher. Lariar's reply convinced Benny Lee that his limited view was wrong; he eventually paid for his son's lessons. Thus early on Johnson was resistant to a narrow view of blackness. The counterexample of his mother reinforced his rejection of that view. Ruby Elizabeth encouraged her son to browse among her shelves, which he described as filled "with books that reflected her eclectic tastes in yoga, dieting, Christian mysticism, Victorian poetry, interior decorating, costume design, and flower arrangement." Johnson's writing too blends materials from divergent sources into a literature that ignores conventional generic and canonical limitations. Furthermore, as he absorbed this diverse information, he came to realize that the only limits to his fusion of ideas were externally imposed.

Johnson experienced a profound challenge to his parents' way of seeing the world when he enrolled at Southern Illinois University in 1966. He found the university relatively friendly territory, although Carbondale and its environs were segregated. The town attitude is not surprising. More unusual is the university history. At the behest of President DeLyte Morris, SIU had integrated in the early 1950s, well before many southern schools did. Morris's egalitarian vision of education made him amenable to integration; however, his paternalistic attitude made him resistant to others' suggestions about how integration should be brought about. The students of Johnson's generation were forced to fight for every concession. As a result, racial tensions, as well as increasing student unrest over Vietnam, made SIU a political hotbed during Johnson's years there. At first staying away from protests over racial conditions at SIU, Johnson pursued his drawing career, working for both the campus and town newspapers, and threw himself into his class work. Majoring in journalism, he was required to take a philosophy course and found in the subject—especially the study of aesthetic questions over the course of human history—another pursuit equal in significance to his artwork.

He also encountered two older artists who would prove influential. The first was the poet Amiri Baraka, who spoke at SIU in 1969. At the time Johnson heard him, Baraka was delivering the message of the Black Arts movement he helped found with a group of peers, including Larry Neal. As the movement gained momentum, more writers took up its fundamental premise, the notion that black artists should make art directed toward blacks and concerned with nurturing the African American community emotionally and spiritually. The Black Arts movement artists also articulated a new critical standard for black art. Claiming that white criticism of black literature had for too long limited black artists' expressive possibilities, the movement's architects advocated developing a Black Aesthetic, a set of critical tools generated from within and controlled by the black literary community. Adherents sought to escape the limitations of white-defined standards, which served to control black art. The impulse to redefine black art is of a piece with the drive to expand conceptions of African Americans' role in the national history, in that both reclaim and revise established perceptions of black being and black accomplishment. Without this reclamation and revision process, Black Aestheticians argued, progress is impossible. Furthermore, from the perspective of the Black Aesthe-

ticians, artists have a primary responsibility to lead the way in the fight for empowerment.

This was the message Baraka brought to Carbondale. Flanked by security guards and refusing to acknowledge white audience members, Baraka charged his listeners to "take [their] talent back to the black community." Inspired, Johnson left the lecture and dropped everything else to draw cartoons that would explore "the history and culture of black America." Working obsessively for a week, he produced what would be the first of his two published collections of comic art, *Black Humor* (1970). Johnson continued his study of philosophy, becoming particularly interested in phenomenology and Buddhism. It was after immersion in these subjects that he began to wrestle with the aesthetic and ontological questions raised in the debate over black identity. Growing less tolerant of the Black Arts and Black Power movements, he sought for ways to transcend essentialism. His second book of cartoons, *Half-Past Nation Time* (1972), makes a pointed statement about the false promise of political approaches to questions of racial being as he mocks the foibles of the Black Panther party.

Once *Half-Past Nation Time* was accepted for publication, Johnson's creative impulse expanded beyond drawing to the writing of novels. He produced six apprentice manuscripts in two years, adhering to a ten-weeks-per-manuscript schedule; each of the novels allowed Johnson to hone a different element of his craft, but ultimately none was satisfying. Working in a mode that evoked Richard Wright, James Baldwin, and John A. Williams, writers he was reading at the time, Johnson assessed his own efforts as formulaic. Setting those texts aside, he began what would become his first published novel, *Faith and the Good Thing* (1974), a story that addressed the various philosophical and personal questions with which he had been wrestling. He sought feedback as he worked from the novelist John Gardner, who also had a strong interest in philosophy. Gardner, who recognized Johnson's emotional commitment to his philosophical project, read every draft and offered commentary and insight that helped Johnson fulfill his artistic objectives of expanding the sense of black identity and black literature. Simultaneously, Johnson read all of Gardner's work, which helped him articulate his aesthetic. With Gardner as mentor, Johnson found a way to blend his growing interest in phenomenology, and its emphasis on experience, with the resistance to racial limits he learned in Evanston. In a 1985 essay ("A Phenomenology of *On Moral Fiction*") on Gardner's prescription for the modern novel, Johnson espouses Gardner's fundamental assertion that the writer must present "an aesthetic vision which, to the best of [his] ability, embodies as many perceptions as possible in a fiction." In *Faith and the Good Thing,* the result was a work that put forth an integrative, universalist vision of human experience.

Johnson finished *Faith and the Good Thing* in nine months, a pace much slower than that for his apprentice novels but much faster than the deliberate crafting of the historical novels he wrote later on, which required substantial background research. The period of writing this novel coincided with Gardner's work on his *On Moral Fiction* (1978), in which Gardner stresses that authors should teach the reader some significant, potentially life-altering lesson. Gardner's emphasis on morality does not imply conventional, Judeo-Christian "goodness." Rather, for Gardner, moral art "ought to be a force bringing people together, breaking down barriers of prejudice and ignorance, and holding up ideals worth pursuing." True to his and Gardner's shared idea of drawing on a variety of older sources to illuminate one's fiction, Johnson uses African American folklore to illustrate the transformation of consciousness through experience in his protagonist, Faith Cross. That evolution is the first manifestation of the new way of seeing that would drive Johnson's fiction throughout his career.

FAITH AND THE GOOD THING

Throughout the nineteenth and twentieth centuries, black writers have drawn on African American oral tradition to articulate a group identity. *Faith and the Good Thing* puts Johnson in the company of such writers as Jean Toomer, Ralph Ellison, Zora Neale Hurston, and Toni Morrison. Yet whereas some writers, such as Hurston and Morrison, use folklore to emphasize the "other" nature of black culture and to celebrate particular group attributes, for Johnson folklore grounded in otherness promotes a divisive and inhibiting understanding of identity. Johnson, like Ellison and Toomer, sees value not in the particularities separating folk traditions but in the commonalities that bind them. This universalist impulse drives Faith's quest for the "good thing," as she embraces, through the guidance of a conjurer, an amalgam of black folklore and classical knowledge that transforms her understanding of both racial and personal identity.

Faith is not alone in turning to black folklore for release from suffering and from the limitations associated with a narrow view of black identity. However, the other characters' experiences with folklore illustrate what Johnson sees as a fundamental flaw in a racially defined way of seeing the world. Because their understanding of blackness is circumscribed, they use folklore primarily to separate themselves from white culture. What Faith Cross learns, however, is a means of transcending the preconceptions and the sense of victimization limiting the other characters. As she comes to understand her connection to all people, things, and traditions, she faces a broader sense of her identity that opens up new definitions of blackness to her.

Faith's father, Big Todd Cross, who populates her childhood with the magical figures of the folk tradition, was lynched years before for resisting two white strangers bent on examining his genitalia. The death of her mother, Lavidia, on Faith's eighteenth birthday leaves her alone in the world. With her dying breath, Lavidia urges Faith, "girl, get yourself a good thing," advice the confused young woman discusses with Reverend Brown, her mother's preacher. Brown insists that the good thing is her Christian salvation, reminding Faith of a conversion experience she had shortly after Big Todd's death. Rejecting that facile assessment, she seeks advice from the Swamp Woman, the feared hoodoo worker of Hatten County, Georgia, a "werewitch" with mythic powers. The werewitch embodies several concepts important to Johnson's aesthetic. A conjure woman steeped in classical philosophy, she celebrates experience as the means of gaining enlightenment, knows things are not what they seem and therefore must not be taken at face value, and understands that learning and life are processes. Although she cannot tell Faith all of this and have her understand it, she plants the seeds of the enlightenment that Faith will eventually experience.

From the first mention of the werewitch, Johnson uses her to emphasize the danger of adhering to rigid preconceptions about reality. The Swamp Woman specializes in altering people's lives, and many Hatten County residents come to her with specific requests. In asking, each petitioner makes the same mistake: viewing the world through a restricted set of received ideas. The werewitch broadens their visions by adding her own twists to their dreams as she grants their wishes. Old plantation masters seeking youth unexpectedly trade bodies with young slaves and suffer the consequences of prior cruelty; men seeking love potions receive powerful charms designed for women and must face pursuit by younger men. Delivering a technically accurate but spiritually skewed version of each request, the Swamp Woman reminds the supplicants that they must see the world more completely to guard against the kinds of suffering she visits on them.

The Swamp Woman also practices this lesson with her universalized folkloric tradition, which Johnson champions over the more restricted belief system Big Todd Cross once adhered to. As artifacts in her hut indicate, she knows that one who interprets the world through the lens of one belief system sees it incompletely. Her collection includes "a rotten ferryboat oar from the Styx, . . . wood . . . from the cross at Calvary, [a] philosopher's stone . . . speckled philosopher's eggs [and] clay, wax, and wooden figures . . . used for divination." Her conjuration method, which draws on all of these artifacts, reflects Johnson's own creative process. The mix of traditions apparent in the Swamp Woman's hut signals the issues of racial and cultural identity present in the moment of the novel's composition. As Johnson moves away from his initial interest in the Black Arts movement, one sees him drawing more broadly on widely varying sources.

Based on the Swamp Woman's advice, Faith goes to Chicago seeking the good thing. She immediately encounters Richard Barrett, a mad philosopher who robs her; her confusion then drives her into the arms of Arnold Tippis. A desperate, broken man twisted by his self-hatred and an ongoing identity crisis, he mistakenly classifies Faith as a prostitute, rapes her, and pays her twenty dollars. Believing herself permanently branded a "whore" by the experience, Faith sells her body, as well as the stories she learned from Big Todd, to survive. During this period of suffering, in which she identifies with the history of black oppression in the New World, she loses sight of her original objective. Her luck and her convictions begin to change, however, when Barrett reappears and returns both her money and the focus she has lost. Like Faith, Barrett seeks the good thing, but unlike her he has made some progress and gained some insight. Spinning the tale of his life, he inspires her to resume the quest. He also encourages her to reconnect with her Hatten County roots by way of her imagination.

Unfortunately, despite all Barrett tries to give her, Faith stumbles onto another destructive path when she marries journalist Isaac Maxwell. An overbearing boor who spouts aphorisms about will power but sees himself fundamentally as a racial victim, Maxwell drags Faith into his own mire of insecurity and self-hatred. He first smothers her, then abuses her, then, when he learns about her past, forces her back into prostitution as a means of advancing his career. Faith remains in this nightmare until Alpha Omega Holmes, a painter and her childhood sweetheart, reappears in her life. When she first visits his squalid apartment, she sees his portrait of the Swamp Woman, which symbolizes everything she believes Alpha can give her—in essence, the key to her liberation. Although he reconnects her to her Hatten County roots and affirms the power of the folkways Maxwell rejects, Alpha holds to a rigid conception of his artistry; though Faith becomes pregnant with his child, this rigidity makes him unable to accommodate her in his world. Unwilling to care for her, he abandons Faith to Maxwell, who beats and rejects her when, although it has been months since their last sexual encounter, she tries to convince him he is the child's father. With nowhere else to go, Faith returns to her old rooming house to have her baby. On a cold, snowy day when the weather knocks out the power, she bears a child, a girl, who she hopes will live more happily than she has. Her landlady, who helps with the birth, accidentally knocks over a candle by the bed and starts a fire. The new baby perishes in the blaze; Faith is badly burned and symbolically purified, a cleansing further figured in her rejection of Tippis and Maxwell, who both appear at the hospital and offer to help her.

Recognizing that there is no one she will accept help from in Chicago, Faith returns to Hatten County. She has one final interview with the Swamp Woman, who strips Faith of her last illusions and explains to her the value of experience. She also delineates the process of self-transformation that is the good thing:

Ya take every path: the oracle's, teacher's, the artist's, and even the path of the common fool, and ya learn a li'l bit from each one. . . . Ya keep right on steppin' and pickin' up the pieces until ya gets the whole thing—the Good Thing.

The Swamp Woman cites conjuration, which involves adopting a different way of seeing, as the only way to reach the good thing; as the Swamp Woman works her spells, she liberates her vision and Faith's from conventional boundaries and engages with the world in terms defined by possibility rather than limitation.

OXHERDING TALE

Johnson came to believe that, although folklore allows for a different way of seeing, it does not defy certain fundamental conventions of Western cosmology, physiology, and linguistics. As he strove to engage these issues in his work, Johnson moved beyond the limits of the African American folk tradition to create a fictional tribe of wizards, the Allmuseri, who stand outside the boundaries that hold the characters in *Faith and the Good Thing,* embracing a synthesizing worldview similar to that of the Swamp Woman. Johnson drew on details from a wide variety of sources to develop the tribe's cosmology, theology, and language. A vehicle for his aesthetic program, the Allmuseri were introduced in his next novel, *Oxherding Tale* (1982), and appear also in later novels and several short stories.

Oxherding Tale presented particular difficulties, as Johnson sought to meld the history of slavery with Eastern and Western philosophical traditions. The novel combines the story of a racially mixed fugitive slave's quest for mental and physical freedom with the history of Eastern and Western thought about the nature of being. In many ways, his journey resembles Faith Cross's search. Both are versions of Johnson's archetypal story: a seeker evaluating numerous teachers' models of perception. *Ten Oxherding Pictures,* a twelfth-century Japanese text, was a primary source for the book; this Zen narrative offered a model of the quest for enlightenment that all of Johnson's protagonists undertake. In *Oxherding Tale,* however, the author expands his inquiry beyond that of *Faith and the Good Thing,* moving from a consideration of various models of black being to questioning the very validity of constructs such as race and identity.

Johnson raises important questions with his opening vignette, in which Andrew, the protagonist, recounts how he came to be. The story is as follows. After a long, riotous evening on his South Carolina plantation house veranda, Jonathan Polkinghorne proposes to his black butler, George Hawkins, that the men should trade beds for the night. Somewhat confused but bound by tradition to obey his master's will, George visits Anna Polkinghorne's bedroom. Their sexual union results in George's demotion to field hand, Jonathan's exile to the lower floor of the house, and the birth of Andrew. By having Andrew recount this episode in detail, Johnson subverts standard elements of the slave narrative tradition. Frederick Douglass, the son of a slave mother and a white father, never knew his father's identity for certain; in his autobiography, he hints at suspicions that his master was his father and records the outrage of his conception. By contrast, Andrew's knowledge of his origins complicates his sense of self; he is more clearly tied to both the black and the white worlds. His challenge will be to negotiate the tensions between racial groups in order to achieve some relief from his psychological torment. As he moves between the two worlds, he encounters various teachers, most of whom are driven by some essentialist agenda. In order to be free, he must reconcile the conflicting impulses of their various lessons.

Feeling unwelcome in his master's house and disconnected from his father's, Andrew must also listen to George's rantings about race. Once reluctant to criticize the Polkinghornes, the butler-

turned-oxherd views his fall from grace as a sign: nothing in the white world is for him. Furthermore, George's change in position brings his racial militancy to the surface. He uses his separation from the big house to solidify his dependence on a dual identity; race automatically invalidates any assertion coming from the other side of the divide. As he proclaims to his son, "If they say *hup,* Hawk, it's gotta be *down.*"

The oxherd's rigid view of racial identity keeps him from examining Andrew's complex racial position. Furthermore, he burdens his son with an enormous responsibility: "Whatever you do, Hawk—it pushes the Race forward, or pulls us back. . . . If you fail, everything we been fightin' for fails with you. Be y'self." As George well knows, Andrew has both black and white ancestors; therefore, truly being himself means something different from what George has in mind. Similarly, George points out to Andrew that he is light enough to pass for white and then tells him that doing so would be a complete rejection of his father. In a sense, George demands that Andrew divide himself, placing primary importance on the facets of his identity that perpetuate George's idea of black manhood. For Andrew, the fallout from his father's conviction that black men must express a collective sense of who they are means he cannot yet meaningfully express any sense of who he might be by looking at himself, his race, and the world differently from his father.

Andrew acquires some of the tools for his struggle against essentialism through the education Jonathan provides him. At the feet of Ezekiel Sykes-Withers, his crazed transcendentalist tutor, Andrew learns the major lessons of Western intellectual history and many fundamentals of Eastern thought. Ezekiel sets Andrew to a program of study that only intensifies his sense of separation from his father's world. George responds by emphasizing how Ezekiel is "ruining" Andrew, teaching him things that threaten his black identity. Unlike George, Ezekiel is not plagued by the issue of race; for him, Andrew's studies are all that matter. This contrast is the source of Andrew's disconnection from George's world. In his father's nationalist consciousness, Andrew's adherence to Ezekiel's lessons makes him a servant of the "white" mind. Like the Black Arts movement's adherents in the late 1960s, George sees this mental domination as evil. His racializing the situation further burdens Andrew, who would ideally like to please both men. Yet he cannot, because neither Ezekiel nor George can accept the other's approach, and neither has room in his worldview for diverse elements. Andrew's solution involves embracing the contradiction between the two men. As he reconciles these influences, he transcends intellectual and racial essentialism, thereby effectively embodying Johnson's creative ideal.

Not surprisingly, his education spoils him for servitude, and Andrew asks Jonathan to free him. Instead, Jonathan sends Andrew to work for Flo Hatfield at Leviathan plantation. She forces Andrew into a sexual servitude so demanding that it threatens to destroy him. She also adheres to a racial essentialism that threatens Andrew's journey to enlightenment. Flo falls prey to this way of seeing by participating in the institution of slavery, which Andrew refers to as her having "epidermalized Being." It is precisely this worldview that Andrew must escape to achieve enlightenment. When he is free from a constricting view of race, Andrew can examine the question of individual identity more carefully and experience a healing connection with the rest of the universe.

What saves Andrew is his friendship with Reb, the plantation coffin maker. Reb teaches Andrew a new way of seeing that protects him from the fragmenting forces of race, education, and sensuality. The coffin maker's worldview comes largely from his Allmuseri heritage. The Allmuseri aim to transcend dualism and conquer the self so as to live nonviolent, creative lives of peace and *ahimsa,* or harmlessness to all sentient beings. Reb understands his identity as a constructed illusion that he can change to maintain harmony with his surroundings. This approach protects him from the suffering Andrew is experiencing. When Andrew inevitably displeases Flo, she sends both men to the nearby salt mines. They escape by posing as a white gentleman and his body servant. The fugitives must elude capture by Horace Bannon, a bounty hunter also known as the Soulcatcher, who, as Johnson explains in his introduction to the novel, "plays upon black fears—and a rigid, essentialist notion of the self—to trap his prey." Bannon believes entirely in his method, so much so that he vows to retire if he ever meets a slave he cannot catch.

Andrew and Reb settle in Spartanburg, where Andrew adopts the name William Harris and takes a teaching position. Concealing his background, he courts and marries Peggy Undercliff. After Andrew's marriage, Reb flees North with the Soulcatcher in pursuit. Andrew and Peggy appear to be settling into a comfortable routine until Andrew finds Minty, a slave woman he had loved as a child at Cripplegate, on the town's auction block. He takes her home, confesses some of his past to Peggy, and tries to save Minty from a fatal case of pellagra. When she dies, Bannon reappears. Andrew thinks the Soulcatcher has finally come to claim him. Bannon, however, has come to tell him that he is free. Unable to capture Reb, whose antiessentialist worldview makes him impossible to trap, Bannon has given up slave catching. He and Andrew have a final conversation, in which Andrew comes to terms with his identity and reconciles the disparate elements of his heritage. He then goes home to Peggy to take up "the business of rebuilding . . . the world," an effort he can successfully engage in because he has achieved a unified way of seeing.

THE SORCERER'S APPRENTICE

Johnson's next major work is *The Sorcerer's Apprentice: Tales and Conjurations* (1986), a collection of eight stories written between 1977 and 1982 that are connected thematically to *Oxherding Tale*. Both the Eastern-influenced, neo-slave-narrative novel and the stories challenged Johnson to master, in keeping with the lessons of Gardner, a broad range of story types. He also wrestled with the difficulties inherent in challenging conventional notions of what black literature might be. As a result, *The Sorcerer's Apprentice* centers on three interrelated ideas: the importance of form to the meaning of fiction, the relationship between literary master and student, and the liberation associated with embracing new ways of understanding racial identity.

The collection contains two historical tales, a beast fable, a stream-of-consciousness narrative, and four stories of "contemporary" life told from divergent perspectives in distinctive narrative voices. This experimentation with story genres allows Johnson to interpret experience in diverse and original ways. The chosen genre must fit the world it seeks to capture; by way of example, in his book on black writing, *Being and Race,* Johnson contrasts the different worldviews presented by Richard Wright's social realist *Native Son* and his own folklore-inspired *Faith and the Good Thing.* Johnson affirms that, because the black experience is in fact not a singular entity, stories about that experience not only can but must take diverse forms.

One certainly sees the imprint of Johnson's literary predecessors, both black and white, in "The Education of Mingo" and "The Sorcerer's Apprentice," the stories that frame the collection. Each recounts the psychological costs of slavery for its survivors, black and white, and for their descendants. In "Mingo," however, one also finds resonances with Edgar Allan Poe's "William Wilson"; "Apprentice" bears the mark of Nathaniel Hawthorne's "The Artist of the Beautiful." As Johnson blends these influences with his stories' messages about race, he achieves the broadening of perspective that is a fundamental goal of his aesthetic.

Although none of the stories in the collection is about writers per se, several engage the basic notion of influence, of mentor and apprentice. These concerns are most clearly presented in "The Education of Mingo," "The Sorcerer's Apprentice," and "China." As Frederick T. Griffiths notes, the frame stories consider the responsibilities that the master and the slave bear when their connection influences either person's creativity. In the story of a slaveholder's tragic attempts to train an Allmuseri tribesman to be his companion, "Mingo" presents a commentary on the relationship between white "master" authors and black "apprentice" writers who internalize their lessons literally. The title story, by contrast, illustrates the dangers facing young black writers who adhere too closely to the single example of their African American predecessors.

"China," a tale of one man's liberation from limiting notions of black identity through immersion in Eastern philosophy, is the most important story of the collection in terms of Johnson's quest for "whole sight." Fifty-four-year-old Rudolph Jackson, an African American postman in Seattle, lives a life burdened by received conceptions of what he as a black man "can" be. Together with his wife, Evelyn, he has settled down to a monotonous existence characterized chiefly by a sense of victimization. Rudolph's life begins to turn around when he sees an advertisement for a kung fu movie. Despite Evelyn's rejection of the movie action, as pictured in the advertisement, as impossible, he goes to see the film and then begins training. His experiences at the training hall are transformative. In addition to the physical benefits of the exercise, he embraces the philosophical foundations of the martial art and begins meditating; through kung fu practice and belief, he finds a way to escape the sense of racial limitation that has held him back for so long. The difficulty in his life at this point is that Evelyn does not understand the changes she sees in him; she tries to turn him back into the man she has become comfortable with, even if that man was a broken one.

Evelyn's reaction arises from her strict adherence to a circumscribed notion of what her life can be. Deeply rooted in the traditions of the black church, she expects that she and Rudolph will grow old together in a predictable way and on a set path. Significantly, Evelyn is gradually going blind: on every level, she cannot see the good in the new Rudolph. His new hobby, as she characterizes it, frightens and confuses her. In response, she tries to undercut everything he does, hoping to get a rise out of him so that she can fight him back into place. Filled with inner harmony, however, Rudolph refuses to argue. Instead, he asks her to support him as he fights in a tournament. She hesitates, but finally arrives at the arena in time to witness Rudolph's success. The vision of him leaping high into the air, figuratively transcending the limitations of all he has been before, convinces her of the value of his new approach to life.

"China" is a kind of bridge between *Faith and the Good Thing* and *Oxherding Tale* in its evocation—and resolution—of the tension between Rudolph's Eastern beliefs and Evelyn's African American Christianity. As it is for Lavidia Cross, Christianity for Evelyn is an important element of African American identity. Rudolph represents Johnson's own philosophical and religious leanings in his exploration of black being along avenues different from the traditional African American path. The success of Rudolph's quest, his recognition of a new source of identity, opens up the manifold possibilities inherent in black being. Rudolph achieves the fusion Johnson aspires to in his fiction. Evelyn is given the potential to grasp what her husband has learned; indeed, she decides that, if she dies before her husband, she will permit him to throw out her old books. She is almost ready to cast off her narrow, restrictive worldview—if not in life, then after life. "China" is the most complete articulation, save *Oxherding Tale,* of the relationship between Johnson's ideas about race and Eastern philosophy. Rudolph, and

to some degree Evelyn, discover the richness and diversity that is the only unchangeable characteristic of blackness. That multifaceted vision of racial identity infuses all the stories in the collection.

MIDDLE PASSAGE

When *Middle Passage* (1990) won the National Book Award, Johnson became only the second African American male to achieve that recognition, the first being Ralph Ellison for *Invisible Man* in 1952. The novel grew initially from his second apprentice text, which, as it was told from the point of view of a white ship captain, failed to evoke the emotions of the slaves onboard. After completing *Oxherding Tale,* Johnson returned to this manuscript and focused his energies on expressing the slaves' experiences. This exercise also enabled him to build upon the descriptions of the Allmuseri that appear in "The Gift of the *Osuo,*" "The Education of Mingo," "The Sorcerer's Apprentice," and *Oxherding Tale.*

Rutherford Calhoun, the protagonist of *Middle Passage,* is a manumitted slave and a petty thief who drifts from Makanda, Illinois, to New Orleans after the death of his former master, Reverend Peleg Chandler, and a falling out with his older brother, Jackson. Once in the Crescent City, Calhoun spends most of his time stealing, drinking, and whoring; the remainder he devotes to the necessarily chaste pursuit of Isadora Bailey, a transplanted Boston schoolteacher. Although he is fond of Isadora, Rutherford sees their relationship as casual. Not so Isadora, who loves Rutherford and aspires to redeem him. Knowing that Rutherford owes money to numerous creditors, she goes to Philippe "Papa" Zeringue, the Creole gangster behind all the establishments where Calhoun has unpaid bills, and arranges to pay his debts in exchange for Papa's forcing Rutherford to marry her. Outraged at Isadora for what he sees as her betrayal, Rutherford stows away aboard the slave ship *Republic,* bound for Africa to claim a cargo of forty Allmuseri.

Once aboard the *Republic,* Calhoun must mediate among numerous conflicting groups seeking to control the ship's destiny. He falls under the spell of Captain Ebenezer Falcon, the monomaniacal dwarf who believes in both the innate superiority of the white race and the inevitability of human separation. Although Falcon's ideas disturb Rutherford, he cannot resist the captain's will and acts as his spy among the crew. At the same time, Calhoun agrees to help the first mate, Peter Cringle, who wishes to seize the ship and put the captain over the side. Finally, as the only black crew member, Rutherford has a bond with the Allmuseri cargo.

Calhoun's experiences, particularly his contact with the Allmuseri, begin to change him from self-serving cynic and victimizer to selfless servant of others' needs. One sees this when he takes one of the Allmuseri children, a girl named Baleka, under his protection. Very soon, however, a new crisis tests his transformation. On the day that Cringle and his cohorts had planned to mutiny, the Allmuseri rebel. Once the Africans take control of the ship, Calhoun must plead with them for the lives of the remaining crew and officers. They agree, offering to spare the captain contingent on Rutherford's ability to make Falcon serve them. He goes below to plead the tribe's case, only to see the captain commit suicide—but not before telling Calhoun that Papa Zeringue is part owner of the Allmuseri cargo.

Untold days of suffering follow, marked by sickness, starvation, and cannibalism, as Cringle sacrifices himself so that the others might eat. Finally, Calhoun, Squibb, and three Allmuseri children escape the sinking *Republic* for a ship returning to New Orleans from a pleasure cruise. Rutherford spends his time recording the *Republic*'s adventures, using the creative act to free himself from the memories that haunt him. He

emerges from his cabin only when he learns that Zeringue is aboard and that on the following day he is planning to marry Isadora, for whom Rutherford has been pining. He confronts the gangster, blackmails him into giving up Isadora, and reconciles with her. The novel closes with an image of their spiritual union as Rutherford explains who he has become during the middle passage.

The most striking feature of the novel is the presentation of the Allmuseri. The tribe members have a profound sense of connection to their environment and a sustained awareness of their responsibility for maintaining that harmony through their every action. Their attitudes are Eastern, reflecting the synthesis of self and surroundings that one sees in the Zen text *Ten Oxherding Pictures.* As Ashraf H. A. Rushdy notes, the Allmuseri worldview also closely resembles the phenomenological *epoche,* the bracketing of preconceptions and suppositions that allows one a more intimate connection with objects and experiences. Johnson's treatment of these phenomenological and Buddhist elements of the Allmuseri belief system bring him, in *Middle Passage,* to a larger issue: that of collective responsibility.

The earlier stories emphasize the individual Allmuseri descendant, who conveys a lesson about unity to the protagonist. *Middle Passage,* however, shows the reader a large group of Allmuseri, whose transformation illustrates the need for group application of the creative ideal. When the tribe plunges into "the world of multiplicity, of *me* versus *thee,*" they undermine their worldview. One can attribute this initiation into separation at least partially to the horrors of the middle passage. Without denying or downplaying the gross injustice of the slave trade, however, Johnson claims that circumstance alone is insufficient explanation for their fall. As Ngonyama, the Allmuseri tribesman whom Rutherford befriends early on in the voyage back to New Orleans, explains to Rutherford, the Allmuseri's responsibility is to resist such divisive impulses; their failure to do so despite the pressures of the middle passage is, in his eyes, a betrayal of their faith.

Their apostasy illustrates one of Johnson's main concerns about racial identity. The Allmuseri fall into a sense of division and suffering in the midst of what Carl Pedersen calls "the defining moment of the African-American experience." The challenge for them, Johnson argues, is to avoid turning this experience into the absolute definition of African American identity. The Allmuseri are understandably angry over the injustice of their bondage; their response, however, is to turn from victims to victimizers as soon as possible. Throughout his life up to the middle passage, Rutherford Calhoun has lived by similar ground rules, as his justification of thievery on racial grounds illustrates. What he learns, however, is what the Allmuseri have at least temporarily forgotten: that one must nurture and maintain a sense of connection to all things in order to escape the trap of racialist thinking. This is the lesson that Andrew learns in *Oxherding Tale* and that Faith learns in *Faith and the Good Thing.* What is different in *Middle Passage,* however, is that Johnson shows with devastating clarity the impact of an individual's actions on the group. The Allmuseri have made a pact to maintain their sense of harmony, and tragedy ensues when they break their vow. Similarly, Johnson suggests, Americans must come to terms with the historical event of the middle passage and ensure that separatist attitudes do not perpetuate the suffering that sprang from the transatlantic voyage. This conviction takes him a step closer to the fullest achievement of his artistic vision in *Dreamer,* which celebrates the fulfillment of human potential through the cohesiveness of community.

In addition to transforming perceptions about individual and group identity with his account of Allmuseri beliefs, Johnson also uses the tribe to make a point about language and literature. As Daniel Scott notes, *Middle Passage* is profoundly a text about writing. Johnson develops the tribe's

significance by giving them a language that defies conventional expectations. The tribe's history, for instance, is mutable, rather than a formalized, factual record of their evolution as a people. This rejection of conventional Western understandings of history implies a refusal to accept the organization and limitation that such an approach necessarily involves. Along with their fluid sense of history, the Allmuseri have a language especially suited to their worldview. They use a written language consisting of pictograms that must be "read" simultaneously and speak a language with no "to be" verb and no nouns. Western language systems order, name, and therefore limit experience; Johnson frees his archetypal tribe from these boundaries.

DREAMER

In *Dreamer* (1998) Johnson moves beyond the idea of a philosophical commitment to the human community to a specific plan of action for improving social conditions. As Johnson recounts the impact of Martin Luther King Jr., on the lives of his narrator, Matthew Bishop, and King's cynical body double, Chaym Smith, he emphasizes the value of "doing well." He defines *doing well* as making a contribution to King's vision of "the beloved community," a unified understanding of humanity unhampered by divisive definitions such as racial identity. In these terms, a new way of seeing the world is not sufficient; one must also behave differently. And in making this claim, Johnson behaves differently as an author as well. Moving beyond the abstractions of his earlier considerations of identity, he calls here for the application of philosophical ideals to everyday life. By doing so, he occupies a role not unlike the one that King, a trained philosopher himself, played in the civil rights struggles.

When King brings his campaign against slums to Chicago in 1966, Matthew Bishop willingly signs on. An aspiring philosopher forced to drop out of college when his mother died, Matthew joins the movement as a tribute to her conviction that King will save the black community. He exists somewhat on the periphery of the movement. He is in love with a fellow worker, Amy Griffith, who has no interest in him. Doubly isolated by her rejection and his self-doubt, Bishop contents himself with service and with chronicling the campaign's events. Fate hands him a more important role, however, when he is on duty to greet Chaym Smith. This disillusioned drifter appears one night at King's Lawndale apartment bearing a hard luck story, a plea for assistance, and a striking physical resemblance to the minister. He eventually convinces King to take him on as a body double; the minister in turn assigns Matthew and Amy to take Smith into hiding in southern Illinois, where he will learn the necessary lessons for playing his new role.

Once away from Chicago, Smith reveals himself to be much more complex and sophisticated than his interview with King suggests. A modern-day Ishmael, Smith has wandered the East, studying for a year in a Japanese monastery; he also, in the course of his travels, has internalized an encyclopedic knowledge of Western philosophy. Nevertheless, despite all he knows, Smith remains convinced that hopefulness and philanthropy are merely illusions. As he tells Matthew and Amy, "There's two kinds of people in this world. Predators and prey. Lions and *lunch*. You see it any other way, buddy, and people will chump you off." Although Amy rejects this assertion, Matthew considers Chaym's points, which speak to his personal sense of loss. As a result, he soon finds himself torn between the minister's and the misanthrope's visions of humanity.

All of that changes, however, when Matthew and Amy bring Smith back to Chicago to stand in for King. In a bizarre reenactment of Izola Ware Curry's assassination attempt on King, an angry old African American man shoots Smith.

Matthew and Amy take him back to their hideout to recuperate; during his physical healing process, Smith undergoes a profound philosophical change. Having looked on death and survived it, he chooses to live differently in the aftermath. For Smith, this means grasping the underlying message of King's vision and celebrating his connection to the universe.

As he changes, Smith also comes to understand his role differently. No longer bemoaning his fate as a victim of circumstance, the body double focuses his energy on service, trying to bring forth King's spiritual ideal through his daily actions. Once a sharp critic of Christianity, Smith volunteers his services as gardener and carpenter at a small church near his Makanda, Illinois, hiding place. His example proves useful also to Bishop, who serves as his assistant in these endeavors. In addition to some rough carpentry, Bishop learns from Chaym how he might also better contribute to creating the "beloved community" despite his personal imperfections. Inspired by Chaym's actions, he makes a personal commitment to love, as he risks rejection in order to forge a permanent connection with Amy. She, in turn, learns to overcome her distrust of black men and reaches out to Matthew when he reappears in Chicago. His visit is all too brief, however. Chaym summons him back south when he sees strangers watching the hideout. These observers turn out to be government agents, who force Smith to participate in their plot against King. The body double has one final interview with Bishop before going into seclusion to prepare for a nefarious assignment.

Before the government can use Smith, however, King is assassinated on April 4, 1968. With the body double gone, Bishop ponders Smith's—and King's—legacy. For Bishop, one inheritance is a heightened awareness of accountability for the civil rights leader's death. As he tells Amy as they march behind King's coffin, they all killed King, "black and white—because we didn't listen when he was alive." Despite that recognition, however, he does not despair, because part of what he gained from his encounter with Smith is a new belief in the possibility of redemption. Bishop realizes that "Chaym had in his covert passage through our lives let us know that, if one missed the Galilean mark, even the pariahs, the fatherless exiles, might sometimes—and occasionally—doeth well." This final hopeful assertion, that not everyone need be as spiritually and philosophically evolved as the slain leader in order to bring his vision to fruition, emphasizes both the need for and the possibility of achieving King's goal. By ending on this note, Johnson encourages the reader to participate in King's vision; in the process, he transforms his literature into a plea for social change.

The idea that the best and the least can all work together to create the beloved community resolves an important tension that operates throughout the novel. Picking up threads interspersed through *Middle Passage,* Johnson weaves the biblical story of Cain and Abel into *Dreamer.* Chaym's name, which derives etymologically from Cain, identifies him as a spiritual heir to the first murderer's suffering. Profoundly aware of the etymology of his name, Smith declares himself (and Bishop) marked. Believing that he is thus stained, he sees no possibility for any sort of connection with others. Chaym must achieve a new way of seeing that will enable him both to overcome his sense of himself as irrevocably ostracized and to claim a place for himself in the beloved community.

This Cain and Abel imagery also has further implications for Johnson's conception of racial identity. Traditionally, scholars associate the mark of Cain with blackness. One result of that identification is a negative view of race arising from within the black community. This attitude, which Smith demonstrates in *Dreamer,* gives rise to the victim-victimizer mentality; Johnson challenges the reductive view that all blacks are

Cainites. As a part of his effort to illustrate the richness and complexity of black being, he demonstrates that the black community contains both Abelites and Cainites. In the moral vision of his fiction, the haves within the community can assist the have-nots toward the realization of a harmonious society. This pattern of action breaks down the stigmatization and separation associated with the mark, or stain, of race in contemporary America.

Although Johnson takes a somewhat different position in *Dreamer* than in his previous novels with regard to the issue of one's responsibility to others, he does not abandon the principle that each person individually must strive to achieve "whole sight." As the characters in *Dreamer* move toward the realization of King's social vision, they must learn to overcome limited understandings of racial and individual identity and to reject narrowly defined models of perception. In effect, he argues, one cannot create the beloved community without such an unlimited way of seeing the world. The question that *Dreamer* asks more explicitly than the previous works is this: Once one has this liberating knowledge, what must one do with it?

Clearly, one thing to do with this awareness is to make art. Chaym's musical and artistic expression of his evolution illustrates Johnson's belief in the artist's ability to help build the beloved community. When Bishop broaches the subject of Smith's art with him, the body double reiterates his desire for acceptance: "I was hoping that if I created something beautiful, I could offer that to others. Something that would live after I was gone. A li'l piece of me, you know, that'd endure." Believing, however, that his inferior status makes his art necessarily inferior, Smith eschews the idea of making objects of beauty to share with others and turns instead to chronicling the desperate conditions plaguing the black community; this in turn confirms his sense of himself as second class. What could be an important gift to others becomes instead a medium for perpetuating his isolation. After Chaym's brush with death, however, he begins to use his art again as a healing tool. As part of Chaym's enlightenment, Johnson has his character come to understand the link between art and action, that art is one of the ways to fulfill one's personal responsibility to help improve social conditions. Searching through Smith's sketchbooks after the government men have taken his friend away, Matthew sees how drawing has become an instrument of hope for Chaym. Smith's decision to reinvent the world in his drawings reflects his attainment of enlightenment, as making art allows him to break out of his negative worldview and adopt a more hopeful stance. From that position comes his inspiration to serve again, which he satisfies by "doing well" at Bethel AME Church. Matthew sees that "even the pariahs, the fatherless exiles, might sometimes—and occasionally—doeth well."

SINGING THE WORLD

For almost three decades, from the drawings in *Black Humor* to the prose of *Middle Passage,* Johnson has worked for a social and a literary ideal: a nation not defined and divided by racialism, and an American canon in which works need not be discussed in racial terms. At a crucial moment in *Dreamer,* Johnson evokes a creative forebear who set an example for addressing the challenges that racial issues pose both to life and literature. When Matthew Bishop returns to Makanda from his visit with Amy, he finds Chaym at Bethel AME Church, where he has been doing well for the congregation by tending their property. As he sits and listens to Chaym explaining his plan for assisting the Bethel congregation, Matthew notes that his face is "splattered with Optic White" paint. The narrator of Ralph Ellison's *Invisible Man* works for a time at Liberty Paints, the manufacturer of Optic White. In that

novel, in a scene symbolizing the importance of American blacks to the nation as a whole, the narrator demonstrates that ten drops of black go into the formula for the white paint. When Johnson marks Chaym with this same paint just as the character is coming to view his status in a different light, he affirms Ellison's unifying vision.

In *Invisible Man* Ellison asks the reader, "Who knows but that, on the lower frequencies, I speak for you?" Johnson's work is an affirmation of a writer's ability to speak in a multiplicity of voices to a multiplicity of readers. In *Being and Race,* Johnson expresses his hope that black writers will "feel at ease both in their ethnicity and in their Yankeeness, and find it the most natural thing, as [the philosopher] Merleau-Ponty was fond of saying, to go about 'singing the world.' "

Selected Bibliography

WORKS OF CHARLES JOHNSON

NOVELS
Faith and the Good Thing. New York: Viking, 1974.
Oxherding Tale. Bloomington: Indiana University Press, 1982.
Middle Passage. New York: Atheneum, 1990.
Dreamer: A Novel. New York: Scribner, 1998.

SHORT STORIES
The Sorcerer's Apprentice: Tales and Conjurations. New York: Atheneum, 1986.
"Kwoon." In *Playboy Stories: The Best of Forty Years of Short Fiction.* Edited by Alice K. Turner. New York: Dutton, 1994.
"The Gift of the *Osuo*"; "The Green Belt: A Play for Television." *African American Review* 30, no. 4:519–526 (winter 1996). Special issue devoted to Johnson's work.
"Executive Decision." In *Outside the Law: Narratives*

on Justice in America. Edited by Susan Richards Shreve and Porter Shreve. Boston: Beacon, 1997.

Africans in America: America's Journey through Slavery, by Charles Johnson, Patricia Smith, and the WGBH Series Research Team. New York: Harcourt Brace, 1998. Twelve short historical fictions by Johnson interspersed with other material. Published in connection with the PBS series.

"The Work of the World." In *I Call Myself an Artist: Writings by and about Charles Johnson.* Edited by Rudolph P. Byrd. Bloomington: Indiana University Press, 1999.

DRAWINGS

Black Humor. Chicago: Johnson Publishing, 1970.
Half-Past Nation Time. Chicago: Aware Press, 1972.

ESSAYS AND LITERARY CRITICISM

"*The Primeval Mitosis:* A Phenomenology of the Black Body." *Ju-ju,* winter 1976, pp. 48–59.

"Philosophy and Black Fiction." *Obsidian* 6, no. 1:55–61 (summer 1980).

"Whole Sight: Notes on New Black Fiction." *Callaloo* 7, no. 3:1–6 (fall 1984).

"A Phenomenology of *On Moral Fiction.*" In *Thor's Hammer: Essays on John Gardner.* Edited by Jeff Henderson. Conway: University of Central Arkansas Press, 1985.

Being and Race: Black Writing Since 1970. Bloomington: Indiana University Press, 1988.

"Where Fiction and Philosophy Meet." *American Visions* 3, no. 36:47–48 (June 1988).

"The Philosopher and the American Novel." In *In Search of a Voice,* by Charles Johnson and Ron Chernow. Washington, D.C.: Library of Congress, 1991.

"Charles Johnson." In *Contemporary Authors Autobiography Series,* vol. 18. Edited by Joyce Nakamura. Detroit: Gale Research, 1994.

"The King We Left Behind." *CommonQuest,* fall 1996, pp. 7–10.

"John Gardner as Mentor." *African American Review* 30, no. 4:619–624 (winter 1996). Special issue devoted to Johnson's work.

"A Capsule History of Blacks in Comics." Foreword to *Still I Rise: A Cartoon History of African Americans,* by Roland Owen Laird Jr., with Taneshia Nash Laird. New York: Norton, 1997.

"The Second Front: A Reflection on Milk Bottles, Male Elders, the Enemy Within, Bar Mitzvahs, and Martin Luther King, Jr." In *Black Men Speaking.* Edited by Charles Johnson and John McCluskey Jr. Bloomington: Indiana University Press, 1997.

"On the Nature of Tales." Introduction to *QPB Treasury of North American Folktales.* Edited by Catherine Peck. New York: Quality Paperback Books, 1998.

"An Ever-Lifting Song of Black America." *New York Times,* Feb. 14, 1999, pp. 1, 34.

CRITICAL STUDIES

Byrd, Rudolph P. "*Oxherding Tale* and *Siddhartha:* Philosophy, Fiction, and the Emergence of a Hidden Tradition." *African American Review* 30, no. 4:549–558 (winter 1996). Special Johnson issue.

———, ed. *I Call Myself an Artist: Writings by and about Charles Johnson.* Bloomington: Indiana University Press, 1999.

Coleman, James W. "Charles Johnson's Quest for Black Freedom in *Oxherding Tale.*" *African American Review* 29, no. 4:631–644 (winter 1995).

Gleason, William. "The Liberation of Perception: Charles Johnson's *Oxherding Tale.*" *Black American Literature Forum* 25, no. 4:704–728 (winter 1991).

Goudie, S. X. " 'Leavin' a Mark on the Wor(l)d': Marksmen and Marked Men in *Middle Passage.*" *African American Review* 29, no. 1:109–122 (spring 1995).

Griffiths, Frederick T. " 'Sorcery Is Dialectical': Plato and Jean Toomer in Charles Johnson's *The Sorcerer's Apprentice.*" *African American Review* 30, no. 4:527–538 (winter 1996). Special Johnson issue.

Hayward, Jennifer. "Something to Serve: Constructs of the Feminine in Charles Johnson's *Oxherding Tale.*" *Black American Literature Forum* 25, no. 4:689–703 (winter 1991).

Little, Jonathan. "Charles Johnson's Revolutionary *Oxherding Tale.*" *Studies in American Fiction* 19, no. 2:141–152 (autumn 1991).

———. *Charles Johnson's Spiritual Imagination.* Columbia: University of Missouri Press, 1997.

Muther, Elizabeth. "Isadora at Sea: Misogyny as Comic Capital in Charles Johnson's *Middle Pas-*

sage." *African American Review* 30, no. 4:649–658 (winter 1996). Special Johnson issue.

Pedersen, Carl. "Middle Passages: Representation of the Slave Trade in Caribbean and African American Literature." *Massachusetts Review* 34, no. 2:225–239 (1993).

Rushdy, Ashraf H. A. "The Phenomenology of the Allmuseri: Charles Johnson and the Subject of the Narrative of Slavery." *African American Review* 26, no. 2:373–394 (summer 1992).

———. "The Prospects of Desire: Forms of Slave Identity in Charles Johnson's *Middle Passage.*" *Arizona Quarterly* 50, no. 2:73–108 (1994).

Scott, Daniel M. "Interrogating Identity: Appropriation and Transformation in *Middle Passage.*" *African American Review* 29, no. 4:645–655 (winter 1995).

Storhoff, Gary. "The Artist as Universal Mind: Berkeley's Influence on Charles Johnson." *African Amer-*
ican Review 30, no. 4:539–548 (winter 1996). Special Johnson issue.

INTERVIEWS

Boccia, Michael. "An Interview with Charles Johnson." *African American Review* 30, no. 4:611–618 (winter 1996). Special Johnson issue.

Little, Jonathan. "An Interview with Charles Johnson." *Contemporary Literature* 34, no. 2:159–181 (summer 1993).

McCullough, Ken. "Reflections on Film, Philosophy, and Fiction: An Interview with Charles Johnson." *Callaloo* 4, no. 1:118–128 (fall 1978).

Nash, William R. "A Conversation with Charles Johnson." *New England Review* 19, no. 2:49–61 (spring 1998).

—*WILLIAM R. NASH*

Susan Minot

1956–

THE NOVELS AND short stories of Susan Minot address the universal themes of desire, death, the self, and memory. Memory, always partial, fragmentary, and only tenuously based in history, nonetheless serves as the controlling narrative of many of Minot's characters' lives, determining their desires, informing their identities, and simultaneously connecting people and isolating them from one another.

Minot's fiction explores human behavior and tries to get at what it means to be alive as an individual in a family and a community—in a maze of human relationships fraught with mysteries and secrets. Secrets, so seamlessly woven into our consciousness, so integral and inevitable a part of our daily lives, result from our need to at once connect with and separate ourselves from others. For Minot, the secrets we keep from each other signal the larger mystery and unfathomable nature of others, the impossibility of ever knowing another completely. Most often her subjects are women and their attempt to achieve wholeness and authenticity, especially as this attempt is complicated by relationships with men and children. Her prose style is marked by its poetic quality, by the writer's ability to distill into a single image a complex array of meaning. This intensity of language, together with Minot's fearless efforts to uncover truths of human behavior and emotion, have secured her place among American writers of fiction.

BACKGROUND

Minot was born on December 7, 1956, to George R. and Carrie Minot, in Manchester, Massachusetts, the second-oldest of seven children in a middle-class family. Surrounded by siblings, she found her sense of self in community even as she struggled to assert her individuality and autonomy. Hiding was a necessary part of growing up: in a large family, "Life wasn't about you and your relation to the world," she told the interviewer Robley Wilson, "it was about you and your relation to other people. . . . You moved your elbow, this way, and you touched someone." Images of concealment pervade her fiction. In several stories it reflects the desire of the individual to escape community in pursuit of peace and solitude, in pursuit of self-knowledge. The idea of retreating from the group has been of signal interest to her. In a scene in her first published story, "Hiding," which was later included in *Monkeys* (1986), a collection of related short stories often referred to as a novel, a group of children hide with their mother in a closet, hoping to lure their distracted father into searching for them. Hiding in that story is a communal act of play, a mother-inspired child's game that reveals the conspiratorial community of mother and children longing, paradoxically, to include an indifferent father.

When Minot was twenty-one years old, newly graduated from college and ready to set off for Europe, her mother died tragically in an accident; that loss, and the way crisis and death push a family in new directions, has found its way into much of her work. She has said that to observe a family under duress is to witness its basic dynamics. Minot returned to Manchester to face the loss with her family. Her mother was beautiful and charismatic; since her father, a stockbroker, was emotionally distant and sometimes physically absent, Carrie Minot was clearly the primary parent. Her loss was keenly felt, and Susan stayed a year at home serving as something of a surrogate mother to her siblings, the youngest of whom was only eight years old at the time. *Monkeys* chronicles the impact on the Vincent family of the mother's life and death. Minot's works explore also the more general ways in which families influence individual personalities and actions. Because of her insights into the family, Minot invites comparison with J. D. Salinger, one of her literary heroes, and Raymond Carver. *Monkeys* certainly established Minot's place in contemporary American literature; yet it also caused considerable pain and tension within her own family.

Growing up in a large family meant that Minot always shared a room with one of her sisters. Writing daily in a journal from the time she was thirteen helped her to define a private territory that enabled her to sift through the chaos of life and clarify her thoughts. It was only when she went to the prestigious Concord Academy that she finally had "a room of her own." Despite the proximity of the family home to Boston, Minot's family traveled only infrequently to the city; other than summers in Maine, Minot spent most of her time close to home. Thus, attending Concord Academy was her first foray into a more independent life. Yet even there she kept her writing to herself. Minot describes herself in her school years as a sullen teenager who would play lacrosse but smoke cigarettes at halftime. She did join the school's literary journal and late at night in her room immersed herself in poetry. Although writing was in fact an integral element of her daily life, it took many years before Minot thought of herself as a writer.

CREATIVE DEVELOPMENT

Minot spent a year at Boston University before transferring to Brown, where she studied art and creative writing. In 1980 she moved to New York City and enrolled in Columbia University's graduate writing program, where she was a contemporary of writers such as Jay McInerney, with whom she became friends. Minot was not particularly encouraged by her writing teachers, but she sold four stories—two to *The New Yorker* and two to the literary journal *Grand Street*—soon after leaving Columbia. Ben Sonnenberg, the editor of *Grand Street,* became her mentor and faithful reader. Several of the stories that would appear in *Monkeys* were written while Minot was canvassing door-to-door for the environmental activist group Greenpeace and working as a carpenter and house painter. She was married to filmmaker Davis McHenry until their divorce in 1992. A peripatetic writer, Minot travels widely. As she noted in a 1999 *Vogue* magazine article, her 1998 novel, *Evening,* "traveled over three different continents, visited five countries, was worked on in six states, five islands, seven cities, [and] fifteen towns."

In 1987 Minot was living and writing in a Tuscan village in Italy when she received the Prix Femina Etranger for *Monkeys;* the novel, translated into a dozen languages, was a best-seller in Italy. Both *Monkeys* and *Evening* were warmly received by critics writing in *The New York Times Book Review*. In 1994, following the publication of the novel *Folly* and revealing her increasing popularity as a contemporary writer, Minot was named September writer-in-residence at the magazine *Victoria*. As a freelance journalist and essayist, Minot has written for publications as varied as *Vogue, Esquire, Skiing, Travel and Leisure,* and *The New York Times Magazine*. Many of her articles have been prompted by her travels outside of the United States, particularly the extended time she spent living and writing in Africa. She has written about contemporary American politics and culture, including gender politics, as well as international affairs. Minot is also the author of the screenplay for Bernardo Bertolucci's 1996 film *Stealing Beauty,* and in the late 1990s she was working on a screen adaptation of her own novel, *Evening.* She has taught creative writing workshops at Columbia University (1988–1989) and as an adjunct professor at New York University, and she has given readings of her work across the United States. A talented painter—her own watercolor provided the jacket art for *Monkeys*—she has written (in a *Vogue* article on the poet Elizabeth Bishop, who also painted) that "the connection [between writing and visual art] is a natural one. The urge to express—to look, to set down, to arrange—spills over into another medium."

Minot is drawn to lyric poetry and the kind of poetic compression that characterizes works by many late-twentieth-century fiction writers, most especially Raymond Carver. Carver, a writer admired for his poetic tenderness and the ability to speak directly to the deepest emotions of the reader, has been one of Minot's greatest influences and sources of inspiration. While studying at Columbia under teachers as different as Elizabeth Hardwick and Richard Price, Minot welcomed the opportunity to experiment with fictional form. She read widely in postmodernist fiction as well as in the works of such masters of the short story and the novel as Marcel Proust,

Henry James, Edith Wharton, Virginia Woolf, William Faulkner, F. Scott Fitzgerald, Ernest Hemingway, and Kathrine Mansfield. Reading Faulkner's experimental modernist novel *The Sound and the Fury* marked a pivotal moment in her life as a writer; it instilled in her the desire to write with a similarly great emotional force. Thus, rather than constructing plot-based narratives, her works are often intimate and intense studies of characters' psychological and emotional states.

The subjects of Minot's fiction are primarily women plagued by unfulfilled desires. In a 1998 interview, Minot speaks of how "desire automatically generates conflict—inner and outer conflict with the self, conflict between people—and conflict is an integral subject for fiction." The subject of her novel *Folly* (1992), set in the drawing rooms and on the sidewalks of Boston in the period between the two World Wars, is Lilian Eliot, a young woman whose choices are circumscribed by her Boston Brahmin social class and her gender. The narrators in *Lust and Other Stories* (1989), Minot's second collection, view the world primarily through a feminine and feminist consciousness; most of the stories investigate the psychological effects of love and loss on women in the aftermath of failed relationships. The title story has been anthologized widely and is probably one of Minot's most popular short stories; it keenly exposes the sexual double standards women continue to be subjected to. Most of the stories in *Monkeys*—a book, like *Lust and Other Stories,* that frequently appears on the reading lists for college courses in contemporary American literature and women's literature—are narrated through the consciousness of Sophie, the second-oldest sister in the family. The narrative sympathies and predilections of *Monkeys* are distinctly feminist, although the work itself is softly nuanced and only quietly resistant to the patriarchal structure of the Vincent family. The narrative mode of *Evening,* her most compelling and sophisticated literary work to date, mixes the rhythms of dreams with the pace of waking life; it is reminiscent of Virginia Woolf's *Mrs. Dalloway* and *To the Lighthouse,* in that it is a penetrating journey through the psychological terrain of a single woman's consciousness, searching the substance of every banal and pedestrian detail, finding the cosmic in the quotidian.

MONKEYS

It is from T. S. Eliot that Minot draws the epigraph for *Monkeys:* "The houses are all gone under the sea." The line establishes at the outset a sense of loss, anticipating Minot's picture of a modern wasteland in which family and its old and familiar structures no longer hold. The epigraph achieves a desolate resonance when, in the final chapter or story of the collection, the Vincent family sails out from the coast of Maine to cast the ashes of their mother into the water. Houses serve as a metonym for mothers—for it is undoubtedly the mother who has kept the house of the Vincents from falling; without her the entire family structure is threatened.

The table of contents for *Monkeys* lists not only the stories but also the years in which they are set, from 1966 to 1979. Thus the chronology of the parts establishes the connectedness of the whole, and renders the collection a novel. Certainly the individual stories can stand alone, and have been anthologized as such, but each finds its greatest meaning and resonance in relation to the others.

The prose of each story is spare, imagistic, and poetic, and this consistency of style further enhances the stories' collective impact as a novel. In the first story, "Hiding," for instance, Minot writes: "We run ahead and hide in a pile of leaves. Little twigs get in your mouth and your nostrils; we hold still underneath listening to the brittle ticking leaves." Later in the same story: "We have the ice pond all to ourselves. In certain places the ice is bumpy and if you glide on it going *Aauuuhhh* in a low tone, your voice wobbles and vibrates. Every once in a while, a crack shoots across the pond, echoing just beneath the surface, and you feel something drop in the hollow of your back. It sounds like someone's jumped off a steel wire and left it twanging in the air." In the third story, "Allowance," Minot describes the family on vacation in Bermuda: "Things were different in Bermuda. The grass was scratchy and rough, not at all like the grass at home, and the air had a thickness that made your bones feel loose. Stepping into the coral caves was like entering a sea shell, with a low wind rushing and the echo of water slaps." In more familiar holiday surroundings, the descriptions resonate with those of Bermuda: "There was a toppled tree up there, with roots that spread out like a fan. When they were younger, the kids used to stand in front of it and hoot and listen for the echo. It was like a half-shell, the way the sounds reverberated. Up close, the roots and moss made intricate designs, like an ancient chart." In the final story, "Thorofare," Minot describes two of the family members in the garden: "There was a narrow window on either side of the door. They clustered to one, to stay out of sight. Dad and Delilah were standing at the end of the lawn. Behind them the spring trees made a light-green screen, and beyond it the ocean was flat. Dad held the box while Delilah reached inside. She pulled back her fist and flung some white bits over the garden and down the hill." These qualities—the poetic impact of the prose and the blurring of the distinction between story and novel—render the work strangely resistant to neat and efficient descriptions of genre. Likewise, the tight focus on family and the domestic domain achieves a certain quaint or old-fashioned flavor while at the same time the author's approach to her subject seems startlingly fresh and new.

Following the table of contents is a list of the characters in the book, all of them members of the Vincent family. (The book proceeds to reveal an extended family in terms of both its history and contemporary context.) The chronological table of contents and the character list recall the apparatus of novels of an earlier era, and thus also a certain notion of family as reliably intact; but it is this facade of family, concealing flaws and sorrows, that is slowly stripped away over the course of the book.

"Hiding" was the first of Minot's stories to be published, and it is the first story of this work, establishing in its title the metaphor that extends throughout Minot's oeuvre. Just as Minot blurs boundaries of genre in *Monkeys,* so too does she play with expectations of consistency of point of view and tense within and between the stories. "Hiding" begins in the first-person plural, establishing the perspective of all the children with the first two words, "Our father . . ." The father dominates the children's perspective; he begins their story. Although the narrative point of view soon narrows to first-person singular, it is from a collective perspective that the father is perceived. The words "Our father" evoke the first words of the Lord's Prayer, but this allusion is immediately and ironically undercut by the words that follow: "doesn't go to church." Thus the very first line suggests contradictory impulses and paradoxes, which are played out throughout this story and the ones that follow.

The mother, on the other hand, is referred to as "Mum," without the "our" to separate the narrator's mother from the reader's; Rosie Vincent becomes immediately familiar. The present tense of the story situates the reader within the chaotic family circle, and the vividness and force of the verbs propel the reader into an intimate proximity with the flurry of movement: "Sherman ripples by, coat flapping, and Mum grabs him by the hood, reeling him in, and zips him up." Out of this domestic realm, this collection of ordinary events and moments, emerges the extraordinary, a lasting and meaningful vision not simply of the Vincent family but of family itself.

In "Hiding" the Vincent family is portrayed as both typical and particular; the reader glimpses both the routine and the unusual elements of their life. Seen from Sophie's childlike perspective and consciousness, a particular moment is etched in its singularity and stretched through the temporal spaciousness of memory, where all moments—past and present—cohere. Minot uses the child's narrative consciousness to collapse temporal and spatial boundaries; the very process of telling a story becomes intimately connected with the processes and products of memory.

Despite the father's clear dominance over the family, he establishes his authority from the periphery, hanging almost always to the side and the back of the family circle, at whose center stands the mother. In the eyes of her children, Rosie Vincent ice skating is lovingly seen as a "tulip," a "twirling whirlpool," a "pillar or tornado"—but Gus Vincent doesn't see her this way, or is too distant to see her at all. Rosie Vincent constantly protects her husband from what she knows he sees as the onslaught of his family on his sensibilities; she keeps the children "in the kitchen a little longer so he can have a little peace and quiet." Mr. Vincent is portrayed in images of darkness and separateness: when he enters the family circle, it is "as if he's emerged from a dark tunnel."

Rosie Vincent is herself playful and childlike, ebullient and delighted to be in her children's company. She appears to be protecting them from their father's indifference, compensating for his absence. When the mother proposes that they all hide in the closet to incite the father to find them, the children are filled with anticipation and excitement, captivated by the imagination and daring of their mother. They are just as filled with disappointment and anticlimax when their father doesn't participate in the game, when he doesn't bother to come and look for them. The children understand that their mother's attempt has failed: "We see the wince on her face like when you are waiting to be hit or after you have been."

In "Allowance" and later stories, Gus Vincent's expectations of his children's behavior are contrasted with his own alcoholic outbursts.

When not flagrantly violating his own standards of decorum, he is simply remote, unable to participate in the life of his own family. At the dinner table in a posh Bermuda holiday hotel, "Dad glanced around the table. Perplexed, he saw six children, six hopeful faces looking back at him. Down at the other end was a woman in a pink dress. What did they want? He stood and excused himself." The father's behavior here anticipates almost exactly that of Gilbert Finch in Minot's later work, *Folly;* the fathers in both works are absent in a profoundly emotional sense.

Rosie Vincent fills her life with a magic found outside of marriage but within motherhood. She also finds her moments of being alone: "On summer nights, she'd stop the car at Booth Cove and get out. The gate in the seawall was as wide as a barn door and creaked when she opened it. The water would be still and inky black and very inviting and, in her pink evening gown, the satin one with the rhinestones, she'd slip into the water, breaking the moon's reflection." "Wildflowers" also captures her essential spirit: "She found fields everywhere shimmering down to the sea, flowers scattered and random, not boxed inside walls." The wildflowers she finds serve as a metaphor for herself and the magical world she insists upon in spite of her husband's obdurate lack of imagination and refusal to acknowledge another dimension to the world. When Rosie passionately announces her sighting of a silver fox, her husband claims that there is "no such thing." But Rosie is unafraid of straying from convention; she is one of only two Democrats in Marshport. She is also unafraid of embracing motherhood as the grand passion of her life; when Miranda Rose is born during the spring after Rosie's fortieth birthday, the baby is her new treasure. Two of the older girls watch their mother watching the baby:

After fixing [her nipple] to the baby's mouth, and satisfied with it, she looked up. Caitlin and Sophie saw it—that wild look—only this time there was something added. It was aimed at them and it said: There is nothing in the world that compares with this. The eye was fierce. The baby stayed fast. There is nothing so thrilling as this. Nothing.

In all of the stories of the collection, as in many contemporary American short stories, absence is inscribed in the narrative structure. Questions are asked but not answered, meaning and understanding suffer constant erasure as the gaps and silences of human contact are revealed. Raymond Carver describes, in *Fires* (1983) the "menace" that unsettles the surface of short fiction through what is left out and through the power suggested by a simple, unexpected detail. As with lyric poetry, which shares some of the qualities of short fiction, the power of Minot's stories lies in what is implied through symbol and image, through a well-selected phrase or sentence, and through what remains unsaid, existing beyond and outside of language. Time passes in the collection without being explicitly signaled; gaps and silences exist within and between the stories. Sophie remains the controlling presence in the later stories even when she is only referred to tangentially by a different narrator; but other points of view are captured within the shifting narrative focus. The past and present tenses are fluidly exchanged, revealing the ongoing presence of the past in individual and collective family memories.

A sorrow that is unspeakable runs through the collection. One afternoon Sophie comes upon her mother apparently taking a nap: "She was lying on her side, facing the wall, and her shoulders were shaking up and down, crying. Sophie turned away quietly, her heart loud inside." Both mother and daughter remain outwardly silent in their grief. Rosie's loss of a baby is muted in the narrative (as is the drowning death of Ann Lord's twelve-year-old son in *Evening*). Rosie's own tragic death is buried within *Monkeys,* remaining undescribed until the last stories; it is referred to in "Accident" as having already happened. Like the characters, the narrative itself is nearly unable to speak the unspeakable sorrow or to make sense of such loss. The aching absence caused by death, and the inability of the characters to speak their grief, is inscribed in narrative absence. The reader receives the news with shock and disbelief, wondering when and how Rosie could have died, why nothing in the narrative leads up to the fact of her death, why it has not been prepared for and explained. Thus the reader experiences shock and disbelief much as the family has. "Accident" is narrated in the present tense: life goes on in all its banality and with all its flux and chaos. "The girls never stopped talking, worrying about their boyfriends, worrying about Dad, always having fits—especially since their mother died." The tone of the narrative is matter-of-fact, stripped of the magic and the imagination associated with the earlier childhood stories so filled with the presence of the mother's indomitable spirit.

The narrative in this story becomes reportorial, informing the reader of each child's doings; but as though slipped into it, certain moments evoke the memory of the accident: "Sherman hears, down at the marsh, the familiar rattle of the train going by, the train that hit Mum's car and killed her. Sherman has certain theories about the accident, and about the family." The sound that signals loss and silent grief returns in the household as in the narrative: "The back door is open behind Mr. Vincent, and with no one talking they can hear clearly the train rattling by down through the woods, along the marsh. Then it clatters off faintly. . . . Everyone keeps on with the meal, ignoring it, acting as if they're used to it by now."

After Rosie Vincent's death Sherman becomes increasingly withdrawn into a world of marijuana and alcohol, and when, in a suicidal drunken stupor, he crashes his car, he finally unleashes his rage against his father: " 'You're my faddah,' he said, oblivious of everyone else. . . . Sherman's voice was eerie and low. 'Are you my faddah or not?' " Gus Vincent refuses to answer his drunken son, apparently unaware that his own alcoholism and emotional distance from his children has precipitated this second accident, this tragic cry for attention. His wife is no longer present to compensate for his ineptitude; the Vincent house has "gone under the sea." As Gus Vincent turns his back on his son's anguish, the true grief the children feel for their mother is finally expressed: "Then from Sherman came a kind of wail, a hollow cry like something heard on a marsh. . . . It was like when their mother died. When you first heard the news, when it first hit you, it was like that—you couldn't breathe." A collective grief descends upon the children, their mother's death like a devil "lingering with them all, hulking in the middle of the table, setting down to stay."

In the final story, "Thorofare," in which the family scatters Rosie Vincent's ashes, the narrative evokes the quiet torpor of the occasion. There is a brief, factual report of the death; finally the narrative can withstand such details. When Gus Vincent goes with Delilah into the garden so that she can scatter some of the ashes on the soil of their family home before setting off for the final tribute at sea, she finds in her father the kindness and compassion she has always longed for. Together on the boat, each family member takes a turn scattering some of the ashes, each gesture revealing their individual grief. However awkward, the Vincent family comes together in this final act of remembering and memorializing. The ritual serves as a cathartic rebirth in which the family is cleansed and unified. "The light had become less opaque and the air was warmer. Sunlight was showing up with the sharpening shadows." Although complete understanding and closure is, of course, elusive, the family has undergone a change, suggesting both hopeful possibility and the fearful unknown: "Up the ramp they went, in single file, feeling something lofty in their procession, hearing flags billow and snap, following at one another's heels, no one with the slightest idea, when they raised their heads and looked around, of where to go next."

LUST AND OTHER STORIES

While Minot was in Italy working on her next collection of short fiction, three months' worth of work vanished, stolen when her rental car was vandalized. She set about rewriting her manuscript, and what resulted was *Lust and Other Stories,* a collection of thematically connected short stories. The central characters in *Lust and Other Stories* are cynical yet sensitive, flippant yet fragile. They are men and women in their twenties and thirties whose experiences force them to pose questions both banal and overwhelming as they try to navigate the waters of relationships and self-definition. The stories build upon one another to create the cumulative sense of the ineffability of desire, the elusiveness of love.

"Lust" establishes for the collection the tensions and anxieties of sexuality and of seemingly irreconcilable differences between the desires of men and women. Minot begins the story with a catalog of the narrator's sexual conquests; each paragraph names a different boy and the sexual memory the narrator associates with him. The tone is cavalier and conversational, carelessly matter-of-fact. The voice is that of a teenager remembering her own experiences, but the pronouns flip back and forth from first to second person, creating the effect of the narrator's simultaneous intimacy with and distance from the experiences, as if she is somehow suspended from herself and her sexuality. Increasingly the specificity of boys and what she remembers about them is lost in the litany of sexual acts, the labyrinth of lust. The boys' identities blur together; certain paragraphs name the act but not the boy with whom the act was done, as the narrator becomes "a body waiting on the rug." Tucked in between the sexual memories that seem to saturate the narrator's consciousness are references to

the other parts of her life, yet these references suggest only anxiety and ambivalence: "I could do some things well. Some things I was good at, like math or painting or even sports, but the second a boy put his arm around me, I forgot about wanting to do anything else, which felt like a relief at first until it became like sinking into a muck."

The one-line paragraph "It was different for a girl" marks a turning point in the narrator's sexual sensibility and thus in the narrative itself; the flippancy changes to a contemplative regret.

> Certain nights you'd feel a certain surrender, maybe if you'd had wine. The surrender would be forgetting yourself and you'd put your nose to his neck and feel like a squirrel, safe, at rest, in a restful dream. But then you'd start to slip from that and the dark would come in and there'd be a cave. You make out the dim shape of the windows and feel yourself become a cave, filled absolutely with air, or with a sadness that wouldn't stop.

The desire to merge with another, to forget the self, to become an undifferentiated whole, surpasses the desire implicit in sexual lust; but the safety of that forgetting, temporarily achieved through an act of lust, gives way to a sad emptiness. The sense of loss intensifies as the narrator, becoming increasingly distanced from herself—the "you" comes to dominate the "I"—realizes that she is invisible to the boys she is with: "After sex, you curl up like a shrimp, something deep inside you ruined, slammed in a place that sickens at slamming, and slowly you fill up with an overwhelming sadness, an elusive gaping worry." By the end of the story she recognizes the objectification—the total annihilation—of the self through countless acts of loveless lust: "You seem to have disappeared."

FOLLY

Folly departs notably from Minot's contemporary focus and her personal experience. The novel explores the narrow and confining world of a young Boston woman, Lilian Eliot, between 1917 and 1939. Minot divides the book into six sections, each named for one of the characters. The reader assumes that each section will focus on that character; yet the first, named for Lilian's father, is not really about him at all; rather, it is about his influence on Lilian. In this way, each of the sections gives the sense that, although the novel's protagonist is Lilian Eliot, her story is defined by her relationships; she cannot exist in isolation. Nor is she given a first-person voice through which to tell her own story. She is spoken of and spoken for by the third-person omniscient narrator, filtered through the perspective of the title character of each section. Her story is her family's story; we come to know her only in relation to them.

The beginning of *Folly* is rendered in spare prose, describing and inscribing a life of exteriors and facades rather than interior, psychological landscapes. The style mirrors the superficiality of the society; inner lives are hidden beneath polite exteriors. Appearances are paramount: the self is concealed behind a mask of propriety and predictability. Because of this deliberate subsuming of the interior by the exterior, the narrative and its action seem to proceed apart from reality, suspended in time and space despite the fact that the chapter titles within the sections locate the story geographically and historically. The book begins in the middle of ongoing action: " 'I'm afraid there's been a change in plan,' Mr. Eliot said." Lilian's father's voice begins the book, and in the politest of ways he demonstrates his position of unwavering authority in changing the plans his eighteen-year-old daughter has made. He silences her protests; his decision is unequivocal. Although Lilian is described as resembling her parents in appearance, "the eyes were her own, liquid brown, pooled and shiny." We have a hint that something lies beneath the mask of conformity Lilian wears.

Disrupting the narrative and social surfaces of the novel is the unspoken tension surrounding

World War I. The war is a point of distant reference that alerts Lilian to an outside world and momentous conflicts that make a mockery of the petty concerns of her social class. Walter Vail, who enters her life only fleetingly before leaving for Europe and the war, connects her to that outside world and precipitates her sexual awakening, feelings that create a permanent conflict in her soul. Life's possibilities are newly apparent to Lilian:

> She felt a welling up inside her: the outdoors made it happen. She breathed deeply to quiet it, trying to coax the feeling into a narrow stream which she might pour into a tiny cup. . . . She felt as wide as the sky. . . . Sometimes she was amazed by the amount of feeling sloshing about inside her. If she let it out there would be a terrible flood, she thought.

Lilian contains the flood; she never reveals it to the outside world, never disrupts the mask of social graciousness. But it exists within her nonetheless. As the novel progresses it becomes clear that Walter Vail, who remains in Europe after the war, will always hover on the periphery of her life; he enters her heart only to leave again, leaving her on the brink of love and of life. Lilian becomes destined to an interior life, never revealing what is going on inside. She realizes that this might be a way of life for everyone in her society: "There was life inside all of them and yet how secretly they kept it." Walter does not keep the life inside of him secret—this is why she is attracted to him—nor will he attach himself to her or anyone else.

The novel treads an uneasy line between a serious study of its subject—women confined to a life without love and passion outside of the strictures of social marriages—and a metafictional satire of itself. Chapter headings such as "You're some girl," "He appears again," and "The rendezvous and its aftermath" purposely echo a theatrical melodrama; they serve as a sardonic and deprecatory undercutting of the seriousness with which the Boston society takes itself but also of the novel's own seriousness. Yet there is no doubt about the seriousness of Lilian's desire for a meaningful life. We see just how severe the damage wrought by societal strictures can be through Lilian's friend Irene, whose slight eccentricity makes it impossible for her to maintain her sanity; her life ends in suicide. The pervasiveness of alcohol, even during Prohibition, also suggests a dangerous instability beneath the surface. We see, in other words, that life will not be contained; the flood will come sooner or later.

Gilbert Finch, Lilian's unlikely husband after her passion for Walter Vail, suffers from clinical depression as a result of the war. Yet even with such clear evidence of a reason for his "sickness," the society struggles to make sense of someone who cannot sustain its standards of grace and decorum. Until Gilbert finally "breaks," when he is taken to England for treatment, Lilian and he live on the edge of his silent and impenetrable world. Children are born, houses are managed, but life leaks through the cracks and souls are hollowed out. Lilian's feelings for Walter assume a space in her interior being that she preserves, at times willingly, at times unwittingly. In Walter's absence and without any knowledge of his whereabouts or whether, indeed, he will ever reenter her life, Lilian feels "the lovely construction which had gone up around her splinter and fall to the ground." The metaphor of her life as constructed, of her own private and interior construction of a room—a space—in which to house her feelings for Walter, is extended throughout the novel. Minot creates an exterior and an interior architecture to Lilian's life, and the two remain in an uneasy and irreconcilable tension with each other. The structure is fragile, and the reader realizes how precariously Lilian, fragmented by the different selves and subject positions she is forced to occupy, manages to sustain her two discrepant worlds.

Lilian is aware of her fragmented self and her fractured marriage: "Lilian couldn't shake the feeling that the life [she and Gilbert] shared was of the most tenuous construction, and running down the center of it was a gauzy wall which kept them quite separate. They were each within shadowy view but in opposite spaces." Whereas with Walter Vail she felt an urgent and strong sense of connection and corporeality—when he holds her hand he quickens her physical and emotional self—Gilbert is a ghostlike presence in her life. Yet Walter leaves—at the last, cruelly—and Gilbert is constant. Of her life, Lilian notes: "There are slivers into which I pack my greatest feeling. . . . The moments with this skittish man who appears now and then in my life are to have more power than all the days with my husband." In another place and era Lilian's choices in love might not be so limited. Gilbert is a good man at heart, and indeed the narrative solicits the reader's sympathy for him. But both he and Lilian are forced to settle, to compromise their truest selves for the sake of a socially acceptable marriage.

Folly explores the ultimate aloneness and loneliness of women and men in a particular time and place; but this aloneness extends to a more general view of human relations. As the novel's epigraph, a quote from Blaise Pascal, puts it: "Man is so necessarily foolish that not to be a fool is merely a varied freak of folly." Lilian's efforts, however muted they may be, to break the mold her world has created for her, to go against the folly of its constraints, are another kind of folly, one that only serves to further emphasize her aloneness. Yet her final epiphany strikes a quietly triumphant (and far more feminist) chord: "So it didn't depend on Walter Vail after all, and it wouldn't depend on Gilbert, either." Lilian's realization is a challenge to the myth of romance, in which a woman must depend on a man for her happiness. A woman must complete herself, achieve her own authenticity and autonomy.

Although the novel received an unfavorable review by Michiko Kakutani in *The New York Times,* Helen Dudar, reviewing *Folly* in *The Wall Street Journal,* praised the novel for the way it "creeps up on a reader, becoming oddly and unexpectedly affecting. It is also, with its sly touches of humor, quite sad—not depressing but laced with melancholy, a mood that pervades some of her other work. In Ms. Minot's fiction, human connections nearly always falter and fail; the chasms between people are unbridgeable."

EVENING

Evening explores the nature of the self—of memory and consciousness, knowledge and desire, and love. It does so by way of Ann Lord, a woman not quite in the autumn years of her life who is suffering from a terminal illness. Minot gives us Ann's thoughts and feelings in her last days, rendering with startling immediacy the effects of the proximity of death on her mind and memories. The novel is prefaced by a quotation from *The Sound and the Fury:* "I give it to you not that you may remember time, but that you might forget it now and then for a moment and not spend all your breath trying to conquer it." In a 1998 interview, Minot remarked that "much of the way we behave in life can be traced to our relationship with time—trying to wrestle it down, control it, even stop it—and, in doing so, trying to reckon with our inevitable death." *Evening* is, above all, a novel that explores the presence of the past in human consciousness and memory. The power and fragility of memory render essentially mutable a world once thought of as solid; the line between the real and the imagined are increasingly blurred. It is important to note that *Evening* is an elegy to an unremarkable—and thus universally resonant—woman's life.

Toward the end of the novel, Ann has an epiphany. She senses a figure swimming alongside her, and in her morphine-induced dream state she hears its message:

> I am here swimming up from this sea beside you I am here I have always been here your true self I was never gone and though you thought it came from him it was really yourself your whole self entire swimming underwater all the time beside you I was always there beside you your gliding boats and your flapping boats and your humming grinding boats all along I have been alongside you I have always been here I never left.

This revelation, which occurs toward the end of Ann's life, is followed soon afterward by Ann's request to see a priest. Is the figure she sees at her side a Christlike symbol of her higher, more constant and spiritual self? Is it simply her inner self, the self she has for so long denied in her roles as wife to three husbands and mother to five children? In either case, Minot clearly is seeking to establish that a woman's happiness and her reason for being should not, cannot, be won through love of a man.

And yet this message, so late in the novel, contradicts almost everything that has preceded it. As Ann lies dying, secrets surface: her mind becomes suffused with memories of a weekend forty years earlier during which she met and fell in love with Harris Arden. The details of this memory eclipse all else in her life. Indeed, so present is the memory of that first love, that passion suppressed and safe and inviolate in her deepest core of being, that *Evening* can be read as a tragic love story. But it is more than that, and, as the final pages suggest, if it is a love story, perhaps it is a lesson in loving the self as much as it is a revelation of Ann's secret love for Harris Arden.

Evening is divided into five sections that can be read as five acts leading toward a denouement. The narrative consciousness is that of Ann, as her sickness provides her with a new lens through which to view her life; ironically, and somewhat perversely, imminent death allows Ann to discern what is truly important to her. The moment of her meeting with Harris Arden at a wedding four decades earlier recurs like a poetic refrain. Sickness calls up from the past the deepest love, the "one true thing" that survives while so much else that she might have expected to stay is erased:

> The images kept coming, vague and scattered, and she thought, how could one's life keep going this way? With more and more images piling up in one's heart and crowding and swelling like music. How was one to make room and to keep all of them? The answer which Ann Lord knew now having lived a life was that one did not. Things were forgotten. An astonishing amount of what one had known simply disappeared.

As Ann tries to make sense of the images that fill and fall from her mind, she realizes that, though meaning "was slipping," it "had always been slipping off to the side only she hadn't noticed it before." Love is the principle that, finally, positions and sustains Ann, but it does so only because it remains in her memory as loss, as unfulfilled, unfinished.

"In her mattress there beat the feather of a wild bird." So begins the novel: the wild bird within Ann is at once the woman longing to fly from the prison of her cancer and the sustaining secrets—the secret love, the secret life—that return to her in the final stages of this death-in-life. "She was undergoing a revolution, she felt split open"; Ann's proximity to death precipitates extraordinary change and upheaval in her desiring consciousness. The bed in which she lies dying suggests "a thousand beds in a thousand other rooms" so that sickness—and the spiritual clarity it evokes—and sexuality are strangely connected in Ann's vision. The morphine moves her mind into unexpected planes and places, allowing simultaneously an astonishing clarity of vision and a blurring of boundaries between reality and fantasy. Woven through the narrative are imagined conversations between Harris and Ann as they discuss, with the wisdom of hindsight, what might have been had Harris not already been engaged to another woman. Ann comes to realize that "it couldn't have been different"; she can hold the memory of this love, this one true thing, because marriage and the mundane aspects of life have not been able to revise its initial intensity, to mar it in any way. Ann has never told her children of her first love; much of her life has been kept private, secret. The drowning death of one of her twin sons, at the age of twelve, is an anguish that she cannot begin to approach or articulate, even in the privacy of her soul, even in this final rush of memories.

The stronger the effects of the morphine on Ann's memory, the further Minot extends her imaginative sweep, and indeed the syntax of her sentences, to encompass the many identities of Ann's life. About Ann's husbands, she writes: "She followed them into the darkness. They were at the office. They were playing golf. The children rode on their shoulders. They threw balls. She was in a box in the window." The three husbands, none of them having allowed Ann the freedom or autonomy she needed, are conflated into one: "She never turned to another place, she never turned away. *Come here they said.* She was their wife. *Come here.*" The question of identity is associated with being understood by others, and such understanding is always partial: "One saw that only bits got recognized, never the whole person, some bits by this person, other bits by that, but one was never completely connected up with another person, one was never altogether recognized, except, she supposed, by oneself."

As Ann's cancer forces her to confront the fact that she will probably not see another autumn, she allows herself finally to linger on a love that could never become marriage; and she grants herself the most important realization of all: that even without Harris, she is not alone. She has herself. It is the self, indomitable and ultimately inviolate in spite of the ravages of cancer, that Minot preserves through the character of Ann Lord. And it is the ability to capture the interior workings of a woman's heart and mind and memory that is Minot's supreme success in *Evening.*

CONCLUSION

Susan Minot's work has met with wide critical acclaim, and yet at the close of the twentieth century it had not received a great deal of scholarly attention. Her narratives invite critical appreciation from a wide variety of contemporary theoretical perspectives, most notably feminist and psychoanalytic. Her fiction is also of critical interest for its adherence to a modernist aesthetic, most notably in *Evening,* in a postmodern context. In her explorations of form, Minot has taken to heart Ezra Pound's famous injunction to the high modernist poets of the early 1900s—"make it new." Yet it is perhaps above all her explorations of timeless universal themes that make her an important and inspiring literary voice.

Selected Bibliography

WORKS OF SUSAN MINOT

NOVELS AND SHORT STORY COLLECTIONS
Monkeys. New York: Dutton, 1986.
Lust and Other Stories. New York: Houghton Mifflin, 1989.
Folly. New York: Houghton Mifflin, 1992.
Evening. New York: Knopf, 1998.

OTHER WORKS
"House of Women" (short story). *Paris Review* 121:140–149 (1991).
"No Woman Is Convinced of Her Beauty." *Esquire,* October 1993, p. 156.
"Ottawa Takes to Its Skates." *New York Times Magazine,* November 14, 1993, p. 52.
"A Poet Who Paints." *Vogue,* October 1996, p. 214.
Stealing Beauty (screenplay). Story by Bernardo Bertolucci. New York: Grove Press, 1996.
"Tanzania on Foot." *New York Times Magazine,* September 13, 1998, p. 18.
"Quick-Change Artist." *Vogue,* March 1999, pp. 146–148.

CRITICAL STUDIES

Dudar, Helen. "A Woman in Old Boston." *Wall Street Journal,* October 12, 1992, p. A8.
Kakutani, Michiko. "It's Your Choice, Lilian: The Cad or the Cluck." *New York Times Current Events Edition,* October 2, 1992, p. C17.
———. "Reviewing a Fading Life Defined by Doomed Love." *New York Times,* October 2, 1998, sec. E, p. 45.

INTERVIEWS

Handschuh, Judith. "Interview with Susan Minot." *The Book Report, Inc.,* 1998.
Pryor, Kelli. "The Story of Her Life." *New York,* June 12, 1989, pp. 52–55.
Wilson, Robley. "Interview with Susan Minot." *Short Story* 2, no.1:112–118 (spring 1994).

—LINDSAY PENTOLFE AEGERTER

Grace Paley

1922—

*I*N THE 1985 story "Midrash on Happiness," Grace Paley's semiautobiographical character, Faith, outlines the elements necessary for her to feel content, that she has "everything":

> By everything, she meant, first, the children, then a dear person to live with, preferably a man, but not necessarily. . . . She required three or four best women friends to whom she could tell every personal fact and then discuss on the widest deepest and most hopeless level, the economy, the constant, unbeatable, cruel war economy, the slavery of the American worker to the idea of that economy, the complicity of male people in the whole structure, the dumbness of men (including her preferred man) on this subject.

Faith's laundry list of desires—and biases—expressed while taking a walk with a friend also summarizes the motivating forces in Paley's life. A longtime feminist and activist, Paley incorporates radical leftist ideas into the playful setting of family life and everyday banter. Her characters' comments and casual manifestos often inspire friction in the short stories, particularly when uttered to other characters of different backgrounds and beliefs. This is just the sort of conflict, however, that Paley cultivates in her fiction; she defines the short story as "a meeting of two events or ideas or experiences or sounds." To Paley this collision is essential to good prose:

"It's that bumping into each other," she has said, "which makes everything in the world happen."

Many of Paley's charged, realistic stories take place on the open-air stage of the streets and parks of New York City. These settings enable her to focus on or "investigate" community life as well as the ways in which women and children fit into the larger society. While keeping an eye on their children, the women converse, offer advice, and philosophize. Sometimes they are visited by charming, but often unreliable, men like Peter, Anna's ex-husband in "The Pale Pink Roast" (1959), and Philip in "Dreamer in a Dead Language" (1977) and other stories, serial smooth talkers and slapdash fathers who flirt with more than one woman on the playground. But the park also is a stage for political activity. By getting involved in demonstrations and picketing, the mothers begin to grasp their solidarity and possibilities. In "Politics" (1968) a group of regulars from the park lobby the board of estimates for a playground fence by serenading the city comptroller. In "Faith in a Tree" (1974) Paley's standby character, Faith Darwin Asbury, has an epiphany in the park that shapes her future philosophy and narrative style: a parade of protesters passes the playground one day, carrying a poster that bears the image of a napalmed, maimed Vietnamese baby. "Would you burn a child?" one of the signs says. "When necessary," replies another.

The neighborhood cop shoos away the demonstrators, and Faith's older son scolds his mother and her friends for not standing up to him. Faith's son then writes the protesters' lines in pink chalk on the nearby blacktop. Watching him, Faith comes to a realization:

> And I think that is exactly when events turned me around, changing my hairdo, my job uptown, my style of living and telling. Then I met women and men in different lines of work, whose minds were made up and directed out of that sexy playground by my children's heartfelt brains, I thought more and more and every day about the world.

This defining episode with the demonstrators was not included in the story's first published version, in 1967. The altered ending likely reflects Paley's increasing commitment to activism and her belief that literature should portray such incendiary issues.

Though Paley's body of work is relatively small—she has written no novels, and *The Collected Stories* (1994), a National Book Award nominee, includes only forty-five short stories— she is considered a writer's writer who records the voices of past generations and different cultures in colloquial speech. Also a poet and essayist, she shows us irreverent characters who range from immigrants to middle-class leftists and junkies. Wit mixed with a sense of grim inevitability permeates her stories, and this tone is reflected in both the titles and the content of her three short-story collections: *The Little Disturbances of Man* (1959), *Enormous Changes at the Last Minute* (1974), and *Later the Same Day* (1985). The different emphases of each book and the considerable intervals between their publications suggest a lot about Paley's progress as an artist and her priorities. Even as she began to win literary awards, such as the PEN/Faulkner Prize for fiction in 1986 and the Senior Fellowship of the Literature Program of the National Endowment for the Arts in 1987, she remained committed to her grassroots affiliations. In the late 1960s, when her stories began to appear in prestigious magazines, including *The New Yorker* and *Atlantic Monthly,* she continued to publish in special-interest publications, such as *Noble Savage* and *WIN,* the magazine of the War Resisters League.

POLITICS AND WRITING

Authors such as David Remnick have praised Paley's political activity; the novelist Rosellen Brown has pronounced her a "good citizen of the world"; and longtime friend and author Donald Barthelme has called her a "wonderful writer and troublemaker." But some critics and reviewers, from such diverse sources as *The Nation, Newsweek,* and *People,* have worried about the effects of her activism on her art. Not only does it allow her less time to work, but there is also a greater possibility of letting, as Laura Shapiro put it in *Newsweek,* "the politics overwhelm the person." It is true that Paley's fiction (and, to a greater extent, nonfiction) expresses overt political messages, such as Faith's impassioned speech about Israel's separatism in "The Used-Boy Raisers" (1959) and Faith's older son's treatise on "the intelligentsia" in "Listening" (1985). These pronouncements generally are balanced, though, by irony and other characters' equally zealous responses. This humorous but realistic look at political movements has continued to layer Paley's writing as well as temper some critics' fears of didacticism. As Walter Kirn wrote in *New York* magazine of *The Collected Stories,* they "are everything the utopian schemes they touch on never were: funny, stylish, eccentric, and aware that cant and jargon take quotation marks."

Since she began writing fiction in the mid-1950s, Paley has continued to pursue her political work and art in tandem, and sometimes both endeavors have proved simultaneously fruitful. In

1961, the same year she helped found the Greenwich Village Peace Center, she received a Guggenheim Fellowship. In 1979, the year she was arrested on the White House lawn for demonstrating against nuclear weapons, she published two short stories in *The New Yorker,* "Love" and "Friends," the latter of which was chosen for *The Best American Short Stories 1980.* As the literary world began to take note of her in the 1960s, the Federal Bureau of Investigation also developed a file on her. Paley's characters are similarly perseverant; even as they fail to rid the world of inequity through protest or art, their bitterness is leavened with a lingering sense of hopefulness. This obstinate naïveté is evident in "Wants" (1971) when her narrator reflects, "I had promised my children to end the war before they grew up."

BACKGROUND

Politics and philosophy have long been part of everyday dialogue for Paley, who was born on December 11, 1922, in the Bronx, New York, to Manya Ridnyik Goodside and Dr. Isaac Goodside, Russian-Jewish émigrés. In the early 1900s both her parents were exiled in Russia and Germany for political-resistance activities against tsarist rule. Upon release in 1906 (when the tsar had a son), they emigrated to the United States. Both Isaac and Manya were twenty-one years old when they arrived in America, and they were soon followed by Isaac's mother and two sisters. Isaac, a self-proclaimed atheist, soon changed the family name from Gutseit to Goodside. The extended family lived together, first in lower Manhattan, with the women supporting Isaac as he studied to be a doctor. Several languages swirled through the household and neighborhood, a cacophony of sound and expressions that later would inform Paley's range of realistic dialogue and teach her to listen for cadence and rhythm.

At home Paley's family spoke primarily Russian; in the street she heard Yiddish. The two languages coexisted so naturally in Paley's mind that "Goodbye and Good Luck" (1956), her second completed story, showcases both cultures and the intersection between them. The protagonist, Rosie Lieber, tells her niece about her long affair with Volodya Vlashkin, the Yiddish theater star of the Russian Art Theater of Second Avenue. Though the story is written in English, the cadence and colloquialisms capture a certain wry sensibility or tragicomic view of the world often associated with the work of Jewish writers such as Isaac Babel, whom Paley has long admired, and others such as Saul Bellow, Bernard Malamud, and Philip Roth, who, as Remnick notes, has praised Paley for having an "understanding of loneliness, lust, selfishness and . . . fatigue that is splendidly comic and unladylike." But Paley adds her own imprint in the frame narrator—a woman speaking to another woman, explaining her life's choices—that is more reminiscent of another Russian-Jewish writer, Tillie Olsen. Rosie, overweight and unmarried for years, is finally getting the chance to confide that she, too, had experienced great passion in her life. Paley has said that the first line of "Goodbye and Good Luck"—"I was popular in certain circles"—was actually uttered by an aunt of her husband Jess's.

The only religious member of Paley's family was her paternal grandmother, whom she called Babushka and with whom she sometimes went to temple. Paley's parents dismissed the religious traditions of Judaism, considering them old-fashioned and probably associating them with trials of the past, but Paley has said that she considers herself a cultural Jew. In her essay "Introduction to a Haggadah" (1984) she points out that "I lived my childhood in a world so dense with Jews that I thought we were the great imposing majority and kindness had to be extended to the others because, as my mother said, everyone wants to live like a person." Though the Goodside family focused on supporting Isaac's work, they remained staunch socialists, or social democrats, as they came to call themselves in the United States, and passed their beliefs on to their three children. "I didn't have to work my way toward a sudden awakening in revolutionary amazement," Paley has said of her political education. When Grace, who was the youngest by fourteen years, was nine, she was a member of the Falcons, a group of socialist youths under the age of twelve. Clad in red kerchiefs and blue shirts, they sang songs, talked about suffering (it was the midst of the Depression) and prejudice, and performed plays that emphasized working-class solidarity. But it was not all bleakness and cant. "At each meeting we paid .05 or .10—not so much to advance Socialism as to be able to eat cookies at four o'clock," Paley wrote in "Injustice" (1955).

By the time Paley was born, her family had reached a fairly comfortable existence; they were one of the few families in their neighborhood to own a Victrola. Despite the Goodsides' increasingly middle-class life, Paley's parents never dismissed their past persecution and remained wary about the future. Paley, who has said that all good writers were once children who listened to grown-ups while sitting under the table, overheard a conversation (presumably in Russian) between her parents in the 1930s that influenced her profoundly. Her mother, who had been reading the newspaper, looked up and said to Paley's father, "It's coming again." She was talking about the advent of Adolf Hitler, Paley later wrote in her essay "Like All the Other Nations" (1988). Because of this legacy, and connection to tragedy, she wrote, "that incident at the kitchen table was so powerful that when I began to write, I thought, Should I really write in English?"

Writers need "two ears" according to Paley—one for literature and one for home, for the streets in which they grew up. Paley's father, whose first language in the United States was Italian—he learned it from a photographer for whom he worked—taught himself English by reading Dickens. His lifelong reverence for literature and authors, such as Guy de Maupassant, Anton Chekhov, and Ivan Turgenev, resonates in Paley's work, especially in the closely autobiographical and widely anthologized story "A Conversation with My Father" (1974). The narrator's eighty-six-year-old father, hospitalized for a weak heart, chides his daughter for not writing "simple" stories like those of his literary icons: "There are in fact Russian writers you've never heard of, you don't have an inkling of, as good as anyone, who can write a plain ordinary story." At the crux of the tale is the father and daughter's inability to agree on form, plot, or the natural lifeline of a story. He accuses her of not being able to write about "recognizable people" and "what happen(s) to them next." Outwardly, Paley's narrator tries to please her father, dutifully spinning cohesive but slyly far-fetched vignettes, but inwardly, she admits to despising plot, which she defines as "the absolute line between two points."

EARLY LITERARY EFFORTS

Paley's own career or path as a writer (she has said she dislikes the term "career," probably because it sounds too deliberate or self-promotional) has been anything but straight or conventional. She did not write fiction until her early thirties, when she was married and had two young children, and did not publish her first collection of short stories until 1958. Even then, her literary reputation was slow to build. It was not until 1966 that she began her twenty-two years of work as a teacher of writing, at Sarah Lawrence College. (She also taught occasional classes at the City College of New York, New York University, and Syracuse University.) But from childhood on, she loved literature, especially poetry. Her family encouraged her in her reading and writing and considered her generally intelligent; as a seven-year-old, she scored high on diagnostic tests at City College of New York. But in her teens she was not a particularly strong student outside of her English courses; in fact, she was expelled from Hunter College for poor attendance during her freshman year, disappointing her parents. Later, she explained that she would arrive at the building, intending to go to class, but would be distracted and leave. As she put it to her biographer Judith Arcana, she suffered from a "lackadaisical, laid-back, premature-sixties attitude."

Concerned about his daughter's ability to support herself, Paley's father insisted she enroll in a stenography and typing course. At Merchants and Bankers Business and Secretarial School, Paley learned to type, a skill that helped shape her future. Over the years it enabled her to work as a secretary for a reinsurance company, the Southern Conference for Human Welfare, the New York Tenants Association, and Columbia University (for science professors). At home she typed her poems and, eventually, stories and essays. Later her children would recall their mother as "always typing." Her fictional women rely on typing as well. In "A Subject of Childhood" (1959) Faith says she has raised her two sons alone "with one hand typing behind [her] back to earn a living."

In the midst of her early clerical jobs and active social life (Paley met her first husband, Jess, in her late teens), her ardor for poetry survived. "I went to school to poetry," she has often said, explaining that she learned to write from reading such poets as Christopher Isherwood, Stephen Spender, Dylan Thomas, and William Butler Yeats. Her own early attempts at poetry, however, mimicked their language too much, and the result was stiff and forced. This fact was pointed out to her by the poet W. H. Auden, with whom she took a course at the New School for Social Research when she was seventeen. One day Auden asked the students in the large lecture hall if any of them were poets and offered to look at their work. Pa-

ley raised her hand. When they met to discuss her poetry, Auden questioned her about the language she was using—that of an "upper-middle-class Englishman," with words like "trousers." By inquiring if she "really talked like that" or had heard others speak that way, the poet helped Paley begin to locate her natural "grammar," or everyday speech, and translate it onto the page. "I do write with an accent," she has said.

Despite her emphasis on fiction, Paley has continued to write poetry and has published several volumes, including *Leaning Forward* (1985), *Long Walks and Intimate Talks* (1991), *New and Collected Poems* (1992), and *Begin Again* (2000). Throughout, her poetry has tended to be more baldly political than her fiction and sometimes more limited in scope. Critics, and Paley herself, have downplayed the significance of her poems; she has pronounced them "mostly about flowers" or "too literary." But some of them display the verve and innuendo that energize her fiction. An untitled poem from *Leaning Forward* begins: "A woman invented fire and called it / the wheel. . . ." Another poem in the same collection opens:

One day lying on my stomach in the afternoon
    trying to sleep
I suffered penis envy (much to
my surprise
and with no belief in Freud for years
in fact extreme
antipathy).

In a clever blending of her genres, several of Paley's poems are incorporated into her stories like song lyrics, expressing characters' preoccupations and prompting conversations. Characters of all ages write poems in her stories, ranging from Faith's son Richard and a black second-grader named Donald in "The Long-Distance Runner" (1974), to Faith's elderly father, Gersh Darwin, a resident poet at the Children of Judea Home for the Golden Ages. Sometimes the poems in Paley's stories even serve as setups for one-liners. "Love" (1979) begins with a poem, after which the narrator tells her husband she has just written a poem about love. "What a good idea," he responds, then proceeds to tell her about his paramours in the past.

CENTRAL THEMES

Love, sex, and marriage are central themes in Paley's stories. Despite her background as a tomboy—she has described herself as being "a former boy" ("in the sense that many little girls reading *Tom Sawyer* know they've found their true boy selves")—in her adolescence she became "boy crazy." Paley has said that her parents tended toward the "puritanical" when it came to sexual matters, but she was strongly drawn to the opposite sex. She enjoyed meeting men and dating, and by her family's standards this active interest made her a bit wild. At age eighteen she obtained a diaphragm from Margaret Sanger's Manhattan clinic, an act that required considerable moxie in 1940. "It was very scary to go there," she wrote in her essay "The Illegal Days" (1991). "The general embarrassment and misery around getting birth control were real." Even at the Sanger clinic, she felt she had to lie and say that she was married. But it would be another year until she married Jess Paley, a young music aficionado and aspiring filmmaker.

Paley's frank, unrepressed interest in the carnal is expressed in her fiction, particularly in some of the young women protagonists. Fourteen-year-old Josephine in "A Woman, Young and Old" comes on strong to her aunt's corporeal boyfriend, trying to convince him that she is ready for marriage. When he asks her how she learned to kiss, she tells him she practiced on her arm. Cindy Anne, a high-school student in "An Irrevocable Diameter," returns the lust of Charles C. Charley, a thirty-two-year-old air-conditioner installer. When her father grills her about the rela-

tionship, she admits that she had sex with Charles because she "wanted to." In Paley's later stories the women characters seek a different kind of liberation by having brief flings or affairs. In "The Expensive Moment" (1983) Faith sleeps with Nick, a "famous sinologist," even though she is involved in a serious relationship with Jack. On the day Faith and Nick sleep together, they have been spending their time talking about poetry and politics, and their sex is presented as part of the "play." As Faith astutely observes, their lovemaking is "ordinary but satisfactory. Its difference lay only in difference."

Faith and even Virginia from "An Interest in Life" (1959) and "Distance" (1967) may be able to parse their sexual motives as a kind of experiment or even currency, but the younger women in Paley's fiction often pay for their perceived brashness in dramatic ways. In Cindy Anne's case, her parents take Charles C. Charley to court for statutory rape, then set up a young, doomed marriage. Sometimes the result is even more dire: in "The Little Girl" (1974), one of Paley's grimmest stories, a young white girl claiming to be from the Midwest eagerly has sex with a black man she meets in the park. Later she is found dead, presumably murdered by the young man.

But for many of Paley's characters sex leads to a more commonplace fate: uneasy domesticity. As Faith explains it, she married Ricardo because, "in happy overindulgence," she had become pregnant. Like Faith, Paley had two children, Nora and Danny, born in 1949 and 1951. But unlike Faith, she did not raise them alone. Her husband, Jess, continued to live with the family until the couple separated in 1967. Paley is clear about her attachment to her children and the importance of her role as a mother and, later, grandmother. Part of this emphasis—even adamancy—may have been influenced by the loss of her own mother, who died of breast cancer in 1944. (She became ill when Paley was thirteen.) In "Mother" (1980) Paley wrote about her tremendous desire to see her again standing in a doorway and scolding her daughter for coming home at four in the morning on New Year's Day. Years later Paley said she still had "an awful lot of feeling" about her mother's death and that her pain likely colored some of her writing about "that long period when I kept trying to think of something else all the time." Paley also points out that her mother lived selflessly in a household of extended family who vied for her husband's attention. In this sense Paley credits her hardworking but often marginalized mother with teaching her about tolerance.

Motherhood and politics are closely linked for Paley; her stories and essays suggest that her relationship with her children and other mothers helped shape her sense of community and fueled her activism. Though she would have liked to have more children—she called their very existence a "life-enhancing, fascinating fact"—when Nora was three and Danny one and a half, she had an abortion. The decision was difficult for her, not because of moral or ethical concerns but because she loved her children and enjoyed being a mother. But the obstacles were considerable— she was exhausted, the family's resources were limited, and she lacked her husband's encouragement; "having children was very low on his list of priorities." Even Paley's father agreed that she should seek an abortion. From a woman in the park she obtained the name of a doctor on Manhattan's West End Avenue. Though Paley was anxious, the procedure went smoothly. The next year the doctor was arrested and sent to jail. Paley writes about her reproductive experiences with candor and some anger at the necessary secrecy of those days, an anger that would turn to activism and most likely led to her demonstrations years later on behalf of such groups as Mobilization for Women's Lives. In "The Illegal Days" she says of antiabortion protesters responsible for actions, sometimes violent, against clinics in the 1990s, "They are determined to reduce women's

normal sexual responses, to end them, really, when we've just had a couple of decades of admitting them."

Ironically, it was either Paley's abortion or her subsequent miscarriage—she cannot recall which—that led directly to her writing fiction. As she recuperated, her doctor told her to take it easy for a while. For the first time in years she had uninterrupted hours to herself. For several weeks her children went after school to day care at a local center called Greenwich House. "Suddenly I was getting time, time for myself," she said later. Alone at home, Paley had time to read some of her favorite authors, James Joyce, Virginia Woolf, and Gertrude Stein. She also found herself trying to write a short story, something she had attempted in the past but at which she had failed partially, because, she said, she "hadn't known how to let women and men into the language." She also began to hear the cadences of her childhood, the mixture of Russian and Yiddish. Soon she found herself writing short stories, then reading aloud what she had written as a means to edit. Literally, she was discovering her voice.

Her first two efforts, which were published, after many rejections, in *Accent,* a literary journal at the University of Illinois, were "The Contest" (1958) and "Goodbye and Good Luck." Both investigate the romantic desires of spirited, resourceful women and the men who often disappoint them. In "The Contest" a young woman named Dotty Wasserman tries to get her boyfriend, Fred, to marry her by enlisting his help in a Yiddish newspaper's competition called "Jews in the News." When they win first prize—five thousand dollars and a trip to Israel—she reveals that they have to be married for him to accompany her.

NEIGHBORHOOD DIALOGUES

Paley's sly, colorful stories might have remained unpublished in book form, or read only by friends, but she says that she came into some "luck" in the form of Doubleday editor Ken Mc-Cormick, the ex-husband of a friend and father of her children's friends. In an act of probable manipulation, his ex-wife urged him to read Paley's work. When he did, he was so impressed with the three stories she showed him that he urged her to write seven more. He promised that Doubleday would then publish the collection. This unconventional entry into publishing—through connections with neighborhood women and children—is in keeping with Paley's subject matter. She has said that when she began to write fiction seriously, she was concerned about the lives of women. Their situations (and probably hers) seemed precarious. During her early years of marriage, she had followed her husband to several army bases (Jess was in the Signal Corps), so she had begun to observe women in a state of curious isolation. When she became a mother in the late 1940s, she found herself in even greater contact with other women, many of them mothers, and suddenly she wanted to understand how they survived physically and intellectually. "I became terribly interested in the lives of women and children, how they were living apart from men," she said. The park and street became her primary places of "paying attention" to what she perceived as "the dark lives of women."

Though she doubted that her subject matter had a place in the world of literature, she found herself writing fiction that focused on the lives of resourceful and intelligent but also wounded women. Their anxiety manifests itself in many ways, including wisecracks and witty laments. As "Faith in a Tree" (1974) begins, "Just when I most needed important conversation, a sniff of the man-wide world, that is, at least one brainy companion who could translate my friendly language into his tongue of undying carnal love, I was forced to lounge in our neighborhood park, surrounded by children." This is more than an expression of frustration with traditional roles; as Paley points out, Faith and most of the women in the park are profoundly attached to their children. But they also are beginning to raise questions about their social status and obligations.

Dialogue becomes a lifeline for these park-bound thinkers, both in conversations with each other and, soon, with the world beyond their close-knit community. For Paley dialogue serves two crucial purposes: it shows us the speaker's unique background and priorities and suggests a relationship with the larger world. Even Faith's style of narration reflects her conflicting desires, her inner conversations. When Alex O. Steele, a visiting father to the park on his third marriage (the men tend to make cameo appearances), asks Faith if she has heard from Ricardo, her itinerant husband, she answers him in "lecture form." In a spiteful fantasy (though not implausible as reality) she makes Ricardo ask about their sons; but then he turns on her and adds, "Just make sure they don't get killed crossing the street. That's your job." The rare diatribe is usually uttered by Paley's characters in frustration or fatigue, and the words most used to convey their disgruntled state are "lousy" and "it stinks." These words and phrases often signal important, momentary departures from the women's (and sometimes men's) bright, everyday determination and practical optimism. If they are to remain resourceful and self-reliant, it seems, once in a while they must be allowed to escape or at least bemoan their questionable choices.

The vulnerability and frustration of Paley's women characters do not stem solely from their relationships with men, but that is where the trouble often begins, especially in her earlier stories. Virginia, in "An Interest in Life" (1959), lets us know from the opening that she has been wronged: "My husband gave me a broom one Christmas. This wasn't right. Nobody can tell me it was meant kindly." Her husband, who may or may not have gone off to join the army, has left her to care for their four children without financial support. As Virginia talks to her neighbor Mrs. Raftery about contacting welfare for the children's Christmas presents, Paley reminds us of the universality of Virginia's plight: "She saw that sadness was stretched worldwide across my face."

FEMINISM AND ANTIWAR ACTIVISM

Paley's sense of sisterhood has grown increasingly strong over the years, both in her writing and in her political work. Often the two concerns have dovetailed; in 1986, for example, she and Meredith Tax founded the Women's Committee of PEN. In the late 1980s she attended a meeting of Jewish writers in Switzerland where something disturbed her. Looking around at the Israelis—who included the poet Yehuda Amichai and the novelist Aharon Appelfeld—Paley was unnerved by the absence of women: as she wrote later, she could not help asking, " 'But where are my Israeli sisters?' " Recounting that meeting in the foreword to *Apples from the Desert* (1998), by Israeli writer Savyon Liebrecht, Paley wrote, "The men, suddenly looking like my Russian-Jewish uncles caught in a not-so-terrible but embarrassing mistake, looked at one another, startled, and said, 'Yes, yes, of course, we should . . . Yes, What about Celia? Dahlia?' "

Paley's stories show women in difficult and sometimes desperate situations, but she has argued that they are not victims; they are, rather, oppressed. In order to maneuver out of their predicaments, they do not always resort to noble methods. After Virginia's husband leaves, she begins an affair with Mrs. Raftery's married son John. Her motive is twofold: in addition to wanting to free herself from physical loneliness, she wants her young sons to be in the company of a man, even if he is only there part-time. Like Faith in "The Used-Boy Raisers," whose boyfriend plays too rough with her sons and then criticizes her parenting skills, Virginia tries to compensate.

But the real comfort for the women in Paley's fiction lies in women friends, relatives, and, in a late story, romantic involvement with other women. "Women have been the pleasure and consolation of my entire life," says the grandmother in "A Woman, Young and Old." Paley, who was raised in a household with a strong female presence—a matriarchy, despite their shared worship of her father—learned about courage and the art of conversation from her mother, unmarried aunt, and older sister Jeanne. This attempt of the young and the old to find a common language is an essential task in her fiction. As Paley grew up, the women surrounding her often dispensed far-ranging advice; her aunt Mira was especially vigilant, warning her as she went to her first political parades and demonstrations never to carry the flag: "The one who carries the flag is sometimes killed," Paley remembers her saying in the essay "Other Mothers" (1995). Her aunt's fears had some historical basis: in the early 1900s in Russia, Mira's brother Rusya was murdered for carrying the red banner of the working class. In the short-short story "In This Country, but in Another Language, My Aunt Refuses to Marry the Men Everyone Wants Her To" (1983), Paley draws the connection between this wariness and her aunt's choice to remain single.

"It's possible to write about anything in the world," Paley writes in "Some Notes on Teaching: Probably Spoken" (1970), "but the slightest story ought to contain the facts of money and blood in order to be interesting to adults." Growing up with women surrounding and advising her, Paley learned to listen to not only what they had to say about their competing desires and concerns but also how they told their stories. This combination of heeding advice while attempting empowerment is evident in her stories. Women meet in the parks and the streets, at PTA meetings, and even in jail. In 1966 Paley was sentenced to six days at the Women's House of Detention (in Greenwich Village) after participating in an antimilitary demonstration at an Armed Forces Day parade. This was one of several arrests in her life, and its details were emblematic of her life's concerns. In the essay "Six Days: Some Rememberings" (1994) she describes the experience, noting that most of the other protesters with her received only two days or were dismissed. But the judge was particularly angry with Paley: "He thought I was old enough to know better, a forty-five-year-old woman, a mother and teacher." In prison she met other women, many of them minorities and some of them prostitutes. From their windows they could observe the goings-on of the neighborhood—Paley recalled that, from a window, she could see her children and their friends on their way to music lessons. Family members and friends made contact with the incarcerated women by standing outside the fourteen-story prison and yelling up toward the windows. Paley cried at one point, not because she was daunted by the confinement (she admits to sleeping surprisingly well on the hard mattress) but because she received a note informing her that, due to her imprisonment, her son could not go to summer camp.

Feminism and antiwar activism were extensions of motherhood for Paley. In the parks and the streets, at PTA meetings, and in jail, the women are bound by a common anxiety about the welfare of children—their own and other women's. In "Friends" (1979) several of her standby characters meet at the deathbed of their friend Selena. Selfishly shaken by the fact that she will not be around to comfort them in their own illnesses some day, they reminisce. Though some of their stories tangentially mention men (Faith makes a crack about one of her friend's "him-itis, the dread disease of females"), most concern the welfare of children. One anecdote, taken from Paley's own life, details how she and a group of neighborhood women tutored Spanish-speaking kids at the local public school "who were stuck in crowded classrooms with exhausted teachers among little middle-class achievers." The principal and the board of education tried to stop them, since they were not formally trained,

but the women slipped into the school anyway and worked with the children. These kinds of hands-on attempts at social change and progress are typical of Paley's life and work. "Most of the women in our P.T.A. were independent—by necessity and disposition. We were, in fact, the soft-speaking souls of anarchy."

Paley's characters channel personal anxieties into social commitment, but in the midst of Central Park sit-ins and sandwich-board-wearing marches, they pause to talk about their families and lovers and make jokes. Solidarity of mothers recurs in the stories, sometimes in an extreme manner. Alexandra, an unwed, pregnant social worker in "Enormous Changes at the Last Minute" (1972), invites similarly unwed and pregnant clients to live with her in her apartment: "She ensured their health and her own and she took notes as well. She established a precedent in social work which would not be followed or even mentioned in state journals for about five years." Alexandra's semi-utopian matriarchy seems to work out, but not all unwed mothers in Paley's fiction care to consort with middle-class mothers. In "Northeast Playground" (1967) a woman narrator (not unlike Faith) goes to the park and encounters eleven unwed mothers on relief. Four are whores, the narrator matter-of-factly points out, and the rest unwed "on principle or because some creep had ditched them." Some are junkies, some "dykey women."

As the narrator observes them, she admires their organization; they resemble a "special-interest group," as one mother points out. Watching them, the narrator reflects on how she and her former cohorts at the playground were not as unified or as accepting of quirks in their children. When the narrator asks this group of mothers why they do not mix with the other mothers and babies and what "this ghettoization will do" to their children, they remain nonplussed. The narrator then recalls her own days at the playground when her children were small:

she explains that women wearing "I Like Ike" buttons sat on the south side of the sandbox, and the rest, revisionist Communists and revisionist Trotskyites and revisionist Zionists, all registered Democrats, sat on the north. "No kidding!" the unwed mothers respond. These "painful divisions" that Paley observed among the mothers prompted her to action. Though her ex-husband later said that Paley did not always consider herself a feminist, her work quickly moved in that direction. Beyond the PTA, women-based organizations she has worked with include the Women's Pentagon Action Group (a 1980 photograph shows her planting a sign in the ground that says "The Unknown Woman"), MADRE (a New York–based nonprofit organization founded to assist the women of Nicaragua and El Salvador), and WIMPs (Women Indict Military Policies). In 1987 she co-founded the Jewish Women's Committee to End the Occupation of the West Bank and Gaza.

Women's oppression by certain personal and societal situations lends them a precarious status: it makes them vulnerable but also privy to the lives of other outsiders or "strangers," as Paley has said such outsiders used to be called. "The writer's natural business is a long stretch toward the unknown life," she wrote in her essay "Thinking about Barbara Deming" (1985), a tribute to a friend who was a writer, nonviolent protester, and lesbian. In addition to speaking up for other marginalized women, the female narrators in Paley's fiction serve as reporters on social change, sometimes literally. In "Demystified Zone" (1980) Faith is sent by the PTA and local school board to a conference in Puerto Rico called "The Bilingual Child and Public Education." When she returns, she goes on record in a local newspaper about the poverty she witnessed and evidence of U.S. exploitation. Paley has written about this story, saying that she sent Faith to Puerto Rico because she thought Faith would "do well with journalistic responsibility."

CROSS-CULTURAL INFLUENCES

Beginning in the late 1960s, Paley—and sometimes her characters—went abroad more often. In 1969 the author traveled to North Vietnam as part of a delegation of filmmakers and peace activists to bring home three prisoners of war. The experience, she has said, changed her life. She recorded her horror at the condition of the country in her nonfiction piece "Report from North Vietnam" (1969). But she also included her visit in her creative work. "Two Villages," one of her poems from that year, ends with a numerical list of the atrocities that the village of Trung Trach had suffered, ranging from 1,201 attacks to 267 time bombs.

In the years that followed, Paley went on other fact-finding missions to such locations as China, Russia, Central America, and Chile. During the 1970s she wrote about her experiences in a column (in which she alternated with Noam Chomsky) in the magazine *Seven Days.* "Somewhere Else" (1978) shows Faith and her friends just back from a journey to China. As they watch slides and talk, they make uncomfortable connections with cultural and racial divisions in their own neighborhood. Cameras and photographs suddenly become tools of colonialism as well as of art.

Motherhood remains a uniting force in Paley's stories that involve politics in developing nations; for example, in "The Expensive Moment" a visiting Chinese woman shares her concerns about her children with Faith and Ruth. Though the circumstances of their mothering have been quite different—Xei Feng had to leave her daughters with her mother when she was sent down to the countryside to dig up stones—as Xei Feng looks around Faith's apartment and photographs her sons' bedroom, the Chinese guest poses a concern that suddenly unites all three women: What is the best way to raise children? "You don't want them to be cruel, but you want them to take care of themselves wisely," she says. Ruth, who has not seen her activist-daughter Rachel in eight years, is silent. Faith, whose sons are passionately involved in politics but are still present in her daily life, agrees that maybe she did not know how to instill in her children a combination of political consciousness and common sense.

Cross-cultural bonding is not always instant, however, with the women in Paley's fiction. Though her characters travel and make friends from other nations, they remain particularly adept at reporting on change in their own community. Language is one of Paley's primary tools for investigating differences between cultures and economies, neighborhoods and nations. In the form of the speaking voice or dialect, which she uses frequently, it becomes an instrumental tool in what she has called the fiction writer's task or "job"—to tell "the story of his or her people, in the life of his or her time." Paley—like Faith—enjoys returning to her childhood neighborhood every few years. For the author, as for her lead protagonist, alterations in the landscape and living conditions take on both personal and sociological implications.

In "The Long-Distance Runner" Faith returns to her childhood home in Brooklyn and finds that her former neighborhood—once primarily white, Jewish, and Irish—is now mostly black. At the door of her former apartment Faith admits to feeling some fear, and this shames her. "Despite my wide geographical love of mankind," she says, "I would be attacked by local fears." In a surreal twist she ends up living three weeks in her former apartment, which is now occupied by Mrs. Luddy, a black woman with four young children. There is a sense that Faith is hiding there, chased by angry neighborhood residents because of her snooping, but also that she is confronting her past. Soon she is part of the household, though not in a sentimental or sisterly way. Together the women share the chores, the diaper changing, the making of coffee. The details of the day are much the same as Faith describes in "The Used-Boy

Raisers": on weekends she plans out the "greedy day" to accommodate her children and the running of her household. As the women get to know each other better, they exchange some views of human nature. Soon their conversations revolve around issues of gender and race, though not in a clinical or academic way. When they discuss sex, Mrs. Luddy says that white women have turned black men "rotten" by giving them the impression "their dicks were made of gold." Faith listens, then counters: "White or black . . . they did think they were bringing a rare gift, whereas it was just sex, which is common like bread, though essential."

RACIAL ISSUES

Paley also returns to her former neighborhood in her nonfiction, where she comments on shifts in race and economics. In "The Unfinished Bronx" (1996), an essay used as the preface to Mel Rosenthal's book of photographs, *In the South Bronx of America,* Paley muses about the changes in the East Bronx. After she left home in 1942, she said, she returned every few years "sentimentally and out of persistent political interest." At first, she said, the neighborhood was mostly the same, except for the fact that the mothers "called to their children in Spanish instead of Yiddish." The local shul had become the Iglesia Pentecostal. But by her third visit home, Paley said, the neighborhood had been ravaged by drugs and rage. On one building she saw some disturbing graffiti: "People Still Live on This Godforsaken Block." Relationships between the races—and economic classes—recur in Paley's work, rarely leading to easy resolutions. When white and black characters have sex, the results are uneasy, sometimes even tragic. Invariably, interracial sex involves risk and takes on multiple layers of meaning. In "The Little Girl" a fourteen-year-old runaway, a "little soft yellow-haired baby chick," flirts with Carter, a young black man, by bragging that she has had sex back home with a "colored boy." The two go back to Carter's friend's place, where he has frequently entertained women, according to his friend Charlie, the narrator: "We just like the UN. Every state in the union stop by." After Charlie finds out that Carter and his drug-addict roommate brutally murdered the young woman, he imagines what she would have been like if she had gone unharmed, like the other "little girls" they had known: "after a while they get to be grown womens, they integrating the swimming pool and picketing the supermarket, they blink their eyes and shut their mouth and grin."

Other unions between the races in Paley's fiction may not be similarly tragic, but they are still complicated. Some produce children who tend to serve as reminders of society's unfinished issues with race. Two of her stories examine a white adult parenting a black child and the complex story behind the situation. In "Northeast Playground" a young white woman who is described as a street whore dandles a beautiful "dark brown" baby. Leni, the white woman, chose her profession despite, as one of the other mothers points out, coming from Brighton Beach and her "age, weight and religion." As Leni forthrightly explains, the baby was payment from a john who owed her money. He gave her "the first little bastard he had," and now Leni stays home and collects from Aid to Dependent Children. Though the negotiation was crass, it is clear that Leni adores her son. After all, he has altered her life and brought her in contact with the other iconoclastic women of the playground.

"Zagrowsky Tells" (1985), another story about race relations, is set on a playground. Izzy Zagrowsky, an elderly Jewish pharmacist who once barred blacks from his store, is the grandfather (and primary caretaker) of his mixed-race grandchild, Emanuel. Faith, who used to picket outside the pharmacy, sees him in the park one day with the enthusiastic, bright child and demands to know the story. Zagrowsky, who obviously dotes

on his grandson, finally reveals the facts: his blond daughter, Cissy, who was committed to a mental institution, had become involved with a black gardener there. As he talks to Faith, Zagrowsky casually announces his altered views: "A person looks at my Emanuel and says, Hey! He's not altogether from the white race, what's going on? I'll tell you what: life is going on." Faith is impressed by his commitment to his grandson, but she also remembers his earlier gestures of goodwill, such as the time he delivered a prescription for one of her sons late at night to her home. As a result, the story shows both Faith and Zagrowsky reconsidering their views of human nature, their literal and metaphoric black-and-white views of the world. As Zagrowsky admits, initially he had to be talked into caring for his grandson. Even when he grew to love the child, however, he faced further, social challenges. Toward the end of the story, for instance, a stranger rudely inquires about Emanuel's parentage.

But in "At That Time, or The History of a Joke" (1981), a near parable, society responds joyfully when a black child is born to a white mother. Here Paley works with hyperbole and overt symbolism—the woman has received a uterine transplant and instantly becomes pregnant (it is implied that the "darling, rolled-up" fetus already existed in the donated organ). She gives birth to a baby girl who is "black as the night which rests our day-worn eyes." Soon she is heralded as a savior, and the announcement of her birth is reenacted on giant theater screens. Her holy status is debated—certain Jews protest—but a doctor confirms that it was, indeed, a virgin birth. The result is nearly utopian, though Paley sneaks in a sobering qualifier: "By that time, sexism and racism had no public life, though they were still sometimes practiced by adults at home."

The act of a white woman mothering a black child resonates for Paley, who as a young woman had a brief but dramatic experience of her own.

In 1943 she traveled by bus from New York to Miami to join her husband on an army base. She was sitting in the last white row, she writes in the essay "Traveling" (1997), and she noticed a black woman standing, holding a large sleeping baby. Paley offered the woman her seat, but the woman was too scared to accept it. Finally, Paley asked to hold the child, and the woman acquiesced. Paley held the little boy close and was closing her eyes when she heard a white man say, "Lady, I wouldn't of touched that thing with a meat hook." Paley's immediate response, she said, was an apocalyptic thought: "Oh, this world will end in ice." At the end of the essay Paley adds an important note. Alluding to her young grandson, who is black, she muses that that bus ride was how she first knew him, though she could only protect him "for about 20 minutes 50 years ago." Not all encounters between the races in Paley's work are so congenial. When Faith first approaches her former neighborhood in "The Long-Distance Runner," she stands in the street in her sloppy running clothes, and young black men toss profanity-laced taunts at her. Undaunted, she retorts, "I like your speech . . . Metaphor and all."

The characters in Paley's fiction seem to be wise to the politics of storytelling itself, and they comment on it from time to time in a way that is both wisecracking and philosophical but just short of metafictional. Early in "The Long-Distance Runner," when Mrs. Raftery accuses Faith of having been "as gloomy as a tick on Sunday," Faith snaps at her about her "folkshit," then reflects on how Mrs. Raftery is an invention of Faith's just as Faith is a creation of Paley's. "Folkshit from bunion to topknot. That's how she got liked by me, loved, invented, and endured." The final section of "Friends" is just as much about writing as about the group of women Paley describes. Almost in defense of her strategy and subject matter, Faith ends the story by saying, "I was right to invent for my friends and our children a report on these private deaths and the con-

dition of our lifelong attachments." And Dotty Wasserman, who makes her first, vibrant appearance in "The Contest" and is alluded to in "Faith in a Tree," is, in the story "Love," acknowledged by Jack, Faith's lover, as a fictional character. By briefly describing Dotty in terms of Faith's life, Jack reminds Faith of his love for the author and her art.

MALE CHARACTERS

Jack is one of the first full, sympathetic (and recurring) male characters in Paley's work. He is sometimes flawed—he has occasional love affairs, as does Faith—but he also has the ability to question her thoughtfully, to challenge her in an admiring way. In addition, he is afforded a complicated family history, as shown in "The Immigrant Story" (1972), and many humanitarian pursuits. Though he is Jewish—he recalls his immigrant father selling brushes, hawking his wares in Yiddish—he probably is based in part on Paley's second husband. In 1972, a year after she and Jess divorced, Paley married Bob Nichols, a non-Jewish writer, poet, and landscape architect. Little is known about Paley's divorce from Jess (it has been mentioned that their careers had taken them in different directions, and, according to Judith Arcana, there was the complication of "at least one new lover"), but the union with Nichols seems to make sense on many levels. First, he was a divorced father of three who involved himself directly in the neighborhood—he even helped design the playgrounds. Second, like Paley, he expressed his political concerns in his art; he was a member of the Village Poets and wrote plays for urban street theater. Jack, in "The Story Hearer" (1982)—an O. Henry Prize winner—and "The Expensive Moment," is similarly involved, as he writes for a magazine called the *Social Ordure* and is a member of an organization called the Other Historian.

Nichols, who spent portions of his boyhood in rural Vermont, introduced Paley to the area, and they have lived there at least part-time since the 1970s. In her essay "Life in the Country: A City Friend Asks, 'Is It Boring?' " Paley details the local political organizations as well as the everyday tasks, such as stacking wood and "keeping mud and hay out of the house." Finally, she describes the beauty of the landscape, the "broad river plains" and "white pink rust black across the wooded hills." In the late 1970s she even served on a Vermont jury. But despite her turn to a sylvan way of life, Paley has remained committed to her beloved New York. In 1987 she was named the first New York State Author and winner of the Edith Wharton Citation of Merit for fiction writers.

Jack is a refreshing character in Paley's stories because he interjects comments in Faith's narratives and poses lively arguments. Not unlike Faith's father, Gersh, Jack debates issues with Faith and teases her. When they exchange ideas, there is a greater sense of dialogue than in many of Paley's previous stories. Philosophy and play intermingle, and the result is compelling and unpredictable. In "The Story Hearer" Faith details her day for Jack, working into the details of errands her ardent opinions or expressions of her "cultivated individualism." For example, she reports that when the butcher asked her, "What'll you have, young lady?" she refused to answer. Jack groans and says, "Oh God no! You didn't do that again," but Faith stands firm. Being referred to as a "young lady" when she is obviously middle-aged is an insult, she says. Faith and Jack debate the point, and though Faith does not change her mind, she adds that the butcher does have a long commute to his job. "I'm sorry for his long journey," she says to Jack, "but I still mean it. He mustn't say it anymore."

Ultimately this is the direction Paley's stories take—more listening and hearing. At the end of "The Story Hearer" Faith and Jack go to bed and sleep, "his arms around me," Faith says, "as sweetly as after the long day he had probably slept beside his former wife (and I as well beside my etc. etc. etc.)." There is a realization here that they have come together after having worked out many, but not all, of the issues of their youth and young adulthood. At the same time, though they still nurse extravagant hopes—Faith even suggests trying to have a child—they seem to realize that the true future (and energy) of their relationship lies in their storytelling. Jack is a particularly good audience for Faith because he, too, is fascinated by women's lives. As he says to Faith in "Listening," "You know I'm more interested in women. Why don't you tell me stories told by women about women?"

In contrast to Jack, the male characters in Paley's earlier stories are often engaged in defending their actions to women. Frederick P. Sims, of "The Contest," offers few apologies about his problems with commitment. In a bitter letter to Dotty, he explains why he cannot marry her: "A happy daddy-and-mommy home. The home-happy day you could put your hair up in curlers, swab cream in the corner of your eyes . . . I'm not sure all this is for Fred." It is clear that Fred will not compromise his beliefs. True, he will reap few tangible rewards, but at the end his confusion and disappointment are somehow believable. Though he may have been selfish in his relationship with Dotty, he is genuinely befuddled at the end. As he says in the beginning of the story, "I am ambitious, but it's a long-range thing with me. I have my confidential sights on a star, but there's half a lifetime to get to it."

Like Fred Sims, the narrator Charles C. Charley in "An Irrevocable Diameter" could hardly be called altruistic. After buckling under pressure to marry the young girl he has slept with, he acquires a position in her family's business but makes it clear that the marriage will be short-lived. Emphasizing the couple's age difference, Charles ends the story on a philosophical note: "It is my opinion that she will be a marvelous woman in six or seven years. I wish her luck: by then we will be strangers." Charles, like Fred, understands his limitations. They both are flawed characters, but they reveal a self-knowledge that makes them at least partially sympathetic.

Dennis, the cabdriver in "Enormous Changes at the Last Minute," shows a bit more responsibility and respect for his lover, Alexandra, but he seems more interested in the mystique of being a father than in actually being one. At the cooperative where he lives, he says, nobody is sure about the children's biological fathers. One child, he says, might be his. "It's far out," he says. The story ends with him singing (along with his folk-rock group) a lullaby that pleads for his son (by Alexandra) to visit him someday when he is in an old-age home. There is irony in his plea, a knowledge that he will crave the company of family as he approaches his own "last minute."

As Paley's stories move away from derelict fathers to those who attempt to reckon with the past, the work grows even richer. Women still tend to control the structure of these later stories, but the men make more substantive contributions. Reading them, one has the sense that relationships such as that between Faith and Jack are ongoing conversations. Imagination and ideals remain central to their lives. Paley also touches on the relationships between the men themselves. In "Listening" Jack asks Richard if he has forgiven his father, Ricardo, for having "run out" on him and his brother years before. Richard responds, "I don't forgive him and I don't not forgive him." Then he quickly distances himself from the conversation by talking about imperialism and political injustice. But Jack persists, asking if Richard thinks Jack's own daughter will ever forgive him for leaving the family. He is met with Richard's poignant evasion.

CONCLUSION

Paley has continued to work in her Vermont community and to travel for a variety of political and literary causes. Her work has received increasing recognition, including, in 1997, a seventy-five-thousand-dollar Lannan Literary Award from the Lannan Foundation. Over the years Paley has been praised and criticized for taking on myriad tasks while also pursuing her art. To her this competition for her time merely reflects the everyday lives she chronicles: "The politics takes from the writing, the children take from the politics, and the writing took from the children," she has said. "Someone once said, 'How did you manage to do all this with the kids around?' and I made a joke; I said, 'Neglect!' But the truth is, all those things pull from each other, and it makes for a very interesting life."

Selected Bibliography

WORKS OF GRACE PALEY

SHORT FICTION
The Little Disturbances of Man. New York: Doubleday, 1959.
Enormous Changes at the Last Minute. New York: Farrar, Straus & Giroux, 1974.
Later the Same Day. New York: Farrar, Straus & Giroux, 1985.
The Collected Stories. New York: Farrar, Straus & Giroux, 1994.

POETRY
Leaning Forward. Afterword by Jane Cooper. Penobscot, Maine: Granite Press, 1985.
New and Collected Poems. Gardiner, Maine: Tilbury House, 1992.
Begin Again. New York: Farrar, Straus & Giroux, 2000.

OTHER WORKS

Long Walks and Intimate Talks: Poems and Stories. With paintings by Vera Williams. New York: Feminist Press, 1991.

Preface to *In the South Bronx of America,* by Mel Rosenthal. Willimantic, Conn.: Curbstone Press, 1996.

Foreword to *Apples from the Desert,* by Savyon Liebrecht. New York: Feminist Press, 1998.

Just As I Thought. New York: Farrar, Straus & Giroux, 1998.

CRITICAL AND BIOGRAPHICAL STUDIES

BOOKS

Arcana, Judith. *Grace Paley's Life Stories: A Literary Biography.* Urbana: University of Illinois Press, 1993.

Bach, Gerhard, and Blaine H. Hall, eds. *Conversations with Grace Paley.* Oxford: University Press of Mississippi, 1997.

Isaacs, Neil David. *Grace Paley: A Study of the Short Fiction.* Twayne Studies in Short Fiction. Boston: Twayne, 1990.

Taylor, Jacqueline. *Grace Paley: Illuminating the Dark Lives.* Austin: University of Texas Press, 1990.

ARTICLES AND ESSAYS

Baba, Minako. "Faith Darwin as Writer-Heroine: A Study of Grace Paley's Short Stories." *Studies in American Jewish Literature* 7:40–54 (spring 1988).

Barthelme, Donald, William Gass, Grace Paley, and Walker Percy. "A Symposium on Fiction." *Shenandoah* 27:3–31 (1976).

Baxter, Charles. "Maps and Legends of Hell: Notes on Melodrama." In his *Burning Down the House: Essays on Fiction.* St. Paul, Minn.: Graywolf Press, 1997.

Bendow, Burton. "Voices in the Metropolis." *Nation,* May 11, 1974, pp. 597–598.

Broner, E. M. "The Dirty Ladies: Earthy Writings of Contemporary American Women—Paley, Jong, Schor, and Lerman." *Regionalism and the Female Imagination* 4:34, 41 (winter 1979).

Brown, Rosellen. "You Are Not Here Long." In *Letters to a Fiction Writer.* Edited by Frederick Busch. New York: Norton, 1999.

Charters, Ann, ed. "A Conversation with Grace Paley." In her *The Story and Its Writer: An Introduction to Short Fiction.* 4th ed. Boston: Bedford Books, 1995.

Criswell, Jeanne Sallade. "Cynthia Ozick and Grace Paley: Diverse Visions in Jewish and Women's Literature." In *Since Flannery O'Connor: Essays on the Contemporary American Short Story.* Edited by Loren Logsdon and Charles W. Mayer. Macomb: Western Illinois University Press, 1987.

Gelfant, Blanche H. "Grace Paley: A Portrait in Collage." In her *Women Writing in America: Voices in Collage.* Hanover, N.H.: University Press of New England, 1984.

Kamel, Rose. "To Aggravate the Conscience: Grace Paley's Loud Voice." *Journal of Ethnic Studies* 11:21–22 (1983).

Klinkowitz, Jerome. "The Sociology of Metafiction." *Delta* 14:290 (May 1982).

McMurran, Kristin. "Even Admiring Peers Worry That Grace Paley Writes Too Little and Protests Too Much." *People,* February 26, 1979.

Park, Clara Claiborne. "Faith, Grace, and Love." *Hudson Review* 38:481–488 (autumn 1985).

Peden, William. "The Recent American Short Story." *Sewanee Review* 81:712–729 (1974).

Remnick, David. "Grace Paley, Voice from the Village." In *Conversations with Grace Paley.* Edited by Gerhard Bach and Blaine H. Hall. Oxford: University Press of Mississippi, 1997.

Shapiro, Harriet. "Grace Paley: 'Art Is on the Side of the Underdog.' " *Ms.,* May 1974, pp. 43–45.

—CAROLYN ALESSIO

Robert Pinsky

1940–

ROBERT PINSKY HAS described himself in his poetry as a soul who "cleaves to circles." In "Biography," a poem from Pinsky's 2000 collection *Jersey Rain,* he refers to a particular event, "My mother's dreadful fall." This image generates what follows: "Her mother's dread / Of all things: death, life, birth." One thing leads to another: "My brother's birth / Just before the fall, his birth again in Jesus." What may seem like a pattern of events in "Biography" is more precisely a pattern of words—a swirl of language that seems at once fateful and arbitrary. The mother's "dreadful" fall leads to the grandmother's "dread." Her dread of "birth" invokes her grandson's "birth again in Jesus." This rebirth allows his brother, who was "born only once," into the poem. Pinsky is a poet who recognizes that his being is determined by ever widening circles of experience, history, and chance—the "unseen multitudes" (as he puts it in "An Alphabet of My Dead," also from *Jersey Rain*) who have determined the shape of his body, his house, the world through which he walks.

Robert Pinsky was born in Long Branch, New Jersey, on October 20, 1940, the son of Milford Simon Pinsky and Sylvia Eisenberg Pinsky. "When you are small," he recalled in a 1986 autobiographical essay, "you do not know that you are a child in a lower-middle-class Jewish family living in an economically depressed, culturally

low backwater. It feels more like being a Renaissance nobleman's son." When Pinsky lived there, Long Branch was a dilapidated resort town populated by Italians, Jews, and African Americans; but it had also been a summer residence both for the U.S. presidents Ulysses Grant and James Garfield and, more recently, for the Mafia. Pinsky's paternal grandfather was the owner of the Broadway Tavern in Long Branch; during Prohibition he had been a bootlegger and a small-time gangster himself. "Circle of causes or chaos or turns of chance," intones Pinsky in "Biography": How *does* one thing lead to another?

When Pinsky graduated from Rutgers University in 1962 he wrote his senior thesis on T. S. Eliot, the reigning literary aristocrat of the time. Moving on to Stanford University for his Ph.D., he wrote his dissertation on the underappreciated Romantic poet Walter Savage Landor. *Landor's Poetry* was published by the press of the University of Chicago, where Pinsky held his first teaching job, in 1968. The first collection of Pinsky's poems, *Sadness and Happiness,* was published in 1975, seven years later. More books of poetry and criticism followed. So did *Mindwheel* (1986), an electronic novel, and a much-acclaimed translation *The Inferno of Dante* (1994). After teaching at Wellesley College and the University of California at Berkeley, in 1988 Pinsky moved to Boston University, where he continued to teach in 2000. In 1997 Pinsky was named poet laureate of the United States.

Part of what has made Pinsky a successful poet laureate (he was appointed to an unprecedented third term in 1999) is his sense that he is something of an interloper—a saxophone-blasting kid from a lower-middle-class Jewish family in Long Branch, New Jersey. He wants both to revere and to ruffle the tradition; more profoundly, he suggests that we cannot possibly revere the tradition—continue it, make it live—without ruffling it. "The poet's first social responsibility, to continue the art" writes Pinsky in his collection of essays *Poetry and the World* (1988), "can be filled only through the second, opposed responsibility to change the terms of the art as given—and it is given socially, which is to say politically."

How does a poet—who spends most of his time alone, pushing words around—actually fulfill these momentous responsibilities? In *The Sounds of Poetry: A Brief Guide* (1998), his guide to the technical aspects of verse, Pinsky notes that both Allen Ginsberg's poem "Howl" (1955) and W. E. B. Du Bois's essay "Of the Training of Black Men" (1902) end with what can be heard as lines of iambic pentameter: "Door of my cottage in the Western night"; "I sit with Shakespeare and he winces not." But he neither upbraids these radical writers for co-opting the western literary tradition nor laments that the tradition is susceptible to radical innovation. To Pinsky, there is nothing ironic about Ginsberg's or Du Bois's use of the great English line. Since the tradition is an ongoing process rather than a static body of achievement, it is available to everyone. And since English is a mongrel tongue, the tradition itself is fruitfully compromised: the sound of Thomas Jefferson's phrase "life, liberty, and the pursuit of happiness" combines the Anglo-Saxon bluntness of "life" and "hap" with the "Roman, legalistic force of Latin 'liberty' " and the "courtly, equestrian connotations of Norman French 'pursuit.' " This is a reticent way of saying that a kid from

Long Branch and the Declaration of Independence are cut from the same ragged cloth.

As the poem "Biography" suggests by its very design, the events of Pinsky's life don't tell us much. What interests Pinsky is the movement between those events, the way in which the sound of one word generates another. Consequently, to discover the "biography" of this poet one has merely to listen to his writings—to hear that his poems feel simultaneously anarchic and well-made, reckless and traditional. In "Shirt," from *The Want Bone* (1990), Pinsky thinks about the innumerable historical forces that have made the very clothes on his back (the "shirt" serves as a kind of emblem for "identity"). The poem's pentameter lines swirl from sweatshops in Korea to Scottish mills, from the seventeenth-century Anglican poet George Herbert to an almost anonymous African American woman in South Carolina.

Wonderful how the pattern matches perfectly
Across the placket and over the twin bar-tacked

Corners of both pockets, like a strict rhyme
Or a major chord. Prints, plaids, checks,
Houndstooth, Tattersall, Madras. The clan tartans

Invented by mill-owners inspired by the hoax of
    Ossian,
To control their savage Scottish workers, tamed
By a fabricated heraldry: MacGregor,

Bailey, MacMartin. The kilt, devised for workers
To wear among the dusty clattering looms.
Weavers, carders, spinners. The loader,

The docker, the navvy. The planter, the picker, the
    sorter
Sweating at her machine in a litter of cotton
As slaves in calico headrags sweated in fields:

George Herbert, your descendant is a Black
Lady in South Carolina, her name is Irma
And she inspected my shirt. Its color and fit

And feel and its clean smell have satisfied
Both her and me. We have culled its cost and
    quality
Down to the buttons of simulated bone,

The buttonholes, the sizing, the facing, the
   characters
Printed in black on neckband and tail. The shape,
The label, the labor, the color, the shade. The
   shirt.

As these lines suggest, Pinsky is deeply interested in the racial and ethnic components of identity, and though all the ingredients for an identity politics are contained in his poems, such a politics never emerges. Far more interesting is the way in which one thing leads unpredictably to another: the rhythm of the phrase "The loader, / The docker, the navvy" generates the phrase "The planter, the picker, the sorter" in the same way that Irma leads us back to George Herbert. Things are themselves because they are made of other things, and the links between them feel simultaneously inexplicable and incontrovertible. In "Window" (also collected in *The Want Bone*) Pinsky gently undermines the easy association of any representative individual with any particular group:

My mother Mary Beamish who came from Cork
Held me to see the snowfall out the window—
Windhold she sometimes said, as if in Irish
It held wind out, or showed us that wind was old.
Wind-hole in Anglo-Saxon: faces like brick,
They worshipped Eastre's rabbit, and mistletoe
That was Thor's jissom where thunder struck the
   oak.
We took their language in our mouth and chewed
(Some of the consonants drove us nearly crazy
Because we were Chinese—or was that just the
   food
My father brought from our restaurant
   downstairs?)

Is this the poet's biography? Rather than asserting the importance of his lower-middle-class Jewish heritage alone, Pinsky wants to emphasize the mongrel heritage of everything. His poems are not often about Long Branch, New Jersey, but their linguistic texture feels like Long Branch, which is to say that they feel like Robert Pinsky:

courtly yet provincial, elegant yet homemade, preserved out of time yet as relentlessly in motion as the waves on the shore. From Pinsky's point of view, his poems could not be otherwise. "Our very sentences," he writes in *An Explanation of America* (1979), "are like a cloth / Cut shimmering from conventions of the dead."

FOUNDATION: *SADNESS AND HAPPINESS* AND *THE SITUATION OF POETRY*

Being the least dogmatic of poet-critics, Pinsky could never lend his name to an age. But in retrospect, it is difficult not to feel that the one-two punch of *Sadness and Happiness* (his first book of poems, published in 1975) and *The Situation of Poetry: Contemporary Poetry and Its Traditions* (his account of American poetry after modernism, published in 1976) had something to do with the swift decline of what was once thought of as the Age of Lowell—the age of high-wire, hard-drinking confessional poets. "But it is all bosh, the false / Link between genius and sickness," Pinsky writes in "Essay on Psychiatrists," the long poem that concludes *Sadness and Happiness*: "The contemporary poets of lunacy— none of them / Helps me to think of the mad otherwise / Than in cliches."

With its provocative blandness, the very title of Pinsky's first book of poems announced his distance from the dramatically personal poetry of Robert Lowell, Anne Sexton, and Sylvia Plath. It was the style (more than the content) of poems like "Essay on Psychiatrists" that made the announcement meaningful. Rather than plumbing his soul in agitated free verse, Pinsky constructed an argument about the world in stately pentameters. In *The Situation of Poetry* he helped to create the taste by which he would be judged, offering the word "discursive" to describe a poetry that might be organized by abstract statement rather than primal images.

Almost overnight, the reception accorded these two books transformed a well-educated kid from Long Branch into the new hope for American poetry. From the start of his career, however, Pinsky has labored to expand the possibilities available to American poetry. It is true that in *The Situation of Poetry* he criticized what we might think of as a strain of attenuated modernist writing that privileges the "image" over more abstract or discursive modes of writing. But Pinsky did not set out to replace one orthodoxy with another; his goal is to resist any vocabulary for poetry that becomes exclusionary and taken-for-granted. The title poem of *Sadness and Happiness,* with its invitation to treat human emotions as abstract categories, is one of Pinsky's most movingly intimate performances: "Sadness and Happiness" is the name of a bedtime game he and his wife played with their daughters. Pinsky could have been describing himself when he said in *Poetry and the World* that the legitimately "post-modernist" poet will be one for whom "formal freedom feels assured, and matters of technique no longer fighting issues in the old modernist sense."

Pinsky rarely needs to shore up his enthusiasms with antagonisms, and in this regard he resembles one of his most influential teachers, the poet-critic Yvor Winters, not at all. During his first semester at Stanford, after reading Robert Lowell's review of Winters' *Collected Poems,* Pinsky decided to show Winters his own poems. In a 1986 autobiographical essay Pinsky described this meeting, with the keen sense of chance—one thing leading unpredictably but inevitability to another—that distinguishes much of his work.

> He asked me to sit down, and he thumbed through the manuscript while I was there. It took him perhaps four minutes, stopping once or twice at certain ones. Then he looked up at me, and said, "You simply don't know how to write."
> He added that there was some gift there, but because I was ignorant of what to do with it, he could not estimate how much of a gift it was. If it was

blind luck or happy fate or smiling Fortune that must be thanked for leading me to Stanford, let me congratulate myself for having the sense not to leave the room when he said that.

Pinsky stayed in the room for several years, taking directed reading courses with Winters and writing poems. He has subsequently expressed his debt to Winters many times, most memorably in the penultimate section of his "Essay on Psychiatrists," much of which is spoken by Winters: *"My friend Hart Crane died mad. My friend / Ezra Pound is mad. But you will not go mad; you will grow up / To become happy, sentimental old college professors / Because they were men of genius, and you / Are not."* But unlike many writers who have identified with Winters, Pinsky has never seemed like a Wintersian, repeating the "Old Man's" idiosyncratic take on literary history. He did inherit Winters' preference for a Jonsonian clarity of statement in poetry; and he did share Winters' skepticism about poetic madness. Ultimately, however, Winters was important to Pinsky as a poet-critic who stressed the necessity of coming to terms with the entire history of poetry: it was Winters' generosity rather than his crankiness that made a forceful impression on the young Pinsky. In addition, Winters stressed in usable terms what Pinsky knew intuitively: that the reading and writing of poetry, however private, is inevitably an act with social consequences.

Three years after he showed Winters his work, Pinsky published his first poems in the October 1965 issue of the *Southern Review,* then a journal in which many of Winters' students and friends appeared. These poems sound almost nothing like the work Pinsky would produce three or four years later, but they are distinguished by a formal clarity and ease. Of the four poems, Pinsky preserved only "Old Woman" in *Sadness and Happiness.*

Not even in darkest August,
When the mysterious insects

Marry loudly in the black weeds
And the woodbine, limp after rain,
In the cooled night is more fragrant,
Do you gather in any slight
Harvest to yourself. Deep whispers
Of slight thunder, horizons off,
May break your thin sleep, but awake,
You cannot hear them. Harsh gleaner
Of children, grandchildren—remnants
Of nights now forever future—
Your dry, invisible shudder
Dies on this porch where, uninflamed,
You dread the oncoming seasons,
Repose in the electric night.

Like one of the poems that accompanied it in the *Southern Review* (another was set in rhymed couplets and the fourth in terza rima), "Old Woman" is organized syllabically, the eight syllables of each line variously accented. The subtlety of their rhythm does stand apart from the lines of the other poems, such as "The Destruction of the Long Branch" ("The marriage bed awakes to hear / A voice reciting, without fear"), but "Old Woman" showed only half of what Pinsky would become: the expert craftsman.

Pinsky published no more poems until 1969–1970, when he appeared again in the *Southern Review* and also in *Poetry:* most of these poems remain uncollected, as do four additional poems that appeared in a 1971 issue of *Poetry*. Pinsky included one of these four, "The Destruction of Long Branch," in *Sadness and Happiness*. In retrospect, the poem seems like a watershed. It begins:

When they came out with artificial turf
I went back home with a thousand miles.

I dug a trench by moonlight from the ocean
And let it wash in quietly

And make a brackish quicksand which the tide
Sluiced upward from the streets and ditches.

The downtown that the shopping centers killed,
The garden apartments, the garages,

The station, the Little Africa on (so help me)
Liberty Street, the nicer sections,

All settled gently in a drench of sand
And sunk with a minimum of noise.

It is tempting to say that the power of these lines comes from Pinsky's focus on the peculiarity of his hometown. And in some sense, the poem does represent the finding of a "subject matter"; Pinsky has subsequently written in sophisticated ways about the importance of subject matter and of poems that are organized by the earnest presentation of their meaning. But this advance happened when it did because Pinsky broke through an earlier idea about poetic language. He has said that "Old Woman" represents a kind of poetry that no longer interests him because of its "overt lyricism." In contrast, the force of the language of "The Destruction of Long Branch" depends not on an extravagance of image or wit or metaphor—not on the sonorous quality of a line like "Deep whispers / Of slight thunder, horizons off, / May break your thin sleep"—but on the unfolding of an argument that includes words like "shopping center." Pinsky has joked that he tends to be suspicious of a poet who hasn't gotten a shopping center into his poems: his point is to stress not only the place of the everyday world but the place of everyday language—language that by itself is not poetic—in poetry. The phrase "shopping center" could never appear in "Old Woman," just as Yeats could never have gotten the words "greasy till" into "To the Rose upon the Rood of Time."

"The Destruction of Long Branch" sounds even more like the mature Pinsky, the poet of "Shirt" and "Biography," because the introduction of phrases like "shopping center," "artificial turf," and "so help me" does not disrupt the formal clarity evident even in his earliest work. In "American Poetry and American Life" (collected in *Poetry and the World*) Pinsky has described the social qualities of the work of the contemporary American poet Anne Winters.

> I don't intend anything as quixotic or odious as prescribing a subject matter, or proscribing one. Rather, the point is that a certain kind of fluidity, a formal and moral quality, seems to have been demanded of American poets by their circumstance. . . . Winters's laundromat with its *I mean to live* seems simultaneously to challenge and embarrass poetic language, and to incorporate it: to defy poetic form, and to demand it.

These sentences offer an apt description of later poems like "Shirt." They also describe the values that give those poems their idiosyncratic movement. Pinsky has no interest in the "freedom" so often associated with the breaking of poetic forms, since he understands that forms are, as part of the historicity of his writing, unbreakable; but he is interested in bending them, testing them against the warp and woof of his experience.

Perhaps it is not coincidental that "The Destruction of Long Branch" embodies thematically this double attitude toward history and form—defying them and demanding them. The poem is not about the slow decay of Long Branch; rather, it is about Pinsky's desire to flood the place and pave it over—an act that he accomplishes, like any Romantic poet, "by moonlight." But the loving specificity of the poem's catalog of everything that disappears belies his desire to destroy, and the poem ends not with destruction but with Pinsky's "cautiously elegiac" re-creation of his hometown. In the process, the words that threatened to make him what he is ("artificial turf," "shopping mall") become the words with which he names the world and makes it his own.

Comparing Elizabeth Bishop with William Wordsworth in "The Idiom of a Self," Pinsky has said that "her great subject is the contest—or truce, or trade-agreement—between the single human soul on one side, and on the other side, the contingent world of artifacts and other peo-

ple." This is Pinsky's subject too, and it accounts for his emphasis on the historicity of his language: it is only through the social structure of language that the self is constituted, and it is only through language that the self asserts its power over the social structure. "Naming and placing things," writes Pinsky apropos of Bishop (though he could have been talking about "The Destruction of Long Branch"), "is an approach to genuine liberty. This is true even though the very means of naming things . . . are also part of the terrain."

This concern unites the poems of *Sadness and Happiness.* If Bishop's "In the Waiting Room" is a poem that dramatizes the difficulty of realizing that the self is a social construction (the individual merely "one of *them*"), then the first poem in *Sadness and Happiness* is about the opposite difficulty of seeing the individual as anything but a product of the categories that constitute it—"an I." The opening stanzas of "Poem about People" offer a comfortable account of other people seen less as individuals than as exemplars of a kind of Johnsonian "general nature." The difficulties begin a little further in:

> But how love falters and flags
> When anyone's difficult eyes come
>
> Into focus, terrible gaze of a unique
> Soul, its need unlovable.

Pinsky offers several examples of this problem, the last of which explores the sentimentality of his remark, stated earlier in this poem, that it is "possible / To feel briefly like Jesus / . . . Crossing the dark spaces" between individuals.

> In the movies, when the sensitive
> Young Jewish soldier nearly drowns
>
> Trying to rescue the thrashing
> Anti-semitic bully, swimming across
> The river raked by nazi fire,
> The awful part is the part truth:

Hate my whole kind, but me,
Love me for myself.

The truth is partial because single selves have meaning only as the parts of whole kinds; the difference is frightening, and difficult to calibrate. But it is not impossible, as the poem's final lines suggest, restating the opening stanzas' hope in darker, more tentative terms: "we / All dream it, the dark wind crossing / The wide spaces between us."

In *The Situation of Poetry: Contemporary Poetry and Its Tradition* (1976), Pinsky provided the term that would most often be used to describe the poems of *Sadness and Happiness:* discursive. "It is speech," wrote Pinsky of discursive poetry, "organized by its meaning, avoiding the distances and complications of irony on one side and the ecstatic fusion of speaker, meaning, and subject on the other. The idea is to have all of the virtues of prose, in addition to those qualities and degrees of precision which can be called poetic." Throughout the most egregiously discursive poems in *Sadness and Happiness,* poems such as "Essay on Psychiatrists" and "Tennis," Pinsky tries to recapture the pre-Romantic sensibility of Dryden and Virgil (the sensibility that was supposedly available, as Yvor Winters is made to say in "Essay on Psychiatrists," before *"the middle / Of the Eighteenth Century"* when *"the logical / Foundations of Western thought decayed and fell apart"*). If Virgil could write poems about the skills of farming, why not poems about the skills of tennis?

> Hit to the weakness. All things being equal
> Hit crosscourt rather than down the line, because
> If you hit crosscourt back to him, then he
>
> Can only hit back either towards you (crosscourt)
> Or parallel to you (down the line), but never
> Away from you, the way that you can hit
>
> Away from him if he hits down the line.

When these lines were first published, they seemed ingeniously innovative. But after twenty-five years, it has become evident that the more egregiously discursive poems are not the crucial achievement in *Sadness and Happiness.* While the textures of "Essay on Psychiatrists" and "Tennis" do encourage the expansion of poetic language, they do so programmatically, making the inclusion in poetry of phrases like "crosscourt" and "down the line" sound like a feat rather than an achievement that later poems will build on. Consequently, the poems seem more like attempts to write like Virgil (no more possible than it is to write like John Keats) than efforts to adapt Virgil's pre-Romantic sensibility to the poetry of today. Pinsky does accomplish the latter challenge in *Sadness and Happiness* with poems such as "Poem about People," "Discretions of Alcibiades," and "The Beach Women." They are the poems that paved the way for "Shirt" and "Biography"—the poems that sound most like Robert Pinsky.

TRANSITION: *AN EXPLANATION OF AMERICA* AND *HISTORY OF MY HEART*

In "Poem about People" Pinsky introduced the problem he continues to write about today: How can we imagine a society that will give an individual person meaning without threatening to dispense with individuality—a society that we might exist *in* without necessarily being thoroughly *of*? In his next book, almost wholly given over to a long poem in three parts, "An Explanation of America," Pinsky examined this question on a grand scale: because of its imperialistic hunger, American culture threatens to swallow us; but because of its vastness, the culture provides a sense of community amorphous enough to sustain us.

Given its subject matter and essayistic tone, *An Explanation of America* is a surprisingly intimate performance; the poem is addressed to one of

Pinsky's daughters. And if *An Explanation of America* is as discursive as "Tennis" or "Essay on Psychiatrists," it is also a poem in which Pinsky has something far more urgent to say. Halfway through, Pinsky offers this hope to his daughter:

> So what I know,
> What you know, what your sister knows
>   (approaching
> The age you were when I began this poem)
> All differ, like different overlapping stretches
> Of the same highway: with different lacks, and
>   visions.
> The words—*Vietnam*—that I can't use in poems
> Without the one word threatening to gape
> And swallow and enclose the poem, for you
> May grow more finite; able to be touched.

This wisdom about language is what Pinsky had learned, writing his first book of poems. But the word that he chooses here, so much more charged than "shopping center," reveals how much he feels is at stake in the expansion of the language of poetry. Pinsky begins *An Explanation Of America* by stressing the vast multiplicity of images in American culture ("Colonial Diners, Disney, films / Of concentration camps, the napalmed child / Trotting through famous newsfilm"), and he wants his daughter to see all these images—just as wants to build a poem ample enough to contain them. Such a poem might satisfy Pinsky's smaller hope:

> The Shopping Center itself will be as precious
> And quaint as is the threadmill now converted
> Into a quaint and high-class shopping center.

The larger hope—the larger word—is not dispatched with so easily:

> Someday, the War in Southeast Asia,
>   somewhere—
> Perhaps for you and people younger than you—
> Will be the kind of history and pain
> Saguntum is for me; but never tamed

> Or "history" for me, I think. I think
> That I may always feel as if I lived
> In a time when the country aged itself:
> More lonely together in our common strange-
>   ness . . .
> As if we were a family, and some members
> Had done an awful thing on a road at night.

These issues concerning the relationship of language and history were crucial for Pinsky's development, but the broadly discursive style in which he addressed them was not: in retrospect, *An Explanation of America* seems like a dangerous undertaking, one that might permanently have stunted a poet too eager to be identified with a small bundle of stylistic signatures. For if *The Situation of Poetry* were merely a polemic (and it is not), then *An Explanation of America* would be the poem that we would all too readily expect the author of that polemic to write. However boldly extended, the poem's discursiveness was never destined to become Pinsky's signature: Where in this relentlessly logical poem can we feel his characteristic obsession with chance, with movement, with surprise, with the mysterious way in which one thing leads to another?

"Modern poetry was created by writers born about a hundred years ago," he writes in *The Situation of Poetry.*

> The premises of their work included a mistrust of abstraction and statement, a desire to escape the blatantly conventional aspects of form, and an ambition to grasp the fluid, absolutely particular life of the physical world by using the static, general medium of language. Those premises are paradoxical, or at least peculiar, in themselves. Moreover, the brilliant stylistic inventions associated with the premises—notably the techniques of "imagism," which convey the powerful illusion that a poet presents, rather than tells about, a sensory experience—are also peculiar as techniques.

If this passage once seemed to justify the shape and feel of "Tennis" or *An Explanation of America,* it now seems like a description of the even more powerful poetry that Pinsky has gone on to write—poems that traffic not so much in abstraction and statement as in paradoxical, and peculiar, stylistic inventions; poems that present rather than explain sensory experience. The poems in his next book, *History of My Heart* (1984), do continue to address Pinsky's signature theme (the dialectical relationship of the self and the social structure), but they do so dramatically, enacting the dialectic as well as explaining it. And while these poems retain the clarity of *An Explanation of America,* they do not sacrifice mystery to clarity. Their narratives seem, even within their considerably smaller compass, more comprehensive and complex, more a dramatization of a mind thinking than the product of thought (to borrow a distinction Elizabeth Bishop favored). Pinsky would later title his collected poems after the first poem in *History of My Heart* ("The Figured Wheel") because this poem not only announces his characteristic theme but also inaugurates his fully mature style: here is the poet who (as "Biography" has it) "cleaves to circles."

"The Figured Wheel" describes the rotation of a great wheel throughout history. A catalog of culture, high and low, familiar and foreign, it begins with a shopping mall rather than a shopping center and ends, somewhat in the manner of "Biography," with the creation of Robert Pinsky's single self.

> Even in the scorched and frozen world of the
>   dead after the holocaust
> The wheel as it turns goes on accreting
>   ornaments.
> Scientists and artists festoon it from the grave
>   with brilliant
>
> Toys and messages, jokes and zodiacs, tragedies
>   conceived
> From among the dreams of the unemployed and
>   the pampered,
> The listless and the tortured. It is hung with
>   devices
> By dead masters who have survived by reducing
>   themselves magically

> To tiny organisms, to wisps of matter, crumbs of
>   soil,
> Bits of dry skin, microscopic flakes, which is why
>   they are called "great,"
> In their humility that goes on celebrating the
>   turning
> Of the wheel as it rolls unrelentingly over
>
> A cow plodding through car-traffic on a street in
>   Iasi,
> And over the haunts of Robert Pinsky's mother
>   and father
> And wife and children and his sweet self
> Which he hereby unwillingly and inexpertly gives
>   up, because it is
>
> There, figured and pre-figured in the nothing-
>   transfiguring wheel.

These lines establish the terms in which the title *History of My Heart* must be understood. As the poem "Biography" suggests, virtually all of Pinsky's poems are autobiographical, but they recognize that any autobiography, like the self it narrates, is constituted by a wide array of cultural and historical forces. To get to the "heart" of these poems is not to find some essential core but to recognize that the heart is on the surface of everything the poet sees or speaks.

The second poem in *History of My Heart* adds a more plainly political charge to this history. "The Unseen" begins with a group of tourists in Krakow, touring the death camp. The scene is "unswallowable," both unbearably familiar and unbearably horrific: "We felt bored / And at the same time like screaming Biblical phrases." Stalled between these extremes, Pinsky remembers a "sleep-time game"—an insomniac's dream of heroic destruction: granted the power of invisibility, Pinsky roams the camp, saves the victims from the gas chamber, and, as a finale, "[flushes] everything with a vague flood / Of fire and blood." As in "The Destruction of Long Branch," Pinsky dreams of having power over his history, remaking what made him.

It is not possible to take that dream too seriously in "The Destruction of Long Branch," of course: its act of destruction serves as a kind of metaphor for the self's struggle with language and history. In "The Unseen" the act is too literal, too historically charged, and Pinsky must back away from it more distinctly.

> I don't feel changed, or even informed—in that,
> It's like any other historical monument; although
> It is true that I don't ever at night any more
>
> Prowl rows of red buildings unseen, doing
> Justice like an angry god to escape insomnia.

Though he feels unchanged, Pinsky describes an important transformation here. Having imagined himself as the "unseen," Pinsky now recognizes a more potent invisible presence.

> And so,
> O discredited Lord of Hosts, your servant gapes
>
> Obediently to swallow various doings of us, the
>   most
> Capable of all your former creatures—we have
> No shape, we are poured out like water, but still
>
> We try to take in what won't be turned from in
>   despair.

In Pinsky's lexicon, this force could be called "history" as easily as "Lord of Hosts." Having earlier found the scene "unswallowable," Pinsky realizes that he has no choice but to take in the past. And as "The Figured Wheel" suggests, the past—however sordid—is already inside him: in this sense, the force of "history" could also be called "my heart." As one thing leads unpredictably but inexorably to another, any distinctions between private and public history become difficult to sustain.

CONSOLIDATION: *THE WANT BONE*

The wheel of history rolls through all of Pinsky's work, beginning with "Poem about People," the first poem in his first collection. But *The Want Bone* represents a point of crystallization—the midcareer moment in which Pinsky's characteristic preoccupations found a verbal music adequate to convey their power. Following on "The Figured Wheel," the poems of *The Want Bone* do not offer an "explanation" of anything; they enact the wheel's movement in the unpredictable leaps and turns of syntax, diction, and metaphor.

"*How can I turn this wheel / that turns my life?*" asks Pinsky in "Shiva and Parvati Hiding in the Rain" in *The Want Bone*. Throughout *History of My Heart* he is amazed by the vast array of images that make up the self; throughout *The Want Bone* he is equally amazed by the images that the self can make. The desire—the want—to turn the wheel of history has certainly been present in Pinsky's work since "The Destruction of Long Branch"; but in *The Want Bone* Pinsky sometimes stands aghast at the potential hubris of the human imagination—or what in "What Why When How Who" he calls

> The old conspiracy of gain and pleasure
>
> Flowering in the mind greedily to build the world
> And break it.

Behind these lines stand Old Testament injunctions against idolatry, but in an essay on the prophet Isaiah (collected in *Poetry and the World*) Pinsky concludes that "all worship, even the most meticulous or elaborate, may be flawed by the spirit of idolatry." Since idolatry is in some way essential to human action, good or bad, Pinsky's fascination is less with greed as such than with the point at which pleasure begins to conspire unhappily with gain.

The astonishing first poem in *The Want Bone*, "From the Childhood of Jesus," is impatient with both Old and New Testament wisdom, both the laws of Judaism and Jesus' revision of them. Pinsky tells the apocryphal tale of a young Jesus who makes a little pond of mud and twigs and models twelve sparrows from clay. The scene seems innocent enough until "a certain Jew" (Pinsky incorporates the language of the anti-Semitic joke or story here) scolds the child for "making images." In response, Jesus makes the sparrows come to life, and, when the son of Annas accidentally ruins the little pond, Jesus makes the boy wither away. The petulant tone of Jesus' anger is familiar from the Gospels ("what did the water / Do to harm you?"), but his actions are merciless, filled with the childish self-importance that the tone suggests. (As Pinsky in "Lament for the Makers" writes, "Worship is tautological, with its Blessed / Art thou O Lord who consecrates the Sabbath. . . . And then the sudden curt command or truth: / God told him, Thou shalt cut thy foreskin off.") "From the Childhood of Jesus" ends like a parable gone wrong.

By dusk, the Jews were all gone from the river.

Small creatures came from the undergrowth to
   drink
And foraged in the shadows along the bank.

Alone in his cot in Joseph's house, the Son
Of man was crying himself to sleep. The moon

Rose higher, the Jews put out their lights and
   slept,
And all was calm and as it had been, except

In the agitated household of the scribe Annas,
And high in the dark, where unknown even to
   Jesus

The twelve new sparrows flew aimlessly through
   the night,
Not blinking or resting, as if never to alight.

Jesus is resolutely human in this story, granted the powers of a god but the emotions of a child, and, like any man, he cannot control the things he has made: the poem's final image is more frightening than the child's petulance. "From the Childhood of Jesus" is astonishing because, while it is ultimately about the consequences of the simple human desire for power, it tells that profane story in the vocabulary of the sacred. Consequently, this poem about hubris is itself startlingly hubristic—a paradox that embodies Pinsky's uneasy double attitude toward the human imagination.

"From the Childhood of Jesus" exemplifies one of the two kinds of poems that make up *The Want Bone*. The other kind, rather than adapting biblical rhetoric, builds on the achievement of "The Figured Wheel" by combining a multiplicity of vocabularies and narratives into a meandering shape that seems at once wild and controlled, random and planned. Structurally, these poems are organized something like a baroque concerto with a ritornello, or repeating motif, that appears (though in a different key) after each episode of new material. In "The Uncreation" various ideas of singing hold the poem's disparate materials together. In "At Pleasure Bay" some version of the phrase "never the same" recurs. And as we've already seen, the repeated motif in "Shirt" is neither a theme nor a phrase but simply a rhythm: "The back, the yoke, the yardage"; "The planter, the picker, the sorter." Similar to those of *History of My Heart* but even more daringly dependent on verbal music rather than logical argument, these poems are what "The Destruction of Long Branch" ultimately made possible.

In "The Hearts" the ritornello is an unsentimental image of the heart: "pulpy shore-life battened on a jetty."

Slashed by the little deaths of sleep and pleasure,
They swell in the nurturing spasms of the waves,

Sucking to cling; and even in death itself—
Baked, frozen—they shrink to grip the granite
   harder.

Between the recurrences of this image comes a catalog of harsh desires, one thing leading to another. The victim of a suffocating lover is equated with a heroin addict who knows, the first time he shoots up, that he will suffer, go to prison, and probably die. But this knowledge doesn't stop the addict, whose consolation is that proposed by Enobarbus in *Antony and Cleopatra* when Antony laments "*Would I had never seen her*": "Then you would have missed / A wonderful piece of work." This passage, in turn, invokes a sentence from Stephen Booth's commentary on Shakespeare's sonnets: "*Shakespeare was almost certainly homosexual, / Bisexual, or heterosexual, the sonnets / Provide no evidence on the matter.*" This link in the chain of associations provokes the poem's central question: Why does human desire fuel, over and over again, the making of images—the singing of songs, the throwing of pots, the writing of poems?

All of these creative acts are invoked as the chain continues, one image leading almost arbitrarily to the next. The question of Shakespeare's sexuality invokes the rhetoric of courtly love (tears, crystals, hearts), which continues to infect the songs (in this case, Lee Andrews and The Hearts—"*My tear drops are / Like crystals*") we sing in the shower (water falling like tears or crystals).

To Buddha every distinct thing is illusion
And becoming is destruction, but still we sing
In the shower. I do. In the beginning God
   drenched

The Emptiness with images: the potter
Crosslegged at his wheel in Benares market
Making mud cups, another cup each second

Tapering up between his fingers, one more
To sell the tea-seller at a penny a dozen,
And tea a penny a cup. The customers smash

The empties, and waves of traffic grind the shards
To mud for new cups, in turn; and I keep one here
Next to me: holding it awhile from out of the
   cloud

Of dust that rises from the shattered pieces,
The risen dust alive with fire, then settled
And soaked and whirling again on the wheel that
   turns

And looks on the world as on another cloud,
On everything the heart can grasp and throw away
As a passing cloud. . . .

The image of the wheel returns here, but unlike "The Figured Wheel," the potter's wheel is turned by a man: the result of all human *making*, Pinsky suggests, is this absurd, this transient—not the potent images with which the Hebrew God drenches the emptiness but the mere images that the Buddha denounces as empty. And yet, as the poem continues to unfold, the wheel continues to turn—perhaps productively. The visions of the Old Testament are dismissed as "too barbarous for heaven / And too preposterous for belief on earth"—here Pinsky rehearses the horrible vision in Isaiah 6, after which the prophet's unclean lips are purified by a live coal—and "The Hearts" ends by returning to Lee Andrews and The Hearts, their record spinning like the potter's wheel.

As the record ends, a coda in retard:
The Hearts in a shifting velvety *ah,* and *ah*
Prolonged again, and again as Lee Andrews

Reaches *ah* high for *I have to gain Faith, Hope
And Charity, God only knows the girl
Who will love me—Oh! if we only could*

Start over again! Then The Hearts chant the
   chords
Again a final time, *ah* and the record turns
Through all the music, and on into silence again.

These lines of the poem answer the song: you can start again, though you will end up in pretty much the same place. Finally, Pinsky's suggestion is that the turning itself—the longing, the singing, the making—must constitute our human value. If this seems like a paltry consolation, the empty images condemned by the Buddha, we should remember in contrast the uncontrollable, unsatisfying images conjured by the Son of Man in "From the Childhood of Jesus."

In "Impossible to Tell," one of the new poems in *The Figured Wheel: New and Collected Poems, 1966–1996* (1996), Pinsky describes (among many other things) the way in which medieval Japanese poets worked together to write linked poems or *renga:* "The movement / Of linking *renga* coursing from moment to moment / Is meaning." This is a good description of what Pinsky tries to accomplish in poems like "Shirt" or "The Hearts," creating the texture not only of one poet's mind but of a culture's accumulating stock of reality. In "Impossible to Tell" Pinsky cuts back and forth between the Japanese poet Bashō, nurturing his disciples, and Pinsky's own friend Elliot Gilbert, who was a consummate teller of ethnic jokes. The jokes Pinsky repeats in "Impossible to Tell" are sidesplitting, but the poem is also deeply moving. A kind of courtly community grows from the conventional yet idiosyncratic work of the joke teller.

> But as the *renga* describes
> Religious meaning by moving in drifting petals
>
> And brittle leaves that touch and die and suffer
> The changing winds that riffle the gutter swirl,
> So in the joke, just under the raucous music
>
> Of Fleming, Jew, Walloon, a courtly allegiance
> Moves to the dulcimer, gavotte and bow,
> Over the banana tree the moon in autumn—
> Allegiance to a state impossible to tell.

Once again, as in "Window," Pinsky wants to emphasize the mongrel, compromised heritage of the world: through poetry, through jokes, through any communal activity, our allegiance is to "a state impossible to tell." At first, this poem might seem to move haphazardly, jumping from the sacred to the vulgar to the commonplace; but as Pinsky suggests in "Impossible to Tell," the

movement (or, as he puts it in "The Hearts," the "turning") of the poem between these elements— more than the elements themselves—is what ultimately satisfies us.

Thinking about this quality of movement in "Poetry and Pleasure" (collected in *Poetry and the World*) Pinsky asks a question that has been implicit in his work since "The Destruction of Long Branch": "If gorgeous, impressive language and profound, crucial ideas were all that poetry offered to engage us, would it seem—as it does to many of us—as necessary as food?" This may be the most provocative question that can be asked of poetry at the end of the twentieth century, and Pinsky's answer is convincing because it neither dismisses nor exaggerates poetry's claim on our attention. What engages us in poetry is not the product (the achieved word or thought) but the process of moving through those thoughts and words: "This movement—physical in the sounds of a poem, moral in its relation to the society implied by language, and the person who utters the poem—is near the heart of poetry's mysterious appeal, for me." In their sinuous investigation of desire, Pinsky's fully mature poems not only describe this appeal: more profoundly, they enact it.

ACHIEVEMENT: *THE FIGURED WHEEL* AND *JERSEY RAIN*

The movement of "Impossible to Tell" seems closer to the poems of *The Want Bone* than to the other new poems in *The Figured Wheel* or the poems in *Jersey Rain,* published in 2000. At first, these poems might seem even more dense and difficult, even more dependent on our willingness to give ourselves over (as Pinsky puts it in *The Sounds of Poetry*) to "the pleasure taken in language that is only partly understood," than the poems of his earlier books. But they are without question the most ambitious and compelling poems of Pinsky's career—the poems he has been writing toward for thirty years. In "The Ice-Storm" (from *The Figured Wheel*) he rephrases the question he has been asking since he wrote "Poem about People": "What is a life? A specimen, or a kind?" The answer, over and over again, is *both.*

The notion of a community's atonement (or, more literally, its desire for "at-one-ment") preoccupies Pinsky in "Avenue," another new poem from *The Figured Wheel.* This poem surveys a crowded city street, a cacophony of voices and images, before it takes on the point of view of one particular human being. This nameless "one"—a man lying drunk in the street—explains how he was rescued by the many.

> Their headlights found me stoned, like a bundled
> sack
> Lying in the Avenue, late. They didn't speak
> My language. For them, a small adventure. They
> hefted
> Me over the curb and bore me to an entry
>
> Out of the way. Illuminated footwear
> On both sides. How I stank. Dead drunk. They
> left me
> Breathing in my bower between the Halloween
> Brogans and pumps on crystal pedestals.
>
> But I was dead to the world. The midnight city
> In autumn. Day of attainment, tall saints
> Who saved me. My taints, day of anointment. Oil
> Of rose and almond in the haircutting parlor,
>
> Motor oil swirling rainbows in gutter water.
> Ritually unattainted, the congregation
> File from the place of worship and resume
> The rumbling drum and hautbois of conversation,
>
> Speech of the granary, of the cloven lanes
> Of traffic, of salvaged silver. Not shriven and yet
> Not rent, they stride the Avenue, banter, barter.
> Capering, on fire, they cleave to the riven hub.

These lines suggest that, through anonymous acts of charity, a multitude of people might imagine a sense of community. But the drama of this poem—as is the case in most of Pinsky's later work—is more resolutely linguistic than thematic. Poems like "The Hearts" or "Impossible to Tell" move down the page phrase by phrase, twisting and turning: in the new poems of *The Figured Wheel* and those of *Jersey Rain,* the syntactical units are shorter, and the poems move almost word by word. In "Avenue" the language almost seems to generate itself, one word leading to another: "atonement," "attainment," "tall saints," "taints," "anointment." Consequently, a threat of randomness enters the poem's movement—as if the sounds of the words alone were determining the direction of the poem's argument. The poems never succumb to this threat. But we need to feel a swirling cloud of language congealing to make the poems, just as the crowd in "Avenue" seems as if it were condensed down to the nameless "one" in the street.

"Tell," "feel," "well": this is the first triplet of rhymes in Pinsky's translation of Dante's *Inferno,* which was published two years before *The Figured Wheel.* Adapting Dante's terza rima (his interlocking pattern of rhyme—aba, bcb, cdc, and so on) into English, Pinsky solved the problem of the English language's relative paucity of rhymes by employing consonantal rhyming—rhymes in which the vowel sound may change while the consonants remain the same: "sleep," "stop," "up"; "night," "thought," "it." This keen focus on sounds that almost (but not quite) coincide helped to consolidate the features of Pinsky's mature style, allowing his poems more powerfully to enact the slippery movement of language: "atonement," "attainment," "tall saints," "taints," "anointment." "The medium of poetry is a human body," Pinsky writes in *The Sounds of Poetry:* "the column of air inside the chest, shaped into signifying sounds in the larynx and the mouth. In this sense, poetry is just as physical or bodily an art as dancing." The power of the poems of *The Figured Wheel* and *Jersey Rain* depends not so much on the unfolding of their meaning than on a beguiling cacophony of sounds—sounds that by raising the specter of chance (one sound of one word leading to another) refuse to allow us to take for granted our ability to make words meaningful.

We have already observed this swirl of language in "Biography," the poem from *Jersey Rain* with which we began.

> My mother's dreadful fall. Her mother's dread
> Of all things: death, life, birth. My brother's birth
> Just before the fall, his birth again in Jesus.
> Wobble and blur of my soul, born only once,
> That cleaves to circles. The moon, the eye, the
>   year,
> Circle of causes or chaos or turns of chance.

Throughout *Jersey Rain,* Pinsky "cleaves to circles" more resolutely then ever before: words are not only repeated or echoed as consonantal rhymes within individual poems; words also reoccur from poem to poem, unifying the entire book. Yet the precise nature of the unity is difficult to specify: we are shown over and over again that one thing leads to another, but the reasons determining these links remain obscure; the threat of the arbitrary is impossible to dispel. Nor does Pinsky want to dispel it. For unlike a poet who insists that aleatory nonsense must be staved off by traditional structures—and unlike a poet who insists that traditional structures must be undermined by aleatory nonsense—Pinsky suggests that nonsense and meaningfulness are unavailable to us except in consort with each other. The phrase "put me up" means something very different from the phrase "put up with me," but both sound exquisitely similar to our ears. The poems of *Jersey Rain* do not lament but thrive on such contingency. The book's very climate—rain falling from sky to ocean, nonsense consorting with meaningfulness—is one of contingency: "I feel it churning even in fair weather," Pinsky writes in the book's title poem, "To craze distinction."

While many of his earliest poems ran through their subject matters with an essayistic aplomb ("Madness itself, as an idea, leaves us confused," he observed in "Essay on Psychiatrists"), Pinsky in his later work courts the very sound of madness—a limpid cacophony that beguiles without begging for comprehension. "Ode to Meaning" is the major poem of *Jersey Rain* and possibly the major poem of Pinsky's career:

> Gesturer, when is your spur, your cloud?
> You in the airport rituals of greeting and parting.
> Indicter, who is your claimant?
> Bell at the gate. Spiderweb iron bridge.
> Cloak, video, aroma, rue, what is your
> Elected silence, where was your seed?

The "you" Pinsky addresses in these lines is meaning itself. Where do you come from, he asks, what provokes you, what receives you? Meaning is everywhere in the poem—everywhere in the world—yet its very abundance is overwhelming; it continually escapes our best efforts to pin it down. We crave meaning, yet once clearly defined, meaning threatens to determine us.

"Dire one and desired one," begins "Ode to Meaning," "Savior, sentencer." In the same way that the sounds of the phrases "dire one" and "desired one" threaten to become identical (while their meanings are opposed), meaning is a force that we cannot help spurning even as we crave it. "In an old allegory you would carry / A chained alphabet of tokens," the poem continues. What force determines the shape of the sentence that follows, giving us a picture of that string of tokens? The alphabet: the words of this sentence appear in alphabetical order.

> Ankh Badge Cross.
> Dragon,
> Engraved figure guarding a hallowed intaglio,
> Jasper kinema of legendary Mind,
> Naked omphalos pierced

By quills of rhyme or sense, torah-like: unborn
Vein of will, xenophile
Yearning out of Zero.

Pinsky is playing here, but he is not merely playing. Throughout *Jersey Rain* the alphabet reoccurs, most powerfully in "An Alphabet of My Dead," in which Pinsky describes the way in which for years he has staved off insomnia by thinking of a name (lost friends, relatives, poets) for each letter of the alphabet. Far from diffusing meaning, this sequence of twenty-six letters offers the backbone of convention that makes meaning possible: the arbitrary is not opposed to meaning—meaning contains it.

"You are the wound," ends "Ode to Meaning," "You / Be the medicine." However much this poetry embraces madness, Pinsky craves sanity. "Let those scorn you who never / Starved in your dearth," he says of meaning, and his poem—turning swiftly from literary history to biography—points to the origins of his hunger.

Untrusting I court you. Wavering
I seek your face, I read
That Crusoe's knife
Reeked of you, that to defile you
The soldier makes the rabbi spit on the torah.
"I'll drown my book," says Shakespeare.

Drowned walker, revenant.
After my mother fell on her head, she became
More than ever your sworn enemy. She spoke
Sometimes like a poet or critic of forty years later.
Or she spoke of the world as Thersites spoke of
   the heroes,
"I think they have swallowed one another. I
Would laugh at that miracle."

The phrase "fell on her head" appears several times throughout the poems of *Jersey Rain;* it names the central event in the biography Pinsky constructs for himself throughout this book: "My mother's dreadful fall," as he puts it in the poem titled "Biography." But it would be too easy to say that Pinsky has long been obsessed with the dialectic of meaning and madness—describing it in "Essay on Psychiatrists," embodying it in "Ode to Meaning"—because his mother suffered a severe concussion from which she never completely recovered. Throughout "Ode to Meaning" Pinsky presents the "fall" into a swirling world of language as a fortunate fall: as he writes in the final lines of "In Memory of Congresswoman Barbara Jordan," the poem preceding "Biography," no one is exempt from "that first painted April when we fell." Every one of us grapples, sometimes expertly, often ineptly, with the sounds of language, and we could not be comforted if we were not confused—and confused again. Meaning, Pinsky insists in "Ode to Meaning," is to be found "not in the words, not even / Between the words, but a torsion, / A cleaving, a stirring." Which is to say that meaning exists in movement, in the ever shifting way in which one thing leads to another, making us who we are, unmaking us so that we might be made again.

"Pathos / Of survival, briskness of destruction, works / And place half abolished, that once I willed / Dead," writes Pinsky in "The Superb Lily," thinking back to "The Destruction of Long Branch," the first poem in which he discovered himself in language.

                    Longing flows now to what

The heart happily would have destroyed:
The boardwalk's mostly gone, the merry-go-round
With its painted scenes of the National Parks

And calliope has been dismantled and sold.

Pinsky's attitude toward Long Branch has changed; a tenderness has replaced the brashness of his earliest work. But he remains fascinated with the ways in which places, people, and poems exist in motion: they are created, they change, disappear, then reappear (as he puts it in "The Cycles") as "particles of energy, cycles, vibrations"—raw materials for new places and people, new poems. And the poems can't help but to commemorate the people and places that made them. An art museum "seems / So separate from the world," he writes in "At the Worcester Museum," a companion poem to "Ode to Meaning." But however artificial, however bound up with convention, the museum quite simply "is / The world, or what we remember of the world." The same could be said of Robert Pinsky's poems.

Selected Bibliography

WORKS OF ROBERT PINSKY

POETRY
Sadness and Happiness. Princeton: Princeton University Press, 1975.
An Explanation of America. Princeton: Princeton University Press, 1979.
History of My Heart. New York: Ecco Press, 1984.
The Want Bone. New York: Ecco Press, 1990.
The Figured Wheel: New and Collected Poems, 1966–1996. New York: Farrar, Straus & Giroux, 1996.
Jersey Rain. New York: Farrar, Straus & Giroux, 2000.

PROSE
Landor's Poetry. Chicago: University of Chicago Press, 1968.
The Situation of Poetry: Contemporary Poetry and Its Traditions. Princeton, N.J.: Princeton University Press, 1976.
Mindwheel. San Rafael, California: Broderbund Software, 1986.
Poetry and the World. New York: Ecco Press, 1988.
The Sounds of Poetry: A Brief Guide. New York: Farrar, Straus & Giroux, 1998.

TRANSLATIONS
The Separate Notebooks, by Czeslaw Milosz. With Robert Hass. New York: Ecco Press, 1984.

The Inferno of Dante. New York: Farrar, Straus & Giroux, 1994.

UNCOLLECTED PROSE
"The Idiom of a Self: Elizabeth Bishop and Wordsworth." *Elizabeth Bishop and Her Art.* Edited by Lloyd Schwartz and Sybil P. Estess. Ann Arbor: University of Michigan Press, 1983. Pp. 49–60.
"Robert Pinsky." *Contemporary Authors: Autobiography Series.* Edited by Adele Sarkissian. Vol. 4. Detroit: Gale Research Company, 1986.
"Mr. Mintser." *Kenyon Review* 4:24–36 (1982).
"American Poetry in American Life." *American Poetry Review* 25:19–23 (March–April 1996).
"Poetry and American Memory." *Atlantic Monthly* 284:60–70 (October 1999).

CRITICAL AND BIOGRAPHICAL STUDIES

Gluck, Louise. "Story Tellers." *American Poetry Review* 26:9–12 (July–August 1997).
Howard, Richard. "Art or Knack?" *Poetry* 129:226–232 (1977).
Longenbach, James. "Figuring Multitudes." *Nation,* April 29, 1996, pp. 25–28.
McClatchy, J. D. "Shapes of Desire." *New Republic,* September 24, 1990, pp. 46–48.
Parini, Jay. "Explaining America: The Poetry of Robert Pinsky." *Chicago Review* 33:16–26 (1981).
Sacks, Peter. " 'Also This, Also That': Robert Pinsky's Poetics of Inclusion." *Agni* 36:272–280 (1992).

INTERVIEWS

Downing, Ben, and Daniel Kunitz. "Robert Pinsky: The Art of Poetry LXXVI." *Paris Review* 144:181–213 (1997).
Halliday, Mark. "An Interview with Robert Pinsky." *Ploughshares* 6:141–169 (1980).
Harry, Thomas. "A Conversation with Robert Pinsky." *TriQuarterly* 92:21–37 (1994/1995).
Sorkin, Adam J. "An Interview with Robert Pinsky." *Contemporary Literature* 25:1–14 (1984).

—*JAMES LONGENBACH*

Reynolds Price

1933–

*I*N AN INTERVIEW published in the September/ October 1999 issue of *Book,* the poet and memoirist Mark Doty said, "I think we need the stories of our lives to be told. They need to be given shape. There's some way in which the story that you don't tell controls you. That story seems to live you." Most writers would agree with Doty; especially, perhaps, those who grew up in the rich oral narrative tradition of the southern United States. The revered "old masters" such as Eudora Welty, William Faulkner, and Tennessee Williams, and younger writers including Kaye Gibbons, Clyde Edgerton, and Josephine Humphreys, found their richest ore when mining their own lives for material. This has also been the case for Reynolds Price, whose very birth was the stuff of the southern literary tradition: biblical, gothic, and miraculous.

CHILDHOOD THROUGH HIGH SCHOOL

Edward Reynolds Price was born on February 1, 1933, in his mother's family home, a large, white, tree-shaded house built by Price's grandfather John Rodwell in the mid-1880s, in Macon, Warren County, North Carolina. Elizabeth Rodwell Price's first pregnancy was uncomplicated but because it was a breech delivery, labor was difficult. Indeed, the family physician declared at

one point that he feared losing both mother and child. This circumstance caused Price's father, William Solomon Price, to leave the home that cold February morning and fall on his knees in prayer in the dark confines of a woodshed. There, he struck a bargain with God: if his wife and child survived, he promised that he would mend his alcoholic ways. In his retelling of this family legend in his memoir *Clear Pictures: First Loves, First Guides* (1989), Price says of his father's vow to quit drinking, "The fact is, in time he did but not at once." Price was named Edward in honor of his paternal grandfather. Reynolds was the family name of his paternal great-grandmother, from Perth, Scotland. There were two additional births for Elizabeth Price: a girl, stillborn when Reynolds was three, and another son, William Solomon Price Jr., born five years later in 1941.

Survivors of near fatal events tend to bond closely, united by their common relief and gratitude. This was the case with Price and his parents. Although they lived in a poor rural area during the difficult years of the Great Depression, with its omnipresent possibility of financial ruin, the family shared a loving happiness that stayed with Price through his adult years. The novelist Anne Tyler, in her reminiscence "Reynolds Price: Duke of Writers," recalled the time when she was a student of his at Duke University in the 1950s: "I remember a thought I had when I was a sopho-more, listening to one of his funny, incisive dis-cussions. *He must have been a very much-loved child,* I thought. I believe that occurred to me because he seemed, sitting in our midst, a natu-rally happy man." The importance of familial closeness in Price's life and the effect it had on his work cannot be overemphasized. Price has written of the union of father, mother, and son as a "triad"—a three-way marriage. He contends that his parents were his greatest influences and greatest loves. Indeed, in a 1991 interview in *Paris Review,* Price said, "They were almost too lovable, which is something I've heard very few people say about their parents. I think both my brother and I, who were their only children to survive infancy, have all our lives been handi-capped by the fact that we seldom meet human beings as loyal, affectionate or continuously amusing as our parents."

Times were tough for the Price family in the late years of the Depression. Price seemed to have more than the usual number of bouts of childhood illnesses, including severe allergic reactions, whooping cough, and mysterious seizures. In ad-dition, his father's job as an appliance salesman for Carolina Power and Light Company required the family to move an average of once a year until his son entered high school, when the family set-tled in Raleigh. Among the memories Price re-calls in *Clear Pictures* is a recurring one of his mother handing him an empty box and instruct-ing him, "Pack your toys, son. We're moving to-morrow to a lot nicer place." These moves were generally upward (however, one was caused by the lack of fifty dollars for a house payment) and were within a small radius of Macon. Living in towns such as Henderson, Warrenton, Roxboro, and Asheboro, Price was never far away from the company of his large extended family of uncles, aunts, and cousins. They provided him with a wealth of family lore and he enjoyed their re-markable storytelling skills. In the preface to

Learning a Trade: A Craftsman's Notebooks, 1955–1997 (1998), Price gave this description of his early childhood:

> Note that, despite my family's slender means in the late Depression years, I had a room of my own from the age of six onward; and that was no negligible privilege. In the absence of brothers and sisters—I was an only child till the age of eight—I not only relished my unique status in the house, I undertook as early as possible to fill the long hours of extreme household silence with engrossing activity.

He goes on to say: "For me, as for many other children who become writers, the first of my se-rious diversions was drawing and painting, which are alternate means for watching the world with close concentration." Price remembered with pleasure writing and illustrating in second grade an assigned poem about rain and, in fifth grade, working on a novel with a female cousin. How-ever, it was in the eighth grade, in December 1946, that he wrote what he has described as his "official first work," *The Wise Men,* a play in five acts.

As a child interested in the fine arts, an unusual diversion for a boy from the standpoint of the midcentury, traditional South, Price suffered re-jection and worse at the hands of his contempo-raries. For companionship and play he turned to the hardworking children of nearby farms. Those children were bused into school and, at the end of the day, returned to their rural homes, several miles away. For most of these farm children a telephone was a luxury their parents could ill af-ford, so interaction with his pals after school was rare. As an adolescent, Price filled the vast amounts of silence and open time perfecting his drawing and writing skills.

In his third year as a student at Needham Broughton High School in Raleigh, Price was fortunate enough, after being guided and encour-aged by some splendid instructors, to encounter a gifted teacher of literature and composition,

Phyllis Abbott Peacock. Mrs. Peacock possessed the remarkable ability, the hallmark of the finest educators, of being able to recognize a student's talents while challenging them, patiently and purposefully, to exceed their limitations. At the end of a year in her class, Price's future was decided. As he wrote in the preface to *Learning a Trade,* "I'd go to college, read and write more; and once I'd entered the world of jobs—there was no family money to fund an author's life in the tropics or elsewhere—I'd begin writing books and I'd teach what I learned to oncoming years of unequipped students."

The religious instruction Price received as a child was ecumenical, to say the least. His paternal grandfather was an Episcopalian married to a Baptist. Price's father, William, attended services with his mother and youngest sister at the Baptist church. Price's mother, Elizabeth, and her family were Methodists. As a result, young Price was witness to heated, albeit civil, debates regarding matters of faith and doctrine, the most hotly discussed issue being that of the rite of baptism—the total-immersion form practiced by the Baptist members of the family versus the application of holy water to the head, practiced by the Episcopalians and Methodists.

The Prices did not attend church together; family loyalties prevented each of Price's parents from adopting the other's religious affiliation. Some Sundays Price would journey with his father to the Baptist church and on others he would attend Methodist services with his mother. For the most part, however, he was allowed the freedom to pursue the holy on his own. It was through his solitary musings and his observations of the natural world that Price developed his own particular creed. He found a place for his beliefs in the Episcopal Church of the Good Shepherd, which stood just three blocks from his home in Asheboro, where he lived from ages six to eleven. In identifying with this institution he was, however, careful to cause no harm to those he loved

and on whose love he thrived. Without strong urging from his family, Price chose to divide his church attendance three ways. He participated in summer-vacation Bible school at the Baptist church, but he also sang in the choir at the Methodist church and served as an acolyte with the Episcopalians. Ultimately, however, organized religion did not satisfy Price's yearnings for the mystery of God and he began to withdraw from church affiliation. In *Clear Pictures,* he wrote,

> The further I moved from organized worship, the more the God of my childhood meant to me. . . . My silent mind knew however, no question or qualm, that in churches I felt increasingly blocked from my best means of understanding. I'd come to believe, and still do, that those means were my own inquisitive eyes and conscience, watching intently for the motions of the spirit, and my study of the ancient texts of the Bible.

Price neither discussed nor defended this action. Nor did he attempt to persuade his "churchly contemporaries" to follow his example. Indeed, Price's pulling back from organized religion, as he went on to explain in *Clear Pictures,* was not total.

> I've visited churches many times, for lone worship, for the chance to share the wine and bread that stand for Christ and for other chances to use that gift I'd once thought useless in pulpits, near altars—the use of words to try to convey a wordless knowledge of the core of light. But I've never yet stayed; I still withdraw. At least till now I've kept good faith with the child I was and may always be.

COLLEGE YEARS AND LOSS

Price graduated from high school in 1951 and entered Duke University in Durham, North Carolina, with a full scholarship, as an Angier B. Duke scholar. He was determined to become a "writer who taught," even though he had produced very little of his own work other than academic papers. During his first three years at Duke, college social life, mysterious and challenging to a young man testing his wings thirty miles away from the nest, and course work, consumed his time and energies. In a 1983 interview with Daniel Voll, Price remembered, "I loved being in college. It was the first time in my life when the things I was good at were prized by the place I was in." To dispel the idea that college was all work and no play, Price went on to say, "I worked like a dog. I was also in a hell-raising fraternity and greatly enjoyed that. It was new and strange to me—like being an honorary member of a zoo for three years."

In 1954, during Price's junior year, the Anglo-Irish novelist and short story writer Elizabeth Bowen visited Duke. Since the death of her husband, Alan Charles Cameron, in 1952, Bowen had made a practice of spending part of every year in the United States, lecturing and working as a writer in residence. Bowen read a rough draft of a story Price had been working on since his freshman year; it had begun as a writing assignment for Philip Williams's advanced composition class. She encouraged him to expand the piece, teaching him the often ignored lesson that a story must have a middle as well as a beginning and end.

In late January 1954 Price received a message asking him to call home as soon as possible; his beloved father was showing symptoms of influenza. Price returned to Raleigh the following weekend to find William Price, a normally robust man, frail and unsteady on his feet. A chest X ray showed a dark patch on his right lung that was thought to indicate pneumonia or, at worst, tuberculosis. Subsequent tests, however, revealed cancer. Surgery to remove William Price's right lung took place on a Wednesday in mid-February 1954. The operation further revealed that the cancer had spread. The prognosis was bleak: William Price's doctors told the family that he did not have long to live; there was nothing to do but try to relieve his pain and wait. Price stayed with his father, camping out in the hospital room, occasionally returning to the family home to rest and wash. The following Sunday evening, Price and his high school friend Patricia Cowden were sitting on either side of his father's hospital bed when Will Price died. To Reynolds Price, the loss of this bighearted and loving man, a man who showed affection openly, who called his sons "darling" and kissed them in front of their peers without embarrassment, was profound. Writing of this time in *Clear Pictures* Price stated, "Unquestionably those days with Will were a fulcrum of my life, the point on which youth tilted into manhood." He viewed his father's death as a gift; a final secret shared, a final skill taught. "I saw that the kindest thing Will Price did for me was to die when he did, when I stood on the doorsill of maturity in an America that was already starting its lethal commitment to the prolongation of youth."

In his senior year at Duke, from the fall of 1954 through the spring of 1955, Price was enrolled in his first creative writing course, English 104 (narrative writing), taught by Professor William Blackburn. Again, as with Phyllis Abbott Peacock, Price was blessed with an instructor who was perfectly suited to provide guidance and encouragement to the unproven and aspiring writer. Blackburn had received his Ph.D. from Yale in 1943. He was a scholar of Elizabethan poetry and taught that subject for many years. He also had a special interest in Joseph Conrad and edited a collection of Conrad's letters. However, his true legacy arises from his instruction in the art of creative writing, and he is credited with the development of the creative writing program at Duke. His students at the university included, in addition to Price, William Styron, Mac Hyman (the author of the 1954 novel *No Time for Sergeants*), the poet James Applewhite, Fred Chappell, and the novelist Anne Tyler. Blackburn's students remember him as dramatic, inspiring, and daunting; a teacher who lived up to the sublimity of what he taught. He encouraged informality by serving tea in his undergraduate classes and created an atmosphere wherein interested students could share their writing, criticism, and ideas with him and each other.

It was Blackburn who read the expanded version of Price's story "Michael Egerton" and passed it on to Eudora Welty. Welty visited Duke in February 1955 to give a celebrated lecture, "Place in Fiction," at the Women's College on East Campus. Price had heard that Welty would be arriving by train, alone, at 3:00 A.M., and he arranged to meet her and escort her to the Washington Duke Hotel. Their lifelong friendship began at that point. Price had been introduced to Welty's writing in high school. He remembered especially her story "A Worn Path," which was in one of his high school anthologies. By the time of their meeting, he had read her work in quantity. It was Welty who had the greatest influence on the budding writer. Price said this about her short stories in a 1966 interview with Wallace Kaufman:

> They were an instantaneous revelation and a revelation about my life, not about literature nor the methods and techniques of fiction. They revealed to me what is most essential for any beginning novelist—which is that his world, the world he has known from birth, the world that has not seemed to him in any way extraordinary is, in fact, a perfectly possible world, base, subject for serious fiction.

Welty considered Price's story to be excellent and thoroughly professional and offered to send it to her agent, Diarmuid Russell. Russell was to become Price's agent as well and championed his work in the early years when no one in America was interested in publishing it. Welty expressed an interest in seeing more of Price's work and encouraged him to become more productive. As he explained to Kaufman, "What she offered me was what any young writer demands in varying ways at various times in his career—adequate judgment. I knew that she was a sound judge; and

I knew it because she was judging my work as *art,* not as the product of a favorite student or a friend."

"Michael Egerton" is a first-person narrative told by an eleven-year-old boy who is attending a Christian summer camp. The first boy the narrator meets at camp is one of his cabin mates, the title character Michael Egerton, a tall boy of around his own age whose facial features make him look much older. Michael's father, a famous war correspondent, leaves Michael at camp on his way to report on events in France. At the end of the camp session, Michael is to stay with an aunt for a while. No mention is made of the boy's mother. The narrator is intrigued by Michael and tries to learn more about him by telling the boy everything there is to say about his own life. Michael responds in bits and pieces; the narrator learns that Michael's mother has not lived with him and his father for nearly a year.

Michael is quite popular with the other boys in the camp. He shows outstanding athletic skills in swimming and baseball. There is hope that with Michael pitching, the Colossians (each of the camp's athletic teams is named for one of the epistles of Saint Paul) will win the junior title. On the day of the semifinals, when the Colossians are to play against the Ephesians, Michael is told by the camp director that he has visitors. From the cabin, the narrator watches as Michael walks toward the main lodge, stopping beside a car near the front steps. A man and woman emerge from the car, and it is obvious by their similarities that the woman is Michael's mother. The narrator watches as the three talk, but since he cannot hear them, he soon grows bored and takes a short nap. When he awakes, the car is gone and so is Michael. The game is about to begin and he is sent to find the team's star pitcher. Unable to locate Michael in time for the start of the game, the narrator returns to take his place on the playing field.

The Colossians, with an inferior substitute pitcher, are defeated. After the game, when the narrator finally finds Michael, he learns that the woman in the car was indeed Michael's mother and that the man is a "new father." The narrator learns that Michael's mother had asked Michael how he liked having two fathers. For the remaining week of camp, Michael withdraws from all activities and companionship. The other boys, who blame him for the loss of the baseball championship and its accompanying prestige, torment him. Camaraderie in the boys' cabin suffers because of Michael's inactivity. On the final night of camp, Michael surprises everyone by dressing to attend the Farewell Banquet. Four of the boys grab him and tie him, his arms outstretched in mock crucifixion, between two of the bunks. Michael does not struggle and he is left there as the others attend the banquet. The narrator slips away from this group and returns to untie Michael, but the boy has freed himself and disappeared. The narrator intuits that Michael is in the bathroom, the place to which he had retreated during the baseball game, but decides to leave him alone and returns to the boisterous crowd at the lodge.

The lean style of this story is reminiscent of the early work of Ernest Hemingway, but the subject matter is pure Reynolds Price. The contrasting need for society and solitude, the fear that reaching for someone will result in loss of freedom, the realization that one is ultimately unable to enter into, understand, or alleviate another's pain—these are the conundrums found in all of Price's writings.

Price graduated from Duke summa cum laude, Phi Beta Kappa, in 1955. He was awarded a Rhodes Scholarship and, from 1955 to 1958, attended Merton College, Oxford University (England). Always fortunate in instructors, he studied under Helen Gardner and Lord David Cecil and became acquainted with the poet W. H. Auden, who was a professor of poetry, and the poet and critic Sir Stephen Spender. His field of study was seventeenth-century English literature and he wrote his thesis on the importance of the Chorus in Milton's *Samson Agonistes.* In addition, he

wrote several of the short stories that would later appear in *The Names and Faces of Heroes* (1963) and first ideas for a novel, *A Long and Happy Life* (1962). In 1958 Price's short story "A Chain of Love" was accepted for publication by Spender's literary magazine, *Encounter.*

THE MUSTIAN STORIES

"A Chain of Love" had begun as a writing assignment for Professor Blackburn's class at Duke. Price was unsure of a subject for his story until one Sunday afternoon when he and a friend went to a Howard Johnson's restaurant near the campus for lunch. While there, Price saw a young lady and her boyfriend walk in and sit at the soda fountain. She was dressed as if she had just come from church, and Price says in his interview with Voll, "I instantly knew a whole story about her and who she was." This woman became the inspiration for one of Price's most memorable characters, Rosacoke Mustian. The unique and unforgettable first name was that of a fellow college student, Rosa Coke Boyle. Price, in "A Place to Stand," the preface to *A Singular Family: Rosacoke and Her Kin* (1999), wrote that he could not remember ever meeting Rosa Coke but knew of her through her sister.

The fictional Rosacoke and her family, Papa (her grandfather), brothers Milo and Rato, Baby Sister, and Mama, make their debut in "A Chain of Love," and their story is the subject of three later novels. The Mustians are quintessential rural North Carolinians; the type of people Price, an artistically inclined city boy who was tormented by his city peers, turned to in his adolescence for friendship. Their values, customs, mannerisms, and language are as old as the hills where they were born. In the art of Price, however, they are never "quaint." Their dignity is preserved at all times and in the few instances of comic behavior or circumstance, Price never allows them to appear ridiculous. The Mustians are not Ma and Pa Kettle or the Beverly Hillbillies.

"A Chain of Love" tells the story of a hospital stay. Papa is suffering from what his physician, Dr. Sledge, calls a "tired heart" ("Tired of what?" Papa asks). The family drives Papa to the hospital in Raleigh for tests, and Rosacoke and her younger brother, Rato, are delighted to set up residence in the hospital room. The older brother, Milo, is needed to run the family farm, and Mama is responsible for a Christmas pageant at church. Rosacoke fills the long stretches of time during her hospital vigil by thinking of her boyfriend, Wesley, whom she loves to distraction, and worrying about the patient in the room across the hall. This man and his family are fashioned after the Price family and their ordeal. Price, as a gesture of farewell to his father, has the character speak what was his father's last request, "Don't forget to give Jack Rowan one of those puppies." Elizabeth Price raised cocker spaniel puppies in the 1940s and Jack Rowan was her nephew. Will Price, near death, was recalling something he had wished to have done nearly a decade earlier.

Rosacoke's desires and fears are the focus of the story. She has a strong desire to be with her grandfather yet fears her absence from home will cause Wesley to be lured into the company of her rival for his affection, Willie Duke Aycock. Rosacoke also desires to extend the "chain of love" to include the patient across the hall and his family but fears that they will not understand her kindness and consider her an intruder during their private time of grief. Yet Rosacoke's virtue and innate goodness overcome what could have been paralyzing fears. She is not passive; her motivation is what Price has called "the ethic of the freely given gesture," the compelling desire to help someone else find happiness.

After receiving his BLitt from Oxford in 1958, Price returned to his younger brother and widowed mother in North Carolina and began his teaching career as an instructor at Duke. Near the

university, he found a small trailer-house that offered easy access to a pond, fields of broomstraw, and woods filled with deer, foxes, and birds. Here he began the arduous task of writing his first novel, the first of the Mustian trilogy, *A Long and Happy Life.* Although he maintained a full teaching schedule, two courses of freshman composition and one in English literature, he arranged these duties on a three-day cycle, thereby allowing three days for writing (he took Sundays off).

A Long and Happy Life, A Generous Man (1966), and *Good Hearts* (1988) chronicle the lives of the Mustians over a period of more than thirty years. The first in this trilogy tells the story of Rosacoke's and Wesley's difficult courtship, Rosacoke's decision to give Wesley what she thinks he wants and what she hopes will bind him to her, and the resulting pregnancy. From beginning to end, *A Long and Happy Life* is a novel about gifts and gift giving; the motivation of the giver often being misunderstood by the recipient. Rosacoke attempts to give a pair of stockings to her friend Mildred Sutton on her twenty-first birthday and to wish her "a long and happy life," only to find out that Mildred has died in childbirth. Mr. Isaac Alton doles out pieces of horehound candy to children, but with the mysterious question, "whose girl [or boy] are you?" Milo gives away his deceased child's clothing. Rato brings home a sack of Christmas gifts. The community searches for the perfect present for Mr. Alton. Rosacoke's gift to Wesley of her own body is perhaps the most problematic offering. Nature's gifts to Wesley of good looks and virile eroticism have taken possession of Rosacoke, though she fervently wishes they had not. She is smart enough to know that these physical attributes attract others, men as well as women. Wesley, in his cruelty, teases Rosacoke about his possible dalliances in Norfolk, Virginia, a few hundred miles away, where he makes his living selling motorcycles. Desperate to keep him in the only way she knows how, she gives herself to him in a field at night. Her gift is momentarily appreciated but the giver clearly is not. Wesley, in his postcoital euphoria, calls Rosacoke by another woman's name, "Mae." He seems unaware of his mistake and Rosacoke, true to her character, retreats into herself. However, another gift, the child that she conceived that night, reunites them.

In the Christmas pageant that concludes this novel, the gifts of the Magi are of some significance. Rosacoke, at the last minute, is called upon to stand in for an ill cast member as the Virgin Mary. Wesley plays the role of the third Wise Man. The two have communicated mostly by letter since the night of their lovemaking and Wesley, learning that Rosacoke is pregnant, has promised to do the right thing. It only remains for Rosacoke to accept or reject his offer of marriage. As he approaches her with the third wise man's gift, he sings the words of the carol "We Three Kings"—"Myrrh is mine, its bitter perfume / Breathes a life of gathering gloom." Rosacoke barely whispers her acceptance of this life to the child she holds in her role as Mary, as well as to the child who holds both her and Wesley. Will they enjoy the gift of a long and happy life? The ambiguous ending offers few clues. Price, however, hinted at an answer to this question in his preface to *A Singular Family: Rosacoke and Her Kin,* a collection of the Mustian stories: "I sat at my new worktable to write what I was already calling *A Long and Happy Life* (the title, though a common phrase, had volunteered some months before when I first saw the film *Bridge on the River Kwai* and heard William Holden wish it for a young soldier doomed to swift destruction)."

Price's debut novel was published by Atheneum in March 1962; *Harper's* magazine printed it in its entirety in its April 1962 issue. The dust jacket on the first edition contained prepublication praise from authors on both sides of the Atlantic: Eudora Welty, Harper Lee, Lord David Cecil, and Sir Stephen Spender. Reviews of the book were, for the most part, positive. One of

Price's earliest and strongest supporters and promoters, the critic Granville Hicks, wrote in *Saturday Review* that the novel was "a love story, and one of the simplest and most poignant I have ever read," and that "to have created Rosacoke Mustian is an achievement that the most mature novelist might envy." Dorothy Parker wrote in *Esquire,* "Meticulously observed, beautifully told, it strikes too deep to fuss around with analysis. You can say only of it that it is indeed a lasting novel . . . a lovely novel." Some reviewers, however, found Price to be nothing more than a Faulkner imitator whose writing was overstylized and artificial. Indeed, Jason Epstein threatened to resign from Random House if the company published the book. In spite of the few negative reactions, the novel won the Sir Walter Raleigh Award and the William Faulkner Award. The Faulkner Award was a mixed blessing in that it fed the perception of Price as a mere imitator ("Faulkner Lite," so to speak). It would take Price nearly two decades to rid himself of that criticism, and to show that it was the Bible, Tolstoy, Milton, Welty, and more importantly his own family and friends that were his true primary influences.

Between the publication of his first novel and his second, Price published a collection of short stories. *The Names and Faces of Heroes* (1963) contained "Michael Egerton," "A Chain of Love," and five others. The collection further identified Price as a new voice of the easily accessible, romantic, southern pastoral tradition. His next novel would shatter that identity. *A Generous Man* is a complex novel that works on many levels: mythical and spiritual, concrete and supernatural. The events occur several years before those in *A Long and Happy Life* and "A Chain of Love." Milo Mustian is fifteen and, at the beginning of the novel, has just been initiated into the mysteries of manhood by Lois Provo. Lois and her aunt, Selma, are members of a traveling carnival, the exhibitors of a monstrous python named Death. Rato, Milo's younger brother, has disappeared and it is suspected that he is searching for his runaway dog, Phillip. Milo, feeling very much the hero with his newly acquired sense of virility and desirability, takes on the quest of finding Rato and returning him safely home, subduing Death, who has escaped, and coming to the aid of the fair maiden, Lois. He feels that there is nothing he can't do for himself and for others. However, the stamina necessary for his forty-eight-hour adventure as a knight-errant, including an encounter with the ghost of Lois's father, Tommy, cannot be sustained. Milo learns early the limits of male potency and, disappointingly, chooses a safe and predictable life on the family farm.

It would be twenty years before Price took up the story of the Mustians again. Despite some high comic occurrences, *A Generous Man* is a dark and troubling work that forecast the tone of Price's next novel.

MAN OF LETTERS

Love and Work (1968) is a departure from Price's former characters and locales. The setting, Fenton, is Anytown, USA. Nature, in the form of woods, trees, and wildlife, so important in Price's previous work, is ignored here; most of the narrative's action takes place indoors. In addition, the two main characters lack the unusual, almost Dickensian, quality of Price's prior fictional names: Rosacoke, Rato, and Milo give way here to Tom and Jane. The story itself is an obviously autobiographical study of Price's coming to grips with the demands of his life as an educator and writer and the loss of his parental generation (Price's mother died in 1967). The novel, considered by some critics to be inaccessible and over-written, was not well received.

A collection of short stories and other pieces written over a period of seven years, *Permanent Errors* (1970) expands upon the same themes as *Love and Work,* though the locales are as varied as Oxford, England, and an Indian reservation in the southwestern United States. In his preface to the collection, Price explains his intention: "The attempt to isolate in a number of lives the central error of act, will, understanding which, once made, has been permanent, incurable, but whose diagnosis and palliation are the hopes of continuance." These are stories of loss and failure and the demands and compensations of art.

After three novels and two collections of short stories, Price brought his readers into his classroom by means of his sixth book, *Things Themselves: Essays and Scenes* (1972). The book marked Price's twentieth anniversary as a writer and the tenth anniversary of the publication of his first novel. He writes in the preface, "During those years, like most novelists, I have written a number of things other than fiction—critical and personal essays, scenes, poems, translations, lectures, reviews, articles—and this book is a drastic selection from those things (a good deal more than this much is omitted)." In other words, this is a collection of what a novelist writes when his muse of fiction is on leave. The publication of this book, and his promotion to full professor at Duke in 1972, added a new dimension to Price's reputation, that of a multifaceted man of letters.

Price's next novel, *The Surface of Earth* (1975), sparked immediate controversy. Richard Gilman, writing for *The New York Times Book Review* in June 1975, described the work as a "great archaic beast" and went on to dismiss Price as being "anachronistic." In the war of words that erupted upon publication of this review, Eudora Welty leaped to the battlements with a strong letter to the editor defending Price, his novel, and southern literature in general.

Price returned to his native soil in this book. The setting is rural North Carolina and Virginia and covers a time span from 1903 to the period just before America's entrance into World War II.

The lives, loves, and losses of multiple generations of the Mayfield and Kendall families are chronicled, but the focus is on the often erotic physical intimacy between fathers and sons. This work is the first installment in what Price called his "Great Circle" trilogy. The Mayfield–Kendall story continued in *The Source of Light* (1981) and reached its climax in *The Promise of Rest* (1995).

In 1977 Price published his first play, *Early Dark*. Although he claimed otherwise in his preface, this drama is essentially a retelling of the story of *A Long and Happy Life*. There is, however, a shift in blame for the situation Wesley and Rosacoke find themselves accepting at the end of the novel. *Early Dark* presents more of Wesley's side of the story; Rosacoke is exposed as a woman living in a dream world, with unrealistic expectations of people and life. The year 1977 was also when Price was named James B. Duke Professor of English at Duke University.

A Palpable God: Thirty Stories Translated from the Bible with an Essay on the Origins and Life of Narrative (1978) is a collection of Price's translations from the Old and New Testaments. The book began as notes for what was to become *The Surface of Earth,* in which the Old Testament stories of Abraham and Isaac and Jephthah and his daughter play significant roles. Price disclosed in his preface that he began these translations at a time of difficulty and questioning. He wondered, at the age of thirty-five, if he could continue writing, and why he had started in the first place. To find the answers to these concerns, he turned to the long-standing narratives of the Bible. Price, with no knowledge of Hebrew and only a little Greek, used literal interlinear translations and Jerome's Latin Vulgate to strip off the glossy veneer of current translations and expose the solid wood of the plain, powerful narratives. The book was well received by the public and by biblical scholars. Anthony Burgess, in particular, stated that the introductory essay should be required reading for students of creative writing. The book was nominated for the National Book Award for translation, which furthered Price's reputation as a scholar.

The Source of Light (1981), part two of Price's trilogy, is considered by some to be Price's "Oxford" novel. The settings for much of the story are European: England, Wales, Italy, and the Isles of Scilly, and it is dedicated to his Oxford friends and teachers David Cecil and Stephen Spender. The wide focus of Price's previous novel is narrowed to examine the father/son relationship of Rob and Hutch Mayfield. This is perhaps Price's most autobiographical work and, indeed, his boldest portrayal of the many varieties of human sexuality. Readers with even the slightest knowledge of Price's life recognized parallels. Unaware that his father is dying, twenty-five-year-old Hutch leaves home to study abroad. While at Oxford, writing his thesis on Andrew Marvell and questioning his own worth as a poet, Hutch is recalled to his North Carolina home by news of his father's impending death. He leaves behind several attractive men with whom he has enjoyed sexual liaisons and his supposed fiancée, Ann Gatlin. Rob's death is rendered in some of Price's most beautiful prose. It is as if Rob were being born into death; indeed, the novel spans the human gestational period of nine months. Hutch feels, as Price did at his own father's death, that with his father's absence, he has, finally, room to grow into himself. What his future holds, however, is veiled in ambiguity at the novel's end.

The Source of Light contains a beautiful poem Hutch wrote for his deceased father. It was the first example of Price's remarkable abilities as a poet that was published for a wide readership. Although he had been writing poetry since before high school, Price's poems were unknown by the general reader. They had appeared in scholarly journals and in beautifully bound limited editions that were given by Price as Christmas presents. In 1982 fifty of Price's poems were collected and published in *Vital Provisions*. Most of the poems are narrative, as might be expected from a novelist and short story writer, and the subjects range from Robert E. Lee to Robert Frost, Jesus Christ to Leontyne Price. Perhaps Price's best poem is the last one in this collection, "The Annual Heron." In this work, the poet spies a heron through his window on a cold morning in late December. The heron has stopped on its annual migration for the past ten years to feed at the poet's pond.

His tenth year with me—the fish or me.
I know because when I saw him first,
I wrote him down in my first novel
Which was ending then. He still stands
There, page 169, proffered oasis
For a couple too gorged on mutual
Misery to take his option—consolation *in situ*
Or an emblem of flight, contented self-service.

The pond freezes and the heron is unable to feed. The poet thaws a trout and slides it across the ice to the bird, but the bird will not eat with him watching. Next morning, the poet goes out, after coffee, to see whether or not the bird has partaken of the meal. He finds dog tracks and heron feathers. Eleven months later, the heron returns. The poet knows it is the same bird, recognizing a knot on its right knee. The bird seems "possessed of new / Grace since his nocturnal skirmish with / The local dingoes." After watching the heron rise and fly away, "trailing legs like crutches," the poet returns home.

I climb to the otherwise
Empty house and make for myself
An oracle from his mute persistence
Through volumes of air, corrosive years—
Endurance is fed: here, in time.
Therefore endure. Then make another—
You hope in vain. The heart is fed
Only where I go when I leave you here.
Follow me.

Henry Taylor, in a mixed review of *Vital Provisions* for the *Washington Times* in February 1983, wrote,

Not . . . all 50 of these poems are successful. A few of the more personal recollections of erotic encounters are slightly embarrassing, not merely because of the subject matter, but because the experiences recounted have not had lavished upon them the full resources of the poetic art; they seem too much like private notes, with too little attention paid to the over-hearers. The bulk of the book, however, made up of longer poems recounting dreams, tense episodes in friendships, and even the life of Christ, are compelling and unobtrusively skillful.

In 1984 Price was commissioned to write a television play for the premiere season of PBS's *American Playhouse.* The play, *Private Contentment,* is the story of a young man who is about to be sent overseas in 1945 when, after attending his mother's funeral, he discovers a family secret regarding his father. The show starred Kathryn Walker, the wife of the singer and songwriter James Taylor, who wrote the score for the production. Price and Taylor later collaborated on such songs as "New Hymn" (written to commemorate the retirement of Taylor's longtime friend Paul Moore, Episcopal bishop of New York City from 1972 to 1989), and "Copperline," which they wrote in 1991 when Price was staying at Taylor's home in Connecticut.

CANCER

In the late spring of 1984 Price began to experience difficulty walking. He entered Duke Hospital on May 31 of that year, the day of a total eclipse of the sun. As Price told S. D. Williams in a 1987 interview, "Certainly no ancient Roman would have gone in under such terrible omens." Tests revealed a ten-inch astrocytoma, a cancerous tumor, wrapped in the core of his spinal cord. His first surgery failed to remove more than 10 percent of the cancer. Five and a half weeks of radiation followed. Three weeks into the treatment, Price began to lose the use of his legs and by September he was a paraplegic. His doctors' prognosis was bleak: eventual quadriplegia followed by death within five weeks. Price returned home to die. In the weeks that followed, his pain became unbearable and medication was prescribed in ever increasing doses. Writing was impossible and he turned to his earliest form of artistic expression, drawing.

In November 1984 Hendrix College in Conway, Arkansas, contacted Price asking him to write a play. Price recalled his feelings at the time to Michael Ruhlman: "I just sort of took that as a tap on the shoulder from the Holy Spirit, and I told them, 'O. K., I'll do it. But here's the danger. I might not live to finish the play.' " Not only did he finish the work, *August Snow,* he completed two other plays that winter. *New Music: A Trilogy,* published in 1990, includes *August Snow, Night Dance,* and *Better Days.* Together they tell the story of two generations of the Avery family in rural North Carolina.

This burst of creativity encouraged Price to return to a novel that he had put aside on the day he entered the hospital, *Kate Vaiden* (1986). In a 1986 interview with Wendy Smith of the *Chicago Sun-Times,* Price explained the genesis of the novel.

Kate Vaiden began because I had become fascinated with lots of questions about the life of my mother. I wanted to write about the way in which a woman from her part of the world would have the kind of life that in some ways my mother was qualified for. I think Mother would have loved to have a great deal more independence than she wound up having in her life.

As I worked with the idea of that kind of woman, it just became inevitable that I was going to have to speak, or want to speak, in the first person, which was a form I had never used before in a novel. I gave Kate essentially my own generation, though, because I didn't want to do a lot of research into the social reality of my mother's early life. Once I knew when she was born and what her name was, it proceeded very smoothly. I simply had to do each day a quick metamorphosis into being another person of another gender.

It was great fun; I was going through a lot of trouble with this spinal tumor, and it made it much easier for me each day to just go into a room and become somebody else for a good part of the day.

Fifty-seven-year-old Kate tells her life story in this novel as a means of rehearsing what she may tell the son she abandoned nearly forty years before and whom she has recently found. Most of the narrative focuses on Kate's adolescent years, from the time of her parents' murder/suicide when she was eleven to just before she turns eighteen. The orphaned Kate develops a belief that it is necessary to one's survival to "leave people before they can plan to leave you." This personal creed allows Kate to depart from towns and people at will whenever they become too comfortable and seemingly permanent. She abandons her illegitimate son soon after his birth and at that point abandons herself and the world. "My life stopped there, my old life as Kate, a girl people thought they knew and could lean on." The novel then shifts to the present. Kate, who has just returned from a tour of Rome and the Vatican, has been diagnosed with cervical cancer and is given five years to live. This prognosis, coupled with a revelation of the possibility of repentance she experienced while viewing the bones of Saint Peter, the "biggest quitter in human history," urges Kate into action. She determines to find her son and tell him her story.

Kate Vaiden was hailed by critics and the reading public as a welcome return of the voice first heard in *A Long and Happy Life;* a voice, many felt, that was lacking in Price's recent works. It won the National Book Critics Circle Award.

During the period of writing *Kate Vaiden,* Price endured two further surgeries. Although the cancer was finally completely removed, it left Price a paraplegic. However, with physical therapy, he was able to return to a fairly normal life.

The success of *Kate Vaiden* was followed by Price's second book of poetry, *The Laws of Ice* (1986) and *A Common Room: Essays, 1954–1987*

(1987). Central to the poetry collection is the sequence "Days and Nights: A Journal," which chronicles Price's bout with cancer. The fifty-seven essays gathered in *A Common Room* are broadly diverse but are clearly the work of a single vision. The subjects range from Jesus to Hemingway, Milton to southern cooking, and a proposal to correct the failure of male/female relations.

Price illustrates the cost of such failure in *Good Hearts.* The popularity of Rosacoke and Wesley's story had not waned in the twenty-eight years since the publication of *A Long and Happy Life.* Price was often asked about these characters at readings and on book tours. Initially, he felt that their story had ended. He says in his book *A Whole New Life* (1994), "I'd occasionally wondered if her and her husband's ongoing lives were interesting enough for another look; but I always concluded they were sadly becalmed in normal existence." He chose, however, to take up their story again as a means of demonstrating the deadly effect of what he calls "benign neglect" in marriage. Wesley and Rosacoke (now Rosa) are middle-aged and drifting apart. Indeed, Wesley, who has displayed a tendency to take his wife for granted, even to the point of mysteriously disappearing from home for a few days at a time, has abandoned Rosa and moved in with a younger woman in another state. In his absence, Rosa is raped by a character named Wave, the personification of the evil that Price suggests can easily enter into and destroy the lives and hearts of those who are not vigilant.

Perhaps it was this return to his early work that inspired Price to write a memoir, *Clear Pictures.* Price had said, in *A Whole New Life,* that the book was the result of memories of his childhood brought to mind in great detail by hypnosis and biofeedback. Price had undertaken both treatments to alleviate the pain of his recent surgeries. *Clear Pictures* is a vivid portrait of a gifted boy growing up in the South during the 1930s, 1940s, and 1950s. Homage is paid to all those who influenced and shaped his life, most notably his parents but also teachers, friends, and household servants. The book was well received both by critics and Price's ever increasing readership.

Price followed his own coming-of-age story with a coming-of-age novel, *The Tongues of Angels* (1990). Again, as in *Kate Vaiden,* Price makes use of first-person narration. The story is told by Bridge Boatner, a successful fifty-four-year-old representational landscape painter, who is recalling the summer of his twenty-first year, the year of his first important painting, *The Smoky Mountains As the Meaning of Things.* Boatner, whose father had recently died, spent the summer as a counselor at Camp Juniper, a boys' camp in North Carolina. In that time of self-discovery, Boatner formed an intense relationship with an angelic, almost Christ-like, fourteen-year-old camper, Rafe Noren. Rafe was a gifted dancer whose art Boatner recognized as a connection with the divine. Price, through Boatner, expounds upon his belief that the life of art, of careful observation and creation, puts one in touch with the secrets of God and is ultimately rewarding and healing. Artists, whether they are painters, dancers, musicians, or authors, are messengers (angels) in the service of holy mysteries. Boatner reappears in Price's short story "An Early Christmas."

Throughout the 1990s, Price maintained a pattern of publication that began early in his career, a pattern of alternating forms of written expression. *The Tongues of Angels* was followed by a collection of poems, *The Use of Fire* (1990), the three plays of *New Music,* and a trilogy of novellas, *The Foreseeable Future* (1991). His next novel, *Blue Calhoun* (1992) is similar to *Kate Vaiden.* Both are eponymous, first-person narratives that consist of personal letters of explanation to a young family member. Blue tells his story, however, in one continuous epistle, 373 pages long. Some critics who were unfamiliar with the loquaciousness characteristic of southern discourse found Blue's enterprise less than credible. The reading public embraced the novel and its narrator, however, and, at the turn of the twenty-first century, it remained Price's best-selling book. Price frequently referred to it as his favorite, although perhaps not his best, novel.

In 1993 Price published *Full Moon and Other Plays.* That same year, *The Collected Stories* was released, nearly forty years after Price's first serious attempt at the short story form, "Michael Egerton." The book contains the works from his first two short story collections in addition to new material. The later stories came about, Price is quoted as saying in a review by George Garrett, as the result of an incentive program he established for students in his writing course. "The hardest thing for young writers to figure out," Price explained, "is how a professional writes a story. So I told them that whenever you hand in an assignment, I'll hand in one. Once I was able to persuade them that I wasn't one of the world's most sensitive men they seemed to find it useful—and I got some very good criticism." Ron Carlson, writing for *Southern Review,* stated, "*The Collected Stories* of Reynolds Price . . . will exist somewhere as a thread in the fabric of twentieth-century American literature." The collection was nominated for a Pulitzer Prize in April 1993.

BOOKS OF RECOVERY AND HEALING

During the years of struggle with his cancer, Price sought a book that could help him better understand what was happening to his body and how to cope with the painful changes that were to come. Believing that such a book did not exist and knowing that he was certainly not the only person who could benefit from it, Price set out to write the remarkable *A Whole New Life.* In this book, Price recounts his harrowing ordeal in minute detail without bravura, self-pity, sentimentality, or anger. Central to his belief that God cured him, by means of skilled surgeons and the recent invention of the laser scalpel, is a pair of startling

visions that came to Price soon after the first surgery failed to remove the entire cancerous growth. In the first vision, Price saw a small gathering of men standing by the shore of a sea or lake. The central figure in this group is clearly Jesus, who motioned Price toward the water. There he bathed Price's raw incision and said, "Your sins are forgiven." As Jesus turned to join his companions, Price called out to him, "Am I also cured?" Jesus replied, "That too." The other vision occurred some time later, when Price was faced with the worst of his pain and despair. He cried out into the darkness of his room asking how much more suffering was to come. He heard a voice reply very clearly: "More."

In addition to his story of recovery, Price included a chapter for those facing circumstances similar to his and a three-page essay on medical ethics. Far from being yet another self-help book created for a specific audience, *A Whole New Life* is indeed a book for everyone, since everyone will eventually have to confront loss, devastation, and dying.

In 1995 Price completed his Mayfield–Kendall trilogy, the so-called "Great Circle," with the publication of *The Promise of Rest.* Hutch, who was twenty-five at the end of *The Source of Light,* is now sixty-two. Like Price, Hutch has returned home from his studies in England and is a professor at Duke University. In the novel's opening scene, Hutch is reading to his class from the works of John Milton, specifically Milton's elegiac "Lycidas." The role of poetry as a healing agent is strongly presented throughout this book, which includes many examples of English verse. Indeed, the remaining members of the Mayfield family sorely need healing. Hutch is estranged from his wife and his son is dying of AIDS.

Throughout the massive undertaking of this trilogy, every pregnant woman dies in childbirth or is put through some living horror. Every father has ambiguous physical desires. Every son seeks his lost father in homosexual liaisons. As if these topics were not compelling enough, Price also addressed the devastation of AIDS and racism. However, the overriding theme in the three novels is love. Love as a blessing and a curse, a rescuer and a killer; love as it is manifested in diverse couplings and the individual self. Love in all its complexity is depicted; it is not always a pretty picture.

Price, who was well aware of the healing and sustaining power of Scripture, returned to the problem of translating the ancient texts in a way that would re-create the "feel" of living in those times and hearing those words when they were first spoken. *Three Gospels* (1996), includes a reworking of his translation of the Gospel of Mark first published in *A Palpable God,* a new translation of the Gospel of John, and Price's own attempt at the story of Christ, "An Honest Account of a Memorable Life."

The Collected Poems, published in 1997, contains Price's three previous books of poetry plus *The Unaccountable Worth of the World,* which consists of new and uncollected poems. The new material is presented in the same strong narrative voice that was lauded by critics of his earlier work. Noteworthy is the preface, in which Price writes about his introduction to poetry and those poets who personally encouraged him to pursue that form of literary expression: Robert Frost, W. H. Auden, and Stephen Spender. He makes mention, also, of a book he was urged to read in his sophomore year at Duke, *Poetry As a Means of Grace* by Charles Grosvenor Osgood. Osgood's essays, especially his essay on John Milton, revealed to Price the healing nature of a life devoted to poetry.

Near the close of the twentieth century, Price published a novel that tells the story of a woman who lived to see most of it. *Roxanna Slade* (1998) is a chronicle of what the narrator, Roxanna herself, considers an uneventful life. Ninety-two-year-old Roxanna's story begins on an outing that took place on her twentieth birthday. Within three

hours, she meets the love of her life, Larkin Slade, becomes engaged to him, and, almost unbelievably, witnesses his death by drowning. She later marries Larkin's brother, Palmer, gives birth to their children and endures her husband's infidelities. Despite these and other soul-shocking events and a long spell of deep depression, Roxanna's story is ultimately a celebration of the extraordinary blessings to be found in the ordinary life.

Forty-two years of journal entries, from Price's early searches for story and poem ideas through his thoughts on his eleventh novel, *Roxanna Slade,* are presented in *Learning a Trade,* published in 1998. Some entries are richly detailed, covering two or three pages; others are quite simple observations, such as the entry for January 1, 1960: "I saw 2 cardinals today." Price's consistent advice to would-be writers, as he wrote in "Letter to a Young Writer," published in *A Common Room,* has been, "If you can stop, you probably should." For those who feel that they have no choice but to continue on in the writing trade, this book gives an over-the-shoulder look at Price's creative process. It is an opportunity to see how ink became the lifeblood of his characters.

In April 1997 Price received a letter from a young medical student who had read *A Whole New Life.* The student, Jim Fox, had recently learned that he had cancer of the liver and colon, and he wrote to Price questioning God's existence and seeming lack of concern for human suffering. Price initially responded by telephone and e-mail but felt that his answers were inadequate. He used the opportunity of being invited to give the Rudin Lecture at Auburn Theological Seminary in New York to expand his thoughts. Price's first draft of his letter to Mr. Fox was presented at Auburn Seminary on November 3, 1997. Further additions were made and the final draft was published as *Letter to a Man in the Fire: Does God Exist and Does He Care?* in 1999. In this slim volume of meditations and personal testimony, Price gave a resounding yes to both questions. However, his frustration and disappointment in trying to express in words a truth that can only be known in the language of the heart and soul is evident. Although Price made many attempts to contact him, Mr. Fox never saw the letter. The dedication reads: For Jim Fox, 1962–1998.

LIFE IN THE NEW CENTURY

In the year 2000, Reynolds Price still lived in the home he had moved into nearly forty years earlier. The ground floor of the two-story structure was adapted and expanded to accommodate Price's wheelchair and the growth of his eclectic collection of artifacts. The home is just outside of Durham, not far from the Duke campus, in piney woods, overlooking a pond. Natural beauty, found in most of Price's prose and poetry, abounds. With the help of a hired assistant, usually a Duke student, Price enjoyed a fairly self-sufficient and active life.

In an editor's note accompanying "Jesus of Nazareth, Then and Now," an article written by Price and published in the December 6, 1999, issue of *Time* magazine, a forthcoming novel for children was mentioned. In response to a written query regarding this curiosity, his first book for children, Price sent the following note:

The children's book is a novel called *A Perfect Friend*. It's about a boy aged eleven whose mother died a year ago. His name is Ben Barks; and he lives out from town with his father, a kindly man who drinks a little on the weekends. Since early childhood, Ben has been fascinated by elephants but has only seen them at a distance in a single visit to a circus. During the time covered by my story, a small circus visits his town for several days, and Ben develops a deeply rewarding intimacy with one particular elephant. That piece of luck goes a long way toward repairing the damage of his mother's absence. The book will have a beautiful jacket drawing, especially provided by Maurice Sendak. Now I've begun work on another novel—one for adults: it would be my dozenth.
Good luck,
RP

Selected Bibliography

WORKS OF REYNOLDS PRICE

NOVELS
A Long and Happy Life. New York: Atheneum, 1962.
A Generous Man. New York: Atheneum, 1966.
Love and Work. New York: Atheneum, 1968.
The Surface of Earth. New York: Atheneum, 1975.
The Source of Light. New York: Atheneum, 1981.
Mustian: Two Novels and a Story. New York: Atheneum, 1983. (Contains *A Long and Happy Life, A Generous Man,* and "A Chain of Love.")
Kate Vaiden. New York: Atheneum, 1986.
Good Hearts. New York: Atheneum, 1988.
The Tongues of Angels. New York: Atheneum, 1990.
Blue Calhoun. New York: Atheneum, 1992.
The Promise of Rest. New York: Scribner, 1995.
Roxanna Slade. New York: Scribner, 1998.
A Singular Family: Rosacoke and Her Kin. New York: Scribner, 1999. (Contains *A Generous Man,* "A Chain of Love," *A Long and Happy Life,* and *Good Hearts.*)

SHORT STORY COLLECTIONS
The Names and Faces of Heroes. New York: Atheneum, 1963.
Permanent Errors. New York: Atheneum, 1970.
The Foreseeable Future. New York: Atheneum, 1991.
The Collected Stories. New York: Atheneum, 1993.

POETRY COLLECTIONS
Vital Provisions. New York: Atheneum, 1982.
The Laws of Ice. New York: Atheneum, 1986.
The Use of Fire. New York: Atheneum, 1990.
The Collected Poems. New York: Scribner, 1997.

ESSAY COLLECTIONS

Things Themselves: Essays and Scenes. New York: Atheneum, 1972.

A Common Room: Essays 1954–1987. New York: Atheneum, 1987.

MEMOIRS

Clear Pictures: First Loves, First Guides. New York: Atheneum, 1989.

A Whole New Life. New York: Atheneum, 1994.

OTHER NONFICTION

Learning a Trade: A Craftsman's Notebooks, 1955–1997. Durham, N.C.: Duke University Press, 1998.

Letter to a Man in the Fire: Does God Exist and Does He Care? New York: Scribner, 1999.

PLAYS

Early Dark. New York: Atheneum, 1977.

Private Contentment. New York: Atheneum, 1984.

New Music: A Trilogy. New York: Theatre Communications Group, 1990.

Full Moon and Other Plays. New York: Theatre Communications Group, 1993.

TRANSLATIONS

A Palpable God: Thirty Stories Translated from the Bible with an Essay on the Origins and Life of Narrative. New York: Atheneum, 1978.

Three Gospels: The Good News According to Mark, The Good News According to John, An Honest Account of a Memorable Life. New York: Scribner, 1996.

BIBLIOGRAPHY

Wright, Stuart, and James L. W. West III. *Reynolds Price: A Bibliography 1949–1984.* Charlottesville: University Press of Virginia, 1986.

CRITICAL AND BIOGRAPHICAL STUDIES

Burgess, Anthony. "Good Books." *New York Times Book Review,* March 12, 1978, pp. 14–15, 22.

Carlson, Ron. "The Collected Stories of Reynolds Price." *Southern Review* 30, no. 2:371–378 (April 1994).

Garrett, George. "Here Is Heartbreak, and Here Is Laughter," *New York Times Book Review,* July 4, 1993, p. 8.

Gilman, Richard. "A Mastodon of a Novel by Reynolds Price." *New York Times Book Review,* June 29, 1975, pp. 1–2

Hicks, Granville. "Country Girl Burdened with Love." *Saturday Review* 45:17 (March 10, 1962).

Kimball, Sue Leslie, and Lynn Veach Sadler, eds. *Reynolds Price: From "A Long and Happy Life" to "Good Hearts."* Fayetteville, N.C.: Methodist College Press, 1989. (Includes bibliography.)

Parker, Dorothy. "Six Collections of Stories and a Lovely Novel." *Esquire* 57:67 (June 1962).

Rooke, Constance. *Reynolds Price.* Boston: Twayne, 1983.

Schiff, James A. *Understanding Reynolds Price.* Columbia: University of South Carolina Press, 1996.

———, ed. *Critical Essays on Reynolds Price.* Boston: G. K. Hall, 1998.

Taylor, Henry. "Price's New Volume of 50 Earns Him His Poet's Spurs." *Washington Times,* February 1, 1983, sec. D, pp. 3, 16.

Tyler, Anne. "Reynolds Price: Duke of Writers." *Vanity Fair* 49, no. 7:82–85 (July 1986).

Welty, Eudora. Letters to the Editor. *New York Times Book Review,* July 20, 1975, pp. 24–25.

INTERVIEWS

Baker, Charles R. Letter to Charles R. Baker from Reynolds Price, January 11, 2000.

Busch, Frederick. "Reynolds Price: The Art of Fiction CXXVII." *Paris Review* 121:150–179 (winter 1991).

Humphries, Jefferson, ed. *Conversations with Reynolds Price.* Jackson: University Press of Mississippi, 1991. (Collected interviews.)

Kaufman, Wallace. "Notice, I'm Still Smiling: Reynolds Price." *Shenandoah* 17, no. 4:70–95 (summer 1966).

Ruhlman, Michael. "A Writer at His Best." *New York Times Magazine,* September 20, 1987, p. 134.

Smith, Wendy. "Staying Power of Reynolds Price." *Chicago Sun-Times,* August 24, 1986, p. 25.

Voll, Daniel. "The Spy That Stayed: A Conversation

with Reynolds Price." *Tobacco Road,* April 1983, pp. 4–6.

Williams, S. D. "Reynolds Price on the South, Literature, and Himself." *Leader Magazine,* June 4, 1987, pp. 4–6.

FILMS ABOUT REYNOLDS PRICE

Clear Pictures. Directed by Charles Guggenheim. Direct Cinema, 1994.

Reynolds Price: A Writer's Inheritance. Directed by Marcia Rock. New York University Journalism Department, 1990.

The Roots of Solitude: The Life and Work of Reynolds Price. Carolina Video, 1992.

—*CHARLES R. BAKER*

Muriel Rukeyser

1913–1980

"WE ARE POETS; we can make the words. . . . For the question is asked in a thousand ways each day: Is poetry alive? Is there a place for poetry? What is that place?" No words serve as a better introduction to Muriel Rukeyser, one of the most prolific and complex poets of the twentieth century, than these from her *The Life of Poetry* (1949). Although she wrote in diverse genres, including biography, autobiography, the essay, and drama, poetry was her principal expressive medium. Eclectic and visionary, Rukeyser sought throughout her long career not only to affirm the "life of poetry" but also to define and secure its place in the modern world. Addressing the complications and suffering of life in the twentieth century, she spoke out against repression of all kinds while affirming the traditional role of the poet to speak for those who cannot speak for themselves. At the same time, she performed out of a complicated aesthetic vision that only began to receive the full appreciation that it merits at the end of the twentieth century. Her confidence in the healing powers of poetry and in poetry's ability to bring together people, ideas, and feelings emerge repeatedly in her writing.

"THE MOTHER OF EVERYONE": BIOGRAPHICAL CONTEXTS

Perhaps the most famous image of Muriel Rukeyser is the 1975 photograph in which she stands outside the gates of the prison where South Korean poet Kim Chi-ha, who was condemned to death for his criticism of the government, was being held. When the Korean authorities refused to let her see her fellow poet, Rukeyser staged an impromptu protest that became a familiar symbol for activist writers. Looking very small but very straight in the center of the photograph, Rukeyser stands between a door and a larger set of gates with a decorative wrought iron motif at the top. These gates inspired her last major poem, the title poem of her 1976 book *The Gates*. In spite of poor health, Rukeyser went to Korea as the president (1975–1976) of the PEN American Center, an international writers' organization that supports the freedom of and free speech for writers around the world. This action is emblematic of Rukeyser's lifelong commitment to activism and social justice.

Muriel Rukeyser was born in New York City on December 15, 1913, to Lawrence B. and Myra Lyons Rukeyser. Her father, about whom she writes in "Sand-Quarry with Moving Figures," cofounded Colonial Sand and Stone and was a builder and engineer who inspired the poet's interest in science, an interest that would emerge in poems ranging from "The Gyroscope" (1935) to "The Conjugation of the Paramecium" (1968). Her mother appears to have lived a fairly conventional life for a woman of her era. Rukeyser's family life seems to have been marked by a measure of detachment on the part of her parents; her father ultimately rejected her for her unconventional life and political beliefs. "Four in a Family" records the alienation typical among family members in the modern era. "Poem out of Childhood" juxtaposes Rukeyser's observations of being born in a time of war and growing up in an atmosphere with low expectations for women; it also records the poet's affirmation to be something larger: " 'Oh, and you,' he said, scraping his jaw, 'what will you be?' / 'Maybe : something : like : Joan : of : Arc.' "

Rukeyser attended Vassar College and in the summers of 1931 and 1932, Columbia University. From another perspective, however, she educated herself. When nine black men were imprisoned in Scottsboro, Alabama, for allegedly raping two white women in the spring of 1931, Rukeyser traveled south to cover the trial for the leftist *Student Review* and was arrested when police found her talking about the situation with black reporters. As her solitary support of Kim Chi-ha indicates, her profound commitment to social justice and peace continued throughout her life; she was arrested again in 1972 for protesting against the Vietnam War.

Shortly after leaving Vassar and Columbia, Rukeyser attended the Roosevelt School of Aviation in New York City, while working on her first book, *Theory of Flight,* which won the 1935 Yale Series of Younger Poets competition. Only twenty-one when she received this major award, Rukeyser throughout her career attracted a peculiar combination of critical praise and disparagement. In 1935 she became involved with the theater; she worked for the Theatre Union and Garrison Films, writing titles and commentaries for foreign films and learning film editing. This experience strongly influenced the cinematic structures of her poems.

In 1936, Rukeyser traveled to England and Spain. She also went to Gauley Bridge, West Virginia, to survey a Union Carbide mining disaster.

Workers digging a hydroelectric tunnel hit a vein of valuable silica ore, whose dust causes silicosis, an incurable lung disease. The company did nothing to protect its mostly black workers and denied charges of corruption and conspiracy, It also refused to pay the workers' staggering health care costs and the claims of miners' widows for compensation. Rukeyser's series of poems "The Book of the Dead" in the first half of her second book, *U.S. 1* (1938), unforgettably documents this tragedy. In 1938 she also published a translation of Erika Mann's *School for Barbarians,* a volume about German education.

The next year saw the publication of a third book of poems, *A Turning Wind,* which contains a complex sequence, "Elegies." The book was completed in September 1939, when Germany overran Poland and England and France entered the war against Germany. Although "Elegies"—which she continued in her next volume, *Beast in View* (1944)—reflects the grim and fragmented tenor of the times, it also reveals glimpses of Rukeyser's characteristic optimism and her sense of responsibility for revealing truth and fostering change. Critical opinion of "Elegies" was widely divided, with some critics praising its aesthetic and philosophical power and others criticizing the poet for obscurity and frequent abstraction.

Rukeyser's work is characterized by complicated and apparently conflicting methods and structures that were unified in her own poetic vision but rarely well understood in her own time. This misunderstanding is ironic, given Rukeyser's own brilliant literary criticism, among the most perspicacious of her time, as shown in her assessment of Walt Whitman's reception: "He speaks of himself as ill-assorted, contradictory. His readers reacted violently from the beginning to his writing about sex—and of course it is not writing *about* sex, it is that physical rhythms are the base of every clear line, and that the avowals and the secrecy are both part of the life of a person who is, himself, a battleground of forces."

A Turning Wind also contains a cluster of Rukeyser's earliest biographical work, including the poems "Gibbs," "Ryder," "Chapman," and "Ives." Continuing this interest, Rukeyser next published the biographical poem *The Soul and Body of John Brown* (1940), which she would also include in *Beast in View,* along with her ninety-four line "Wake Island" (published in 1942 as a fifty-cent pamphlet). In 1942 she also published her lyrical biography *Willard Gibbs,* about one of the greatest scientists of the nineteenth century; considered the father of American physics, the Yale-educated Gibbs (1839–1903) received one of the first doctorates in engineering in the United States. As Louise Kertesz points out in *The Poetic Vision of Muriel Rukeyser* (1980), "Gibbs's work on the changing phases of matter gave the poet 'a language of transformation,' which she translated into poetic language and apprehended as humanly significant. . . . Thus in writing the biography of Gibbs that she needed to read, she created a source of power" for herself and her poetry This impetus may also have fostered her later biographies of Wendell Willkie, the 1940 Republican presidential candidate (*One Life,* 1957), and Thomas Hariot, the English Renaissance naturalist and scientist (*The Traces of Thomas Hariot,* 1971). With their lyricism and fractured structures, these biographies were far from conventional, again drawing a wide range of responses from her contemporaries.

One of the central, transformative events in the poet's life was personal, not political: the birth of her son, William, in 1947. After a brief marriage in 1945 to the painter Glynn Collins, Rukeyser formed other romantic alliances. She gave birth to William as a single mother in a time when to do so meant great shame for both mother and child. As William Rukeyser explains in Anne F. Herzog and Janet E. Kaufman's *How Shall We Tell Each Other of the Poet* (1999), "On a personal level she rejected the life of a suburban, married matron her parents had designed for her."

He also rather wryly notes, "It is . . . impossible to say whether there was affection between her and her mate. Some indications are that she went searching for a father for her child the way people go to The Gap: she was shopping for genes." He indicates Rukeyser's ambivalence about her decision, or perhaps her awareness of social realities, for she often made up stories about having been widowed and used "Mrs." in front of her name. In being a mother, she lived out her social beliefs, finding a school for William where he would feel comfortable among his mostly Jewish but also black, Puerto Rican, Catholic, and WASP classmates. Her pregnancy and motherhood transformed her perspective, perhaps bringing home even more concretely the horrors of modern life, with its wars, genocide, and racism. In the 1940s and early 1950s, Rukeyser lived in San Francisco, trying to earn a living, teaching a poetry workshop at the California Labor School, participating in poetry readings, and enjoying the company of other writers, artists, and intellectuals. After the birth of her son, she was rescued from financial disaster by an anonymous benefactor.

Continuing her pattern of enormous productivity, Rukeyser published an acclaimed volume of poetry, *The Green Wave,* in 1948, and three additional books in 1949: *Elegies,* a collection of her ten poems in the elegy series; *Orpheus,* a long poem; and *The Life of Poetry,* an important set of meditations on the necessary role of poetry in human life. In contrast to fellow poets like Robert Lowell, Randall Jarrell, and John Berryman, Rukeyser sought to find hope and redemption out of nearly a decade of war. Rejecting the ironic and alienated perspective growing increasingly prevalent among writers, especially in the academy, she articulated a sense of possibility. This attitude emerges plainly in such poems as "Mrs. Walpurga," "A Certain Music," and "Crayon House," as well as "This Place in the Ways," where she affirms her feelings of "Rage for the world as it is / but for what it may be / more love now than last year." Unquestionably informed by her status as a mother, such a positive vision—even though it was tempered by reality and, as always, a commitment to intervention into pressing social problems—would ultimately damage her reputation among the New Critics who held power in literary critical circles.

Although the 1950s should have been a time of triumph for Rukeyser, with the publication of *Selected Poems* in 1951, this period was one in which the poet was forced to remain relatively invisible. Her participation in leftist causes made her vulnerable to the McCarthyism and cold war sentiments sweeping the country, and as a single mother with a young child, she could not afford to become a victim of the period. Nevertheless, in addition to her collection, she published the verse biography of Willkie in 1957 and an important new volume of poetry, *Body of Waking,* in 1958. The latter reflected both the repression of the times—as we see in her elegy for the famous gay literary critic, her friend F. O. Matthiessen, who committed suicide in 1950—and the hope fostered by her perspective as a mother. In their movement toward greater openness about the body, the poems that energize this collection, including "Unborn Song," "Children, the Sandbar, That Summer," and " 'Long Enough,' " anticipate the frank poems of her last years. During this difficult political period, she found employment and pleasure in teaching young writers at Vassar and Sarah Lawrence colleges. Although she was a superb teacher, she characteristically refused the security (and potentially stultifying convention) of tenure at Sarah Lawrence, resigning in 1967.

In 1962 she published another collection of poems, *Waterlily Fire: Poems, 1935–1962,* and in 1963 translations of two works by Octavio Paz. Although she suffered a stroke in 1964, she continued to publish, including *The Orgy* (1965), a lyrical, autobiographical "book" that is difficult to characterize, and *The Speed of Darkness* (1968). In the 1970s, Rukeyser added to her ac-

complishments with a biography of Thomas Hariot (1971); two more books of poetry, *Breaking Open: New Poems* (1973) and *The Gates* (1976); and *The Collected Poems of Muriel Rukeyser* (1978). These last volumes of poetry reveal a writer whose political involvement never diminished and whose idiom became in many poems more accessible and more candid. These years also brought renewed visibility and honors: in 1961 she was awarded an honorary doctor of letters degree from Rutgers University, in 1967 she was elected a member of the National Institute of Arts and Letters, and in the spring of 1977 the American Academy of Arts and Letters awarded her the Copernicus Prize. The citation for the latter reads in part: "From her first book . . . through her recent collection . . . the work of Muriel Rukeyser has been committed to ideas of freedom. Throughout her life she has been sensitive to encroachments on the freedom of individuals or peoples."

William Rukeyser speaks of his mother's self-invention, her playfulness, her stringent standards for life and art, and her willingness to embrace opposites. He affirms, "Muriel Rukeyser was proud of what she was: Jewish, fat (in her view that equated to strong), independent—a free woman, long before society was ready for free women. But she was also fascinated by what she wasn't." Weakened by another stroke in 1977, the poet whom Anne Sexton called "the mother of everyone" died on February 12, 1980.

"IF I COULD WRITE": LITERARY BACKGROUND

In order to understand Rukeyser's poetry as well as her character it is helpful to consider the critical responses to her writing. Today's readers are more open to the poet's complexity and understanding of her struggle. In her important 1992 essay "A World that Will Hold All the People,"

Suzanne Gardinier writes frankly that Rukeyser's transformations of experience into poetry "are not uniformly successful," but her work includes "the most interesting and alive poetry we have." The poet and critic Kate Daniels provides the most concise account of the vagaries of Rukeyser's reputation over the years in "Muriel Rukeyser and Her Literary Critics" (1996). An individualistic writer whose work conformed to no school, although it frequently crossed the boundaries of several, Rukeyser was often caught in the middle of vitriolic critical debates both for and against her idiosyncratic style and vision, and critics often seemed to respond either with enthusiastic praise or personal attack. The measure of her integrity was her steadfast refusal to be swayed by reviews and criticism.

In the 1930s, Rukeyser's work seemed to fit most readily into such categories as "proletarian" or "social realist." Her first book, *Theory of Flight,* was framed by many critics, including Kenneth Burke and John Crowe Ransom, as allied with the vision of the Communist Party. But she also refused to condemn writers, like William Faulkner, whom the left criticized for "decadence." As Daniels observes, "Throughout her life, [Rukeyser] found herself astonished at the inability of most literary critics to consider work that departed from the conventions of a particular school or norm, and in her own critical writings she demonstrated her ability to transcend the contemporary and topical contexts of a work in favor of what she considered its more enduring artistic qualities." William Rukeyser observes, "In the thirties she didn't fear to embrace the Communists. . . . But she wasn't timid about rejecting Communist dogma or thought control. For her pains she was vilified by both sides . . . because she wouldn't follow anybody's party line except her own."

Despite her early commitment to a leftist worldview, Rukeyser's first two volumes of poetry revealed a decided emphasis on the aesthetic that fits more readily into the older tradition of Romanticism or the emerging one of modernism. Such an emphasis emerged in both the structure and language of her poetry, transforming what was on the surface purely "political" and topical poetry into another literary dimension. This crossing of boundaries between the political and the aesthetic made her work unpopular with the New Critics, who dominated the literary scene both in and out of the academy from the 1940s to the early 1960s. Moreover, beginning in the early 1940s, powerful periodicals such as the *Partisan Review* and *The New Yorker,* where Louise Bogan held sway as poetry critic from 1931 to 1968, consistently reviewed her work with scorn. In 1943 the *Partisan Review* published an unsigned personal attack on the poet, entitled "Grandeur and Misery of a Poster Girl," that made such claims as "the lines of her verse often seemed to resemble a bathrobe." Such criticism reveals not only the intense personal tone characteristic of some of Rukeyser's detractors but also some critics' misinterpretation of her innovative open punctuation and idiosyncratic style as slovenly.

As Rukeyser herself acknowledges indirectly in *The Life of Poetry,* such attacks were often gendered in nature. It was only with the reemergence of a politicized, feminist criticism that Rukeyser's work began to regain currency and attract renewed attention. Beginning in the mid-1970s, several Ph.D. dissertations with Rukeyser as their theme were completed; the *American Poetry Review* produced a retrospective of her entire body of work in 1974; and Kertesz published the sustained study *The Poetic Vision of Muriel Rukeyser* in 1980. Notwithstanding this renewed, affirmative attention, and despite poems that spoke powerfully to many feminist readers, Rukeyser nevertheless declined the label of feminist, asserting her individual activist vision.

Although Rukeyser always followed her own aesthetic perspective, her work possesses clear alliances with other poets, including, as Kertesz points out, such near-contemporaries and contemporaries as W. H. Auden, Genevieve Taggard, Lola Ridge, Robert Lowell, and Allen Ginsberg. Her work also emerged from the much earlier transcendentalist tradition of Ralph Waldo Emerson, Henry David Thoreau, and Walt Whitman. Characteristically affirming her independence from Whitman, Rukeyser acknowledged her affinities with and admiration for her precursor in *The Life of Poetry.* She observes, "People have been comparing me to Whitman and although I love and adore and am a child of Whitman, both of us come from the Bible and from the religious writings where the parallelism enables contradictions to be contained and synthesis to be achieved." Here she emphasizes a perspective that permeates her work as it did Whitman's: the reconciliation of apparent opposites. Rukeyser would reaffirm over and over during her career Whitman's great claim: "Do I contradict myself? Very well then I contradict myself."

This emphasis on the necessity to synthesize contradiction, separation, and paradox is apparent throughout her work, both in content and in theme. It is figured, for example, in the early poem "Effort at Speech between Two People," which draws its inspiration from a famous love poem in the Chinese *Book of Songs.* In "Effort at Speech," Rukeyser imagines two lovers attempting to communicate across a great psychic distance. Emphasizing openness, she articulates the need of different people to "conceal nothing," to "be open" and to "be close." One of the speakers urges the other, "Grow to know me," while the other asks, "Speak to me. Talk to Me." Using spaces within the lines of her poetry and between stanzas, Rukeyser separates the speakers and their words; she embodies and performs the fact of difference and envisions a world where "these our separate entities could come to grips." Recalling Whitman's intimate voice at the end of "Song of Myself," in which he affirms to the reader that "I stop somewhere waiting for you," Rukeyser's poetry attempts to mend ruptures between people.

This metaphoric rendition of separateness reappears in the well-known poem, "Who in One Lifetime," where Rukeyser's speaker describes a world with "inexorable armies and the falling plane." Herself "introspective and whole, / She knows how several madnesses are born, / Seeing the integrated never fighting well, / The flesh too vulnerable, the eyes tear-torn." It is the imagination of the poet that is able to reconcile the violence of the present world with the hope of the future; in her eyes, "the camps of ambush" become "chambers of imagery. / She holds belief in the world." Describing herself and the possibilities she contains, the speaker closes the poem with a final, affirmative paradox that signals the reconciliation of opposites: "A childless goddess of fertility." It is the largeness of the poet's vision that is able to encompass loss and hope, life and death; sharing his optimism, Rukeyser evokes Whitman's famous affirmation, "I am large, I contain multitudes." Part of her detractors' dislike for Rukeyser's work was the apparent audacity of a woman poet making claims to this kind of Whitmanesque inclusiveness and sweeping vision.

Rukeyser's optimism and her lifelong effort at social amelioration continue not only the work of Whitman but also that of a powerful tradition of nineteenth-century activist women's poetry that is still being reevaluated by literary critics. A brief examination of these poets' work makes it evident that Rukeyser is not as anomalous as many twentieth-century critics have asserted. The earliest and perhaps best-known activist poet was Lydia Sigourney (1791–1865), whose efforts on behalf of Native Americans and other marginalized groups have garnered attention from late-twentieth-century critics of American women's writing such as Nina Baym, Paula Bennett, and Karen L. Kilcup. In the second half of the nineteenth century, poets as diverse as the African American writer Frances E. W. Harper (1825–1911), the working-class writer Lucy Larcom (1824–1893), and the Jewish writer Emma Lazarus (1849–1887) would take up all of the great social causes of the time, among them the abolition of slavery, women's rights, worker's rights, temperance, immigration reform, and peace.

Beginning in the 1920s, poetry and poetry criticism rejected strongly the political bent of the preceding century for several reasons. First was the affiliation of such political poetry with women writers. As modernist male poets like T. S. Eliot and Ezra Pound sought to achieve recognition and to distinguish themselves from their predecessors, they defined their work in aesthetic terms, rejecting as "impure" the writing that emerged from political concerns. Because much of this political writing was authored by women, such poets sought effectively to reclaim poetry as a "masculine," intellectual terrain. In addition, the association of political poetry with mass audiences—who were often themselves female—further feminized the writing of poetry. Modernist poets, both male and female, attempted to elevate their work "above" that of the common man and woman. Some of the writers and critics who sought a new, "purer" form of poetry, like Louise Bogan, would be sharply critical of Rukeyser's verse activism. Moreover, the stylistic characteristics of nineteenth-century poetry that included straightforward treatment of a subject and accessible language came to be regarded as naive. Sincerity was out, ironic detachment was in. But the new poets neglected or were unable to perceive Rukeyser's profound investment in modernist aesthetics.

"NOT SAPPHO, SACCO": RUKEYSER'S VERSE ACTIVISM

Theory of Flight inaugurates almost all of Rukeyser's characteristic concerns, including class and race differences, social inequality, the relationship between technology and art, the promise of American culture, and the impulse to situate opposites in productive relation. The book's first section brings together poems focusing on the writer's childhood and adolescence; one of the most important is "Poem out of Childhood," which reveals the poet working "out of" her early experience. Here Rukeyser initiates her paradigmatic relationship to the world: "Breathe-in experience, breathe-out poetry." In "Song of Myself," Whitman used the words "The smoke of my own breath . . . / My respiration and inspiration, the beating of my heart, the passing of blood and air through my lungs." Like Whitman, Rukeyser envisions that her work will connect experience and art in an organic and affirmative manner. This romantic vision is undercut later in Rukeyser's poem by the disillusionment endemic to adolescence, where she discovers that her idealism about America is not warranted. This discovery sparks what would become her lifetime vision of the poet: "Not Sappho, Sacco." The execution of the anarchists Nicola Sacco and Bartolomeo Vanzetti in 1927 became an emblem for the politicized, activist perspective that her work articulated, as she affirmed the necessary ethical stance of the poet.

Theory of Flight was built around the 950-line title poem that extended many of the ideas that emerge in "Poem out of Childhood." Unlike Hart Crane's *The Bridge* or T. S. Eliot's *The Waste Land,* to which it has often been compared, "Theory of Flight" articulates a more optimistic vision of technology. As the title suggests, the poem attempts to synthesize the putative disjunction between technology and artistic vision; "flight" encompasses both the Wright brothers' actual effort and the flights of imagination traditionally assigned to the poet. The poet's transcendental optimism emerges in the speaker's exhortations to the reader, which again echo Whitman's calls to his reader:

Look! Be : leap ;
paint trees in flame
bushes burning
roar in the broad sky

know your color : be :
produce that the widenesses
be full and burst their wombs
. . . .
put up your face to the wind
FLY

Almost mystical in nature and suggestive of the divine qualities within human beings, this flight also evokes the necessary participation of women in imaginative and actual growth, a theme that would emerge much more explicitly in Rukeyser's later work, especially after the birth of her son.

Power, and the abuses of power, are important themes in both "Theory of Flight" and the volume as a whole. In "The Trial," the poem's third section, Rukeyser considers the state's injustice toward the Scottsboro boys. Echoing her earlier accusation about the failure of justice for Sacco and Vanzetti—and for all members of the social underclass—this section offers images that are concrete, even lovely ("The South is green with coming spring"), and harshly judgmental ("all the people's anger finds its vortex here / as the mythic lips of justice open, and speak"). Throughout the poem Rukeyser balances the tensions between exalted and indignant, concrete and imaginative, and political and aesthetic, as she makes visible the injustices and ambiguities in modern American culture. At the end of "Theory of Flight," she reaffirms the possibility of the future, provided that all of the people, not just elites, participate in its creation; she urges, "Say yes, people. / Say yes. / YES."

As a whole, *Theory of Flight,* like most of Rukeyser's work, emphasizes relationships. "Sand-Quarry with Moving Figures," for example, explores the relationships between family members, emblematized in a father-daughter relationship; "Sundays, They Sleep Late" critiques middle-class individuals who reject connections outside their comfortable existence.

Rukeyser's second book, *U.S. 1,* which contains what is perhaps her emblematic "political" poetry, explores the relationship between races and classes in powerful detail. A group of her most powerful poems emerged from the Gauley Bridge, West Virginia, mining disaster. "The Book of the Dead" is a long composite poem, reminiscent of film in its pictorial juxtapositions, that vividly explores the place where the disaster occurred, the miners' lives, and the corruption of company officials and physicians. Highlighting the potential universality of the disaster, the realistic poem "Gauley Bridge" depicts sympathetically an essentially "ordinary" town, with its "postoffice window, a hive of private boxes," "the bus station and the great pale buses stopping for food," and "the little boy [who] runs with his dog." Other details provide subtle clues about the paradoxical uniqueness of this largely black community: "the tall coughing man stamping an envelope" and "the deserted Negro standing on the corner." Though still restrained, the poet's anger and outrage emerge in the final stanza, only after the relatively detached, journalistic description that precedes it:

What do you want—a cliff over a city?
A foreland, sloped to sea and overgrown with
   roses?
These people live here.

Comparing the privilege of a seaside town, lovely and romantic with flowers, to this working community, the speaker affirms the right of the inhabitants of Gauley Bridge not only to "live here," but to *live.*

"Praise of the Committee" performs a version of the Senate hearings that surrounded the disaster, including the efforts of "crooked lawyers" to block Union Carbide's responsibility and the leadership of miner George Robinson in seeking justice. The speaker of "Absalom" is a mother whose husband and three sons have died from silicosis; in this poem, Rukeyser evokes Whitman's task of giving voice to the voiceless. Similarly, Rukeyser articulates the suffering of the women who were left behind by the catastrophic illness, as well as their powerful resistance to the forces of corporate money and power. Dying, the mother's eighteen-year-old son urges her, " 'when I die, / 'I want you to have them open me up and / 'see if that dust killed me. / 'Try to get compensation.' " The mother's heroism emerges in her prophetic rejoinder: "He shall not be diminished, never; / I shall give a mouth to my son."

"The Disease" reveals the forces arrayed against the mother: here we see a doctor explaining the path of the illness to the Senate investigating committee. The speaker's detached, unemotional—though ironically "poetic"—voice provides a vivid and painful counterpart to that of the mother:

> Now, this lung's mottled, beginning, in these
> areas.
> You'd say a snowstorm had struck the fellow's
> lungs.
> About alike, that side and this side, top and
> bottom.
> The first stage in this period in this case.

The poem concludes with the doctor's response to the investigator's question: "Does silicosis cause death? / Yes, sir." The poem gains power by the disembodiment of the Senate questioner, whose words, hanging in midair in brief one-line stanzas, underscore that disembodiment.

Rukeyser's ability to admire the paradox of beauty in ugliness and suffering—to construct relationships between opposites—emerges not only in "The Disease" and in the incomparable "Alloy," which describes the whitened landscape, but also in the dramatic poem "George Robinson: Blues." Robinson describes the landscape from an insider's perspective:

> Looked like somebody sprinkled flour all over the
> parks and groves, it stayed and the rain

couldn't wash it away and it twinkled that
white dust looked really pretty down around
our ankles.

> As dark as I am, when I came out at morning
> after the tunnel at night, with a white man,
> nobody could have told which man was white.
> The dust had covered us both, and the dust was
> white.

Commenting indirectly on the leveling effect of death across race, Rukeyser powerfully accuses the white men who have created the tragedy of Gauley Bridge. As Gardinier writes, " 'The Book of the Dead' . . . offers that rare thing in the poetry of this nation of many races: a vision of the bonds that tie these two different men together."

"POWER NOT DOMINION": GENDER, POWER, AND POETRY

The activist vision of Rukeyser's first two books reappears throughout her body of work. "Ceremonies," from *A Turning Wind,* critiques the century's violence as World War II unfolds: "the century had its rites, its politics, / machineries whose characters were wars. / Ceremonies of further separation." "Who in One Lifetime," from *Beast in View,* is also a reflection on the destruction of war, though it seeks hope through the poet's vision. "Body of Waking," from the volume with the same title, addresses the loss of American ideals: "America, / Did you think only of wars and luxury? / Can you remember your early dreaming?" "Flying to Hanoi," based on the poet's experience, affirms, "I thought I was going to the fighters, but I am going to the men and women who are inventing peace."

In addition to her attention to social inequalities based on race and class difference, another cluster of concerns emerges, principally in the 1940s: gender relations, women's bodies, and women's social power. These concerns mesh with Rukeyser's class consciousness in the early poem, "More of a Corpse Than a Woman," in which the poet critiques the passive, conventional women whose presence is deadly: "I went to the movies with that one, / feeling the weight of their death where she sat at my elbow." This "death" is a product of middle-class life, she suggests, full only of things such as boats, "a seashell from the faltering monarchy," and "the nose of a marble saint," which Rukeyser calls "the souvenirs of boredom" for the "expensive girls," "the well-protected woman," "the ice-cream girl." Recalling Emily Dickinson's "What Soft—Cherubic Creatures— / These Gentlewomen are—," Rukeyser demands change:

> When your women are ready and rich in their
>   wish for the world,
> destroy the leaden heart,
> we've a new race to start.

Published in 1935 in her first book, "More of a Corpse than a Woman" forecasts the full flowering of Rukeyser's woman-centered consciousness in the decades of the 1960s and 1970s.

Although we see the poet's interest in women's concerns and perspectives continued by such poems as "Ann Burlak" (from *A Turning Wind*) and "Wreath of Women" (from *Beast in View*), *The Green Wave* (1948) displays them in more detail. "Nine Poems for the Unborn Child" is distinguished by its willingness to open for poetic discourse subjects that had been repressed in American culture and that the stolid postwar period would delete from the public record: women's bodies, especially related to the subjects of sexuality, pregnancy, and childbearing. In some sense, Rukeyser again has more in common with some of her nineteenth-century women precursors than her contemporaries. For example, in 1861 Harriet Prescott Spofford (1835–1921) published the romantic and erotic long poem, "Pome-granate Flowers," which depicts a woman seamstress, possibly a prostitute, in an erotic setting that may involve masturbation. Similarly, Rose Terry Cooke (1827–1892) published the autoerotic "In the Hammock" (1866) and the frightening "Blue-Beard's Closet" (1861), which evokes powerfully the affiliation between sexuality and death for women. Writers such as Margaret Fuller (1810–1850), Frances Kemble (1809–1893), and Sophie Jewett (1861–1909) published work with a relatively overt homoerotic content.

It was not until Amy Lowell began writing her lesbian love poems in the 1920s that the subject of female eroticism emerged, plainly, in the twentieth century. Not surprisingly, Lowell's work often shocked the sensibilities of conservative critics, but her writing opened the field for later twentieth-century poets like Rukeyser, who herself may be exploring same-sex eroticism in such poems as "Orgy" and "Looking at Each Other."

By the late 1940s, when "Nine Poems for the Unborn Child" was published, many women were still ignorant about their bodies and divorced from the processes of birth, as Adrienne Rich explains in *Of Woman Born: Motherhood as Experience and Institution* (1976). Polite society still suppressed discussion of women's bodies—except as art objects—and many women were unconscious while giving birth. Attempting to re-establish women's relationships with their bodies, Rukeyser's poem blends concrete and elevated images and language to intervene in this silence. The poem opens with an evocation of the poet's feelings:

> The childless years alone without a home
>   flashed daily with the world's glimpse,
>   happiness.
> Always behind was the dark screen of loss
> Hardly moving, like heavy hardly-moving
>   cloud.

This complicated statement combines a sense of the poet's distance from an inaccessible happiness coupled with a sense of loss for her childlessness. At the same time, the passage intimates the effort it takes her to move her pregnant body.

The second section of the poem conjures up the announcement by the angel Gabriel to the Virgin Mary that she is pregnant with Jesus. By invoking this association, Rukeyser elevates motherhood generally, mythologizing and spiritualizing the process of pregnancy: "Trees struck their roots as deep and visible / As their high branches, the double planted world." This section also addresses one of the most difficult elements of her pregnancy for Rukeyser: her unmarried status and the "illegitimacy" of her child. For the "fatherless children"—connected here implicitly with God's children—"their choice is death or the world." Such children, she affirms, "do choose. / Earn their brave set of bone, the seeking marvelous look / Of those who lose and use and know their lives." In 1947 the stigma attached to unmarried motherhood was enormous; Rukeyser negotiates with social norms as she refigures the meaning of single motherhood here and in subsequent sections.

As in much of her poetry, the political becomes her concern in the seventh section, for the warring world into which the child will be born, "the world where death by fear and explosion / Is waited." Imagining the amniotic fluid, she addresses the child directly: "You in your dark lake moving darkly now / Will . . . / Enter the present, where all the deaths and all / The old betrayals have come home again." Nevertheless, her characteristic optimism emerges, most plainly in the last two sections. Recalling her dreams of the unborn child, she affirms that "in my belly be a birth, will keep / All delicacy, all delight unclouded." The poem's conclusion insists, "And at this daylight, praise / To the grace of the world

and time that I may hope / To live, to write, to see my human child." Like many American women poets connecting the birth of poetry with human birth, Rukeyser echoes the seventeenth-century poet Anne Bradstreet's much earlier claim in "The Poet to Her Book" to a feminine and maternal creativity. As in much of Rukeyser's poetry, the key ideas in "Nine Poems for the Unborn Child" are connections and the construction of relationships amid apparent paradox, fragmentation, and loss.

In *One Life,* the section Rukeyser calls "Power Never Dominion" advances the poet's interest in gender concerns; here the poet affirms that male religion has translated "some fleshly girl" into an animal: "She will appear / In textbooks as a sacrificed antelope / Guilt running shiny over the short fur." Concealing her power, male-dominated religion seeks dominion over the powerful girl who is unforgivably affiliated with birth. Later poems such as "The Birth of Venus" (from *Body of Waking*), "The Poem as Mask," and "Painters" (from *The Gates*), continue Rukeyser's exploration of gender relations, which emerges most frankly in *The Speed of Darkness* (1968), *Breaking Open* (1973), and *The Gates* (1976). "Anemone" speaks even more frankly of the connection between women's erotic power and poetic creativity: "My sex is closing, my sex is opening. / You are singing and offering: the way in." "Ms. Lot" and "Myth," two of her most frequently anthologized poems, retell traditional myths from a woman's perspective.

"Myth" brilliantly retells the story of Oedipus. Imagining a dialogue between him and the Sphinx—who may represent a version of the crafty poet—Rukeyser has the Sphinx tell Oedipus that he "gave the wrong answer"—"Man"—to her question, "What walks on four legs in the morning, two at noon, and three in the evening?" Defending himself, Oedipus asserts his power and privilege, but the Sphinx has other ideas:

"When you say Man," said Oedipus, "you include
   women too. Everyone knows that."
She said, "That's what you think."

The humor and subversive power of this poem, which emerged at virtually the same time as the mid-twentieth century movement for women's rights, are characteristic of her later work.

Adrienne Rich praises Rukeyser "because she would not trim her sails to a vogue of poetic irony and wit, an aesthetics of the private middle-class life, an idea of what a woman's poetry should look like." As early as 1949 Rukeyser had acknowledged the affiliation of poetry with gender: "One will say it is willfully obscure. . . . And almost any man will say that it is effeminate: it is true that poetry as an art is sexually suspect." In addition to underscoring the charged nature of gender relations at the time, she also highlights the potentially damaging charge of homoeroticism to which male poets were vulnerable, a vulnerability that may have informed the determination of many male poets to construct a hard, detached, unemotional poetry. Such a poetic standard required women writers who sought to enter the increasingly masculinized literary tradition of the 1920s onward to write in ways that felt inauthentic. In the nineteenth century women writers used emotion—culturally acceptable for women to this day—to condone their entrance into the public sphere in the service of social reform. Late in the century, however, the dominant voices in publishing and literary criticism damned the sentimentality of these earlier women, and by the early twentieth century any expression of emotion was often considered retrograde and weak.

This attitude, increasingly enforced during the time that Rukeyser's work first appeared, ensured that poets like Edna St. Vincent Millay, Genevieve Taggard, and Lola Ridge—who were, not coincidentally, invested in social reform like their nineteenth-century precursors—would be diminished, disparaged, and ultimately excluded from the canon of "great" poetry. In *The Life of Poetry* Rukeyser notes the difficult atmosphere for openness in American culture ("its hunger for conformity") and the harsh criticism against strong women: "The repressive codes are everywhere. Our movies are censored before they are plotted; our radio comedy is forbidden its list of themes; have you noticed how our bestselling books are written in reaction to the dominating woman?" With the emergence in the 1950s of what became known as "confessional" poetry by such writers as Anne Sexton, Sylvia Plath, and Robert Lowell, emotion in poetry regained some currency. Raw and personal, such poetry reauthorized women to articulate their experiences.

Into the space opened by such confessional poetry, Rukeyser interposed graphic, explicit poems, often emerging out of the female body, that connected body and spirit. Poems such as "What Do We See " and "Despisals" make explicit the connection between the hatred of the body and the hatred of marginalized people, including women, in American culture. Echoing Whitman's affirmation that "the scent of these armpits" is "aroma finer than prayer" ("Song of Myself"), "Despisals" makes stern requirements of its readers:

            In the body's ghetto
never to go despising the asshole
nor the useful shit that is our clean clue
to what we need.   Never to despise
the clitoris in her least speech.
. . . .
         . . . To make this relation
with the it : to know that I am it.

At the same time that she affirms women's particular experience, however, Rukeyser emphasizes, like Whitman, her desire to speak for both men and women. In "Double Ode," for example, she outlines her "female powers," but at the same time articulates her "eternal double music male and female."

AESTHETICS: LIFE AND ART IN DIALOGUE

One frequent refrain throughout Rukeyser's career, and an important factor in the diminishment of her critical reputation between the 1940s and mid-1960s, is the difficulty that critics have in categorizing her writing. In a 1963 response to her collection of poems *Waterlily Fire: Poems, 1935–1962,* the poet and critic Hayden Carruth considered this difficulty in relatively affirmative terms: "Although I have known Miss Rukeyser's poems for a long time, I shall need to know them much longer still before I can decide whether or not they are, taken as a whole, really good. Possibly I will never decide. Must one stuff every book one reads into a category?" Rukeyser's work often so skillfully weaves together activism and art that it is difficult to pull apart single threads as representative. But we can trace some recurring patterns in her work if we are guided by her masterful critical meditation, *The Life of Poetry.*

The title of this work suggests the multiplicity of the poet's perspective, for it refers both to a life lived as a poet and the powerful animation of the art itself. *The Life of Poetry* identifies some of the central strands of Rukeyser's aesthetic. For example, an important concern is the integration of all elements of human experience, good and bad, and all ways of knowing, from the scientific to the poetic. The opening sentence of the book's "Note from the Author" underscores this concern: "A way to allow people to feel the meeting of their consciousness and the world, to feel the full value of the meanings of emotions and ideas in their relations with each other, and to understand, in the glimpse of a moment, the freshness of

things and their possibilities." Constructing poetry as a form of "knowledge," "feeling," and "truth," the poet seeks to reinvigorate what she sees as a diminished way of knowing in American culture and to counterbalance the common fear of poetry that she describes here passionately.

This emphasis on constructing connections and relationships appears indirectly in her biographies *Willard Gibbs, One Life,* and *The Traces of Thomas Hariot;* her "autobiographical" text *The Orgy* (1965); and her biographical poems such as "Käthe Kollwitz," "Suite for Lord Timothy Dexter," "Ryder," and "Ives." In each of these works, poetry and narrative, often combined with the associative or montage techniques of film or collage, fuse to create an imaginative, fictionalized narrative that defies categorization. *The Orgy,* for example, recounts an event in County Kerry, Ireland, called Puck Fair, which is a country fair of possibly pre-Christian origin, historically centered on the celebration of a male goat (or "Puck"), a pagan symbol of fertility. Describing her arrival at the fair and its three-day progress, Rukeyser offers a broad range of personal associations, but the book as a whole constitutes what the poet's introduction calls "a free fantasy on the event." Some reviewers were frustrated by their inability to situate the book formally; others criticized its eroticism; still others appreciated the more vivid, even "truthful" description offered by the volume's imaginative approach.

Such an eclectic approach both to literature and experience was an early characteristic of Rukeyser's work. For example, the Gauley Bridge mining disaster poems of *U.S. 1* combine lyrics, reportage, and description. In addition, a stock quotation for Union Carbide appears near the end of "The Dam," while the testimony of a social worker during a congressional hearing emerges in "Statement: Phillipa Allen." Like much of her "factual" work, Rukeyser's biography of the post–Civil War scientist Willard Gibbs blurs the boundaries between literal and imaginative truth.

Perhaps the clearest statement of Rukeyser's complex formal inventions comes from her long poem on the German artist Käthe Kollwitz:

> Woman as gates, saying :
> "The process is after all like music,
> like the development of a piece of music.
> The fugues come back and
>   again and again
> interweave.
> A theme may seem to have been put aside,
> but it keeps returning—
> the same thing modulated,
> somewhat changed in form.
> Usually richer.
> And it is very good that this is so."

In her frequent use of the techniques of film, music, and collage, Rukeyser proposes a different and more "organic" form of poetry; these strategies of incorporation encompass both the subjects and forms of Rukeyser's work.

Anne F. Herzog and Louise Kertesz suggest that Rukeyser's techniques anticipate postmodern aesthetic strategies; as Kertesz points out, postmodernism was first identified among the poets of the San Francisco renaissance of the late 1950s, including Allen Ginsberg, Gregory Corso, and Lawrence Ferlinghetti. Nevertheless, postmodernism does not entirely encompass Rukeyser's method; nor would the poet have been amenable to yet another label applied to her idiosyncratic writing.

Her complex reception history was certainly influenced by the advent of a masculine modernist poetry that valued detachment from emotion and from political advocacy. Nevertheless, her simultaneous investment in modernist aesthetics and activism demands some consideration. In her formal structures as well as her language, Rukeyser not only forecasts the disjunctiveness of postmodern literature but also displays many affinities with her more famous modernist counterparts. For example, if we reexamine "Effort at Speech between Two People," we see Rukeyser's innovative use of punctuation and spacing to convey the "effort" that is the poem's subject. Opening with a colon, each stanza suggests a pretext that informs the speech that follows; the reader is invited to imagine what fills this gap, as Rukeyser not only depicts communication between two people but also enacts it with the reader. The spaces in the poem perform a similar function, at once suggesting the difficulty of speech—let alone communication—and the necessary imaginative work that different individuals need to complete.

As she breaks with the standard line, rhythm, punctuation, and meter here and elsewhere, Rukeyser also uses traditional forms when they advance her purposes, including, as Rich observes, "elegies, odes, lyrics, documentary poems, epigrams, ballads, dramatic monologues, biographical narratives." She also uses one of the most traditional forms, the sonnet—from "Sonnet" in *Theory of Flight* to a series of reinventions in "Nine Poems for the Unborn Child." In the latter work, only section five diverges completely from the sonnet form, while sections three and nine have fifteen lines, and section eight inverts the octave and sestet. Virtually all of the lines (except in section five) are pentameter in length; many rhyme. With this renewal of the sonnet form, Rukeyser also recreates the love poem with which it is identified: here the beloved is not a man or woman but her unborn child. Rukeyser uses a range of formal strategies in her poetry, selecting those that she considered most appropriate for the subject matter at hand, offering a poetic opus that is formally as well as substantively broad.

Although she is most often identified as a political poet, this discussion of form suggests Rukeyser's additional alliances with lyric poetry, which characteristically avoids historically situated subject matter, choosing instead to focus on timeless subjects such as love, death, and beauty. We have seen how the poet powerfully synthesizes an activist perspective with lyrical description in the Union Carbide poems, and *U.S. 1*—one of her most famously "political" volumes—itself includes a section of lyrics. Rukeyser writes poems that are more amenable to interpretation within the framework of the socially detached modernist poem. For example, "Wooden Spring" considers the psychic consequences of spring's absence. The poem begins:

> How horrible late spring is, with the full death
> of the frozen tight bulbs brownly rotting in
> earth; and each chord of light rayed into slivers,
> a bunch of grapes plucked grape by grape
> apart, a warm chord broken into the chilled
> single notes.

Echoing not only Edna St. Vincent Millay's "Spring" but also T. S. Eliot's *The Waste Land,* "Wooden Spring" articulates an alienated perspective often considered characteristic of modernist verse, even though the poem's conclusion seeks to affirm "life in this lack of death, / comfort on this wide ground." The only residue of a political perspective here emerges retrospectively from the reader's association between this poem and other Rukeyser poems that affiliate the sterility and absences of "Wooden Spring" with (for example) her antiwar observations.

Like many other poems, "Wooden Spring" often relies on characteristically difficult modernist language and complex images; from this perspective, she has alliances with her more famous female modernist counterparts, Marianne Moore, Louise Bogan, and H. D. Many of these early modern women's poems, however, engage with contemporary social issues, including gender relations, much less directly than Rukeyser's work, if they do so at all; more "purely" aesthetic concerns of style, language, and structure dominate. Emerging from a later generation of women poet

activists, including Margaret Walker, Tillie Olsen, Kay Boyle, and Millay, Rukeyser also negotiates with the aesthetics of modernism. Poems such as "Suite for Lord Timothy Dexter" and "Waterlily Fire" place enormous demands on the reader's capacity to construct meaning out of diverse images and shifting voices. Rukeyser herself acknowledges this difficulty at the end of *Waterlily Fire* by providing explanatory footnotes for these poems; but even with the notes, the reader faces a significant challenge. "Waterlily Fire," ostensibly about the burning in a 1958 fire of one of Claude Monet's paintings of waterlilies, encompasses not only the actual event, but, as the poet explains, "the history of Manhattan Island and my lifetime on the island." Drawing on her characteristic cinematic techniques, it also includes "an actual television interview with Suzuki, the Zen teacher," a protest against a nuclear war practice drill, and "an idea from India of one's lifetime body as a ribbon of images, all our changes seen in process." Incorporating such wide-ranging materials, "Waterlily Fire" emblematizes the modernist difficulty—even, at times, obscurity—of the writer's work.

Perhaps Rukeyser's most accessible work is contained in her last three volumes of poetry. "The Poem as Mask," another frequently anthologized poem, seems to testify to her desire to seek a more open, less metaphoric language:

> When I wrote of the women in their dances and
>   wildness, it was a mask,
> . . . .
> it was myself, split open, unable to speak, in
>   exile from myself.

She credits the birth of her child with her new commitment to explicit truth, including the truth of the body, affirming, "No more masks! No more mythologies!" This affirmation is reflected in the relative simplicity of "Song: Love in Whose Rich Honor," "Anemone," "Looking at Each Other,"

"Welcome from War," and "St. Roach." Even the longer poems, such as "Breaking Open," "Double Ode," and "The Gates," reflect a commitment to more concrete images and a more direct portrayal of experience than in her earlier work.

As she explicitly acknowledges in *The Life of Poetry,* Rukeyser is acutely aware of her relationship with the reader, acknowledging that her writing challenges the reader to perceive experience in a different way. The relationship begins with openness on the part of the poet: "[Poetry is] the confession to oneself made available to all. This is confession as a means to understanding, as testimony to the truths of experience as they become form and ourselves." Again like Whitman, she seeks a form of interaction: "the poet, intellectually giving form to emotional and imaginative experience, with the music and history of a lifetime behind the work, offers a total response . . . in a most human communication." Although Rukeyser was often (not always unfairly) accused of obscurity, she sought throughout her career to construct dialogues across difference. The end of "Waterlily Fire" reinforces this theme: "I speak to you   You speak to me."

From start to finish, Muriel Rukeyser's work has been demanding of the poet and the reader, both politically and aesthetically. Writing according to her own vision, Rukeyser never followed literary or political trends, at times alienating both the left, with whom she was often identified, and the literary elites. Rich has called her "our twentieth-century Coleridge; our Neruda; and more." Taken as a whole, Rukeyser's vision never fails in optimism, despite war, racial hatred, illness, the Holocaust, fascism, and class differences. Her career encompassed some of the most destructive and constructive moments of the twentieth century, emerging from the Great Depression and concluding after the Vietnam War. Echoing Whitman's inclusive vision in "Song of Myself," she affirms in *The Life of Poetry* a statement as true for her in 1980, at the end of her life, as it was for the young poet of the 1930s or

the mature woman of 1949, the year the book was published: "If we believe in the unity and multiplicity of the world, if we believe in the unity and multiplicity of man, then we believe too in the unity and multiplicity of imagination. And we will speak across the barriers, many to many."

Selected Bibliography

WORKS OF MURIEL RUKEYSER

POETRY

Theory of Flight. New Haven, Conn.: Yale University Press, 1935.

U.S. 1. New York: Covici, Friede, 1938.

A Turning Wind: Poems. New York: Viking, 1939.

The Soul and Body of John Brown. New York: Rukeyser, 1940.

Wake Island. New York: Doubleday, Doran and Co., 1942.

Beast in View. Garden City, N.Y.: Doubleday, Doran, 1944.

The Green Wave. Garden City, N.Y.: Doubleday, 1948.

Elegies. New York: New Directions, 1949.

Selected Poems. New York: New Directions, 1951.

Body of Waking. New York: Harper, 1958.

Waterlily Fire: Poems, 1935–1962. New York: Macmillan, 1962.

The Speed of Darkness. New York: Random House, 1968.

Breaking Open: New Poems. New York: Random House, 1973.

The Gates. New York: McGraw-Hill, 1976.

The Collected Poems of Muriel Rukeyser. New York: McGraw-Hill, 1978.

A Muriel Rukeyser Reader. Edited by Jan Heller Levi. New York: Norton, 1994.

BIOGRAPHIES

Willard Gibbs. Garden City, N.Y.: Doubleday, Doran, 1942.

One Life. New York: Simon & Schuster, 1957.

The Traces of Thomas Hariot. New York: Random House, 1971.

LITERARY CRITICISM, REVIEWS, AND THEORY

Review of Faulkner's *Dr. Martino and Other Stories.* *New Masses,* May 22, 1934, pp. 25–26.

Review of Edith Sitwell's *The Pleasures of Poetry.* *New Masses,* February 12, 1935, p. 26.

Review of Archibald MacLeish's *Land of the Free.* *New Masses,* April 26, 1938, pp. 26–28.

"In a Speaking Voice." Review of Robert Frost's *Collected Poems, 1939. Poetry* 54:218–224 (July 1939).

"Under Forty." *Contemporary Jewish Record* 7:3–36 (February 1944).

"Myth and Torment." Review of Robert Duncan's *Heavenly City, Earthly City. Poetry* 72:48–51 (April 1948).

The Life of Poetry. New York: Current Books, 1949; Williamsburg, Mass.: Paris Press, 1996.

"Lyrical 'Rage.' " Review of Kenneth Rexroth's *In Defense of the Earth. Saturday Review,* November 9, 1957, p. 15.

"The Rhythm Is the Person." Review of Marianne Moore's *O to Be a Dragon. Saturday Review,* September 19, 1959, pp. 17–18.

"On John Crowe Ransom's 'Master's in the Garden Again.' " In *The Contemporary Poet as Artist and Critic.* Edited by Anthony Ostroff. Boston: Little, Brown, 1964.

"A Crystal for the Metaphysical." Review of Marianne Moore's *Tell Me, Tell Me: Granite, Steel, and Other Topics. Saturday Review,* October 1, 1966, pp. 52–53.

"Thoreau and Poetry." In *Henry David Thoreau: Studies and Commentaries.* Edited by Walter Harding et al. Rutherford, N.J.: Fairleigh Dickinson University Press, 1972. Pp. 103–116.

"Glitter and Wounds, Several Wildnesses." Review of Anne Sexton's *The Book of Folly. Parnassus* 2:215–221 (fall/winter 1973).

"The Life to Which I Belong." Review of Franz Kafka's *Letters to Felice. American Poetry Review* 3:8–9 (May/June 1974).

TRANSLATIONS

Paz, Octavio. *Selected Poems.* Bloomington: Indiana University Press, 1963.

Paz, Octavio. *Sun Stone.* New York: New Directions, 1963.

Ekelöf, Gunnar. *Selected Poems.* With Lief Sjöberg. New York: Twayne, 1967.

Paz, Octavio. *Early Poems, 1935–1955.* With others. New York: New Directions, 1973.

OTHER WORKS

The Orgy. New York: Coward-McCann, 1965; London: Deutsch, 1966.

Houdini. A play produced by Lenox Arts Center, 1973.

CRITICAL AND BIOGRAPHICAL STUDIES

Barber, David. "Finding Her Voice: Muriel Rukeyser's Poetic Development." *Modern Poetry Studies* 11: 127–138 (1982).

Brinnin, John M. "Muriel Rukeyser: The Social Poet and the Problem of Communication." *Poetry* 61: 554–575 (January 1943).

Carruth, Hayden. "The Closest Permissible Approximation." *Poetry* 101:358–360 (February 1963).

Cooper, Jane. " 'Meeting Places': On Muriel Rukeyser." *American Poetry Review* 25.5:11–16 (1996).

"Craft Interview with Muriel Rukeyser." In *The Craft of Poetry.* Edited by William Packard. Garden City, N.Y.: Doubleday, 1974.

Daniels, Kate. "Muriel Rukeyser and Her Literary Critics." In *Gendered Modernisms: American Women Poets and Their Readers.* Edited by Margaret Dickie and Thomas Travisano. Philadelphia: University of Pennsylvania Press, 1996. Pp. 247–263.

Davidson, Michael. " 'Not Sappho, Sacco': Postmodern Narratives / Modernist Forms in Muriel Rukeyser and Charles Reznikoff." Chapter 5 of his *Ghostlier Demarcation: Modern Poetry and the Material Word.* Berkeley: University of California Press, 1997.

Dayton, Tim. "Lyric and Document in Muriel Rukeyser's 'The Book of the Dead.' " *Journal of Modern Literature* 21:223–240 (winter 1997–1998).

Flynn, Richard. " 'The Buried Life and the Body of Waking': Muriel Rukeyser and the Politics of Literary History." In *Gendered Modernisms: American Women Poets and Their Readers.* Edited by Margaret Dickie and Thomas Travisano. Philadelphia: University of Pennsylvania Press, 1996. Pp. 264–279.

Gardinier, Suzanne. " 'A World that Will Hold All the People': On Muriel Rukeyser." *Kenyon Review* 14: 88–105 (summer 1992).

"Grandeur and Misery of a Poster Girl." *Partisan Review* 10:471–473 (September–October 1943).

Herzog, Anne F., and Janet E. Kaufman, eds. *How Shall We Tell Each Other of the Poet?: The Life and Writing of Muriel Rukeyser.* New York: St. Martin's Press, 1999.

Kalaidjian, Walter. "Muriel Rukeyser and the Poetics of Specific Critique: Rereading the 'Book of the Dead.' " *Cultural Critique* 20:65–88 (1992).

Kertesz, Louise. *The Poetic Vision of Muriel Rukeyser.* Baton Rouge: Louisiana State University Press, 1980.

Miller, James E., Jr. "Whitman's Multitudinous Poetic Progeny: Particular and Puzzling Instances." In *Walt Whitman: The Centennial Essays.* Edited by Ed Folsom. Iowa City: University of Iowa Press, 1994. Pp. 185–200.

Rich, Adrienne C. "Beginners." *Kenyon Review* 15.3: 12–19 (summer 1993).

Rukeyser, William L. "Inventing a Life." In *How Shall We Tell Each Other of the Poet?: The Life and Writing of Muriel Rukeyser.* Edited by Anne F. Herzog and Janet E. Kaufman. New York: St. Martin's Press, 1999. Pp. 299–301.

Terris, Virginia R. "Muriel Rukeyser: A Retrospective." *American Poetry Review* 3:10–15 (May/June 1974).

Thurston, Michael. "Documentary Modernism as Popular Front Poetics: Muriel Rukeyser's 'Book of the Dead.' " *Modern Language Quarterly* 60:59–83 (March 1999).

Turner, Alberta. "Muriel Rukeyser." In *American Poets, 1880–1945, Second Series.* Vol. 48 of *Dictionary of Literary Biography.* Edited by Peter Quartermain. Detroit: Gale, 1986. Pp. 369–375.

Untermeyer, Louis. "The Language of Muriel Rukeyser." *Saturday Review,* August 10, 1940, pp. 11–13.

Ware, Michele S. "Opening the 'Gates': Muriel Rukeyser and the Poetry of Witness." *Women's Studies: An Interdisciplinary Journal* 22.3:297–308 (1993).

Wechsler, Shoshana. "A Mat(t)er of Fact and Vision: The Objectivity Question and Muriel Rukeyser's 'The Book of the Dead.' " *Twentieth-Century Literature* 45.2:121–137 (1999).

BOOK REVIEWS

THEORY OF FLIGHT (1935)

Benét, William Rose. *Saturday Review,* December 7, 1935, p. 47.

Burke, Kenneth. "Return after Flight." *New Masses,* 18, February 4, 1936, p. 26.

Jack, Peter Munro. *New York Times Book Review,* January 12, 1936, p. 15.

Matthiessen, F. O. *Yale Review,* n.s. 25:604 (spring 1936).

Ransom, John Crowe. *Southern Review,* 1:615–16 (winter 1936).

U.S. I (1938)

Benét, William Rose. *Saturday Review,* April 30, 1938, p. 16.

Maas, Willard. "Lost Between Wars." *Poetry* 52:101–4 (May 1938).

Untermeyer, Louis. *Yale Review,* n.s. 26:608 (spring 1938).

Williams, William Carlos. *New Republic,* March 9, 1938, pp. 141–42.

A TURNING WIND (1939)

Bogan, Louise. *New Yorker,* December 16, 1939, p. 120.

Wilson, T. C. *Poetry* 55:214–16 (January 1940).

WILLARD GIBBS (1942)

Kazin, Alfred. "Another Ancestor." *New Republic,* December 7, 1942, p. 752.

Northrop, F. S. C. "A Poet Discovers the Mathematical Physicist." *Saturday Review,* December 5, 1942, p. 10.

Smith, Henry Nash. *New England Quarterly* 16:525 (September 1943).

Time, January 4, 1943, p. 90.

BEAST IN VIEW (1944)

Flint, F. C. *New York Times Book Review,* September 3, 1944, p. 4.

Miles, Josephine. *Accent* 5:60–61 (autumn 1944).

THE GREEN WAVE (1948)

Caldwell, J. R. "Margins of Terror." *Saturday Review,* March 20, 1948, p. 16.

Jarrell, Randall. *Nation,* May 8, 1948, pp. 512–13.

Myles, Eileen. "Fear of Poetry." *Nation,* April 14, 1997, pp. 30–32.

ELEGIES (1949)

Caldwell, J. R. "Invigoration and a Brilliant Hope." *Saturday Review,* March 11, 1950, p. 26.

Rosenberg, Liz. *New York Times Book Review,* October 26, 1997, p. 52.

Rosenthal, M. L. *New Republic,* February 6, 1950, p. 21.

THE LIFE OF POETRY (1949; reprinted 1974; 1996)

Cusac, Anne-Marie. "The Best Books of 1996." *Progressive* 61:34–36 (January 1997).

Myles, Eileen. *Nation,* April 14, 1997, pp. 30–32.

Rolo, Charles J. *Atlantic* 185:81 (March 1950).

Wolfert, Helen. *New York Times Book Review,* April 23, 1950, p. 28.

SELECTED POEMS (1951)

Bogan, Louise. *New Yorker,* November 3, 1951, pp. 150–51.

Eberhart, Richard. *New York Times Book Review,* September 23, 1951, p. 30.

Ferlinghetti, Lawrence. San Francisco *Chronicle,* November 18, 1951, p. 19.

Salomon, I. L. "From Union Square to Parnassus." *Poetry* 80:52–57 (April 1952).

ONE LIFE (1957)

Booth, Philip. *Saturday Review,* August 3, 1957, p. 12.

Eberhart, Richard. *New York Herald Tribune Book Review,* April 28, 1957, p. 4.

Engle, Paul. *New York Times Book Review,* April 14, 1957, p. 16.

Rolo, Charles J. *Atlantic* 199:82 (May 1957).

BODY OF WAKING (1958)

Rexroth, Kenneth. *New York Times Book Review,* October 19, 1958, p. 4.

Rosenthal, M. L. "Closing in on the Self." *Nation,* March 21, 1959, pp. 259–60.

WATERLILY FIRE (1962)

Adkins, Joan F. "The Esthetics of Science: Muriel Rukeyser's 'Waterlily Fire.' " *Contemporary Poetry* 1:23–27 (1973).

Carruth, Hayden. "The Closest Permissible Approximation." *Poetry* 101:358–60 (February 1963).

Swenson, May. "Poetry of Three Women." *Nation,* February 23, 1963, pp. 164–66.

THE ORGY (1965)

Bergonzi, Bernard. *New York Review of Books,* April 22, 1965, p. 15.

Lynd, Helen M. *American Scholar* 34:668–72 (autumn 1965).

Times Literary Supplement, August 11, 1966, p. 728.

THE SPEED OF DARKNESS (1968)

Eberhart, Richard. *New York Times Book Review,* June 23, 1968, p. 24.

Dee, John. *Times Literary Supplement,* May 19, 1972, p. 579.

Hollander, John. *Harper's* 242:109 (February 1971).

BREAKING OPEN (1973)

Bernikow, Louise. *Ms.* 2:35–36 (April 1974).

McGann, Jerome. *Poetry* 125:44 (October 1974).

Meinke, Peter. *New Republic,* November 24, 1973, p. 25.

Times Literary Supplement, March 29, 1974, p. 340.

THE GATES (1976)

Coles, Robert. "Muriel Rukeyser's *The Gates.*" *American Poetry Review* 7:15 (May/June 1978).

Wagner, Linda. "Song of the Sun." *Nation,* March 19, 1977, p. 348.

THE COLLECTED POEMS OF MURIEL RUKEYSER (1978)

Aldan, D. *World Literature Today* 54.3:437–38 (1980).

Schulman, G. *Partisan Review* 47.4:636–38 (1980).

A MURIEL RUKEYSER READER, EDITED BY JAN HELLER LEVI (1994)

Gray, Richard. *Modern Language Review* 90:990–91 (October 1995).

Howe, Florence. *The Women's Review of Books* 12:12–13 (November 1994).

Jordan, June. *Ms.* 4:70–73 (March–April 1994).

—KAREN L. KILCUP

Jane Smiley

1949–

JANE SMILEY CAME of age during the 1960s and 1970s, when she and her generation energetically reexamined many of the social and political assumptions of American society. While studying creative writing and earning a Ph.D. in English literature, she continued to pursue the social and political ideas she developed during her early twenties. Her novels reflect both these ideas and her academic background: they use traditional literary forms such as the Norse saga, the picaresque romance, and Shakespearean tragedy to address themes such as harm to the environment, apocalyptic terror, destructive family relationships, unpredictable marriages, racial prejudice, and above all the use and abuse of power.

BACKGROUND AND DEVELOPMENT

Although Jane Smiley might resist being called an autobiographical writer, a quick survey of her life reveals the sources for much of the recurring material that she uses in her work. She was born September 26, 1949, in Los Angeles to Frances Graves and James Smiley. Her father soon developed emotional problems, and when she was four her parents divorced. To be near her mother's family, Frances Graves moved with Jane to St. Louis and worked there as a journalist. It was during these early years that Jane acquired

her lifelong love of horses. In 1960 her mother married a man with two children; the family moved to Webster Groves, Missouri, where her mother and stepfather had two more children. At school Jane was most interested in history and English.

Smiley left the Midwest for Vassar College, in Poughkeepsie, New York, where she studied English literature. She found a mentor in Harriet Hawkins and began reading literature from a feminist perspective. As a sophomore Smiley met John B. Whiston, a Yale student, and the two moved into a radical student activist commune in New Haven, where they lived for some months. Many of Smiley's political ideas were formed during this period.

In 1970 she and Whiston were married, and after Smiley graduated from Vassar in 1971, they moved to Iowa. Whiston studied medieval history at the University of Iowa, while Smiley, who was turned down by the Iowa Writers' Workshop, settled in as a graduate student's wife, living in a farmhouse and pursuing a lifestyle in keeping with the back-to-the-land movement. She also took classes at the university, beginning with a course in Old Norse; she then enrolled in the doctoral program in English, continuing her study of languages—Gothic, Sanskrit, Old Irish, Old and Middle English. Two years later she finally enrolled in the prestigious Writers' Workshop at

Iowa. In 1975 she and Whiston were divorced, but for Smiley the return to the Midwest would be the seminal event of her career. She lived in Iowa for the next twenty years as student, wife, mother, horse breeder, professor, and writer, and set most of her novels in the Midwest.

In 1976 Smiley won a Fulbright fellowship to write her dissertation on the Icelandic sagas. Although the year she spent in Iceland was desolate and miserable, she conceived the ideas for several novels, including *The Greenlanders* (1988). Returning home with this backlog of creative inspirations, she burst into a flood of productivity. She wrote three novels—*Barn Blind* (1980), *At Paradise Gate* (1981), and *Duplicate Keys* (1984)—many short stories, and the novella *The Age of Grief* (1987), the story of a troubled marriage. In 1981 she began teaching English at Iowa State University in Ames. Her eight-year marriage to William Silag, with whom she had two daughters, Lucy and Phoebe, ended in divorce in 1986. She married Stephen Mortensen in 1987, and they had a son, Axel. Smiley completed the novel *The Greenlanders* in 1988. This monumental work based on Icelandic sagas can be seen as the culmination of the initial burst of creative energy ten years before. It is by far the most complex and carefully wrought of the novels she produced in that period.

Two more novellas, *Ordinary Love* and *Good Will,* published together in 1989, established Smiley as a master of that often neglected and underappreciated form. Her next project was a series of three novels, a tragedy, a comedy, and a romance. The tragedy was *A Thousand Acres* (1991), a contemporary reimagining of Shakespeare's *King Lear.* The novel won the Pulitzer Prize in 1992, and in 1994 Smiley was named a Fellow of the American Academy of Arts and Letters. The comedy, *Moo* (1995), is a satire of academia set on the campus of a large Midwestern university. Finally, *The All-True Travels and Adventures of Lidie Newton* (1998) is a picaresque historical novel set in Kansas in the 1850s. The appearance of *Lidie Newton,* which completed Smiley's projected series of three novels, was followed by dramatic changes in her life. She left the Midwest and moved to Carmel, California, to live on a horse farm, and in 1998 she and Mortensen were divorced.

In much of her work Jane Smiley has created a world in which the core of predictability in marriage is small and the destiny of a family remarkably uncertain. Regardless of the certitudes posited by, for example, Freud and Christianity, or pictured in fairy-tale worlds from "Cinderella" to *Leave It to Beaver,* people reinvent their families daily, even hourly, as the balance of love, power, and commitment shifts; outside forces such as religion, locale, work, and friends turn the dynamic of family relationships upside down. Smiley questions how, on a larger scale, the unique, unstable, private interactions of a family serve as the basis for large, stable, public institutions. Her work is an attempt to tell the truth about these complex and obscure relationships.

BARN BLIND

Set on a horse farm in Illinois, *Barn Blind* initiates Smiley's radical reexamination of marriage. To an outside observer, the Karlson family—Kate, Axel, and their four children—at home on their farm offer a portrait of human and pastoral harmony:

Behind them as they sat there expertly controlling their horses, around them as they trotted down one side of the ring, were their own trees, their own fences, their own rolling fields, as far as the eye could see. The place was, even this late in the summer, so green, so breezy, so refreshing: streams, ponds, fruit trees, horses, cats, geese, pastoral order on every hand. . . . Kate smiled her glorious smile, Axel shaded his eyes. . . . Who, at this moment, did not want to be them?

All this seeming perfection, however, masks an intense and destructive power dynamic. Smiley dramatically reverses the expected roles of husband and wife: Kate is a charismatic, aggressive, tyrannical woman, whereas Axel is kind, flirtatious, and ineffectual.

Kate wants to produce a horse and rider for the U.S. Equestrian Team, and she pursues this ambition with the same spiritual and moral ardor as she invests in her Catholic faith, which has displaced her husband in her life. Axel vainly tries to flirt his way back into her affections. Commanding her children to help her, Kate imposes on them lists of chores, schedules, regulations, and admonitions worthy of a monastery. Although she has the bad-mother ability to balance their fear of her disapproval with their desire for her attention, it is the tension between these motivations that destroys the children's will; Axel, who adores his wife, is too weak to help them. When the three older children are in their teens, Kate chooses one to train for the U.S. Equestrian Team. Ignoring the complexity and unhappiness of these emotionally stunted children, she evaluates them, as though buying a horse, according to how well they suit her purpose: Peter too tall, John too temperamental, Margaret too sentimental, Henry too careless. Each member of the family tells part of the story. As the narrative progresses, however, Kate tells less and less of the story; the children tell more. As this happens, they become the center of interest in the novel.

Margaret, the firstborn, home from college, stays on over her mother's objections. She spends her time weeping and doing chores such as cleaning out closets. (Her father laughingly asks her if she has found the "Sweater of Invisibility.") Peter, the eldest and most handsome son, who is most like his mother, internalizes her every rule and thereby wins her attention and approval; he comes to envision a kind of monklike existence of total contentment on the horse farm. Trapped

between rivalry with Peter for his mother's attention and resentment of her authority, and unable to withdraw from the contest the way his younger brother Henry does, John is the most spectacular casualty of his mother's regime. When his mother chooses to groom Peter for the Equestrian Team, John realizes that she has no more use for him. He curses her, flagellates himself and the horse his mother bred for him, and nearly kills Peter. Finally, at a horse show, John recklessly rides his horse into a difficult jump, killing himself. Kate remains blind to her responsibility for the act, relentlessly pursuing perfection, power, and control. Two days after John's death, Kate experiences tremendous pleasure at Peter's skill in handling his horse.

Henry, the youngest and the clearest-eyed observer, refuses to ignore Margaret's crying jags, watches John's midnight wanderings, and comments that John and Peter are getting "weirder and weirder." After John's death Henry says, "I don't think we should be happy." With a canny instinct for self-preservation, he opts out of the deadly competition for his mother's approval and identifies with his almost invisible father, who makes the money to support the farm. Henry's confidence in the future inspires in Margaret a vision of freedom and life away from the farm, but Kate's tyranny may well have left her too damaged to make that vision a reality. The novel ends on this ambiguous and tenuous note.

AT PARADISE GATE

In sharp contrast to *Barn Blind,* an action-filled, outdoor novel, *At Paradise Gate* is an interior, quiet story. The marriage it portrays is more typical, with a passive wife and a domineering and abusive husband. Anna Robinson nurses Ike through the last hours of his life, joined in the deathwatch by their three middle-aged daughters, Helen, Claire, and Susanna, and an adult granddaughter, Christine, who is pregnant. This is a closed, interior world, small and getting smaller, of waiting, watching, talking, and thinking—five women of three generations trying to make sense of their lives and their marriages. The daughters retell stories of their lives so contradictory and quarrelsome that Anna carries on a silent, contrapuntal reconstruction of the past, an exercise that she has until then avoided because of Ike's distortions: "Ike had turned so many of the incidents of Anna's life into tales that usually she tried to avoid recollection."

The daughters agree on only one thing: that Christine must not abort her baby and preferably not divorce her husband, Todd. For Christine to do either would be to devalue the institution for which they have sacrificed their independence and individuality and suffered humiliation and abuse. The dully opinionated sisters annoy their mother; their sacrifices and disappointments appear to have deprived them of the air and light they would need to generate fresh thoughts, and meaningful words, about *their* experience. Christine, who as her name implies will be the sacrificial lamb, alone commands the language well enough to describe her feelings about her marriage. She cries out to her grandmother, "The very word *marriage* is this atomic explosion that wipes out every idea in the vicinity!" Of her husband Todd she exclaims, "Todd is like an open book to me, but he's not a novel or a volume of philosophy, he's more like an auto repair manual or something. Detailed but without a lot of levels."

Anna Robinson has shied away from memories of how Ike beat her and other contradictions of family life for so long that she cannot tell them to her granddaughter. Instead of the complex truth, Anna tells an admiring story of how Claire cared for her dying husband. The truth would destroy what Anna calls "compromises for the sake of companionship and daily friendship." This astonishingly false description of what has gone on between Anna and Ike, and by extension the daughters and their husbands, sounds as though it was drawn straight from the *Woman's Day* magazine on the coffee table, and it prevails like sacred writ. This family lacks a truth teller like John Karlson to shout obscenities over the drone of lies. But if Anna's experience cannot be marshaled to help Christine, her review of the past expands her own vision of herself. An intensely symbolic dream after Ike's death suggests a poetic rebirth. Once awake, Anna's vision is less poetic. She sees herself as free to plan a trip to her childhood home. Still, at seventy-six, Anna finally has a vision of a freer and less isolated future.

DUPLICATE KEYS

Duplicate Keys, Smiley's third novel, was conceived during a break from her study period in Iceland. She stayed in New York for three weeks with a friend who had lost track of the number of people to whom she had given keys to her apartment. The novel, a murder mystery, is Smiley's only book set in a city.

Aside from solving a murder, Alice Ellis, who is thirty-one, outgrows her identity as a flower child and becomes a responsible adult over the course of this narrative. By the 1980s Smiley's generation had achieved some perspective on the hippie period of their lives, and many writers were addressing the transition to adulthood—some comically, some with pathos and nostalgia. In Smiley's case, the murder mystery plot served her well as a vehicle for a discussion of the secrets and lies that Alice must discard before she can grow up. Particularly, Alice must let go of her friendship with six Midwesterners who have moved to New York to maintain a social network around a failed rock band called the Deep Six. In *Duplicate Keys* the explosive transition to adulthood motivates the murder of two of the band members, whose deaths mark the end of youthful illusions.

Alice finds the bodies and proceeds to look for the killer. But because Smiley adapts the whodunit to her own ends, the emphasis is not so much on finding out who killed the two men as on revealing Alice. Alice's acknowledgment that "it was hard for her to rate points of view or to decide between them" shows just how immature she is. After a recent divorce, Alice is just beginning to construct a life and a home for herself. A passionate affair develops between Alice and Henry, her neighbor, who knows nothing of Alice's friends. Her discovery of the corpses threatens her progress in her new life and pushes her back toward the security of the familiar. While trying to reorder the group of friends she has depended on for so long, gradually discovering hard truths about them, she keeps them and the murders secret from Henry. Detective Honey, the investigating officer, offers this warning to Alice:

> A violent crime is the beginning of a train of events, and a sign that whatever balance a given social network has achieved is strained. The crime is a change, and the change is always sudden and profound, affecting every member of the network in unforeseen ways and often violently.

While Alice is not the narrator of the novel, she is very much the center of consciousness. The bright polished prose in which Smiley recounts Alice's growing awareness of her friends' foibles—their infidelities, rivalries, drug deals, and beatings—reflects the psychic distance Alice maintains from these nasty realities. She judges the group's seriously antisocial behavior none too harshly and finds Detective Honey intrusive and morally obtuse. In a state of dreamy denial, Alice misses all the clues and ignores Detective Honey's warnings that she is in danger. Even as she uncovers the dying marriages, misunderstandings, and violence of her friends, Alice clings more tightly than ever to Susan, the center of the group, whose domesticity provides physical comfort and whose friendship provides emo-

tional security. Alice's identification with Susan is solidified in an intense moment during a shopping expedition when Alice's eyes slide from her own reflection in the mirror to Susan's in "absolute love and familiarity." Even her desire to suck Susan's breasts seems more infantile narcissism than adult eroticism. Her past self and her potential future self have struggled almost to a standstill.

Early in the novel Alice discovers that the plants which she had come to Susan's apartment to water are already wet. She suspects that Susan had been in town at the time of the murder instead of away on vacation. Later Susan tells her that she had often thought of leaving her boyfriend Denny, one of the murder victims, and that she and Denny were not the devoted couple they appeared to be, which confirms Alice's suspicion that Susan is the murderer. At this point Alice's moral and psychological complexity taxes the structure of the murder mystery. She "had apparently overestimated her capacity for moral outrage. Homicidal drunk drivers and cheating landlords . . . outraged her more. . . . Her adoration of her friend, and her anticipation of lasting, comfortable intimacy were greater than ever." What Alice fails to intuit is that Susan hates the friendship that Alice thrusts upon her. In the end Susan decides to use her duplicate key to enter Alice's apartment and kill her to escape the suffocating intimacy and to prevent her exposure as a murderer should she break off their friendship. Alice halfheartedly and belatedly tries to change the lock on her door, but one night Susan gets into the apartment.

The dramatic and terrifying chase that ends the novel works as a device in the murder mystery genre. Alice is, indeed, attempting to preserve her life, but the scene also depicts Alice's final struggle to escape her unrealistic and irresponsible past. She eludes Susan and the next day tells the police what she knows about the murders. Thus with one ingenious stroke Smiley maintains the integrity of the form she has adopted and the plot and character she has created: the murderer is caught, the unwholesome friendship splinters, and Alice develops an adult sense of justice.

THE GREENLANDERS

The Greenlanders, the novel Smiley wrote after *Duplicate Keys,* is the first of a series of complex and dense works that revisit the subjects and themes of Smiley's previous novels but take her further and deeper into them. A massive and heroic undertaking in the tradition of the epic, this novel in the form of a Norse saga was the culmination of years of study and passionate interest. While at the University of Iowa, Smiley had translated from Old Norse the longest and grandest of the Icelandic sagas. During her year in Iceland, she learned of the Greenland settlements established in 985, which had died out sometime around the middle of the fourteenth century. Smiley held off writing about the Greenlanders until she felt that she had mastered her craft; three novels later, she was ready for the undertaking. Written at a rate of twelve to twenty pages a day, the novel ultimately came to eleven hundred pages. Such zeal took a fearful toll on Smiley's personal life. In his *Understanding Jane Smiley,* Neil Nakadate quotes the author as saying that "what [working on the novel] had done to my life, my routine, and my sense of myself appalled me, and I thought, though I loved *The Greenlanders* . . . I never wanted to go through that again, even for another masterwork. I learned . . . that literature wasn't everything, didn't deserve to be everything."

Smiley's character, Gunnar Asgeirsson, the last literate person in Greenland, tells wonderful stories to entertain people during long winter evenings. He protests, "I would not be sorry to [write them], but indeed, the pen goes so slowly that as I make the words, first I lose the thread of the tale, and then I lose the pleasure of the telling. Those tales are meant for speaking, perhaps, while those duller things are meant for writing

down." Gunnar is several times shown contemplating and recording the history of the civilization that he sees deteriorating around him. Of course, *The Greenlanders* is fiction, and Smiley never suggests that she is basing her story on any text, real or imagined. That there is no historical record of the end of this civilization on the fringe of Christendom six hundred years ago adds to the pathos of Smiley's fictional account. That a history might have been written only to be lost is doubly sad.

But the hypothetical existence of such a history adds another dimension to the relationship between history and sagas. It gives weight to the rich details that Smiley adapted from the authentic narratives of other Norse civilizations. In a style adopted from those texts, she chronicles the Greenlanders' travels, feuds, seal hunts, church rituals, housekeeping, parties, fights, courtships, and civic meetings. She describes the farms, the houses, the animals, the bleak landscape, the clothes, the weapons, the boats, the games, the feasts, the hunger, and the births and deaths of a dozen families, in the manner of the following passage.

> Now it happened that the men had spread out, and had their longest spears ready in their hands, and they looked to Hauk, who gave them a signal, and . . . the men leaped up and began to run among the walruses, spearing them in their chests and drawing forth their heart's blood, for this is the way a walrus must be killed, not with blows to the head, like seals, for every walrus has a head like a stone, and is invulnerable there. And as soon as the first blows were struck, the walruses all roused themselves and began to heave about, with a great bellowing and scraping of flesh over rock. . . . And it was the case that Sigrud Sighvatsson stumbled and fell in front of two bull walruses, and he was speared with their tusks and crushed with their weight, but all the other Greenlanders kept their feet and no other men were lost.

The writers of sagas, Smiley has said (as quoted by Nakadate), "almost never used subordination in a sentence. . . . I'd always envisioned them as seeing the world as some kind of phenomenal movie that's just rushing past, that they don't particularly understand." The sense of cause and effect, responsibility, and priorities that subordination imposes on events was alien to the Greenlanders. Their vision of the world requires the paratactic style; God lurks in the "ands" and "buts" of simple declarative and compound sentences, the assumed but unstated cause, agency, and purpose of events in this world and the next. This style not only reflects a sense of fatalism but flattens the Greenlanders' perception of the passing of time and their own past. Thus the novel, written in a direct, measured, and unforgiving prose, keeps the reader, like the Greenlanders, ever focused on the present. Not even remarkable events, which are, after all, the handiwork of God and thus inevitable, are allowed to stand out from the flat surface of the tale. As soon as they are over, these events simply become markers of passing time rather than climaxes or turning points in the colony's destiny.

The style of the sagas themselves offers clues as to why the Greenlanders' settlements failed. With few exceptions, the Greenlanders had only the most fragile grasp of the concept of change, much less the idea of cause and effect. Thus Gunnar's wife, Brigitta's, pragmatic recollections of the past, such as of the time when, because there was enough grass, cattle did not have to be carried to pasture in the spring, seem to her husband indications of a sort of genius. When from present observations she predicts the future, she herself considers her insights visionary. But Brigitta is exceptional. For the most part the Greenlanders' deep-seated fatalism has deprived them of the intellectual tools that might have improved their chances for survival.

In a 1993 interview with Mickey Pearlman, Smiley remarked: "With *The Greenlanders* I wanted to write the saddest book anybody ever read, but I didn't want it to be depressing." To achieve this Smiley creates a slowly disintegra-

ting world whose daily scenes are yet rendered in lively detail and vivid imagery: a dusty loom, a poorly attended town meeting, a shabby church banner, an accidental killing, a theft, a piece of red silk, and always the specter of starvation:

> The story that Kollgrim and the shepherd told was just like every story in Greenland—the food had run out, Finn had gone off to snare partridges or find something else and had not yet returned. . . . Two days ago they had taken to their beds, for keeping the fire was beyond their strength and if Thorkel had not come Lavrans Stead would have quickly become their tomb. Thorkel let everyone eat and talk a while before again approaching Gunnar's bedcloset, for he had some dread of this, and it seemed as he neared the moment of uncovering Gunnar's death that his cousin had been a great friend and ally to him for many years. . . . And it also seemed to him that each friend buried in a hunger time or a sickness time comes to a man as a fresh and painful injury.

The enemies of this civilization, whose family steadings, once jealously tended and guarded, are left neglected or abandoned to fall into the hands of fewer and fewer people, are clannishness, superstition, shortsightedness, bigotry, impulsiveness, violence, and a failure of leadership. Gunnar himself tells admiring tales, such as that of Gudrun out of Norse myth, of bigotry, clannishness, and revenge. Although the priest Sira Pall Hallvardson points out that these tales are "only fit as an exemplum of the lives of men before the coming of Christ as their Savior," Gunnar argues that "Gudrun's tale is a fine one for when I tell it, my breast swells for the injuries done to her, and her bold resolve in avenging herself." He seeks vengeance for himself and his clan more often than he follows the advice of the priest or seeks justice at the society's seasonal court and civic meeting. Literate and imaginative, Gunnar, like his illiterate and unimaginative society, is unable to change, to adopt either a renewing religious faith or a redeeming civic virtue.

When all of the representatives of the Catholic Church and Sweden, the mother country, die within a year, the colony is left without a religious or political tie to the outside world. Local religious and political leadership is also failing. First the colony selects a generous and charming "lawspeaker" who does not know the law. Then the priest Sira Jon goes mad. When Sira Pall inherits Sira Jon's meticulous records of the community's decline in population, livestock, and food, he sees the desperate condition of his flock, but he cannot act. Although Sira Pall has seen something of the world, he is bound to the Church's traditions as Gunnar is bound to society's traditions. He remains too passive to defy the Church for the sake of the people or to defend it when it is threatened by heretical prophets and pseudo-saints. Sitting helplessly in the church, once the pride of the community, Sira Pall contemplates the shabby condition of its banners; these have been repaired so often that there are stitches sewn to stitches and there is nothing of the original banner left.

Perhaps the most egregious moral as well as pragmatic error the Greenlanders make is in demonizing the skraelings, the indigenous people of Greenland who have lived for generations on the land. The Greenlanders believe that the skraelings have learned their adaptive ways from the devil; thus during the bleak arctic winter the colonists starve in their coffinlike bedclosets while the skraelings stand poised with spears for hours over a hole in the ice waiting to kill a seal. Greenlanders who are curious about the skraelings or who learn their skills are ostracized. Gunnar's brother Hauk is rumored to have learned uncanny hunting skills from the skraelings. He sometimes eats raw meat and wears warm practical clothing, as do the skraelings. Although his skill provides a steady supply of seals, walruses, and whales, Hauk is so marginalized that no woman will marry him. Hauk's nephew Kollgrim, who also has learned to hunt from the skraelings, is burned at the stake for enchanting a dying Greenlander woman with arts he learned from the devil—or the skraelings. And his daughter Margret, who marries the brutish but productive Olaf to save her family from want, warns Asta, who is considering marrying a skraeling man to avoid the dreadful hunger, "It is not for us to walk with demons in order to have full bellies." But fearful as the Greenlanders are of the skraelings, it is not they who destroy the colony.

The problem for the Greenlanders is that they stand poised between the pagan hunting and gathering culture of the skraelings and the Christian agricultural mode of the Europeans. The European community, source of the Greenlanders' economic, religious, and political institutions, neglects and ignores the Greenlanders. The Church and the Swedish state fail to send a bishop or a representative to prop up their ailing institutions. Greenlanders are awed by stories of the grandeur of European courts and cities and seduced by luxurious goods. But as the Greenlanders grow poorer, even material ties of trade are broken. English and Icelandic traders laugh at the Greenlanders' primitive commercial goods; and as the colony grows weaker, raiders loot the settlements along the coast and steal or destroy the Greenlanders' property. When Gunnar's sister Margret is murdered by raiders, Gunnar curses her killers, but recognizes that he, too, is a killer of eight men who have done him harm. At the end of the story, he alone among the Greenlanders arrives at an existential understanding of his condition. "And then he saw what he was, an old man, ready to die, pressed against the Greenland earth, as small as an ashberry on the face of a mountain, and he did the only thing that men can do when they know themselves, which was to weep and weep and weep." Gunnar weeps for his condition; he believes that one winter soon they will all die. For his desolate children he offers the only solace that he can: he tells them a story.

THREE NOVELLAS

Before *The Greenlanders* reached print, Smiley wrote and published *The Age of Grief: A Novella and Stories* (1987). The short stories are concerned with the transition from youthful unrealistic views of the world and the self to realistic, responsible, and sometimes disappointing ones, including views of marriage. But it was in *The Age of Grief* and in two subsequent novellas, published together as *Ordinary Love; and Good Will* (1989), that Smiley demonstrates once again the virtuosity with which she can turn from one literary form to another. Anne Bernays, writing in the *New York Times Book Review,* called *The Age of Grief* "a triumph of the craft of narrative." Smiley's publisher was surprised by the popularity of the novellas; the form's chief advantage, according to the author, is that the reader's attention is focused on one theme, without distracting subplots or characters. Smiley also finds that the novella lends itself more readily than the short story or the novel to more meditative narratives. It is long enough to allow the author to contemplate a complex theme but short enough to head off the reader's expectations for more action or characters.

Unlike the characters who populate *The Greenlanders,* with their lack of introspection and meditation, the novellas feature a woman and two men who respond to nuances of human behavior like a wind chime to a summer breeze. They tell stories of families in various states of disrepair: In *The Age of Grief* a troubled marriage is saved by the wife's concealment of her adultery; in *Ordinary Love* the marriage ended long ago, when Rachel Kinsella's confession of an affair caused her husband to strike her, sell their house, and take their children abroad; in *Good Will* a family stays together, but unrecognizably reconfigured. In theme, character, and structure these three novellas play off each other like a sophisticated puzzle of past and present, actions and consequences,

repair and destruction. In a 1989 interview with Laurel Graeber, Smiley explained how *Ordinary Love* and *Good Will* work together: "I consciously constructed one of these novellas as a more masculine narrative—essentially linear—and the other as more feminine, in which things are hidden then revealed."

Despite Smiley's general confidence in the value of confessing the truth, the marriage of David and Dana Hurst in *The Age of Grief* survives precisely because the adulterous wife does not confess. She is in fact ready to; however, her frantic but wise husband makes it impossible for her to do so. The story is narrated by David, a dentist and a meditative man, charming, rueful, and affectionate. Like Axel Karlson and Alice Ellis, he is a passive observer. But unlike them, he is quick both to perceive the significance of his observations and to formulate successful strategies based on them. Realizing that Dana loves risk and adventure, he woos her with hair-raising bike rides. Years into their marriage he intuits to the hour when Dana falls in love with somebody else. Desperate and grief stricken, he turns his reluctance to face his wife's infidelity into a saving device. Sensing that confrontation would probably lead to her leaving him, he chooses to ignore her behavior and fills the silence with talk about teeth or patients or children. Still avoiding confrontation, he nurses the family through a desperate bout of the flu, saving their lives as he is saving the marriage. But David Hurst can never be as he was. He is too vulnerable; "the barriers between the circumstances of oneself and the rest of the world have broken down, inevitably break down, regardless of the care one takes."

The motivation for and consequences of revealing secrets are almost equally convoluted in *Ordinary Love.* Years after her marriage has ended, Rachel Kinsella tells her grown children about her adulterous affair, which ended her "perfect" marriage to their father; she explains that she confessed because "I wanted him to know I wasn't his." She felt that her husband's "enthusiasm for family life was the passion . . . of a true egomaniac whose wife, children, dogs are the limbs of his own body." Her admission established her separateness from her husband. Twenty years later, the truth will also distance her from her grown children. However, Rachel's confession gives the eldest daughter, Ellen, permission to tell her mother some secret and ugly stories of what happened to Rachel's small children after the divorce—among other things their father's abandoning them in London for six days while he pursued an affair in Holland. In this story revelation is the chief action. The outcome of revelation is knowledge; the consequence of knowledge is a sense of responsibility, an awareness that others may be forced to pay the price for one's own self-centered pursuits.

If David Hurst, narrator of *The Age of Grief,* exemplifies instinctive good will, the narrator of *Good Will* mistakes good intentions for good actions. Robert Miller is an aging flower child who clings to the belief that with enough determination and imagination he can isolate himself and his family from ordinary twentieth-century America. On his small, self-sufficient farm Robert makes or builds everything himself. Filled with contempt for self-indulgence and materialism, he betrays in his language an obsession with power. His wife, Liz, and son Tom act and think as he wishes. Liz says that Robert's vision has given meaning to her life, that there is not enough room in her life for both him and God. Although he observes, looking out over his land, that "from the house everything was perfect," he nevertheless broods over the mistake of building on an old foundation that prevented him from constructing a house as large as he wanted. "Sometimes I can see the structure I might have built so clearly that the frustration of what I have done is explosive." Our creations are inevitably raised on a foundation of the past; our present and future cannot escape those limitations.

Yet in his hubris, Robert imagines that he can create an Eden of his own design independent of the past. His desire echoes America's founding fathers' vision of a new Eden; yet Robert's vision is limited by the same moral flaw—a strain of racial bigotry that clouded that earlier vision. Robert's educational theory, which is intended to turn Tom into a version of himself, works only too well. Tom learns not only what his father thinks is right and what he knows how to do, he also perceives and learns what Robert doesn't know even about himself—that he is a bigot. At school Tom taunts and harasses a guileless and pampered African American child, calling her names and destroying her pretty new coat, so unlike his own austere possessions. When Robert invites the little girl and her mother, Lydia, to visit to cure Tom's prejudice, Robert himself feels an unexpected surge of hostility toward the little girl and recognizes his own bigotry at the same time he acknowledges his desire for the girl's mother. The visit does not cure Tom of bigotry. His cruel and erratic behavior accelerates. When he finally burns down the African American family's house, a panoply of social authorities—social workers, psychologists, police, teachers—descend on the Millers. Threatening to take Tom into custody unless the family abandons the counterculture lifestyle they see as the source of Tom's delinquency, they cast Robert out of his Eden and into the materialistic society from which he has isolated himself.

The Millers buy a car and a television. Tom goes to a new school, makes friends, rides a bike, reads comics, plays games of territorial defense, perhaps king of the mountain or football. Liz gets a job at the university bookstore and has lunch with her colleagues. Robert works in construction at the new biotechnology center at the university. They go through intensive counseling aimed at "recovery," working through steps including "denial," "anger," and "bargaining," always with the threat that Tom could be taken from them if they don't comply. But privately Robert refuses to make a whole out of the various contradictions that now inform his family. Tom's innocence will remain unreconciled with his envy and fury, Liz's grief for the farm unreconciled with her happiness in town, Robert's bigotry unreconciled with his desire for Lydia. Robert will look back on their life on the farm as his work of art, even while the present and the future remain in fragments.

A THOUSAND ACRES

Ecological responsibility, race relations, freedom, power, and the family, subjects central to *Good Will,* are reconfigured and reconsidered at length in *A Thousand Acres.* A long novel set in Iowa, it presents the farmer Larry Cook as a modern-day King Lear. Like King Lear dividing his kingdom, Cook abruptly decides to divide his thousand-acre farm among his three daughters. When the youngest daughter, Caroline, hesitates to take her share, the old man cuts her out of the legacy. The two elder daughters, Ginny and Rose, and their husbands, Ty and Pete, seize the opportunity. As in the Lear story, Cook goes mad and dies, and the family is destroyed. Smiley, who studied the play as an undergraduate, has explained, as quoted by Nakadate, that Larry Cook's villainy erupted from her "longstanding dissatisfaction with an interpretation of *King Lear* that privileged the father's needs over the daughters'. . . . I felt, viscerally, that a habit of mind exists in our culture of seeing nature and women in much the same way. . . . Lear's always talking about nature and his daughters, conflating the two."

Smiley adapts many elements from Shakespeare's play: like Cordelia, Caroline marries a good man; like Goneril and Regan, Ginny and Rose take care of their bossy father while pressing the contrary old man to adjust to their wishes;

like Lear, Cook grows furious at his daughters, calling them bitches and whores; in one scene he stubbornly stays out in a storm. Harold Clark, a Gloucester-like neighbor, denounces the daughters for taking the farm away from their father. Clark, in a parallel of Gloucester's relationship with Edmund, his scheming son, and Edgar, his good and loyal son, also pretends to consider leaving his farm to his long-absent son Jess, who wants to practice organic farming, instead of Loren, who has remained on the farm. Clark, like Gloucester, is blinded. Like Cordelia, Caroline returns to defend her father and take care of him in his senility. Like Goneril and Regan with Edmund, Ginny and Rose both fall in love with Jess, have adulterous affairs with him, and quarrel over him. The list of parallels is remarkably long. Yet, whereas in Shakespeare's play Lear and Cordelia command nearly all our sympathy, the two older daughters remaining almost interchangeably viperous, Smiley forces us to look again at Goneril and Regan through the characters Ginny and Rose.

A Thousand Acres is a first-person narrative delivered by the eldest daughter, Ginny, a docile woman with no will of her own; she controls the story but not her own life. On family outings, Ginny recollects, her father would tell histories of the farms they saw:

> Each acre was something to covet, something hard to get that enough of could not be gotten. Any field or farm was the emblem of some historic passion. On the way to Cabot or Pike or Henry Grove, my father would tell us who owned what indistinguishable flat black acreage, how he had gotten it, what he had done and should have done, with it, who got it after him and by what tricks or betrayals.

She has internalized her father's viewpoint while ignoring the memory of the beatings her father gave her and forgetting that he routinely raped her during her adolescence. It is only when Rose prods her to remember that she allows the truth

302 / AMERICAN WRITERS

into her consciousness. Her chief regret is that, having had a series of miscarriages, which she keeps secret from her husband, Ty, she has no children.

Ginny's life of forgetting, secrets, and lies is emblematic of the larger society, for beneath a carefully cultivated appearance of affability and respectability, the patriarchal Cook family throbs with greed, ambition, lust, incest, and violence. The land, Ginny observes, is as "exposed as any piece of land on the face of the earth," and thus the property itself as well as the house, fences, barns, silos, animals, and equipment are groomed and maintained not only to be productive but to look productive to the neighbors. The family, too, makes every attempt to appear stable, united, and well maintained. Underneath the perfectly groomed land controlled by Larry Cook, the most prosperous, powerful, and respectable man in Zebulon County, however, lies water that has been systematically poisoned by the fertilizers and pesticides that keep those fields so green and productive. It is the poisoned water, the secret by-product of those lush fields and that prosperity, that is responsible for Ginny's inability to bear children and the cancer that killed Cook's wife and that now afflicts Rose as well. Like the poisoned and poisonous water, Cook also hides the secret that he raped and beat his two eldest daughters. Ginny and Rose have never told Caroline, whom they protected from their father's predation, about the incest. For Cook, women are like nature: they were created to serve him and his public image. It is as much his prerogative to have sex with his daughters as it is to plow the land or poison the water.

The society around Cook supports him in his egotism. His neighbor Harold Clark, father of Jess, lures Cook's daughters to a community dinner only to humiliate them by accusing them of stealing the farm and neglecting their father—public lies that displace ugly family secrets. When Ginny's amenable husband refuses to defend her against her father, who calls her "whore"

and "bitch," she realizes that Ty's peace-loving manner of soothing her father's wrath covers a consuming desire to control the farm and abide by its traditions. Ultimately, Ty, having lost his marriage as well as the farm, whimpers, "I was on the side of the farm, that's all." What Ty wanted was the grand history of the farm—the power that accumulates as one man after another inherits the land, expands the holdings, grows more crops, builds more buildings, buys more machinery, and above all controls every living creature on it.

The tragedy of the novel lies in the terrible abuse of power that destroys nature as it destroys people. Larry Cook—cross, self-indulgent, drunk, immoral—is not himself a tragic figure, nor is Cook's relinquishing of his property the book's tragic moment. The tragedy has been years, generations, in the making. As nature has been systematically corrupted, children have been beaten and abused; the tragedy resides in the daughters' ineradicable scars from this brutal exercise of power.

When Ginny learns that Rose has betrayed her with her lover Jess and is scheming to get the farm, like Goneril she concocts an awful plan: consumed with jealousy, she prepares a jar of poisoned sausage and sauerkraut for Rose before leaving Ty and the farm. Although Rose does not eat the poisoned food, her breast cancer recurs. Ginny returns to nurse her until she dies. Speaking of their abuse by their father, Ginny tells Rose that Larry Cook represents the system. The rape of the land and the rape of children—especially daughters—parallel each other. Ultimately none of the daughters inherit the land—a multinational agribusiness enterprise acquires the farm—although they inherit the legacy of abuse.

In the end the three daughters remain largely unchanged. Caroline's innocence (or blindness) remains intact and she defends it against information that she suspects would force her to abandon her memories of a happy childhood—the memories that Ginny and Rose have struggled to create. "You're going to tell me something terrible about Daddy, or Mommy, or Grandpa Cook or somebody," Caroline tells Ginny. "You're going to wreck my childhood for me. I can see it in your face. You're dying to do it, just like Rose was." She finishes with, "I realize that some people are just evil." Ginny understands that Caroline is *not* referring to their father.

But Ginny cannot bring herself to tell Caroline that their father abused her older sisters and that they protected her from the same abuse. She finally protects the illusion that she and Rose created. Caroline remains ignorant, and she and Ginny remain unreconciled. Before she dies, Rose reiterates her conviction that truth, however harsh, is all she has ever had.

> I have no accomplishments. . . . I was as much of a nothing as Mommy or Grandma Edith. I didn't even get Daddy to know what he had done, or what it meant. . . . So all I have is the knowledge that I saw! That I saw without being afraid and without turning away, and that I didn't forgive the unforgivable. Forgiveness is a reflex for when you can't stand what you know. I resisted that reflex. That's my sole, solitary, lonely accomplishment.

MOO

By the time she published *Moo,* in 1995, Jane Smiley had assumed her place in the literary establishment. In *Moo,* the comedy in her projected series of three novels in three moods, Smiley displays all her powers of invention, creating a comic Dickensian universe in a huge land-grant university, Moo U., in the middle of Iowa. The characters include professors of several different subjects, provosts, deans, departmental secretaries, cafeteria workers, and half a dozen students. Beyond the university, the novel includes a billionaire, an inventor, and the governor, all of them with stories to tell.

The book teems with evocative descriptions of meals, sexual encounters of various kinds, cam-

pus buildings, and class discussions; scenes are embellished and elaborated on by way of catalog entries, classroom assignments, administrative memos, and student themes; tossed into the mix are a magical garden, a drug deal in a parking lot at dawn, and an overweight pig. The plot is woven of many strands. The philistine governor slashes the university's budget; McDonald's sets up a franchise on the campus common; three freshmen roommates, one of whom was Warren County Pork Queen, struggle to adjust to college life; the provost Ivar Harstad fears that deconstruction is Marxism gone underground; his religious brother decides to marry and reproduce himself in a petri dish; Dr. Gift, the star of the university, promulgates an economic theory of unmitigated capitalism that destroys many small countries; a pair of advisers to the administration refer to students as "customers"; and Mrs. Walker, secretary to the provost and a lesbian, manipulates the computer system and the provost's signature to right wrongs, transfer money and people, and make herself unacknowledged queen of the university. All is spiced with countless love affairs. The rich variety of characters in this novel is matched by the variety of voices. Smiley uses a mélange of narrators—female and male, young and old, black and white, gay and straight—that reflect the makeup of the university, which in turn reflects the makeup of society.

Whether or not this novel is a roman à clef, it clearly springs from Smiley's twelve years of teaching at Iowa State. *Moo* activates all the recognizable voices of a university and then some. At the center of the campus, hidden illegally in an old and empty slaughterhouse, is a mysterious superhog called Earl Butz, who gets to tell his story just as does any other character. This hog, bred to consume as many calories per day as is physically possible—to eat himself to death—has his human counterpart in Dr. Gift, whose first principle is that "all men, not excluding himself, had an insatiable desire for consumer goods." Earl dies appropriately and gracefully at the feet of the Warren County Pork Queen. This comically sterile and dead-end experiment with the superhog parallels the university's ridiculously conflicted ambitions and absurd academic undertakings. Moo U. is buffeted by shifting public policy, shifty politicians, and unprincipled billionaires. Perhaps most egregiously, academic integrity is no match for big money when tycoon Arlen Martin pays Dr. Gift to write an article supporting a plan for a gold-mining operation in Costa Rica that would destroy the country's cloud forest. Moo U. teeters on the brink of moral and intellectual debasement and social dissolution.

Leaks to the Eastern press, provided by Mrs. Walker and disseminated by the novelist and creative writing teacher Tim Monahan, together with a 1960s-style student riot organized by Chairman X, a passionate hippie environmentalist, wreck the gold-mine project and save the cloud forest. The deus ex machina arrives in the form of Loren Stroop, a paranoid farmer and inventor who wills the university his mysterious and priceless invention that will revolutionize farming. Stroop conveniently dies before his faith in the school can be shattered. With the influx of cash from Stroop's bequest, a kind of normalcy is reinstated: professors turn from corrupt, destructive experiments to harmless, quixotic academic projects; the full curriculum is restored; lovers return to their proper mates and relationships ripen; a series of marriages ends the novel.

Moo has been compared to other satires of academia. Jonathan Yardley notes that "Moo is— or attempts to be—a satirical novel of university life in the tradition of Mary McCarthy's *The Groves of Academe* and most particularly, Randall Jarrell's *Pictures from an Institution.*" Michiko Kakutani and an anonymous reviewer in *The Economist* compared the book to David Lodge's satires of academia. Although the students in *Moo* are more likely to study animal husbandry or engineering than history or English

literature, and find themselves on a large Midwestern campus rather than at an elite Eastern college, the novel paints a picture of a familiar academic world, with vivid strokes of pomposity, lunacy, petty ambition, greed, lechery, and social and academic hierarchies. Indeed, through hypocrisy, self-interest, and venality, Moo U., perfectly suited to lead a campaign to protect the environment, threatens to become the agent of its destruction. A state university under the control of the legislature provides an ideal subject for a satire that skewers society as a whole. Blended with the academic satire is a strong element of the pastoral comedy, with the students as rustics, the faculty as foolish if well-intentioned lovers, the provost and administration as the benign if sometimes misguided aristocracy, and the governor as the wicked ruler, with Dr. Gift as his henchman.

As critics have observed, Smiley's art is not of the slash-and-burn variety. Alison Lurie observed, "For a satirist, Ms. Smiley is remarkably fair-minded and kind." Jonathan Yardley commented, "Smiley is ill-equipped to follow in Jarrell's train. This is not because she lacks humor but because, more tellingly, she lacks malice." Indeed, the characters are too complex to be all bad or all good. Bad guy Dr. Gift, who loves food, drink, sex, and all the goodies money can buy, has invented a philosophy to justify his self-indulgence. Only people who have plans to exploit their neighbors take Dr. Gift's preposterous philosophy seriously. Good guy Chairman X, the keeper of the social conscience, is a skirt chaser. No one totally escapes Smiley's ridicule, just as no figure is reduced to pure villainy or sainthood; rather, some characters are morally superior to others and thrive in the end. Smiley creates a pluralistic society-within-a-society that bumbles along because of rather than despite its conflicting points of view. The academy is not just the subject of this novel, it is the arena in which power, money, and ecological responsibility are juggled and momentarily balanced in a happy, comic conclusion.

LIDIE NEWTON AND BEYOND

The All-True Travels and Adventures of Lidie Newton is a romance set in the nineteenth century in which the title character goes on a journey, has many adventures, sees astonishing things, and learns about herself and the world. Based on journals kept by women in the late nineteenth century, the novel is also a vivid recreation of an infamously violent period in American history. The novel is set in what was then called Bleeding Kansas, where the ideologies of slavery and abolition faced off in riotous anarchy. If the novel begins with ironic hints of the Cinderella story, Lidie, the homely and unfeminine narrator, depends on quite another book for guidance in her life: Miss Catherine E. Beecher's *A Treatise on Domestic Economy, for the Use of Young Ladies at Home,* a widely read book during the nineteenth century. Having already gained some sense of herself from a brief stay at Miss Beecher's school, she now carries the book with her and uses sentences from it as headings for each section of her diary. Although Beecher's *Treatise* becomes useless as a guide through the upheavals in Kansas in the 1850s, it gives some insight into a conventional woman's life in a conventional setting. But Lidie's life is far from conventional. As her sense of herself expands through her adventures and her experience with slavery, she leaves Miss Beecher far behind. Lidie confronts one situation after another in which race and gender are matters of life or death.

In *Harper's* in 1996, two years before *Lidie Newton* appeared, Smiley had published a radical critique of Mark Twain's *The Adventures of Huckleberry Finn.* Upon rereading the narrative as an adult, she writes, she was "stunned" by the idea that anyone could think it "a great novel . . .

even a serious novel." She argues that the needs of Jim, the runaway slave, are neglected and his voice shortchanged; she goes on to charge that "the last twelve chapters are boring, a sure sign that an author has lost the battle between plot and theme and is just filling in the blanks." Furthermore, she contends, "It undoubtedly would have been better for American literature, and American culture, if our literature had grown out of . . . *Uncle Tom's Cabin,* which for its portrayal of an array of thoughtful, autonomous, and passionate black characters leaves *Huck Finn* far behind." The article provoked a storm of critical controversy, most notably in a reply to Smiley's essay by Justin Kaplan that appeared in the *New York Times Book Review:* "The issue here, in part, is whether you want certainty or conflict in the literature you value—closure or risk, instruction or exploration, right-mindedness or free-mindedness." *Lidie Newton* at least partially answers Smiley's critics; it is a novel that invites comparison with Twain's.

Unlike Huck, Lidie becomes a thoroughgoing abolitionist. Huck is reconstructed as Frank, Lidie's scavenger nephew; Lorna, a slave more assertive than the malleable Jim, presses Lidie to help her escape, which Lidie risks her life to do. Unlike the "mainly" true story that Huck tells in Twain's novel—Huck says that telling lies ("stretchers") is "nothing" and that only women tell the truth—*Lidie Newton* is an "all-true" story replete with historical facts. In Smiley's view, achieving historical accuracy demonstrates understanding of historical conditions and situations.

Smiley's details make the society creating itself in Kansas in the 1850s as convincing as the disintegrating society of *The Greenlanders.* With a largely untested political system and a romantic vision of the possibilities of the West with its untapped resources, Americans swallowed whole the propaganda handbills about opportunities for a better life and moved to the frontier. Lidie herself reads those deceptive handbills and imagines moving to a tidy, peaceful town complete with a library. This illusion dissolves for Lidie upon arrival at the dock in Kansas City, where she sees a scene of bullying and disorder that epitomizes everyday life in Kansas. Simple disorder turns into vicious hostility and chaos as the quarrel between abolitionists and pro-slavery factions simmers. Ruffians and other pro-slavery sympathizers prowl, burn, and loot their way across the prairie, harassing, beating, and murdering abolitionists as they go. As Lidie records these events, her eyes are gradually opened to political reality.

Lidie's love for adventure first manifests itself when she swims across the Mississippi—a feat that her nephew Frank relishes in the retelling and that Lidie herself uses as a precedent for her further adventures. Having shirked household drudgery in her half sisters' homes, she hunts, rides, and fishes. Neither beautiful nor womanly, and having turned down three widower suitors, she gives her sisters no reason to think she will ever marry until she meets Thomas Newton, who perceives that her skills in hunting, fishing, and managing horses will be more useful on the frontier than beauty and domestic graces. Unfortunately, he fails to value her sensitivity to danger when he smuggles a load of carbines to his friends in Lawrence, Kansas, an abolitionist settlement at the heart of the violence. In a town of roughnecks, braggarts, loudmouths, and villains, Thomas remains calm, fair-minded, philosophical, and distant. By contrast, Lidie is practical, decisive, and productive. She buys an excellent horse, makes friends, hunts for food, chinks the cracks in their house, and loves a man whose intellectual and emotional range is far more limited than hers. Less than ten months after her marriage to Thomas, Lidie watches as ruffians murder him and kill her horse. Thomas and Lidie have tried to create a civilized life combining morality and domesticity—the nineteenth-century ideal. But that life is over, and so is Lidie's life as more-or-less conventional woman and wife.

Lidie sets out to avenge Thomas's murder or perhaps just to have more adventures. Against the advice of slippery and ubiquitous Mr. Graves, a wagoner who provides transportation to newly arrived settlers, Lidie slips off the boat that would take her home to safety in Illinois and crosses into the dangerous slave state of Missouri. In Thomas's clothes she finds a simple disguise that reveals how confined women's lives are. She works briefly for a newspaper and follows false leads to the murderers on a thirty-mile walk. When she collapses on the lawn of a slaveholder's plantation house, Lorna, a slave of about thirty, nurses her through a miscarriage. During her stay, Lidie shamefacedly enjoys the luxuries and leisure of plantation life. Recognizing her as an abolitionist sympathizer, Lorna presses Lidie to help her escape. The two leave together as woman with maid. But Lorna fails to understand that a lone white woman's position is only marginally more secure than a slave's. Betrayed to the police by Mr. Graves, Lorna is sold down the river; Lidie goes to jail but is spared hanging. After returning to Illinois, Lidie visits Massachusetts once to see Thomas's mother and makes a speech about trying to free Lorna. She feels challenged by the complexity of the question of slavery. Unlike Huck, Lidie never condones lying but remains a believer in the truth. But Smiley does not portray Lidie as another Harriet Beecher Stowe. Lidie has no confidence that she can tell the truth about her experience. After giving one lecture to abolitionists in Massachusetts, she feels "that every word about Lorna seem[ed] like a betrayal of her, every word about Papa and Helen a betrayal of myself." Ultimately she concludes, "No one could describe what was true in Kansas and Missouri." The profound muddle that Lidie experienced left her wordless. All Lidie and

Frank are able to conclude is that "nothing ever surprised either of us again."

Smiley's skill in creating a vivid and trustworthy narrator and her respect for historical accuracy make *The All-True Travels and Adventures of Lidie Newton* a bold and persuasive depiction of the social and physical manifestation of America's deepest moral crisis. Without either legal or political systems to structure the conflict, even the wise and well-intentioned fail to find the language to express its complexities. In the anarchical society of Kansas, with its embryonic social structures, as in the dying society of *The Greenlanders,* with its disintegrating social structures, the two articulate main characters are unable to tell the truth about what they have seen and so they tell imaginary stories, weep, or fall silent.

In her fiction Smiley explores a remarkable variety of both subject and form. From intimate portraits of crumbling marriages to epic portrayals of entire societies, the scope of the subjects of Smiley's fiction is impressive. Equally impressive is the range of traditional genres she has mastered—a different one for every major novel. While this variety of form and subject is a notable characteristic of Smiley's writing, the true bedrock of her work lies in her conviction that there are social responsibilities concomitant with her art. Whatever the genre, Smiley tackles those responsibilities anew in each work.

Selected Bibliography

WORKS OF JANE SMILEY

NOVELS AND COLLECTED SHORT STORIES

Barn Blind. New York: Harper and Row, 1980.

At Paradise Gate. New York: Simon and Schuster, 1981.

Duplicate Keys. New York: Knopf, 1984.

The Age of Grief: A Novella and Stories. New York: Knopf, 1987.

The Greenlanders. New York: Knopf, 1988.

Ordinary Love; and Good Will: Two Novellas. New York: Knopf, 1989.

The Life of the Body: A Story. Limited ed., with six hand-colored linoleum cuts by Susan Nees. Minneapolis: Coffee House Press, 1990.

A Thousand Acres. New York: Knopf, 1991.

Moo. New York: Knopf, 1995.

The All-True Travels and Adventures of Lidie Newton. New York: Knopf, 1998.

SHORT STORIES

"And Baby Makes Three." *Redbook,* May 1977, pp. 231–234.

"I in My Kerchief and Mama in Her Cap." *Redbook,* January 1978, pp. 157–161.

"The Blinding Light of the Mind." *Atlantic Monthly,* December 1983, pp. 48–58.

"The Nickel Plan." *McCall's,* October 1990, pp. 112ff.

"Fahrvegnugen." *Playboy,* December 1991, pp. 102ff.

"Turnpike." In *Voices Louder than Words: A Second Collection.* Edited by William Shore. New York: Vintage, 1991.

"Gregor: My Life as a Bug." *Harper's,* August 1992, pp. 36–37.

"A Quarrelsome Peace." *New York Times Magazine,* December 20, 1992, pp. 26–28, 46.

"Creative Writing 101." *Esquire,* March 1995, pp. 129–130.

"The Life of the Body." In *Prize Stories 1996: The O. Henry Awards.* Edited by William Abrahams. New York: Doubleday, 1996.

ARTICLES AND ESSAYS

"Imposing Values." *New York Times Magazine,* September 20, 1992, pp. 28–29.

"The Undresser." *Allure,* October 1992, pp. 96–97.

"Can Mothers Think?" In *The True Subject: Writers on Life and Craft.* Edited by Kurt Brown. Saint Paul, Minn.: Graywolf Press, 1993. Pp. 3–15.

"Something Extra." *New York Times Magazine,* October 10, 1993, p. 8.

"Borges, JCO, You, and Me." *Antaeus* 73/74:56–57 (spring 1994).

"Can Writers Have Friends?" In *Between Friends: Writing Women Celebrate Friendship.* Edited by Mickey Pearlman. Boston: Houghton Mifflin, 1994. Pp. 44–45.

"So Shall We Reap." *Sierra* 79, no. 2:74–83 (March/April 1994).

"A Novel Encounter." *Harper's Bazaar,* March 1995, pp. 168–169.

"Jane Austen's Heroines." *Victoria,* May 1995, pp. 28–29.

"Confess Early and Often." *New York Times Magazine,* October 8, 1995, pp. 62–63.

"Getting into Character . . . Psyche." *New York Times Magazine,* October 29, 1995, p. 50.

"And Moo to You Too." *Civilization* 2:75 (November/December 1995).

"The Bathroom." In *Home: American Writers Remember Rooms of Their Own.* Edited by Sharon Sloan Fiffer and Steve Fiffer. New York: Pantheon, 1995. Pp. 106–115.

"Full Cry." In *Women on Hunting.* Edited by Pam Houston. Hopewell, N.J.: Ecco Press, 1995. Pp. 186–198.

Introduction to *Best American Short Stories 1995.* Edited by Jane Smiley with Katrina Kenison. Boston: Houghton Mifflin, 1995.

"Say It Ain't So, Huck: Second Thoughts on Mark Twain's 'Masterpiece.' " *Harper's,* January 1996, pp. 61–67.

"Afterword: Gen-Narration." In *Family: American Writers Remember Their Own.* Edited by Sharon Sloan Fiffer and Steve Fiffer. New York: Pantheon, 1996, pp. 241–247.

"Making Enemies: Your Bad Review." *Hungry Mind Review* 40:21 (winter 1996/1997).

"Taking It All Back." *Washington Post Book World,* June 21, 1998, p. 8.

"Two Plates, Fifteen Screws." In *The Healing Circle: Authors Writing of Recovery.* Edited by Patricia Foster and Mary Swander. New York: Plume, 1998. Pp. 99–106.

CRITICAL STUDIES

Bakerman, Jane S. "Renovating the House of Fiction: Structural Diversity in Jane Smiley's *Duplicate Keys.*" *Midamerica* 15:111–112 (1988).

Bernays, Anne. "Toward More Perfect Unions." *New York Times Book Review,* September 6, 1987, p. 12. (Review of *The Age of Grief.*)

Carlson, Ron. "King Lear in Zebulon County." *New York Times Book Review,* November 3, 1991, p. 12. (Review of *A Thousand Acres.*)

Conrad, Peter. "Expatriating Lear." In *To Be Continued: Four Stories and Their Survival.* New York: Oxford University Press, 1995. Pp. 131–134, 141, 143, 151.

Eder, Richard. "Moo U.: The Superheated Life of a University Community." *Los Angeles Times Book Review,* April 2, 1995, p. 5.

Fuller, Edmund. "Kind and Unkind Daughters." *Sewanee Review* 101:50–52 (spring 1993).

Heller, Dana. "Father Trouble: Jane Smiley's 'The Age of Grief.' " In *Family Plots: The De-Oedipalization of Popular Culture.* Philadelphia: University of Pennsylvania Press, 1995. Pp. 94–112.

Humphreys, Josephine. "Perfect Family Self-Destructs." (Review of *Ordinary Love; Good Will.*) *New York Times Book Review,* November 5, 1989, p. 1.

Kaplan, Justin. "Selling *Huck Finn* Down the River." *New York Times Book Review,* March 10, 1996, p. 27. (Response to Smiley's "Say It Ain't So, Huck," *Harper's,* January 1996.)

Lurie, Alison. "Hog Heaven." *New York Times Book Review,* April 2, 1995, p. 26. (Review of *Moo.*)

Mallon, Thomas. "Bleeding Kansas." *New York Times Book Review,* April 5, 1998, p. 10. (Review of *Lidie Newton.*)

Marsh, Kelly A. "The Neo-Sensation Novel: A Contemporary Genre in the Victorian Tradition." *Philological Quarterly* 74:99–123 (winter 1995).

Moore, Lorrie. "Fiction in Review." *Yale Review* 83, no. 4:135–143 (October 1995).

Nakadate, Neil. *Understanding Jane Smiley.* Columbia: University of South Carolina Press, 1999.

Schine, Cathleen. "The Way We Live Now." *New York Review of Books,* August 10, 1995, pp. 38–39.

Yardley, Jonathan. "Wallowing in Hog Heaven." *Washington Post Book World,* March 26, 1995, p. 3.

INTERVIEWS

Graeber, Laurel. "The Problem Is Power." *New York Times Book Review,* November 5, 1989, p. 45.

Neubauer, Alexander. "Jane Smiley." In *Conversations on Writing Fiction: Interviews with Thirteen Distinguished Teachers of Fiction Writing in America.* Edited by Alexander Neubauer. New York: Harper-Perennial, 1994. Pp. 209–227.

Pearlman, Mickey. "Jane Smiley." In *Listen to Their Voices: Twenty Interviews with Women Who Write.* New York: Norton, 1993. Pp. 99–111.

Ross, Jean W. "Smiley, Jane (Graves) 1949–, CA Interview." *Contemporary American Authors.* New Revision Series 30. Edited by James G. Lesniak. Detroit: Gale Research, 1990. Pp. 411–413.

Schneider, Bethany. "A Few Words with Jane Smiley." *Elle,* March 1995, p. 190.

—NANCY COFFEY HEFFERNAN

W. D. Snodgrass

1926–

Born in Wilkinsburg, Pennsylvania, on January 5, 1926, to Bruce D. and Jessie Helen Murchie Snodgrass, William De Witt Snodgrass, known to his friends as De (pronounced "Dee"), entered Geneva College in nearby Beaver Falls, but his studies there were interrupted when he was drafted into the U.S. Navy during World War II and sent to the Pacific. After his hitch in the service, he returned to Geneva College but then transferred to the University of Iowa Writers' Workshop, where John Berryman and Robert Lowell were teaching under the direction of Paul Engle. After completing his work for the bachelor's degree in 1949, Snodgrass continued at the workshop, receiving an MA in 1951 and an MFA in 1953. Just as important as his academic accomplishments were the first appearances of his poems in such magazines as *Botteghe Oscure, Partisan Review, Paris Review, Hudson Review,* and *The New Yorker.* In 1957 five sections from a sequence entitled "Heart's Needle" were included in the important anthology *New Poets of England and America,* edited by Donald Hall, Robert Pack, and Louis Simpson.

SINCERITY WITH CONSTRAINTS: *HEART'S NEEDLE* AND *REMAINS*

Snodgrass was married four times, and the vicissitudes of his family life and the trauma of his separation from his children were central concerns in his early work. His 1946 marriage to Lila Jean Hank ended in divorce in 1953, and his child by that marriage, Cynthia Jean, is the subject of the "Heart's Needle" suite of poems, which is dedicated to her and which gave his first book its title, from the epigraph of an old Irish story, "The Frenzy of Suibne," in which that character observes, "An only daughter is the needle of the heart." The book was amazingly successful for a volume of poetry, winning its author the Pulitzer Prize in 1960—when he was thirty-four years old—along with a National Institute of Arts and Letters award; the British Guinness Award followed in 1961.

The Pulitzer, with its three-thousand-dollar stipend, is not a major prize in purely monetary terms but is extremely prestigious, not least of all, perhaps, because most of its categories are for achievement in journalism, and newspapers and other media pay it a disproportionate amount of attention. It is unusual, moreover, for the Pulitzer to be given to a first book of poems. The poet Karl Shapiro, who also won the prize for his first book, referred to it as a millstone.

What was startling about Snodgrass's work was what M. L. Rosenthal first called its "confessional" quality, a term that Robert Phillips adopted in 1973 for his book-length study *The Confessional Poets.* The undisguised use of intimate autobiographical information by Snodgrass and other poets writing at the time may seem unremarkable now but was then a breaking of the traditions of what had been the conventional symbolist and metaphysical poetic practice.

Robert Lowell's *Life Studies,* which won the National Book Award in 1960, was similarly liberating. Lowell had disliked some of the *Heart's Needle* poems when he'd first seen them at Iowa, but later came to admire them and perhaps even to imitate them; he praised Snodgrass in letters to such writers as Randall Jarrell and Elizabeth Bishop, comparing him with Jules Laforgue and Philip Larkin. Snodgrass in turn acknowledged his debt to Lowell, while also referring on several occasions to a characteristically provocative remark Jarrell once made to him: "Snodgrass, do you know you're writing the very best second-rate Lowell in the whole country?" In truth it can be argued—and some critics have done so—that Snodgrass's poems are more accomplished than Lowell's, more in control and truer in their responses to the awkward demands of the time and the occasions than those of his slightly older contemporary.

There was in Snodgrass's early work a powerful presentation of emotion that was all the more affecting because of its formal constraints. Poem number 7 in the "Heart's Needle" sequence, for example, takes the moment of pushing his daughter on a playground swing and makes of it a figure not only of the difficulties of the parent-child relationship but also of much of our imperfect human intercourse. It begins:

> Here in the scuffled dust
>   is our ground of play.
> I lift you on your swing and must
>   shove you away,
> see you return again,
>   drive you off again, then,
> stand quiet till you come.
>   You though you climb
> higher, farther from me, longer,
>   will fall back to me stronger . . .

The poet is divorced and is taking his daughter to the playground not merely on a visit but as a visitation to which he is entitled under a court order—information that we cannot imagine Snodgrass's modernist predecessors T. S. Eliot or Ezra Pound confiding—but what strikes us now, more than the confession itself, is the rhetorical sophistication and calibration of the statement. The decorum of literature was not so much violated by the Beat poets in the 1960s as it was erased, and Snodgrass, from the vantage point of the twenty-first century, looks to us to be more paleface than redskin, to use the literary critic Philip Rahv's politically incorrect but still useful terminology. Snodgrass's practice did not change but the boundaries moved, so that his place in the literary landscape seems quite different now from what it was in the mid-twentieth century.

His description of that poetic practice is available for us to inspect, most particularly in the essays in *In Radical Pursuit: Critical Essays and Lectures* (1975), in which he records the happening of a poem, even though, as he says, "To do this, I shall have to become, for the moment, a sort of earnest graduate student of my own poem." He gives early and later versions of a poem in the "Heart's Needle" sequence, demonstrating that a craftsmanly and rhetorical fastidiousness has a moral dimension, as it forces the poet to confront an early stage of a work in progress and challenge its accuracy and authenticity.

Of the first version of the poem, which alludes to his asthmatic sister—his child's aunt—he observes the following:

> I can now see that it was sentimental and insincere. For, in the structure which it built (or jerrybuilt), it pretended that my feelings of grief were very important; they were not. Of course I had such feelings, but I had put them at the climactic point of my poem, not because they were actually important climactic feelings in my mind, but rather because . . . they seemed an obvious (because stereotyped) climax for a poem.

What he goes on to remark is central not only to his own work but to the practice of most poets in our time:

> I am left, then, with a very old-fashioned measure of a poem's worth—the depth of its sincerity. And it seems to me that the poets of our generation—those of us who have gone so far in criticism and analysis that we cannot ever turn back and be innocent again, who have such extensive resources for disguising ourselves from ourselves—that our only hope as artists is to continually ask ourselves, "Am I writing what I *really* think? Not what I think is acceptable; not what my favorite intellectual would think in this situation; not what I wish I felt. Only what I cannot help thinking."

Lowell was perhaps luckier, starting out as he did as a paleface and then moving ever further into the redskin camp with work that became not only more and more confessional but was at the same time less and less artificed—as if artifice and technical accomplishment were not aids to achieving the kind of sincerity Snodgrass described but obstacles to authenticity, impediments to the honest expression of the poet's feelings.

Whether because of the poems' sincerity or technical merit, the critics responded to *Heart's Needle* (1995) with enthusiasm, recognizing the authority and originality of that collection. Writing in *Poetry,* Hayden Carruth observed, "I think it is only fair to say that Snodgrass seems to me by far the best poet to have appeared so far in this decade and probably one of the best of any age now practicing in America."

That kind of praise and a Pulitzer Prize can be dangerous, bringing with the admiration an equal measure of scrutiny that can be, for a young man or woman, intimidating. Snodgrass's early success seems to have been a burden of some weight, for he was all but silent for almost a decade, and those poems he did publish appeared under a pseudonym—S. S. Gardons, an anagram for "Snodgrass."

In the "second selection" of *New Poets of England and America,* which appeared in 1962, along with poems under his own name there are two poems attributed to Gardons, who is identified in the contributors' notes as follows: "Born in Red Creek, Texas, 1929. Works as a gas station attendant in Fort Worth. He has published in *Hudson Review.*" By the time the Gardons poems appeared in book form in 1970 in a handsome limited edition (only two hundred copies were issued and none was sent out for review) titled *Remains,* Snodgrass had embellished this fictive bio beyond the bounds of plausibility:

> S. S. Gardons lived most of his life in and near Red Creek, Texas. For years he worked as a gas station attendant, although he took a few university classes in Houston, and later became an owner of a cycle shop. Also a musician, he played lead guitar in the well-known rock group, Chicken Gumbo. This sequence of poems was collected by his friends after his disappearance on a hunting trip in the mountains. From the condition of his abandoned motorcycle, it was impossible to determine whether he suffered foul play, was attacked by animals, merely became confused and lost, or perhaps fell victim to amnesia. At present, the case is listed as unsolved.

It was only after the death of his parents that Snodgrass revised and republished the Gardons work as his own, but by that time his life and career had developed in quite different ways. These poems about the lives of—and his love-hate relationship with—his parents and about the death of his sister from complications resulting from asthma—but more generally from having been emotionally smothered—are pieces he might well have wanted to keep his mother from seeing. J. D. McClatchy has shrewdly noted a question that Snodgrass asked in an essay about John Crowe Ransom that is relevant to these *Remains* poems: "How could one be a first-rate artist without offending, deeply, those he most loves?"

The family drama is dreadful in Snodgrass's rendering but not unusual. As Robert Phillips observed, what differentiates Snodgrass's confessional poems from Lowell's is that in *Life Studies* we get "venerable stone porches, Edwardian clocks, pedigreed puppies, Rogers Peet pants, chauffeured autos, home billiard tables, and wall-to-wall leather-bound books. At times the sheer weight of possessions burdens Lowell's volume. Snodgrass, on the other hand, happily wears his relative poverty on his shirt-sleeve. Experience has taught him 'That all the ordinary / Surrounds of social life are futile and vain.' " The Snodgrass of that period sees both marriage and divorce as traps, his own wretched experience different from but not better than that of his parents who stayed together. In Snodgrass's world, there are few choices and all of them may be bad.

Finally, to compare Snodgrass and Lowell in another way, we may consider their uses of a strikingly similar image. We can admire the battiness of Lowell's lines in "Sailing Home from Rapallo":

> In the grandiloquent lettering on Mother's coffin,
> *Lowell* had been misspelled *LOVEL.*
> The corpse
> was wrapped like *panetone* in Italian tinfoil.

It is certainly a striking and even suggestive picture—the life of the deceased parent was, the poem suggests, rich, exotic, but unpalatable in more than delicate nibbles. But there is no organic connection with the rest of the poem of the kind that Snodgrass engineers in "Disposal," in which, as he explained in *After-Images,* he considers the dismal business of cleaning out his sister Barbara's drawers and closets after her death. He refers to her body which, like so many other precious but useless items, is now wrapped up:

> Spared all need, all passion,
> Saved from loss, she lies boxed in satins
>
> Like a pair of party shoes
> That seemed to never find a taker;

> We send back to its maker
> A life somehow gone out of fashion
> But still too good to use.

EARLY EXPLORATION: *AFTER EXPERIENCE*

Snodgrass's second book, *After Experience,* appeared in 1968, and while it continued with his personal and confessional poetry, it also introduced elements that turned out to be harbingers of the new directions his work would take. For one, there is the broad political satire of "Exorcism," a kind of ghastly fun to which Snodgrass returned later in the poems of *The Fuehrer Bunker: The Complete Cycle* (1995), which had been begun as *The Führer Bunker: A Cycle of Poems in Progress* two decades earlier in 1977. There are the translations from the German poet Rainer Maria Rilke and others, which would prove to be instructive and productive; and there are poems about art, the considerations of paintings by Matisse, Vuillard, Manet, Monet, and Van Gogh, which extended his range and allowed him to find new registers of an ever deepening voice.

"Exorcism" is almost but not quite a series of jokes, about the American diplomat John Foster Dulles, the influence peddler Bernard Goldfine, and Richard Nixon, then vice president of the United States. The poem itself is no great work (Snodgrass does not even include it in his *Selected Poems: 1957–1987* [1987]), and yet it opened up a new vein of poetic practice from which he would extract great riches. The Dulles stanza reads:

> Out, out, you Dullard in the nerves,
> Gray brinkman, tingling through the blood,
> Numb-fingered, dulled in the taste bud,
> Who can't eat cake, would not dare kiss,
> So Chickensteers around Love's curves
> Teasing the intimate abyss.

What perhaps gives this work more point is that it immediately follows the volume's title poem,

"After Experience Taught Me . . ." which is a contemplation of what the poet learned in the navy, how to kill a man bare-handed by poking him in the eyes and ripping off the facial mask. It concludes:

> Wishing to be, to act, to live. He must ask
> First, in other words, to actually exist.

> And you, whiner, who wastes your time
>   Dawdling over the remorseless earth,
> What evil, what unspeakable crime
>   Have you made your life worth?

People like Dulles sit at desks in Washington, D.C., playing their brinkmanship games, Snodgrass seems to say, while out in the field men must commit heinous acts. Snodgrass's treatment of Nixon is even more harsh because Nixon was a fellow lapsed Quaker:

> And you, Nixmaster of the tongue,
> Soft wordsman, scrambling in the mind,
> Unsilent Quaker who can find
> True facts belying your own doubt
> Till all walls fall; ruler among
> The ruins of affection; out!

The poet explained in a 1998 interview with Philip Hay that his service in the Pacific did not include combat. It was nonetheless difficult duty. He was for a time a brig guard, and as he recalled, the prisoners "were made to do heavy labor. They were also made to sleep in an absolutely bare room, under bright lights, with no furnishings of any kind, just a bucket for shitting in. And as if that weren't bad enough, I had to go in every night, every hour on the hour, get these guys on their feet, bring them to attention, dismiss them, and then leave." Snodgrass had to do this for a week or so, as the prisoners grew steadily more exhausted and more angry. And then, "one night, I arrived late, which meant that I had to call them on the half-hour rather than on the hour, and, the next day, someone told them I'd wakened them once too often. That wasn't true. In fact, I'd wakened them one time too few." When asked by the interviewer whether he ought to have refused this duty, Snodgrass, referring to his inability to claim conscientious objector status, replied: "I should have, but I didn't have the courage. By then, it would have meant my going to prison because I'd lost my religious beliefs."

The translations, although Snodgrass did not choose to reprint them in his *Selected Poems,* were almost certainly a kind of liberation, for as a poet looks about for likely pieces to attempt, what he or she is really exploring are alternative ways of seeing and speaking, new tonalities that might be an expression of an important but hitherto unrealized aspect of the constantly changing and developing self. In retrospect, it is clearer than it could have been at the time, but Snodgrass's decisions—or instinctive responses—were mostly in the direction of simplification, a progress toward the voice that would emerge in his Cock Robin poems and in another way in some of the pieces of *The Fuehrer Bunker.* To take one example, his treatment of Rilke's poem "Der Panther" shortens the lines, which is difficult to do, requiring intensity and efficiency that are not easy to manage, for the sake of the *faux naif* tone that is his ultimate goal. Below is the first stanza of Rilke's poem in the original German:

> Sein Blick ist vom Vorübergehn der Stäbe
> so müd geworden, daß er nichts mehr hält.
> Ihm ist, als ob es tausend Stäbe gäbe
> und hinter tausend Staben keine Welt.

This becomes, in the translator Stephen Mitchell's rendition:

> His vision, from the constantly passing bars,
> has grown so weary that it cannot hold
> anything else. It seems to him there are
> a thousand bars; and behind the bars no world.

Snodgrass, as seen below, gives us four-beat rather than five-beat lines:

Always passing bars has dulled
His sight so, it will hold no more.
For him, there are a thousand bars;
Behind the thousand bars, no world.

Snodgrass's lines are perhaps too crisp and hard-edged to be the ideal representation of the Rilke stanza, but the attempt was for him a useful step toward his later work.

The other novelty of *After Experience* is the sequence of poems about paintings. Art proved to be an important source of vision for the poet's subsequent work. As Snodgrass explained in the essay "Poems about Paintings," in *In Radical Pursuit:*

Once, for a single evening, I had taught a course in modern art. I had warned my employers beforehand that I knew nothing about art. "But," they said, "this is Adult Education; you don't need to know anything!" Since the class was to meet in a small lovely mansion and would include excellent dinners, warm sherry, and high pay for me, I overcame my scruples.

This was, it turned out, the ideal situation for the right poet—an occasion in which a sophisticated sensibility could confront serious work without the academic training and socialization that can be useful but also deadening and counterproductive. No one is going to be corrupted or co-opted by a comfortable setting, a good dinner, and a rate of pay that is not, for a change, insulting.

"The Red Studio" by Henri Matisse was one of the paintings Snodgrass discussed with his "class." (There were only two students, both of them housewives whom Snodgrass described as "exquisitely beautiful young women, willing to say just what they thought, intelligent, lively, and totally ignorant.") One of the students found this

painting "absolutely terrifying." Snodgrass reports:

To her, it made the room insubstantial and dangerous; if you set your foot down there, you would surely crash through. The only solid things there, showing the colors of real objects in the real world, were the art objects—paintings, ceramics, etc. It was as if all the rest—walls, floors, furnitures—had somehow been energized.

What Snodgrass had seen as "quite gay, lively, energetic," this young woman found to be frightening. And in a telling comment, Snodgrass says, "I never decided that I was wrong; I certainly decided she was right. Now, I hoped that if I could discover how we were *both* right, I might have my poem."

He describes how he sat and looked at the slide for long periods of time, free-associating.

The first thing that came to mind was a very dangerous and energetic rug in my psychiatrist's office several years before. Talking to him, I often sat on the couch with my legs folded up under me. Meantime his rug would glow a ferocious and threatening red. If I had put my foot down, it would surely have crashed through, might have been devoured or burned to a crisp. Actually, in its natural state, at rest, that rug had been green. Yet I never discovered that, never saw the rug in its normal state, until the therapy was nearly finished. Apparently, my mere entry into that room was all it took to induce a raging, bloody red in the fibers of that green and inoffensive rug.

The emotional and intellectual pressures of this encounter were sufficient to allow Snodgrass to discard the fastidious metrical schemes that were characteristic of much of his early work and to plunge into the choppier waters of free verse. His "Matisse: 'The Red Studio' " begins:

There is no one here.
But the objects: they are real. It is not
As if he had stepped out or moved away;

There is no other room and no
Returning. Your foot or finger would pass
Through, as into unreflecting water
Red with clay, or into fire.
Still, the objects: they are real. It is
As if he had stood
Still in the bare center of this floor,
His mind turned in in concentrated fury,
Till he sank
Like a great beast sinking into sands
Slowly, and did not look up.
His own room drank him.

The poem is, of course, a consideration of the famous Matisse painting, but it is also an exploration of the tension between gaiety and fear. A feeling of apprehension is clear at the opening, conveyed by telegraphic punctuation and hard line breaks ("it is not / As if"; "and no / Returning"; "It is / As if he had stood"). But the poet works through the material to a more cheerful engagement with it, which the poem's concluding lines help us share. Observing some of the figures within the picture, he notes:

These stay, exact,
Within the belly of these walls that burn,
That must hum like the domed electric web
Within which, at the carnival, small cars bump
 and turn,
Toward which, for strength, they reach their iron
 hands:
Like the heavens' walls of flame that the old magi
 could see;
Or those ethereal clouds of energy
From which all constellations form,
Within whose love they turn.
They stand here real and ultimate.
But there is no one here.

It is a strange set of associations, but Snodgrass's essay explains how even the most peculiar had their place in the mental landscape he was exploring. The dodgem car ride, for instance, was, as he tells us, "contained in a highly charged cage, an electrical fence. Strange now to think of the little cars as planets circling inside their own closed system, all contained (like Dante's friendly little universe) in a grid of benign energy—a close and spark-filled heaven to which they must reach for the power they needed. They might almost be praying."

On the other hand, the emptiness in the picture's center also spoke to him:

Where was the man who painted himself? Or painted his studio in place of himself? Why should we have that empty space at the center of the canvas, the very place where the artist *should* stand? I found myself imagining that perhaps he *had* put his foot down there, had been buried or swallowed up by his room. Perhaps he had devised this way to give his surroundings such energy, to fertilize them so they might give birth. So, he has become his paintings. But at the very center of his world is an empty space, an absence. Perhaps the matter he has dissolved and destroyed in order to create new forms, new orders, is himself.

THE MATURE VOICE: *THE DEATH OF COCK ROBIN* AND *THE FUHRER BUNKER*

At about the same time as Snodgrass was putting together the poems of *After Experience,* he brought out a translation in collaboration with Lore Segal of the German poet Christian Morgenstern's *Gallows Songs* (1967), which are mordant burlesques and were exactly the kind of thing that would prove useful in the writing of one of his most important works, *The Death of Cock Robin* (1989). Snodgrass and Segal had met, as they make clear in their acknowledgment, at the artists' colony Yaddo, and the idea of doing Morgenstern was more likely than not Segal's (the volume is dedicated to one Paul Stern, "who taught the poems to Lore in German when she was a child and helped to translate them into English"). They are jazzy, sassy pieces the rendering of which into English loosened up whatever remained of Iowa's formalist constraints in Snodgrass's practice. His version of "Die Behörde," which he called "The Questionnaire," is one of those he liked well enough to include in his 1998 volume *Selected Translations.* It begins:

> Korf gets a printed questionnaire
> From the police, sternly worded,
> Demanding who he is and how and where?
>
> Where was his last home? Precisely what
> Day of what year was he born?
> Divorced, married, or single? If not why not?

This is satisfactory, but still perhaps too polite. My own version of "Die Behörde" (commissioned for the Norton *World Poetry* anthology and reprinted in *PS3569.L3*), included here as a point of comparison, translates these lines as:

> Korf receives one day from the coppers
> one of those B-9 forms, so-called because they
>   aren't:
> *Who? Where? How? Why?* And other such
>   stumpers and stoppers.
>
> *Married? Single? Divorced? Separated? Other?*
> (Supply all relevant and requisite documentation
> to support these claims.) *And the Maiden Name of
>   your Mother?*

The breezy irreverence that is one of Snodgrass's great gifts would emerge more completely and unashamedly in his collaboration with the painter DeLoss McGraw, with whom he began his Cock Robin poems, work that takes as its starting point the nursery rhyme, which is a cheerful and naive recitation, after all, of the facts of a murder investigation, or, in other words, a pastoral. Children's poems have a peculiar capacity to make light of catastrophe, blocking out what is disagreeable and yet, somehow, admitting it, too. "Ring-a-ring-a-roses, / A pocket full of posies" is a ritual reenactment of the rosy rash of the plague from which, in the end, "All fall down." (There

was a similar jump-rope song during the influenza pandemic of 1919–1920: "I had a little bird. / Her name was Enza. / I opened up the window. / And in flew Enza.")

The heartless clarity of vision of Mother Goose poetry appealed to Snodgrass but there was a further attraction in that these pieces carried with them an established visual convention, so that he could consider these subjects in the way that he had learned to brood and free-associate for his poems about painting. The Morgenstern volume he and Lore Segal did together used images from the work of Paul Klee. In DeLoss McGraw, Snodgrass found a way to collaborate directly with a painter with whom he shared tastes and interests. McGraw had read some of Snodgrass's work and, as he has written (in "Two Statements on Collaborating with W. D. Snodgrass," in *The Poetry of W. D. Snodgrass,* edited by Stephen Haven),

> It was a statement in his prose work *In Radical Pursuit* that I found especially unusual. It relates the story of his sister, who, having asthma, was nowhere near death physically but, in W. D.'s view, woke up one fourth of July morning and merely decided not to live anymore.
>
> To me there was something unusual about this view of death that was perplexing and to which I could not see how to make a visual statement. Finally, I realized what struck me was its simplicity and innocence—an almost childlike quality. Immediately, the nursery rhyme "Who Killed Cock Robin" came to me. This nursery rhyme introduces a child to the theme of death, and I knew I had a venue.

McGraw's work is naive, even primitive, and curiously suited to the timbre of voice that Snodgrass's impish anarchism needed in order to express itself. One can see examples of McGraw's paintings either in the University of Delaware Press publication of *The Death of Cock Robin* or on the covers of the BOA Edition volumes of Snodgrass's *Selected Translations* and *After-Images: Autobiographical Sketches* (1999).

The poems have a range of registers, from dignified elegy to in-your-face horseplay, and the truth Snodgrass seems to be intent on conveying is not in the straightforward white keys or the mordant black keys, but in the cracks. He can do a brisk vaudeville turn, as in "W. D. Tries to Warn Cock Robin," which opens with these lines:

> The Brutish are coming, the Brutish,
> The Rude-Coats with snares and bum-drumming!
> The Skittish and Prudish
> The Brattish and Crude
> Who'll check on your morals
> And find your song's lewd
> Then strip off the bay leaves and laurels
> That garnished your brows and your food.
> All tongues and all tastebuds benumbing,
> They'll dull all your senses
> Then lull your defenses
> And rule you through blue-nosed and tasteless
>   pretenses:
>   The Brutish!

But it is his ability to shift from one tonality to another that is most striking. "Cock Robin Takes Refuge in the Storm House" begins with these three stanzas, dignified and even elegant, but whose end rhymes seem to wink at us and at the poem itself:

> The sky's unsettled; hawk-winged shadows
> Swoop overhead all day long, scrawling
> Their logo on the tarnished meadows.
> Blood-bright, a leaf reeled past me, falling.
> Did I hear my storm family calling?
>
> And no bird sings. These weeds keep bristling.
> A chill wind hisses at my ear
> Trying to tell me something, whistling
> Like a consistent, heart-felt jeer.
> They don't live all that far from here.
>
> Like trains colliding, or deep thunder,
> I heard a heavy tree-trunk buckle,
> Crack in the green woods and go under.
> From someplace else, a greasy chuckle.
> They'll need a fourth to play pinochle.

The rhythms, syntax, and rhetorical strategies of Morgenstern are clearly in evidence here, particularly in a piece like "W. D. Sits in Kafka's Chair and Is Interrogated Concerning the Assumed Death of Cock Robin," which opens with moves that are clearly adapted from "Die Behörde":

> Now "W"—we'll call you "W,"
>   Okay? We like the friendly touch.
> Just a few questions that won't trouble you
>   For long; this won't hurt much.
> First: name, age, sex, race, genus,
>   Specific gravity and species;
> Hat size, color of hair and penis;
>   Texture and frequency of feces?

It is a livelier performance than his version of the Morgenstern, and darker than Morgenstern's original. The naiveté allows him a sinister suggestiveness that is altogether unsuitable for children, particularly in its conclusion:

> Have you changed sperm count or IQ
>   Within six months? Signed a confession?
> Why are we holding you? If you
>   Don't know, then why ask you this question?
>
> A simple yes or no is all
>   we want; the truth always shines through.
> Thank you. Please wait out in the hall
>   Until somebody comes for you.

The unspecified menace of *The Death of Cock Robin* is only a half-step from the even profounder bleakness of *The Fuehrer Bunker: The Complete Cycle,* which is Snodgrass's altogether unique achievement, a poem nobody else could have written, although it is not without precedent: Aeschylus did something quite similar in his earliest play, *The Persians.* As Snodgrass observes in "The Battle of the Bunker," an essay in *After-Images,* "What actor wouldn't rather play Iago than Othello? Edmund rather than Albany? If Hardy could write a play about Napoleon only a century after the British had defeated him, and Aeschylus one about Xerxes and Darius only eighteen years after helping defeat them at Marathon, why not take those examples?"

He had been picking at the subject for a long time. He had worked on a dramatization of Hugh Trevor-Roper's *The Last Days of Hitler* (1947) when he was at the University of Iowa Writers' Workshop. Some years later, at a conference at Duke University, he heard Ralph Ellison wonder whether, in her place, he might have behaved any better than Madame Nhu, the sister-in-law and acting first lady of the dictatorial Vietnamese president Ngo Dinh Diem, and Snodgrass responded with interest to what was for him the tantalizing idea that "there might be a positive value, a self-recognition in that identification with evil which art may offer." In one of the essays in *After-Images* he explains the reason for this enthusiasm: "I found this a marvelously decent and (ironically) humane statement—just what I'd have expected from Ellison. I am not a Christian but felt I had finally met one—a man who could admit that his enemies' evils were, at least in part, at least potentially his own." Having recently heard a gamelan orchestra for the first time, he considered changing the setting and the characters of a work about the dark side of human nature from Germany to Vietnam, but as he admits, "I could not learn enough about [Madame Nhu] or her family to put together a drama."

His reading of *Inside the Third Reich,* the memoir of Albert Speer, the architect who was Hitler's armaments minister, prompted him to try a monologue in Speer's voice, and this piece came easily and went well enough, as he guessed at "any guilts beyond those [Speer] reveals." Snodgrass thought about a series of monologues that might turn into another cycle, perhaps on the same scale as the title sequence of *Heart's Needle.* Then, in 1972, when he was on a Guggenheim fellowship in Germany, he was able to visit Speer, who had just been released from Spandau prison and was living in his family's home in Heidelberg. The conversation the poet had with the war criminal was unpredictably direct and

forthcoming. As Snodgrass recalled in *After-Images,* he asked Speer how Hitler "could order out units everyone else knew were in ruins, men who were dead." He then described Speer's response and his own reaction to it.

> Hitler had been like a doctor he'd known, a cancer specialist who could merely look at a patient and tell whether they had cancer; the doctor had, besides, predicted that he himself would die of cancer, yet when he fell victim, he alone did not know. "He neglected his knowing," Speer said in his slightly unorthodox English. That self-deception seemed so central, so crucial, not only to Hitler, but to Speer as well, that I formed another poem around his sentence.

To distinguish the characters in the bunker in the last days of World War II, Snodgrass invented curious and bizarrely playful verse forms. The poems in Speer's voice appear on the page as emblematic triangles, representations of architectural constructions, as in the following example:

> Paul,
> My old
> Schoolmate,
> My own doctor—
> Last week I was there.
> Propped in his armchair;
> No nurse. The needle, used,
> By his armrest. Talking, smoking;
> Our most acute diagnostic mind. What
> He would have seen at first glance in his
> Patients, he can explain away, can talk it all
>
> To
> Death.
> He who once
> Told us all he
> Himself would die by
> Cancer, now he describes
> All this once more and he sees
> Nothing. Nothing. Well, so he may
> escape the guns, escape acknowledging
> What it is his cells have been preparing,
> Step, by step, in darkness, beyond all control.

The playfulness of the enterprise is perhaps its most striking quality and a reason for the success of the work. The heartlessness of nursery rhymes that Snodgrass had put to such unlikely but apposite uses in the Cock Robin poems reappears in these elaborate formal displays of linguistic dexterity. As he explained in *After-Images:*

> Since the triangulated shapes appeared to work for Speer's poems, it seemed reasonable to try similar forms for the other characters. For Himmler, head of the SS and Gestapo, probably the most vile of all, I devised the most rigidly arbitrary form possible: capital letters printed on graph paper, thirty letters and spaces to the line, with an alphabet acrostic (omitting "X") down the left-hand margin. I called this form the "platoon"; on the page it breaks into five "squads" of five lines each. There is no indication where sentences begin and end, so adding to the tonelessness of this "idealistic" weakling and fuddy-duddy who administered the murder of millions.

In a remarkable flight of (in both senses) fancy, he gives Magda Goebbels, "who had always traded on her beauty and been notably unfaithful to those who loved her," a variety of French love forms, "rondels, triolets, villanelles, etc." so that she seems absurdly overdressed:

> No one would dare stay constant to
> The sort who've kept good faith with me.
>   They hang on, need to lean on you;
> No one would dare stay constant to
>   Weaklings. With *your* life to squeak through,
>   What use could some such milksops be?
> No one would dare stay constant to
> The sort who've kept good faith with me.

For most of the other characters, Snodgrass uses free verse, but there are characteristic rhetorical tropes, so that the pieces in the voice of Eva Braun, Hitler's mistress, are often about snapshots and frequently use snatches of songs or hymns. Hitler's ruminations involve regressions to memories, and the indentations represent how far back in time these memories go.

The objections to the poem—and there were a number of them, some quite heated—were based on the notion that Snodgrass had "humanized" the Nazis in the bunker. This is a philosophical or even a theological criticism more than a literary one, and the further question that animated it is that of the uniqueness of the Holocaust. Were the National Socialists freaks and devils whose actions were altogether outside the norms of human behavior? Or, perhaps more disturbingly, were they an extreme instance of a more general tendency in the sorry history of the past couple of centuries?

Snodgrass's essay about the work in *After-Images* sets forth at least partly his own response—that he is not "sympathetic" to Hitler, Himmler, Goering, Goebbels, and the rest, and that although "one of the chief Nazi crimes was to deny humanity to the Jews; that gave us no right to deny theirs." His position is not much different from that of Richard L. Rubenstein's in *After Auschwitz: History, Theology, and Contemporary Judaism* (1966), which sees the Holocaust as continuous with a number of other genocidal efforts, more ruthless and efficient, perhaps, but not for that reason discontinuous with the Turkish massacre of the Armenians, the killings in Cambodia, or those in Rwanda, or, for that matter, the American displacement of Native Americans or the Australian expropriation of their territory from its aboriginal inhabitants.

If "never again," is to be more than an empty slogan, a recognition is required that such horrors as the Nazis perpetrated are by no means beyond human imagination or capability. As Snodgrass declares, "People recognize that the poems won't support any accusation of Nazi sympathies. Yet they feel threatened, themselves accused by any admission that we too have committed shameful acts, that nothing human is foreign to us. In place of answerable accusations, there have been rumors, innuendos, and unspoken blame."

It is a powerful cycle of poems and much of the impact comes from the stylization and reduction that results from Snodgrass's rhetorical choices. How can anyone imagine, let alone attempt to convey, the tonality of the moment in which Magda Goebbels passes out to each of her children ampoules of potassium cyanide? What Snodgrass offers is a dozen heartlessly intricate stanzas that begin:

This is the needle that we give
Soldiers and children when they live
Near the front, in primitive
        Conditions or real dangers;
This is the spoon we use to feed
Men trapped in trouble or in need,
When weakness or bad luck might lead
        Them to the hands of strangers.

This is the room where you can sleep
Your sleep out, curled up under deep
Protective layers that will keep
        You safe till all harm's past.
This is the bed where you can rest
In perfect silence, undistressed
By noise or nightmare, as my breast
        Once held you soft but fast.

By the end of the piece, she has arrived at at least a glimmering of self-awareness, for her passage concludes:

You needn't fear what your life meant;
You won't curse how your hours were spent;
You'll grow like your own monument
        To all things sure and good,
Fixed like a frieze in high relief
Of granite figures that our Chief
Accepts into His fixed belief,
        His true blood-brotherhood.

You'll never bite the hand that fed you,
Won't turn away from those that bred you,
Comforted your nights and led you
        Into the thought of virtue.
You won't be turned from your own bed;
Won't turn into the thing you dread;
No new betrayal lies ahead.
        Now no one else can hurt you.

It is, in its awful way, moving. And because it is moving, as Aeschylus' grieving Persians are

moving, it allows us to experience even more keenly the satisfaction of schadenfreude as these characters come to ruin.

Snodgrass reports in *After-Images* that the book was "picked for but did not receive the National Book Critics Circle Award in 1978. One of the judges later told me that they had agreed to give my book the award, but before this was announced, Robert Lowell had died—so they gave it to *Day by Day,* which I thought not up to his best work." He goes on to explain how the whole purpose for the creation of this prize had been to provide a kind of correction, "because the other awards—the Pulitzer and the National Book Award—had been given so often, for nonliterary considerations, to inferior books." This may sound like sour grapes, but there is a note of bewilderment in the poet's words as well. As Snodgrass makes clear, he was "shocked when [Lowell's] death deprived us all of an astonishing sensibility, deprived me of an irreplaceable friend, and, at the same stroke, of that award which might have profoundly affected the reception of my work."

It may not be the most tactful observation a writer could make, but there is that undeniable note of subversive truth that redeems it. The tone of the remark is also softened by Snodgrass's amusement, expressed elsewhere in *After-Images,* at the intricacies and repercussions of his getting the Pulitzer Prize, when he says that "even then [in 1960] I knew that such prizes meant nothing about the quality of my work. Much later I learned of the actual maneuvers and pressures behind my own award. Most of the judges—newspapermen who knew nothing of poetry—had tried to force Louis Untermeyer, the chief judge, to choose a book, any book, of light verse." The word apparently was out that Phyllis McGinley was going to get it, but Untermeyer insisted on his prerogative and, with the help of Caleb Bingham, a southern newspaper editor who was a reader of poetry, gave the prize to Snodgrass.

"Picking my book," Snodgrass says, "cost Untermeyer the judgeship; the following year he was ousted and the prize was given to Miss McGinley for another book which had a preface by W. H. Auden."

RESPITE AND REVELATION: LATE WORK

It is too early to tell whether *The Fuehrer Bunker* is the major work that Snodgrass had in mind or only an earnest if eccentric reaction to the great moral question of our time. What will no doubt keep the text alive is Snodgrass's ongoing career, his further exploration of the possibilities that were evident from the beginning of a lively intelligence, an acute ear, and a depth of psychological understanding that can, with luck, make for great work. When his *Selected Poems* came out in 1987, there was not only a reprise of his famous early work but also an offering, for the first time, of the Gardons poems, some other verse that had been available only in limited editions, in particular the fine sequence "A Locked House" (to which he appended the very quirky "D. D. Byrde Callyng Jennie Wrenn"), and many of the Cock Robin poems, as well as the brilliant "A Darkling Alphabet," a similar exercise in wisdom poetry in the pastoral mode of the conventions of children's verse. The first two letters of the alphabet provide a fair sample of the poem's ingenious strengths and charms:

A is for Atom, the source
of the matter. Within it,
childlike, primal forces
meet, pivoting their courses
as unlike poles attract, submit
to power's laws, commit
themselves to form and limit.
For good or evil, it,
like humans, can be split.

B is for Brain, which helps us cope,
sometimes, with theories, art,

math, cataclysms, styles,
passions and affections.
Its networked scope
and tally of connections
exceed the sum of all
particles in this universe.
There *are* imperfections:
all fall
short; some, apart;
its core is still a reptile's
and we don't know
what that rules. Still, it's the one hope
of human being. And the curse.
At birth, you *did* have one
with all its nerve cells, though
if you start
using it, new circuitries can grow.
With luck, that's scarcely begun;
if it's done, we're done.

The voice is a convenient one for terse, direct statement, the playfulness of the form preventing him from becoming too serious and preachy. Later Auden sometimes manages this trick, and for Snodgrass, it is comfortable enough for him to comment, by the by, on what he thinks his readers might have missed in *The Fuehrer Bunker.* When we get to the letter H, we read:

H is for Hitler, the great
purveyor of Glamour and of Hate
who promised heaven on earth, then tossed
us all to hell and holocaust
and fifty millions dead—a cost
that might seem small, suppose we'd lost.
Some who survived suspect
he hides among us still. Correct.
Their post-war histories
prove his victorious enemies
harbor him, in whole or part,
locked in the heart
of every living man or woman.
Hate this: he still is human.

Although the reaction to that book was more than respectful, nothing astonishing happened. There weren't even any rumored prizes that failed to materialize. Its most important review was a notice in *The New York Times Book Review* by Gavin Ewart, which began with the grand announcement, "On the evidence of his *Selected Poems 1957–1987,* W. D. Snodgrass is one of the six best poets now writing in English—though who the other five are would be arguable." But it then deteriorated to a more qualified approbation and fainter praise. There were other reviews and notices, the two best (most intelligent and also most favorable) being those by Robert McDowell in *The Hudson Review* and Larry Levis in *American Poetry Review,* who observed that "the best of the poems in this collection are so central to our lives and to our thought that I think the book should be read by anyone interested in poetry at all."

Snodgrass may, indeed, have been better served by this solid though unspectacular success. He has written in *After-Images* of poets of his generation and what dreadful things happened to them—particularly to Lowell, John Berryman, and Jarrell, with all of whom he had been on friendly terms. Personal turmoil and psychic stress are not the best conditions for a writer, or indeed for any human being. Snodgrass had been teaching at the University of Delaware from 1979. He had met and, in 1985, married Kathleen Brown, and he was happy, which allowed him to continue with what he loved and was good at.

In the 1980s, he did the two Cock Robin books with DeLoss McGraw (*Lullaby: The Comforting of Cock Robin* and *The Death of Cock Robin*) and then, in 1993, brought out a substantial new collection, *Each in His Season,* which shows a light at the end of the emotional tunnel, or at least a quiet settling in for the long haul. What was now in evidence was a scrupulous close-focused attention to natural wonders—the changing seasons and different kinds of flowers—and even the cautious assertion, pleasant both for the poet and his readers, of moments of joy, which can be, in a poet like Snodgrass, every bit as complicated as misery. In the title sequence, for instance, a series of poems about the seasons, there is a poem (in the section titled "Snow Songs") that could be taken for mere mimesis, albeit uncannily accurate, of the coming on of a snowstorm. It begins:

> one. now another. one
> more. some again; then done.
> though others run
> down your windshield when
> up ahead a sudden
> swirl and squall comes on
> like moths, mayflies in a swarm
> against your lights, a storm
> of small fry, seeds, unknown
> species, populations—every one
> particular and special; each one
> melting, breaking, hurling on . . .

In his remarkable essay, "The Music of 'Each in His Season' " (in *Tuned and under Tension,* edited by Philip Raisor), Fred Chappell observes the similitude between these lines and those of the adagio of Antonio Vivaldi's "Summer"—which Snodgrass had translated and which appears in his *Selected Translations.* The Vivaldi "Four Seasons" poems were not only originally printed as prefaces to the concertos but appeared directly above those parts of the music that represented or embodied their contents. Snodgrass, as Chappell reports, "is an accomplished musician and an ardent amateur musicologist," and the particular line Chappell offers for our consideration is "E de mosche, e mossoni il stuol furioso!" describing the agitation of swarms of gnats and flies, which the famous music represents with "repeated dotted notes in violins and cellos while the sullen whine of the insects sounds from a languorous solo violin." Chappell calls our attention to how "Snodgrass employs repetitious droning rhythm and slant rhyme . . . to reinforce his metaphor of the swarm-storm of insect species, while the base rhyme-word *one* . . . emphasizes the uniqueness of each individual life 'particular and special.' "

Chappell also refers in passing to one of the most striking features of this collection and, indeed, of Snodgrass's entire oeuvre, the extraordinary range of his technical accomplishment in which he "often intersperses his elaborate and sometimes persnickety forms with looser lines; the contrast points up the virtues of both poetic idioms and offers some of the same tension/relaxation qualities we find in the musical counterposing of allegro and adagio tempos and melodic lines."

The remarkable "In Flower" sequence with which the volume concludes is less complicated but hardly less accomplished, a display of small poems of close observation, cheerful pastorals of mostly agreeable responsiveness to the natural world. In "Tulips," for instance, he likens these flowers to

> opened halves of
> some bright eggshell
> or the gaping bills
> where young birds squall
> and trill above their
> mud-dull nest and still
> unfolding petals
> stretch up, out and over
> backwards: a stemmed
> and blown glass goblet's
> spread lips that outspill
> their brimming overflow
> to wish you well.

This poem is not, all by itself, going to change anything, but it is an indication that, for the moment at least, nothing needs to be changed. The challenge in such modest beauty is to the receptivity of our eyes and our souls. We can, if we are not preoccupied or in pain, respond to such occasions and realize that the tulips and the world of which they are a part may offer in "their brimming overflow" a benediction, a blessing. The contrast with some of the poems of earlier books, and indeed with some of the enraged or an-

guished or disgusted poems that appear in this collection, is drastic, so that one understands and appreciates all the more what may not be resolution but is at least respite.

Snodgrass's *Selected Translations* appeared in 1998, a collection of his renditions into English of a wide variety of poetry and, in separate sections, the lyrics of folk songs and art songs. The timbres of his own work allow him to address himself to such a diverse group of texts. The sophisticated poems he can manage quite handily; the deceptively simple but equally demanding *faux naïf* voice of the Cock Robin poems equips him for the *vrai naïf* of the folk songs. Translation, for a practicing poet, can be instructive, restorative, exploratory, or all of those at once. As Snodgrass remarked in the introduction to this work, "Robert Lowell . . . said, as nearly as I can recall, 'Sometimes your own work gets so painful you have to set it aside for a while. At those times, try some translations—you don't have to know the language. Take one of Mrs. Norton's prose versions of Rilke, for instance, and kick it around to see if you can make an English poem out of it. That at least keeps your hand in.' "

For a reader, these exercises are especially revealing of the habits of mind and craft of the poet. One can consult the source text, either in the original language or in a word-for-word trot version, and then see what the poet has done to recreate the work, not just in his own language and idiolect but in his own sensibility, so that the words and phrases resonate correctly in his voice box and sinuses with the pace and texture conformable to the requirements of his own nervous system.

The mature Snodgrass is able to endorse the truth of Lowell's encouraging remark to the student writer about how "you don't have to know the language," and even to go beyond it, for he says now, "half joking, but *only* half," that "it's easier to translate poems from a language you don't know." The reason for this, he goes on to explain in the introduction to *Selected Translations,* is as follows:

> Bilingual translators face a difficulty: having translated a poem, they cannot read their own version without hearing, simultaneously, the original still stored elsewhere in the brain. This offers a compounded experience—to *them.* Alas, translations aren't made for the bilingual. Though translating a poem should teach you much about its original— its textures, sound effects, formal workings, language and image constructions—you will almost never be able to recreate the same effects in another language. And you can waste years trying. Meantime, you may overlook the new language's possibilities. Transcribing the mere tune without drawing on your new orchestra's range of instruments, harmony and tone color, you deprive your audience of the rich complex of meaning and feeling we bargain for in a poem.

Conversely, with a rich enough linguistic orchestration, one can be altogether persuaded of the authenticity of a performance of a work with which one is unfamiliar in the original, and Snodgrass manages this over and over again. One such convincing rendition is Guilhem IX of Poitiers's "The Nothing Song," the breeziness of which is immediately winning. It starts:

> Sheer nothing's all I'm singing of:
> Not me and no one else of course;
> There's not one word of youth and love
>   Nor anything;
> I thought this up, once, on my horse
>   While slumbering.
> I don't know my own sign at birth;
> I'm neither native here nor strange;
> I don't feel gloom, I don't feel mirth.
>   Don't blame me, though—
> One night a fairy worked this change
>   That's made me so.

The poem's contemporary feel is never anachronistic but rather an indication of Snodgrass's skill in bringing these earliest extant troubadour lyrics to life in the language of our time.

In 1999 Snodgrass published *After-Images,* a collection of autobiographical essays, which is essential for an understanding of the ground from which the poems have grown and blossomed. Some of it, particularly the descriptions of his parents and the house in which Snodgrass grew up, can be depressing, but the book is also instructive, as one sees what the poet had to work through—in part through psychotherapy, which "consisted, really, of stating the problem over and over until I dropped the learned terminology and got it down into my own voice." It is also enlightening to read about the peculiar combination of intellectual dedication and sordid behavior that characterized the Iowa Writers' Workshop in its best days. Of Paul Engle, its founder and director, Snodgrass wrote:

> Engle enlisted many students who had more promise, were on the verge of more achievement, than his own. This must have been hard to live with. He was. Subtle and energetic, he held the purse strings for graduate students—as the young men's wives were supporting them, there were ready ways to destabilize their psyches. . . . People moved to Iowa City, perhaps with families, on the promise of grants or fellowships which never materialized. "Ongoing" fellowships might suddenly be canceled.

There are other distressing pieces of information that Snodgrass offers or alludes to—Jarrell's jealousy, Berryman's drunkenness and madness, Lowell's fame, self-indulgence, and descent into madness. "In time," Snodgrass wrote, Lowell "became the center of an industry, surrounded by sycophants or those founding careers on his. Acclaim grew as the poems diminished and he declined, I thought, into a public figure." But if one reads *After-Images* closely, what is impressive is Snodgrass's restraint.

He has been called a "confessional poet," although he heartily dislikes the term and it isn't even applicable to the work beyond his first few books. As he writes in the preface to *After-Images:*

> I am in no sense religious, and I have no interest in the lurid revelations of afternoon TV shows or of "true confessions" publications. I believe that no subject matter should be barred from poetry, but that those matters usually considered personal or private should not be broached for their own sensational sake, where they could damage people still living, or might lead to self-display or self justification. Autobiographical details, if they appear, should satisfy the poem's needs, not the author's hankering for notice or admiration.

The confessionalist label has, nevertheless, stuck to him the way labels often do, despite the fact that Snodgrass has expressed disapproval of the methods employed by confessionalism's most noted practitioners. For example, Lowell's use in his poems of Elizabeth Hardwick's private letters Snodgrass characterized as "an act which I, like many others, thought execrable." In his account of Lowell's death in a taxicab on the way from the airport to Hardwick's apartment, Snodgrass admits, "It is no doubt a failing that I have never ended a marriage amicably—love converts too easily into hatred—but I, too, would have died before going back into the apartment of someone I had once loved but then had so profoundly injured." That "too" represents a generous gesture on Snodgrass's part, for Lowell didn't die of shame but of banal physiological causes.

Snodgrass may not be a conventionally religious poet, but in his work he has allowed for—and sought after—transcendence, an almost Buddhist investment in the sources of pain and wonder that animate the phenomenal world. He approaches this serious subject most directly in his playful poems, which are never *merely* playful. Thus, in "W. D. Sees Himself Animated," in *Each in His Season,* he addresses a version of the self we can recognize from the essays in *After-Images:*

> You are yourself who stands aside
> To watch and witness, petrified,
> While vast universal powers collide
> In archetypal conflicts to decide
> Whether good fortune or ill betide,
>   Whether the robin with green face
>   Would clench its claws in the wriggling, base
>   Adder, then soar, all craft and grace,
>   Over your checkerboard of days
> Or should the serpent, sleek and wily,
> Slink through to its goal where it might slyly
> Envenom the growing young boy vilely,
>   Who sits like a stone grown soft with moss
>   Seeming to take no thought of loss
>   And making no move toward victory.
>   This is your life if such there be.

The move toward victory, or at least acceptance and accommodation, is slow and painful, but it happens, and Snodgrass's body of work is the record of that progress.

Selected Bibliography

WORKS OF W. D. SNODGRASS

BOOKS
Heart's Needle. New York: Knopf, 1959; reprint, 1983.
Gallows Songs by Christian Morgenstern. Translation. With Lore Segal. Ann Arbor: University of Michigan Press, 1967.
After Experience. New York: Harper and Row, 1968.
In Radical Pursuit: Critical Essays and Lectures. New York: Harper and Row, 1975.
Remains: A Sequence of Poems. Brockport, N.Y.: BOA Editions, 1985.

The Führer Bunker: A Cycle of Poems in Progress. Brockport, N.Y.: BOA Editions, 1977.

Selected Poems: 1957–1987. New York: Soho, 1987; reprint, 1991.

W. D.'s Midnight Carnival. With DeLoss McGraw. Encinitas, Calif.: Artra, 1988.

The Death of Cock Robin. Paintings by DeLoss McGraw. Newark: University of Delaware Press, 1989.

Each in His Season. Brockport, N.Y.: BOA Editions, 1993.

The Fuehrer Bunker: The Complete Cycle. Brockport, N.Y.: BOA Editions, 1995.

Selected Translations. Brockport, N.Y.: BOA Editions, 1998.

After-Images: Autobiographical Sketches. Brockport, N.Y.: BOA Editions, 1999.

LIMITED FINE PRESS EDITIONS

Remains: Poems by S. S. Gardons. Mount Horeb, Wis.: Perishable Press, 1970.

If Birds Build with Your Hair. New York: Nadja, 1979.

These Trees Stand. Portrait series by Robert Mahon. New York: Carol Joyce, 1981.

Heinrich Himmler: Platoons and Files. Cumberland, Iowa: Pterodactyl, 1982.

The Boy Made of Meat: A Poem. Wood engravings by Gillian Tyler. Concord, N.H.: William B. Ewert, 1983.

Magda Goebbels. Winston-Salem, N.C.: Palaimon, 1983.

D. D. Byrde Callyng Jennie Wrenn. Concord, N.H.: William B. Ewert, 1984.

A Locked House. Concord, N.H.: William B. Ewert, 1986.

A Colored Poem. Color lithographs by DeLoss McGraw. San Diego: Brighton, 1986.

The House the Poet Built. Color lithographs by DeLoss McGraw. San Diego: Brighton, 1986.

The Comforting of Cock Robin. Paintings by DeLoss McGraw. New York: Nadja, n.d.

The Kinder Capers: Poems. Illustrations by DeLoss McGraw. New York: Nadja, 1986.

The Midnight Carnival. Original etchings by DeLoss McGraw. San Diego: Brighton, 1988.

To Shape a Song. Illustrations by DeLoss McGraw. New York: Nadja, 1988.

Autumn Variations. New York: Nadja, 1990.

PAMPHLETS

Spaulding Distinguished Lectures. Durham: University of New Hampshire Press, 1969.

Lullaby: The Comforting of Cock Robin. New York: Nadja, 1988.

BIBLIOGRAPHY

White, William. *W. D. Snodgrass: A Bibliography.* Detroit: Wayne State University, 1960.

CRITICAL STUDIES

Ewart, Gavin. "One Poet, Many Voices." *The New York Times Book Review,* September 13, 1987, p. 52.

Gaston, Paul L. *W. D. Snodgrass.* Boston: Twayne, 1978.

Haven, Stephen, ed. *The Poetry of W. D. Snodgrass: Everything Human.* Ann Arbor: University of Michigan Press, 1993.

Hay, Philip. "Interview with W. D. Snodgrass." *Between the Lines* (London) 1 (1998).

Levis, Larry. "Not Life So Proud to Be Life: Snodgrass, Rothenberg, Bell, and The Counter-Revolution." *American Poetry Review* 18.1:9–20 (January-February 1989).

Raisor, Philip, ed. *Tuned and under Tension: The Recent Poetry of W. D. Snodgrass.* Newark: University of Delaware Press, 1998.

Phillips, Robert. "W. D. Snodgrass and the Sad Hospital of the World." In *The Confessional Poets.* Carbondale and Edwardsville: Southern Illinois University Press, 1973.

—DAVID R. SLAVITT

Index

Index

Arabic numbers printed in bold-face type refer
to extended treatment of a subject.

Red Pony, The (Steinbeck), **IV,** 50, 51, 58, 70

Red Roses for Bronze (Doolittle), **Supp. I, Part 1,** 253, 268, 271

Red Rover, The (Cooper), **I,** 342–343, 355

"Red Silk Stockings" (Hughes), **Retro. Supp. I,** 200

"Red Wheelbarrow, The" (Williams), **IV,** 411–412; **Retro. Supp. I,** 419, 430

"Red Wind" (Chandler), **Supp. IV, Part 1,** 122

Redbook (magazine), **III,** 522–523; **Supp. IV, Part 1,** 354

"Redbreast in Tampa" (Lanier), **Supp. I, Part 1,** 364

Redburn: His First Voyage (Melville), **III,** 79–80, 84; **Retro. Supp. I,** 245, 247–248, 249

Redding, Saunders, **IV,** 497; **Supp. I, Part 1,** 332, 333

Reddings, J. Saunders, **Supp. IV, Part 1,** 164

"Redemption" (Gardner), **Supp. VI,** 72

"Redeployment" (Nemerov), **III,** 267, 272

Redfield, Robert, **IV,** 475

Redgrave, Lynn, **Supp. V,** 107

Red-headed Woman (film), **Retro. Supp. I,** 110

Redrawing the Boundaries (Fisher), **Retro. Supp. I,** 39

Redskins, The (Cooper), **I,** 351, 353

"Redwings" (Wright), **Supp. III, Part 2,** 603

Reed, Ishmael, **Supp. II, Part 1,** 34

Reed, John, **I,** 48, 476, 483

Reed, Rex, **IV,** 401

"Reed of Pan, A" (McCullers), **II,** 585

Reedy, William Marion, **Supp. I, Part 2,** 456, 461, 465

Reef, The (Wharton), **IV,** 317–318, 322; **Retro. Supp. I,** 372, **373–374**

Rees, Robert A., **II,** 125; **Supp. I, Part 2,** 425

Reeves, George M., Jr., **IV,** 473

Reeves, John K., **II,** 292

Reeves, Paschal, **IV,** 472, 473

Reeve's Tale (Chaucer), **I,** 131

Reflections at Fifty and Other Essays (Farrell), **II,** 49

Reflections in a Golden Eye (McCullers), **II,** 586, 588, 593–596, 604; **IV,** 384, 396

Reflections of a Jacobite (Auchincloss), **Supp. IV, Part 1,** 31

Reflections on Poetry and Poetics (Nemerov), **III,** 269

"Reflections on the Constitution of Nature" (Freneau), **Supp. II, Part 1,** 274

"Reflections on the Death of the Reader" (Morris), **III,** 237

Reflections on the End of an Era (Niebuhr), **III,** 297–298

"Reflections on the Life and Death of Lord Clive" (Paine), **Supp. I, Part 2,** 505

Reflections: Thinking Part I (Arendt), **Supp. I, Part 2,** 570

Reflections on the Revolution in France (Burke), **Supp. I, Part 2,** 511, 512

"Reflex Action and Theism" (James), **II,** 345, 363

"Refugees, The" (Jarrell), **II,** 371

Regan, Robert, **III,** 432

Régnier, Henri de, **II,** 528–529

Regulators, The (King), **Supp. V,** 141

Rehder, Robert, **Supp. IV, Part 1,** 69

Reichart, Walter A., **II,** 317

Reichel, Hans, **III,** 183

Reid, B. L., **II,** 41, 47

Reid, Randall, **IV,** 307

Reid, Thomas, **II,** 9; **Supp. I, Part 1,** 151

Reign of Wonder, The (Tanner), **I,** 260

"Reincarnation" (Dickey), **Supp. IV, Part 1,** 181–182

Reiner, Carl, **Supp. IV, Part 2,** 591

Reinfeld, Linda, **Supp. IV, Part 2,** 421

Reisman, Jerry, **Supp. III, Part 2,** 618

Reiter, Irene Morris, **II,** 53

Reivers, The (Faulkner), **I,** 305; **II,** 57, 73

Reivers, The: A Reminiscence (Faulkner), **Retro. Supp. I,** 74, 82, 91

Relation (Banks' genre), **Supp. V,** 13

Relation of My Imprisonment, The (Banks), **Supp. V,** 8, 12–13

"Relations between Poetry and Painting, The" (Stevens), **Retro. Supp. I,** 312

Relearning the Alphabet (Levertov), **Supp. III, Part 1,** 280, 281

"Release, The" (MacLeish), **III,** 16

Reles, Abe ("Kid Twist"), **Supp. IV, Part 1,** 382

"Relevance of an Impossible Ethical Ideal, The" (Niebuhr), **III,** 298

"Religion" (Dunbar), **Supp. II, Part 1,** 199

"Religion" (Emerson), **II,** 6

Religion of Nature Delineated, The (Wollaston), **II,** 108

"Religious Symbolism and Psychic Reality in Baldwin's *Go Tell It on the Mountain*" (Allen), **Supp. I, Part 1,** 69

"Reluctance" (Frost), **II,** 153

Remains (Snodgrass), **Supp. VI,** 311, **313–314**

"Remains, The" (Strand), **Supp. IV, Part 2,** 627

"Remarks on Spencer's *Definition of Mind as Correspondence*" (James), **II,** 345

Remarque, Erich Maria, **Retro. Supp. I,** 113; **Supp. IV, Part 1,** 380

Rembar, Charles, **III,** 192

Rembrandt, **II,** 536; **IV,** 310; **Supp. IV, Part 1,** 390, 391

"Rembrandt, The" (Wharton), **IV,** 310

Rembrandt Takes a Walk (Strand), **Supp. IV, Part 2,** 631

A Complete Listing of Authors in *American Writers*

Sandburg, Carl   Volume 3

Santayana, George   Volume 3

Schwartz, Delmore   Supplement II

Sexton, Anne   Supplement II

Shapiro, Karl   Supplement II

Shepard, Sam   Supplement III

Silko, Leslie Marmon   Supplement IV

Simon, Neil   Supplement IV

Sinclair, Upton   Supplement V

Singer, Isaac Bashevis   Volume 4

Smiley, Jane   Supplement VI

Snodgrass, W. D.   Supplement VI

Sontag, Susan   Supplement III

Stegner, Wallace   Supplement IV

Stein, Gertrude   Volume 4

Steinbeck, John   Volume 4

Stevens, Wallace   Volume 4

Stevens, Wallace   Retrospective Supplement I

Stone, Robert   Supplement V

Stowe, Harriet Beecher   Supplement I

Strand, Mark   Supplement IV

Styron, William   Volume 4

Swenson, May   Supplement IV

Tate, Allen   Volume 4

Taylor, Edward   Volume 4

Taylor, Peter   Supplement V

Thoreau, Henry David   Volume 4

Thurber, James   Supplement I

Toomer, Jean   Supplement III

Trilling, Lionel   Supplement III

Twain, Mark   Volume 4

Tyler, Anne   Supplement IV

Updike, John   Volume 4

Updike, John   Retrospective Supplement I

Van Vechten, Carl   Supplement II

Veblen, Thorstein   Supplement I

Vidal, Gore   Supplement IV

Vonnegut, Kurt   Supplement II

Walker, Alice   Supplement III

Warren, Robert Penn   Volume 4

Welty, Eudora   Volume 4

Welty, Eudora   Retrospective Supplement I

West, Nathanael   Volume 4

Wharton, Edith   Volume 4

Wharton, Edith   Retrospective Supplement I

White, E. B.   Supplement I

Whitman, Walt   Volume 4

Whitman, Walt   Retrospective Supplement I

Whittier, John Greenleaf   Supplement I

Wilbur, Richard   Supplement III

Wilder, Thornton   Volume 4

Williams, Tennessee   Volume 4

Williams, William Carlos   Volume 4

Williams, William Carlos   Retrospective
    Supplement I

Wilson, Edmund   Volume 4

Winters, Yvor   Supplement II

Wolfe, Thomas   Volume 4

Wolfe, Tom   Supplement III

Wright, Charles   Supplement V

Wright, James   Supplement III

Wright, Richard   Volume 4

Wylie, Elinor   Supplement I

Zukofsky, Louis   Supplement III